Pelican Books
Marxists on Literature
An Anthology

David Craig is a Senior Lecturer at
the University of Lancaster. His major
publications are *Scottish Literature and the
Scottish People, 1680–1830* (1961) and
The Real Foundations (1973). He has also
edited several books for Penguins, including
Hard Times by Charles Dickens and Hugh
MacDiarmid's *Selected Poems* and is
co-editor of *Fireweed*.

D0716861

EDITED BY DAVID CRAIG

Marxists on Literature
An Anthology

PENGUIN BOOKS

Penguin Books Ltd,
Harmondsworth, Middlesex, England
Penguin Books Inc.,
7110 Ambassador Road, Baltimore, Maryland 21207, U.S.A.
Penguin Books Australia Ltd,
Ringwood, Victoria, Australia
Penguin Books Canada Ltd,
41 Steelcase Road West, Markham, Ontario, Canada
Penguin Books (N.Z.) Ltd,
182–190 Wairau Road, Auckland 10, New Zealand

First published 1975

Introduction and selection copyright © David Craig, 1975

Made and printed in Great Britain by
Hazell Watson & Viney Ltd,
Aylesbury, Bucks
Set in Linotype Granjon

This book is sold subject to the condition that
it shall not, by way of trade or otherwise, be lent,
re-sold, hired out, or otherwise circulated without
the publisher's prior consent in any form of
binding or cover other than that in which it is
published and without a similar condition
including this condition being imposed on the
subsequent purchaser

WITHDRAWN

CONTENTS

ACKNOWLEDGEMENTS

For permission to use copyright material acknowledgement is made to the following:

Lawrence & Wishart Ltd for 'Speech and Thought' from *The First Philosophers* and 'The Art of Poetry' from *The Prehistoric Aegean*, both by George Thomson; for '*Othello* and the Dignity of Man' by Geoffrey Matthews from *Shakespeare in a Changing World*, edited by Arnold Kettle; for 'Report on the Journals *Zvezda* and *Leningrad*, 1947' from *On Literature, Music and Philosophy* by A. A. Zhdanov; for 'English Poets: (1) The Period of Primitive Accumulation' from *Illusion and Reality* by Christopher Caudwell.

V. G. Kiernan for 'Wordsworth and the People', his own essay in *Democracy and the Labour Movement*, edited by John Saville, published by Lawrence & Wishart Ltd.

Arnold Kettle for 'Dickens and the Popular Tradition', his own essay in *Zeitschrift für Anglistik und Amerikanistik*, 1961, No. 3, published by V.E.B. Deutscher Verlag der Wissenschaften, Berlin.

Jack Mitchell for 'Aesthetic Problems of the Development of the Proletarian-Revolutionary Novel in Nineteenth-Century Britain', his own essay in *Zeitschrift für Anglistik und Amerikanistik*, 1963, No. 3, published by V.E.B. Deutscher Verlag der Wissenschaften, Berlin.

The Merlin Press Ltd for 'Tolstoy and the Development of Realism' from *Studies in European Realism* and 'Franz Kafka or Thomas Mann?' from *The Meaning of Contemporary Realism*, both by Georg Lukács.

Methuen & Co. Ltd for 'Theatre for Pleasure or Theatre for Instruction', 'The Popular and the Realistic', 'On Rhymeless Verse with Irregular Rhythms', all by Bertolt Brecht, taken from *Brecht on Theatre*, edited by John Willett; © 1957, 1963 and 1964 by Suhrkamp Verlag; translation © 1964 by John Willett.

Vlady Kibalchich for 'The Writer's Conscience' by Victor Serge from *Now*, No. 7.

Victor Gollancz Ltd for 'What is *Littérature Engagée*?' from *Commitment in Modern French Literature* by Max Adereth.

Econ Verlagsgruppe for 'The Loss and Discovery of Reality' from *The Necessity of Art* by Ernst Fischer, translated by Anna Bostock (Penguin Books, 1963).

This anthology has been compiled because I and other Communists working in literature are often asked for reading lists that give 'the Marxist view' of the subject. There is no unified view. Marxist interpretations of literature are rich and various, but they are scattered through all manner of sources. With a few exceptions – for example, Caudwell's *Illusion and Reality*[1] and Fischer's *The Necessity of Art*[2] – Marxist critics have not drawn their thoughts together in systematic works, as have their comrades in such other fields as economics, politics, history and philosophy. Nevertheless this book will have failed unless it convinces its readers that during the past century there has grown up a body of thought in which Marxism yields insights into literary creation and immediately kindred human activities such as cannot be got from other sources. I cannot but be aware of saying this in the teeth of an opinion widespread in Britain and the United States that the link between 'Marxism' and 'literature' has been on the whole a forced and barren one. Ten years ago in a small town on the Yorkshire coast I was meeting an evening class in Modern Literature, run by the WEA, to revise their syllabus which I had had to take over at short notice from another tutor who had left. *Doctor Zhivago* was on the list (along with a good deal of Bellow, Murdoch, Angus Wilson, and so on) and I suggested, to bring the work nearer what I was most able and interested to teach, that we could compare Pasternak's novel with the 'main Soviet literary tradition'. 'I didn't know there was one,' said one of the members right away. In fact we went on to spend some good hours discussing the novels of Sholokhov and Konstantin Fedin along with Pasternak. But that woman's remark typifies the general view: that in the

1. See below, Text 4.   2. See below, Text 26.

countries where Communist governments have organized literary work on what they consider Marxist lines, the results have been on the whole the sterilization, or outright suppression, of good writing and the forcing down the public throat of a great deal of old-fashioned, conformist hackwork in the name of 'moulding socialist consciousness'.

This view, for which there is much justification, cannot be brought *nearer* to what has actually happened by any single book like this anthology. Readers sceptical whether Marxism has anything human to say to them should at least read Engels's *Condition of the Working Class in England in 1844* and his *Socialism Utopian and Scientific*, Lenin's *Imperialism*, Mao Tse-tung's 'Report on the Peasant Movement in Hunan', and Castro's speeches (now anthologized in a Penguin). Readers sceptical whether writers working by the light of Marxism have created anything of human significance should at least read the Don novels by Sholokhov and his story 'A Man's Fate', the middle-period poems of Hugh MacDiarmid, Brecht's poems and plays, the novels and histories of Victor Serge. Without some such minimum of pondered material in common between all parties to the discussion, we will not get beyond the catcalling and defensive aggressiveness of the Cold War. Literary criticism is strictly secondary to the kinds of writing just mentioned, but it has its necessary function, all the more so amidst the fevered scene of Communist and anti-Communist controversy. This anthology is therefore offered to be read in conjunction with those major pieces of theoretical and creative writing.

Because of the fairly scattered and as yet unsystematic state of Marxist literary work, there is no piece in this anthology which is authoritative in a theoretical way. Yet there is now a nucleus of Marxist cultural theory which readers should have at the back of their minds as they try the various samples which make up this book. Marxism is best known for its theory, first expressed in the *Communist Manifesto* of 1848, that 'The history of all hitherto existing society is the history of class struggles.' The link between this and its less directly political implications is given in what Engels calls 'the fundamental proposition' of the *Manifesto* 'which forms its nucleus':

... in every historical epoch, the prevailing mode of economic production and exchange, and the social organization necessarily following from it, form the basis upon which is built up, and from which alone can be explained, the political and intellectual history of that epoch...[3]

From these ideas and the whole body of thought they belong to, we may infer the following idea of literature :

The deepest-rooted forces acting in history – that is, the struggle between sections of society for the means of life – transform the way of life, that is, people's relations as they work together to subsist (which includes psychological well-being, sexual satisfaction, as well as food, clothing, and shelter). This transforming gives rise to new networks of communication (oral performance for a one-class audience, commodity circulation of printed work for a mixed public, or whatever). Out of this arises literature, the expression in words (often closely fused with music and graphics) of the new, pressing life-concerns of people in a particular place and time (concerns that overlap to a degree with the life of our species in all its places and times). And this expression is in styles that adapt in a personal way – according to the innate and conditioned natures of the individual artists and artistes – the media available in the community at the time.

Theory at so general a level is in danger either of turning into platitudes which few would bother either to take seriously or to refute or else of being treated to the academic Death by a Thousand Cuts : each specialist goes lovingly through his files until he has found enough tiny items to expose the large theory for the elephantine and out-dated thing he takes it to be. Yet general ideas are indispensable – 'Without theory, action is blind; without action, theory is barren', as Lenin once remarked – and the very fact that many kinds of revolutionary socialist can be called by the name of a fairly technical philosophy first worked out by a German thinker in the nineteenth century shows how

3. *Manifesto of the Communist Party* (Moscow ed., 1957), p. 46; Preface to English ed. of 1888, in *Manifesto*, p. 23. Marx's most elaborated version of this idea is the passage beginning, 'In the social production of their life . . .', from the Preface to his *Critique of Political Economy*, which is in most selections of his writings.

needful it is to be clear about the *ideas* uppermost in the minds of the people who wrote the critical pieces that follow. Still, Marxism has always insisted on the test of action; and this, along with the common Western view that, however true it may be in an ideal kind of way, Marxism has been a bloodstained travesty in practice, makes it best to take the discussion further by studying a particular area of Marxist literary activity. It is clear from the history and the principles of Marxism that the area most in dispute is socialist realism.

For Western readers 'socialist realism' means little more than the novels and plays which Soviet writers produce to the orders of their government, the sort of art that highlights the good features of Soviet life and glosses over the malignant ones. Even socialists in the West tend to be sceptical as to whether 'socialist realism' has any meaning at all – whether there has been a school of writing that measures up to the blueprints given out in various pronouncements by the Communist Establishment. The hostility to the idea is part of that ignorance of socialist practice which our rulers and their media are so good at fostering. It is also a tragically inevitable result of the distortions of literary work and critical thought which occurred in the Stalin era and are still occurring nearly twenty years after the twentieth Congress of the Soviet CP at which many of the wrongs done by Stalin's government were admitted and denounced.

In practice I find socialist realism, if I take it according to its ablest practitioners and theoreticians, a fruitful idea and a necessary one. The best explanation of it is in Lukács's *Meaning of Contemporary Realism*. He argues that the main novelists of the first modern stages, for example Dickens, Tolstoy, and (unmentioned by Lukács) Conrad, were 'critical realists' : they were able, as Chekhov put it, to 'raise the reasonable question' but not to envisage a perspective in which answers might arise.[4] To take an example, Dickens and Conrad were wonderfully good at presenting (in *Little Dorrit* and *The Secret Agent*) the insulating divisions between people and how these arise on the basis of unequal access to the means of life. Yet they avoid – they almost visibly

4. Georg Lukács, *The Meaning of Contemporary Realism* (Merlin, 1963), p. 69.

back away from – imagining what it might be for the under-men to rise and claim their own.

By 1910 or so, in the work of Gorky, Robert Tressell, Upton Sinclair and others, there began to emerge a school or new tradition which would presently be called socialist realism because it aimed 'to describe the forces working towards socialism *from the inside*'. Its purpose was 'to locate those human qualities which make for the creation of a new social order'.[5] Lukács's work is painfully thin in discussion of substantial examples of such work and his phrasing tends to be philosophical instead of critical. Those pages of his need to be supplemented by a note on socialist realism which Brecht jotted down in 1954:

> In the case of Socialist Realism a large part of the pleasure which all art must provoke is pleasure at the possibility of society's mastering man's fate...
>
> A Socialist Realist work of art lays bare the dialectical laws of movement of the social mechanism, whose revelation makes the mastering of man's fate easier...
>
> A Socialist Realist work of art shows characters and events as historical and alterable, and as contradictory...
>
> The Socialist Realist performance of old classical works is based on the view that mankind has preserved those works which gave artistic expression to advances towards a continually stronger, bolder and more delicate humanity.[6]

This palpably has Brecht's own theatre practice behind it, and elsewhere in the same note he gives a brief mention to the stylistic side of the matter: 'A serious effort has to be made to find new means of representation.' Yet this does little to answer a question that must arise for any socialist concerned with literature: *how* must one write so as to describe the forces and locate the human qualities which make for a new social order?

Since Marxists have always held that it is the workers of the world who are instrumental in overthrowing existing social systems, it follows for us that the human qualities concerned are embodied especially in the working people, with their language and idiom, their views, emotions, and typical experiences – their

5. *The Meaning of Contemporary Realism*, pp. 93–4.
6. *Brecht on Theatre*, ed. John Willett (Methuen, 1964), p. 269.

life-style. Therefore socialist realism must draw most heavily on the workers' and peasants' culture if it is to rise to its historical task and make a new sort of art which is equal to evoking what it takes to create a new way of life.

Some Marxists have denied or missed this, apparently through falling over backwards to avoid being doctrinaire in the bad old Stalinist way. So Ernst Fischer writes:

> Against the definition of socialist realism as a method or style, the question immediately comes to mind: whose style, whose method? Gorky's or Brecht's? Mayakovsky's or Eluard's? Makarenko's or Aragon's? Sholokhov's or O'Casey's? The methods of these writers are as different as can be . . .[7]

In fact all those writers have a main quality in common: they excel at turning idioms, styles, modes from vernacular, popular, and public sources to creative effect.[8] They have all 'watched the people's mouth' – to use a phrase that had special value for Brecht.[9] This is the main specific way in which artists can take part in the struggle to change the world. As Mao Tse-tung puts it:

> Our artists and writers should work in their own field, which is art and literature, but their duty first and foremost is to understand and know the people well. How did they stand in this regard in the past? . . . They failed to understand language, i.e. they lacked an adequate knowledge of the rich and lively language of the masses of the people. Many artists and writers, withdrawing themselves from the people into a void, are of course unfamiliar with the people's language, and thus their works are not only written in a language without savour or sap but often contain awkward expressions of their own coinage which are opposed to popular usage . . . all artists and writers of high promise must, for long periods of time, unreservedly and whole-heartedly go into the midst of the masses, the masses of workers, peasants and soldiers; they must go into fiery struggles, go to the only, the broadest, the richest source to observe, learn, study and analyse all men, all classes, all kinds of people, all the vivid

7. Ernst Fischer, *The Necessity of Art* (Penguin, 1963), p. 110.
8. More detailed grounds for this point are given in my 'The New Poetry of Socialism': *The Real Foundations* (Chatto & Windus, 1973), pp. 215–23.
9. He quotes it in Text 23 below.

patterns of life and struggle and all raw material of art and literature, before they can proceed to creation. Otherwise, for all your labour, you will have nothing to work on and will become the kind of 'empty-headed artists or writers' against whom Lu Hsun, in his testament, so earnestly cautioned his son.[10]

Western readers tempted to think that this applies only to a backward country in a state of turmoil should ponder the fact that the finest novelists – the Tolstoys, Conrads, Lawrences – have led lives which put them in active touch with all walks of life in their society.

It is no accident that the age which has seen the first successful socialist revolutions has also been rich in novels and poems, films and plays, which have for the first time expressed the experience of working people in their own language or styles based on it. In Scott and Dickens, working men and women were brought on from time to time, for laughs or sob-stuff. In such novels as *The Quiet Don*, *A Scots Quair*, and *The Grapes of Wrath*, in such plays as *Juno and the Paycock*, *Mother Courage*, and *Roots*, in such poems as Brecht's 'Legend of the Dead Soldier' and MacDiarmid's 'The Seamless Garment', the medium of the work, its language and the consciousness in which it is felt to be situated, is given over to the infantrymen, peasants, factory hands, small traders, housewives – to people whose experiences are typical of *the majority*.

This is not to say that a socialist realist more familiar with life among the well-to-do would not want to deal with the world of such people, particularly as it has been affected by cultural shifts and insecurities. When Louis Aragon was asked why he, France's leading Communist writer, had put so many middle-class characters into his novels (to which, after all, he had given the title *The Real World*), he answered, 'I know them better.' And the same applies to the trilogy by Fedin, *Early Joys*, *No Ordinary Summer*, and *The Conflagration*, which to my knowledge is unique among major Soviet works with a contemporary theme in having a bourgeois (the fashionable playwright, Pastukhov) as a major character. But for writers and critics who are part of

10. 'Talks at the Yenan Forum on Art and Literature': *Selected Works of Mao Tse-tung*, IV (Bombay, 1956), pp. 66–7, 77.

the revolutionary movement to change the world in the interests of the many and against the rule of the propertied, the first priority goes to the people at large. Arturo Barea was the one person broadcasting from besieged Madrid during the Spanish Civil War who brought to the fore the experiences of ordinary people, and he later defined his belief as a writer in the foreword to *The Track* (1943), the middle part of his trilogy of auto-biographies:

A very distinguished critic [has objected] that 'the conversations ... the discoveries ... and the disillusionments of experience are such as could be described by millions...' This is ... as I think it should be... The millions who shared the same experiences and disap-pointments do not usually write, but it is they who are the rank and file in wars, revolutions and 'New Orders', they who carry on in the Old Order, helpless, restless, and disillusioned ... They are usually called the common people or the 'little men' or the 'lower orders'. As I was one of them, I have attempted to be vocal on their behalf, not in the form of propaganda, but simply by giving my own truth.[11]

Socialist poets have the problem of speaking for people at large in a way that is authoritative, the voice of the vanguard, while avoiding hectoring from on high. Socialist novelists and play-wrights have the problem of being in the shoes of their characters and expressing their partial vision of things while suggesting to the reader or viewer that there is a longer perspective which he should attain. None of the characters in Brecht's *Caucasian Chalk Circle* is concerned to change society. They want to lead their own lives. It is not as an act of class-conscious struggle but sheerly out of maternal protectiveness that Grusha looks after the noble-woman's child when its mother has fled from the city after the *coup d'état*. Afterwards all she wants is to keep the child who is now in effect hers. It is in the trial scene when the issue of motherhood comes up that Brecht shows himself a great socialist realist. Justice is never a matter of absolutes – abstract good or abstract wrong – it inevitably involves class. At first the judge, Azdak, is tempted to side with the class that pays him. But he is

11. Arturo Barea, *The Forging of a Rebel* (Davis-Poynter, 1972), p. 234. The wonderfully telling concrete evidence of what Barea said in his broad-casts and what ordinary people thought of them is on pp. 676–81 and 695.

a man of the people and Grusha tongue-lashes him to remind him of it. It is then that he hits on the device of putting the two women's love for the boy to the test of the chalk circle and it is the peasant girl who wins the boy because she cannot bear to risk injuring him by grabbing and hauling at him. By the end of the play no-one has become a revolutionary or a premature socialist. The audience has been given insight into the class system and how power is held. We are made to think how society imposes roles on us, which are hit off comically or satirically in every scene. And we have seen enacted the great axioms of socialist humanism:

> ... what there is shall belong to those who are good for it, thus
> The children to the motherly, that they thrive;
> The carts to good drivers, that they are driven well;
> And the valley to the waterers, that it shall bear fruit.[12]

The tragedy was that, in the countries which were struggling towards socialism, instead of encouraging artists to enter into the new life with a will and hence develop in their own way the styles and themes of a new literature, the Party censored, intimidated and decreed. In the USSR Zhdanov took it upon himself to harangue artists and philosophers about what they must do for the socialist motherland.[13] Mayakovsky, the most popular poet in the ten years after the October Revolution, in a burst of revolutionary fervour tried to 'trample on the throat of his own song'. He wrote:

> I want the pen
> to equal the gun,
> to be listed
> with iron
> in industry.
> And the Politbureau's agenda
> Item 1
> to be Stalin's Report on
> 'The Output of Poetry'...[14]

12. Brecht, *Plays*, I (Methuen, 1960), p. 96.
13. See Appendix A.
14. *Mayakovsky and his Poetry*, ed. Herbert Marshall (Pilot Press, London, 1945), p. 62.

This was almost literally fulfilled. The artist's responsibility and practical link with society, in itself desirable and necessary for socialist-realist work, came to be conceived in purely administrative terms. Conformism was enforced, on pain of death or withdrawal of the right to publish, and few writers were brave enough to resist relapsing into the hackwork expected of them.

After the twentieth Congress of the CPSU the official policy, as administered by Khrushchev until he lost power in 1964, encouraged greater freedom in the arts. The critical side of socialist realism was given some rein: the journal *Novy Mir* was allowed to publish Solzhenitsyn's *One Day in the Life of Ivan Denisovich* and so, at a stroke, the great taboo subject in Soviet experience, the Terror that had deformed so much of life, was thrown up into the light of artistic representation. After a year or two of such work (mainly memoirs, novels, and Akhmatova's poem-sequence *Requiem*) the coercion and suppression closed in again. But it seems that the socialist countries, after a first puritanical phase, can never quite re-establish the most rigorous control. The Party agencies are forever exhorting themselves, as it were, to try and unbend their more rigid practices.[15] Some Soviet critics are now able to conceive of socialist realism in more flexible terms and formulate a socialist view of literature that should be useful to readers anywhere in the world, especially those who see the need to link literature with the struggle to do away with the unbearable and anti-human in the present life of mankind.

To enter this struggle, even if only imaginatively, is to be committed, and since such commitment is of the essence for Communists, it might be thought that this would come out as bias in Marxist critics. We do badly want there to be excellent novels, poems, and plays by writers who share our views, and we may well warm more to these than to the best work of non-socialist writers. But since a Marxist is also specially aware of history, he tries to *explain* any shortcomings in the literature he

15. E.g. *Pravda*, 19 May 1963: 'The Party sees no necessity to act as watchdog over every step taken by our artistic intelligentsia, to state in detail how people must write books, make a film, compose music. While fixing the principal objective, it calls the masters of literature and art to boldness and creative independence.' (See also Appendix B.)

considers progressive, since he is concerned to understand their social causes. For example, Jack Mitchell's fellow-feeling for nineteenth-century workmen-novelists (see Text 11) doesn't blind him to, but enables him to understand, that backwardness in terms of awareness of where their class stood which made their novels wishful and weakly romantic. I also believe that candid and witting partisanship is a more satisfactory position than disguising your bias towards the old order as a belief in some ideal civilization outside history or using your scholarly detachment as an excuse for making no distinction between books that help the wretched of the earth to get on their feet and books fitted only to kill time for the well-to-do. In any case, a critic, the Marxist as much as any, must ground his thought in the scrutiny of particular works and be able to test his conclusions against this. It is then up to other readers either to fault his analysis or to take seriously the ideas which this analysis has been used to support.

The concern of Marxists with the workings of society might seem to entail that we favour the more public sorts of theme and, in our critical methods, make heavy use of social history. There is notable Marxist literary criticism which shows that we have learned from modern ways of close analysis [16] and that we realize as well as any other kind of critic that a work of art 'contains within itself the reason why it is so and not another thing'. This doesn't mean that we think a work of art is self-sufficient, that in reading literature we ought to try and approach it in a frame of mind from which all considerations but the 'aesthetic' have been excluded. But if a novel throws a clear and intense light on some walk of life, if it goes in detail into the workings of a law court or a factory or a block of flats in Rome just after the War or a Russian landed family in 1812, and if it succeeds artistically, it will contain within itself the knowledge needed to appreciate it and authenticate its truth to reality. Artistic success may be defined by the degree to which the internal structure of a work

16. Text 5 below, for example, by Geoffrey Matthews, fairly represents the kind of scrupulous critical relevance typical of the best books by English Marxist critics. See also Arnold Kettle's two volumes on the English novel and Alick West's *The Mountain in the Sunlight*.

is both integrated and convincing. What it convinces us of, finally, is its truth to life. Working on Dickens, for example, has shown me that his novelistically most intense passages – whether hilarious, scathing, or darkly coloured – are usually the most exact. The better the writing, the more likely he is to qualify as a reliable historian of the society he lived in as it formed itself through the breakneck growth of the Industrial Revolution. To verify what he conveys about the workhouse or the Court of Chancery, you can go, if you like, to the factual sources, the memoirs and Blue Books. You will probably find that the facts were already there, dramatized and poetically evoked, in Dickens's art. Marxists are not prostituting literature when they use it as a source of *historical knowledge* (and 'history' includes yesterday and last year), they are paying it the attention it calls for.

So far the stress has been on the 'social' (although, as a Marxist, I can't accept the linguistic habit which suggests there is some break in the continuum including what is inside us and what is 'out there'). It is true that this has been a lop-sided tendency of Marxism so far. Engels admitted it in a letter of 1890 :

Marx and I are partly to blame for the fact that the younger people sometimes lay more stress on the economic side than is due to it. We had to emphasise the main principle *vis-à-vis* our adversaries, who denied it, and we had not always the time, the place or the opportunity to give their due to the other elements involved in the interaction.[17]

This pioneering type of fault presently fused with another difficulty, the problem of *popularization* – usually in the teeth of terrible material shortages – to give rise to the imbalance defined by Gramsci in 'Marxism and Modern Culture' :

Marxism was confronted with two tasks: to combat modern ideologies in their most refined form in order to create its own core of independent intellectuals; and to educate the masses of the people whose level of culture was medieval. Given the nature of the new

17. To C. Schmidt, 27 October 1890: Marx and Engels, *Selected Correspondence* (Moscow, n.d.), p. 500.

philosophy, the second and basic task absorbed all its strength, both quantitatively and qualitatively. For 'didactic' reasons the new philosophy developed in a cultural form only slightly higher than the popular average (which was very low) . . . Marxism has itself become 'prejudice' and 'superstition' . . .[18]

In many countries which are now trying to apply Marxism, these earlier difficulties no longer exist. We may hope that the *anti-psychological* legacy of Stalinism will presently wither away. It is surely significant that the recent thinker who seems to count most for radical people today as they work out their view of life is the psychologist and psychiatrist Wilhelm Reich, whose books and thoughts have survived – narrowly – the efforts of Establishments round the world, from the National Socialist Party in Germany in the Thirties to the American State Department in the Fifties, to burn and pulp them like so much garbage. It is a sorry fact that his own party, the German CP, did all it could to gag him in the early Thirties although he was doing more than anyone else in Europe at that time to take Marxism into new channels. His psycho-social explanations of Nazism in *The Mass Psychology of Fascism* and of the coercive anti-sexuality of the Soviet government in *The Sexual Revolution* are classic examples of the power of Marxism to evolve as it grapples with new social happenings. The centre of Reich's attention was the inner self of the person, whose unhealth or deformity and society's are inseparable. This is perfectly compatible with 'classic' Marxism: the second section of the *Communist Manifesto* ends by envisaging a society 'in which the free development of each is the condition for the free development of all'. A creative socialist of our own time, Arnold Wesker, was expressing a kindred point in a *Daily Worker* article ten years ago when he defended the preoccupation with loneliness in recent theatre (including the Theatre of the Absurd) on the ground that it is a duty of socialist writers to help each person cope with his sense, which is both natural and intensified by certain modern conditions, that ultimately he is on his own.

18. Antonio Gramsci, *The Modern Prince and Other Writings* (Lawrence & Wishart, 1957), pp. 85, 87.

21

Everything said so far about commitment, actual practice, and the functions and duties of writers must suggest that Marxists believe in the power of literature to help change the world. A rare case where this seems definitely to have happened is Upton Sinclair's novel *The Jungle* (1906), which raised an outcry about the Chicago meat-packing industry and helped bring about some pure-food legislation in the United States. The effects of literature cannot usually be ascertained in such tangible terms. If you expect so practical an outcome from it you are liable to be disheartened, as Sartre seems to be in recent remarks on the futility of literature, or even to repudiate some of your best work, as Auden did in dropping 'Spain' from the canon of his poetry while saying that 'not a poem of his had saved a single Jew from the gas chamber'. I can hardly believe that he expected his writing to do this even in 1937. Surely, if literature affects action or changes someone's life, it is not by handing out a recipe for the applying but rather by disturbing us emotionally, mentally, because it *finds* us (in Matthew Arnold's word), so that, after a series of such experiences and along with others that work in with it, we feel an urge to 'do something' or at least to ask ourselves the question (the great question put by Chernyshevsky, Lenin, and Silone): 'What is to be done?'[19] There is no one factor that leads to action. It is the whole of your personality that is involved when you act, and literature helps to mould or re-align your personality by widening and by sorting your experience.

The criterion for choosing the pieces that follow was that each should be highly interesting and cogent in its own right, written by an avowed Marxist, and able to hold the attention and deepen the insight of readers regardless of whether they have any prior interest in Marxism. The selection has not been angled to try and typify 'the Marxist view' of literature nor to 'cover' the periods and authors of which literature consists. If there seem to

19. The references are to Chernyshevsky's novel of that name (1863), Lenin's pamphlet of the same name (1902), and the closing pages of Silone's classic novel *Fontamara* (1930; trans. 1934).

be gaps in the coverage, it is because, in my view, Marxists have not done important work in those areas so far; and if some writers seem to be missing, I can only reply that I have my areas of ignorance and that, in any case, differences of opinion are bound to occur over so wide a field. Some readers will miss Walter Benjamin: I have found his work, in *Illuminations* and *Understanding Brecht*, disappointingly slight and bitty, and the biographical record suggests that the upheavals of his time (which finally killed him) stopped him from settling to the work he had in him. Others will miss Lucien Goldmann: I found the more anthologizable parts of his work, for example the introductory essay in *The Hidden God* called 'The Whole and the Parts', too obvious and over-general to be of much use. Others again may think it narrow in a sectarian way to have left out Sartre and Raymond Williams, yet neither man has unambiguously avowed Marxism and this along with their demurrals at some Marxist axioms persuaded me that theirs was a tradition rather different from the ones represented in this book.

The pieces chosen are certainly not offered as unanswerably true or exactly in accord with my own views. For example, Lukács's argument in Text 18 that Kafka's real subject was life under the capitalism of the later Austro-Hungarian Empire is rather speculative and debatable,[20] yet the general effort in that part of *The Meaning of Contemporary Realism* to feel through to a historical basis for modernism is so suggestive that it seemed worth including. Again, George Thomson's theory (in Text 2) that music originated in labour chants has probably to be replaced or very much changed to take account of the theory developed by the German musicologist Hornbostel that the first music was totemistic imitation of animal sounds through wooden masks so made that they altered the human voice as much as possible.[21] But such debates are rarely quite finished, least of all the debate between myself and other comrades (I would like to name above all Max and Victor Adereth) that has gone into the making of

20. I have debated it in my chapter in G. H. R. Parkinson (ed.), *Georg Lukács: The Man, His Work and His Ideas* (Weidenfeld & Nicolson, 1970), pp. 209–10.

21. I owe this point to the composer Alan Bush.

this book. The twenty-six pieces that follow seem to me to demand serious consideration for their power to help us understand literature anew, especially its part in the general effort of our species to 'make ourselves at home in the world'.[22]

DAVID CRAIG

Lancaster, September 1973

22. The phrase is Engels's, from his discussion of religion in *The Condition of the Working Class in England in 1844*.

Speech and Thought*

1. Man and the Animals

'The first premiss of all human history is of course the existence of living human individuals. Thus, the first fact to be established is the physical organization of these individuals and their consequent relation to the rest of nature.' So Marx and Engels [1] wrote in their first full statement of Marxism. 'Thought and consciousness,' wrote Engels many years later, 'are products of the human brain.' [2] The truth of these statements is so plain that it might almost seem to be obvious; yet philosophers have piled tome upon tome in order to deny, distort, or obscure it.

In one of his dialogues Plato puts into the mouth of Protagoras a fable about the origin of man. Living creatures were made by the gods out of earth and fire. After they had been created, Prometheus and his brother Epimetheus bestowed on them their appropriate faculties, giving them hoofs or wings or underground dwellings, so that each species might have the means of self-defence; wrapping them in furs and skins for shelter against the cold; ordaining that some should be the natural prey of others and at the same time ensuring their survival by making them exceptionally prolific. All this was done by Epimetheus under his brother's direction, but at the end of his task he found that he had inadvertently bestowed all the available faculties on the animals, leaving none for man. In order to save man from extinction Prometheus gave him fire.

This is a myth. The question, what a myth is, will arise later. No myth is true in the form in which it is presented, but many myths contain truth. In the present instance, man did not receive

---

* From *The First Philosophers* (1955).
1. *The German Ideology* (1938 ed.), p. 7.
2. *Anti-Dühring* (1934 ed.), p. 44.

fire as a gift from Prometheus or any other god. He discovered it for himself by his own wits. The Greeks themselves recognized this, for they interpreted the figure of Prometheus as a symbol of human intelligence. Moreover, they recognized that intelligence was inseparable from another faculty, also distinctively human, the faculty of speech. Man differs from the animals in possessing *lógos*, which is reason, understanding, and also speech. It is this that has made him the lord of creation, the master of nature, swifter than the eagle and stronger than the lion. How did he get it? The answer given in the myth is that he got it because he was deficient in those bodily developments, offensive and defensive, possessed by other animals. Lacking these, he was faced with extinction, and so forced to develop as he did. This, the kernel of the myth, is a scientific truth.

In general, the various forms of animal life have evolved over an immense period of time by natural selection, through which they have become differentiated by adapting themselves, with varying degrees of success, to different environments and to successive changes of environment. Not only do climatic conditions differ in different parts of the earth, but in all parts they have undergone a long series of more or less profound changes. No species of animal can ever be perfectly adapted to its environment, because the environment changes; and a species which has adapted itself exceptionally well to the conditions of a given period may later be incapacitated for that very reason, while other species, less highly specialized, increase and multiply.

Man is one of the primates, the highest order of animals, which includes, besides him, the apes and monkeys. Other mammalian orders are the carnivora, including the dog and cat, and the ungulates, including the horse and cattle. The earliest mammals lived in trees. From this ancestral stock the ungulates and carnivora branched off by adapting themselves in various ways to living on the ground. Losing the finer articulation of their limbs, they learnt to stand firmly and move rapidly on all fours, and they developed various offensive and defensive organs, such as horns, hoofs, spines, tusks, teeth for chewing grass or for tearing flesh, and long snouts for smelling at a distance. Meanwhile another group, ancestors of the primates, remained in the trees and so preserved on the whole the primitive mammalian structure. Their conditions of life required good eyesight rather than a keen scent, agility and cunning rather than speed and strength, and their diet of fruit and leaves made no great demands on the teeth. The snout dwindled, while the eyes developed full stereoscopic vision. The claws shrank into flattened nails imbedded in sensitive pads; the digits became more flexible, with the thumb and big toe moving in opposition to the others, so that they could grasp and handle small objects; and finally, in keeping with these developments, the brain became larger and more complex. Since the function of the brain is to control the other bodily organs in their interaction with the external world, it is the one organ whose growth is free from the risks of over-specialization. Thus, the primates evolved in such a way as to become more, not less, adaptable.

Man's nearest living relatives are the anthropoid apes. From these he differs in his upright gait and posture and his larger brain. In certain features he is actually more primitive than they. Their long arms, short legs, small hindquarters, and stub-like thumbs are comparatively recent developments due to their habit of swinging from bough to bough.[3] These features are absent from the fossil types discovered in Kenya, from which the large anthropoids of the present day are believed to be descended, and they are absent also from the Australopithecus of South Africa. This is a closely related group of fossil types, which have comparatively small brains and heavy jaws, like the apes, but resemble man not only in the absence of the above-mentioned characters, but also in their upright posture, indicating that they were accustomed to walking on open ground; and this is confirmed by geological evidence, which suggests that their habitat was not densely wooded. Whether they had tools of any sort is still an open question.[4]

Even more important are the remains of Pithecanthropus, especially those discovered near Peking. Here again the brain is comparatively small and the skull has many ape-like features, but the body is of human shape. It has been established that

3. W. E. Le Gros Clark, *History of the Primates* (1953), pp. 33-4.
4. ibid., pp. 63-5.

these primitive men dwelt in caves, hunted deer, made tools of quartz, and were well acquainted with the use of fire.[5]

It seems, therefore, that the first step in the differentiation of man from the animals was taken when, in response to some change of environment which has not yet been defined, some of the apes abandoned their arboreal habits and began living on the ground. This is what the first ancestors of the carnivora and ungulates had done millions of years before; but, when man followed their example, he did so at a far higher evolutionary level, and hence the consequences of the change were entirely different. He was already, as we have seen, in possession of a better brain than any other animal; and in learning to walk on the ground he committed himself to a way of life in which his only chance of survival lay in further development of his brain. At this point we are reminded of another myth :

> There wanted yet the master-work, the end
> Of all yet done – a creature who, not prone
> And brute as other creatures, but endued
> With sanctity of reason, might erect
> His stature, and upright with front serene
> Govern the rest, self-knowing . . .[6]

2. Hand and Brain

The animals are part of nature. The interaction that takes place between them and their environment is, on their part, entirely passive and adaptive. In this respect there is no difference in quality between them and the lower forms of organic life. It is true that they react on nature, as when the flora of some region is transformed by the depredations of grazing herds of cattle; but the animals themselves are no more conscious of what they are doing than the rivers which carve out valleys in their course. Beehives, birds' nests, and beavers' dams are no exception. Such activities are forms of adaptation biologically inherited.

Nevertheless, there are differences of degree between the

5. ibid., pp. 80–83; Pei Wen-chung, 'New Light on Peking Man', *China Reconstructs*, Vol. 3, No. 4 (Peking, 1954), p. 33.

6. Milton, *Paradise Lost*, Bk 7, l. 505.

lowest animals and the highest. They are more or less adaptable. The non-human primates, the highest of the animals, owe their superiority to the fact that, thanks to the relatively large size of the brain, rendered possible by lack of specialization in the other organs, they became, of all animals, the most adaptable. They were able to evolve in this way because they lived in trees, which provided them with food ready to hand and a refuge from their enemies.

When man's first ancestors abandoned these natural advantages, there opened a new stage in the evolution of organic life, in which the relation between animal and nature underwent a qualitative change. In respect of teeth, arms, legs, they were utterly defenceless; and, had they been dependent on them, they would certainly have perished. But they were endowed with a brain, which, though smaller than ours, was larger than those of the anthropoid apes; and moreover, thanks to their erect posture, they had a pair of hands, which, guided by the brain, enabled them to adapt nature consciously to their needs instead of merely adapting themselves to natural conditions. Unlike the animals, man is 'self-knowing', and accordingly his relation with nature is not merely passive, but active, a relation between subject and object. As Engels wrote:

In short, the animal merely *uses* external nature, and effects changes in it merely by his presence. Man changes it so as to make it serve his ends; he *masters* it.[7]

Having thrown the whole weight of his body on his feet, man lost the prehensility of his toes, but, with his hands free, his fingers became capable of the most delicate movements. This was a gradual process. The first effect of the new posture was to relieve the pressure on the jaws by transferring from them to the hands such tasks as tearing and crushing food and other objects. Accordingly, the jaws began to contract, thus leaving room for further expansion of the brain; and, as the brain expanded, so it became capable of subjecting the hands to an ever closer control.

It is to this parallel development of hand and brain that we must look for the physiological origin of man's two cardinal

7. Engels, *Dialectics of Nature* (1940 ed.), p. 291.

characteristics – the use of tools, and speech. The non-human primates can manipulate natural objects, and even use them as missiles; but only man has learnt how to fashion them into tools. Tool-making requires both manual dexterity and intelligence, or rather, as we shall see later, a new sort of intelligence, inseparable from speech. Now, the motor organs of the hand and the speech organs are controlled from two adjacent areas of the brain.[8] For this reason we commonly find what is called a 'spread' from one area to the other. Children learning to write roll the tongue, or even pronounce the words aloud, in the concentrated effort necessary to control the movements of the hand; and, conversely, they tend to gesticulate more freely than adults when they are talking. These are primitive characteristics. Among savages gesticulation is lavish and elaborate. In some languages it is so closely bound up with speech that words are hardly capable of conveying their full meaning without the appropriate gesture.[9] Indeed, we have only to watch ourselves talking to see that the 'spread' has never been completely eliminated. From this we may infer that the manual operations of early man were accompanied to a greater or lesser degree, in proportion to their difficulty, by a reflex action of the vocal organs. Later, in collective labour, these vocal movements were developed consciously as a means of directing the manual operations; and finally they emerged as an independent medium of communication, supplemented by reflex movements of the hands.

3. Consciousness

In the course of evolution the various forms of animal life have adapted themselves structurally and functionally to their changing natural environment; and the highest of them are marked off from the rest by the size and complexity of the brain, which enables them to react to their environment with greater versatility: in a word, they are more intelligent.

8. F. R. Winton and L. E. Bayliss, *Human Physiology* (Churchill, London, 1948), pp. 432–3.

9. George Thomson, *The Prehistoric Aegean* (1954 ed.), pp. 445–6; Ernst Cassirer, *Philosophie der symbolischen Formen* (Berlin, 1923–9), I, p. 130.

To equate intelligence with brain power might seem to be common sense; yet the point needs to be insisted on, or we shall find ourselves ascribing intelligence where it does not belong. Certain species of bees, wasps, ants, and termites live in highly organized communities, which behave with so much apparent intelligence that they have often been compared to human society. On examination, however, we find that their so-called intelligence does not rest on brain power at all, but on an elaborate division of purely physiological functions. In the higher animals these functions, apart from sexual reproduction, are combined in each individual of the species; in these insects they are distributed and coordinated in a system of behaviour which bears a superficial resemblance to social relations, but differs from them in the absence of the activity which we call production.[10] Again, the migration of birds reveals a sense of direction which, if it were a feat of intelligence, would be superhuman; but it is really nothing more than a crude and wasteful form of physiological adaptation to the environment.

It may be said that the working of the brain is also a physiological process. This is true, but of all such processes it is the most subtle and refined. It is an instrument which enables the members of a species to react to their environment as individuals. Confronted with a difficult situation, different individuals of the species deal with it with greater or less success by using their brains. This can be seen in the behaviour of the higher mammals. Placed in the same position, any two fowls will behave in exactly the same way; but some dogs are plainly more intelligent than others. Such individual differences are even more conspicuous among the apes. Thanks to their brains, the non-human primates stand, as it were, on the threshold of an active relation to their environment.

But they cannot speak. Speech is peculiar to man. The difference does not lie in the structure of the vocal organs. Most apes and monkeys have a wide phonetic range amply sufficient for a language. They chatter volubly, and their cries are undoubtedly expressive, but only of passive or subjective attitudes, such as hunger, misery, fear, anger, desire, satisfaction. They are incap-

10. W. M. Wheeler, *The Social Insects* (1928), p. 308.

able of using sounds as words to designate an object.[11] And, since they are unable to express ideas in articulate speech, we may infer that they are unable to form any definite ideas inside their heads. Incapable of speech, they are also incapable of thought.

As the controlling organ of the body, the brain is the mechanism which receives messages from the other organs, such as the eyes and ears and hands, and coordinates them in such a way as to initiate the appropriate reaction. Its power of coordination depends on the complexity of its structure. Now, if the human brain is compared with the ape's, the greatest expansion is seen to have taken place in the cortex, which controls the higher nervous system, including speech. It should, therefore, be possible to learn something about the physiological mechanism of speech and thought by investigating the behaviour of the higher animals. This study was taken up more than fifty years ago by Pavlov, who conducted a series of observations under controlled conditions. The results, formulated in his theory of conditioned reflexes, have proved the correctness of the Marxist theory of consciousness and more particularly of Lenin's theory of reflection.[12] In bourgeois circles, the importance of his work is acknowledged by physiologists, but our psychologists and philosophers still shut their eyes to it. The subject is too technical to be treated here, except in general terms sufficient to lay a foundation for the ensuing argument.

A reflex, as Pavlov used the term, is a reaction to a stimulus. When food is admitted into our mouths it becomes enveloped in saliva, which lubricates it and so makes it easier to swallow. By a series of systematic observations carried out on dogs he showed that the contact of food with the mouth starts a chain of movements passing along the nerve fibres to the brain and back to the mouth, where it sets in motion the salivary glands.

11. W. Köhler, *The Mentality of Apes* (1927 ed.), p. 305.

12. Lenin, *Materialism and Empirio-Criticism* (1908), Ch. 1. In 1894 Lenin wrote in the pamphlet *Who the Friends of the People Are*: 'You cannot argue about the soul without having explained the psychical processes in particular; here progress must consist in abandoning general theories and philosophical constructions about the nature of the soul, and in being able to put the study of the facts on a scientific footing.'

Reflexes are conditioned or unconditioned. The example just given is unconditioned. An unconditioned reflex is inborn. The conditions requisite for its development are present in every normal individual of the species from birth. A chick does not learn to peck; a child does not learn to suck. These are unconditioned reflexes. They correspond broadly to what psychologists call instincts, which are ill-defined groups of reflexes. The difference is that for the psychologist an instinct is a process whose real nature is unknown, whereas, when a neurologist speaks of a reflex, he refers to a process which can be recorded like any other material phenomenon. The term reflex is the better of the two, because, as Pavlov said, 'it has had from the beginning a purely scientific connotation'.[13]

The saliva can be made to flow without actual contact. As we know, the sight or smell of food is sometimes enough to 'make the mouth water'. A reflex of this kind is conditioned. There are certain sights or smells which we have learnt to associate with food. What do we mean by 'learnt'? One of Pavlov's dogs was fed at regular intervals, and, after it had become accustomed to the procedure, a bell was rung just before each feeding-time. It was then found that the salivation took place at the sound of the bell. The stimulus had been transferred to the sound in accordance with the conditions created by the experiment. In the next stage, the bell was sounded, but no food was given, and in time the salivation ceased. It had been inhibited: that is, a contrary stimulus had been set up, corresponding to the new conditions, and the reflex previously established was suppressed. Pavlov showed that such conditioned reflexes did not operate in the absence of a properly functioning cortex. Further research has confirmed his conclusions, and progress has been made in recording the nervous processes involved.

It has just been said that, in contrast to unconditioned reflexes, which are inborn, conditioned reflexes are acquired. The distinction is not absolute. It is valid for the life of the individual, but not for the evolution of the species. The habit of sucking, which characterizes the young of mammals, is inborn in the individual, and has been inborn in innumerable generations of

13. I. P. Pavlov, *Lectures on Conditioned Reflexes* (1927 ed.), p. 276.

individuals, but it was none the less acquired by the first mammalian species in emerging from the pre-mammalian stage. In the course of evolution conditioned reflexes have become unconditioned. It is the acquisition of such reflexes, together with their cumulative effects on the structure of the organism as a whole, under the influence of natural selection, that constitutes the evolutionary process. Lysenko, whose views are in full agreement with Pavlov's, has put the matter thus:

Changes in heredity, the acquisition of new characters and their augmentation and accumulation in successive generations are always determined by the conditions of life of the organism. Heredity changes and increases in complexity through the accumulation of new characters and properties acquired by organisms in successive generations.[14]

The earliest invertebrates made their appearance on earth more than 500 million years ago; the fishes, nearly 400 million; the reptiles, about 250 million; the mammals, less than 200 million; man, 1 million.[15] We see from these figures that the rate of accumulation of new characters increases as we ascend the evolutionary scale, at the head of which stands man, the lordly parvenu. His appearance is marked by an increase in the rate of evolution so rapid that it can only be explained as the result of a qualitative change. It was Pavlov's crowning achievement to show how this change can be analysed in terms of the actual functioning of the brain.

The aggregate of unconditioned and conditioned reflexes in a given animal constitutes an organic unity of the type which Pavlov called the primary signalling system. This is the system characteristic of the animals, more or less developed according to their evolutionary level. In man it became so complex as to create the basis for reflexes of an entirely new kind, which, operating together with the rest, constitute the secondary signalling system.

14. T. D. Lysenko, 'On the Situation in Biological Science', *Proceedings of the Lenin Academy of Agricultural Sciences of the USSR*, July–August 1948, p. 34.
15. Le Gros Clark, *History of the Primates*, pp. 13–16.

One of his pupils conducted the following experiment.[16] An electric current was applied to a child's finger. The child withdrew its finger. The procedure was repeated. After a time, before the current was applied, a bell was rung; and when this had been repeated, the child withdrew its finger at the sound of the bell. Next, instead of ringing the bell, the experimenter uttered the word 'bell'; and the child withdrew its finger instantly at the sound of the word. Then, instead of uttering the word, he showed it written on a card; and the child withdrew its finger at the sight of the word. Finally the child was made to withdraw its finger at the mere thought of a bell. These results have been confirmed by hundreds of experiments conducted in all parts of the world.[17]

This experiment began with an unconditioned reflex – the withdrawal of the finger in response to the stimulus of the electric charge; and it proceeded to a conditioned reflex – the withdrawal of the finger at the sound of the bell. These were passive responses, arising from external associations. But when the child reacted to the sound, sight, and thought of the *word*, the responses were of a different order. In these cases, through the use of the word, the child has generalized actively, 'electively'. The word is not merely another signal; it is 'a signal of signals'. As Pavlov wrote:

The word is for man just as much a real conditioned response as all the other responses which he has in common with the animals. At the same time this response is more complex than any other, and in that respect cannot be compared, qualitatively or quantitatively, with the conditioned responses of animals. Words, which are bound up with the whole of the mature person, with all the external and internal stimuli which affect the cerebral cortex, signify all these, take their place, and cause the organism to react in the same way as to the original stimuli themselves.[18]

16. W. Hollitscher, 'The Teachings of Pavlov': *Communist Review* (1953), p. 23.
17. A. McPherson, 'Recent Advances in Conditioned Reflexes': Society for Cultural Relations with the USSR: Science Section (1949), p. 2.
18. Hollitscher, 'Pavlov', p. 21. Pavlov's theory of conditioned reflexes was anticipated by Spinoza, *Ethics*, Part II, Prop. xviii: 'If the human body has once been affected at the same time by two or more bodies, when the

In this way man developed, on the basis of the primary signalling system, common to him and the animals, a secondary signalling system, which we call speech. This differs from the other in that its characteristic stimulus is not an objective natural phenomenon acting on the sense organs but an artificial sound invested socially with a subjective value.

'Speech,' said Marx, 'is the direct reality of thought.'[19] It is true that deaf mutes can be taught to think by means of sign language, which serves as a substitute for speech, but only if they have a normally developed cortex. Thought is an internal process which takes place on the basis of the cortical movements established normally by the development of speech, and it is communicated externally by means of speech, or else by writing, which is speech in visible form. Speech and thought both rest on a complex process of synthesis and analysis operating through an intricate network of cortical nerve connections. How complex the process is may be judged from the fact that, whereas the latest mechanical calculator contains 23,000 valves, the human cortex contains nearly 15,000,000,000 cells.[20] We are only beginning to understand how the system works, but its general character is becoming clear. As Plekhanov said, 'consciousness is an internal state of matter'.[21]

In the primary signalling system the stimuli are material phenomena which in particular conditions set up conditioned reflexes. Words, too, are physical stimuli, but of a different kind.

In the first place, as we have remarked, the material form of

---

mind afterwards remembers any one of them it will straightway remember the others . . . And hence we can clearly understand why the mind from the thought of one thing should immediately fall upon the thought of another which has no likeness to the first; e.g. from the thought of the word *pomum* a Roman immediately began to think about fruit, which has no likeness to that articulate sound nor anything in common, save that the body of that man was often affected by these two, that is, the man frequently heard the word *pomum* while looking at the fruit; and thus one passes from the thought of one thing to the thought of another according as his habit arranged the images of things in his body.'

19. J. V. Stalin, *Concerning Marxism in Linguistics* (1950 ed.), p. 29.
20. J. Z. Young, *Doubt and Certainty in Science* (Oxford, 1951), p. 37.
21. Quoted by Lenin in *Materialism and Empirio-Criticism*.

a word is determined, not naturally, but socially. The same is true of its content. The word *bell* signifies, besides the sound of a bell, the shape of a bell and the function of a bell, and not only of this or that bell, but of all bells; it signifies the sum-total of common properties abstracted from the concrete properties of particular bells. Of words, as 'signals of signals', Pavlov wrote:

They represent an abstraction of reality and admit of generalization, which is our compound, specifically human, higher form of thought, which first makes possible common human experience and then science itself, the instrument for perfecting human orientation in the environment and in itself.[22]

In the second place, as this observation of Pavlov's implies, the word serves to organize our sense impressions, not only in relation to previous impressions of the same kind, but in relation to the collective experience of society accumulated and transmitted through speech. The human consciousness is far more than a simple relation between the individual and his natural environment; it is, even in its simplest forms, a social product – the relation between society and its environment as reflected in the individual. It has been observed that, when a small child is drawing or painting an object, it tends to omit those parts of it which it cannot name; and similarly, persons born blind and subsequently cured find difficulty at first in distinguishing even the most obvious shapes and colours.[23] In both cases certain features are missed because they have not yet acquired for the observer a social value.

As Marx wrote: 'It is not the consciousness of men that determines their being, but, on the contrary, their social being determines their consciousness.'[24]

4. Cooperation

Another characteristic of the higher animals, connected with the expansion of the brain, is the lengthening of the period of im-

22. Hollitscher, 'Pavlov', p. 23.
23. Young, *Doubt and Certainty*, p. 91.
24. *Contribution to the Critique of Political Economy*, in Marx and Engels, *Selected Works*, I (Moscow, 1958 ed.), p. 363.

maturity.[25] Most of the ungulates grow very fast. A young hartbees can follow its mother a few hours after birth, a young elephant when it is two days old. The carnivora, on the other hand, are born helpless and remain dependent for several months. Among the primates, the gibbon remains clinging to its mother's body for seven months; the orang-utang spends the first month on its back, then slowly learns to walk, becomes independent at three years, and full-grown at ten or eleven. The human baby takes about a month to learn how to focus the eyes, and can seldom walk before the end of the first year.

Not only do the primates grow more slowly than the lower mammals, but of all their bodily organs the slowest in growth is the brain.[26] In man this disparity is even greater. His brain puts on weight after birth more rapidly and for a longer time than the rest of the body; and the increase is mainly due to the growth of a network of fibres connecting the cells of the cortex, especially the two areas which control, first, the hands and fingers, and, second, the tongue and lips. These areas are very large in proportion to the other motor areas, and much larger than the corresponding areas in the non-human primates. It is the communications established by these fibres in the cortex that constitute the signalling system, and it is during the period of immaturity, when they are being formed, that the most vital and enduring of the conditioned reflexes are established. Thus, the human organism has evolved in such a way as to enjoy exceptional opportunities for the accumulation and elaboration of conditioned reflexes. We have already remarked that, apart from his brain, early man was almost destitute of bodily defences, and to this we must now add the exceptionally prolonged period during which the adults were occupied in rearing helpless infants. It seems probable that this condition both necessitated and assisted the development of collective labour, involving tools and speech.

The formation of conditioned reflexes is, as we have seen, a description in physiological terms of what we call learning. A young animal learns by imitation. It clings to its mother, follows

25. R. Briffault, *The Mothers* (1927), I, pp. 96–110.
26. ibid., I, pp. 100–103.

its mother, copies its mother. It acquires by this means many habits which are commonly supposed to be hereditary. For example, a puppy brought up on milk does not salivate when meat is offered to it for the first time.[27] If puppies normally eat meat, it is because they have learnt to do so from their mothers. Among animals the capacity to learn is limited, for the most part, to the period of immaturity. When they have grown up, they are much slower to learn even simple things, and many things which they could have learnt earlier are beyond them.

To this rule there is one important exception. Monkeys are proverbially imitative. The extent to which the animals are capable of conscious imitation has been much discussed. After a careful investigation Chalmers Mitchell concluded:

Notwithstanding the innumerable anecdotes about the intelligence of other animals, and the great difficulty of describing or even thinking over one's personal experience in taming and training animals without slipping into language that implies conscious imitation, I do not think there is any real evidence of it outside the group of monkeys.[28]

The development of this faculty among the primates was no doubt assisted by their habit of living together in bands, composed usually of the females and their offspring.

Conscious imitation is the first step towards cooperation, as can be seen in children. After imitating the action of an adult for its own sake, as though it were an end in itself, the child comprehends in time the purpose of the action, modifies its imitation accordingly, and so learns to cooperate. It might be supposed, therefore, that, after the faculty of conscious imitation had been acquired, cooperation would follow almost as a matter of course. But this is not the case. Apes and monkeys are great mimics, but, except casually and ineffectually, they do not cooperate.[29]

From this we may infer that the development of cooperation was closely connected with those two faculties which we have already recognized as distinctively human – the use of tools, and

27. Young, *Doubt and Certainty*, p. 115.
28. P. C. Mitchell, *The Childhood of Animals* (1912), p. 253.
29. Köhler, *Mentality of Apes*, p. 169.

speech. Without cooperation there could have been no speech, which is its medium. What, then, was the function of co-operation? The answer is, quite simply, that many brains are better than one. Having advanced so far in developing the brain as to adopt the upright posture, our ape-like ancestors entered on a new stage, in which their only prospect of survival lay exclusively in the further development of that organ. They had to go forward or perish; and, as the archaeological record shows, many breeds of them did perish. They were driven by the struggle for existence to expand their brain power beyond its natural limits. They organized it collectively. This gave them a new weapon. Instead of merely changing themselves so as to conform to their environment, they began slowly but surely to change their environment according to their needs by *producing* their means of subsistence. Thus, the three characteristics we have distinguished – tools, speech, cooperation – are parts of a single process, the labour of production. This process is distinctively human, and its organizing unit is society.

5. *The Sentence*

'First came labour; after it, and then side by side with it, articulate speech.' So Engels.[30] In *The Prehistoric Aegean*[31] it was shown that the human sense of rhythm is derived through the labour song from the labour cry, which is in its simplest form a twofold signal coordinating the muscular efforts of a group of labourers. The question to be considered now is whether the elements of the labour process can be discovered in the structure of articulate speech.

It is characteristic of production, as of other forms of co-operation, that the actions of the individual labourers are integrated as parts of a whole, the labour process, which, accordingly, can only be carried out if the labourers maintain the appropriate relations with one another. This is true even where a particular process may be performed by a single labourer; for in such cases the requisite degree of skill has only been reached by division of

30. *Dialectics of Nature*, p. 284.
31. Ch. XIV, section 2; see below, pp. 59–60.

labour, which is a wider form of cooperation. Thus, in production, man's action on nature is not simple and direct but mediated through his relations with his fellow labourers. The principle has been explained by Marx:

> In production, men act not only on nature but on one another. They produce only by co-operating in a certain way and mutually exchanging their activities. In order to produce, they enter into definite connections and relations with one another, and only within these social connections and relations does their action on nature, does production, take place.[32]

These relations are maintained by means of the secondary signalling system, which as we have observed, differs from the primary signalling system precisely in this, that the interaction between the individual organism and the natural environment is mediated through social relations.

A further characteristic of production is the use of tools. To quote again from Marx:

> An instrument of labour is a thing, or a complex of things, which the labourer interposes between himself and the subject of his labour, and which serves as the conductor of his activity. He makes use of the mechanical, physical and chemical properties of some substances in order to make other substances subservient to his aims.[33]

A tool is a natural object which man has taken and shaped deliberately to be operated by his hands as an artificial hand for the more effective control of his environment:

> Thus, nature becomes one of the organs of his activity, one that he annexes to his own bodily organs, adding stature to himself in spite of the Bible.

In production, therefore, not only is the labour process as a whole a complex of social relations, mediated by speech, but each labourer's part in it, his individual action on nature, is also indirect, being mediated by instruments whose use and manufacture presuppose a body of knowledge such as could only have been accumulated by means of social relations.

32. 'Wage Labour and Capital', in *Selected Works*, I, p. 89.
33. *Capital*, I (1946 ed.), p. 158.

Accordingly, we may say that there exists between speech and production an intrinsic connection, pointing to their common origin in the moment at which man's relation to nature became social, and so ceased to be merely natural. Production made man human.

Marx identified three elements in the labour process: first, work, the personal activity of the labourer; secondly, the subject of labour, which consists in its simplest form of the earth and its natural products; and thirdly, the instruments of labour.[34] Let us consider what relation, if any, can be traced between this process and the structure of the simple sentence.

The languages of the world are so bewildering in their diversity that some philologists have despaired of finding the clue to the origin of speech. The explanation is that the essential constituents of speech were formed long before the oldest of our linguistic records. Man is about a million years old; the earliest written documents are less than six thousand years old, and the great majority of languages are known to us over only a fraction of that period. All the linguistic changes that we can trace have arisen from changes in social relations, not from the origin of society itself. For light on the origin of speech we must concentrate our attention on those basic features which all languages have in common.

The principles of grammar have been the subject of prolonged discussion among philologists, much of it vitiated by a tendency to invest the principles peculiar to a particular language, or group of languages, usually the philologist's own, with an absolute validity. In particular, many European scholars of the last century treated the structure of Greek and Latin as a universal ideal or norm, by which other languages were measured and judged to be immature or decadent. In recent years, however, thanks to the development of comparative linguistics, much has been done to clear the ground.

Of the eight parts of speech distinguished by the classical grammarians, only two are now regarded as fundamental, the noun and the verb.[35] Apart from them, there are only interjec-

34. *Capital*, I, p. 157.
35. J. Vendryes, *Language* (1925 ed.), pp. 115-24.

tions and morphemes, which, strictly speaking, are not words at all. Let us begin with these.

Interjections are characterized by the fact that they have no place in the morphological or syntactical structure of the language, and some of them stand outside the phonetic system as well. They are inarticulate cries. Those which are purely affective, such as cries of pain, are indistinguishable in principle from animal cries. They belong to the primary signalling system. They are the raw material from which speech was made.

Many of them have an active function, like 'Ssh!' used as a call for silence; and, just as 'Ssh!' may be replaced by a word, such as 'Quiet!' or 'Silence!', so it has been fashioned into a word, *hush*. Other words of similar origin are *boo, pop, tick, quack, tick-tock, quack-quack, pooh-pooh, ding-dong, see-saw,* etc.

As these examples show, many interjections are onomatopoeic, that is, imitated from natural sounds, and many are reduplicated. Further, they are specially common in baby talk and in the languages of primitive peoples. This is not an accident. Just as the growth of the embryo reveals a sequence corresponding to successive phases in the evolution of the species, so baby talk reproduces certain features of primitive speech.[36]

The early philologists were right in recognizing onomatopoeia as a prolific source of word material, but, for the most part, they failed to see that the medium through which this material was fashioned into speech was labour. Reduplication, which we have just noted as characteristic of interjections, is deeply imbedded in the structure of the Indo-European languages, and indeed of all languages,[37] and it has an elementary function. For the child, a disyllable composed of two identical or similar sounds is easier to pronounce and to remember than a monosyllable, because it is rhythmical; and, as we have seen, the human sense of rhythm can be traced back to the labour cry, which in its typical form is disyllabic. Standing as it does on the fringes of articulate speech,

36. Le Gros Clark, *History of the Primates*, p. 7; Engels, *Dialectics of Nature*, p. 291.
37. Cassirer, *Philosophie der Symbolischen Formen*, pp. 43-4.

the interjection has preserved two features which point back to the origin of speech.

Let us now turn to the morpheme. If the interjection has a purely concrete function, not grammatical at all, the morpheme is purely abstract, a mere grammatical instrument. In the expression 'John's father' the suffix -*s* is a morpheme, marking the syntactical relation. So, in 'father of John', is the element *of*. This *of* is conventionally treated as a word; yet it serves the same function as the suffix and is equally devoid of concrete meaning. They are both morphemes.

The English *I am*, Latin *sum*, Greek *eimi*, have a common ending -*m* or -*mi*. In English it is a meaningless vestige, but in Latin and Greek it was still active as a morpheme marking the first person singular of the verb; and it was originally identical with the pronoun *me*. It is probable that most morphemes originated in this way, that is, in the agglutination and absorption of independent words.[38] Such formations are common in all languages, and can still be followed in our own : *like a man*, *man-like*, *manly*. The process is very clear in Chinese, in which most of the morphemes, or 'empty words' as they are called, are also used as 'full words'. For example, the word *kei* serves, according to the context, either as a verb, the English *give*, or as a morpheme, the English *to* or *for*. The 'full word' is converted into a morpheme by being 'emptied' of its concrete meaning.

It must, however, be noted that morphemes, being derived from full words, belong of necessity to an advanced stage in the development of speech. Sentences can be formed without them, the syntactical relations being indicated by position : 'Sheep eat grass.' Different languages construct their sentences in different ways, but in all the organic unit is the sentence. It is the arrangement of words in sentences that constitutes articulate speech.

There are two types of simple sentence, nominal and verbal. The nominal sentence is composed, in English, of two nouns connected by the copula : 'The stream is full.' The verbal sentence consists of a noun and a verb or of two nouns connected by a verb : 'The stream rises,' 'The stream floods the field.' Even this distinction is partly arbitrary. A slight change, introducing

38. Vendryes, *Language*, p. 170.

the copula, will bring the last two examples into line with the first: 'The stream is rising,' 'The stream is flooding the field.' In other languages this variation is not possible. In some, however, such as Greek, the nominal sentence, in its simplest form, has no copula: 'Full the stream.' This shows that the copula is not indispensable; it is only a morpheme.[39] If we want to reduce these sentences to their essential elements, we must get rid of all the morphemes: 'Stream full,' 'Stream rise,' 'Stream flood field.' These expressions are quite intelligible in English, and they represent the normal form of the simple sentence in many languages, such as Chinese.

At this point, with the removal of the morphemes, even the distinction between noun and verb begins to disappear. In languages with few inflections or none, such as English and Chinese, nouns may be used as verbs and verbs as nouns: 'to stream past', 'paid in full', 'to get a rise', 'in flood', 'they field well'.[40] Even in languages so highly inflected as Latin and Greek, the vocative singular of the noun and the imperative singular of the verb are uninflected, that is, have no morphemes. Why did these two forms remain in this rudimentary condition? Their form is rudimentary because their function is rudimentary. They are, in origin, interjections, the one a call to attention, the other a call to action.

We are left with a sentence of two terms, connected either by simple juxtaposition or by a third term; and these two types of sentence correspond to the two types of musical form, binary and ternary [see below, Text 2, pp. 62–3]. The distinction between the verbal sentence and the nominal sentence is reduced to this, that in the former our attention is concentrated on the action or process, in the latter on the state or result. The idea of change is inherent in both, but in the second it is implied rather than expressed.

It is true, of course, that we habitually use simple sentences from which all idea of change is excluded: 'The earth is round.' But these are abstract notions, and therefore not primitive. There

39. ibid., p. 22.
40. In the Arunta language there is no distinction between noun and verb: A. Sommerfelt, *La Langue et la société* (Oslo, 1938), p. 109.

45

is ample evidence to show that historically the abstract has been preceded by the concrete, which, moreover, is constantly re-asserting itself. Even in our own language, such abstract ideas as rest, dependence, expectation, obedience, virtue, wicked, heavy, round, bear on the face of them the marks of their concrete origin : to rest is to resist movement, to depend is to hang on, to expect is to watch out for, to obey is to listen to, virtue is manliness, wicked is bewitched, heavy is hard to lift, round is wheel-like. In the Tasmanian languages there were no words for such simple qualities as round and hard, these ideas being conveyed by reference to concrete objects – 'like the moon', 'like a stone' – accompanied by appropriate gestures.[41]

We are now at the conclusion of our argument. In the first place, production is cooperation in the use of tools, which serve as conductors, transmitting the labourers' activity to the subject of their labour :

In the labour process, man's activity, with the help of the instruments of production, effects an alteration, designed from the commencement, in the material worked upon. The process disappears in the product; the latter is a use-value, nature's material adapted by a change of form to the wants of man. Labour has incorporated itself with its subject: the former is materialised, the latter is transformed.[42]

In the second place, just as the instruments of production are interposed between the labourer and the subject of his labour as conductors of his activity, so speech is interposed between him and his fellow labourers as a medium of communication effecting those mutual exchanges of activity without which production cannot take place. Consequently, it may be suggested that, as a reflection of the external world acquired through social production, and as the organic unit of articulate speech, the sentence, in its elementary forms of two terms, the one being incorporated in the other, or of three terms, the third mediating the action of the first upon the second, embodies in its structure the three elements of the labour process – the personal activity of the labourer, the subject of his labour, and its instruments.

41. R. B. Smyth, *The Aborigines of Victoria* (1878), II, p. 413; cf. J. Dawson, *The Australian Aborigine* (Melbourne, 1881), i–xlvii.
42. Marx, *Capital*, I, p. 160.

The Art of Poetry*

1. Speech and Magic

The subject of this chapter is the origin and nature of poetry, and it will be treated as a scientific problem. To those who are content to enjoy poetry for its own sake this approach may seem inappropriate or unattractive; but studied scientifically poetry is more, not less, enjoyable. To enjoy it fully we must understand what it is, and to understand what it is we must inquire how it has come into being and grown up.

Our object in raising this problem is to seek light on the prehistory of Greek poetry, but it can only be solved by collating material from as wide a field as we can. Accordingly, our examples will not be confined to Greek poetry. I shall draw freely on English poetry, which is useful because it is the most familiar, and on Irish poetry, which illustrates an earlier stage in the development of modern European poetry, and also on the songs and dances of primitive peoples.

One of the most striking differences between Greek and modern English poetry is that in ancient Greece poetry was wedded to music. There was no purely instrumental music, and much of the finest poetry was composed for musical accompaniment. In Irish too there is a close union between poetry and music, and here it is not just a matter of inference. It is still a living reality. I shall never forget the first time I heard some of the Irish poems I had long known in print sung by an accomplished peasant singer in the traditional style. It was an entirely new experience to me. I had never heard anything like it, in poetry or music.

Irish poetry has another characteristic. To most English people English poetry is a closed book. They neither know nor

* From *The Prehistoric Aegean* (1954 ed.).

care about it. And even the few that take an interest in it – there are not many even of these of whom it can be said that poetry enters largely or deeply into their daily lives. Among the Irish-speaking peasantry it is different. For them poetry has nothing to do with books at all. Most of them are, or were till recently, illiterate. It lives on their lips. Everybody knows it. Everybody loves it. It is constantly bubbling up in everyday conversation. And it is still creative. Whenever a notable event occurs, a song is composed to celebrate it. I say composed, but the word is hardly applicable. These songs are not composed in our sense of the word. They are improvised. In many Irish villages there was till recently a trained traditional poet, who had the gift of producing poems, often in elaborate verse forms – far more elaborate than ours in modern English – on the inspiration of the moment. In the village I knew best there was a famous poet, who died about forty years ago. His poems were nearly all improvised and occasional. I remember being told by his family how on the night he died he lay in bed with his head propped on his elbow pouring out a continuous stream of poetry.

This man was of course exceptionally gifted. He was a professional poet, who had learnt his craft under some poet of the preceding generation. But I soon found that no sharp line could be drawn between the professional poet and the rest of the community. It was only a matter of degree. To some extent they were all poets. Their conversation is always tending to burst into poetry. Just as extant poetry is more widely known than it is in our society, so the ordinary person is something of a poet. Let me give an example.

One evening, strolling through this village perched high up over the Atlantic, I came to the village well. There I met a friend of mine, an old peasant woman. She had just filled her buckets and stood looking out over the sea. Her husband was dead, and her seven sons had all been 'gathered away', as she expressed it, to Springfield, Massachusetts. A few days before a letter had arrived from one of them, urging her to follow them, so that she could end her days in comfort, and promising to send the passage money if only she would agree. All this she told me in detail, and described her life – the trudge to the turf stack in the hills, the loss of her hens, the dark, smoky cabin; then she spoke of America as she imagined it to be – an Eldorado where you could pick up the gold on the pavements – and the railway journey to Cork, and the transatlantic crossing, and her longing that her bones might rest in Irish soil. As she spoke, she grew excited, her language became more fluent, more highly coloured, rhythmical, melodious, and her body swayed in a dreamy, cradle-like accompaniment. Then she picked up her buckets with a laugh, wished me good night, and went home.

This unpremeditated outburst from an illiterate old woman with no artistic pretensions had all the characteristics of poetry. It was inspired. What do we mean when we speak of a poet as inspired?

To answer this question we must turn to primitive poetry as it still lives on the lips of savages at the present day. But we cannot understand the poetry of these peoples unless we know something about their society. Further, poetry is a special form of speech. If we are to study the origin of poetry, we must study the origin of speech. And this means the origin of man himself, because speech is one of his distinctive characteristics. We must go right back to the beginning.

We are still a long way from understanding fully how man came into existence, but there is one fundamental point on which scientists are agreed. Man is distinguished from the animals by two main characters – tools and speech.

The primates differ from the lower vertebrates in being able to stand upright and use their forefeet as hands. This development, involving a progressive refinement of the motor organs of the brain, arose from the special conditions of their environment. They were forest animals, and life in trees demands close co-ordination of sight and touch and delicate muscular control. And once developed the hands presented the brain with new problems, new possibilities. Thus, from the beginning there was an integral connection between hand and brain.[1]

Man differs from the anthropoid apes, the next highest of the primates, in being able to walk as well as stand. It has been

1. G. Elliot Smith, *Evolution of Man* (Oxford, 1924), pp. 17–46; G. Clark, *From Savagery to Civilization* (Central Books, 1946), pp. 1–6.

suggested that he learnt to walk as a result of deforestation, which forced him to the ground. Be that as it may, in him the division of function between hands and feet was completed. His toes lost their prehensility; his fingers attained a degree of dexterity unknown among the apes. Apes can manipulate sticks and stones, but only human hands can fashion them into tools.

This step was decisive. It opened up a new mode of life. Equipped with tools, man produced his food instead of merely appropriating it. He used his tools to control nature. And in struggling to control it he became conscious of it as something governed by its own laws, independent of his will. He learnt how things happen, and so how to make them happen. As he came to recognize the objective necessity of natural laws, he acquired the power of operating them for his own ends. He ceased to be their slaves and became their master.[2] On the other hand, in so far as he failed to recognize the objective necessity of natural laws, he treated the world around him as though it could be changed by a mere assertion of his will. This is the basis of magic.

It its initial stages the labour of production was collective. Many hands worked together. In these conditions the use of tools promoted a new mode of communication. The cries of animals are severely limited in scope. In man they became articulate. They were elaborated and systematized as a means of co-ordinating the actions of the group. And so in inventing tools man invented speech.[3] Again we see the connection between hand and brain. Speech merged as part of the actual technique of production. It assisted the muscular movements of the body by prefiguring the labour process; and being indispensable to that process it appeared subjectively as its cause – in other words, it was magical. In primitive thought the spoken word is universally invested with a magical power.[4]

As technique improved, the vocal accompaniment ceased to

2. Engels, *Dialectics of Nature* (1940 ed.), pp. 279–96.

3. B. Malinowski, 'The Problem of Meaning in Primitive Languages', in C. K. Ogden and I. A. Richards, *The Meaning of Meaning* (1927), p. 310; Malinowski, *Coral Gardens and their Magic* (1935), II, p. 235.

4. Briffault, *The Mothers* (1927), I, pp. 14–23; cf. Malinowski, *Coral Gardens*, II, p. 232.

be a physical necessity. The workers became capable of working individually. But the collective apparatus did not disappear. It survived in the form of a rehearsal, which they performed before beginning the real task – a dance in which they reproduced the collective movements previously inseparable from the task itself. This is the mimetic dance as still practised by savages today.

Meanwhile speech developed. Starting as a directive accompaniment to the use of tools, it became language as we understand it – a fully articulate, fully conscious mode of communication between individuals. In the mimetic dance, however, where it survived as the spoken part, it retained its magical function. And so we find in all languages two modes of speech – common speech, the normal, everyday means of communication between individuals, and poetical speech, a medium more intense, appropriate to collective acts of ritual, fantastic, rhythmical, magical.

If this account is correct, it means that the language of poetry is essentially more primitive than common speech, because it preserves in a higher degree the qualities of rhythm, melody and fantasy inherent in speech as such. Of course it is only a hypothesis, but it is supported by what we know of primitive languages. In them the differentiation between poetical speech and common speech is relatively incomplete.

The common speech of savages has a strongly marked rhythm and a lilting melodic accent. In some languages the accent is so musical, and so vital to the meaning, that when a song is composed the tune is largely dictated by the natural melody of the spoken words.[5] And further, the speaker is always liable to break into quasi-poetical flights of fantasy, like that Irish peasant woman. The first two of these characteristics cannot be illustrated here, but the last one can.

A Swiss missionary was once camping in Zululand close to the Umbosi railway. For the natives the Umbosi railway signifies the journey to Durban, Ladysmith, Johannesburg – the journey made year after year by the boys of the kraal, driven from home by the poll-tax to wear out their youth in the mines, and by the girls too, who suffer many of them an even worse fate in the

5. I. Schapera, *The Bantu-speaking Tribes of South Africa* (1937), pp. 282–3, 286, 401–2; R. S. Rattray, *Ashanti* (Oxford, 1923), pp. 245–7.

back-street brothels. One of the servants was in the camp clean-
ing the pots, when a train approached, and he was overheard
muttering these words:

> The one who roars in the distance,
> The one who crushes the young men and smashes them,
> The one who debauches our wives.
> They desert us, they go to the town to live bad lives,
> The ravisher! And we are left alone.[6]

Here is another artless soliloquy. It is only an old black servant
mumbling to himself, and yet it is poetry. The train catches his
attention. He forgets the pots. Then he forgets the train. It ceases
to be a train and becomes a symbol for the force that is destroying
all he holds most dear. The dumb resentment of his subconscious
being finds a voice. Then the roar of the train dies away, and he
returns to his pots.

Thus, the common speech of these savages is rhythmical,
melodic, fantastic to a degree which we associate only with
poetry. And if their common speech is poetical, their poetry is
magical. The only poetry they know is song, and their singing is
nearly always accompanied by some bodily action, designed to
effect some change in the external world – to impose illusion on
reality.

The Maoris have a potato dance. The young crop is liable to
be blasted by east winds, so the girls go into the fields and dance,
simulating with their bodies the rush of wind and rain and the
sprouting and blossoming of the crop; and as they dance they
sing, calling on the crop to follow their example.[7] They enact in
fantasy the fulfilment of the desired reality. That is magic, an
illusory technique supplementary to the real technique. But
though illusory it is not futile. The dance cannot have any direct
effect on the potatoes, but it can and does have an appreciable
effect on the girls themselves. Inspired by the dance in the belief
that it will save the crop, they proceed to the task of tending it
with greater confidence and so with greater energy than before.

6. H. A. Junod, *The Life of a South African Tribe* (1927 ed.), II, pp.
196–7.
7. K. Bücher, *Arbeit und Rhythmus* (Leipzig, 1919 ed.), pp. 409–10.

And so it does have an effect on the crop after all. It changes their subjective attitude to reality, and so indirectly it changes reality.

The Maoris are Polynesians. So are the islanders of the New Hebrides. These have a traditional song-form consisting of two alternating stanzas in different rhythms. The first is termed the 'leaf', the second the 'fruit'.[8] In Tikopia, another Polynesian island, there is a song-form of three stanzas. The term for the first means properly the 'base of the tree'; for the second, the 'intermediate words'; for the third, the 'bunch of fruit'.[9] The terminology shows that these song-forms have evolved out of mimetic dances like the dance of the Maori girls. Poetry has grown out of magic.

Let us carry the argument further. This is one of the incantations collected by Malinowski in the Trobriand Islands:

> It passes, it passes,
> The breaking pain in the thighbone passes,
> The ulceration of the skin passes,
> The big black evil of the abdomen passes,
> It passes, it passes.[10]

The subject of this poem is not what we should call poetical, but the form is. As Malinowski remarks, the language of these incantations is distinguished 'by its richness of phonetic, rhythmical, metaphorical and alliterative effects, by its weird cadences and repetitions'.[11] By asserting the truth of what you wish to be true, you make it come true; and the assertion is couched in language that echoes the ecstatic music of the mimetic dance, in which you enacted in fantasy the fulfilment of the desired reality.

Here is a song from the New Hebrides, addressed to two women who were said to live in a stone:

8. J. Layard, *The Stone Men of Malekula* (1942), p. 315.
9. R. Firth, *We, the Tikopia* (1936), p. 285.
10. Malinowski, *Coral Gardens*, II, pp. 236-7.
11. Malinowski, *Coral Gardens*, II, pp. 213, 222; cf. R. H. Codrington, *The Melanesians* (Oxford, 1891), p. 334; Layard, *Stone Men of Malekula*, p. 285; J. H. Driberg, *The Lango: a Nilotic Tribe of Uganda* (1923), p. 245.

> The song sings, the song cries,
> The song cries, Let her be my wife!
>   The woman who is there,
>   The two women, they two
>   Who are in the sacred stone,
>   Who sit inside, who live in the stone,
> The song cries, Let both come out![12]

Here instead of a statement confusing fact with fancy we have a command. But the command is not addressed directly to the persons concerned. It is conveyed through the compelling magic of the song. The song is externalized as a supernatural force.

The next example is a German foresters' song:

> Klinge du, klinge du, Waldung,
> Schalle du, schalle du, Halde,
> Halle wider, halle wider, Hainlein,
> Töne wider, grosser Laubwald,
> Wider meine gute Stimme,
> Wider meine goldne Kehle,
> Wider mein Lied, das lieblichste!
>
> Wo die Stimme zu verstehen ist,
> Werden bald die Büsche brechen,
> Schichten sich von selbst die Stämme,
> Stapeln sich von selbst die Scheiter,
> Fügen sich zum Hof die Klafter,
> Häufen sich im Hof die Schober
> Ohne junger Männer Zutun,
> Ohne die geschärften Aexte.[13]

The foresters call on the trees to fall to the ground, break up into logs, roll out of the forest and stack themselves in the yard in answer to their singing. They know very well that all this is not going to happen, but they like to fancy that it will, because it helps them in their work. Poetry has grown out of magic.

My next is from an Old Irish mantic poem:

Good tidings: sea fruitful, wave-washed strand, smiling woods; witchcraft flees, orchards blossom, cornfields ripen, bees swarm, a cheerful world, peace and plenty, happy summer.[14]

12. Layard, *Stone Men of Malekula*, p. 142.
13. Bücher, *Arbeit und Rhythmus*, p. 473.
14. K. Jackson, *Early Celtic Nature Poetry* (Cambridge, 1935), p. 170.

It was chanted by a prophet as an augury of a good season. The desired future is described as though already present.

And so by almost imperceptible degrees we reach a type of poetry with which we are all familiar:

> Sumer is icumen in,
> Lhude sing cuccu!
> Groweth sed and bloweth med
> And springth the wude nu –
> Sing cuccu!

The statement here is a statement of fact, but even here it is accompanied by a command. These seasonal songs, which have deep roots in the life of the European peasantry, were composed to celebrate the realization of communal desires. But the celebration still carries with it the echoes of an incantation. Poetry has grown out of magic.

'Bright star, would I were stedfast as thou art!' *Den lieb' ich, der Unmögliches begehrt.* Why do poets crave for the impossible? Because that is the essential function of poetry, which it has inherited from magic. In the wild transport of the mimetic dance the hungry, frightened savages express their weakness in the face of nature by a hysterical act of extreme mental and physical intensity, in which they lose consciousness of the external world, the world as it really is, and plunge into the subconscious, the inner world of fantasy, the world as they long for it to be. By a supreme effort of will they strive to impose illusion on reality. In this they fail, but the effort is not wasted. Thereby the psychical conflict between them and their environment is resolved. Equilibrium is restored. And so, when they return to reality, they are actually more fit to grapple with it than they were before.

Keats was twenty-four, on his way to Italy in a last effort to recover his health. He had seen Fanny Brawne for the last time. Down the Channel his ship was driven by bad weather into Lulworth Cove, where he went ashore – his last walk on English soil. He returned to the ship in the evening, and it was then he composed this sonnet and wrote it out in a copy of Shakespeare's poems. Four months later he died in Italy of consumption.

> Bright star, would I were stedfast as thou art!

That is a conscious wish – the wish of a dying man. But already it is charged with poetical memories:

> But I am constant as the northern star
> Of whose true-fix'd and resting quality
> There is no fellow in the firmament.

This sets his own fantasy in motion. He identifies himself with the star, and then with the moon, which, as we saw in an earlier chapter, has been worshipped from the earliest times as a symbol of everlasting life. And from the moon, still faintly conscious of the ship rocking gently in the swell running into the Cove, he looks down on the movement of the tides creeping to and fro across the contours of this planet:

> Not in lone splendour hung aloft the night,
>   And watching with eternal lids apart,
>   Like nature's patient, sleepless Eremite,
>   The moving waters at their priestlike task
>   Of pure ablution round earth's human shores,
>   Or gazing on the soft new-fallen mask
>   Of snow upon the mountains and the moors –

Then, having withdrawn thus into infinity, still responsive to the drowsy swaying of the ship, he descends, immortalized, to earth:

> No, yet still stedfast, still unchangeable,
>   Pillow'd upon my fair love's ripening breast,
> To feel for ever its soft fall and swell,
>   Awake for ever in a sweet unrest,
> Still, still to hear her tender-taken breath,
> And so live ever –

But it is impossible. There could be no love without death, and so his prayer for immortality turns into its opposite:

> And so live ever, or else swoon to death.

He wakes up. It is like a dream stirred by the rocking of the boat – a dream in which the white breast of his sleeping love is symbolized in the moving waters and the snow on the mountains. But through the dream he has thrown off what was oppressing him. He has recovered his peace of mind. The world is still objectively the same – the world

> Where youth grows pale, and spectre-thin, and dies –

but his subjective attitude to it has changed. And so for him it is not the same. That is the dialectics of poetry, as of magic.

2. *Rhythm and Labour*

Rhythm may be defined in its broadest sense as a series of sounds arranged in regular sequences of pitch and time. Its ultimate origin is of course physiological, but at that level it is something that man shares with the animals. We are not concerned here with the physical basis of rhythm, but with what man has made of it. I am going to argue that human rhythm originated from the use of tools.

We all know that, when children are learning to write, they often roll the tongue in time with the hand, or even pronounce the words aloud – not because there is anyone to listen but to help the fingers guide the pen. What actually happens is that there is a 'spread' from the motor organs of the hand to the adjacent area of the brain, which controls the tongue. As the child improves with practice, the spread is eliminated.

Similarly, when a man is doing heavy work, such as lifting a log or stone, he pauses before the height of each muscular effort for an intake of breath, which he holds by closing the glottis; then, as he relaxes after the effort, the glottis is forced open by the pent-up air, causing a vibration of the vocal chords – an inarticulate grunt.

Savages, like children, gesticulate when they talk. The function of gesticulation is not merely to help others to understand. They gesticulate just as much when talking to themselves. It is instinctive, like the other movements just described. The movement of the vocal organs overlaps, as it were, with the other muscular movements. For us, speech is primary, gesticulation secondary, but it does not follow that this was so with our earliest ancestors. The inherent interdependence of speech and gesture in primitive psychology is an attested fact.[15]

On the strength of these considerations it was argued half a century ago by Bücher that speech evolved from reflex actions of the vocal organs incidental to the muscular efforts involved in the use of tools.[16] As the hands became more finely articulated, so did the vocal organs, until the awakening consciousness seized on these reflex actions and elaborated them into a socially recognized system of communication.

In working out his hypothesis Bücher made an extensive study of labour songs. The function of these songs is to expedite the labour of production by imparting to it a rhythmical, hypnotic character. The spinner sings in the belief that her song will help the spinning-wheel to go round, and since it helps her to turn it, it does help the spinning-wheel to go round. This is very near to magic. In particular instances it can be shown that these songs originated as incantations.[17]

Labour songs abound at all stages of culture all over the world – except where they have been silenced by the hum of machinery. They spring spontaneously to the lips of savages whenever they are engaged in manual work, providing, especially among the women, an irrepressible continuo to the routine of daily life.[18] And they have a special importance for the origin of poetry, because in them, with certain significant modifications, the

15. L. H. Gray, *Foundations of Language* (New York, 1939), p. 155; R. B. Smyth, *The Aborigines of Victoria* (1878), II, p. 412; Rattray, *Ashanti*, p. 247. Many savage peoples have elaborate 'deaf-and-dumb' languages which they use to circumvent taboos of silence: B. Spencer, *The Arunta* (1927), pp. 433, 600–608; A. W. Howitt, *Native Tribes of South-East Australia* (1904), pp. 723–35; Smyth, *Aborigines*, II, pp. 4, 308.

16. Bücher, *Arbeit und Rhythmus*, p. 395. Cf. Cicero, *Tusculan Disputations*, 2.23.56, '*profundenda voce omne corpus intenditur venitque plaga vehementior*'. Since Bücher a somewhat similar hypothesis, worked out more fully on the physiological side but showing less insight into the other aspects of the problem, has been advanced by Paget.

17. H. M. Chadwick, *The Growth of Literature* (Cambridge, 1932–40), III, p. 783.

18. Bücher, *Arbeit und Rhythmus*, pp. 63–243; cf. Chadwick, III, pp. 583, 648, 783; Schapera, *Bantu-Speaking Tribes*, p. 285; G. S. Orde Brown, *The Vanishing Tribes of Kenya* (1925), p. 167; E. J. Krige, *Social System of the Zulus* (1936), p. 338; Junod, *South African Tribe*, II, pp. 207–9.

original relationship between language and labour has been preserved. This was perceived by Bücher, whose main conclusion, that the rhythm of human speech is derived from the labour process, is undoubtedly sound. He attempted to support it by identifying particular rhythms with particular processes.[19] This part of his argument was mistaken, and I have abandoned it. The clearest proof of his conclusion lies in an analysis of the principles of song structure, and for this I am responsible.

The work of rowing a boat involves a simple muscular operation, repeated at regular intervals without variation. The time is marked for the oarsmen by a repeated cry, which in its simplest form is disyllabic: *O—op!* The second syllable marks the moment of exertion; the first is a preparatory signal.

Hauling a boat is heavier work than rowing. The moments of exertion are more intense and so are spaced at longer intervals. This leaves room for expansion of the preparatory syllable, as in the Irish hauling cry: *Ho—li—ho—hup!* Sometimes the cry ends with a syllable of relaxation, as in the Russian hauling cry: *E—úch—nyem!* And in many cases it has become partly or wholly articulate: *Heave—o—ho! Haul away!*

These two elements, variable and constant, which constitute the simple, disyllabic labour cry, can be recognized in the arsis and thesis of prosody, which denote properly the raising and lowering of the hand or foot in the dance.[20] And so the ictus or beat of rhythm is rooted in the primitive labour process – the successive pulls at the log, or the strokes of the tool on stick or stone. It goes back to the very beginning of human life, to the moment when man becomes man. That is why it stirs us so deeply.

The following ditty was recorded by Junod, the Swiss missionary mentioned above, from a Thonga boy, who sang it extempore at the roadside while breaking stones for his European employers:

> Ba hi shani-sa, ehé!
> Ba ku hi hlupha, ehé!
> Ba nwa makhofi, ehé!
> Ba nga hi nyiki, ehé!

19. Bücher, *Arbeit und Rhythmus*, p. 407.
20. ibid., pp. 25, 402.

> They treat us badly, ehé!
> They are hard on us, ehé!
> They drink their coffee, ehé!
> And give us none, ehé![21]

The repeated *ehé!* is the labour cry, marking the hammer-strokes. This is the constant. Each time it is prefaced with a few articulate words improvised to express the worker's subjective attitude to his task. The song has grown out of the cry, just as the cry has grown out of the work itself.

> Heave on, cut deep!
> How leaps my fluttering heart
> At the gleam that flashes from thine eyes,
> O Puhi-huia!
> Heave on, cut deep![22]

That is a Maori rowing song. The boatswain uses the cries intermittently, and between them he improvises a compliment to the chief's daughter travelling in the boat. During the improvisation the time is marked by the rhythm of the words. The cry is still functional, but it is on the way to becoming a refrain.

My next example is the Volga Boat Song:

> E-uch-nyem! e-uch-nyem! Yeshcho razik! yeshcho da raz!
> Razovyom my beryozu, razovyom my kudryavu!
> Aida da, aida! razovyom! aida da, aida! kudryavu!
> E-uch-nyem! e-uch-nyem! Yeshcho razik! yeshcho da raz![23]

Here an improvised exhortation to the task is prefaced and concluded with the hauling cry, which contains it and defines it.

The labour song was developed by expanding the improvised variable between the moments of exertion. The workers ran over dreamily scraps of traditional lore or passed desultory comments on current events – whatever was uppermost in their minds. We possess an ancient Greek milling song – 'Grind, mill,

21. Junod, *South African Tribe*, II, p. 284.
22. J. C. Andersen, *Maori Life in Ao-tea* (Wellington, N.Z., 1907), p. 373.
23. Bücher, p. 235. There are many versions, because the middle of the stanza is still improvised.

grind' – interspersed with allusions to the tyrant Pittakos;[24] and there is another with the same refrain in modern Greek, improvised by a woman forced to grind barley for a police squad searching for her husband.[25] The constant, tied to the task in hand, tends to remain unchanged; the variable varies indefinitely from day to day. Many of the obscurities in our folk-songs probably arise from our ignorance of the circumstances that inspired the particular form in which they survive. Other examples of the same type will be found among the Negro spirituals, which inculcate Bible teaching at the same time as they soothe the labourers at their task,[26] and in the English sea-shanties, like this one from the end of the eighteenth century:

> Louis was the King of France afore the Revolution,
>   Away, haul away, boys, haul away together!
> Louis had his head cut off, which spoilt his constitution,
>   Away, haul away, boys, haul away together![27]

Meanwhile the art of song had broken away from the labour process. Songs were improvised at leisure, when the body was at rest. But they conformed to the traditional pattern. This is from Central Africa, where it was sung one evening round the camp fire by the porters attached to a white man's caravan:

> The wicked white man goes from the shore – puti, puti!
> We will follow the wicked white man – puti, puti!
> As long as he gives us food – puti, puti!
> We will cross the hills and streams – puti, puti!
> With this great merchant's caravan – puti, puti![28]

And so on, one after another round the fire, till they all fell asleep. The improvisations were rendered in turn by individuals, while the repeated *puti* (which is said to mean 'grub') was sung by all in unison. This gives us the familiar, universal structure of

24. *Carmina Popularia*, No. 23, in D. L. Page (ed.), *Poetae Melici Graeci* (Oxford, 1962), p. 460.
25. N. G. Polites, 'On the Breaking of Vessels as a Funeral Rite in Modern Greece': *Journal of the Anthropological Institute*, Vol. 23, p. 29.
26. Bücher, *Arbeit und Rhythmus*, pp. 263–73.
27. Bücher, p. 239.
28. R. F. Burton, *The Lake Regions of Central Africa* (1860), pp. 361–2.

solo and chorus.[29] The labour cry is now nothing but a refrain.

Severed from the labour process, the constant too is expanded. It becomes fully articulate, and is varied so as to diversify the rhythmical pattern, but without destroying the sense of regular repetition, on which the unity of the whole depends.

> Why does your brand sae drop wi' blude,
>> Edward, Edward?
> Why does your brand sae drop wi' blude,
>> And why sae sad gang ye, O?
> O, I hae kill'd my hawk sae gude,
>> Mither, mither.
> O, I hae kill'd my hawk sae gude,
>> And I had nae mair but he, O.

And so we reach the ballad quatrain, in which the refrain has disappeared as such, but is still embedded in the rhythmical structure, which rests on a continual alteration of thesis and antithesis, announcement and responsion:

> There liv'd a lass in yonder dale,
>> And down in yonder glen O,
> And Kathrine Jaffray was her name,
>> Well known by many men O.[30]

In the ballad measure, the stanza is a musical 'sentence', the couplet a musical 'phrase', the verse a musical 'figure'. There are two figures in each phrase, two phrases in each sentence. The members of each pair are complementary, similar yet different. This is what musicologists call binary form: AB.

This musical anatomy of the ballad measure is not merely an analogy. It is the only proper method of analysis. The prosody of our textbooks is as remote from the living history of poetry as conventional grammar is from the living history of language.

29. H. Basedow, *The Australian Aboriginal* (Adelaide, 1929), p. 376; R. H. Codrington, *The Melanesians* (Oxford, 1891), p. 335; Layard, *Stone Men of Malekula*, pp. 315, 611; Orde Brown, *Vanishing Tribes*, p. 167; P. A. Talbot, *The Peoples of Southern Nigeria* (1926), p. 808; Driberg, *The Lango*, pp. 127, 129, 245; Chadwick, *The Growth of Literature*, III, pp. 353, 355-6, 581; W. J. Entwhistle, *European Balladry* (Oxford, 1939), pp. 19, 35.

30. F. B. Gummere, *Old English Ballads* (Boston, 1894), pp. 169, 263.

The ballad was originally a dance, as it still is in some parts of Europe, like this one from the Faroe Islands:

The precentor sings the ballad and the rhythm is stamped with the feet. The dancers pay close attention to his words, which must come clearly, since the characteristics of the narrative are brought out by the mime. Hands are tightly clasped in the turmoil of battle; a jubilant leap expresses victory. All the dancers join in the chorus at the end of each stanza, but the stanza itself is sung only by one or two persons of special repute.[31]

The analytical principles of musicology belong to the study of rhythm as such, that is, to the common foundation of poetry, music and dancing.

Most of our folk-songs are in binary form, but some are more elaborate. In the Volga Boat Song, for instance, the stanza consists of an improvised passage preceded and followed by the verse containing the traditional hauling cry. In musical terminology, the first subject is followed by a second, and then the first is repeated or resumed. This is ternary form: ABA. In skilful hands A2 becomes something more than a repetition of A1: it is A1 in a new form conditioned by B. And so ternary form is more organic, more dialectical than binary. That is why it has been so highly cultivated in modern music.[32] Both forms were used by the Greeks. The melody of Greek music has perished; but since most of their poetry, apart from epic and dramatic dialogue, was composed for singing, its rhythm can be recovered from the words. I have discussed this in my *Greek Lyric Metre*, where the Greek strophe is shown to be an organism of exactly the same type as the modern stanza.

To resume. The three arts of dancing, music and poetry began as one. Their source was the rhythmical movement of human bodies engaged in collective labour. This movement had two components, corporal and oral. The first was the germ of dancing, the second of language. Starting from inarticulate cries marking the rhythm, language was differentiated into poetical speech and common speech. Discarded by the voice and repro-

31. Entwistle, *European Balladry*, p. 35.
32. S. Macpherson, *Forum in Music* (1915), pp. 61–90.

duced by percussion with the tools, the inarticulate cries became the nucleus of instrumental music.

The first step towards poetry properly so called was the elimination of the dance. This gives us song. In song, the poetry is the content of the music, the music is the form of the poetry. Then these two diverged. The form of poetry unaccompanied by music is its rhythmical structure, which it has inherited from song but simplified so as to develop its logical content. Poetry tells a story, which has an internal coherence of its own, independent of its rhythmical form. And so later there emerged out of narrative poetry the prose romance and novel, in which poetical speech has been replaced by common speech and the rhythmical integument has been shed – except that the story itself is cast in a balanced, harmonious form.

Meanwhile there has grown up a type of music which is purely instrumental. The symphony is the antithesis of the novel. If the novel is speech without rhythm, the symphony is rhythm without speech. The novel derives its unity from the story it tells, taken from perceptual life; the symphony draws its material entirely from fantasy. It has no internal coherence apart from its form. Hence all those structural principles which have disappeared in the novel have been elaborated in music to an unprecedented degree. They have come to be regarded as the special province of music. We speak of them habitually as 'musical form'. Yet they can still be traced in poetry – in the arrangement of its subject matter, I mean, not merely in its metrical structure – if we study it with a sense of music. Let us examine two examples, which, besides illustrating the point at issue, will show once again how poetry is related to magic.

Sappho's Ode to Aphrodite is the oldest European lyric; and it is a lyric in the full sense – a song sung to the lyre. Sappho was head of a religious society of young ladies, dedicated to Aphrodite. One of these girls, to whom she is passionately devoted, has failed to reciprocate her love.

> Aphrodite, goddess enthroned in splendour,
> Child of Zeus Almighty, immortal, artful,
> I beseech thee, break not my heart, O Queen, with sorrow and
>   anguish!

Rather come, O come as I often saw thee,
Quick to hear my voice from afar, descending
From thy Father's mansion to mount thy golden chariot
    drawn by

Wings of sparrows fluttering down from heaven
Through the cloudless blue; and a smile was shining,
Blessed Lady, on thy immortal lips, as standing beside me

Thou didst ask: 'Well, what is it now? what is that
Frantic heart's desire? Do you need my magic?
Whom then must I lure to your arms? Who is it, Sappho,
    that wrongs you?

On she flies, yet soon she shall follow after;
Gifts she spurns, yet soon she shall be the giver;
Love she will not, yet, if it be your will, then surely she shall
    love.'

So come now, and free me from grief and trouble!
Bring it all to pass as my heart desires it!
Answer, come, and stand at my side in arms, O Queen, to
    defend me!

Sappho begins by stating her prayer. She goes on to recall how similar prayers had previously been answered. And then the prayer is repeated. This is ternary form, treated dynamically by a conscious artist. The prayer opens negatively, tentatively; it ends positively, confidently, as though, thanks to what has come in between, a favourable answer were assured.

What does come in between? She reminds Aphrodite of the past: 'If ever before ... so now.' That was traditional. When you prayed to the gods, you reinforced your appeal by reminding them of previous occasions when you had received their help or earned their gratitude.[33] It was a ritual formula. And ritual takes us back to magic. In magic you enact in fantasy the fulfilment of the desired reality. And that is what Sappho does here, except that there is no action, no dancing, only a flight of the imagination. She beseeches the goddess to come; then envisages her as

33. For the full Classical sources of the above paragraphs, the reader is referred to George Thomson's book *The Prehistoric Aegean*, p. 453n.

coming – sees her, hears her; and then, inspired by this imaginative effort to greater confidence, she repeats her prayer. It is magic transmuted into art.

In English poetry, being less close to music, such survivals of musical form are only sporadic, and so the literary critics, who are not interested in origins, have failed to notice them. And yet they are all familiar with this sonnet of Shakespeare's, which is as perfect an example of ternary form as any to be found in Greek:

> When, in disgrace with fortune and men's eyes,
>   I all alone beweep my outcast state,
> And trouble deaf heaven with my bootless cries,
>   And look upon myself, and curse my fate,
> Wishing me like to one more rich in hope,
>   Featur'd like him, like him with friends possest,
> Desiring this man's art and that man's scope,
>   With what I most enjoy contented least,
> Yet in these thoughts myself almost despising,
>   Haply I think on thee, and then my state,
> Like to the lark at break of day arising
>   From sullen earth, sings hymns at heaven's gate;
> For thy sweet love rememb'red such wealth brings
> That then I scorn to change my state with kings.

Only one critic has explained the structure of this poem, and he was a musicologist.[34] In fourteen lines the poet revolutionizes his attitude to the world. At the beginning he is an outcast, crying to deaf heaven; at the end a king, singing hymns at heaven's gate. And the revolution turns on the word *state*. At first it connotes despair – the minor key; but when it returns its tone is modulated, and so we are carried forward to the ringing triumph of the close.

A revolution in our attitude to the world. Arguing from the content of poetry – incantations, seasonal songs, that sonnet of Keats – we concluded that this was the essential function of poetry. The same conclusion has now been reached from our study of its form.

34. W. H. Hadow, *A Comparison of Poetry and Music* (Cambridge, 1926), pp. 10–12; cf. G. Thomson, *Aeschylus, Oresteia* (Cambridge, 1938), I, p. 14.

3. Improvisation and Inspiration

With us poetry is seldom, if ever, improvised. It is a matter of pen and paper. There must be many contemporary poets whose melodies are literally unheard. They have been written down by the poet, printed, published, and read in silence by individual purchasers. Our poetry is a written art, more difficult than common speech, demanding a higher degree of conscious deliberation.

It is important to remember that this feature of modern poetry is purely modern. In antiquity and the middle ages, and even today among the peasantry, the poet is not divided from his audience by the barrier of literacy. His language is different from common speech, but it is a spoken language, common to him and his audience. He is more fluent in it than they are, but that is only because he is more practised. To some extent they are all poets.[35] Hence the anonymity of most popular poetry. Generated spontaneously out of daily life, it passes, always changing, from mouth to mouth, from parents to children, until the faculty of improvisation decays. Only then does it become fixed, and even then it preserves a distinctive quality, which we describe by saying that, however perfect it may be in point of craftsmanship, it lacks the quality of conscious art. That is just what it does lack – the stamp of an individual personality; and inevitably so, because it is the product not of an individual but of a community. The primitive poet is not conscious of his medium as something different from common speech; and in fact, as we have seen, the

35. Chadwick, *The Growth of Literature*, III, pp. 65, 178, 659; Layard, *Stone Men of Malekula*, pp. 314–15; Schapera, *Bantu-Speaking Tribes*, p. 285. On improvisation see Chadwick, I, p. 578, III, pp. 64–5, 152, 156, 174, 181–3, 187, 213, 412, 529, 583, 616, 647–8, 659–63, 868; A. Jeanroy, *Les Origines de la poesie lyrique* (Paris, 1904 ed.), p. 357; Schapera, p. 405; Driberg, *The Lango*, p. 129; H. P. Junod, *The Bantu Heritage* (Johannesburg, 1938), p. 85; Orde Brown, *Vanishing Tribes*, p. 167; J. Bonwick, *Daily Life and Origins of the Tasmanians* (1870), p. 29; W. Bateson, *Letters from the Steppe* (1928), pp. 165–6; Layard, pp. 314–15; Talbot, *Peoples of Southern Nigeria*, p. 808. Greek drama originated in improvisation: Aristotle, *Poetics*, 4.14; Thomson, *The Prehistoric Aegean*, p. 467.

difference is less. Hence he is able to improvise. As he succeeds in objectifying his medium, he loses the gift of improvisation, but at the same time acquires the power of adapting it to his own personality, and so becomes a conscious artist.

On the other hand, the effect of poetry is still, as it has always been, to withdraw the consciousness from the perceptual world into the world of fantasy. In comparing poetical speech with common speech we saw that it was more rhythmical, fantastic, hypnotic, magical. Now, in our conscious life, all the factors that make up our distinctive humanity – economic, social, cultural – are fully active : individual differences are at their maximum. Hence, just as the mental processes of conscious life reveal the greatest diversity between individuals, so common speech, which is their medium, is marked by the greatest freedom of individual expression. But when we fall asleep and dream, withdrawing from the perceptual world, our individuality becomes dormant, giving free play to those basic impulses and aspirations, common to all of us, which in conscious life are socially inhibited. Our dream world is less individualized, more uniform than waking life.

Poetry is a sort of dream world. Let me quote from Yeats :

The purpose of rhythm is to prolong the moment of contemplation, the moment when we are both asleep and awake, which is the one moment of creation, by hushing us with an alluring monotony, while it holds us waking by variety, to keep us in that state of perhaps real trance, in which the mind liberated from pressure of the will is unfolded in symbols.[36]

One might quarrel with the word 'liberated', but that does not matter now. The language of poetry, being rhythmical, is hypnotic. Not so hypnotic as to send us to sleep altogether. If we analyse any metre in any language, we find in it precisely that combination of monotony and variety, that interplay of like and unlike, which, as Yeats perceived, is needed to hold the mind suspended in a sort of trance, the special spell of poetry, caught between sleep and waking in the realm of fantasy.

And so, when we say a poet is inspired, we mean that he is

36. W. B. Yeats, *Essays* (1924), pp. 195–6.

more at home than other men in this subconscious world of fantasy. He is exceptionally prone to psychical dissociation. And through this process his inner conflicts – the contradictions in his relationship to society – are discharged, relieved. The discords of reality are resolved in fantasy. But, since this world into which he retires is common to him and his fellow men, the poetry in which he formulates his experience of it evokes a general response, expressing what his fellows feel but cannot express for themselves, and so draws them all into a closer communion of imaginative sympathy:

> Und wenn der Mensch in seiner Qual verstummt,
> Gab mir ein Gott, zu sagen, wie ich leide.[37]

His fellows are tormented by unsatisfied longings which they cannot explain, cannot express. He too is unable to explain them, but thanks to the gift of inspiration he can at least express them. And when he expresses them they recognize his longings as their own. As they listen to his poetry they go through the same experience as he did in composing it. They are transported into the same world of fantasy, where they find the same release.

In the mimetic dance, directed by their leader, the savage huntsmen pre-enact the successful prosecution of the hunt, striving by an effort of will to impose illusion on reality. In fact all they do is to express their weakness in the face of nature, but by expressing it they succeed to some extent in overcoming it. When the dance is over, they are actually better huntsmen than they were before. In poetry we see the same process at a higher level. Civilized man has succeeded to a large extent in mastering nature, but only by complicating his social relations. Primitive society was simple, classless, presenting a weak but united front against nature. Civilized society is more complex, richer, more powerful, but, as a necessary condition of all this, it has always hitherto been divided against itself. Hence the conflict between society and nature – the basis of magic – is overlaid by a conflict between the individual and society – the basis of poetry. The poet does for us what the dance-leader does for his fellow savages.

The primitive poet does not work alone. His audience col-

37. Goethe, *Tasso*, ll. 3432–3.

laborates. Without the stimulus of a listening crowd he cannot work at all. He does not write, he recites. He does not compose, he improvises. As the inspiration comes to him, it produces in his listeners an immediate response. They surrender to the illusion immediately and wholeheartedly. In these circumstances the making of poetry is a collective social act.

When we read a poem, or hear one being read, we may be deeply moved, but we are seldom completely 'carried away'. The reaction of a primitive audience is less sublimated. The whole company throw themselves into the world of make-believe: they forget themselves. I have seen this many times in the west of Ireland. Or listen to this account of a Russian minstrel reciting in a hut on one of the islands on Lake Onega:

Utka coughed. Everybody became silent. He threw his head back and glanced round with a smile. Seeing their impatient, eager looks, he at once began to sing. Slowly the face of the old singer changed. All its cunning disappeared. It became childlike, naïve. Something inspired appeared in it. The dovelike eyes opened wide and began to shine. Two little tears sparkled in them; a flush overspread the swarthiness of his cheeks; his nervous throat twitched. He grieved with Ilya of Murom as he sat paralysed for thirty years, gloried with him in his triumph over Solovey the robber. All present lived with the hero of the ballad too. At times a cry of wonder escaped from one of them, or another's laughter rang through the room. From another fell tears, which he brushed involuntarily from his lashes. They all sat without winking an eye while the singing lasted. Every note of this monotonous but wonderfully gentle tune they loved.[38]

These people were illiterate; yet poetry meant something for them which it certainly does not mean for English people today. We have produced Shakespeare and Keats, it is true, and they were greater than Utka. But Utka was popular, and that is more than can be said of Shakespeare or Keats in our country today.

Let us push on from Russia into Central Asia and see how, sixty years ago, the Turkmens listened to their poetry:

When I was in Etrek, one of these minstrels had a tent close to ours, and as he visited us of an evening, bringing his instrument with him,

38. Quoted in Chadwick, *The Growth of Literature*, II, p. 241.

there flocked around him the young men of the vicinity, whom he was constrained to entertain with his heroic lays. His singing consisted of forced guttural sounds, more like a rattle than a song, and accompanied at first with gentle touches on the strings. But as he became excited the strokes grew wilder. The hotter the battle, the fiercer the ardour of the singer and his youthful listeners; and really the scene assumed the appearance of a romance, as the young nomads, uttering deep groans, hurled their caps into the air and dashed their hands in a passion through their hair, as though they were furious to combat with themselves.[39]

These Turkmens, poet and listeners alike, were literally entranced.

Turning to ancient times, we may recall a Byzantine writer's visit to the court of Attila :

When dusk fell, torches were lit, and two Huns came out in front of Attila and chanted songs in honour of his victories and martial prowess. The banqueters fixed their eyes on the singers, some of them enraptured, others greatly excited as they recalled the fighting, while those whom old age had condemned to inactivity were reduced to tears.[40]

This is the context in which we must study the *Iliad* and *Odyssey*. How did the ancient Greeks react to Homer? We are apt to assume that they behaved just like ourselves, but this is a mistake. In one of Plato's dialogues a Homeric minstrel describes the effect of his recitals on himself and his audience :

When I am narrating something pitiful, my eyes fill with tears; when something terrible or strange, my hair stands on end and my heart throbs ... And whenever I glance down from the platform at the audience, I see them weeping, with a wild look in their eyes, lost in rapture at the words they hear.[41]

When such poets are questioned about the nature of their art, they all give the same answer. They all claim to be inspired in the literal sense of the word – filled with the breath of God :

39. A. Vaubéry, *Travels in Central Asia* (1864), p. 322.
40. Priscus, part 8, in *Fragmenta Historicorum Graecorum*, ed. C. Müller, IV (Paris, 1851), p. 92.
41. Plato, *Io*, No. 535.

A skilled minstrel of the Kirghiz can recite any theme he wants, any story that is desired, extempore, provided only that the course of events is clear to him. When I asked one of their most accomplished minstrels whether he could sing this or that song, he answered: 'I can sing any song whatever, for God has implanted this gift of song in my heart. He gives the words on my tongue without my having to seek them. I have learnt none of my songs. All springs from my inner self.'[42]

We remember Caedmon, inspired by an angel that visited him in dreams,[43] and Hesiod, who was taught by the Muses while tending his flocks on Helikon,[44] and Phemios and Demodokos, the minstrels of Ithaca and Phaecia: 'I am self-taught,' says Phemios, 'for God has implanted all manner of songs in my heart.'[45]

For primitive peoples everywhere the poet is a prophet, who being inspired or possessed by a god speaks with the god's voice. For the ancient Greeks the connection between prophecy (*mantiké*) and madness (*manía*) was apparent in the words themselves. To them the magical origin of poetry and prophecy was self-evident, because the symptoms of both reminded them of the orgiastic dances that survived in their cults of Dionysus:

All good epic poets are able to compose not by art but because they are divinely inspired or possessed. It is the same with lyric poets. When composing they are no more sane than the Korybantes when they dance. As soon as they engage in rhythm and concord, they become distracted and possessed, like the Bacchants who in their madness draw milk and honey from the streams.[46]

These religious devotees were subject under the influence of music to hysterical seizures, which were explained by saying that they were *éntheoi*, that they had 'a god in them'.[47] At this

42. V. V. Radlov, *Proben der Volkslitteratur der türkischen Stämme und der Dsungarischen Steppe* (St Petersburg, 1866–96), V, xvii.

43. Bede, *Ecclesiastical History*, IV, p. 24.

44. Hesiod, *Theogonia*, ll. 22–3.

45. *Odyssey*, XXII, ll. 347–8; VIII, ll. 479–81.

46. Plato, *Io*, No. 533.

47. G. Thomson, *Aeschylus and Athens* (1946 ed.), pp. 374, 377–8.

level we can no longer speak of art. We have reached its roots in magic.

Inspiration and possession are the same thing. In primitive society mental disorders involving loss of consciousness and convulsions are attributed to possession by a god or animal or ancestral spirit.[48] This idea emanates from the ecstasy of the mimetic dance, in which the performers lose consciousness of their identity as they impersonate the totemic animal – the symbol of the heightened common ego evoked by the dance.

Hysteria is a neurosis – a conflict between the individual and his environment which issues in a revolt of the subconscious. It is common among savages, not because they are more prone to such conflicts than we are, but because their consciousness is shallower, less resilient. It is treated by magic. When the first symptoms appear, a song is chanted over the patient. This facilitates the psychical dissociation, precipitates the fit.[49] Here, then, we have poetry at a purely magical level, or rather not poetry at all but the form of therapeutic magic out of which poetry evolved. For magic too is a revolt of the subconscious, cured in the same way. The difference is that in the mimetic dance this hysterical propensity is organized collectively – it is organized mass hysteria; whereas these individual seizures are sporadic. But the treatment is essentially the same. The patient is exorcized. The possessing spirit is evoked and expelled by the magic of the song. The exorcist who administers the treatment – the shaman, medicine-man or witch-doctor, as he is variously called – is usually himself a hysterical subject who has undergone a special training.[50] The relation of the exorcist to the patient is

48. Junod, *South African Tribe*, II, pp. 479–503; E. W. Smith and M. Dale, *The Ila-speaking Peoples of Northern Rhodesia* (1920), II, pp. 136–52; Schapera, *Bantu-speaking Tribes*, p. 253; J. Roscoe, *The Baganda* (1911), pp. 274, 318, 320–22; Codrington, *Melanesians*, p. 218; Chadwick, *Growth of Literature*, III, pp. 449, 454; M. A. Czaplicka, *Aboriginal Siberia* (Oxford, 1914), pp. 307–25; R. Karsten, *The Civilization of the South American Indians* (1926), p. 18; E. D. Earthy, *Valenge Women* (Oxford, 1933), p. 199; H. Webster, *Primitive Secret Societies* (New York, 1932 ed.), pp. 151, 175; Fallaize in J. Hastings, *Encyclopedia of Religion and Ethics* (Edinburgh, 1908–18), X, p. 122.

49. Fallaize, as cited; Smith and Dale, *Ila-speaking Peoples*, II, pp. 137–8.
50. Thomson, *Aeschylus and Athens*, p. 375.

thus similar to that of the leader to his followers in the mimetic dance.

Prophecy is a development of possession. One of the commonest conditions of exorcizing a patient is that the possessing spirit should be forced to reveal its name, and often, after revealing its name, it demands to be propitiated in return for releasing its victim. In this way the procedure becomes a means of proclaiming the will of the gods and so of predicting the future. The hysterical seizure assumes the form of a prophetic trance, in which the patient becomes a medium in the modern spiritualistic sense – a vehicle for the voice of a god or spirit.[51] In this condition he expresses fears, hopes, anticipations of the future, of which in his conscious life he is unaware. We still say that coming events cast their shadows before. They impinge on our subconscious, causing an indefinable unrest, and in the prophet, whose subconscious, being abnormally active, is constantly liable to erupt, they rise to the surface.

And finally the prophet becomes a poet. In primitive thought there is no clear line between prophecy and poetry. The minstrels described in the Homeric poems are credited with second sight, and their persons are sacrosanct.[52] The poet is the prophet at a higher level of sublimation. The physical intensity of the trance has been mitigated, but it is a trance all the same. His psyche is precipitated into fantasy, in which his subconscious struggles and aspirations find an outlet. And just as the prophet's predictions command general acceptance, so the poet's utterance stirs all hearts.

In this way we are able, with Caudwell, to define the essential nature of art:

Art changes the emotional content of man's consciousness so that he can react more subtly and deeply to the world. This penetration of inner reality, because it is achieved by men in association and has a complexity beyond the power of one man to achieve, also exposes the hearts of his fellow men and raises the whole communal feeling of society to a new plane of complexity. It makes possible new levels

51. ibid., p. 376.
52. Hesiod, *Theogonia*, ll. 31–2; *Odyssey*, VIII, ll. 479–81; XXII, ll. 345–6.

of conscious sympathy, understanding and affection between men, matching the new levels of material organisation achieved by economic production. Just as in the rhythmic introversion of the tribal dance each performer retired into his own heart, into the fountain of his instincts, to share with his fellows not a perceptual world but a world of instinct and blood-warm rhythm, so today the instinctive ego of art is the common man into which we retire to establish contact with our fellows.[53]

There is one other aspect of inspiration that may be mentioned here. Just as magic was for a long time the special province of women, so we find all over the world that inspiration in prophecy and poetry belongs especially to them.[54] The evidence is all the more striking because their part in primitive life is not nearly so well documented as the men's.[55] I am not going to enlarge on this subject now. The reader may study it in the pages of Bücher, Briffault, and Chadwick. It was more than a poet's fancy that prompted Homer and Hesiod to invoke the aid of female deities. The woman's part in the origin of music is commemorated in the word itself.

53. C. Caudwell, *Illusion and Reality* (1946 ed.), p. 155.
54. Bücher, *Arbeit und Rhythmus*, pp. 434–52; Briffault, *The Mothers*, II, pp. 514–71; Chadwick, *Growth of Literature*, III, pp. 186–8, 413, 663, 895–8. Of 1,202 songs collected in Estonia, Latvia and Lithuania, 678 are women's songs, 355 are men's, and 169 are indeterminate (Bücher, p. 450). The history of ballad poetry in southern and western Europe points to a similar conclusion: Entwistle, *European Balladry*, pp. 37–8.
55. Thomson, *Prehistoric Aegean*, p. 241, and cf. Bücher, pp. 435–6; Chadwick, III, xxii.

On the Social Basis of Style *

The laxity of aristocratic morals in the second half of the seventeenth century was, as we know, reflected on the English stage, where it assumed truly incredible proportions. Nearly all the comedies written in England between 1660 and 1690 were almost without exception what Eduard Engel calls pornographic.[1] In view of this, it might be said *a priori* that sooner or later, in accordance with the principle of antithesis, a type of dramatic works was bound to appear in England whose chief purpose would be to depict and extol the domestic virtues and middle-class purity of morals. And in due course this type really was produced by the intellectual representatives of the English bourgeoisie. But I shall have to speak of this type of dramatic works later, when I discuss the French '*tearful comedy*'.

As far as I know, the importance of the principle of antithesis in the history of aesthetic concepts was noted most keenly and defined most cleverly by Hippolyte Taine.[2]

In his witty and interesting *Voyage aux Pyrénées*, he describes a conversation he had with a 'table companion', Monsieur Paul, who, to all appearances, expresses the views of the author himself: 'You are going to Versailles,' Monsieur Paul says,

---

* From *Unaddressed Letters and Art and Social Life* (Moscow, 1957 ed.).

1. *Geschichte der englischen Literatur* (Leipzig, 1897 ed.).

2. Tarde had an excellent opportunity to investigate the *psychological* operation of this principle in his *L'opposition universelle, essai d'une Théorie des Contraires*, which appeared in 1897. But for some reason he did not utilize the opportunity, and confined himself to very few remarks on the subject. True, he says (p. 245) that this book is not a sociological essay. But he probably could not have coped with the subject even in an essay specifically devoted to sociology unless he had abandoned his idealist outlook.

and you cry out against seventeenth-century taste... But cease for a moment to judge from your needs and habits of today... We are right when we admire wild scenery, just as they were right when they were bored by such landscapes. Nothing was more ugly in the seventeenth century than real mountains.[3] They evoked in them many unpleasant ideas. People who had just emerged from an era of civil war and semi-barbarism were reminded by them of hunger, of long journeys on horseback in rain and snow, of inferior black bread mixed with chaff, of filthy, vermin-ridden hostleries. They were tired of barbarism, as we are tired of civilization... These ... mountains give us a respite from our sidewalks, our offices and our shops. Wild scenery pleases us only for this reason. And if it were not for this reason, it would be just as repulsive to us as it was to Madame de Maintenon.[4]

A wild landscape pleases us because of its contrast to the urban scenes of which we are tired. Urban scenes and formal gardens pleased seventeenth-century people because of their contrast to wild places. Here the operation of the 'principle of antithesis' is unquestionable. But just because it is unquestionable, it is a clear illustration of the way psychological laws may serve as a key to the history of ideology in general, and to the history of art in particular.

The principle of antithesis played the same role in the psychology of the people of the seventeenth century as it plays in the psychology of our contemporaries. Why, then, are our aesthetic tastes the opposite of those of seventeenth-century people?

Because we live in an entirely different situation. We are thus brought back to our familiar conclusion, namely, that it is because of man's nature that he may have aesthetic concepts, and that Darwin's *principle of antithesis* (Hegel's 'contradiction') plays an extremely important and hitherto insufficiently appreciated role in the mechanism of these concepts. But why a particular social man has particular tastes and not others, why certain objects and not others afford him pleasure, depends on the surrounding conditions. The example given by Taine also provides a good indication of the character of these conditions; it

3. Do not forget that this conversation took place in the Pyrenees.
4. *Voyage aux Pyrénées* (Paris, 1858 ed.), pp. 190–93.

shows that they are social conditions which, in their aggregate, are determined – I put it vaguely for the time being – by the development of human culture.[5]

Here I foresee an objection on your part. You will say: 'Let us grant that the example given by Taine does point to *social* conditions as the cause which brings the basic laws of our psychology into operation; let us grant that the examples you yourself gave point to the same thing. But is it not possible to cite examples that prove something quite different? Are we not familiar with examples which show that the laws of our psychology begin to operate under the influence *of surrounding nature?*'

Of course we are, I answer; and even the example given by Taine relates to our attitude towards impressions produced on us by *nature*. But the whole point is that the influence exerted upon us by these impressions changes as our attitude towards nature

5. Already, on the lowest rungs of civilization, the psychological principle of contradiction is brought into operation by division of labour between man and woman. V. I. Jochelson says that 'typical of the primitive system of the Yukagirs is the opposition between men and women, as two separate groups. This is likewise to be seen in their games, in which the men and the women constitute two hostile parties; in their language, certain sounds being pronounced by the women differently from the men; in the fact that descent by the maternal line is more important to the women, and by the paternal line to the men; and in that specialization of occupation which has created a special, independent sphere of activity for each sex.' (*On the Rivers Yasachnaya and Korkodon. Ancient Yukagir Life and Literature*, St Petersburg, 1898, p. 5.)

Mr Jochelson does not appear to observe that specialization in the occupations of the sexes was the cause of the contrast he notes, not the other way round.

That this contrast is reflected in the ornaments of the different sexes, is attested by many travellers. For example: 'Here, as everywhere, the stronger sex assiduously tries to distinguish itself from the other, and the male toilet is markedly different from the female' (Schweinfurth, *Au coeur de l'Afrique*, II, p. 281), 'and whereas the men devote considerable labour to their hairdress the coiffure of the women is quite simple and modest' (ibid., II, p. 5). For the influence *on dances* of division of labour between men and women, see von den Steinen, *Unter den Naturvölkern Zentral-Brasiliens* (Berlin, 1894), p. 298. It may be said with confidence that man's desire to distinguish himself from *woman* appears earlier than the desire to contrast himself to the *lower animals*. Surely, in this instance, the fundamental properties of human psychology find rather paradoxical expression.

changes, and the latter is determined by the development of our (that is, social) culture.

The example given by Taine refers to *landscape*. Mark, sir, that landscape has not by any means occupied a constant place in the history of painting. Michelangelo and his contemporaries ignored it. It began to flourish in Italy only at the very end of the Renaissance, at the moment of its decline.

Nor did it have an independent significance for the French artists of the seventeenth and even the eighteenth centuries. The situation changed abruptly in the nineteenth century, when landscape began to be valued for its own sake, and young artists – Flers, Cabat, Théodore Rousseau – sought in the lap of Nature, in the environs of Paris, in Fontainebleau and Melun, inspiration the possibility of which was not even suspected by artists of the time of Le Brun or Boucher. Why? Because social relations in France had changed, and this was followed by a change in the psychology of the French. Thus in different periods of social development man receives different impressions from Nature, because he looks at it from different viewpoints.

The operation of the general laws of man's psychical nature does not cease, of course, in any of these periods. But as in the various periods, owing to the different social relations, the material that enters man's head is not alike, it is not surprising that the end results are not alike either.

One more example. Some writers have expressed the thought that everything in a man's external appearance that resembles the features of lower animals seems to us ugly. This is true of civilized peoples, though even with them there are quite a number of exceptions: a 'leonine head' does not seem unsightly to any of us. But notwithstanding such exceptions, it may be affirmed that when man comes to realize that he is an incomparably higher being than any of his kindred in the animal world, he fears to resemble them and even endeavours *to underline, to exaggerate* the dissimilarity.[6]

6. 'In its idealization of Nature, sculpture was guided by the finger of Nature itself: it chiefly overvalued features which distinguish man from the animal. The erect stature led to greater slenderness and length of leg, the increasing steepness of the cranial angle in the animal kingdom, to the

But this assertion is not true of primitive peoples. We know that some of them knock out their upper incisors in order to resemble ruminating animals, others file them in order to resemble beasts of prey, others still plait their hair into the shape of horns, and so on almost *ad infinitum*.[7]

Often this tendency to imitate animals is connected with the religious beliefs of primitive peoples.[8]

But that does not alter things in the least.

For if primitive man had looked on lower animals with *our* eyes, they would probably have found no place in his religious ideas. He looks at them differently. Why differently? Because *he stands on a different level of culture*. Hence, if in one case man strives to resemble lower animals and in another to differentiate himself from them, this depends on the state of his culture, that is, again on those *social* conditions to which I have referred. Here, however, I can express myself more precisely: I would say that it depends on the degree of development of his productive forces, on his *mode of production*. And in order not to be accused of exaggeration and 'one-sidedness', I shall let von den Steinen, the learned German traveller I have already quoted, speak for me. 'We shall only then understand these people,' he says of the Brazilian Indians, 'when we regard them as the product of the

---

evolution of the Greek profile, while the general law, already formulated by Winkelmann, that when Nature breaks surface she does so not bluntly but decisively, led to a preference for sharply rimmed eye-sockets and nose bones, as well as for a sharply curved cut of the lips.' Lotze, *Geschichte der Aesthetik in Deutschland* (Munich, 1868), p. 568.

7. The missionary Heckewelder relates that he once went to see an Indian of his acquaintance and found him preparing for the dance, which, as we know, is of important social significance with primitive peoples. The Indian had painted his face in the following intricate manner: 'When we viewed him in profile on one side, his nose represented the beak of an eagle ... When we turned round to the other side, the same nose now resembled the snout of a pike ... He seemed much pleased with his execution, and having his looking-glass with him, he contemplated his work, seemingly with great pride and exultation.' Jean Heckewelder, *Histoire, moeurs et coutumes des nations indiennes, qui habitaient autrefois la Pensylvanie et les états voisins* (Paris, 1822), p. 324.

8. cf. J. G. Frazer, *Le Totémisme* (Paris, 1898), pp. 39 ff.; Schweinfurth, *Au cœur de l'Afrique*, I, p. 381.

hunter's way of life. An important part of their experience is associated with the animal world, and it was on the basis of this experience that their outlook was formed. Correspondingly, their art motifs, too, are borrowed with tedious uniformity from the animal world. It may be said that all their wonderfully rich art is rooted in their life as hunters.'[9]

Chernyshevsky once wrote, in his dissertation on *The Aesthetic Relation Between Art and Reality*: 'What pleases us in plants is their freshness of colour and luxuriant abundance of form, for they reveal a life full of strength and freshness. A withering plant is unpleasant; so is a plant which has little vital sap.' Chernyshevsky's dissertation is an extremely interesting and unique example of the application of the principles of Feuerbachian materialism to aesthetic problems.

But history was always a weak point with this materialism, and this is clearly to be seen in the lines I have just quoted: 'What pleases us in plants . . .'

Who is meant by '*us*'? The tastes of men vary extremely, as Chernyshevsky himself pointed out many a time in this same work. We know that primitive tribes – the Bushmen and Australians, for example – never adorn themselves with flowers although they live in countries where flowers abound. It is said that the Tasmanians were an exception in this respect, but it is no longer possible to verify the truth of this statement: the Tasmanians are extinct. At any rate, it is very well known that the *ornamental art* of primitive – more exactly, *hunting* – peoples borrows its motifs from the *animal* world, and that plants have no place in them. And modern science attributes this, too, to nothing but the state of the productive forces.

'The ornamental motifs borrowed by hunting tribes from nature,' says Ernst Grosse,

consist exclusively of animal and human forms. Thus they select those things which are to them of greatest practical interest. The primitive hunter leaves the gathering of plants, which is also of course necessary for him, to his womenfolk, as an inferior occupation, and shows no interest in it whatever. This explains why we do not find in his ornaments even a trace of the plant motifs which are so richly de-

9. *Unter den Naturvölkern Zentral-Brasiliens*, p. 201.

veloped in the decorative art of civilized peoples. Actually, the transition from animal to plant ornaments is symbolical of a great advance in the history of civilization – the transition from hunting to agriculture.[10]

So clearly does primitive art reflect the state of the productive forces that in doubtful cases the state of these forces is now judged from the art. The Bushmen, for example, draw human and animal forms very readily and comparatively well. Some grottoes in their places of habitation are regular picture galleries. But the Bushmen never draw plants. In the only known exception to this general rule – a depiction of a hunter hiding behind a bush – the clumsy way in which the *bush* is drawn shows most effectively how unusual this subject was for the primitive artist. Some ethnologists conclude from this that if the Bushmen did at one time stand at a somewhat higher level of culture than they do now – which, generally speaking, is not impossible – they were certainly never familiar with *agriculture*.[11]

If all this is true, we can now modify as follows the conclusion we drew from Darwin's records: it is the psychological nature of primitive man which determines that he may have aesthetic tastes and concepts generally, but it is the state of his productive forces, his hunter's mode of life, which leads to his acquiring particular aesthetic tastes and concepts, and not others. This conclusion, while throwing vivid light on the art of the hunting tribes, is at the same time another argument in favour of the materialist view of history.

With civilized peoples the technique of production exercises a direct influence on art far more rarely. This fact, which would seem to testify against the materialist view of history, actually provides brilliant confirmation of it. But we shall leave this point for another occasion.

I shall now pass to another psychological law which has played a big role in the history of art and which has likewise not received the attention it deserves.

Burton says of certain African Negroes he knew that they had

10. *Die Anfänge der Kunst*, p. 149.

11. See Raoul Allier's interesting introduction to Frédéric Christol's *Au sud de l'Afrique* (Paris, 1897).

a poorly developed sense of music, but were nevertheless astonishingly sensitive to rhythm: 'The fisherman will accompany his paddle, the porter his trudge, and the housewife her task of rubbing down grain, with song.'[12] Casalis says the same thing of the Kaffirs of the *Basuto* tribe, whom he studied very thoroughly. 'The women of this tribe wear metal rings on their arms which jangle at every movement. They not infrequently gather together to grind their corn on the handmills, and accompany the measured movement of the arms with a chant which strictly corresponds to the rhythmical sound emitted by the bracelets.'[13] The men of this tribe, Casalis says, when they are at work softening hides, 'at every movement utter a strange sound, whose significance I was unable to elucidate'. What this tribe likes particularly in music is rhythm, and they enjoy most those songs in which it is most strongly marked. In their dances the Basutos beat time with their hands and feet, intensifying the sound thus produced with the help of rattles hung around their bodies.[14] The Brazilian Indians likewise reveal a strong sense of *rhythm* in their music, but are very weak in *melody* and apparently have not the slightest idea of *harmony*.[15] The same must be said of the Australian aborigines.[16] In a word, rhythm has a colossal significance with all primitive peoples. Sensitivity to rhythm, and musical ability generally, seem to constitute one of the principal properties of the psycho-physiological nature of man. And not only of man. Darwin says that the ability at least to perceive, if not to enjoy, musical time and rhythm is apparently common to all animals and is undoubtedly connected with the physiological nature of their nervous system.[17] In view of this, it might be presumed that the appearance of this ability, which man shares with other animals, was not connected with the conditions of his

12. R. F. Burton, *The Lake Regions of Central Africa* (1860), p. 602.
13. E. Casalis, *Les Bassoutos* (Paris, 1863), p. 150.
14. *Les Bassoutos*, pp. 141, 157–8.
15. Von den Steinen, *Unter den Naturvölkern*, p. 326.
16. See E. J. Eyre, 'Manners and Customs of the Aborigines of Australia', in *Journal of Expeditions of Discovery into Central Australia and Overland* (1847), II, p. 229. Cf. also Grosse, *Anfänge der Kunst*, p. 271.
17. *The Descent of Man*, [Russ. trans.], II, p. 252.

social life in general, or with the state of his productive forces in particular. But although this presumption may appear very natural at a first glance, it will not stand the criticism of facts. Science has shown that such a connection does exist. And mark, sir, that science has done so in the person of a most distinguished *economist* – *Karl Bücher*.

As is apparent from the facts I have quoted, it is because of man's ability to perceive and enjoy rhythm that the primitive producer readily conforms in the course of his work to a definite time, and accompanies his bodily movements with measured sounds of the voice or the rhythmical clang of objects suspended from his person. But what determines the time observed by the primitive producer? Why do his bodily movements in the process of production conform to a particular measure, and not another? This depends on the *technological character of the given production process, on the technique of the given form of production*. With primitive tribes each kind of work has its own chant, whose tune is precisely adapted to the rhythm of the production movements characteristic of that kind of work.[18] With the development of the productive forces the importance of rhythmic activity in the production process diminishes, but even with civilized peoples – the German peasants, for example – each season of the year, according to Bücher, has its own work sounds, and each kind of work its own music.[19]

It should also be observed that, depending on how the work is done – whether by one producer or by a body – songs arise either for one singer or for a whole choir, and the latter kind are likewise divided into several categories. And in all cases, the rhythm of the song is strictly determined by the rhythm of the production process. Nor is this all. The technological character of the process has a decisive influence also on the *content* of the song accompanying the work. A study of the interconnection between work, music and poetry leads Bücher to the conclusion that 'in the early stage of their development work, music and poetry were intimately connected with one another, but the basic element in

18. K. Bücher, *Arbeit und Rhythmus* (Leipzig, 1896), pp. 21, 22, 23, 35, 50, 53, 54; Burton, loc. cit., p. 641.
19. Bücher, ibid., p. 29.

this trinity was work, the other elements having only a subordinate significance'.[20]

Since the sounds which accompany many production processes have a musical effect in themselves, and since, moreover, the chief thing in music for primitive peoples is *rhythm*, it is not difficult to understand how their simple musical productions were elaborated from the sounds resulting from the impact of the *instruments* of labour on their *object*. This was done by accentuating these sounds, by introducing a certain variety into their rhythm, and generally by adapting them to express human emotions.[21] But for this, it was first necessary to modify the *instruments of labour*, which in this way became transformed into *musical instruments*.

The first to undergo such transformation must have been instruments with which the producer simply *struck* the object of his labour. We know that the *drum* is extremely widespread among primitive peoples, and is still the only musical instrument of some of them. String instruments originally belonged to the same category, for the primitive musicians *play* upon them *by striking the strings*. Wind instruments hold a minor place with them: the most frequent to be met with is the flute, which is often played as an accompaniment to work performed in common, in order to lend it a rhythmic regularity.[22] I cannot discuss here in detail Bücher's views concerning the origin of poetry; it will be more convenient to do so in a subsequent letter. I shall only say briefly that Bücher is convinced that it originated from energetic rhythmical movements of the body, especially the movements which we call work, and that this is true not only of poetical *form*, but also of *content*.[23]

If Bücher's remarkable conclusions are correct, then we are entitled to say that man's nature (the physiological nature of his nervous system) gave him the ability to perceive musical rhythm and to enjoy it, while his technique of production determined the subsequent development of this ability.

The close connection between the state of the productive forces of the so-called primitive peoples and their art had been recog-

20. ibid., p. 78. 22. ibid., pp. 91–2.
21. ibid., p. 91. 23. ibid., p. 80.

nized by investigators long ago. But as the vast majority of them adhered to an idealist standpoint, they, as it were, recognized this connection despite themselves and explained it incorrectly. For example, the well-known historian of art, Wilhelm Lübke, says that the art productions of primitive peoples bear the stamp of *natural necessity*, whereas those of the civilized nations are infused with *intellectual consciousness*. This differentiation rests on nothing but idealist prejudice. In reality, the art of civilized peoples is no less under the sway of necessity than primitive art. The only difference is that with civilized peoples the *direct dependence* of art on technology and mode of production disappears. I know, of course, that this is a very big difference. But I also know that it is determined by nothing else than the development of the social productive forces, which leads to the division of social labour among different classes. Far from refuting the materialist view of the history of art, it provides convincing evidence in its favour.

I shall also point to the 'law of symmetry'. Its importance is great and unquestionable. In what is it rooted? Probably in the structure of man's own body, likewise the bodies of animals : only the bodies of cripples and deformed persons are unsymmetrical, and they must always have produced an unpleasant impression on physically normal people. Hence, the ability to enjoy symmetry was likewise imparted to us by nature. But we cannot say how far this ability would have developed if it had not been strengthened and fostered by the very mode of life of the primitive peoples. We know that primitive man was principally a hunter. One effect of this mode of life, as we have already learned, is that motifs borrowed from the animal world predominate in his ornamental art. And this induces the primitive artist – already from a very early age – to pay attentive heed to the law of symmetry.[24]

24. I say from a very early age, because with primitive peoples children's games likewise serve as a school for the training of artistic talent. According to the missionary Christol (*Au sud de l'Afrique*, p. 95 ff.), children of the Basuto tribe themselves fashion from clay toy oxen, horses, etc. Needless to say, these childish sculptures leave much to be desired, but civilized children cannot compare in this respect with the little African 'savages'. In

That man's sense of symmetry is trained precisely on these models, is to be seen from the fact that savages (and not only savages) have a preference in their ornamental art for *horizontal*, rather than *vertical* symmetry:[25] glance at the figure of the first man or animal you meet (not deformed, of course), and you will see that its symmetry is of the former, not the latter type. It should also be borne in mind that weapons and utensils often required a symmetrical shape because of their very character and purpose. Lastly, as Grosse quite rightly observes, if the Australian savage, when ornamenting his shield, is just as cognizant of the importance of symmetry as were the highly civilized builders of the Parthenon, then it is obvious that the sense of symmetry cannot in itself explain the history of art, and that we must say in this case as in all others: it is nature that imparts an ability to man, but the exercise and practical application of this ability is determined by the development of his culture.

Here again I deliberately employ a vague expression: *culture*. You will, on reading it, exclaim with heat: 'Nobody has ever denied this! All we say is that the development of culture is not determined solely by the development of the productive forces, by economics!'

Alas, I am only too well acquainted with this kind of objection. And I confess that I have never been able to understand why even intelligent people fail to observe the frightful logical blunder that lies at the bottom of it.

For indeed, you, sir, would like the development of culture to be determined by other 'factors' as well. I ask: is art one of them? You will, of course, say that it is, whereupon we get the following situation: the development of human culture is determined, among other things, by the development of art, and the development of art is determined by the development of human culture. And you will be constrained to say the same thing of all the other 'factors': economics, civil law, political institutions,

_____

primitive society the amusements of the children are intimately associated with the productive pursuits of the adults. This throws vivid light on the relation of '*play*' to social life.

25. See the designs of the Australian shields in Grosse, *Anfänge der Kunst*, p. 145.

morals, etc. What follows? Why, this: the development of human culture is determined by the operation of all the foregoing factors, and the development of all the foregoing factors is determined by the development of culture. This is the old logical fallacy for which our forebears had so strong a propensity: What does the earth rest on? Whales. And the whales? On water. The water? On the earth. And the earth? On whales – and so on in the same astonishing rotation.

You will agree that one must try, after all, to reason a little more seriously when investigating serious problems of social development.

I am deeply convinced that criticism (more exactly, scientific theorizing on aesthetics) can now advance only if it rests on the materialist conception of history. I also think that in its past development, too, criticism acquired a firmer basis, the nearer its exponents approached to the view of history I advocate. In illustration, I shall point to the *evolution of criticism* in France.

There its evolution was closely linked with the development of historical thought generally. As I have already said, the eighteenth-century enlighteners looked upon history from an idealist standpoint. They saw in the accumulation and dissemination of knowledge the chief and most profound cause of man's historical progress. But if the advance of science and the development of human thought generally really are the chief and paramount cause of historical progress, it is natural to ask: what determines the progress of thought itself? From the eighteenth-century point of view, *only one answer* was possible: the nature of man, the immanent laws governing the development of his thought. But if man's nature determines the *whole* development of his thought, then it is obvious that it also determines the *development of literature and art*. Hence, man's nature – and it alone – can, and should, furnish the key to the development of literature and art in the civilized world.

Because of the properties of human nature, men pass through various ages: childhood, youth, adulthood, etc. Literature and art, in their development, pass through the same ages.

'Was there ever a people that was not first a poet and then a thinker?' Grimm asks in his *Correspondence littéraire*, wishing to say thereby that the heyday of poetry coincides with the child-hood and youth of peoples, and the progress of philosophy with their adulthood. This eighteenth-century view was inherited by the nineteenth century. We even meet with it in the celebrated book of Madame de Stael, *De la littérature dans ses rapports avec les institutions sociales*, where at the same time there are quite substantial rudiments of an entirely different view. 'Examining the three different periods in Greek literature,' Madame de Stael says,

we observe a natural movement of the human mind. Homer is characteristic of the first period; in the age of Pericles, we remark the rapid progress of drama, eloquence and morals and the beginnings of philosophy; in the time of Alexander, a more profound study of the philosophical sciences became the principal occupation of men dis-tinguished in literature. Of course, a definite degree of development of the human mind is required to attain the highest peaks of poetry; nevertheless this branch of literature is bound to lose some of its brilliance when the progress of civilization and philosophy corrects some of the errors of the imagination.[26]

This means that if a nation has emerged from its youth, its poetry is bound in one degree or another to pass into decline.

Madame de Stael knew that the modern nations, despite all their intellectual achievement, had not produced a single poetical work that could be ranked above the *Iliad* or the *Odyssey*. This fact threatened to shake her confidence in the constant and pro-gressive perfection of mankind, and she was therefore unwilling to discard the theory of the various ages she had inherited from the eighteenth century, with the help of which the difficulty in question could be easily resolved.

For as we see, from the standpoint of this theory the decline of poetry was a symptom of the intellectual adulthood of the civilized nations of the modern world. But when Madame de Stael abandons these similes as she passes to the history of the literature of modern nations, she is able to look at it from an entirely different standpoint. Particularly interesting in this respect are the chapters in her book which discuss French litera-

26. *De la littérature, etc.* (Paris, 1800), p. 8.

ture. 'French gaiety and French taste have become proverbial in all the European countries,' she observes in one of these chapters.

This taste and this gaiety were commonly attributed to the national character; but what is the character of a nation, if not a result of the institutions and conditions which have influenced its prosperity, its interests and its customs? In these past ten years, even at the calmest moments of the revolution, the most piquant contrasts failed to prompt a single epigram or a single witticism. Many of the men who acquired great ascendancy over the destiny of France possessed neither elegance of expression, nor brilliance of mind; it may even be that their influence was in part due to their moroseness, taciturnity and cold ferocity.[27]

Whom these lines are hinting at, and how far the hint accords with the facts, is not of importance to us here. The only thing we have to note is that, in Madame de Stael's opinion, *national character is a product of historical conditions*. But what is national character, if not human nature as manifested in the spiritual characteristic of the *given nation*?

And if the nature of any nation is a *product* of its historical development, then obviously it could not have been the *prime mover* of this development. From which it follows that *literature*, being a reflection of a nation's spiritual character, is a product of the same historical conditions that begot the national character. Hence, it is not human nature, nor the character of the given nation, but its history and its social system that explain its literature. It is from this standpoint that Madame de Stael considers the literature of France. The chapter she devotes to seventeenth-century French literature is an extremely interesting attempt to explain its predominating character by the social and political relations prevailing in France at the time, and by the psychology of the French nobility, regarded from the standpoint of its attitude to the monarchical power.

Here we find some very subtle observations on the psychology of the ruling class of that period, and some very penetrating ideas concerning the future of French literature. 'With a new political order in France, no matter what form it may take,' Madame de Stael says, 'we shall see nothing like it [the litera-

27. *De la littérature*, II, pp. 1–2.

ture of the seventeenth century], and this will be a good proof that the so-called French wit and French elegance were only a direct and necessary product of the monarchical institutions and customs which had existed in France for many centuries.'[28] This new opinion, which holds that literature is a product of the social system, gradually became the predominant opinion in European criticism in the nineteenth century.

In France, it was reiterated by Guizot in his literary essays.[29]

28. ibid., p. 15.

29. Guizot's literary views throw such a vivid light on the development of historical thought in France that they deserve to be mentioned if only in passing. In his *Vies des poètes français du siècle Louis XIV* (Paris, 1813), Guizot says that the history of Greek literature reflects the natural development of the human mind, but that the problem is far more complicated in the case of modern peoples; here 'a host of secondary causes' must be taken into account. When, however, he passes to the history of French literature and begins to investigate these 'secondary' causes, we find that they are all *rooted in the social relations* of France, under whose influence the tastes and habits of her various social classes and strata were moulded. In his *Essai sur Shakespeare*, Guizot regards French tragedy as a reflection of class psychology. Generally, in his opinion, the history of drama is closely associated with the development of social relations. But the view that Greek literature was a product of the 'natural' development of the human mind had not been discarded by Guizot even at the time the *Essay on Shakespeare* appeared. On the contrary, this view found its counterpart in his views on *natural history*. In his *Essais sur l'histoire de France*, published in 1821, Guizot advances the idea that the political system of every country is determined by its *'civic life'*, and civic life – *at least in the case of the peoples of the modern world* – is related to landownership in the same way as effect is related to cause. This *'at least'* is highly noteworthy. It shows that, in contrast to the civic life of the peoples of the modern world, the civic life of the antique peoples was conceived by Guizot as a product of *'the natural development of the human mind'*, and not as a result of the history of landownership, or of economic relations generally. This is a complete analogy with the view that the development of Greek literature was exceptional. If it be added that at the time his *Essais sur l'histoire de France* appeared Guizot was ardently and resolutely advocating in his journalistic writings the thought that France had been 'created by class struggle', there cannot be the slightest doubt that the class struggle in modern society became apparent to modern historians before the class struggle in the states of antique times. It is interesting that the ancient historians, such as Thucydides and Polybius, regarded the struggle of classes in the society of their time as something natural and self-understood, just as our communal peasants regard the struggle between the large and small landholders in their village communities.

It was expressed by Sainte-Beuve who, it is true, accepted it only with reservations. Lastly, it was fully and brilliantly reflected in the works of Taine.

Taine was firmly of the persuasion that 'every change in the situation of people leads to a change in their mentality'.

But it is the mentality of any given society that explains its literature and its art, for 'the productions of the human spirit, like the productions of living nature, are only explicable in relation to their environment'. Hence, in order to understand the history of the art and literature of any country, one must study the changes that have taken place in the situation of its inhabitants. This is an undoubted truth. And one has only to read his *Philosophie de l'art, Histoire de la littérature anglaise*, or *Voyage en Italie* to find many a vivid and talented illustration of this truth. Nevertheless, like Madame de Stael and others of his predecessors, Taine adhered to the idealist view of history, and this prevented him from drawing from the unquestionable truth that he so vividly and so talentedly illustrated, all the benefit that might be drawn from it by an historian of literature and art.

Since the idealist regards the advance of the human mind as the ultimate cause of historical progress, it follows from what Taine says that the *mentality* of people is determined by *their situation*, and that *their situation* is determined by *their mentality*. This led to a number of contradictions and difficulties, which Taine, like the eighteenth-century philosophers, resolved by appealing to *human nature*, which with him took the form of *race*. What doors he sought to open with this key may be clearly seen from the following example. We know that the Renaissance began earlier in Italy than anywhere else, and that Italy, generally, was the first country to end the medieval way of life. What caused this *change in the situation* of the Italians? The properties of the Italian race, Taine replies.[30] I leave it to you to judge how satisfactory this explanation is, and shall pass

---

30. '*Comme en Italie la race est précoce et que la croûte germanique ne l'a recouverte qu'à demi, l'âge moderne s'y développe plus tôt qu'ailleurs.*' ['As the Italians are a precocious race, and as the Germanic crust only half covered it, the modern age developed there earlier than in other countries.'] *Voyage en Italie* (Paris, 1872), I, p. 273.

to another example. In the Sciara Palace in Rome, Taine sees a landscape by Poussin, and he observes in this connection that the Italians, because of the specific qualities of their race, have a peculiar notion of landscape; to them, it is nothing but a villa, only a villa of enlarged dimensions, whereas the German race love nature for its own sake. Yet in another place Taine himself says in reference to Poussin's landscapes: 'To really appreciate them, one must be a lover of (classical) tragedy, classical poetry, of ornate etiquette and signoral or monarchical grandeur. Such sentiments are infinitely remote from those of our contemporaries.'[31] But why are the sentiments of our contemporaries so unlike those of the people who loved ornate etiquette, classical tragedy and Alexandrine verse? Is it because the Frenchmen of the time of Le Roi Soleil, say, were people of a *different race* than the Frenchmen of the nineteenth century? A strange question! Did not Taine himself emphatically and insistently reiterate that the mentality of people changes when their situation changes? We have not forgotten this, and repeat after him: the situation of the people of our time is extremely unlike that of the people of the seventeenth century, and therefore their sentiments are very different from those of the contemporaries of Boileau and Racine. It remains to learn why the situation has changed, that is, why the *ancien régime* has given place to the present bourgeois order, and why the Bourse now rules in the country where Louis XIV could say almost without exaggeration: *'L'état c'est moi'*? And this question is answered quite satisfactorily by the economic history of the country.

You are aware, sir, that Taine's opinions were contested by writers of very different views. I do not know what you think of their contentions, but I would say that none of Taine's critics succeeded in shaking the thesis which is the sum and substance of nearly everything that is true in his theory of aesthetics, namely, that art is the product of man's mentality, and that man's mentality changes with his situation. And similarly, none of them detected the fundamental contradiction which rendered any fruitful development of Taine's views impossible; none of them observed that, according to his view of history, man's

31. ibid., I, p. 330.

mentality is determined by his situation, yet is itself the ultimate cause of that situation. Why did none of them observe this? Because their own views of history were permeated by this same contradiction. But what is this contradiction? Of what elements is it composed? It is composed of two elements, one of which is called the *idealist* and the other the *materialist* view of history. When Taine said that people's mentality changes with a change in their situation, he was a materialist; but when this self-same Taine said that the situation of people is determined by their mentality, he was repeating the idealist view of the eighteenth century. It need scarcely be added that it was not this latter view that suggested the best of his opinions on literature and art.

What conclusion is to be drawn from this? It is that the contradiction which ruled out any fruitful development of the intellect and profound views of the French art critics could have been avoided only by a man who said: The art of any people is determined by its mentality; its mentality is a product of its situation, and its situation is determined in the final analysis by the state of its productive forces and its relations of production. But a man who had said this would have been enunciating the materialist view of history.

4. CHRISTOPHER CAUDWELL

English Poets : (I)
The Period of
Primitive Accumulation*

I

Capitalism requires two conditions for its existence – masses of capital and 'free' – i.e. expropriated – wage labourers. Once the movement has started, capitalism generates its own conditions for further development. The sum of constant capital grows by accumulation and aggregates by amalgamation, and this amalgamation, by continually expropriating artisans and other petty bourgeoisie, produces the necessary supply of wage-labourers.

A period of primitive accumulation is therefore necessary before these conditions can be realized. This primitive accumulation must necessarily be violent and forcible, for the bourgeoisie, not yet a ruling class, has not yet created the political conditions for its own expansion : the State is not yet a bourgeois state.

In England during this period the bourgeoisie and that section of the nobility which had gone over to the bourgeoisie seized the Church lands and treasure and created a horde of dispossessed vagrants by the enclosure of common lands, the closing of the monasteries, the extension of sheep-farming, and the final extinction of the feudal lords with their retainers. The seizure of gold and silver from the New World also played an important part in providing a base for capitalism. This movement was possible because the monarchy, in its fight with the feudal nobility, leant on the bourgeois class and in turn rewarded them for their support. The Tudor monarchs were autocrats in alliance with the bourgeoisie and bourgeoisified nobility.

In this period of primitive accumulation the conditions for the growth of the bourgeois class are created lawlessly. To every bourgeois it seems as if his instincts – his 'freedom' – are intoler-

* From *Illusion and Reality* (1946 ed.).

ably restricted by laws, rights and restraints, and that beauty and life can only be obtained by the violent expansion of his desires.

Intemperate will, 'bloody, bold and resolute', without norm or measure, is the spirit of this era of primitive accumulation. The absolute-individual will overriding all other wills is therefore the principle of life for the Elizabethan age. Marlowe's Faust and Tamburlaine express this principle in its naïvest form.

This life-principle reaches its highest embodiment in the Renaissance 'prince'. In Italy and England – at this time leaders in primitive accumulation – life reaches its most poignant issue in the absolute will of the prince – this figure of the prince expresses most clearly the bourgeois illusion, just as in real society the prince is the necessary means of realizing the conditions for bourgeois expansion. To break the moulds of feudalism and wrench from them capital requires the strength and remorselessness of an absolute monarch. Any established bound or let to the divine right of his will would be wrong, for such bounds or lets, being established and traditional, could only be feudal, and would therefore hold back the development of the bourgeois class.

Elizabethan poetry in all its grandeur and insurgence is the voice of this princely will, the absolute bourgeois will whose very virtue consists in breaking all current conventions and realizing itself. That is why all Shakespeare's heroes are princely; why kingliness is the ideal type of human behaviour at this time.

Marlowe, Chapman, Greene, but above all Shakespeare, born of bourgeois parents, exactly express the cyclonic force of the princely bourgeois will in this era, in all its vigour and recklessness. Lear, Hamlet, Macbeth, Antony, Troilus, Othello, Romeo and Coriolanus, each in his different way knows no other obligation than to be the thing he is, to realize himself to the last drop, to give out in its purest and most exquisite form the aroma of self. The age of chivalry appears, not as it sees itself, but discredited and insulted, as the bourgeois class sees it, in the person of Hotspur, Falstaff and Armado, English cousins of Don Quixote.

Even the meanest creature, the empty, discredited, braggart Parolles, realizes this unbounded self-realization to be the law of his stage existence and in some sort the justification of his character:

> Simply to be the thing I am
> Shall make me live.

In this intemperate self-expression, by which they seem to expand and fill the whole world with their internal phantasmogoria, lies the significance of Shakespeare's heroes. That even death does not end their self-realization, that they are most essentially themselves in death – Lear, Hamlet, Cleopatra and Macbeth – in this too is both the secret of their death and the solution of the tragedy.

The depth with which Shakespeare moved in the bourgeois illusion, the greatness of his grasp of human society, is shown by the fact that he is ultimately a tragedian. This unfettered realization of human individualities involves for him the equally unfettered play of Necessity. The contradiction which is the driving force of capitalism finds its expression again and again in Shakespeare's tragedies. In *Macbeth* the hero's ambitions are realized – inverted. In *King Lear* the hero wrecks himself against the equally untempered expression of his daughters' will and also against Nature, whose necessity is expressed in a storm. The power of the storm symbolism lies in the fact that in a thunderstorm Nature seems to conduct herself, not as an inexorable machine but like a human being in an ungovernable passion. In *Othello* man's love realizes the best in himself, yet by the free play of that realization 'kills the thing it loves'. In *Hamlet* the problem of a conflict of unmeasured wills is posed in yet another form – here a man's will is divided against itself, and therefore even though nothing 'external' can oppose or reflect it, it can yet struggle with itself and be wrecked. This 'doubleness' of a single will is aptly symbolized by the poisoned swords and goblet in which the one aim is as it were two-faced, and secures opposite ends. In *Antony and Cleopatra* and in *Romeo and Juliet* the fulfilment of the simplest and most violent instinct is to love without bound or compass, and this love ensures the destruction of the lovers, who are justified simply because the love is unbounded, and scorns patriotism, family loyalty, reason and self-interest. Such deaths are tragic because at this era the intemperate realization of the self is heroic; it is the life principle of history. We feel that the death is necessary and is what must have been: 'Nothing is here for tears.'

At this stage the strength and vigour of the bourgeois depends on his cohesion as a class under monarchist leadership. In many parts already a self-armed, self-acting commune, the bourgeoisie in England has as its spearhead the court. The court is the seat of progress, and its public collective life is for the moment the source of bourgeois progress and fountain of primitive accumulation. The court itself is not bourgeois: it seeks the coercive imposition of its will like a feudal overlord, but it can only do so by allying itself with the bourgeoisie for whom the 'absoluteness' of the monarch, although feudal in its essence, is bourgeois in its outcome because it is creating the conditions for their development.

Hence we find Shakespeare, although expressing the bourgeois illusion, is an official of the court or of the bourgeois nobility. Players are the 'Queen's Servants'. He is not a producer for the bourgeois market or 'public'. He has a feudal *status*. Hence his art is not in its form individualistic: it is still collective. It breathes the collective life of the court. As player and as dramatist he lived with his audience in one simultaneous public world of emotion. That is why Elizabethan poetry is, in its greatest expression, drama – real, acted drama. It can still remain social and public and yet be an expression of the aspirations of the bourgeois class because of the alliance of the monarchy with the bourgeoisie.

Elizabethan poetry tells a story. The story always deals with men's individualities as realized in economic functions – it sees them from the outside as 'characters' or 'types'. It sites them in a real social world seen from the outside. But in the era of primitive accumulation, bourgeois economy has not differentiated to an extent where social 'types' or 'norms' have been stabilized. Bourgeois man believes himself to be establishing an economic role by simply realizing his character, like a splay foot. The instinctive and the economic seem to him naturally one: it is only the feudal roles which seem to him forced and 'artificial'. Hence the story and poetry are not yet antagonistic: they have not yet separated out.

In this era of primitive accumulation all is fluid and homogeneous. Bourgeois society has not created its elaborate division of labour, to which the elaborate complexity of culture corresponds. Today psychology, biology, logic, philosophy, law, poetry, history, economics, novel-writing, the essay, are all separate spheres of thought, each requiring specialization for their exploration and each using a specialized vocabulary. But men like Bacon and Galileo and da Vinci did not specialize, and their language reflects this lack of differentiation. Elizabethan tragedy speaks a language of great range and compass, from the colloquial to the sublime, from the technical to the narrative, because language itself is as yet undifferentiated.

Like all great language, this has been bought and paid for. Tyndale paid for it with his life; the English prose style as a simple and clear reality, fit for poetry, was written in the fear of death, by heretics for whom it was a religious but also a revolutionary activity demanding a bareness and simplicity which scorned all trifling ornament and convention. Nothing was asked of it but the truth.

These facts combined make it possible for Elizabethan poetry to be drama and story, collective and undifferentiated, and yet express with extraordinary power the vigour of the bourgeois illusion in the era of primitive accumulation.

Shakespeare could not have achieved the stature he did if he had not exposed, at the dawn of bourgeois development, the whole movement of the capitalist contradiction, from its tremendous achievement to its mean decline. His position, his feudal 'perspective', enabled him to comprehend in one era all the trends which in later eras were to separate out and so be beyond the compass of one treatment.[1] It was not enough to reveal the dewy freshness of bourgeois love in *Romeo and Juliet*, its fatal empire-shattering drowsiness in *Antony and Cleopatra*, or the pageant of individual human wills in conflict in *Macbeth*, *Hamlet*, *Lear* and *Othello*. It was necessary to taste the dregs, to anticipate the

1. In the same way More, from his feudal perspective, anticipates the development of capitalism into communism in his *Utopia*.

era of *surréalisme* and James Joyce and write *Timon of Athens*, to express the degradation caused by the whole movement of capitalism, which sweeps away all feudal loyalties in order to realize the human spirit, only to find this spirit the miserable prisoner of the cash-nexus – to express this not symbolically, but with burning precision :

> Gold! yellow, glittering, precious gold! No, gods,
> I am no idle votarist. Roots, you clear heavens!
> Thus much of this will make black white, foul fair,
> Wrong right, base noble, old young, coward valiant.
> Ha! you gods, why this? What this, you gods? Why this
> Will lug your priests and servants from your sides,
> Pluck stout men's pillows from below their heads:
> This yellow slave
> Will knit and break religions; bless the accurs'd;
> Make the hoar leprosy ador'd; place thieves,
> And give them title, knee, and approbation,
> With senators on the bench; this is it
> That makes the wappen'd widow wed again;
> She, whom the spital-house and ulcerous sores
> Would cast the gorge at, this embalms and spices
> To the April day again. Come, damned earth,
> Thou common whore of mankind, that putt'st odds
> Among the rout of nations, I will make thee
> Do thy right nature.

James Joyce's characters repeat the experience of Timon :

> all is oblique,
> There's nothing level in our cursed natures
> But direct villainy. Therefore, be abhorred
> All feasts, societies, and throngs of men!
> His semblance, yea *himself*, Timon disdains.
> Destruction, fang mankind!

From the life-thoughts of Elizabethan poetry to the death-thoughts of the age of imperialism is a tremendous period of development but all are comprehended and cloudily anticipated in Shakespeare's plays.

Before he died Shakespeare had cloudily and phantastically

attempted an *un*tragic solution, a solution without death. Away from the rottenness of bourgeois civilization, in the island of *The Tempest*, man attempts to live quietly and nobly, alone with his thoughts. Such an existence still retains an Elizabethan reality; there is an exploited class – Caliban, the bestial serf – and a 'free' spirit who serves only for a time – Ariel, apotheosis of the free wage-labourer. This heaven cannot endure. The actors return to the real world. The magic wand is broken. And yet, in its purity and childlike wisdom, there is a bewitching quality about *The Tempest* and its magic world, in which the forces of Nature are harnessed to men's service in a bizarre forecast of communism.

2

As primitive accumulation gradually generates a class of differentiated bourgeois producers, the will of the monarch, which in its absoluteness had been a creative force, now becomes anti-bourgeois and feudal. Once primitive accumulation has reached a certain point, what is urgently desired is not capital but a set of conditions in which the bourgeois can realize the development of his capital. This is the era of 'manufacture' – as opposed to factory development.

The absolute monarchy, by its free granting of monopolies and privileges, becomes as irksome as the old network of feudal loyalties. It is, after all, itself feudal. A cleavage appears between the monarchy and the class of artisans, merchants, farmers and shopkeepers.

The court supports the big landowner or noble who is already parasitic. He is allied with the court to exploit the bourgeoisie and the court rewards him with monopolies, privileges or special taxes which hamper the development of the overwhelming majority of the rising bourgeois class. Thus the absolute 'will' of the prince, now that the era of primitive accumulation is over, no longer expresses the life principle of the bourgeois class at this stage.

On the contrary the court appears as the source of evil. Its glittering corrupt life has a smell of decay; foulness and mean deeds are wrapped in silk. Bourgeois poetry changes into its opposite and by a unanimous movement puritanically draws its skirt's hem away from the dirt of the court life. The movement which at first was a reaction of the Reformed Church against the Catholic Church is now a reaction of the puritan against the Reformed Church.

The Church, expressing the absolute will of the monarch and the privileges of the nobility, is met by the individual 'conscience' of the puritan, which knows no law but the Spirit – his own will idealized. His thrift reflects the need, now that primitive accumulation is over, to amass the capital in which freedom and virtue inheres by 'saving' and not by gorgeous and extravagant robbery.

Donne expresses the transition, for he is torn by it. At first captivated by the sensuality and glittering brilliance of the court, the insolent treatment he receives produces a movement away from it, into repentance. The movement is not complete. In Donne's last years, filled as they are with death-thoughts and magniloquent hatred of life, the pride of the flesh still tears at his heart.

Poetry, drawing away from the collective life of the court, can only withdraw into the privacy of the bourgeois study, austerely furnished, shared only with a few chosen friends, surroundings so different from the sleeping and waking publicity of court life that it rapidly revolutionizes poetic technique. Crashaw, Herrick, Herbert, Vaughan – all the poetry of this era seems written by shy, proud men writing alone in their studies – appealing from court life to the country or to heaven. Language reflects the change. Lyrics no longer become something that a gentleman could sing to his lady; conceits are no longer something which could be tossed in courtly conversation. Poetry is no longer something to be roared out to a mixed audience. It smells of the library where it was produced. It is a learned man's poetry : student's poetry. Poetry is read, not declaimed : it is correspondingly subtle and intricate.

But Suckling and Lovelace write court poetry, the simple, open poetry of their class. They stand in antagonism to puritan poetry, and maintain the tradition of the Elizabethan court lyric.

The collective drama, born of the collective spirit of the court, necessarily perishes. Webster and Tourneur express the final corruption, the malignantly evil and Italianate death of the first stage of the bourgeois illusion.

3

The transitional period moves towards Revolution. The bourgeoisie revolt against the monarchy and the privileged nobility in the name of Parliament, liberty and the 'Spirit' which is nothing but the bourgeois will challenging the monarchical. This is the era of armed revolution, of civil war, and with it emerges England's first openly revolutionary poet, Milton.

Revolutionary in style, revolutionary in content. The bourgeois now enters a stage of the illusion where he sees himself as defiant and lonely, challenging the powers that be. With this therefore goes an artificial and *consciously* noble style, an isolated style, the first of its kind in English poetry.

Bourgeois revolutions, which are only accomplished by the help of the people as a whole, always reach a stage where it is felt that they have 'gone too far'. The bourgeois demand for unlimited freedom is all very well until the 'have-nots' too demand unlimited freedom, which can only be obtained at the expense of the 'haves'. Then a Cromwell or Robespierre steps in to hold back coercively the progress of the Revolution.

Such a bourgeois halt must always lead to a reaction, for the bourgeois class thus destroys its own mass basis. A Robespierre gives place to a Directory and then a Napoleon; at an earlier stage a Cromwell gives place to a Monk and a Charles II. The wheel does not come back full circle: there is a compromise.

To those who expressed directly the interests of the petty bourgeois, the puritans, this final stage of reaction is a betrayal of the Revolution. Therefore in *Paradise Lost* Milton sees himself as Satan overwhelmed and yet still courageous: damned and yet revolutionary. In *Paradise Regained* he has already rejected power in this world in exchange for power in the next. He scorns the temples and towers of this world; his reward is in the next because he will not compromise. Hence this poem is defeatist, and lacks the noble defiance of *Paradise Lost*. In *Samson Agonistes* Milton recovers his courage. He hopes for the day when he can pull the temple down on the luxury of his wanton oppressors and wipe out the Philistine court.

Did he consciously figure himself as Satan, Jesus and Samson? Only consciously perhaps as Samson. But when he came to tackle the bourgeois theme of how man, naturally good, is everywhere bad, and to give the familiar answer – because of Adam's fall from natural goodness as a result of temptation – he was led to consider the tempter, Satan, and *his* fall. And Satan's struggle being plainly a revolution, he filled it with his revolutionary experience and made the defeated revolutionary a puritan, and the reactionary God a Stuart. Thus emerged the towering figure of Satan, which by its unexpected disproportion shows that Milton's theme had 'run away with him'.

In *Paradise Regained* Milton tries to believe that to be defeated temporally is to win spiritually, to win 'in the long run'. But Milton was a real active revolutionary and in his heart he finds this spiritual satisfaction emptier than real defeat – as the unsatisfactoriness of the poem shows. In *Samson Agonistes* he tries to combine defeat and victory.

Of course the choice was already made in *Comus,* where the Lady spurns the luxury of the court and allies herself with the simple virtue of the people.

Note how already the bourgeois illusion is a little self-conscious. Milton is consciously noble – Shakespeare never. The Elizabethans are heroic: the puritans are not, and therefore have to see themselves as heroic, in an archaistic dress. The verse and vocabulary of the Latin secretary to the Provisional Government well expresses this second movement of the illusion. The theme of the poems cannot be at once noble and in any sense contemporary. Poetry is already isolating itself from the collective daily life, which makes it inevitable that the prose 'story' now begins to appear as an opposite pole.

Of course the transition from the court, like all other movements of the bourgeois illusion, is foreshadowed in Shakespeare. In *The Tempest* Prospero withdraws from corrupt court life to the peace of his island study, like a Herbert or a Milton. Shakespeare did the same in life when he retired to Stratford-on-Avon.

But he could not write there. His magic wand was a collective one. He had broken it with the breaking of his tie with the court, and the cloud-capp'd palaces of his fancy became empty air.

4

The atmosphere of a period of reaction such as that which followed the Puritan Revolution is of good-humoured cynicism. A betrayal of the extreme 'ideals' for which the battle had been fought appeared prudent to the majority. Unrestrained liberty and the free following of the spirit, excellent in theory, had in practice been proved to involve awkwardnesses for the very class of whom it was the battle-cry. The bourgeois illusion went through a new stage, that of the Restoration.

Such a movement is cynical, because it is the outcome of a betrayal of 'ideals' for earthly reasons. It is luxurious because the class with whom the bourgeoisie, having taught it a sharp lesson, now allies itself again – the landed nobility – has no need of thrift to acquire capital. It is collective because there is a return to the public court life and the play. It is not decadent in any real sense; true, the bourgeoisie has allied itself with the old doomed class – but it has breathed new life into that class. Webster, expressing the decadence of the court, gives way to Dryden, expressing its vigour. And Dryden, with his turn-coat life, so different from Milton's rectitude, exactly expresses the confused and rapid movement of the bourgeoisie of the time, from Cromwell to Charles II and from James II to William III. It is a real alliance – there is no question of the feudal regime returning. James II's fate in the 'Glorious Revolution' clearly shows the bourgeoisie have come to rule.

The poet must return from his study to court, but it is now a more citified, sensible, less romantic and picturesque court. The court itself has become almost burgher. The language shows the same passage from study to London street, from conscious heroism to business-like common sense. The sectarian bourgeois revolutionary, a little inclined to pose, becomes the sensible man-of-the-world. This is the transition from Milton to Dryden. The idealization of compromise between rival classes as 'order' and 'measure' – a familiar feature of reaction – leads to the conception of the Augustan age, which passes by an inevitable transition into eighteenth-century nationalism, once the Glorious Revolution has shown that the bourgeoisie are dominant in the alliance.

The self-valuation of this age as Augustan is in fact singularly fitting. Caesar played the role of Cromwell and Augustus of Charles II in a similar movement in Rome, where the knightly class at first rebelled against the senatorial and, when it became dangerous to go farther, entered on a road of compromise and reaction.

Elizabethan insurgence, the voice of primitive accumulation, thus turns into its opposite, Augustan propriety, the voice of manufacture. Individualism gives place to good taste. In its early stages bourgeoisdom requires the shattering of all feudal forms, and therefore its illusion is a realization of the instincts in freedom. In the course of this movement, first to acquire capital, and then to give capital free play, it leans first on the monarchy – Shakespeare – and then on the common people – Milton. But because it is the interests of a class it dare not go too far in its claims, for to advance the interests of all society is to deny its own. It must not only shatter the old forms which maintained the rule of the feudal class, but it must create the new forms which will ensure its own development as a ruling class. This is the epoch of manufacture and of agricultural capitalism. Land, not factories, is still the pivot.

This epoch is not only opposed to that of primitive accumulation, it is also opposed to that of free trade. Capital exists, but the proletariat is as yet barely in existence. The numerous artisans and peasants are not yet proletarianized by the very movement of capital : the State must therefore be invoked to assist the process. The expansive period of capitalism, in which the rapid expropriation of the artisan hurls thousands of free labourers onto the market, has not yet arrived. The vagrants of Elizabethan days have already been absorbed. The bourgeoisie finds that there is a shortage of wage labour which might lead to a rise in the price of labour-power over and above its value (i.e. its cost of reproduction in food and rent).

Hence there is need for a network of laws to keep down wages and prices and regulate labour in order to secure for the bourgeois class the conditions of its development. It now sees the 'impracticable idealism' of its revolutionary demands for liberty. Order, measure, law, good taste and other imposed forms are necessary. Tradition and convention are valuable. Now that the feudal state has perished, these restraints ensure the development of bourgeois economy. Free Trade seems the very opposite of desirable to the economists of this era. The bourgeois illusion betrays itself.

5

Therefore, during the eighteenth century, bourgeois poetry expresses the spirit of manufacture, of the petty manufacturing bourgeoisie, beneath the wings of the big landowning capitalists, giving birth to industrial capitalism. The shattering expansion of capitalism has not yet begun. Capitalism still approximates to those economies where 'conservation is the first condition of existence' and has not yet fully entered into the state where it 'cannot exist without constantly revolutionizing the means of production'. Capitalism is revolutionizing itself, but like a slowly growing plant that needs protection, instead of like an explosion in which the ignition of one part detonates the rest. By the compromise of the Glorious Revolution, the Whig landed aristocracy were prepared to give that protection because they had themselves become bourgeoisified.

It was only when the separation between agricultural and industrial capitalism took place as a result of the rise of the factory that the cleavage between the aristocracy and the bourgeoisie began to have a determining effect on the bourgeois illusion. While the woollen-mill was still no more than a hand-loom and an appendage of the agricultural capitalist's sheep-farm, there was no direct antagonism between the classes: it was only as the woollen-mill became a cotton-mill, depending for its raw material on outside sources, and when sheep-farming developed in Australia and provided wool for English mills, that there arose a direct antagonism between agricultural and industrial capitalism which expressed itself ultimately on the side of the industrialists as a demand for Free Trade and the repeal of the Corn Laws.

Pope's poetry, and its 'reason' – a reason moving within singularly simple and shallow categories but moving accurately – with its polished language and metre and curt antitheses, is a reflection of that stage of the bourgeois illusion where freedom for the bourgeoisie can only be 'limited' – man must be prudent in his demands, and yet there is no reason for despair, all goes well. Life is on the up-grade, but it is impossible to hurry. The imposition of outward forms on the heart is necessary and accepted. Hence the contrast between the elegant corset of the eighteenth-century heroic couplet and the natural luxuriance of Elizabethan blank verse, whose sprawl almost conceals the bony structure of the iambic rhythm inside it.

Pope perfectly expresses the ideals of the bourgeois class in alliance with a bourgeoisified aristocracy in the epoch of manufacture.

It is important to note that even now the poet himself has not been bourgeoisified as a producer. He does not produce as yet for the free market. Almost a court or aristocratic official in the time of Shakespeare, poet is a parson's or scholar's occupation in the ensuing period, and even as late as Pope he is dependent on being patronized, i.e. he has a 'patriarchal' or 'idyllic' relation to the class of whom he is the spokesman in the time of Pope.

Such an 'idyllic' relation means that the poet writes non-idyllic poetry. He still sees himself as a man playing a social role. This was the case with the primitive poet; it remains true of Pope. It imposes on him the obligation to speak the language of his paymasters or co-poets – in the primitive tribe these constitute the whole tribe, in Augustan society these are the men who form his patron's circle – the ruling class. Johnson – dependent on subscribers – bridges the gap between the poet by status and the poet as producer. Thus poetry remains in this sense collective. It talks a more or less current language, and the poet writes for an audience he has directly in mind, to whom perhaps he will presently read his poems and so be able to watch their effect. Poetry is still for him not so much a poem – a self-subsisting work of art – as a movement from writer to reader, like the movement of emotion in a publicly acted drama or the movement of a Muse in the minds of men. Hence he realizes himself as playing a social role: inspirer of humanity or redresser of the follies of mankind. He has not yet become a self-conscious artist.

5. G. M. MATTHEWS

Othello and the Dignity of Man*

The most important feature of *Othello* is the colour of the hero's skin. This is superficially obvious enough, but most critics have avoided treating Othello's colour as the essence of the play for two good reasons: first, that it is unhistorical to suppose that 'colour', as we understand the term, had much meaning for the Elizabethans or early Jacobeans; and second, that to interpret *Othello* as a play about race would be like saying that *Henry IV* is a play about fatness. The real preoccupations of the tragedy, critics say, are incomparably wider and deeper than the nationality assigned to the characters, and sooner or later Dryden is quoted on the subject of Shakespeare's comprehensive soul.

I agree about Shakespeare's soul, and that racial differences were, ultimately, irrelevant to it; but I do not think this irrelevance was a premiss which the dramatist took for granted in taking over the hero of this play, nor is the irrelevance easy to deduce from the events of the play, which suggest that Desdemona might have done better to marry a white man. For the example chosen is inescapably specific. Shakespeare had no need to borrow Cinthio's original story if all he wanted was a tragedy of jealous love; it was not a very good story, and nobody in the audience would have known it except a few highbrows who read Italian. In borrowing, he had to alter it more fundamentally than the originals of his other tragedies. One change he made was to modernize: the events dramatized in *Othello* took place in 1544, Cinthio's account of them appeared in 1565, but Shakespeare based the threatened Turkish attack which takes Othello to Cyprus on a historical event of 1570. This sharply distinguishes *Othello* from the earlier *Hamlet*, set in ancient Scandinavia, and from the later *King Lear* and *Macbeth*, both set in ancient

* From *Shakespeare in a Changing World*, ed. Arnold Kettle (1964).

Britain; the time of action corresponds roughly to that of a present-day play based on Mussolini's invasion of Ethiopia. *Othello* is not a vaguely timeless story of jealousy, but a modern instance of a black man's love for a white woman.

R. B. Heilman has shown how strongly the imagery, and even the structure of the play, emphasize the contrast between light and dark.[1] Othello is far more than black, because his visage is in his mind; Iago will make the blonde Desdemona begrimed and black by turning her virtue into pitch: 'Iago's business is to confuse the opposites.' The first and last Acts are set in darkness, broken in one case by torches and in the other by Othello's fatal candle as he speaks the soliloquy 'Put out the light, and then put out the light'. 'While Iago is trying to bring darkness into the happy light of Othello's life, there is an opposing force which tries to bring light into the surrounding darkness.' The bearing of this symbolism on the moral opposition between 'good' and 'evil' is obvious, but Shakespeare does not start with symbols and then attach complexions to them, and the inevitable effect of this opposition (though Heilman does not make the point) is to stress the racial contrast between Othello and his associates. I believe it is right, therefore, to see this contrast as the core of the play, its ultimate determinant (which is not, of course, to say it is the whole of the play), and the present essay will try to show that in Shakespeare's hands this determinant is not a limiting one.

Naturally it would be wrong to approach *Othello* as if it had been written after several centuries of imperialist relations with Africa. 'Colour-prejudice' could not possibly have been a current problem in Shakespeare's day in the modern sense of economic, political, and sexual rivalry within a competitive society, conditioned by the hangover from slavery and by movements for African independence. Elizabethans would, however, have had first-hand contact with Moors. Trade with North Africa had long flourished; and on two occasions when there was an explosion of Moors from Spain, in 1598 and 1609, they were carried back to Africa in English ships, apparently with much sympathy from the crews.[2] As England backed the Moors against a com-

1. 'Light and Dark in Othello': *Essays in Criticism*, Oct. 1951.
2. C. J. Sisson, *Shakespeare's Tragic Justice* (Methuen, 1961), p. 37.

mon enemy, Spain, it is perhaps significant that the form of Iago's name is Spanish. In 1600, only four years before the first recorded performance of *Othello*, many theatregoers would have seen 'noble Moors' lodging in London, members of an embassy from the Barbary Coast to Queen Elizabeth.[3] There is little doubt that Moors were generally credited with savagery as well as splendour. Elizabethan processions might be lent magnificence by a 'King of the Moors',[4] but many of the words associated with 'Barbary' (1596) are also Elizabethan: for instance, *barbarity* (= uncivilized condition, first recorded in 1570), *barbarism* (same meaning, 1584), *barbarous* (= cruelly savage, 1588). Shakespeare's earlier Moor, Aaron in *Titus Andronicus*, had been an atheist and an 'inhuman dog' (in some respects interestingly like Iago), who went to death by torture saying defiantly,

> If one good deed in all my life I did,
> I do repent it from my very soul.
>
> (v, 3, 189–90).

There was evidently a contradiction between the theory of 'order and degree', which enjoined the marriage of class-equals, and a deep suspicion of the alien. Although the Prince of Morocco in *The Merchant of Venice* is eligible to marry Portia, she is glad to get rid of him and 'all of his complexion'; and the King of Naples in *The Tempest* is bitterly reproached for marrying his daughter to the King of Tunis after the whole court had begged him not to 'loose her to an African'. Again, the force of Hamlet's pun when he is making his mother compare her first husband with her second,

> Could you on this fair mountain leave to feed,
> And batten on this Moor? ha, have you eyes?

depends on the double antithesis not only between *mountain* and *moor*, but between *fair* and *Moor*. All these are reasonable tests of audience-response. The unfamiliarity of the colour-problem would even tend to increase its impact: marriage between

3. Bernard Harris, 'A Portrait of a Moor': *Shakespeare Survey*, II (1958).
4. Malone Society, *Collections*, III (1954), xvii–xviii, xxv.

Othello and Desdemona must have been very startling to an audience that had never even seen a coloured boy walking out with a white girl. Professor Dover Wilson goes further and says: 'If anyone imagines that England at that date was unconscious of the "colour-bar" they cannot have read *Othello* with any care.'[5] Tension, it is clear, could quickly be generated by confronting white with black under certain conditions, although *Othello* cannot be a product of existing tension in Elizabethan society.

It looks as though the colour-difference in *Othello*, while topical and even prophetic in form, may draw some of its emotional intensity from other antagonisms, not necessarily racial, for example those involving puritan, heretic, and crypto-Jew, and even those created by the hierarchical system itself. Othello's royal lineage was not valid in Venice, and it is notable that his enemies (even discounting Iago) tend to assimilate him with the lower orders, as in Roderigo's complaint that Desdemona had been conducted

> with a knave of common hire, a gondolier,
> To the gross clasps of a lascivious Moor.
>
> (I, I, 126–7).

Othello presents, in extreme form, the situation of the alien (including the class-alien) in a hierarchical, predatory and therefore not yet fully human society. Othello's colour is thus representative of a much wider human protest than concerns race alone, and Paul Robeson was right in maintaining that

Shakespeare meant Othello to be a 'black moor' from Africa ... But the colour is essentially secondary – except as it emphasizes the difference in *culture*. This is the important thing ... Shakespeare's Othello has learned to live in a strange society, but he is not *of* it – as an easterner today might pick up western manners and not be western.[6]

In another way, however, the colour is of crucial importance in focusing the irrational feelings associated with that difference, as a remarkable footnote by A. C. Bradley illustrates. He is

5. *Othello* (New Cambridge Shakespeare, 1957), xi.
6. Quoted from Marvin Rosenberg, *The Masks of Othello* (Berkeley, California, 1961), p. 195.

agreeing with Coleridge that Othello should be 'sunburnt' rather than black on the modern stage:

Perhaps if we saw Othello coal-black with the bodily eye, *the aversion of our blood, an aversion which comes as near to being merely physical as anything human can, would overpower our imagination* and sink us below not Shakespeare only but the audiences of the seventeenth and eighteenth centuries.[7]

Whatever we make of this, it reminds us that Shakespeare forced his audience to see Othello first with the 'bodily eye' of Iago. This hero is a great human being who, differing *physically* as well as *culturally* from the community he has entered, recognizes (within the limits of his social role) only universal humane values of love and loyalty; but when in his equalitarian innocence he assumes full human rights in a society where other values are dominant, he makes himself and his personal relationships vulnerable to irrational, un-human forces, embodied in Iago, that try to reduce him to a level as irrational as themselves and almost – but not quite – succeed.

Othello's commanding personality and the glamour of his poetic idiom tend to make his actual social position seem much higher than it really is. He is employed by the Venetian republic as a professional soldier, a mercenary, and has become its most reliable and popular general. In his own country he was descended 'From men of royal siege', and he can say without boasting that he merits the position he has reached. Yet in Roderigo's words he is 'an extravagant and wheeling stranger' (where *extravagant* means 'straying outside his proper place'), who has lived in Venice, as distinct from the camp, for less than a year (1, 3, 84–5). The precarious anomaly of Othello's status is vividly dramatized in what are perhaps the most brilliant opening scenes in any Shakespeare play. In the second scene two parties of men are searching for him independently through the streets of Venice: one from the Duke's senate to require his urgent service against the 'enemy Ottoman', the other to imprison him for marrying a senator's daughter. Ironically, one party is at first mistaken for the other in the darkness.

7. *Shakespearean Tragedy* (1904), p. 202n. My italics.

Othello himself, not without irony, comments on the paradox; if I obey the prison party, he says, 'How may the duke be therewith satisfied?' Othello's prestige rests on his indispensability, but being indispensable does not make him socially acceptable in governing circles. Brabantio invited him home and 'loved' him while he recounted his past adventures, but as a future son-in-law he is decidedly *persona non grata*, a 'thing' that no Venetian girl could possibly look at with affection except by some preposterous error of nature. Brabantio never does reconcile himself to the match, the grief of which kills him. There were, of course, 'fortunates' at stake, and the runaway marriage (in contrast to Cinthio's version, which takes place with the reluctant consent of the girl's parents) signifies not rashness but purity of motive. Their secret union, in contempt of the 'many noble matches' available to Desdemona, is to make it quite clear that no material interests were involved in what was a free love-match. Othello gets nothing from it, while as Desdemona says:

> That I did love the Moor to live with him,
> My downright violence and scorn of fortunes
> May trumpet to the world.

(I, 3, 248–50.)

Desdemona affirms her choice in public and with devastating simplicity – devastating because when her father asks her to say where her obedience lies, she answers:

> here's my husband,
> And so much duty as my mother show'd
> To you, preferring you before her father,
> So much I challenge that I may profess
> Due to the Moor, my lord.

(I, 3, 185–9.)

She makes no distinction whatever, that is, between her parents' marriage and her own. Brabantio retorts in effect that in that case he is no longer related to her: 'I had rather to adopt a child than get it.' And Desdemona finds, without dismay, that her act has isolated her with Othello, for her father will not admit her into his house, even alone. Desdemona's childlike simplicity, dramatically so effective at the end of the play in heightening the pathos of her helpless isolation, has the effect in this scene of positing the spontaneous, instinctive naturalness of her love for Othello (to Iago her act means the opposite: 'If she had been blest she would never have loved the Moor'). Unlike her father, Desdemona entertains no consideration 'of years, of country, and of credit', only of direct human relationships: parents, lover, husband, friend.

Othello's commitment complements hers. Shakespeare shows that this is the first relationship he has experienced since childhood (Cassio's friendship apart) that was not based on military or political expediency but purely on human feeling. Yet in staking his emotional life on Desdemona he has put his free condition into a 'circumscription and confine' which makes him vulnerable, and that is why the supposed loss of her love exhausts his capacity for suffering. There is nothing egotistical in this attitude; on the contrary. Disease, poverty, slavery, even public disgrace – the loss of all he has valued up to now – he could bear 'well, very well',

> But there, where I have garner'd up my heart,
> Where either I must live or bear no life,
> The fountain from the which my current runs,
> Or else dries up – to be discarded thence!

> (IV, 1, 58–61.)

Thus both lovers assert 'humane' values against the conventions that debase them; but 'humaneness', so isolated, is itself an abstraction and reliance on it leaves them fatally vulnerable. The emotional innocence of the hero and heroine (like the extreme youth of Romeo and Juliet) reflects both their protest against the social environment and their ultimate helplessness before it.

It is of course between Othello and Iago that the main issue is fought. Here Shakespeare made another significant change in Cinthio's original story. Cinthio's equivalent of Iago did not hate the Moor at all, but deceived him in order to revenge himself on his wife for her refusal to commit adultery. It was only after having her murdered that the Moor, regretting the deed, turned on its instigator and demoted him, and they then began *to hate each other*. In Shakespeare Iago's hatred, which fills the entire play from line 7 to the end, is one-sided, obsessive, and single-minded. Yet Othello, like all the other characters, has no reason to suspect its existence. Cassio and Roderigo are of marginal importance to Iago, and when he actually has Desdemona at his mercy in Act IV Scene 2 he is perfectly indifferent to her suffering and makes no attempt either to prolong or to exploit it. It looks as if Iago's interest in Desdemona is solely on account of her relationship with Othello. 'Peradventure' lust has something to do with it, he says, but his chief anxiety is to get even with the lusty Moor for supposed adultery with Emilia, the thought of which

> Doth like a poisonous mineral gnaw my inwards;
> And nothing can or shall content my soul
> Till I am even'd with him, wife for wife.

(II, 1, 291–3.)

Indeed, revenge by proxy would do just as well; he tells Roderigo, whom he keeps going 'For his quick hunting' as well as for the money in his purse, 'If thou canst cuckold him, thou dost thyself a pleasure, me a sport.' Desdemona is simply the best means of getting at Othello; and Roderigo, like Cassio, a means of getting at Desdemona. To Cassio, Othello's only friend, Iago extends the same fantastic suspicion of adultery with Emilia: 'For I fear Cassio with my night-cap, too.' That *too* is revealing. If Iago has an obsession about sex it is clear that Othello is somewhere at the centre of it.

Why does Iago hate Othello? This has always been the crux of the play. The characters themselves are baffled by hatred of such intensity; the dying Roderigo calls Iago an 'inhuman dog', and to Lodovico he seems 'More fell than anguish, hunger, or the sea' – more implacable than the blind forces of nature. Yet when Othello asks him point-blank why he acted as he did, he shuts up completely. Not that Iago has ever been unwilling to talk, indeed he has just 'part confessed his villainy': all he refuses to explain is the motive of his hatred. 'What you know you know.' What could he possibly say? 'I was passed over for the lieutenancy'? 'Some people thought Othello had seduced my wife'? The possible rational motives are so ludicrously incommensurate with the effects. But although the quick-witted Iago cannot explain his conduct rationally, Coleridge's verdict of 'motiveless malignity' overlooks the first scene of the play, which shows that his conduct was powerfully motivated. He is no devil from hell, except metaphorically. We learn within twenty lines that he is sensitive to aliens, because one of his first objections to Cassio is that he is a foreigner, 'a Florentine'. And although Iago's avowed policy is to thrive by Othello until he has lined his coat, his first dramatic action is to stir up an unprofitable racial riot against Othello merely in order to 'poison his delight' in his marriage, which is described to Brabantio in bestially obscene language:

IAGO: Even now, now, very now, an old black ram
           Is tupping your white ewe ...
  ... you'll have your daughter cover'd with a Barbary horse; you'll
  have your nephews [=grandchildren] neigh to you; ... your
  daughter and the Moor are now making the beast with two backs.
BRABANTIO: Thou art a villain.
IAGO: You are – a Senator.

                                              (I, I, 89–119.)

The moment is crucial. The profane wretch and the magnifico suddenly recognize, behind their hostile confrontation, a kind of mutual identity: Brabantio is face to face with his own unconfessed reaction to the news of his daughter's elopement with a black man. Before the Duke that reaction becomes explicit, and Iago afterwards uses it as an invaluable source of quotation in baiting Othello. When Brabantio's 'loved' visitor is also loved by Desdemona he is immediately regarded as a heathen dealer in witchcraft and aphrodisiacs, and the senator's class-prejudice and religious intolerance are revealed in his horrified fear that if such unions are permitted, 'Bond-slaves and pagans shall our statesmen be.' These early scenes demonstrate, therefore, that Iago's view of Othello is not – except in pathological intensity – a unique aberration, but an attitude held by the Venetian ruling class when forced into human relationship with a Moor. The

Duke and the rest of his council who are conciliatory and tolerant cannot afford to be otherwise, 'cannot with safety cast him': they need Othello's professional services.

Iago hates Othello because he is a Moor. This irrational but powerful motive, underlying the obsessive intensity of his feeling and the improvised reasons with which he justifies it, continually presses up towards the surface of his language. It breaks through into action at the opening of the play in order to give the audience the key to his character; after this its energies go into the intrigue that will bring the hated object and all its associates to destruction; but it often nearly betrays itself. Iago's 'motive-hunting' has been much discussed, but the fact is that he never gives a direct reason of any kind for his hatred. He tells Roderigo the story of Cassio's appointment and then asks whether this gives him any reason to *love* the Moor? Later he reflects: 'I hate the Moor; And it is thought abroad that twixt my sheets He's done my office' – the hatred and its possible cause are unconnected. Again he tells himself: 'The Moor, howbeit that I endure him not, Is of a constant, loving, noble nature,' where this phrase *I endure him not* ('I just can't stand him') is even more revealing than *I hate*, especially when accompanied by an acknowledgement of his true qualities. 'I have told thee often, and I re-tell thee again and again, I hate the Moor.' Iago's mind broods constantly over Othello's colour. After the disembarkation at Cyprus, when Cassio drinks 'To the health of our general' Iago drinks 'to the health of black Othello'. But it is in conversation with Othello himself that the hidden disgust most nearly betrays itself. One exchange is of particular importance. Othello's trust in Desdemona is just beginning to waver:

OTHELLO: And yet, how nature erring from itself –
IAGO: Ay, there's the point: as – to be bold with you
    Not to affect many proposed matches
    Of her own clime, complexion, and degree,
    Whereto we see in all things nature tends –
    Foh! one may smell in such a will most rank,
    Foul disproportion, thoughts unnatural.
    But pardon me –

                    (III, 3, 231–8.)

Othello has been judged stupid for failing to see that this is an open insult, but it is *not* an open insult; Iago is repeating what Brabantio had said in council:

> she – in spite of nature,
> Of years, of country, credit, every thing –
> To fall in love with what she fear'd to look on!
> It is a judgement maim'd and most imperfect
> That will confess perfection so could err
> Against all rules of nature
>
> (i, 3, 96–101.)

The points lies in two antithetical interpretations of 'nature'. For Othello, as for Desdemona, what was 'natural' was a marriage between two lovers, involving the same duties as their parents had owed each other, and by *nature erring from itself* Othello meant 'a wife forgetting her proper loyalty'. To Brabantio it was against all rules of nature for a Venetian girl to love a Moor, and Iago therefore inverted Othello's phrase *nature erring from itself* to mean 'a woman flouting the laws of colour and class' ('clime, complexion, and degree'). The tragedy is epitomized in this exchange. Human love is what Othello stands by. But for Iago Othello is not a human being at all, he is an animal: a ram, a horse, an ass; his sexual union with Desdemona will produce not children but colts. Since Iago himself admits Othello's qualities ('a constant loving, noble nature'), he is involved in complete irrationality, forced to argue that it is the very virtues of men that make them beast-like:

> The Moor is of a free and open nature
> ... And will as tenderly be led by th' nose
> As asses are.
>
> (i, 3, 393–6.)

This particular beast is loved by his wife and honoured as a brilliant military commander. The real relationship between him and Iago was established at the beginning of the play when Othello quelled the uproar Iago had raised by saying: 'For Christian shame put by this barbarous brawl'; Othello is the civilized man, Iago the barbarian. Iago's task is to reduce him in actuality to a shape that at first exists only in Iago's fantasy, that of an irrational beast, by

> making him egregiously an *ass*,
> And practising upon his peace and quiet
> Even to *madness*.

(II, I, 303–5; my italics.)

So when Othello exclaims, at the beginning of his ordeal, that Iago would have to 'exchange [him] for a goat' before he would make jealousy the business of his soul, he is describing with unconscious irony exactly what Iago proposes to do. This is not a study of a civilized barbarian reverting to type (for Othello has never been a barbarian, though he has been a slave), but the more subtle one of a white barbarian who tries to make a civilized man into his own image.

The psychology of the Nazi underlings who ran the concentration camps has been similarly explained. By reducing intelligent human beings to the condition of animals they could enjoy a superiority that inverted the real relation between them: it was a fantasy enactment, resembling magic as magic has been defined by Professor Gordon Childe, 'a way of making people believe they are going to get what they want'.[8] The element of fantasy and the reliance on magic is one of the 'realist' Iago's most striking characteristics. Some of his logic, even when it is not designed to mock the half-witted Roderigo, shows an opportunism that is simply bizarre. He will postulate almost anything for immediate effect, not just on others but even on himself, and then back it up with moralizings that sound shrewd only because they are cynical, like a sort of lunatic Polonius. It is a superb study of an irrational mind, lucid and cunning on the surface but mad just underneath; and in this it contrasts directly with Othello's, which is deeply rational but guileless on the surface.

Other characters find Iago's surface convincing, but when they describe him as *honest* they are in effect confessing that all they see in him is surface. The main function of the famous

---

8. *History* (Cobbett Press, 1947), p. 37.

epithet is of course ironic: the pitiless deceiver is the man everybody turns to for help and everybody trusts. But the word *honest*, constantly repeated, is eventually felt to express a definite limitation; Iago is imprisoned within the boundaries of the epithet as a modern commodity is imprisoned within the slogan advertising it. When Othello says 'Iago is most honest,' the honesty is that of an NCO who is thoroughly reliable at his own job but never in the running for a commission. Iago seems to recognize the limiting force of the description so automatically attached to him by the savage way he quotes it himself when undertaking to make discord of the lovers' harmony:

> O, you are well tun'd now!
> But I'll set down the pegs that make this music,
> As honest as I am.

> (II, 1, 197–9.)

Thus there is an ironical parallel between Iago who, though lavishly praised for honesty, is not in fact able enough even for minor promotion, and Othello, the truly 'noble Moor', who is not considered good enough to marry into the Venetian ruling class. And the parallel almost converges in the end, for Othello's nobility deceives everyone and becomes, in its effects, practically indistinguishable from Iago's honesty.

The weapon Iago uses is systematic unreason, magic. Brabantio's first assumption on learning that his daughter had fallen in love with a Moor was that she must have been corrupted by sorcery:

> thou hast practis'd on her with foul charms,
> Abus'd her delicate youth with drugs or minerals ...

> For nature so preposterously to err, ...
> Sans witchcraft could not.

> (I, 2, 73–4, 62–4.)

The Duke's council soon realizes that mutual love was the only 'witchcraft' in the case. Shakespeare is careful to show that the advances came equally from both sides, though at first he plays down the sensual element in Othello's love because men from hot climates were traditionally hot-blooded and this must not be supposed of Othello. The perfect equality of the lovers is symbolized in their playful exchange of roles on arrival in Cyprus, where Othello is Desdemona's 'dear' and Desdemona is Othello's 'fair warrior', while the imagery of Cassio's benediction on them is rich with fertility-feeling:

> Great Jove, Othello guard,
> And swell his sail with thine own powerful breath,
> That he may bless this bay with his tall ship,
> Make love's quick pants in Desdemona's arms,
> Give renew'd fire to our extinguished spirits,
> And bring all Cyprus comfort!

(II, I, 77–82.)

It is hard to see how Shakespeare could have made the case clearer. It is not their union but their disunion that is effected by 'drugs or minerals', as the imagery now begins to demonstrate. Iago curbs Roderigo's impatience by reminding him that 'we work by wit and not by witchcraft', meaning 'the job can't be done without planning'; but in this most ironical of Shakespeare's tragedies the statement carries an opposite implication: 'I work by witchcraft, not by reason.' The degrading of Cassio in Act II is a kind of symbolic rehearsal of the method Iago will use with his principal victim. Betrayed into drunkenness and senseless violence Cassio cries in self-disgust: 'To be now a sensible man, by and by a fool, and presently a beast!' The 'medicine' that so 'unwitted' Cassio was alcohol; the drug used on Othello will be more subtle and instead of wine into his mouth Iago will pour pestilence into his ear, but the sequence of results is to be identical. 'The Moor already changes with my poison,' Iago says after his first insinuations, and for this the victim has no counter-drug:

> Not poppy, nor mandragora,
> Nor all the drowsy syrups of the world,
> Shall ever medicine thee to that sweet sleep,
> Which thou owed'st yesterday.

(III, 3, 344–7.)

This poetry, it has been noticed, is in Othello's own style: Iago is putting on the verbal habits of his victim, as Othello's later 'Goats and monkeys!' will adopt Iago's; but its *content* is quite alien to Othello's thinking, who is not a drug-addict. Othello's characteristic images are of achieved perfection: Desdemona is a pearl, she is as smooth as monumental alabaster, he would not exchange her for a world made of chrysolite; and it is this integrity of love that Iago attacks with the solvents and corrosives of unreason.

The two exceptions are Othello's description of the handkerchief, and his request for poison in order to kill Desdemona. The *actual* virtue of the handkerchief is simply that both lovers valued it as Othello's first remembrance and to lose it might have been interpreted as a 'symptomatic act' (even Desdemona fears that such a loss might put some men to 'ill thinking'), but Iago's plot loads it with fictitious *mana* as a symbol of infidelity. Naturally Desdemona cannot see it like that, and Othello, mentally unbalanced after his latest interview with Iago, piles more and more on to the supposed properties of the handkerchief in order to scare her into some sense of the enormity of her offence. She feels his urgency but is sceptical of the details ('Sure there's some wonder in this handkerchief' is the furthest she will go), which are evidently new to her; all Othello's previous stories have been factual. Thus it is Iago's magic that went into the web, the absurdity of the hallowed worms and maidens-heart dye corresponding to the irrational significance he has made Othello attach to it. Iago's refusal to agree to the use of poison has been explained as reluctance to implicate himself, but more is implied than mere caution. If Romeo could get poison without signing a register Iago certainly could. Othello surely thinks first of poison because he wants to do the right thing: isn't this the way (his request implies) in which good Italians dispose of unfaithful wives? But Iago cannot allow him to kill Desdemona at a distance, like a civilized Venetian; he must 'strangle her in her bed' with his bare hands, like a savage. Poison is Iago's speciality. 'Work on, my medicine, work!' Just before advising Othello to strangle Desdemona, Iago succeeds in goading him to the point of complete mental breakdown; in the Folio text he 'falls in a trance', and Iago has the satisfaction of telling Cassio that he sometimes 'breaks out to savage madness' and foams at the mouth. As he recovers his reason, it is with loss of manhood that Iago taunts him. 'A passion most unsuiting such a man'; 'Good sir, be a man'; 'Would you would bear your fortune like a man!' *Like a man* in this context carries a double irony because the fortune Othello is being advised to bear is that of cuckoldry, so it really means 'like a monster'. From this point on, Othello is absorbed more and more into Iago's mental world. His vicious 'I will chop her into messes' shows him becoming as barbarous as Iago wishes.

How is it that what is rational and human, personified in the hero, is so nearly turned into its opposite by this medicine-man? The classic dilemma of *Othello* criticism has been that if the hero is as noble as he seems, a villain of superhuman intelligence would be needed to break him down. There are therefore critics who make Iago superhuman: a symbol or embodiment of Evil. Alternatively, if Iago is as ignoble as he proves, the hero must be a very poor type to be taken in by him. This (broadly speaking) is the line followed by critics from F. R. Leavis to Laurence Lerner. Both views depend ultimately on the Aristotle–Bradley doctrine of the 'tragic flaw' – a doctrine that has obscured the true nature of Shakespearian tragedy far more than any over-emphasis on 'character'. Indeed, it is only when a man's 'character' is pictured as a sort of hard, fixed core somewhere inside him (rather as the essential particles of matter were once pictured as miniature billiard-balls) that looking for 'flaws' in it makes any sense. The idea is that if a dramatic character changes into something different from what he was, he must really have been like that all along; or, at least, he must always have shown some incipient weakness which could lead to that result. In one way this is a truism, for a man obviously cannot develop in any direction unless he is capable of doing so; but the theory is a nuisance because the potentialities of men are infinite, and whatever the greatness of a dramatic hero, any number of potential 'flaws' can be found, or invented, to account for his downfall. Yet in all Shakespeare's tragedies except, perhaps, *Macbeth*, the determining 'flaw' is in society rather than in the hero's supposed distance from perfection. Tragedy does not occur in *Hamlet* because the hero has a bad habit of not killing people at once, but because the power of the Danish court is founded on violence and adultery. No personal idiosyncracy can alter the tragedy inherent in this situation, though it may of course affect the special form the tragedy takes. The 'tragic flaw' theory means that it is a punishable offence to be any particular kind of man. Moreover it shifts the emphasis from *men in conflict* to the *private mind*; J. I. M. Stewart has even interpreted *Othello* as a debate in which Iago and Othello are at times the two halves of one mind, 'abstractions from a single and, as it were, invisible protagonist'.[9] This seems perversely un-Shakespearian.

Far from being self-centred or stupid, Othello is not presented as having any particular moral or intellectual weakness, though he is fully individualized. Certainly Othello has very different qualities of mind from Hamlet. But Hamlet's superiority lies mainly in the other meaning of the word 'intelligence'. Hamlet is equipped to face the treachery around him because all the facts have been revealed to him, so that throughout the play the dramatic irony works entirely on his side. If Claudius had told the audience the facts, and not the Ghost Hamlet, would Hamlet seem so very bright when his uncle patronized him?

Some impression of cleverness in a plotter and of stupidity in his victim is inevitable when the dramatic irony works the other way. Iago knows something essential that Othello does not know; the audience share the knowledge and so are implicated with Iago whether they like it or not. Iago's knowledge is not objective knowledge of real human relations, which Othello ought in reason to share, for Iago has invented the situation that puts Othello at a disadvantage; but the power it confers is real enough, and this is why the audience find themselves tied to Iago by a bond of complicity. The effect is intentional; *Othello* is not a play for making consciences comfortable. A rather similar effect occurs in Patrick Hamilton's thriller *Rope*, where a young moron who has committed a motiveless killing gets the victim's father to share a meal with him on top of the box con-

9. *Character and Motive in Shakespeare* (Longmans, 1949), p. 108.

taining his son's body. This gruesome situation inevitably causes the father's perfect ignorance to appear as stupidity and his own knowledge (which the audience share) to appear as wit. Hamilton is said to have been thinking of the psychology of fascism when he wrote *Rope*.

Even if Othello's 'stupidity' is partly a dramatic illusion, it would still seem a paradox to say that because he was rational he failed to notice that he was being led by the nose, and this needs explanation. Some recent criticism has blamed Othello's credulity on his immature attitude towards his wife, or on some inadequacy in their relationship. A marriage that ends in murder certainly ends inadequately, but again it would be wrong to deny the fact of change, especially in a play where change is constantly stressed; and if the marriage was inadequate from the beginning, its destruction is not so very regrettable. But 'immature', in modern critical jargon, often turns out to mean 'not adjusted to the existing social order', and in this sense both the lovers were emphatically immature, since they disregarded the convention of the arranged marriage as well as the 'natural' laws of clime, complexion, and degree, and married for love. It is the flaw in society that breaks Othello down and destroys the marriage. In purely human terms his bond with Desdemona is strong, and it is hard to imagine any of the wealthy curlèd darlings of Venice forging a stronger one, but the phrase 'purely human' is an admission of the price paid in isolation and vulnerability. Othello's pathetic defence in the last act, sword in hand, of a dead body in an empty bedroom – in fact, the whole claustrophobic movement of the play – reflects this isolation and confinement. *Socially* speaking, the union of what Iago called 'an erring barbarian and a supersubtle Venetian' was genuinely frail, and although his words were a parody not a description of the difference between them, he was accurately foreshadowing his line of attack. *Supersubtle*, the opposite of what Desdemona really is, comes from Iago's sardonic fantasy, but it is fantasy he makes Othello share; *erring* in its primary sense means 'wandering', for Othello is a soldier of fortune, but *erring barbarian* also suggests a savage who has strayed from his proper station in life by embracing Christianity and a white wife. Iago puts it to him, after some preliminary softening-up, that he is unfamiliar with the local customs:

IAGO: I know our country disposition well:
  In Venice they do let God see the pranks
  They dare not show their husbands . . .
OTHELLO: Dost thou say so?
IAGO: She did deceive her father, marrying you;
  And when she seem'd to shake and fear your looks,
  She lov'd them most.

(III, 3, 205–12.)

The deadliness of these first reasonings lies in the fact that they are not Iago's, but endorsements of what Desdemona's own father had said; they voice a social attitude already expressed to Othello. For example: 'She has deceiv'd her father, and may thee' (1, 3, 293), and 'To fall in love with what she fear'd to look on!' (1, 3, 98.) Only now, when Iago quotes Brabantio as saying: 'He thought 'twas witchcraft –', he imputes the witchcraft to Desdemona's skill in deceit, not Othello's power of attraction as Brabantio had done.

Under this combined pressure, Othello discovers very quickly that he has overrated his own emotional security. However well he knows his wife, this difference of race is the one factor in their relations in which he is necessarily ignorant, and through this irrational door the prompting of a Venetian supposed to be experienced in 'all qualities of human dealings' gains entry.[10] Consequently the first and principal thing Othello considers in weighing the possibility of Desdemona's unfaithfulness is his own colour: 'Haply, for I am black ... She's gone'. He is persuaded, in fact, that he *cannot* know her, and all his tragic blindness stems from that persuasion.

Iago's aim has been not Othello's overthrow but his total degradation as a human being: that he should kill what he loved most, in jealous madness, with his bare hands. This aim is

---

10. Iago would seem still more convincing if, as Paul A. Jorgensen maintains (*Redeeming Shakespeare's Words*, Berkeley, 1962, pp. 14–19), the audience took him to be posing to Othello as Honesty, a professional smeller-out of knaves.

almost realized. At least once Othello has broken down into actual madness under Iago's mental drugs; he has solemnly dedicated his heart to hatred and vengeance; and in his insults to Desdemona he has become indistinguishable from the bond-slave Brabantio once compared him to: 'a beggar in his drink Could not have laid such terms upon his callet'. Yet he does not actually commit the murder in jealous revenge but as an act of objective justice, even of civic and religious duty. In a way this makes it worse; but it means that Iago has already partly failed. Othello kills in persisting love, not hate ('O balmy breath, that dost almost persuade Justice to break her sword!'), and even against his will: for every two lines of the soliloquy 'It is the cause, it is the cause, my soul' there is a word of nega-tion or qualification, *not, nor, yet, but*. Action has restored his self-command and reasserted his public responsibility at the ex-pense of his private inclination. In Desdemona's actual presence, instead of behaving like a mad beast he has to force himself to go through with it. When he says, weeping over the girl he intends not to murder but to sacrifice,

> this sorrow's heavenly;
> It strikes where it doth love,
>
> (v, 1, 21–2.)

he is recognizably trying to administer the same impersonal jus-tice as when he dismissed Cassio:

> Cassio, I love thee;
> But never more be officer of mine.
>
> (ii, 3, 240–41.)

There too, ironically enough, he had been tricked into his act of justice, and here it is a horrible delusion, as Desdemona tries to tell him with her unanswerable 'That death's unnatural that kills for loving'; but from now on Othello is deluded but responsible, capable of summing himself up with complete self-awareness after his enlightenment as 'an honourable murderer'.

This second change in Othello raises one question of im-portance for an Elizabethan audience at least. Iago has not only destroyed all that Othello valued on earth but has consigned him to eternal punishment by trapping him into murder and suicide. Othello was a Christian convert, and by killing himself he knowingly accepts the fate of being 'damned beneath all depth in hell' for what he has done; to the dead Desdemona he says:

> When we shall meet at compt,
> This look of thine will hurl my soul from heaven,
> And fiends will snatch at it.
>
> (v, 2, 276–8.)

If Shakespeare as an orthodox Christian believed the same, what can be the point of emphasizing Othello's recovery of human integrity? Speculation on Shakespeare's religious beliefs is of course unprofitable, but the text does make one broad hint. Some thirty lines after Desdemona has been left for dead, she speaks again, and her last words, in answer to Emilia's question 'O, who hath done this deed?' are: 'Nobody: I myself ... Commend me to my kind lord: O, farewell!' This attempt to take the blame for her own murder (which provokes Othello into a furious avowal of responsibility: 'She's like a liar gone to burning hell. 'Twas I that killed her') is so piteously absurd that its dramatic point has been queried; but the point is surely obvious. There is a precedent for Desdemona's absurdity in the Christian doctrine of the Atonement. This does not mean that Desdemona is a 'Christ-figure'. In letting her speak as it were from beyond the grave, Shakespeare is suggesting to his audience that whatever might happen 'at compt', one voice at least – his victim's – was unlikely to be raised against Othello.

It is Emilia who, after the murder, takes over from Othello as representative of common humanity. Deluded herself for most of the play (like every single character in it), once she sees the truth she refuses to compromise either with the misleader or the misled, and her magnificent outbursts first against Othello and then against her husband reassert what is human and rational in a world almost completely given over to unreason. The human relation was valid after all: 'she loved thee, cruel Moor'. For the last time Iago tries to control the course of events by witchcraft:

IAGO: Go to, charm your tongue.
EMILIA: I will not charm my tongue; I am bound to speak.

(v, 2, 186-7.)

So he silences commonsense by another murder; but it is too late: she has brought the issues into the plain light of day, and Othello's judges as well as Othello himself have at least partly understood them.

Othello's behaviour in the final scene is governed by the way Lodovico discriminates between him and Iago in allotting punishment. Iago has been unmasked, and the Venetian delegation joins with Othello in execrating him. He is sentenced out of hand to be tortured to death – the most savage punishment in Shakespeare, or indeed, anywhere else. Othello is relieved of his post and remanded in custody 'Till that the nature of [his] fault be known To the Venetian state'. The customary Elizabethan class-distinction whereby, for example, noble traitors were gracefully beheaded while commoners were hanged, drawn, and quartered may have something to do with this. But the truth is that among the Venetians as in the audience there is strong sympathy for him, and some reluctance to condemn:

> O thou Othello, that was once so good,
> Fall'n in the practice of a damned slave,
> What shall be said to thee?

(v, 2, 294-6.)

While Iago is called 'demi-devil', a 'hellish villain', Othello is a 'rash and most unfortunate man'. In Cinthio's story, where the Moor's deed is far less excusable, he escapes with his life. The deferment of judgement, when the facts are so plain, clearly implies that Othello's life may well be spared in view of the circumstances and of his own past merit. So at least Othello understands the position, for as soon as Lodovico's decision is announced he says:

> I have done the state some service, and they know't –

(v, 2, 342.)

an ironic repetition of his confidence in Act I that his usefulness to the state would outweigh Brabantio's objections to his marriage: 'My services which I have done the signiory Shall out-tongue his complaints.' He can hardly be 'cheering himself up', as T. S. Eliot oddly interprets; he is recognizing, and rejecting, the possibility of avoiding the death-penalty. He refuses to throw himself on the mercy of the Venetian senators, even though the most powerful of those that might seek vengeance on him, Brabantio, is known to have died. Instead he repudiates the deed – for which his sterile tears flow like the secretions from trees in his native Africa that can restore life to the phoenix – and also dissociates himself from those who would judge him for the deed. They are offered, almost contemptuously, 'a word or two before you go'. Othello is now seeing himself and his social environment with complete objectivity: 'Speak of me as I am; nothing extenuate, Nor set down aught in malice,' and his own comments are not expressed subjectively but in detached clear-cut images. Whether it is to the 'base Judean' of the Folio or to the 'base Indian' of the Quarto that he compares himself (v, 2, 350), Othello's final image of his relationship with Desdemona is of a white pearl in a black hand. And his self-assessment just before he pronounces sentence on himself broadens the implications of the play in an image that brings its ironies into sharp focus:

> say besides that in Aleppo once,
> Where a malignant and a turban'd Turk
> Beat a Venetian and traduc'd the state,
> I took by th' throat the circumcisèd dog
> And smote him – thus.

> (v, 2, 355–9.)

Overtly Othello presents himself as a servant of the State, avenging an insult by a foreigner: he is the Turk, the heathen barbarian Iago has tried to make him, who has committed violence on a Venetian citizen and betrayed a public trust, having defiled his human relations with Desdemona and his soldier's honour alike. But the words *malignant, turbaned*, and *circumcisèd dog* are bitterly ironic, because *turbaned* and *circumcisèd* tend to identify the Turk with Othello rather than provide an insulting analogy (for circumcision could be a mark equally of Christian, Moor, Turk and Jew), while *malignant* and *dog* do not fit Othello at all, only Iago. Hence Othello's apparent tit-for-tat in killing the Turk can also be taken in the opposite sense: that he had acted to suppress racial violence in the trading-centre of Aleppo, just as when the play opens we see him suppressing Iago's 'barbarous brawl'. As a final irony, Othello's analogy reminds the Venetians that in dealing with himself as he dealt with the Turk he is in fact depriving them of their main bulwark against Turks. Some of Shakespeare's audience might have remembered that the historical Turkish attack on Cyprus in 1570 had been successful.

Othello's final speech, therefore, though it cannot mitigate what he has done, demonstrates the complete recovery of his integrity as a human being. He will not beg for mercy on the strength of his past greatness, but sums up himself and others with objective self-knowledge, and carries out his own sentence, offering himself by his last gesture as a sacrifice to his victim, since this is the only act of reunion open to him:

> I kiss'd thee ere I kill'd thee. No way but this –
> Killing my self, to die upon a kiss.

(v, 2, 361–2.)

All that Iago's poison has achieved is an object that 'poisons sight': a bed on which a black man and a white girl, although they are dead, are embracing. Human dignity, the play says, is indivisible.

6. DAVID CRAIG

Towards Laws of Literary Development*

'. . . the historical element is still what is most conspicuously
lacking in the way critics approach their given tasks.' –
'English Literary Criticism', *Times Literary Supplement*,
27 November 1970

It seems reasonable to suppose that the media we group as
'literature' change over the years according to laws – that there
are sequences and distinctive sorts of qualitative leap in the
processes that we group as 'tradition'. Most of us cannot avoid
from time to time resorting to some ideas, often tangled and
sketchily formulated, of how literature grows, ideas that usually
relate literature to other lines of growth and especially the history
of ideas and social history. I doubt, however, if we can perceive
literature clearly enough for what it is – let alone *explain* it –
unless we become more conscious and more precise in our theory,
and to explain it is, it seems to me, the main work of criticism
now asking to be done.

Criticism and scholarship have flowed out so abundantly in
the past half-century, so much has been reprinted, anthologized,
discussed, and revalued, that in most areas of British literature
there is little left to be done. Literature can be analysed – its
detail and structure made clear. It can be evaluated – its quality
assessed by one's touchstones of the significant and fine. And it
can be explained – the emergence of forms, styles, themes, motifs,
and individual talents accounted for in terms of their timing,
their appearance in strength and their dying away. Properly,
these 'three' approaches are scarcely separable aspects of understanding literature as a human product. But it strikes me forcibly
that the stress or weight of critical effort in our time has leaned
very little towards the explanatory aspect: that is, the historical.
Writers such as Lukács have speculated boldly on certain inter-

* From *Mosaic*, Vol. V, No. 2 (Winnipeg, 1972).

connections: for example, between peaks of political activity and the emergence of the historical novel and of realism. But the one work that seems to me both clear yet supple in its theoretical guidelines and richly detailed in its historical facts is in a field remote from our own place and time, namely George Thomson's work on ancient Greek literature and society.[1] It may be that it is Thomson's kind of work, which is both empirical and theoretically articulate – in effect, specific chapters of literary history – that can best further what I am calling the explanation of literature, and that a search for anything like 'laws' is foredoomed. At least, however, some misconceptions and fallacies can be cleared away if we consider what sorts of question might be answered if we were clearer in our theory of literary history; what efforts at explaining have been made so far; and what sorts of objection have been made against the explanatory or historicist approach.

Here is the type of question that I have in mind: Would it be agreed, and if so how would we explain, that no love poetry with the candour and richness of, say, Donne's Elegy XIX was written between the 1650s and the 1780s; and that human sexuality was not truly or fully expressed from early in the seventeenth century until early in the twentieth? Would it be agreed, and if so how would we explain, that a very considerable part of the best British fiction since early this century has been set overseas? There are also questions which one can't pose without putting into them an element of evaluation: Why is there no prose fiction to speak of, in English, before the 1720s? And why do novels remain psychologically elementary and formally mixed and uncertain until 1818 (when *Persuasion* was published)? Following closely from that, would it be agreed, and if so how would we explain, that the 1820s and 1830s are a barren lull in our tradition, followed almost at once, from about 1848 to 1865, by a great burst in which the supreme modern form, the novel, comes of age?

It is matters as central as these that we have to explain, and I am persuaded that they are genuine and pressing questions by

1. *Aeschylus and Athens* (1941, 1946); *Studies in Ancient Greek Society*, I: *The Prehistoric Aegean* (1949, 1954); II: *The First Philosophers* (1955).

the fact that one's students and colleagues seem normally not distinctly aware of those lulls and peaks and that when they are brought to their attention, they will resort to all manner of ingenious details, minor or unique exceptions, rather than admit, and then try to explain, these salient aspects of literary history.

To ask how such matters are to be explained amounts to asking: what might the axioms of literary development be like? If I now sketch my own explanation for one of those aspects, namely the emergence of fiction as and when it did, we will then be able to see what implications of principle arise from it.

The long story had of course existed from prehistoric times (so far as we can tell by inference from the legends of sur iving 'stone age' peoples such as the original people of Australia). The stylistic ingredient necessary to transform the long story into the novel proper – that is, a down-to-earth prose steeped in the detail of contemporary life – sprang up out of an England shaken and as it were mobilized by the seventeenth-century revolution. This gave rise directly to the printed speech, the newspaper, detailed lives of people in the public eye, and histories in the sense of narrative of recent happenings that went closely into social and personal motives. By 1700 or a little later our culture had evolved a new thing – narrative and commentary grounded in the present, referring to it directly and not by way of allegory or oblique analogy, and cast in a form that appealed to as many people as possible, regardless of class or specialized training. Of course there had been for generations forerunners of such media. But the essays, satires, and novels that come flocking in the age of Defoe, Swift, Dryden, Addison, Pope, Fielding, and Johnson amount to a new wave in the growth of our media; and it can be shown that the impetus comes from the main events of the English revolution.

The axiom implicit in this would be as follows: The literary forms and specific works are to be thought of, not as pearls secreted by special individuals, though that does enter into it; nor as emanations of the *Zeitgeist*, though that too enters into it; but rather as working parts of the culture, forms that people find necessary because of the conditions in which they live their lives.

If this were accepted, the *prima facie* case would then be that the course of literary development – its lulls, peaks, dying branches and new shoots – is determined by the main course of history. Yet it is the case that expert literary opinion, when it must enter onto the plane of history, tends to brush aside, cursorily or defiantly, this dependence of the literary on the historical. Saintsbury remarks blandly in his often reprinted *History* that 'The best explanation why there is no poet in English who is the equal of Chaucer between Chaucer himself and Surrey, is that, as a matter of fact, no such poet appeared.'[2] Plainly, such an approach makes the writing of history proper – that is, the sequential explanation of phenomena – impossible. No one bothers with Saintsbury now. But it was just recently that a very senior and leading authority ended his survey of seventeenth-century prose by saying: 'It is no doubt beyond the wit of any man to say why the novel should have been born in the eighteenth century and not earlier.'[3] If such an approach had its way, literature would be the one phenomenon in the universe without either a cause or a subsequent explicable evolution. This may be what the experts want. One common view is typified by this passage from Graham Hough's book on modernism:

Literature, by a fortunate dispensation, does not reflect very accurately the convulsions of the social order. Its revolutions sometimes precede the social ones, sometimes follow them, sometimes, it would seem, overlap them quite pointlessly... But as soon as we begin to look closely at a particular patch of literature we are likely to see it developing according to its own principles, which have their own interest, and are likely to be at least partly fortuitous in their relations to the wars, technologies or movements of classes that are their temporal accompaniments. The dispensation is fortunate, for it is a happy instance of what we mean by the freedom of the spirit.
　... In short, a literary revolution must be a *literary* revolution if it is to be anything. It may accompany or be accompanied by almost any other kind of revolution, at almost any distance... But unless we are

2. George Saintsbury, *A Short History of English Literature* (1929), p. 154.
3. F. P. Wilson, *Seventeenth Century Prose* (University of California Press, 1960), pp. 21–2.

looking at literature as a symptom of something else (a possibly respectable occupation, but not that of the literary critic) what must be
attended to is the behaviour of literature itself.[4]

In this anti-historical climate – backed, as we can see in Hough,
by the overwhelming prestige of notions like 'the freedom of the
human spirit' – attempts to explain literature coherently have
been rather rare. Three sorts crop up: The critic notes striking
likenesses between works of an epoch but stops short of explaining their emergence together. The critic offers a model of literary
development which sounds well as a metaphor but is only
pseudo-explanatory. The critic offers to sketch a theory of literary
development but it is liable to go for nothing unless it is put to
work – verified – in specific literary fields.

As an example of the first, various efforts have been made to
explain the emergence of modernism – that extraordinary burst
of innovating which showed marked likenesses (collage, pastiche,
borrowings from 'primitive' art, deliberate disruption of the
beautiful) even between arts as different as fiction, music, and
painting. In one recent essay Alan Bullock, the historian, drew
together many of these innovations, in science and machinery
as well as in the arts, from around 1900 and tried to formulate
them as a qualitative leap in the growth of civilization. But his
conclusion was a wistful anti-climax: 'Surely, the break-up of
the old patterns in so many different spheres at roughly the same
point of time cannot have been accidental,' and there the matter
trailed off.[5] It could be that a modern historian, biographer of
Hitler and Ernest Bevin, is out of his element in the history of
art. Yet what help could he have got from his literary colleagues?
I had had hopes of Ellman and Feidelson's massive compilation,
The Modern Tradition (1965), with its sub-title *Backgrounds of
Modern Literature*. But it is only another reader in philosophies,
in the proliferation of words about words. Their main headings
are: Symbolism, Realism, Nature, Cultural History, the Uncon-

4. Graham Hough, *Reflections on a Literary Revolution* (Catholic University of America Press, Washington, D.C., 1960), p. 1.
5. Alan Bullock, 'The Double Image', *Listener* (19 March 1970), p. 373.

scious, Myth, Self-Consciousness. I find missing here (among the areas next door to literature) social history and the sciences. I find missing from inside literature itself the idea of function and the genre of documentary. The effect is to treat literature as a kind of condensing from mid-air of that old gas, the Spirit of the Age. In the section on 'Artist and Society' I find missing: art as a persuader, art as the voice of a group, art as a bearer of information. From among the authors' range of sociological terms – which do include 'manners', 'class', and 'fact' – I find missing: the city, party and partisanship, and work ... In short, the muscle and bone of life have been filleted out, which leaves, presumably, the soul. In another book, now much in use, *Tradition and Dream* by Walter Allen, the critic offers much the same cluster of modernist innovations as in Bullock's essay; he briefly raises the question whether they arose from the ferment of the Great War, and concludes from the dates that it cannot have been the War – Stravinsky, Picasso, Chekhov, Joyce, Freud had all set out on their new paths well before 1914. So he falls back on Virginia Woolf's epigram, 'On or about December 1910 human nature changed.'[6] Once again a critic, in his theoretical innocence, has been unable to take the following steps of reasoning: (1) If upheavals or qualitative leaps occur nearly simultaneously in literature and in social life, it is more likely than not that they are causally connected. (2) But the one cannot be a 'reflection' of the other, for how could artists transform their modes and styles so quickly as to be able to catch the essence of a new way of life a few bare months or years after it had dawned? (3) The probability, therefore, is that they are connected by a common root, which clearly must be looked for in the generations immediately before the change itself. This conclusion may seem a platitude, yet it is necessary, in order to rebut the notion of literature as the 'reflection' of its age without entirely uprooting it from history. What we have to recognize is that evidently kindred developments on the planes of history and literature are more likely than not to be *cognate*.[7]

6. Walter Allen, *Tradition and Dream* (Phoenix House, 1964), pp. 1–3.
7. I have expanded on this, in relation to Scott and Wordsworth, in my chapter in G. H. R. Parkinson (ed.), *Georg Lukács*, pp. 202–7.

Secondly, critics have tried to make sense of literary development by means of models or metaphors. For years the most popular was that of the pendulum: writers and public tire of the established mode, for example the Augustan 'formality', and the pendulum swings to the other end of its arc, in this case the natural language and spontaneous emotion of the Romantics. This is what Cazamian presumably means by 'the oscillation of the moral rhythm of the English national soul'.[8] It is true that modes are presently felt to be outworn and art has to be made new. But the pendulum model fails to explain why the new generation of artists choose this or that group of modes from the infinite range at their disposal – it appears to postulate pairs of opposite qualities, so that if age 1 goes in for x, then age 2 will necessarily swing to minus x. This would make prediction easy. Yet the fact is that usually we have had no idea of what form the new wave will take. Even retrospectively the pendulum model fails to work. Consider the opening of Turberville's *English Men and Manners in the Eighteenth Century* (and I take so out-of-date a book because the traces of its half-truths are still to be seen on all sides, both in the assumptions made by young students and in scholarly work on the subject such as Sutherland's *Preface to Eighteenth Century Poetry*):

... every age in developing its own distinctive genius is to a certain extent in reaction against its predecessor. Such is the explanation of the literary school which dominates the first part of the period – the school of Pope. Its work was extraordinarily chaste in expression and highly polished; it was also notably devoid of enthusiasm. This was because it thoroughly disliked and disapproved of the florid, extravagant language and forced involved ideas and conceits which had marred some of that so-called 'late Elizabethan literature which is really Jacobean. The Classical school condemned that style as unnatural and in bad taste, and demanded greater restraint, correctness, and purity of diction. It made literature 'gentlemanly', and it appealed to a small educated class composed of London society.[9]

8. Quoted from René Wellek and Austin Warren, *Theory of Literature*, 3rd ed. (Penguin, 1963), p. 253.

9. A. S. Turberville, *English Men and Manners in the Eighteenth Century*, 2nd ed. (Oxford, 1929), pp. 1–2.

All the questions are here left begged. The reasons for the dislike of 'enthusiasm', which were at bottom a fear of popular upheaval, the democratic sects, and other such forces that had emerged in the seventeenth-century revolution, are made exclusively stylistic – a distaste for florid and extravagant language. And this cannot be true, for the poetry of the time was heavily influenced (disabled, I would say) by the magniloquence it learned from Milton. Then the swing of the stylistic pendulum is supposed to have 'made literature "gentlemanly" ' – and lo and behold! there the gentlemen were, waiting for the literature. This simply stands the process on its head and, worse, insulates from each other the evolution of the class and the evolution of the medium. How much truer it would have been to the real interaction of cultural forces if Turberville had been able to see as *cognate* the two things – urbane style and the affluent metropolitan upper-middle class dependence of monarchy and aristocracy on the City of London.

The axiom implicit in this would be as follows: It is certainly proper to postulate a degree of autonomy for the literary forms: once the essay or the satire or the novel is there, artists will seek to develop the form to its uttermost, and stale forms will need to be replaced by something fresh and different. But their emergence in the first place, and the precise forms taken by their later growth and by what it is that evolves to replace them, cannot be explained in isolation from their environment.

Thirdly, critics have attempted ambitious sketches for a theory of literary development, often by taking up the language of a relevant science – fifty years ago that of Darwin, more recently that of Karl Mannheim. Around the turn of the century there appeared things like Brunetière's *Evolution des genres* and John Addington Symond's 'On the Application of Evolutionary Principles to Art and Literature'.[10] Too often this work never got beyond the truism that the art forms wax and wane. The agents of change were not identified. But there is one piece from that phase, on the origin of the drama in England, which goes so deeply into literary change that it could be that it has in it, by

10. These references are taken from Part 3, 'The Extrinsic Approach to the Study of Literature', of Wellek and Warren's *Theory of Literature*.

analogy, something of what is needed for other forms and ages. Its author, Manly, writes that he did not set out to be Darwinian about literature but was brought by the facts of his specialism to see that

it is practically impossible to speak or think of any unified body of facts showing progressive change as men habitually spoke and thought before 1860. That we should still speak and think as if the needs of human thought could be met by a mere chronological record is not to be wished ... [11]

Manly then discusses the various seemingly embryonic forms of drama all of which failed to evolve into the drama proper – the ritual of the mass, the dialogic element in epic and in sermons – and shows how the take-off came with the unauthorized variations, both musical and verbal, that crept into the liturgy. These tropes presently grew out from every important feature of the mass, and one of them was an antiphonal lyric which the two halves of the choir sang during the Introit at Easter. The question-and-answer form of it was potentially dramatic and it became fully and formally so when it began to be sung by two priests impersonating the angels at the tomb and three other priests impersonating the three Marys (pp. 5, 7–8).

This is profoundly suggestive and wants to be applied to all the major forms and changes of form in literary history. But as theory it is not yet complete. Trope into drama, or Newgate criminal's confessions into novel as in Defoe, is the literary equivalent of the biologist's mutation – it happens under the momentum of the organism. But what can be the equivalent for literature of the biologist's natural selection, the process whereby some forms take and flourish while others die out? Manly writes:

... particular species seem to have special periods of mutation. During these periods, variations, mutations resulting in new species, are produced in great abundance ... And in each case we can find a probable cause of the period of productiveness, of variability, in the fact

11. J. M. Manly, 'Literary Forms and the New Theory of the Origin of Species', *Modern Philology*, IV, No. 4 (April 1907), p. 4.

that each follows hard upon, and is part of, a great intellectual or artistic movement [pp. 17–18].

But what caused these great movements? Manly's argument here unfortunately is circular. It turns back on itself and explains nothing, and this seems to be typical of the theories that treat intellectual movements or the history of ideas as prime movers in cultural growth. One critic who uses Mannheim writes as follows on the problem of explaining a cultural period:

First, select a period for study and pick the problem to be treated, setting up the leading concept and its opposite. Second, on the initial level of imputation analyse all the works involved, trace them to the central common idea, for example, transcendentalism, and produce a structural type which makes the *Weltanschauung* clear. Third, analyse the works and see to what extent they fit the construction … [12]

But already the fatal circularity has entered in, for of course the works will 'fit the construction' once they have been chosen according to the 'central concept' or 'central common idea' from which the inquiry started! Kern goes on:

Fourth, on the level of sociological imputation, by going behind the *Weltanschauung*, seek to derive the structure and tendencies of thought style from the composition of the groups, classes, generations, occupations, sects, parties, regions, cliques, or schools which express themselves in that mode.

By this time we are surely feeling that it would have been better if the *Weltanschauung* had never been there to be groped through or past in the first place, and equally that it is probably obfuscating to think of the main impulse of a period as something abstract like 'transcendentalism'. Unfortunately, ideas are repeatedly in this way treated as prime movers – the student who feels called upon to read something more than just the text and one or two critics is all too likely to turn to Basil Willey's potted histories of English philosophy. This, as we have seen already, merely throws us back on the prior question: What caused the

12. Alexander Kern, 'The Sociology of Knowledge in the Study of Literature', *Sewanee Review*, L (1942), p. 507.

ideas? For presumably they did not start into being by a kind of virgin birth. Consider two cases where ideology might seem prior to the literary developments. The devotee of *Weltanschauung* would presumably make utilitarianism prime for the period 1800–1860 and existentialism prime for the period 1940–1960. For the former, it seems to me that if Bentham and James Mill had never written a word and Chadwick had never worked for the Poor Law Commission, the best work of Wordsworth, Shelley, and Dickens would still have been as it was, for what they confronted in their day was the closing in of rigid systems – genteel taboos and prohibitions and the enclosures, factories, workhouses, and grid-plan towns. From this environment sprang the Romantic revolt and the condition-of-England novels and from it too sprang the utilitarian philosophy. The two sorts of work are cognate. The ideology is in no sense prior. But the case of existentialism seems to enforce the opposite conclusion, which shows how needful it is to be undogmatic in the framing of literary laws. For it seems *not* to be the case that Sartre's trilogy and Camus's *Outsider* and Beckett's *Waiting for Godot* would have been as they were even if the young Marx, Nietzsche, Heidegger, and the rest had never written a word. The death of God had brought home to people that man is in a state of *Geworfenheit ins dasein*; we are thrown into existence by a physical process we do not choose and must thenceforward fill our lives by projects that are forever sapped by our awareness that they are provisional. Certainly, the notion of man anguished at his own freedom because he has nowhere to turn as he makes his choices has sunk so deeply recently because the writers, along with everyone else, have had to confront the workings, on a scale that could engulf the world, of those faceless powers – powers controlled from hundreds or thousands of miles away – that have given rise to the Displaced Person, the Occupied Country, the men or women who are robbed, under hideous extremes of stress, of all their attributes and, almost, of themselves. But it seems likely that this experience has been dealt with so often in modes of fantasy or fable that treat the matter apart from specific social circumstances – Beckett's and Pinter's plays, Camus's novels, Ted Hughes's 'Crow' poems – because it had been worked over so intensively in an abstract form by the philosophers.

In this latter case, then, the thought and the literature are not cognate – two among many offshoots of the one root. The thought has helped mould in advance how the writers will take the experience when it comes. But so far as my knowledge goes such cases are outnumbered by those in which the literary development is part of a whole cultural process, historically caused, in which *Weltanschauung* is one among many factors and not a prime mover or fountainhead.

Of course the lack of satisfactory historicist theory doesn't preclude extremely valuable work which explains how literature has developed over particular phases. This point can be made most briefly by saying that Leavis's *Revaluation* is the only history of English poetry that I find useful when I need more than facts and references. In this same field there is another book, Rodway's *Romantic Conflict*, which brings out well how possible it is for a critic to spell out boldly the historical causes of developments in literature without at all abating his discrimination as a critic. The opening section of the book is a seamless historicist account of why the Romantic poetry emerged as and when it did, and from the start it is clear that this critic is fully aware of the kind of explanation he is offering:

Chance could hardly ordain that in England all those coming to maturity between 1789 and 1830, and possessed of poetic genius, should have been born with a romantic temperament while the genius of, say, 1689 to 1730 was born Augustan. We are forced to the conclusion that the milieu probably encouraged one type of genius and inhibited another. The art-form is inseparable from the circumstances of the age.[13]

Put so clearly it may even sound trite – 'mere commonsense'. Yet it is very uncommon: Leavis, for example, while epitomizing admirably the social conditions that account for the difference between the poetry of before and after the Restoration, is silent on the equivalent causes for the emergence of the Romantics and

13. Allan Rodway, *The Romantic Conflict* (Chatto, 1963), p. 4.

can even single out as the best of Shelley those intensely revolutionary poems of 1819 without even a hint to the effect that it was the political crisis in the year of Peterloo which at last matured his art.

As Rodway gets into the poetry itself, we see that he is in no danger of oversimplifying to fit a thesis. Romanticism he defines as the poetry that 'enfranchised psychological states, including some subconscious ones, by giving them thenceforward the status of fact' (p. 3), and he explains this phenomenon as follows:

Romanticism grew as reform came to seem more desirable than stability ... the literary revolt was symptomatic of a wide-spread social conflict and a deep-seated psychological one connected with it ... a sudden increase in social pressures seems to have resulted in a corresponding increase of force in the poetry ... The later romantic writers [i.e. later than Chatterton, Smart, Cowper] revolted radically against their society because they were revolted by it, and this provoked a daring, a heart-searching, a struggle both deeper and more directed than anything their predecessors got into their poetry [pp. 13–14].

Implicit in this is the idea – vital for the historicist approach – that the social and the psychological should not be thought of as mutually exclusive entities: they are two aspects of the human condition. The same flexible attention to the 'two' aspects is at work in Rodway's account of the pre-Romantic phase, that of Sensibility, which he interprets as 'unpurposive pity, which seems, psychologically speaking, to be a sign of guilt and a substitute for reformism' (p. 22). The phases or waves inside the Romantic period are then defined with a clarity that is equally historical and literary. 1789 stands as the date of the French Revolution and of Blake's *Songs of Experience*, 1824 as the date of Byron's death and of the repeal of the Combination Acts. 1804–15 is viewed as a stasis – a time of religious revival, some hopes for reform, and the release of emotion against the now outright enemy, France. In literary terms Rodway calls this the 'period of the pseudo-romantics', such as Moore and Campbell, and of the 'traditionalist' Scott – to which he might have added that it also marked virtually the end of Wordsworth as a creative force. Renewed tyranny by government and struggle against it, from

1815 to 1824, he views as a phase of 'unattained liberty', characterized by poets of 'European vision' – Byron and Shelley, who now supplanted Coleridge and Wordsworth as talents capable of making innovations in their art that heightened its responsiveness to changes in contemporary experience.

This seems to me a model of how to explain a period, and as such it should be (what it certainly is not) the kind of thing which literary people, by which one means students, teachers, critics, and interested readers generally, have at their fingertips. There are just two things which leave me afraid that such single explanatory works may fail to make the headway they deserve. The first is Rodway's tendency occasionally to lose sight of his usually clear vision of how the history determines the literature. For example, he argues that the phase from 1760 to 1790 makes 'romanticism a psychological necessity, but does not otherwise further its expression' because there were various remedial forces that kept people lulled – the outlet offered by Methodism, the rise of Cabinet government which seemed as though it might be a check on the oligarchy of the landowners. But he then blurs this by adding: 'More important than these reasons, however, is the fact that the poets have no theory, and therefore, so to speak, don't know they are romantic' (pp. 21–2, 31). This verges on the fault of making ideology prior, for it begs the question: Why had they no theory – that is to say, no developed awareness that they 'spoke for great causes' (as Rodway later puts it)? Surely because the causes themselves were still latent, seeds just under the surface. The poets' lack of theory – the fact that the Preface to *Lyrical Ballads* was not yet written – is itself a symptom of a society still lulled by the sense that piecemeal changes would suffice.

My second reason for wishing the laws of literary development to be spelled out more fully than they are even by Rodway (or Leavis) is that if they are not given serious status in literary opinion, it is always possible for people to say, 'Well yes, of *course* from time to time one gets these schools of writers who are so involved in social movements that obviously *their* work can be explained historically,' and historicism is written off as at best a circular argument, and even so of limited application. If there is an orthodoxy in literary studies, it is this ahistorical or anti-historical bias. As Wellek and Warren put it, there are two sorts of literary historian, those who 'treat literature as mere documents for the illustration of national or social history' and those who do treat it as an art but 'appear unable to write history ... lacking any conception of real historical evolution'.[14] Indeed it seems that this state spreads well beyond literature. In his 'Digression on Art History' Karl Mannheim has to report that while modern art-historians have moved on to a 'wider conception of art history as an aspect of the religious and philosophical modulations of ideas', they still haven't 'advanced to the cardinal questions of art history':

whose mentality is recorded by given art objects? ... what action, situations and what tacit choices furnish the perspectives in which artists perceive and represent some aspect of reality? If works of art reflect points of view, beliefs, affirmations, who are the protagonists and who are the antagonists? Whose reorientation is reflected in the changes of style? Such questions do not arise within the fragmentary view of art objects. The conceptual vacuum between them will only be concealed, not bridged, by such traditional concepts as 'the spirit of the times'.[15]

In the literary field most of the closely argued works in which the question of literary development is raised either explain it wholly from within itself – it unfolds; or else they deal polemically in a dismissive way with the historicist approach. There is room here to discuss in detail one of each kind – Josephine Miles on the evolution of poetry and Diana Spearman on the evolution of fiction.

For convenience Miles's work, which is now formidably influential in at least some circles, must be represented by a single essay, 'Eras in English Poetry', in which she uses a method akin to such other works of hers as *Eras and Modes* and *The Continuity of Poetic Language*. At the start of the essay she remarks

14. *Theory of Literature*, p. 252.
15. Karl Mannheim, *Essays on the Sociology of Culture* (Routledge, 1967), pp. 32–3.

that 'neither diction nor metrics alone seems to provide a pattern regular enough to mark change' but sentence structure 'does reveal a sequential pattern'.[16] Her types of sentence are: substantival or phrasal – more adjectives than verbs; clausal – more verbs than adjectives; and balanced – averaging one verb and one adjective per line. Applying these criteria in her undoubtedly thorough word-count of the British and American poets from 1500–1900, she finds a sequence of four groups, one in each century, 'each begun by an extreme and terminated by a balance' (pp. 854, 858). As soon as this is turned into particulars, doubts arise. For example, she says that 'some poetic sense of century seems undeniable'; yet of the Classical period she says that 'The eighteenth century began with Prior and Thomson' (p. 855), and we know that Thomson, poet of *The Seasons*, was not a force in poetry (if 'force' is the word for work so enfeebled by artifice) until 1730. Since Blake and Burns already counted in poetry by 1790, and Burns became rapidly and widely influential, this reduces the eighteenth century to sixty years, and years not at all neatly fitted into the century proper. Again, her phase of balance – what she calls the 'levelling, composing, classicizing of what had gone before' – is supposed to come at the end of each century. Her sixteenth-century example is Shakespeare's sonnets, which is all right by dates (though hardly a sample of major Shakespeare), but her nineteenth-century example is Swinburne, who flourished a full generation before that century came to an end. The centuries, therefore, as one would have expected, don't turn out to be actual phases in the development of poetry.

The next objection begins to create doubts of principle as well as of detail. She refers to 'the phrasal extreme of adjectives twice verbs in mid-eighteenth century' (p. 859). I take it that the middle eighteenth century which matters to us is the completed *Dunciad* and the satires 'On the Use of Riches' and Johnson's 'Vanity', and since these don't strike us as at all 'adjectival', whom can she mean? Her tables show that she means John Dyer (author of *The Fleece*), with a typical count of 13 adjectives/20 nouns/8

16. *Proceedings of the Modern Language Association*, LXX (1955), p. 853. It is unconsciously revealing that the only change she finds significant is apparently that which can be expressed in a *regular* pattern.

verbs, and Thomson, with a count of 15/18/7. Pope's count is 11/20/11 and Johnson's is 10/21/11 (p. 872). It begins to look as though the poets of 'balance' in this sample are the best poets and the 'phrasal' ones are the less dynamic and varied talents. A check through the rest of the tables confirms this. Poets who are either balanced or clausal are: Donne, Herbert, Wyatt, Jonson, Chaucer, Pope, Johnson, Burns, Dryden, Hopkins, Yeats, and T. S. Eliot. Phrasal poets are: Dyer, Thomson, Spenser, Milton, Shelley, Keats, Tennyson.[17] Inside single poets, Blake's *Songs* are clausal, his *Prophetic Books* are phrasal. So all that has been done is to produce a laborious confirmation by statistics of what was already, I trust, our view: good poetry seems alive with activity, experience enacts itself in the words, whereas weak poetry strives for its effects by applying qualities like labels, by means of adjectives, to an essentially static or inert vision.

If one then scrutinizes Josephine Miles's method of sampling, it turns out to show how needful it is to keep active the evaluative aspect, *whatever* type of analysis one is making. Since she is counting up the occurrences of key words, the validity of her findings depends on what poetry she picks to count. A poet is allowed into only one slot: for example, Shakespeare counts only for 1570–1600, which leaves out the bulk of the work for which we remember him. Donne too is pre-1600 only, which leaves out his religious poetry. Marvell is in only for 1670–1700, for the *Poems on Affairs of State* – precisely those which are least read. Wordsworth is only in 1770–1800, i.e. he is represented by *Lyrical Ballads* and not by 'Michael', 'The Brothers', and *The Prelude*. Sassoon, Owen, and Rosenberg are not in at all, though Edna St Vincent Millay and Edith Sitwell are. Cleveland is in but not Butler, Roscommon but not Rochester ... In short her judgement of value – of what poets can reasonably to taken to represent their period – is out of touch with the consensus of modern literary opinion. Now, her criterion in drawing up the lists of the favourite words used in each period is their frequency of occurrence in four or more poets (p. 868). Since we have just seen that she chooses poets

17. This is not, obviously, a complete listing of the poets she uses; it is a selection from the various types as they emerge according to her clausal/balanced/phrasal classification.

neither according to their sales – an objective criterion but impossible to ascertain for large areas of the field – nor according to their quality as evaluated by modern readers, and since insipid poets are measured on a par with important ones, it follows that she is not really measuring the *incidence* of words over a meaningful cultural area. An insipid poet, or a good one who for some reason gained little currency, would contribute comparatively few instances of his words being read, uttered, cited, or reprinted to the total usage in his society over a given time. An excellent one whose repute matched his quality, or a poor one who for some reason caught on, would of course contribute far more such instances. Josephine Miles has therefore measured neither the frequency of key words used in the significant poetry of our tradition nor the frequency of key words in all the poetry. It seems, therefore, that the critic should either work by the usual method of developing, on the basis of his own taste, his own view of the tradition, which he then offers for the use and interest of readers, or else he must go thoroughly statistical and process nothing less than the whole of the data in the given medium.

The remaining aspect of Josephine Miles's method is crucial for my argument, since it bears on the defining of epochs – that is, the drawing of date-lines. Because each poet can get into only one slot, she cannot take into account his possible effects either as a transitional figure or as an abiding contemporary influence on more than one generation of writers. She also says that 'poets seem to use one sentence structure ... predominantly through their work' (pp. 858–9). So if Wordsworth was balanced after 1800 (as he was before), and if she *had* allowed in his best poems up to 1805, balanced poets for the first phase of the nineteenth century would have outnumbered clausal ones by 2:1. Yet she counts this phase as clausal. Hardy is only in 1870–1900, yet at that time his reputation was as a novelist; his best poems mostly have dates and these dates are mostly between 1900 and 1912. Since he is clausal, putting him in 1900–1940 would have yielded equal numbers of clausal and balanced for that phase. Yet she has told us that a century is typically 'begun by an extreme'. It becomes plain that epochs cannot be delimited – let alone explained – by such data or such an analysis of it, any more than the Jehovah's

Witnesses have managed to foretell the end of the world by juggling the numbers in the Book of Ezekiel.

How can so minute and industrious a researcher come up with results so invalid? Apparently because her kind of approach irresistibly leads her to find regularities – it would cause her intellectual discomfort not to. But all she has to make patterns with is the language of poetry. And it seems that there is no reason inherent in it – so long as it is treated in isolation from all else – why it should manifest pattern. It is not a homogeneous material, like ice or nucleic acid, which could not exist were it not for their regular patterns. 'Poetry' is a highly mixed entity – it is a term given to different things by different ages and cultural groups. It can be used to cover forms of philosophy, propaganda, prayer, and a host of directly functional forms that include lullabies, work-songs, weather rhymes, and the bits in the 'In Memoriam' columns of the newspapers. Since it is so mixed or hybrid, we should not expect there to be a set of laws that apply to it alone or could be derived from it alone. And since its hybrid nature results from crossing with other media and materials, of a non-'artistic' or directly socially functional kind, it follows that whatever laws we can find for poetic and other literary development should recognize this by including elements that represent the integral being of the literary and the social-historical (see p. 160 below for my suggested 'laws'). As Mannheim puts it: 'Only society as a structured variable has a history and only in this social continuum can art be properly understood as a historical entity.'[18]

Diana Spearman's book *The Novel and Society* (Routledge, 1966) is a much more rigorous challenge to the historicist approach. It amounts to a handbook of all those methods and specific points that one must be able to meet or rebut if one is to maintain the position that laws of literary development necessarily involve history. Her first step is to put together from several critics a simplified, and thus vulnerable, form of the historicist theory of the early novel in Britain, which even becomes 'a sort of class manifesto' (p. 49). She then tries to show that the novels of

18. *Essays on the Sociology of Culture*, p. 33.

Defoe and Fielding and Richardson were not particularly for the middle class, nor about them, nor was their heyday a heyday also of the middle class. Before entering into the detail of this, two points from among the assumptions stated in her Introduction need to be dealt with. First, she writes that the 'assertion that the style and content is determined by the social context ... fails to explain why people ... enjoy reading [authors] who speak from so different a world that it is not necessary to fit them into the political spectrum' and she cites the kind of personal experience, such as *déja vu*, which was known in twelfth-century Japan as in our own place and time (pp. 3, 12–13). The explanation isn't hard to find, and I don't pretend that it is exclusively historicist. What exists in society is an organism, an animal, a species, named *homo sapiens*, which over millennia has scarcely changed. So we can respond with delight or wonder to the bulls of Lascaux or of Picasso, the stories of Homer or Lawrence. What the 'social context' determines is the stressing and selecting of specific fibres out of that whole nature and the bringing of them into prominence through particular styles or linguistic forms.[19] Again Mrs Spearman writes: 'If literature is tied to a particular social setting, how is it that no literature which is incomprehensible to us has been found?' (p. 5). Partly, again, because the behaviour patterns and environments of our species don't differ utterly over the years, and partly because to understand a piece of literature is partly to learn facts about a condition – perhaps a temperament, perhaps a social way of life – different from one's own. The information that we need to make sense of the work comes to us in the imaginative work itself. Clearly this does not exclude the social, for in adjusting our

19. This point is well put by Barrington Moore in the section on 'Reactionary and Revolutionary Imagery' in his *Social Origins of Dictatorship and Democracy*: 'There is always an intervening variable, a filter, one might say, between people and an "objective" situation, made up from all sorts of wants, expectations, and other ideas derived from the past. This intervening variable, which it is convenient to call culture, screens out certain parts of the objective situation and emphasizes other parts ... what looks like an opportunity or a temptation to one group of people will not necessarily seem so to another group with a different historical experience and living in a different form of society.' (Penguin ed., 1969), p. 485.

responses to what may at first reading be an alien convention, we are at the same time and by this very process seeing through to the society which had needed to create this medium of art in the first place. Finally, she writes: 'The persistence of certain themes also seems hard to understand' (p. 5) – that is, if literature is the product of particular societies. The persistence of motifs and themes (her example is the Arthurian legends) can be explained by the comparative continuity of human nature, while the difference in treatment, which makes Malory and Tennyson so unlike as artists, is presumably due to the quite different sorts of audience and role for the artist that the late-medieval and the early-industrial cultures called into being.[20]

The particular form of her anti-historicist thesis, then, is to refute the 'generally accepted [notion] that the society of eighteenth-century England in some way produced or moulded the eighteenth-century novel' (p. 7). First she finds what are certainly clear cases of novels well before the eighteenth century, for example *Don Quixote* and *La Princesse de Clèves*, and from this argues that the lengthy prose fiction cannot have been a distinctive out-growth of the age of Defoe. Of course there would be forerunners – there always are, since the whole of human development is latent or potential from the beginnings of the species. Whatever cultural features we choose, we find cases of the 'modern' outcropping long before our age. Municipal drainage and two-storey houses with bathrooms existed in the Indus Valley nearly five thousand years ago.[21] So in literature: there was realistic narrative in Bronze Age Crete and medieval Japan, yet those were not ages of the novel because prose narrative of everyday incident was still uncommon, whereas in Britain fiction now accounts for about 5,000 of the 22,000 titles published annually. This point is in fact a crux of the many-sided debate between the progressives and the conservatives, which means also the historicists and the empiricists. For example, a common defence of the early industrial revolution against the indictment

20. The different treatments of this material over the years have been analysed by A. L. Morton in his paper 'The Matter of Britain', *Zeitschrift für Anglistik und Amerikanistik* (Berlin, 1960), I, pp. 1–24.

21. Gordon Childe, *What Happened in History* (Penguin, 1954), p. 127.

brought by Engels, Marx, the Hammonds, and others has been that, really, the effects were not so very terrible and in any case there was no such thing as an industrial *revolution*. J. U. Nef, the historian of the coal industry, brings figures to show that mining was a much more productive and highly capitalized industry in Tudor times than had been realized. No doubt. But what Nef never does and could not prove is that mechanized work was at any time before 1800 on a scale that could transform the family life, working habits, settlements, and population distribution of entire nations. The major forerunners in England by which Spearman tries to prove that the novel was not specially an eighteenth-century thing are the prose romances, especially Malory's *Morte d'Arthur*, with their comparatively lifelike settings, dialogue, and details of behaviour. But as she herself has to note, 'none of the realistic romances attracted much of an audience' and 'Neither Malory nor de la Sale [author of the main French realistic romance, the *Petit Jehan de Saintré*] found much of an audience' (pp. 84, 100). In short, the situation about 1500 was that people were already inclined to pay some attention to stories of likely or possible experiences but that this was still greatly overshadowed by their fascination with fantasy, whether in the religious, the romantic, or the heroic mode.

As for the nature of the eighteenth century considered as an epoch, Spearman has to strain to make out that it was not particularly 'bourgeois' (her own term). In politics, she implies, the old fundamentals remained little changed. This is not the view of the leading authorities, who see the later seventeenth century as a political watershed.[22] As for the nation's work, of

22. Spearman points out that people still invoked medieval precedents to justify curtailing the monarchy's powers, the House of Commons still didn't dominate Parliament, and the City of London, though powerful, had always been politically influential. The facts are that for the first time the monarch had to have his budget voted after hard debate in Parliament and that the members doing the debating included from the 1690s those men who were nicknamed 'the Puritan Usurers of Grocer's Hall' – the governors of the newly founded Bank of England. 'In 1660,' says our leading historian of the seventeenth century, 'the City had probably played the decisive part in restoring Charles II; in 1688 its leading role was formally recognized'; and inside the City itself, its Council 'was no longer checked by the richer and

course corn and wool still bulked largest in our trading but (even according to her own figures) manufactures were *expanding faster*, and here as so often what counts culturally is the thrust of the new factor, which begins to change people's sense of the possibilities open to them.[23] It must be for this reason that the supreme poetry of the later seventeenth century, Dryden's *Medall* and *Absalom and Achitophel*, reaches its intense points, its clusters of organic imagery, when the poet has visions of disorder engendered from the rich slime of London's commercial artery, the Thames. That is why Pope, a generation later, reaches a peak when satirizing the abuses of affluence. That is why in popular song by the last quarter of the seventeenth century 'references to economic conditions ... money or the lack of it ... had a way of getting in everywhere'.[24] That is why the new fashionable medium, the essay, goes off into rhapsodies on wealth when Addison (in the *Spectator* for 19 May 1711) conjures up a kind of dance of the commodities in honour of the Stock Exchange.

If the age, then, was indeed coloured and moulded by trade and the people taken up with it, what was the class position of

---

more conservative aldermen'. (See Max Weber, *The Protestant Ethic and the Spirit of Capitalism*, [London, 1930], p. 186, n. 6; Christopher Hill, *The Century of Revolution, 1603–1714*, [Nelson, 1961], pp. 275–6).

23. According to Spearman herself, the contemporary comment on Henry Pelham (who was the most successful politician of the time apart from Walpole) that he was 'a good man of business' could not have been made 'about an aristocratic statesman in any other country', for trade was 'not a class preserve but an interest of the whole nation' (pp. 25–7). Precisely. Here we have the typical outlook of a country anxious to put well behind it the turbulence of the previous century, when a king had been beheaded, power changed hands through *force majeure*, rich landowners were expropriated, and at times (as between Cromwell's death and Charles II's Restoration) neither shops nor law courts could do business because of the unrest and violence. Now was the time, in the words of a Scottish nobleman in the 1700s, 'to live at peace and ease, and mind their affairs and the improvement of their country – a much better employment than in the politics'. (See H. W. Meikle, *Scotland and the French Revolution* [Glasgow, 1912], p. xvii.)

24. C. V. Wedgwood, *Poetry and Politics under the Stuarts* (Cambridge, 1960), p. 194.

the novelists themselves? Here is Spearman's way of expressing what she takes to be the historicist view:

> From constant references by literary critics to the optimism of the rising middle class and Puritan commercial morality, it might be supposed that Defoe was the pattern of a successful and upright businessman. In reality, not only was he a failure in business, but his life was so unusual as to make it impossible to regard him as the representative of any class [p. 29].

This makes the elementary mistake of reducing the typical to the average. For surely when we say that someone is 'typically American' or 'a real Londoner', we mean that he has *some* of what are accepted as the usual features of the group concerned.[25] In the case of Defoe and the other early novelists, what stands out is that they came, not from the richer or more powerful sections of society (the nobility and gentry), but from the less well off, usually the middle class. In France (according to Spearman herself) the first novels were *Le Roman comique* and *Le Roman bourgeois*, which 'deal with the life of the middle class'. The first German novelist, Grimmelshausen, was a mercenary (pp. 50, 56, 58). In Britain, as a matter of the novelists' conscious aims, Fielding and Richardson objected 'to the high rank of the characters' in popular fiction before their time (p. 107). As for their origins – the experiences they were able to drink in during their formative years – the changing state of affairs becomes clear if one studies the social circumstances of writers over the generations. The majority of 'standard' writers born between 1630 and 1680 were from the nobility and gentry, and the larger part of them went to Oxbridge. In the next generation, which includes the early novelists, the majority came from professional

25. Compare Marx on France in 1848: 'Just as little must one imagine that the democratic representatives are indeed all shopkeepers or enthusiastic champions of shopkeepers . . . What makes them representative of the petty bourgeoisie is the fact that in their minds they do not get beyond the limits which the latter do not get beyond in life, that they are consequently driven, theoretically, to the same problems and solutions to which material interest and social position drive the latter practically. This is, in general, the relationship between the *political* and *literary representatives* of a class and the class they represent.' (*The Eighteenth Brumaire of Louis Bonaparte*, [Moscow ed., 1954], pp. 65–6).

families of a mainly middle-class kind, and for the first time (in a record stretching back to 1480) less than half went to Oxbridge.[26]

So the evidence from both social and literary history suggests that the view of the eighteenth century as a middle-class heyday is no travesty but the truth. The culture that arose from this was one in which it became more and more natural to view experience, not under the aspect of eternity, but on the ground of one's own actual life. In terms of convention and the media, ceremony and mystique and tradition and ritual counted for less and less; the hallowed and remote – whatever might be the preserve of the elect or the privileged – counted for less. And this is the type of change in ethos, institutions, and media that the historicist is interested in. He does not confine himself to factors artificially isolated, such as trade by itself or politics by itself. He believes, with Marx, that the deepest-lying motive force of change in history is the struggle among sections of people for the means of life. What this changes is the culture as a whole, by 'culture' meaning that which is to the actual mass of people concerned very much what one's personality is to one's body. And from this culture – this new social frame of mind, cluster of habits, or life-style – emerge specific works which are thus representative of their epoch.

This is, unavoidably, so general that it may sound like a mere set of words whereby the theorist could bend any data to suit his bias. It needs to be checked against particular works and particular styles. On style, for Spearman, the eighteenth-century novel would typify a 'bourgeois' age only if it dealt repeatedly with money matters, average commercial careers, and the like. This is again her simplifying tactic but in this case it makes a point which needn't be rejected outright. Consider the matter both generally and specifically. In general, the seventeenth century had been remarkable for poetry and prose that worked out in a subtle, often a devious way the eternal – or more accurately the long-standing – issues of man in the universe, and the writers had tended to take their materials from any place and time. By

26. Raymond Williams, *The Long Revolution* (Penguin, 1965), pp. 257–8.

the later seventeenth century, and very clearly by the eighteenth, writers were tending to create a lifelike or readily recognizable image of life as it was there and then, in order to light up the problems, hazards, and distinctive flavours of our daily conduct. To make the case specifically: few critics would deny that *Moll Flanders* is the book that launches, that sets the first mode and tone for, the fiction of that century. It seems to be equally undeniable that *Moll Flanders* epitomizes a businesslike ethos in every fibre of its texture, whether it is the incessant stress on the mercenary (to the exclusion of most other human drives), or the rough-and-ready movement from episode to episode (typical of the producer of soap opera in any age), or its journalistic way of establishing authenticity by means of small circumstances. It is on the basis of this kind of literary evidence that critics of the finest perception have viewed Defoe as a typically 'bourgeois' writer. As Leslie Stephen put it: 'Defoe for the most part deals with good tangible subjects, which he can weigh and measure and reduce to moidores and pistoles.' Or Q. D. Leavis:

> The public for which *Roxana* was written was being indulged with a day-dream carefully moulded to its heart's desire: but a day-dream in which the solid unromantic interests ruled. Hence the stress in all the novels on 'portable property', the lists of stolen goods, booty, and possessions generally, the tiresome balancing of pros and cons in every possible situation, and the mental stock-taking which is a substitute for both psychology and emotion. And so, too, the running moral commentary. The reader is only interested in what touches his own daily life, and with all the opportunities of providing Count of Monte-Cristo attractions one observes in *Roxana* nothing of the kind: the middle station in Defoe's day was satisfied with its own way of living, and self-respecting enough to see no reason for coveting the splendours of high life.[27]

This focuses more sharply on the fiction itself than any passage in *The Novel and Society* and that is why it is able at the same time to grasp the book as an entity situated in history.

Whether full-fledged laws, thoroughly verified and with a predictive value, can be formulated by means of the historicist

27. Leslie Stephen, *Hours in a Library* (London, 1890 ed.), I, p. 20; Q. D. Leavis, *Fiction and the Reading Public* (London, 1932), pp. 103–4.

approach is something we will only know after much more work, preferably done by a team, and a team that includes social historians and sociologically trained critics of the mass media as well as literary critics. Throughout this paper I have used 'axiom' instead of the more imposing 'law'. But there are six hypothetical laws that I have formulated after working mainly with British literature from the sixteenth century to the present and it is possible that they may stand the test of being put to work in different fields. They are these:

The rise of a genre is likely to occur along with the rise of a class (e.g. in average wealth, in the proportion of the population belonging to it).

The waning of a genre (e.g. enervation and derivativeness of style, a shrinking number of leading writers expressing themselves through it) is likely to occur along with the waning of a class (e.g. one that is being supplanted by another in its influence on government).

A new genre is likely to piece itself together out of motifs, styles, means of circulation that had belonged to some medium not thought of as art proper.

Such an emergence is likely to take place at a time of social upheaval and rapid change.

A change in literature and a change in history that resemble each other (e.g. an emphasis on control, a seeking after spontaneity) are likely to be related, not directly, but by deriving from the same cause further back in history.

Clusters of works that have strong family likenesses yet whose authors differ in social position, outlook, etc., are particularly sensitive indicators of the feel and tendency of their culture.

Wordsworth and the People *

> My heart was all
> Given to the People, and my love was theirs.
>
> – *The Prelude*, Book IX

Wordsworth devoted the greater part of his life to the study of political and social questions, and Marx a great part of his to the study of poetry. For both men the French Revolution and the Industrial Revolution were supreme facts; and of the other chief ingredients of Marxism the poetry of the Romantic age is at least as important as the German metaphysics. Marx himself was once a young romantic poet, and if later on he and his friends were notably silent about the nature of their ideals, it was because they took these for granted and could confine themselves rigorously to building the road across chaos to the new world that the poets had seen in the distance. Today it may be time for Marxism to defend not only the economists of that age against their erring successors, but its writers, as men of revolutionary hopes and therefore in bad colour now, though in good company, with Milton.[1]

That in modern society intellectual and artist are separated from any genuine contact with their fellow men has come to be a matter of course. Only in epochs of great and volcanic energy is a high enough temperature generated to melt down this stony isolation, even partially. For the Romantics of Europe the fall of the Bastille was a wonderful event, above all because it made it seem possible for men like them to be brought back into the circle of humanity, as if returning to Eden. Of the English

---

* From *Democracy and the Labour Movement*, ed. John Saville (1956).

1. 'What Byron saw already – that Pope was a greater poet than Byron himself or any of his contemporaries – is now generally recognized. The Romantics are now under a cloud . . .' (S. Spender, *Shelley* [Longmans, 1952], p. 44.)

Romantic poets Wordsworth was the only important one who saw the Revolution as it were face to face; he experienced longer and more urgently than any of the others the problem of the relation between artist and people, art and life, individual and mass. 'Society has parted man from man';[2] he searched for a means of overcoming this morbid division, and his task was at bottom the same as that of finding a bridge between himself and the world of men. He failed; but if it is true that he has meant little to modern poets,[3] most of these have perhaps not even attempted what he failed in; and his work in the years round 1800 may still be, both for example and for warning, one of our chief starting-points for a new literature.[4]

In Wordsworth's *Descriptive Sketches*,[5] written in 1791–2 on the banks of the Loire, can be found a surprising number of what were to be the dominant themes of his later work. Prominent among them was that of Freedom, always to remain, though in diverse forms, one of his leading thoughts. Ages ago man was 'entirely free, alone and wild', 'none restraining, and by none restrained', unless by God. Even now, 'traces of primeval Man', of a bygone society not divided into classes, could be found in remote valleys like those of Switzerland, or of Cumberland. There, the argument implied, men felt no need of any government and ran no risk of misgovernment; all they wanted was to

2. *The Prelude*, II, 219. This and all later quotations from this poem are from the Text of 1805 edited by E. de Selincourt (1933). All references to the long poems are to the book and the line.

3. D. Bush, in *Wordsworth Centenary Studies*, ed. G. T. Dunklin (Oxford, 1951), p. 9.

4. With this work Blake's *Songs* might of course be coupled, and the resemblances and contrasts between these two poets are highly instructive.

5. Both the 1793 and the later versions are printed in the Oxford one-volume edition of Wordsworth (1904). All passages referred to here occur in the earlier text, if not in both. The earlier text is often the less polished; but Coleridge was to say of it: 'Seldom, if ever, was the emergence of an original poetic genius above the literary horizon more evidently announced.' (*Biographia Literaria*, 1817, chapter IV); cf. De Quincey's appreciation, in *Reminiscences of the English Lake Poets* [Everyman], pp. 129–30. G. M. Harper remarks that here already Wordsworth was describing common people with a novel freedom from condescension (*William Wordsworth, His Life, Works and Influence* [1916], I, p. 95).

be left alone. There was another side to the picture, however, in the cutting poverty of the free mountain-folk, poverty in which Wordsworth saw reflected 'the general sorrows of the human race'. His early pessimism was much more than a youthful pose; he was never to shake it off for very long. And this thought led directly to the conclusion of the poem, in which he saw the Revolution arming for battle against the leagued despots of Europe and prayed for the triumph of the good cause. He believed in the Revolution because he felt that it promised to bring Freedom down from the mountains, where she had been hiding like a timid chamois, onto the fertile plains. France had made the grand discovery that 'Freedom spreads her power Beyond the cottage-hearth, the cottage-door'.

Poverty could thus be abolished, for most of mankind were only poor because they were enslaved. In Wordsworth's later account of these days in *The Prelude*, the most poignant moment is the one where his friend Beaupuy points to the starving country girl and exclaims ' ''Tis against *that* Which we are fighting.' [6] Wordsworth was haunted all his life by the image of an outcast, suffering woman. It occurs first in the earliest of his poems that reached publication, 'An Evening Walk' of his college days – a sick woman dragging herself along the Lakeland roads with her starving infants: a single painful episode in an idyllic poem. [7] It reappears in *Descriptive Sketches*, and in all the succeeding long

6. *Prelude*, IX, 509 ff. The French Revolution and Wordsworth's interpretations of it are among the relevant topics which there is only space to mention briefly in this essay. He was a sort of 'Girondin', but his 'Apology' of 1793 could be at least as well described as 'Jacobin' in temper. In general, he may be forgiven for not having fully understood an upheaval whose complex forces we are still trying to understand today, after a hundred and fifty years.

7. The 'Evening Walk' was a rewriting of the still earlier 'Vale of Esthwaite', and the picture of the forlorn woman was originally borrowed from a poem by Langhorne. (See H. Darbishire, *The Poet Wordsworth* [Oxford, 1950], p. 20; E. de Selincourt, *Wordsworthian and Other Studies* [Oxford, 1947], pp. 15 ff.) For criticisms of the 'psychoanalytical' view that this theme was inspired by nothing more than a guilty conscience in Wordsworth himself, see W. L. Sperry, *Wordsworth's Anti-Climax* (1935), p. 95; H. Sergeant, *The Cumberland Wordsworth* (Williams & Norgate, 1950), pp. 28 ff.

poems, including *The Borderers*, as well as many short ones, down to 1800; it has other reincarnations after that, especially in *The White Doe*, and finally it dwindles away into those chocolate-box martyrs, the Russian Fugitive and the Egyptian Princess. In this figure we have a key to Wordsworth's social problem, that of poverty, as in the idea of Freedom we have a key to his political thinking. The Revolution brought the two together.

His politics in the period after his unpublished 'Apology for the French Revolution' of 1793 can be seen most clearly in two letters to Matthews in 1794, when they were planning a political journal.[8] His views were very radical indeed: he thought, though reluctantly, that things might soon become so bad as to make even the terrible event of a revolution in England welcome; not agitation, but a villainous Government, was driving the country towards it. He was above all outraged by what in his eyes was the monstrous wickedness of the Government in going to war with France; war, indeed, seemed to him the characteristic crime of States. He was doubly isolated. He wanted France to win, as she did; he was revolted by the Terror, the Jacobin dictatorship of the crisis; at home those in power seemed to him eager to imitate so far as they could the crimes though not the virtues of the Revolution, and to degrade law into 'A tool of Murder'.[9] The middle-class progressive movement towards Parliamentary reform was blocked; abstract radical theorizing among Godwinian intellectuals was no substitute for healthy activity. Wordsworth, a practical countryman, always wanted to come to grips with something concrete. He was growing disgusted with his own sort of people, as well as with his country; he 'Fed on the day of vengeance yet to come'.[10]

8. *The Early Letters of William and Dorothy Wordsworth, 1787–1805*, ed. E. de Selincourt (1938), pp. 114, 119.

9. *Prelude*, X, 648.

10. *Prelude*, X, 275. 'Wordsworth, as the course of his life shows, had not a *real* confidence in himself. He was curiously compounded of timorousness and courage.' (Harper, op. cit., II, p. 323; he emphasizes that Wordsworth was 'the most political of all our great poets' except Milton; I, p. ix.) This inner uncertainty in Wordsworth is to be connected with his isolation from any organized movement.

Hence his turning away from the educated classes to the 'common people', towards whom history was, as it were, forcing him all through his years as a great poet. The impulse had stirred in him earlier than this time. In his first vacation from Cambridge he had looked at his plain rustic neighbours with a new sense of 'love and knowledge', a new 'human-heartedness', and it was then that he had his nocturnal meeting with the old soldier whose 'ghastly figure', 'solemn and sublime' in its simplicity, was to throw a long shadow over his poetry.[11] In France he had loved 'the People', but a foreign people, and in part a figment of political rhetoric. Now he wanted to know his fellow beings as they really were.

How far he could get on this new road would depend on many things beside his own resources. He began, necessarily, with remnants of an older, pre-1789 way of looking at things, in which the philosopher or sage (or 'intellectual', as we say) virtuously dedicated himself to the happiness of his less fortunate fellows. In phrases like 'the labours of benevolence', 'the labours of the sage', 'Heroes of Truth',[12] we can see that attitude peeping out. From it to a real enrolment of the intellectual in a progressive mass movement was to be a very long-drawn historical process, far from completed a century and a half later. He found no organized movement to gravitate towards; and he was living near the end of the pre-Copernican epoch in political thought – with the Revolution, action had for the time left theory far behind – and had no serviceable analysis of classes or the State to help him. A radical error lurked in him from the beginning: he was turning to the common people, not so much in search of a force capable of carrying to success the lofty hopes fostered and disappointed since 1789, as in search of a consolation in the sight of humble virtue for the 'Ambition, folly, madness' of the world's rulers. He wanted to satisfy himself that 'real worth', 'genuine knowledge', 'true power of mind', could be found in the labouring poor, in spite of an unjust society, and that the basic human

11. *Prelude*, IV, 200 ff, 400 ff.

12. 'Lines left upon a Seat in a Yew-tree' (*Lyrical Ballads*, I), and cancelled stanzas of 'Guilt and Sorrow' (see Selincourt, *Wordsworthian and Other Studies*, op. cit., pp. 27–9).

qualities could thus survive in an iron age in the common people who – he agreed with Robespierre – were free of the corruptions of their superiors.[13]

These ideas must have been growing in his mind for a considerable time before he came to systematize them in the *Preface* of 1800. In the *Prelude* he associated them with, for instance, his walk on Salisbury Plain in 1793, when he felt again a fresh stirring of his poetic energy.[14] This was the decisive moment in the moulding of his next long poem, 'Guilt and Sorrow'.[15] It is a very impressive, though it may not be a dazzling poem. It moves firmly, with a strong cumulative effect; Wordsworth was never to achieve greater success along this line, or rather was never again to undertake anything quite like it. It owes its firmness of outline, and the solidity of its two chief characters, to the fact that the sufferings of these two homeless outcasts are rooted in the reality of social injustice. As before, Wordsworth keeps his two problems of government and poverty close together, under the shadow of his prime evil, unjust war. In 'An Evening Walk' the poor woman's husband was a soldier, far away 'on Bunker's charnel hill'. Here the man is a sailor, press-ganged and made to serve for years as 'Death's minister'; maddened by ill-usage, and so hurried into the crime of murder. His fellow vagrant is the daughter of a poor man ruined by oppression, the widow of an artisan ruined by war and unemployment and

13. *Prelude*, XII, 71, 98–9. Cf. Robespierre: 'I bear witness ... that in general there is no justice or goodness like that of the people ... and that among the poor ... are found honest and upright souls, and a good sense and energy that one might seek long and in vain among a class that looks down upon them.' (Speech of 22 August 1791; see J. M. Thompson, *Robespierre* [1935], p. 168.)

14. *Prelude*, XII, 312 ff.

15. According to Wordsworth's Note on this poem (see *The Prose Works of William Wordsworth*, ed. A. B. Grosart [1876], III, p. 10) the story of the 'Female Vagrant', forming the second part, was taken from life. The poem was begun in 1791, completed in 1794, and re-worked later; for instance in Germany in 1799 Wordsworth was thinking of inserting another improbable coincidence (*The Early Letters*, op. cit., p. 223). It was not published as a whole till 1842. With its range of ideas it may be compared with that of the *Religious Musings* (1794) of Coleridge, whose development was in many ways parallel to Wordsworth's.

driven by hunger into the army, where he perished. She too has been forced by misery into crime.[16]

Wordsworth comes closest here to reaching, but does not quite reach, a recognition of State and law as things not foreign and extrinsic to society, but integral parts of an unjust social order. His band of gypsies are happy because they have no chiefs or separate property among them, but they too stand outside society and can do nothing to remedy it – they are free men astray and soiled in a bad world. War is an unexplained evil; and in later years, when Wordsworth came to accept the war with France, he came to accept the British Government with it. At present, though this is a radical and 'progressive' poem, Wordsworth has not succeeded in making it a revolutionary one. Its atmosphere belongs to Dostoyevsky rather than to Gorky, or even to Tolstoy. At the bottom of these forlorn creatures a fundamental goodness remains, a light glimmers in the darkness. They, unlike their rulers, have sinned involuntarily, and it is better, the sailor tells the brutal peasants, to suffer than to inflict injuries. Wordsworth feels overpoweringly the guilt of society, but he is not strengthened by any active movement towards setting it right. It seems irremediable; and because of this it transfers itself to its own victims, who become its scapegoats. The sailor's obsessive memory of his own crime is what the poem succeeds most vividly in presenting. Haunted and paralysed by this sense of guilt, the sufferers of the social order are powerless against what has ruined them. It ends in that turning away from earth to heaven, later to become the fatal habit of Wordsworth's thinking.

In September 1795 he went to live with his sister Dorothy at Racedown in Dorset; from there he moved in July 1797 to Alfoxden in Somerset, in September 1798 to Germany, and finally in December 1799 to Grasmere. This 'healing time of his spirit'[17] has been much dwelt on by biographers, and he has been given much credit for shaking off his revolutionary nonsense and settling down sensibly like a middle-class poet to write

16. This version of 1798, as the 'Female Vagrant' stood in *Lyrical Ballads*, was later somewhat toned down.

17. J. C. Shairp, *Preface* to the 1874 edition of Dorothy Wordsworth's *Scottish Journal*, xvii.

middle-class poetry. This is misleading in several ways. He was not exactly retiring to the countryside, for he had already been spending nearly all his time there. In the region he was moving to in 1795 he would be likely to see a good deal more of the poverty and distress that beset his thoughts than he had been seeing in Penrith. 'The peasants are miserably poor,' wrote Dorothy in one of her first letters from Racedown.[18] The works he now set about writing (*The Borderers*, late 1795-6, and *The Ruined Cottage*, a slower growth) were still of an extremely gloomy cast, and continued the wrestling with his problems where 'Guilt and Sorrow' had left off. He was not throwing down his shield and flying from the battlefield like Horace at Philippi; he was only turning away from a 'fretful stir unprofitable', which included the uproar of war propaganda as well as vexation at his own unavailing efforts to find an active part to play. He still hated the Government and the condition of society, though it may be with less of urgency in his opposition as the war changed its character. The Revolution was over, France was out of danger after the Basle treaties of 1795, and on both sides the Anglo-French contest was falling back into its old rut, the quarrelling of two empires over markets and slave-plantations.

Wordsworth's opposition did, in the years 1795-1800, acquire more of a passive and negative character. In these five years he was to turn over many new leaves in English literature, and produce much work of high value. Other parts of his output were to be less good. He was losing as well as gaining, declining as well as advancing; and what he lost politically through being out of touch with any movement was of ill omen for his poetical future.

He began - simplifying his task for the moment and complicating it for the future - by separating his 'political' from his 'social' problem. *The Borderers* is an intellectual study of politics,

18. *The Early Letters*, op. cit., p. 148. The passage goes on: 'their cottages are shapeless structures . . . indeed they are not at all beyond what might be expected in savage life'. In many parts of Dorset whole parishes were being engrossed into one or two hands, and this 'fatal blow' was reducing the small farmer to a labourer, considered by the wealthy farmer as 'a mere vassal'. (J. Claridge, *General View of the Agriculture in the County of Dorset* . . . [1793], pp. 22-3.)

based on Wordsworth's understanding (necessarily limited and fragmentary) of the French Revolution; more exactly, a study of the psychology of action, and particularly – in the character of Oswald – the psychology of terrorism. In it he moved towards a conviction that the troubles of mankind were insoluble by *action*, which was more likely than not to lead to worse than failure. 'Action is transitory,' its consequences incalculable. A tragic fatality seemed to overshadow even 'the motion of a muscle this way or that', as it had overshadowed the sailor's crime in 'Guilt and Sorrow'.[19] Here, growing upon Wordsworth's mind, was the mode of thinking of the isolated spectator of events, to whom the possibility seemed remote of any activity being both good and successful. 'The world is poisoned at the heart.' [20]

The Ruined Cottage is removed from the world of action altogether. A cottage-weaver, reduced to misery by unemployment following bad harvests and war, deserts his wife and infants and joins the army; she dies slowly of a broken heart and of want. Wordsworth tells this story, taking many of its touches from the life of the people around him, with profound sympathy, and the quality of the poetry is very high. It is so partly because Wordsworth takes a more limited canvas than in the woman's story in the earlier poem. His new heroine Margaret is a stationary figure, not a wanderer over the earth; she is a passive victim of misfortunes that squeeze her life out inch by inch. She has no contact with other victims, though it is a time of mass distress that the poem refers to; this is a step back from even the half-formed idea in *Descriptive Sketches*, that in 'life's long deserts' it is better to be joined with others in the 'mighty caravan of pain: Hope, strength and courage social suffering brings'. The writer is now looking at his theme more from outside, as a fine painting of human grief. War is attributed to the will of Heaven, rather than to iniquity. Attention has moved from the social to the individual; and Wordsworth's inability to see any remedy for the ills he describes is taking shape in the philosophical narrator of the story, the old Pedlar. As the poem gradually grew and

19. See the lines from *The Borderers* which Wordsworth later prefixed to *The White Doe*.
20. *The Borderers*, 1036.

unfolded like a plant, this part of it expanded, until by March 1798 Dorothy could speak of the Pedlar having come to play the *largest* part in it.[21] This throws a long shadow forward; for the Pedlar of 1798 was to grow into the Wanderer of *The Excursion*, and he already embodied the negative, quietist tendency in Wordsworth's mind – much as Coleridge's later decrepit self was prefigured by the reformed churchgoer at the end of the 'Ancient Mariner'. Through the Pedlar, Wordsworth was groping for moral instead of political solutions; he was trying to extract from 'mournful thoughts' and sights 'A power to virtue friendly', and coming closer to the quagmire of Resignation that was one day to swallow him up.

He was not satisfied; he went on for years and years tormenting himself over this poem, trying to cobble it into something more convincing. He had now written a good deal since 1793, but had got nothing into a shape for publication, which was a symptom of his frustrated condition. Now, in 1798, came the change marked by the first volume of *Lyrical Ballads*. For him the short poem was a novelty, and always remained something of a condescension, a bagatelle; but it allowed him to express feelings as they arose, to strike sparks where he could not kindle a bonfire, and thus to recover himself now as a poet with something to say to the public. He had Coleridge to admire and stimulate him, and in some ways this was, as it has often been called, his springtime and rebirth. Spring was in his thoughts, his powers were expanding, he heard the 'mighty sum of things' speaking to him in fresh tones. 'Never did fifty things at once Appear so lovely, never, never.'[22]

In preparation for the giant life-work now floating before his eyes, he felt again the need to learn more of himself (he was soon to begin *The Prelude*), and more of his fellows. These two studies were still closely related. He was going in search of the People again, not hiding from them; the voice of Nature included the voice of simple, natural man. But as before there was loss as well as gain. Neither Coleridge nor Dorothy, nor the

21. *The Early Letters*, op. cit., pp. 176 ff, containing a draft of the poem in the form described here.
22. 'Expostulation and Reply' (*Lyrical Ballads*, I), 'Peter Bell', Prologue.

'wise passiveness' they were helping to foster in him, could be an altogether reliable guide for such a man. In the Prologue to 'Peter Bell' (summer 1798) it is possible to read a dual meaning into the poet's return from his imaginary voyaging among the stars to 'the dear green Earth' where alone he could feel 'I am a man', and his rejection of 'the realm of Faery' in favour of the humdrum tale of a potter beating a donkey. He was banishing fantasy and choosing reality as the theme of his poetry; but fantasy was beginning to include the limbo of political strife and faction, as Wordsworth thought of it in those moods when he turned away too indiscriminately from 'the sages' books' to the running brooks.[23] 'Reality' was thus in danger of impoverishment.

However lovely the face of Nature might seem, the subjects that attracted him were often far from lovely. Fewer than half of the 1798 *Ballads* leave a cheerful impression. Nearly half are concerned with Wordsworth's own feelings and interests – those of a young romantic suffering chronically from bad nerves, indigestion, headaches, fevers, insomnia, irregular hours; not of a sober, well-disciplined moralist. He was seeing himself anew, in new relations with his environment; but it is noteworthy that he succeeded much better in his more personal poems, with which six of the eight successful new poems of the volume[24] may be classed, than in the others. In these latter there was a distinct falling off, instead of an advance, in point of imaginative realism, and it corresponded with a loosening of the framework of ideas in which his pictures of humanity were set. Compared with the characters in 'Guilt and Sorrow', those of these *Ballads* tend to be flat and dull, or else melodramatic and unconvincing.[25] There is a practically complete absence of normal human beings; Words-

23. 'The Idle Shepherd Boys' (*Lyrical Ballads*, II), cf. 'A Poet's Epitaph', ibid.

24. 'Expostulation and Reply'; 'The Tables Turned'; 'Anecdote for Fathers'; 'Lines written at a small distance . . .'; 'Lines written in early Spring'; 'Tintern Abbey'.

25. It is hard to agree that 'the prevailing notes are exultant and happy' (Darbishire, op. cit., p. 34). Wordsworth was soon finding fault with 'The Female Vagrant' (see *The Early Letters*, op. cit., pp. 268 ff); perhaps, though not ostensibly, for political reasons.

worth is alone with his sister in a circle of children, ancients, beggars, imbeciles. Only in these poems, not about himself, did he make much use of the new and soon famous style that may fairly be labelled the *idiot style*.

Prominent among their characters is a bevy of unfortunate females, whose hard lot wrings few tears from the reader: the deserted Red Indian woman; the mad mother (not too mad to assure us that she is legally married); the erring penitent of 'The Thorn' (very little removed from the 'super-tragic' mourners whom Wordsworth remembered with amusement in his juvenile efforts);[26] Goody Blake, the doddering old spinner; and the two unbearable gossips of 'The Idiot Boy'. Then we have Simon Lee limping tediously on his swollen ankles in front of the final quatrain of a poem that has no need of him, and the old man of 'Animal Tranquillity and Decay'. It is a set of bad poems, offering an unappetizing picture of the deserving poor. 'The Thorn' was composed 'with great rapidity', and 'The Idiot Boy' 'almost extempore'; what is more surprising is that the latter was written 'with exceeding delight and pleasure', and its author continued to read it with the same complacency.[27] Evidently he believed himself to have accomplished something significant in enlarging the circle of poetry to include such waifs and strays, when he seemed to others to be making a caricature of life. Social injustice – as if he was now left bewildered and helpless by it – had descended to the farcical level of Goody Blake's tale where her oppressor, the grasping farmer, is punished, not by a combination of the labouring poor against him, but by an old woman's curse; a 'true' story told by Wordsworth in the manner of one relating an edifying though improbable anecdote to a Sunday-school class.[28]

Extravagance of subject in these poems is only exaggerated by ultra-literal diction. In 'Guilt and Sorrow' and *The Ruined Cottage* the language had been quite simple enough; in 'Michael' it was to be so in perfection. Wordsworth's theory of diction, a

26. *Prelude*, VIII, 531.
27. See Notes to *Lyrical Ballads*, and *The Early Letters*, op. cit., p. 295.
28. In the Preface he tries to rationalize in psychological terms the effect of the curse.

democratic one, grew out of his political radicalism.[29] But there was in the sectarian lengths to which he pushed it at this stage an element of compensation for what was missing – any practical remedy or protest against 'what man has made of man';[30] and with it a touch of self-mortification, as of one wilfully refusing to stand well with his public. Having discarded the 'artificial' life of the city in favour of the cottage, he was proposing to revive English poetry by ridding it of artificial conventions. But this was in any case a negative reform, and no reform of diction could take the place of a regeneration of the social order.

The theory which he fancied to be broad and liberating was in fact narrow and restrictive. He had been clinging to his trust 'In what we may become';[31] but to limit poetry to the everyday language of ordinary men and thereby to their everyday thoughts would condemn him to see people and things as fixed and unchanging – as, ultimately, all existence was to seem to him. This was to fall into the same arid 'realism' that he complained of in Crabbe.[32] He was incurring this danger because he had turned away from the people in arms to the people in rags, squalor and helplessness, and now he was inclined to project into them his own sensations of gloom and defeat, blind to the power that was still in them of struggling against their fate. Tempted to seek the bedrock of their own experience in himself in solitary abstraction, he was looking for it in the poor also as detached individuals, the *disjecta membra* of humanity, and coming to seek in them a refuge instead of a source of energy. Contemplating a very old man, alive only by the faintest flicker, he was

29. The assumptions he was working on belonged to the medley of progressive ideas, 'mingled somewhat vaguely in the brain of the average English "Jacobin" ', that are described by C. Brinton in *The Political Ideas of the English Romanticists* (1926), p. 29 (cf. K. MacLean, *Agrarian Age: A Background for Wordsworth* [1950], pp. 100–101). Cf. Hazlitt on Wordsworth in *The Spirit of the Age* (Bohn's Standard Library [1904], p. 152): 'the political changes of the day were the model on which he formed and conducted his poetical experiments'; and Stopford Brooke, *Theology in the English Poets* (1874), pp. 166–7.

30. 'Lines written in early Spring'.

31. *Prelude*, VIII, 806.

32. *The Life of George Crabbe*, by his son (World's Classics edition, 1932), p. 164, shows that Crabbe reciprocated the criticism.

fascinated by the thought of an absolute immobility, a Nirvana, of thought. In the dim recesses of an idiot boy's mind, and the mother's near-animal affection, he could find an impregnable shelter from life at the very moment when he supposed himself to be grappling most closely with life – 'Thou art the thing itself!' It was often in future to happen to Wordsworth to be furthest from 'reality' at the point where he believed himself nearest.

There are other children in these and the later *Ballads,* seeming to symbolize new beginnings, though quite often it is the memory of dead children that he is thinking of. From these young minds he felt that he could and must learn; and so too from common humanity at large. But he was losing sight too completely of the People as a collective thing, and what he needed most was something that could not be learned – though many valuable smaller lessons could – from fragmentary talk with wayfarers on the roads of Somerset or Cumberland,[33] any more than from the peasant-pilgrims Tolstoy talked with on the road to Kiev. It had to be learned with, not from, the people, and on the highroad of history. Failing to see that 'real life' must be rooted in a collective life, and one still in development, he fell into the error he denounced in mechanistic science: 'we murder to dissect'.[34] When he came to write his own history he missed much of what had gone to make him, because he lacked an understanding of the process of history in the wider sense; in the same way now he was failing to see how many of the qualities he admired in the poor were the outcome of an active, purposeful social existence and centuries of social conflict – which might be said also of their vocabulary. He was losing sight even of any close links between individuals, except those of the family, which he was coming to see as the only shelter in a bleak world.[35]

If previously Wordsworth had thought of an educated *élite* guiding an inert popular mass, he was now involved in the converse error of wanting to merge himself in the mass, at the cost of ceasing to be himself; whereas the true task for such a

33. *Prelude,* XII, 161 ff.
34. 'The Tables Turned'.
35. cf. 'Guilt and Sorrow', stanza LVII.

man was to find ways of contributing his own special resources to a common struggle in alliance with the people. His new notion meant living among the poor, and like the poor, in a somewhat mechanical fashion, and thinking and writing only such things as a humble neighbour might think or say. It would mean, if persisted in, a sacrifice not merely of Wordsworth's worldly prospects, but of his inmost self and business in life, of the talent which is death to hide. He could only make the effort spasmodically, and while he did so there was bound to be an element of pastoral masquerade in his work, of the intellectual awkwardly bringing himself down to the level of the people. He dabbled at times in verse meant to be read by the poor themselves,[36] but he was not finding much to say to them. When Cobbett wrote in the *Political Register* for his 'Chopsticks', the same south of English labourers Wordsworth was now living among, he wrote a language a good deal less simple than that of some of the *Ballads*, without ever puzzling his head about the matter, and they understood him. Wordsworth's still sad music was leading him astray, by leading him towards those who suffered most, not those who had most to give to the future. An artist needs to hear drums as well as dirges. In the England of 1798 the drums of the future were indeed thickly muffled. The new factory proletariat was taking decades, even generations, to form out of the debris of an older society. It was still half a century before Marx and Engels would open the leaden casket of the industrial slums from which Wordsworth (and Cobbett not much less) recoiled in horror.

Usually Wordsworth was writing about the poor for his own class. There seems to have been floating in his mind the dream that was to visit Tolstoy and Gandhi of opening the eyes of the

36. See *Prose Works*, op. cit., I, p. 336. Literacy was widespread in Lakeland; and there was the example of Burns. L. Abercrombie (*The Art of Wordsworth* [Oxford, 1952], p. 78) recalls that *We are Seven* was sold in the countryside as a broadsheet. Engels (*The Condition of the Working Class in England in 1844*, trans. by F. K. Wishnewetzky [1892], pp. 239–40) believed that Shelley and Byron were read chiefly by the proletariat. Cf. Scott: 'I am persuaded both children and the lower class of readers hate books which are written *down* to their capacity.' (Sir H. Grierson, *Sir Walter Scott, Bart.* [1938], p. 272).

better-off classes and giving them a change of heart, so that they would stop despising and ill-treating the poor: they would become as little children, and society would be a happy family again as in the golden age gone by – if a poor and primitive family; humanity reduced to the ancient, indestructible core of its material.[37] In harmony with this was the concern for goodwill in private relations as forming the 'best portion of a good man's life'.[38] But belief in such a programme could not come easily to a man of Wordsworth's native shrewdness, and the effort and strain involved may be seen as one cause of the 'extremism' of the *Ballads*.

What the idea must mean in practice was of course reconciliation of jarring classes within the prevailing order for the benefit of its rulers. In 'Peter Bell' Wordsworth can be seen drifting towards the weir, though as yet the idea remained in an allegorical shape, not reasoned out as it was later. In this fable, moreover, he strained every nerve to keep within the limits of rational possibility – instead of throwing the responsibility on to Providence – a change of heart in a villain guilty of callously ill-treating women and animals; in effect, in the terms of Wordsworth's symbolism, an oppressor of mankind. Peter's consciousness of guilt is powerfully developed, as in 'Guilt and Sorrow'; his conversion, with the aid of a donkey and a Methodist hymn, is ludicrously unconvincing – much more than if the means of grace were avowedly supernatural as in the parallel poem, 'The Ancient Mariner'. Wordsworth had bowdlerized the problem of reform into a silly parable. He turned away at present from this path, only to come back to it later. 'Peter Bell' was published in 1819, in the most reactionary period of Wordsworth's political life. In his respectable old age it was precisely with class harmony and conciliation that he came to be associated, as the Public Orator at Oxford did not fail to note when rewarding him with a degree.[39]

37. *The Early Letters*, op. cit., p. 295.
38. 'Tintern Abbey'.
39. See G. H. Healey, *Wordsworth's Pocket Notebook* (1942), p. 65; cf. Lady Richardson's account of the celebration of his 74th birthday by all ranks (*Prose Works*, op. cit., III, p. 444). There is a heated condemnation of all the ideas of class struggle in Coleridge's *The Friend*, Section 1, Essay 5.

Wordsworth's quest for the People seemed to have petered out. There was, however, another 1798 poem, 'The Old Cumberland Beggar' (published 1800), that pointed another way. Here, refreshed by a breeze from his native hills, he wrote with restraint and effect, at once realistically and – because he saw the old man's existence as interwoven with that of the society around him – imaginatively. In the 'vast solitude' of extreme age, this beggar still seemed to him to play a useful part on the earth, through the charitable impulses he called forth in the cottagers, themselves poor enough, thus providing a moral cement for a rural community where he, like Scott's Bluegown, had a distinct place of his own, more as a pensioner than as a vagrant.

Here was an image, death and life intertwined in a way characteristic of him, that Wordsworth could fasten on to. The social and moral disintegration of the English countryside, with its capitalistic agriculture and pauperized labourers, was equally disintegrating to his poetry, where it engendered the unreal or dying creatures of the *Ballads*. At Goslar in the winter of 1798–9, living with Dorothy in complete solitude, he was turning his eyes back towards Lakeland, as an oasis where a decent human existence still went on, and he was making sketches for the first two books of the *Prelude*, on his boyhood days. Among the other 'German' poems that were to appear in Volume II of the *Ballads* (1800), the Lucy poems, as well as 'Lucy Gray' and 'To a Sexton', show him preoccupied with thoughts of death. In 'Hart-Leap Well', with its hill-country setting, he again gave an allegorical, but this time a much more sober, version of the world's cruelty, drawing a moral of non-violence, or brotherly love.

Writing at this period of the poisoned atmosphere of the times – 'This melancholy waste of hopes o'erthrown', fear or apathy or defection on all sides – Wordsworth thanked 'Nature' for his own ability to hold fast, with 'more than Roman confidence', to his faith in humanity.[40] When in December 1799 he settled at Dove Cottage, to live henceforward close to the source of his inspiration, it was not a question of getting back merely to the hills, considered as rock and bracken : what he was seeking was

40. *Prelude*, II, 248 ff.; a passage suggested by a letter from Coleridge in 1799 (see note by Selincourt).

the 'natural' order of society that he associated with the hills, where he could see 'Man free, man working for himself',[41] and breathe freely. His return, decided on with many heart-searchings and hesitations, as *The Recluse* (Book I, 1800) shows, was a quest, not an escape. The sentimental tourist's notion of 'peace, rusticity, and happy poverty' in Grasmere [42] was not for Wordsworth, who was well aware that Lakeland poverty was not always happy. Dorothy's early Grasmere Journal is full of accounts of tramps and beggars on the roads, outsiders from Ireland or Manchester; misery could be found among the native peasantry too, as when the Wordsworths and Coleridge, basking in the summer beauty of the waterside, were suddenly broken in on by the sight of an old, infirm, hungry man trying to get something to eat out of 'the dead unfeeling lake'.[43] None the less, there was still a core of the old rural order left; and poverty did not usually appear as man-made (which later was to encourage Wordsworth to view it as made by Heaven). Here was little of a resident gentry; he had scarcely ever in youth seen a human being who claimed anything on the score of birth or rank;[44] social oppression was out of sight, and 'no people in the world are more impatient under it', a contemporary wrote.[45] Labourers were few, and lived with the farmers' families. Wordsworth could feel that there was at least no 'extreme penury', no suffering beyond what good neighbourship could relieve.[46] In Grasmere vale, with its forty or fifty scattered cottages, he and

41. *Prelude*, VIII, 152. The Journal of the Scottish tour of 1803 shows much interest in society as well as scenery. The idea of retirement to cottage seclusion was an old one; cf. the 'Evening Walk', and a poem of 1794 to Mary Hutchinson (Selincourt, *Studies*, op. cit., pp. 21–3).

42. Gray, quoted by W. Hutchinson, *History of the County of Cumberland* (1794), p. 233 n.

43. 'Poems on the Naming of Places', IV (*Lyrical Ballads*, II). Two of the first individuals in Grasmere who fixed his attention were a crippled workman and a paralytic (see *The Recluse*, Appendix A in the edition of *The Excursion* by E. de Selincourt and H. Darbishire [Oxford, 1949], pp. 329–30. All references to *The Excursion* are to this edition).

44. *Prelude*, IX, 217 ff.

45. J. Housman, *A Topographical Description of Cumberland, Westmoreland, Lancashire . . .* (1800), pp. 103–5.

46. *The Recluse*, op. cit., pp. 324–5.

Dorothy found the old ways 'little adulterated' and the people 'kind-hearted, frank and manly, prompt to serve without servility'.[47] Unlike the pauperized masses of the south, a great many of them were still small independent farmers, rather hugging the chains of sentiment that bound them to a poor soil than hating their condition, and thus seeming to prove that for the spirit of man poverty – which Wordsworth was accepting for himself too – was not the worst, or an unbearable, evil.

He loved the combination of individual pride and tenacious spirit of neighbourhood. It underlay his own conception of the combined independence and civic responsibility of the artist. These Lakeland small-holders, part farmer and part shepherd, had only of late years been emerging from a 'natural economy'. Each household was an almost self-sufficient unit, rooted in the thin soil like a gnarled tree – or like Wordsworth's genius – growing out of the rocks. Each household was drawn close about the spinning-wheel and loom that occupied all its free hours; the hum of the wheel had something sacred in Wordsworth's ear, which linked it with all the decencies of a stable family life.[48] Better than any other great poet he understood how the moral as well as the economic life of a free peasantry is bound up with the patrimonial acres that unite each individual with ancestors and descendants, form the repository of all his memories and emotions, and stand to him for history, art, and religion. Folk-art and popular imagination had been largely uprooted from the rest of England when the land was taken away from those who tilled it.

Like any other writer trying to overcome his isolation by finding a framework of living ideas wider than his own self, Wordsworth was identifying his outlook with that of a particular class, and supposing that he had achieved a 'universal' viewpoint. With this class of smallholders, among whom he had spent his early years, he shared many qualities, for instance a sense of humour more hearty than subtle.[49] In particular the shepherd of the high moorlands was a man through whose eyes he felt he could look

47. *The Early Letters*, op. cit., p. 236.
48. See e.g. 'Song for the Spinning-Wheel', 1812.
49. As, e.g. in 'The Waggoner' (1805).

at life; they had in common days made up of toil, hope, danger, and the 'majestic indolence' of freedom,[50] and perhaps he felt an analogy between shepherd and poet, as teacher of mankind. In the series of great years now opening before him he owed very much to the strength he drew from living side by side with a sturdy self-respecting race.[51] It gave him his rugged quality of endurance, as the Revolution had given him a soaring energy. He needed both, and under extreme adverse pressures his genius maintained itself for longer than that of most of the Romantic poets of Europe; because he was able, as *The Prelude* asserts over and over again, to maintain his faith in the common man and the qualities lurking in him.

The renewed integration of his mind found expression at once in the remaining *Ballads* of the 1800 volume. Hardly anything of the 'idiot' style survives here. There is less of the crudely painful; less of death; less of old age and more of childhood (though still not very much in between). More of the successful poems are concerned with things outside the poet. In general the literary quality is a good deal higher.[52] If there is a hint once more of something lost as well as gained, in the practically complete absence now of any reference to social injustice, at present this does not stand out; for Wordsworth has got away from his helpless weaklings to real men, men like old Michael of the 'stern and unbending mind'. This means also that he is throwing off his recent musings about conciliation between the classes. Lakeland knows only a rudimentary division of classes, and the shepherd fights his battles with storm and mist knowing and caring nothing about what educated folk may think of the poor. Wordsworth is grasping at the idea of rescuing the old peasant proprietorship, as the solution of England's problem of pauperism.

This is the point of his letter of January 1801, with a copy of

50. *Prelude*, VIII, 388; see this whole passage on shepherd life, and the long cancelled passage of *The Excursion* (op. cit., pp. 432 ff).

51. Even the woman begging on the roads in 'The Sailor's Mother' (1802) – drawn from life – had a bearing 'like a Roman matron's'.

52. Of forty-one poems altogether in volume II, twenty-five may be reckoned successful; but the improvement in quality is greater than this figure suggests.

the *Ballads*, to Charles James Fox. He laments the 'rapid decay of the domestic affections among the lower orders of society', with the uprooting of the peasantry, and calls on the statesman to arrest this vicious process. (How, he does not explain; and it is a bad omen that he is calling on Fox to save the people, instead of on the people to save themselves.) He sends him the book exclusively on account of two poems, 'The Brothers' and 'Michael', written 'to shew that men who do not wear fine cloathes can feel deeply'.[53] These two long 'pastoral poems' are remarkable achievements, and the second in particular is Wordsworth's finest tribute to the old way of life. What is good in it, and what is painful, are realized with equal intensity, though it is the good that he wants to bring forward. He insists, as earlier in *Descriptive Sketches*, that these rude shepherds do acquire from long familiarity and force of association a genuine love, akin to his own, for the mountain scenery they live amidst. There is an austere simplicity, dignity, pathos in these beings, so different from the hysterical creatures of earlier *Ballads*. They live in a hard, bleak, masculine world where women and Heaven have little part to play. Michael's cottage has never been 'gay', scarcely even 'cheerful'. When he inherited his acres they were mortgaged; until he was forty he had a hard struggle to free them of debt. Now, through a nephew's 'unforeseen misfortunes', he is crippled again, and the struggle must be faced anew. Such is the bitter inheritance he would hand on to his young son Luke, separated from him, as if symbolically, by so many years. Luke, infected and ruined by 'the dissolute city', never returns to take it up. Toiling to the end, dying in extreme age, Michael has no one to follow him, the land passes to a stranger, the plough turns up its grass.

'The Brothers' – a dialogue in the churchyard that was to become within a dozen years Wordsworth's spiritual home – likewise concerns the breaking up of a family, one that has clung to its patch of land for generations until at last the load of debt grew too heavy to bear. Lakeland was now exposed to the rough airs of a commercial age, and we read in a 1794 account: 'These small properties ... can only be handed down, from father to son,

53. *The Early Letters*, op. cit., pp. 259–63; cf. p. 266, to Poole.

by the utmost thrift, hard labour, and penurious living.'[54] Many of the younger sort were sucked away by the attractive power of the new towns. To Wordsworth this was a desertion of the post of freedom for the lure of sordid comfort.[55] He himself, preparing to undergo 'solitary and unremitting labour, a life of entire neglect perhaps',[56] for the sake of his creed, saw in the stern and unbending Michael a brother-spirit.

This lonely stoicism – this *surly virtue* – could not for long be a substitute for the 'soul-animating strains' of an active movement of progress. Lakeland was, at best, on the defensive. Moreover, while each dalesman waged his desperate struggle against circumstances, they were not as a body carrying on any fight against anything so tangible as a body of landlords. Such a fight might have drawn Wordsworth in on the right side, and his pen could have contributed to it. The need was not lacking. Although in these dales there might be little visible oppression, there were man-made evils which, as often in peasant regions, were hardly recognized as grievances, because they were matters of immemorial use and wont. Neither in the 'pastoral poems' nor in

54. J. Bailey and G. Culley, *General View of the Agriculture of the County of Cumberland* (Board of Agriculture, 1794), p. 44. Cf. the story of Wordsworth's neighbours, the Greens (see the memoir by Dorothy, in E. de Selincourt, *Dorothy Wordsworth* [1933], pp. 227 ff.), or that of the old woman of eighty-four in Portenscale who lived by spinning, scorned charity, and kept two guineas locked up for her funeral (Hutchinson, op. cit., p. 158 n.). See also the Lakeland parish reports in Eden's *State of the Poor* (1797), and on the effects of the price-fall here in the depression after 1815, *Agricultural State of the Kingdom* (Board of Agriculture, 1816), pp. 64–5.

55. cf. 'Repentance', a poem of 1804 on a family 'frivolously' giving up its land: Wordsworth's Note (*Prose Works*, op. cit., III, p. 58) shows that much of it was 'taken *verbatim* from the language' of the daleswoman concerned, Margaret Ashburner. Dorothy found it hard to get a servant, because 'the country is drained by the cotton works and the manufactories, and by the large towns whither they are tempted to go for great wages'. *The Letters of William and Dorothy Wordsworth, 1806–11*, ed. E. de Selincourt (1937), p. 26.

56. 'Advice to the Young', (*Prose Works*, I, pp. 316–17); cf. in a letter of 1806: 'a man of letters . . . ought to be severely frugal' (*Letters, 1806–11*, p. 60). Wordsworth may have thought of himself, as well as Milton, as 'almost single, uttering odious truth' (*Prelude*, III, 285).

the letter to Fox did he speak of the vices of an archaic tenurial law in this old Border country, still burdened with 'numerous and strong remains of vassalage', covered with customary manors demanding heriots, boon services, and worst of all those arbitrary *fines* on succession which did as much as anything to make it hard for families to cling to their little holdings.[57] Yet the poet's father had been legal agent to one of the worst of the manorial lords, and himself a victim of his master's injustice.

Lingering decline rather than a galloping consumption was to befall Lakeland. Cobbett found many of the old patriarchal ways still alive in 1832.[58] But whatever survived here could be only an odd fragment of the national life. Peasantry and cottage industry were vanishing before capitalism and the machine. Wordsworth, whose long span of years coincided exactly with the long-drawn extinction of the independent craftsmen, was writing gloomily in 1819 on the passing of his beloved spinning-wheel, and again in 1827 on this 'Venerable Art Torn from the Poor'.[59] Only by transformation into a new pattern could something of the good of the old days be preserved. Sucked into factory towns the once independent craftsmen could contribute a militant element to the battle for reform. Wordsworth, refusing to follow them, was left

57. Hutchinson, op. cit., pp. 36–9; cf. Bailey and Culley, op. cit., pp. 11, 44 ff.; Housman, op. cit., pp. 59–66. MacLean, op. cit., p. 101, is one of the very few writers who have taken notice of this aspect of Lakeland. Elsewhere he points out the tendency of Wordsworth and the other 'rustic' poets 'to neglect the part the landlords and improvers had in creating distress' in the counties affected by the Agricultural Revolution (p. 38; cf. p. 95). The tale of injustice at the beginning of the 'Female Vagrant' had a Lakeland setting.

58. 'The land-owners are very numerous in Cumberland; the farms generally small . . . the people look very neat and clean.' (Cobbett, *Tour in Scotland and in the Four Northern Counties of England* [1833], p. 245.)

59. Sonnets: 'Grief, thou hast lost . . .' (1819), and *To S.H.* (1827); the Note to the former (*Prose Works*, op. cit., III, p. 55) says 'I could write a treatise of lamentation upon the changes brought about among the cottages of Westmorland by the silence of the spinning wheel'. Wordsworth did not perhaps observe how immensely laborious the old cottage industry was. Wages in Kirkoswald parish, Cumberland, are 'very inconsiderable', we read: 'a woman must labour hard at her wheel 10 or 11 hours in the day, to earn 4d.' (Eden, op. cit., II, p. 84.) In Cumwhitton parish none of the poor spent as much as 3d. on a day's food (ibid., p. 74).

with more and more of the husk and less and less of the spirit. Insensibly his mountain fortress turned into a snug summer-house. His 'common man' grew all too uncommon, and he gradually came to attribute to bare hills, by a sort of imputed righteousness, the moral influences that he had known as the property of a simple social system; while conversely he grew to hate in towns their smoke rather than their slavery.[60]

Settling in Grasmere, he was still blaming 'an unjust state of society' for men's troubles,[61] but he was receding from the conception that had come to him in 1792 of expanding and organizing freedom, and marrying freedom to plenty. Now as before the Revolution he felt that a life worthy of human beings could be lived only in secluded valleys. Because his idea of freedom came back to this negative, primitive level – similar to the Anarchism of Europe's surviving craftsmen-communities later in the century – he could have no idea of a State power taken over and used by the People, and he was unlikely to develop that of a constructive popular movement; which meant that in the end he must be drawn into a reactionary current. Such a phenomenon has been seen in various parts of Europe analogous to Wordsworth's. A democratic society is the last that will think of creating a democratic State.

It is to *The Excursion*, especially its later (1810–14) books, that we must look for the record of Wordsworth's decline. Hints of what was to come are thickly scattered over his work after 1800, when the initial recovery conferred by his return to Lakeland had worn off, and he was being left stranded between his two worlds, that of Michael and the hills and that of books, London, Napoleon. Michael was dead, and no other such towering, rock-

60. Mountains, he had written earlier, 'are good occasional society, but they will not do for constant companions' (*The Early Letters*, op. cit., p. 128). As Bowra says, the consolation he now found in a new attitude to Nature could not solve his problems (C. M. Bowra, *The Romantic Imagination* [Oxford, 1950], pp. 100–102). Cf. C. Caudwell, *Illusion and Reality* (1937), p. 98: 'Wordsworth's "Nature" is of course a Nature freed of wild beasts and danger by aeons of human work, a Nature in which the poet . . . lives on the products of industrialism . . .'

61. *The Early Letters*, op. cit., p. 306. But there is no 'injustice' in volume II of the *Lyrical Ballads*.

hewn figure took his place. In 1802, once more oppressed with thoughts of decay and desertion 'And mighty Poets in their misery dead', Wordsworth's imagination caught for comfort at a much lesser figure, the Leechgatherer, endowed with no more than a passive tenacity of life. (It was his imagination, grappling with reality, that created all his significant figures – not his pocket-book jottings from reality. There was no Leechgatherer, as there had been a Simon Lee.) To live long was to live wretched, he reflected at the graveside of Burns.[62] Every living thing's heart was an 'impenetrable cell' of loneliness.[63] Death hung about his thoughts. The age he had been reserved to was a 'degenerate' one.[64]

From the renewal of war in 1803 until its end in 1815 his poetic moods were largely conditioned by the situation of Europe, since that of Lakeland was static. When he wrote of Toussaint, the black man born in slavery defying and morally defeating the master of Europe – or again in 1808–9 when all Spain rose against the tyrant and he wrote *The Convention of Cintra* – Wordsworth could identify himself with struggling people far away; but enthusiasm for freedom and justice abroad could not for long take the place of struggle for freedom and justice at home.[65]

In 1804–5, in a superb burst of energy, he completed *The Prelude*, ending it on a curiously mingled note of hope and pessimism. Free now to embark on his serious life-work, in 1806 he wrote, or put together, the first part of *The Excursion*, whose opening sections had been planned or sketched in 1804 and even earlier. It was not the poem he and Coleridge had dreamed of in 1798. Book I was the old *Ruined Cottage* of that year, in a new guise. This was followed in Book II and the beginning of Book III by the story of the Solitary, which as regards Wordsworth and the French Revolution is better autobiography than most of *The Prelude*. The Solitary was his old self, as the Wanderer (the

62. 'At the Grave of Burns' (1803).
63. 'The Kitten and Falling Leaves' (1804).
64. *Prose Works*, op. cit., I, p. 322.
65. Wordsworth's interest in the affairs of Napoleonic Europe, and his new concept of Nationalism, are not discussed here, for want of space, though they have a greater importance in his development.

former Pedlar, grown into a 'venerable Sage') was his new – or rather they were moods still conflicting in him.[66] Thus he was throwing together the dual problems of his earlier years, of poverty and of freedom. They stand side by side in the Solitary's tremendous catalogue of evils –

> Wrongs unredressed, or insults unavenged
> And unavengeable, defeated pride,
> Prosperity subverted, maddening want . . .[67]

This disappointed revolutionary is a splendidly Byronic character : the finest ever invented, in fact – Byron could never make his heroes speak as this man does. But he is alone, frustrated, impotent; he can denounce oppression and misrule, but all he can *do* is to weep for an old pauper's death and console a child by telling him the old man is in Heaven.[68] What Wordsworth himself could do was dwindling to little more.

By 1806 he was rationalizing the failure of the Revolution into one leading idea : the men of his generation had committed the sin of *hubris* by their 'proud and most presumptuous confidence In the transcendent wisdom of the age', when really they were no better than their fathers, nor their age wiser than any before it.[69] The answer to Wordsworth's view is that men in his day had in fact gone beyond all their predecessors, and with the help of science and industry got onto higher ground from which more of the universe past, present and to come was discernible. Wordsworth would not have admitted this : for him the sky was still 'unvoyageable',[70] when balloons had begun to rise into it. All he could see of that 'new and unforeseen creation', machine in-

66. On Mr Fawcett, the ostensible model for the Solitary, see Harper, op. cit., I, pp. 261–6. On the chronology of *The Excursion*, see op. cit., pp. 369 ff.

67. *Excursion*, III, 374–6. The passage originally belonged to *The Tuft of Primrose*, a lengthy sketch of 1808 (op. cit., Appendix C).

68. *Excursion*, II, 508–11; cf. III, 983–6, on the futility of action. The Solitary began as a *political* figure only; his domestic misfortunes were a much later addition to Book III. (See Notes, op. cit., pp. 418–19.)

69. II, 235–6; IV, 278 ff, and 418 ff. Pride was the 'false fruit' that had corrupted men (IV, 289–93).

70. V, 342.

dustry, was the 'vice, misery and disease' it produced.[71] He missed the good side because he had no faith in men's ability to control what they had created. He knew nothing of factory workers, and even when he had asserted most ardently the survival of virtue in the rustic poor, he had been thinking too much of passive resistance to life, too little of active control of circumstances. He saw industry turning more and more of the country into an arena of blind, brutish forces, men and machines almost equally inhuman, equally intractable to intelligence. Effort to remodel society seemed futile. The problems he was setting himself to wrestle with were more than ever insoluble. He could not even bring them really together. Margaret, the dead woman of Book I, and the embittered rebel of Book II, remained in separate worlds. Their troubles could not be cured separately; mass poverty and intellectual isolation could only be overcome with and through each other, in the process of social advance. The duality of Wordsworth's thinking ran through all his experience: self and mankind, people and law, soul and body, freedom and wealth, intuition and logic, Mary Hutchinson and Annette Vallon, the mountains of Cumberland and the Mountain of Paris: and from now on the dividing walls were to grow thicker and higher.[72]

Wordsworth could not turn away and luxuriate in 'world-excluding groves' and 'voluptuous unconcern'. Only now the idle hedonism he despised included any Utopian kind of poetry made up 'to improve the scheme Of Man's existence, and recast the world'.[73] His problems were really coming down to this: Life being what it was and must be, was it worth living, or should men give themselves up to despair? If fate could not be sent to their will, it must be a question of men bending to the will of fate. In Book IV (sketched, with a further part of Book III, in

71. VIII, 90; VII, 854. Cf. H. L'A Fausset, *The Lost Leader* (1933), p. 205; by rejecting the Industrial Revolution altogether, 'he turned his back upon the ideas and forces which for good and evil were to determine human development during the next hundred years . . .'

72. Hazlitt noticed in Wordsworth 'a total disunion and divorce of the faculties of the mind from those of the body' (*Lectures on the English Poets* [World's Classics edition, 1924], p. 203).

73. *Excursion*, III, 332 ff.

the same year, 1806) he groped towards an answer in terms of a philosophy just at the point of hardening into a religion : belief in Providence was the one 'adequate support',[74] since the world as seen and felt by man was inexplicable. With this answer the debate hung fire, and Wordsworth was for long at a standstill. He had conjured up spirits he could not exorcise. Meanwhile he went on sinking into deeper abstractions from life. How far he was drifting away from any sense of identity (not of sympathy) with the people can be seen in his essay on them, addressed to an Archdeacon, where he reviewed their educational needs with benevolent detachment.[75] Another essay was on epitaphs and immortality. In his poetry he reached the furthest degree of isolation, or mid-channel between his former and his later self, in *The White Doe* (winter 1807–8), in which his quietism hardened into what Harper calls an 'almost oriental renunciation', and his poetry declined to what Jeffrey called, nearly as fairly, 'a state of low and maudlin inbecility'.[76]

From the North Pole all roads run south, and after his 1808 freezing-point (and the interlude of the Spanish war) Wordsworth could only begin sliding from despair of progress towards distrust of progress. For himself he was not only accepting his isolation but making a virtue of it; when he took up *The Excursion* again he was always pausing in the poem to congratulate himself on his cloistered seclusion from a world whose soil was 'rank with all unkindness',[77] and he could indulge the thought that 'in these disordered times' it might be well for a few men, 'from faction sacred' – impartial philosophers – to resume the life the ancient anchorites once led.[78] Inevitably, he carried the poem on by deepening its religious side. He wanted to fill the gap he had left between earth and Heaven, and he filled it chiefly with a collection of stories from the Grasmere churchyard. The germ

74. IV, 10 ff.

75. *Prose Works*, op. cit., I, pp. 335 ff. (June 1808). In *Excursion*, IX, 327, he was to appeal on behalf of the poor to 'the State's parental ear' : cf. *Prose Works*, I, p. 275 (1835).

76. Harper, op. cit., II, p. 155; A. B. Comparetti, *The White Doe of Rylstone* (1940), pp. 253–4.

77. VI, 635.

78. V, 29–36; the same idea pervades 'The Tuft of Primroses'.

of this theme of the graves can be found near the beginning of 'The Brothers', where the village pastor remarks that he could make a 'strange round' of stories out of the graves he is looking at. Wordsworth had forgotten little in these years, but he had not learned enough. This second part of his poem bears some analogy with *Paradise Lost*, and its spiritual ascent and poetical descent from Hell to Heaven. If the first part stands like a sombre Sphinx staring out across the nineteenth century, the second is a sand-heap half burying it. Yet even now, in these last few years remaining to his inspiration, Wordsworth is not less than Archangel ruined; his 'creeping' tale, to use his own simile, still catches every now and then 'The colours of the sun'.[79]

In its outward forms the poem he was writing was still of the people, democratic. Wordsworth did not shrink from proclaiming his belief in 'the aristocracy of nature'[80] by confronting the polite world with a philosophical poem (costing two guineas) whose Socrates was a retired Scots pedlar, like his creator an 'advocate of humble life'.[81] Yet the choice of 'nature's unambitious underwood'[82] for his main theme was bringing him round by a back door to reaction. Contenting himself with the kind of ideas that could be supposed intelligible to humble virtue, fatigued with the toil of searching for undiscoverable truth, he was coming to acquiesce in the necessity of ignorance. From here it was only a step to the obscurantist notion that 'the lowly class' whose station exempted them from doubts or questionings, as

79. IV, 1122–26. Lamb called *The Excursion* 'a vast and magnificent poem' (letter to Southey, 20 October 1814, *The Letters of Charles Lamb*, ed. G. Pocock [Everyman revised edition, 1945], I, p. 347); Keats thought it one of the three wonders of the age (letter to Haydon, 10 January 1818, *The Letters of John Keats*, ed. M. B. Forman [Oxford, 4th ed., 1952], p. 78). Byron saw much talent wasted in it, like rain on rocks or sand (letter to Hunt, September–October 1815, *The Letters of George Gordon, 6th Lord Byron*, ed. R. G. Howarth [1933], p. 134), and Hazlitt compared it neatly to Crusoe's canoe: 'noble materials thrown away' (*Lectures on the English Poets*, op. cit., pp. 240–41).

80. Wordsworth's Note on I, p. 341.

81. II, 628. As Coleridge pointed out (*Biographia Literaria*, chapter XXII), this Socrates was a pedlar only in name. The 'democratic' character was becoming merely formal.

82. VI, 653.

they pursued 'The narrow avenue of daily toil', were really the luckiest.[83] The 'lowly class' would have enough troubles without those of the intellect; such troubles as befell Margaret. On her fate Wordsworth had pondered for years, and it preyed on his mind the more morbidly because he could find no practical answer to it. Religious history is full of examples of how simply feeling sorry for the poor breeds reactionary attitudes. It was only 'natural wisdom', Wordsworth concluded, not to let the mind dwell too long on irremediable calamity.[84] The only remedy, and the only lesson a sage could teach, was resignation.

Margaret's cottage stood by itself on an 'open moorland',[85] out of sight of either landlord and merchant to oppress or fellow workers to defend. Wordsworth had not forgotten that there was 'misrule' on the earth, whose nations groaned under their 'unthinking masters'.[86] But by now these rulers had receded into an indistinct distance. Every breath of social conflict had been hermetically excluded. There was only Heaven above, misery below, philosophy looking on. Wordsworth laid great store by

> the line of comfort that divides
> Calamity, the chastisement of Heaven,
> From the injustice of our brother men;[87]

his Wanderer, journeying from village to village, had been wont to point out this line to poor men chafing under their misfortunes, and thus help to allay social discontent. From this it was easy to drop little by little into the habit of thinking of all human ills as due to Providence, and losing sight of what was wrong with society. In order to cherish this comfort Wordsworth had to remove the towns from his field of vision (though by another contradiction he saw their wealth as necessary for beating Napoleon and keeping England great and free), and in effect

83. V, 593–601. (The Solitary makes a trenchant rejoinder to this rigmarole.) In the same vein is Wordsworth's Note (*Prose Works*, III, pp. 153–4) to *In the Firth of Clyde* (1833).

84. I, 602.

85. I, 26.

86. I, 379–81.

87. II, 72–4. The same distinction had been drawn in the *Apology* of 1793 (*Prose Works*, I, p. 8), but there the stress was on repelling human injustice.

most of the countryside too, because there also, as the Solitary insisted, conditions were deplorable. The 'old domestic morals' were 'Fled utterly! or only to be found In a few fortunate retreats like this'.[88] In Lakeland poverty could still be thought of as 'wholesome', because it kept temptation away and made men more sensible of their need of help from above,[89] while the 'true equality' of virtue was accessible to all; the rustic benefited from his few and simple wants also in learning from them 'patience and sublime content'.[90] This is a point of view congenial to landlords and bishops. There is a *facilis descensus* from praise of the poor to praise of poverty. But Lakeland's 'fortunate retreat' was itself shrinking and decaying. Wordsworth turned instinctively now, for its soul and centre, to the graveyard, an inmost sanctuary where history could not penetrate. Here were true peace, equality, fraternity, with no tombstone or monument to make one man different from another, and the justice of Heaven. All that Wordsworth had once hoped for on earth now stood in his mind as 'the sublime attractions of the grave'.[91]

Hence the long collection of churchyard anecdotes. Like those of the old pauper in Book II, and of the lonely couple in the mountain cottage in Book V, they are mostly, as the Fenwick notes show, true stories. Some of them had been written years earlier, in the same Lyrical Ballad mood whose errors were now magnified into a system; the seeds of this melancholy harvest had long been sprouting in Wordsworth's mind.

In his case-book, as in the graveyard itself, the dead lie indiscriminately, but they can be arranged to illustrate four propositions.

First and foremost, a quiet country life is the best for mould-

88. VIII, 142–7; 236, 253–4.

89. I, 306; IV, 786–9.

90. IX, 248; IV, 818. Yet in practice Wordsworth saw that there were woeful differences between man and man, and vaguely attributed them to 'injustice' (IX, 253–4). Mary Lamb, reading *The Excursion*, felt 'it was doubtful whether a Liver in towns had a Soul to be Saved'. (Charles Lamb, op. cit., p. 339; letter to Wordsworth, 9 August 1814.)

91. *Excursion*, IV, 238; cf. III, pp. 220–24, and 'George and Sarah Green' (1808), where the grave is seen to represent, in Wordsworth's instinctive thinking, escape from trouble into annihilation.

ing character. Half a dozen of the fifteen cases fall under this heading. The restless clergyman (Wordsworth's old crony, Mr Simpson) had resented his banishment to a small country cure, but it had preserved him from frivolity or vice. It shows how much the family bond had replaced all others for Wordsworth that he counts it to Providence for righteousness, instead of complaining of the state of medical science, that this clergyman and his whole family all died within a few months, and thus were not separated for long. Then we have a model rustic, a fine sturdy intelligent young fellow, leader of the local volunteers. He was buried amid the patriotic regrets of the whole valley, which seems to make Wordsworth view the tale as a striking vindication of his main argument: for him now, little but death could bring men's hearts together in such a flow of feeling. Equally characteristic of him, though less edifying, is the case of the mining prospector, a rugged individualist who succeeded by years of lonely persistence, and then drank himself to death. A neighbour still alive, but soon to join the happy band, is a poor, aged, cheerful labourer, so close to Nature as to be barely distinguishable from the animal kingdom – just rational enough to attend church.[92]

Secondly, with Heaven's grace the worst trials can be borne without repining. A man deaf from infancy, and a blind man, are the examples. Wordsworth has the archaic thought of God sending blindness as a parable to teach sublime truths.[93]

Thirdly, time and patience soften misfortunes, such as the loss of wife or child, or disappointment in love.[94]

Lastly, sin can be atoned for by suffering and repentance. We hear of a talented, strong-minded girl who, cramped and thwarted by her narrow rut, grew into a hard and avaricious

92. Of the four cases referred to here, the third book belongs to Book VI, and the others to Book VII.

93. *Excursion*, VII, 395–515. Cf. *Prelude*, XI, p. 375, where God 'corrected' a fit of boyish impatience in him by killing his father – an idea revealing the streak of peasant superstition in Wordsworth. With these two cases compare the subjects of 'The Matron of Jedborough and her Husband' and 'The Blind Highland Boy' (1803).

94. Here may be placed the unhappy lover (VI, 95 ff.), the old Jacobite and Whig (VI, 392 ff.) and the bereaved family (VII, p. 632 ff.).

woman. Wordsworth dwells, not on a pathetic waste of human promise, but on resignation achieved before death under stress of illness and unhappiness. A story – the longest of all – of a poor village Gretchen he tells with sympathy, tolerance, and delicacy; but it is all in the mode of a bygone age: the girl is to forgive her betrayer, turn her thoughts upward, lose her infant, and die of a broken heart. The whole affair is an instance of Heaven's kindness – a good specimen of the sort of heart-rending cheerfulness that Wordsworth is working himself up to.[95]

Wordsworth was trying to answer great public questions from the data of private experience. He offered his stories as 'solid facts', 'plain pictures' of real human beings.[96] These beings were indeed too, too solid, with none of the 'visionary' character of such a figure as the Leechgatherer; Wordsworth's imagination breathed little life into them. He was seeing the People as a collection of halt, lame, or senile individuals, each creeping on his separate way and groaning in his separate key; victims of spiritual or physical infirmity who seem to stand in place of the social disorders that Wordsworth no longer wanted to think of – but that broke in on him again in the final Book in spite of himself. Compared with the eccentrics of the 1798 *Ballads* they are flesh and blood folk; compared with the Michael of 1800 they are feeble, ailing creatures.

Wordsworth keeps them as far apart as possible, like a careful nurse separating children so that they can do one another no harm.[97] Deafness, blindness, old age reinforce his barriers. The prospector digs alone; the quarryman is never heard of at work with his fellows, but only in the inaccessible nook where his old wife spends her eventless days with her peaceful pious thoughts.[98]

95. Also in Book VI are the prodigal son returning to die in his parents' arms, and the husband who dies of remorse after going astray under pressure of bad luck.

96. V, 637–8.

97. The treatment of the old man in Book II, and of Ellen in Book VI, brings about the death of both, but the cause is no more than a little rustic ill-nature.

98. *Excursion*, V, 670 ff.; with his idyllic picture may be compared another that has survived of the same Betty, beating her drunken husband home from the Black Bull. (A. C. Gibson, quoted in G. S. Sandilands, *The Lakes, an Anthology of Lakeland Life and Landscape* [1947], p. 144.)

Wordsworth's rustics have become as solitary as himself, or the sole-sitting lady of the lake, or the shepherd whom his fancy calls up whenever he thinks of Greece, alone in the hills with his meditations and concocting Greek mythology out of them.[99] The one positive quality left in these characters is a dumb, tenacious, peasant endurance: even this, since the class as a whole is beginning to disintegrate, requires in its members more of a religious substitute for the old cement. They all die without any resentment against their fate; the reader, contemplating their patience, is to learn to feel ashamed of his own discontents.[100] Religious consolation for helpless suffering had been one more of the ideas floating loose in the *Descriptive Sketches* twenty years before.[101]

Wordsworth had not turned into a 'reactionary', but as a discouraged 'progressive' he had come near the brink, and would in fact tumble over before long. An artist who does not feel the People as a force positively on his side may soon come to feel them as something against him. The People need allies, not patrons; to gain allies they need strength. Wordsworth was too little conscious of their collective strength, too much of their individual weakness. The weakness, not the strength, of the People frightens an artist in such a position as his, by conjuring up in his fears a blind, anarchical monster incapable of rational purpose. Wordsworth in 1812 was in fear of social war breaking out in the towns.[102] Near the close of *The Excursion* he advocated universal education, as a universal right, but also as a means of counteracting the 'ignorance' that was breeding dis-

99. IV, 846-87.   100. VII, 1051-7.

101. Religion to Wordsworth was a 'natural' consolation. As Hale White points out, there is no *theology* in *The Excursion* (*An Examination of the Charge of Apostasy against Wordsworth* [1898], pp. 36 ff.).

102. Harper, op. cit., II, p. 201, quoting Crabb Robinson. Southey was talking of 'the imminent danger in which our throats are at this moment from the Luddites' (letter to Capt. Southey, 17 June 1812, *Letters of Robert Southey*, ed. M. H. Fitzgerald [1912], p. 202). So far as this goes, there is some point in the contention that Wordsworth's anti-popular attitude of 1818 was spontaneous (E. C. Batho, *The Later Wordsworth* [1933], pp. 59-60). But his need of patronage from the Lowthers (Harper, II, p. 204) was helping him along the same road, towards his place in 'The Black Book: or, Corruption Unmasked' of 1820 (I, p. 89).

content,[103] a highly illiberal notion, exactly opposite to the principle of learning 'from the People'. Growing away from them, he was growing closer – there being no third direction in politics – to their masters.

As always, excessive concentration on the individual self had bred in him its counterpart, a morbid sense of the helpless frailty of the individual amid the 'deserts infinite' of time and space.[104] Deserts, an old image with him, were taking on a more sinister quality, as of barbarism menacing the little oasis of civilization. He saw them within the soul as well as all round it. A favourite adjective of his – *dread* – came to him instinctively now when he peered into the 'dark foundations' of man's nature, embedded in a gulf 'Fearfully low';[105] as low, we might add for him, as memories of guilty love, or the depths of the Faubourg St Antoine. In 1818 he would be waking the echoes of Keswick with warnings of the approach of 'A FEROCIOUS REVOLUTION'.[106] By then he only wanted the People to lie peacefully in the graveyard where he had taken leave of them, while he, hiding behind his mountains like a King of Prussia behind his bodyguard of giants, continued to play the part of Poet of Nature.

At the end of *The Excursion* Wordsworth dodged all the problems he had raised, culminating in the final Book in the passionate denunciation of industrial society (for which we may read capitalism), by going out on the lake for a picnic with the charming clergyman and his family: not a bad forecast of how the rest of his life was to be spent. He never continued the poem, as he had intended: it had been too much for him. As an essay in consolation it is laborious taskwork; as a monument to the pessimism of modern man it is incomparable. It is also the funeral monument of Wordsworth's genius, to which by now 'Night is than day more acceptable', sleep than waking, death than sleep.[107] Its greatest passage of all has a frozen majesty as of Fate answering the Revolution –

103. IX, 293–335, 346. 104. *Excursion*, V. 1107; cf. 500–514.
105. IV, 970; V, 296. 106. *Prose Works*, op. cit., I, p. 255.
107. III, 275–81.

Amid the groves, under the shadowy hills,
The generations are prepared; the pangs,
The internal pangs, are ready; the dread strife
Of poor humanity's afflicted will
Struggling in vain with ruthless destiny.[108]

Settling in Grasmere, Wordsworth had still been hopeful of a 'milder day' to come.[109] But he settled down to look at life through the eyes of a moribund class and a decaying order, and his mind shared in their decline; he came to resemble the sentinels in his poem, set 'between two armies' in the chill night with nothing better than 'their own thoughts to comfort them'.[110] He no longer saw life in the Revolutionary crucible, all its elements melting, running, re-combining, and he no longer felt as if poetry were an active part in an apocalyptic transformation of the world. Things cooled down into separate, inert blocks, fundamentally because he came to see the structure of society as a rigid hierarchy of classes. Human nature, having no warmth of action to transform it, was unalterable; duty abstract and changeless; suffering irremediable.[111] No room was left for imagination as an active, working force. It came down to merely laying a varnish of verse over a worm-eaten surface. After 1814 scarcely anything but the deaths of those he had loved could rouse his imagination again, because only death could knock holes in the walls round him and let him see out.

It was not that he was turning into a bad man. In 1815 Haydon found him a man he could 'worship as a purified spirit'.[112] At

108. VI, 553–7.

109. 'Hart-Leap Well' (*Lyrical Ballads*, II). The same phrase recurs in an allusion to this poem in a cancelled passage from *The Recluse*. (See notes on p. 319 of Selincourt and Darbishire's *The Excursion*.)

110. *Excursion*, VI, 535–8. Both the absence of *action* from Wordsworth's philosophy, and the tendency of much of his best poetry towards a bare, grim, wintry austerity (noticed e.g. by G. W. Knight, *The Starlit Dome* [1941], pp. 4–5), are connected with the fact of his drawing his nourishment from a dying social order.

111. IV, 71–6, 205–14.

112. B. R. Haydon, *Autobiography*, 13 April 1815 (World's Classics edition, 1927), p. 278; cf. Southey: 'in every relation of life, and every point of view, he is a truly exemplary and admirable man' (letter to B.

Rydal Mount bread and cheese were kept ready for all who knocked. Nor was he habitually, after this date, the frightened reactionary of 1818 and 1831; he mellowed into a cheerful, loquacious, amiable, humane and reasonable householder, not averse to cautious reforms. But the bread-and-cheese of charity was no diet for the Muses, nor timid reformism breath for the trumpets that sing to battle. Wordsworth suffered for intellectual, not moral, errors. An artist has to understand as much as to feel.

Though Wordsworth's finest work still lay ahead of him when he came to Grasmere, nearly all of it was to be about his own or the social past. Before long he was troubled with fears that the lease on which he held his poetic gift was running out, like a peasant's lease of his farm. He began writing a lament on the vanishing of something from his world: rainbow and rose came and went, but the 'celestial light' that had touched common things like a dream shone no more.[113] As so often happened with him, he stopped for several years – he could not find out what it was that he had lost. Then in 1806 in his deepening isolation he added the famous stanzas on childhood and a life before birth. Caught in the 'prison-house' of life he clung to half-imaginary memories of his earliest years, and saw them fading like a lost inheritance; he looked further back still, into an earlier existence, and credited to it the sensations that can only belong to man in an elaborated society. That he was weaving private myth out of public reality he might have guessed by recalling those lines in *Descriptive Sketches* on the tradition, still handed down in the Alps from father to son, of an ancient golden age free from labour and hardship. His prison-house was a divided society, the 'fen of stagnant waters'[114] that was his England; his poem

Barton, 19 December 1814, *Letters*, op. cit., p. 235). It was Wordsworth as a public man that Hazlitt attacked with savage irony in his article of December 1816 (*Collected Works*, ed. A. R. Waller and A. Glover, III [1902], pp. 157 ff.), and that Shelley called 'a beastly and pitiful wretch' (Harper, op. cit., II, p. 295).

113. cf. Abercrombie, op. cit., p. 25: 'Perhaps the great Immortality Ode, the climax of his art, marks the turning-point in his psychological history.' It was begun in 1802 and finished in 1806.

114. Sonnet: 'London', 1802.

achieved its immense power through its tragic sense of the loss and laying waste of human value by this captivity. His infancy, about which Heaven lay, was the infancy of mankind, of which a relic lingered in the primitive democracy and fraternity of Grasmere. Not the individual child playing with its toys, but the human race grappling with its tasks, could claim those lofty and inextinguishable gifts, those 'truths' of an early unbroken social bond that men in later ages must 'toil' painfully to rediscover, and could hear the 'mighty waters' of history.

A poem that should have been a hymn to humanity and a splendid memorial of the Revolution turned into an enigma, almost a splendid absurdity, because Wordsworth could now only think of the mind's contact with other minds in social life as cramping and strangling, instead of moulding and fertilizing; because he could see no road forward out of a dismal present, but only a road receding into the mists of a bygone age. It was left to Shelley and Marx to rebuild his 'imperial palace' on new foundations, in the future instead of in the past.

Since Marx, the problems that baffled Wordsworth have begun to be, in principle, soluble. Any poetry that neglects to try and solve them will go wrong, not so much by being untrue, as by being irrelevant, and therefore in danger of being ridiculous. There will not be another great poet who has not learned much from Marx. Marxism also has much to learn, that it has not yet learned, from poetry.

A POSTSCRIPT (1973)

That Marxism and poetry both stand in need of each other's aid seems to me, after nearly twenty years, more true than ever, but its fulfilment harder than ever. In 1954 I was writing as a member of a party; today as an independent Marxist I am more conscious of the obstacles – which communist parties seemed to have found means to overcome – in the way of any genuine coming together of writers or scholars with 'the People'. This pre-Marxist and less uncomplimentary name for 'the masses' links Wordsworth with the long tradition, much studied of late, of Populism, still an active force in the newly developing lands. In the ideas of 'the People' there have always lurked ambiguities and contradictions, many of which revealed themselves, as he might have recognized more clearly, in the French Revolution. But the 'masses', or the 'proletariat', of Marxist thinking have also turned out to be far less simple and comprehensible than we used to suppose.

Since 1955, when my essay was written, the Cultural Revolution has sought to unite thinking individual and mass mind in a newer, more organic fashion, and this accounts for much of its appeal to the West, particularly to the student movement it helped to generate. Whatever the political value of that grand upheaval, however, it would not seem to have had much value for the arts, or 'culture' in any traditional sense; rather it seems to have called on artists and intellectuals to become good Chinese by ceasing to care about being themselves. Wordsworth's 'peasant' style would have been highly acceptable to Mao, but not that of *The Prelude*, nor the themes Wordsworth treated in either medium. There is peril for the writer in being cut off from popular feeling, but there is at least an equal artistic risk of being sucked too deeply into a movement, of being reduced to the role of propagandist, first for a cause, then for a party, finally for a leader. An intellectual who seeks to lose himself in the mass is too much like the mystic who craves to lose himself in the world-spirit, to be a lump of salt dissolving in the ocean.

In England in the 1790s there was more than my essay allowed for of a radical 'movement', and Wordsworth's retreat from London was in one way an instinctive flight from its demands on him. It could not be easy for him to find a congenial place in any movement, because of his autarchic temperament, his impatience of routine, his loafing propensity; the same qualities, bred by a boyhood in the hills and by a nascent sense of destinies of his own, that prevented him from working hard at college, or choosing any profession. (The one he had a hankering for – the army – was the one which would have imposed on him the most constraint, the discipline he could not impose on himself.) But for these qualities we should not have had his poetry, but they made also for the self-absorption that was to startle so many who knew him, and would later help to drag him into Toryism. It would then be his ironic nemesis to have to worry his head over petty official papers and the distribution of stamps in Westmorland.

Ideally a poet should be a man of action too. The French Revolution, while it charged Wordsworth's mind with so much electric fire, also left him with haunting doubts of the validity of action, as a means to change the world. As a means to preserve it, he could come to believe in action in its conventional, respectable form of war; it is characteristic of the freakish logic of history which transposed so many of his convictions into their opposites that from the condemnation of war in his early poems he arrived at the doctrine of 'Carnage is God's daughter'. But for Wordsworth in his own person, as for any writer, to *act* should mean action through the practice of his art. For this he required an audience, one both sympathetic and critical, and responsive on both a literary and a social plane. His isolation from the 'People', which in the end reduced him to a thinking cymbal, began as isolation from any such reading public. He could not write for a peasantry, even if he tried briefly to borrow its language. He could for a while, like Shelley, by withdrawing into solitude write for a half- or more than half-imaginary audience of ardent young listeners, men and women worthy of his highest inspiration. It was for them, with Coleridge as their fittingly elusive representative, that *The Prelude* was written, but it is one of the astonishing facts of literary history that he was to die with his greatest poem still unknown. Appropriately enough it came out at last, in 1850, close after another thunderclap of European revolution, and partly no doubt for that reason struck readers as desperately radical.

That Wordsworth was able to write so splendidly for ten years, and this poem above all, is more notable than his subsequent decay. Unpolitical admirers, among them his latest and excellent biographer Mrs Moorman,[1] have continued to think of his genius as awakened and sustained by withdrawal to the

1. I may refer to my review of the first volume of Mrs Moorman's biography, and of two other new works on Wordsworth, in *The New Reasoner*, No. 7, Winter 1958–9.

peaceful countryside. Clearly this leaves the later decay more inexplicable, but even for the years of inspiration it fails to do justice to what 'Nature' meant to Wordsworth. As a portrayer of scenery he was far from being a pioneer; he marks the culmination of a long English development of landscape verse and painting. His innovation, and what made him great then and gives him meaning now, was his attempt to trace interacting influences of Nature and society on man's being. He was not withdrawing to the countryside in order to shut his eyes to the human condition, like many 'Nature poets' before and since, but to seek a fresh comprehension of it. His success was, indeed, limited. Racedown belonged to the same county of Dorset as Tolpuddle and its martyrs of the next generation. Wordsworth would not have guessed at this banding together of miserable farm labourers against their tyrants. He knew too little about a class which had a smaller place in France, hardly any in Lakeland, and it must be said that he made too little effort to learn about it. His was the same humanitarian sympathy for the unresisting poor as for the suffering animals that appear in the *Lyrical Ballads* beside his human waifs and strays. Peter Bell's donkey never takes it into its head to kick its brutal master. Fellow-feeling with the waifs and strays came all the easier because Wordsworth himself, having thrown off the shackles of convention and respectability, was a kind of outcast. It has been remarked of Orwell and his tramps and destitutes that such figures, unlike the working class as a mass, find a ready response in the romantic middle-class mind by virtue of being unattached atoms, 'casual, masterless, integral, spontaneous men'.[2]

Removal to Cumberland meant withdrawal to a quite different social climate, a fortress protected by mountains and by their inhabitants, like himself sturdy individualists but with strong social ties. When William and Dorothy set up house at Grasmere in 1799 they were founding a miniature utopia, a settlement in the wilderness such as Coleridge and Southey had been planning to found in America. Wordsworth was hitting on the right place for it on his own doorstep, in his native hills which he felt a sort

2. P. Thirlby, 'Orwell as a Liberal', in *Marxist Quarterly*, Oct. 1956, pp. 241–2.

of shame at having ever abandoned, like old Michael's son, for the distractions of the busy world. Here he had the freedom and solitude necessary to him, and could still have hope and confidence in mankind, even if now this was a somewhat disembodied or symbolic mankind, a race of past or future more than of the present. He had belonged to the Left, and would later belong to the Right; in his great years his mind was close to the centre of a vortex of conflicting currents, and it was this vital involvement in Britain's, and still more in Europe's, contradictions, this state of being neither partisan nor indifferent looker-on, that lifted his genius to the heights.

Irreconcilable things outside forced him to postpone from year to year his grand philosophical poem: he was only able to write this, or begin it with *The Excursion*, when he was clear of his maelstrom, a party spokesman once more. Writing *The Prelude* he was driven inward, to search within himself for clues to the mysteries of man's private and social self. There was egotism in his laborious tracking of his own mental growth, but he was at the same time finding a fresh identity between himself and his 'people', humanity on the long pilgrimage of which his own secret history seemed to him an illustration. In what was healthy in himself he could proclaim the work of Nature allied with a right social order, whose blessings he still thought could be extended to all, and mankind thus regenerated. The poetry of *The Prelude* stands as proof that he was not altogether wrong.

Wordsworth's dalesmen as he saw them were, like his Leech-gatherer, in part figments of his imagination; they were in any case a 'reactionary' class, in the sense in which Marxism has – often too hastily – used the word of an obsolete social group impeding the march of history by its unwillingness to disappear. In this light his later desire to preserve England's landed aristocracy might be called a morbidly logical replacement of his earlier desire to keep its peasant-proprietors and shepherds on their farms. It had some affinity with his choice of a Scots pedlar, a straggler from his old poems of common folk, to expound the conservative philosophy of *The Excursion*, and this combination of democratic façade and reactionary core entitles him to count as a forerunner of Tory Democracy. Another Scot of humble origin, Carlyle, was soon taking it up; Disraeli would be a third recruit from far away. It has been pointed out that radical embers were still aglow in him as late as 1809, and what in the end pushed him into panic and reaction was the rioting of 1810 and similar symptoms of mass unrest.[3] His fits of patriotic excitement about the long-drawn war were intermittent: the menace on the home front, the newly spawned English proletariat, frightened him more than Napoleon, because he knew of no answer to it. His 'People' was turning into something alien, cut off from all the old associations, a denizen of slum cellars instead of green hills, far more unknowable than even the farm labourers of the south. If from now onwards he was drifting further and further away from the People, it was he who felt that he was being abandoned. His solitariness, which formerly helped him to have faith in his fellow-men, now helped to distort them into malignant, inhuman shapes.

On a spring evening a year or two ago a knot of youngsters passing Wordsworth's grave was to be heard grumbling comically about how he had bored them at school. Yet ours is, for youth above all, an age of revolutionary change, and no writer has ever expressed more vividly than the young Wordsworth the sensation of drawing breath in such times. Literary Criticism, as much accustomed as any other science to 'murder to dissect', must be credited with robbing him of much of the political passion that belonged to his being, or with failing to rediscover it after the long Victorian torpor. We may wonder how different an image we should have of him, and how differently English poetry might have evolved, if *The Prelude* had come out in those decades of ferment to which the younger Romantics belonged, and *The Excursion* been kept locked up instead. It has never come to be fully grasped as the finest political poem ever written, of which it may be said that to be able to feel its climactic passages with all their vibrations is to belong truly to European history, to the onward-moving conflict of the centuries. Scarcely ever has

3. F. M. Todd, *Politics and the Poet: A Study of Wordsworth* (Methuen, 1957), pp. 132, 141, 151 ff.

Toryism had better cause than in the long burial alive of this poem to congratulate itself on a damaging blow at England's soul – to call it so for want of a better word. It is typical of our situation that the richest of languages has not yet found a better expression, 'cultural life' being the private domain of the academies, 'spiritual life' of the churches.

There may at present be more prospect of Wordsworth the conservative being reprieved by Wordsworth the conservationist. He could not rescue the English peasantry, but he went on trying to save England's scenery, which we today, stifling and suffocating in our monstrous heaps of concrete, are being compelled to regard as one of the planet's precious and irreplaceable resources, daily ravaged and looted for private profit. Wordsworth thought too readily of the cures he found for his own spiritual ills, seclusion and 'wise passiveness' and visionary moorlands, as cures for society too. In the longer run, two centuries after the start of the Industrial Revolution, we can perceive more of practical social wisdom in the gospel he took over from the physicians and gave a fresh meaning, of the *vis medicatrix naturae*, Nature's healing power. Even the bundle of reluctances that kept Wordsworth from winning college prizes and throwing himself into a career, while vaguely dedicating himself to a *mission*, takes on a novel aspect today. 'Getting and spending, we lay waste our powers', he complained to his contemporaries: in our more prosaic speech he was opting out of the rat-race, the pursuit of rewards and dignities to which the rest of the Wordsworth clan – a rising middle class in itself – devoted themselves so ardently.

When Wordsworth accused his generation of 'presumptuous confidence' in its own superior wisdom, he was condemning the illusions of 1789 in almost the same words as Metternich, but his charge lay also, and far more justly, against the power and ambition of a greedy and soulless capitalism; and the two things were, more than he ever understood, parts of the same historical process, the better and worse sides of the same penny. Turning his back on industrialism, he turned away from progress, but he repudiated also the capitalism in which Marx too was to find only present ill, though future good. The social patterns that Wordsworth fell back on in his own environment for bulwarks against its spirit of blind competition, its thirst for *getting on* at all costs, were primitive and archaic: the peasant eking out a bare living from his narrow plot, the family keeping itself, and keeping itself together, by cottage industry. He over-idealized them, especially cottage industry which he made a cult of very much like Gandhi's of the spinning-wheel, failing to realize what crippling toil it often implied.

In a larger historical vista, none the less, these old-world modes of livelihood can be seen as enshrining values, transmuted and preserved in Wordsworth's poetry, that we today feel painfully the lack of. Marxism has concerned itself too exclusively with their 'reactionary' features. Already in 1955 I felt misgivings, some of them prompted by Wordsworth, about the collectivization of land being pushed on in Eastern Europe. Events since then have shown one communist regime after another compelled to come to terms with a tenacious peasant individualism. This is not merely, though it may be largely, *kulak* selfishness and greed: as against the anonymity of big mechanized agriculture it has a kinship with the craftsman's satisfaction in work done by himself, or by his small group. In Western factories in the past few years the workman's impulse to make something himself has collided more and more with the juggernaut conveyor-belt that reduces him to a mere cog. A search has begun for less automatic methods of production, to restore autonomy to small working teams, and resurrect the old skill of the handicraftsman on a higher level. This is a dilemma confronting big industry, whether capitalist or socialist. Socialism simply as 'public ownership of the means of production' cannot put an end to the intricate problems of relationship between individual and collective, of which that between artist and people is another instance.

Wordsworth would have had need of an Ariadne's thread to guide him through the labyrinth of such a span of history as the one he lived through. The historian who tries to trace his poetic and political evolution has need of it equally. And both verse and virtue, such as the stoic endurance Wordsworth shared through long years of neglect with his dalesmen, though they can only grow in very special soil, once grown escape from their points of origin in history and take on a wider significance. All these questions about Wordsworth still seem to me worth studying, perhaps more than ever before, because as an English poet he is second only to Shakespeare, and because we have reached a time when what is authentic in his poetry both of revolution and of preservation has potent meanings, somehow to be reconciled.

Letter to Lassalle*

London, 19 April 1859

I am now coming to *Franz von Sickingen*. In the first instance I must praise the composition and action, and that is more than can be said of any other modern German drama. In the second instance, leaving aside the purely critical attitude to this work, it greatly excited me on first reading and it will therefore produce this effect in a still higher degree on readers who are governed more completely by their feelings. And this is a second and very important aspect.

Now the other side of the medal: *First* – this is a purely formal matter – now that you have written in verse, you might have polished up your iambs with a bit more artistry. But however much *professional poets* may be shocked by such careless-ness I consider it on the whole as an advantage, since our brood of epigonous poets have nothing left but formal gloss. *Second*: The intended collision is not simply tragic but is really the tragic collision that spelled the doom, and properly so, of the revolu-tionary party of 1848-9. I can therefore only most heartily wel-come the idea of making it the pivotal point of a modern tragedy. But then I ask myself whether the theme you took is suitable for a presentation of this collision. Balthasar may really imagine that if Sickingen had set up the banner of opposition to imperial power and open war against the princes instead of concealing his revolt behind a knightly feud, he would have been victorious. But can we subscribe to this illusion? Sickingen (and with him Hutten, more or less) did not go under because of his cunning. He went under because as a *knight* and a *representative of a moribund class* he revolted against that which existed or rather

---

*From Marx and Engels, *Selected Correspondence* (Moscow, n.d.).

against the new form of what existed. Strip Sickingen of his idiosyncrasies and his particular training, natural bents, etc., and what is left is – Götz von Berlichingen. Embodied in adequate form in that last-named *pitiable* fellow is the tragic contrast between knighthood on the one side and Kaiser and princes on the other; and that is why Goethe rightly made a hero of him. In so far as Sickingen – and even Hutten himself to a certain extent, although with him, as with all ideologists of a class, such utterances should have been considerably modified – fights against the princes (after all, he takes the field against the Kaiser only because he transformed himself from a kaiser of the knights into a kaiser of the princes), he is in actual fact only a Don Quixote, although one historically justified. Beginning the revolt under colour of a knightly feud means nothing else but beginning it in *knightly* fashion. Had he begun it otherwise he would have had to appeal directly and from the very beginning to the cities and peasants, i.e., precisely to the classes whose development was tantamount to the negation of the knighthood.

Therefore, if you did not want to reduce the collision to that presented in Götz von Berlichingen – and that was not your plan – then Sickingen and Hutten had to succumb because they imagined they were revolutionaries (the latter cannot be said of Götz) and, just like the *educated* Polish nobility of 1830, on the one hand, made themselves exponents of modern ideas, while on the other they actually represented the interests of a reactionary class. The *noble* representative of the revolution – behind whose watchwords of unity and liberty there still lurked the dream of the old empire and of club-law – ought not, in that case, to have absorbed all interest, as they do in your play, but the representatives of the peasants (particularly these) and of the revolutionary elements in the cities should have formed a quite important active background. You could then have had the most modern ideas voiced in their most naïve form and to a much greater extent, whereas now, besides *religious* freedom, civil *unity* actually remains the main idea. You would then have had to *Shakespearize* more of your own accord, while I chalk up against you as your gravest shortcoming your *Schillering*, your transforming of individuals into mere speaking tubes of the spirit of the time. Did you not yourself to a certain extent fall into the diplomatic error, like your Franz von Sickingen, of placing the Lutheran-knightly opposition above the plebeian Muncerian opposition? ...

Letter to Lassalle*

Manchester, 18 May 1859

... Now as far as the historical content is concerned, you have depicted with great clarity and justified reference to subsequent developments the two sides of the movement of that time which were of greatest interest to you: the national movement of the nobility, represented by Sickingen, and the humanistic-theoretical movement with its further development in the theological and ecclesiastical sphere, the Reformation. What I like most here is the scene between Sickingen and the Kaiser and that between the legate and the archbishop of Treves. (Here you succeeded in producing a fine specimen of character drawing – a contrast between the aesthetically and classically educated and politically and theoretically far-seeing legate, a man of the world, and the narrow-minded German priest-prince – a portrayal which all the same follows directly from the *representative* nature of the two characters.) The pen picture in the Sickingen-Karl scene is also very striking. In Hutten's autobiography, whose *content* you rightly described as essential, you certainly picked a desperate means of working these facts into the drama. Of great importance is also the talk between Balthasar and Franz in Act V, in which the former expounds to his master the *really revolutionary* policy he should have followed. It is here that the really tragic manifests itself; and it seems to me that just because of the significance that attaches to this fact it should have been emphasized somewhat more strongly already in Act III, where there are several convenient places. But I am again lapsing into minor matters.

The position of the cities and the princes of that time is also set forth on several occasions with great clarity and thus the

* From Marx and Engels, *Selected Correspondence* (Moscow, n.d.).

official elements, so to speak, of the contemporary movement are fairly well accounted for. But it seems to me that you have not laid due stress upon the non-official, the plebeian and peasant, elements and their concomitant representatives in the field of theory. The peasant movement was in its way just as national and just as much opposed to the princes as was that of the nobility, and the colossal dimensions of the struggle in which it succumbed contrast very strongly with the frivolous way in which the nobility, leaving Sickingen in the lurch, resigned itself to its historical calling, that of lickspittles. It seems to me, therefore, that also in your conception of the drama which, as you will have seen, is somewhat too abstract, not realistic enough for me, the peasant movement deserved closer attention. While the peasant scene with Fritz Joss is, true enough, characteristic and the individuality of this 'agitator' presented very correctly, it does not depict with sufficient force the movement of the peasantry – as opposed to that of the nobility – which already at that time was a swelling torrent. In accordance with *my* view of the drama, which consists in not forgetting the realistic for the idealistic, Shakespeare for Schiller, the inclusion of the sphere of the so superbly variegated plebeian society of that day would have supplied, in addition, quite other material for enlivening the drama, a priceless background for the national movement of the nobility playing in the foreground, and would have set this movement in the proper light. What wonderfully expressive types were produced by this period of the dissolution of feudal bonds as illustrated by the roaming beggar kings, breadless *lansquenets* and adventurers of every description – a Falstaffian background which in an historical drama of *this* kind would have even greater effect than it did in Shakespeare! But apart from this, it seems to me that this relegation of the peasant movement to the rear is precisely the point that erroneously induced you, I believe, to misrepresent also the national movement of the nobility in one respect and at the same time to allow the *really* tragic element in Sickingen's fate to escape you. As I see it, the mass of the nobility directly subject at that time to the emperor had no intention of concluding an alliance with the peasantry. The dependence of their income on the oppressing of the latter did not permit this. An alliance with the cities would have been more feasible. But no such alliance was effected, or was effected only to a very limited extent. But a national revolution of the nobility could have been accomplished only by means of an alliance with the townsmen and the peasants, particularly the latter. Precisely herein lies, in my opinion, the whole tragedy of the thing, that this fundamental condition, the alliance with the peasantry, was impossible, that the policy of the nobility had therefore to be a petty one, that at the very moment when it wanted to take the lead of the national movement, the *mass* of the nation, the peasants, protested against its leadership and it thus necessarily had to collapse. I am unable to judge to what extent your assumption that Sickingen really did have some connection with the peasants has any basis in history. Anyhow, that is wholly immaterial. Moreover, as far as I remember, wherever Hutten in his writings addresses the peasants, he just lightly touches on this ticklish question concerning the nobility and seeks to focus the wrath of the peasants on the priests. But I do not in the least dispute your right to depict Sickingen and Hutten as having intended to emancipate the peasants. However, this put you at once up against the tragic contradiction that both of them were placed between the nobles, who were decidedly *against* this, and the peasants. Here, I dare say, lay the tragic collision between the historically necessary postulate and the practically impossible execution. By ignoring this aspect you reduce the tragic conflict to smaller dimensions, namely, that Sickingen, instead of at once tackling emperor and empire, tackled only a prince (although here too you tactfully bring in the peasants) and you simply let him perish from the indifference and cowardice of the nobility. Their cowardice would, however, have been motivated quite differently if you had previously brought out more emphatically the rumbling movement of the peasantry and the mood of the nobility, become decidedly more conservative on account of the former 'Union Shoes' and 'Poor Konrad'.[1] However, all this is

1. The *Bundschuh* and the *Armer Konrad* were underground movements of peasants and town workers in the late fifteenth and early sixteenth centuries. Their aims were the abolition of serfdom and the partition of Church and monastic lands.

only *one* way in which the peasant and plebeian movement could have been included in the drama. At least ten other ways of doing this just as well or better are conceivable ...

Dickens and the Popular Tradition*

I

By *Socialist Realism*, in the field of literature, I assume we mean literature written from the point of view of the class-conscious working class, whose socialist consciousness illuminates their whole view of the nature of the world and of the potentialities of mankind. By *Critical Realism* I assume we mean literature written in the era of class society from a point of view which, while not fully socialist, is nevertheless sufficiently critical of class society to reveal important truths about that society and to con-tribute to the freeing of the human consciousness from the limita-tions which class society has imposed on it.

That the division between Critical Realism and Socialist Realism is a tricky business, which though basic is seldom clear-cut, should not surprise us, for the socialist revolution begins many years and even centuries before it can actually take place. As Lenin reminds us : between the bourgeois-democratic revo-lution and the socialist revolution there is no Chinese wall. Which does not mean that between the bourgeois-democratic revolution and the socialist revolution there is no essential dif-ference. What Lenin is warning us against is the expectation of a simple process, a black-and-white picture.

I should like to make two points about Critical Realism which I feel may be worth bearing in mind. One is that it covers a great deal of literature which varies very much not only in quality and subject-matter but also in the point of view from which it is written. To take one or two examples only from the field of English literature : Defoe, Fielding and George Eliot are all, I think correctly, described as critical realists, but though they all three adopt a point of view deeply critical of British bourgeois

* From *Zeitschrift für Anglistik und Amerikanistik*, 1961, No. 3.

society the three points of view have *almost* as much that distinguishes them as they have in common and their individual contributions to the liberation of British consciousness, though not incompatible, are certainly very different. It is important therefore to define, within the general context of Critical Realism, the particular point of view of particular writers and of particular tendencies within this general picture.

My second general point is that when we speak of point of view in relation to creative literature we are referring to something somewhat different from a man's consciously held, or fairly easily abstractable, ideas. We all know from experience that a writer may have very curious, illogical and even reactionary opinions and yet be a pretty good writer, and conversely that there are writers whose philosophical and political opinions are enlightened and 'correct' and yet who are not very good writers. The explanation, of course, is not that the processes involved in the exploration of the world through art and those involved in the formulation of scientific laws are contradictory but that they are not as a rule the same. You may well have appreciated in general terms the correctness of a certain principle but not have understood very fully the actual ways that principle operates : or you may have a remarkable grasp of the way it operates in a specific case or area but yet fail to see its general significance. This can happen to scientists as well as artists. I am not, heaven knows, trying to press some great general distinction between Science and Art or between the make-up of the Scientist and the Artist; but it seems that, just because he is dealing with human material of an exceptionally high degree of complexity, it is particularly possible for the artist to have very valuable specific insights without being able to transform them into general or theoretical ones. To cut short a complicated and difficult (though to me fascinating) subject, I think we should remember that when we refer to the point of view of a writer and use the adjectives 'socialist' or 'critical', we are using adjectives which, though valid and necessary, are normally used in contexts in which the texture of thought is rather more abstract and theoretical than the habitual processes of art. The words 'socialist' and 'critical' are never of course to the Marxist *purely* abstract words. Marxism, which teaches us that reality is more basic than what we think about it, must itself always be a counteracting force to any tendency to 'pure' abstraction, 'pure' theory. Yet – to over-simplify a bit – when in everyday life we refer to a man as 'socialist' or 'critical' we are usually referring to his formulated *opinions*, whereas the important thing about an artist is not his opinions (on that level) but his *sensibility*, his all-round appre-hension and comprehension of things. I am not for a moment meaning to pose the concept of sensibility *against* that of intel-ligence or reason or science. This is a fatal error in much bour-geois thinking. But I am suggesting that it may be useful to remind ourselves that when we refer to a writer's point of view in the artistic sense we are referring to his sensibility rather than to his opinions or intentions, though of course both these are relevant factors.

That is why I am presuming to use in this paper the term 'popular' more often than the term 'critical'. Within the general movement of Critical Realism, it seems to me, there are certain writers who – though certainly critical of bourgeois society – remain in their overall sensibility essentially attached to the ways of thinking and feeling of that society. I would put Charlotte Brontë, Mrs Gaskell, Thackeray and George Eliot within that category. They are honest writers, they have many insights and attitudes highly inconvenient to the ruling class : I do not want to underrate their value. But their sensibility, for all its pro-gressive aspects, seems to me in the end to be exercised, however critically, within the confines of petty-bourgeois feeling : it does not, even in the case of George Eliot (the best of them), burst the buckles of bourgeois consciousness, though it certainly strains them. Whereas, in a basic and essential way, Emily Brontë and Dickens and Hardy *do* burst the buckles. The view of the world they express, the feelings they generate, are not socialist but they are more than what is generally meant by critical. And it would seem that the essential difference between these two groups of critical realist writers is that the latter write from a point of view which can be described not merely in somewhat negative terms as critical but in positive terms as popular, that is to say expressive of the sensibility of progressive sections of the people other than the petty-bourgeois intelligentsia. Hardy is a popular writer in this positive sense because his sensibility is essentially a peasant sensibility. Emily Brontë and Dickens reflect, as it seems to me, that great popular alliance of working class and petty bourgeoisie which *might* – up to about 1848 – have succeeded in giving the bourgeois-democratic revolution in Britain a different and more revolutionary content and thereby in bringing the socialist revolution very much nearer. The might-have-beens of history are, of course, mere speculation. To the literary critic and cultural historian, however, they have a sort of reality, for he is concerned with the expression of forces which, though they may in the actual power-struggle be for the time defeated, yet remain powerful and fruitful. Dickens was not a Chartist, but he could not, I think, have been the novelist he was without Chartism, and in the eighteen-fifties and sixties Dickens's novels carry forward the spirit of Chartism and in some ways even deepen it and bring it nearer the spirit of Socialism.

2

There is a striking contrast between Dickens's general reputation, by no means confined to Britain, as one of the great writers – one of the dozen or so writers of the world whom almost every literate person knows something about – and his treatment by literary specialists in his own country and America. Even among critics who have taken the novel seriously there has been little disposition to recognize him as a supremely great writer, a writer in the category of Shakespeare and Chaucer. The most serious modern English academic literary critic, Dr Leavis, can find no central place for him in his great tradition of the English novel. And even though in the last thirty years – thanks largely to the work of Professors Edgar Johnson, Sylvère Monod, John Butt and Kathleen Tillotson and the admirable pioneering monograph of T. A. Jackson – the position has improved somewhat, there is still nothing like a general recognition in 'respectable' literary circles of Dickens's stature.

Even among those who have done something to fight for the novelist's reputation one has the uneasy sense of the right thing being done for the wrong reason. We must all be grateful for Mr Edmund Wilson's famous essay 'The Two Scrooges', which made it impossible for the sentimental-hearty view of the great writer to be maintained, yet it has to be said that one of the chief effects of Mr Wilson's essay was to provide the stuffy, respectable Dickens-figure with a few good sadistic neuroses very much to the taste of the post-Freudian western reader. And much as one must welcome the debowdlerizing of the Dickens legend which Georgina Hogarth and the Dickens Clubs had for long succeeded in maintaining, there has been a tendency for recent biographical work simply to replace the image of Dickens the Victorian fuddy-duddy by that of the Edwardian sugar-daddy. Among the highbrow literary critics the situation has not been much better. It is now fashionable to refer to the novels as 'symbolic' and certainly this often reflects a more serious and rewarding approach than that of a few decades ago; but 'symbolic' is a word which has at best to be used with the greatest care and can more easily lead away from than towards a just assessment of Dickens's art, especially if its use betrays – as it so often does – a preoccupation with Jungian metaphysics.[1]

Why is it that twentieth-century western literary criticism has so singularly failed to come to terms with Dickens's art? I think the reason has little to do with objective artistic merit but is almost entirely a matter of the historical development of capitalist society over the last hundred years and of the position of the intellectual within that society.

To say that Dickens was very unlike a twentieth-century intellectual is, in a sense, to say something all too obvious, yet it is perhaps worth saying because it explains at least in part why so many twentieth-century intellectuals have either despised Dickens or praised him for off-centre reasons. Specifically, to catalogue the dissimilarities, one might say that Dickens, unlike most twentieth-century western literary intellectuals, was very vulgar,

1. A good example of the sort of thing I mean are some recent interpretations of *Great Expectations* by Dorothy Van Ghent (in *The English Novel Form and Function*) and G. R. Stange (*College English*, XVI, October 1954), admirably commented on by Julian Moynehan in *Essays in Criticism* Vol. X, No. 1, Jan. 1960.

very practical and very optimistic. Perhaps it should be added that, though habitually living beyond his income, he was, by professional middle-class standards, very rich. Also that he was in the more formal, academic sense, quite unintellectual.

None or all of these qualities, of course, however admirable, in themselves make Dickens a great writer; but they do involve his being, when we come to take stock of him, a great writer of a particular and – by modern standards – peculiar kind. And if I use the word 'popular' to describe the kind I do so with my eyes open.

3

There are various reasons for using the word 'popular' in connection with Dickens's novels and some of them, though by no means irrelevant, are not, in my opinion, among the conclusive reasons.

(i) In the first place there is the fact that Dickens was, and has on the whole continued to be, very widely read. There had never been anything like the success of *Pickwick*. And the public that read Dickens was, from the first, remarkably wide, ranging from the aristocracy (including later on the dear Queen herself) to countless not highly educated working-class people. It is improbable that any subsequent serious British novelist, even George Eliot at the height of her fame, had so large or so wide-ranging a reading public, though a contemporary best-seller like John Braine's *Room At The Top*, with its vast Penguin printing, might come within a comparable distance. But though a large circulation over a long period must be seen to be in the end a *sine qua non* of popular literature, yet the obverse is not true and I think it essential to insist that a satisfactory use of the word 'popular' cannot permit of its identification with circulation. It is indeed precisely this identification that has led to the debasing of the word 'popular' in a country like Britain where it is most often used as a synonym for 'commercially successful'.

(ii) More important, perhaps, is the question of Dickens's *relation* with his public. There is no doubt that, both as an adherent of serial publication and as Editor of *Household Words*,

Dickens enjoyed an unusually close relationship with his readers. We all know about the letters begging him to spare Little Nell and it is all too easy to see only the ridiculous side of this kind of thing. Professor John Butt has put the matter into perspective very effectively in *Dickens at Work*:

> To the author [serial publication] meant a larger public, but also a public more delicately responsive, who made their views known during the progress of a novel both by writing to him and by reducing or increasing their purchases. Through serial publication an author could recover something of the intimate relationship between story-teller and audience which existed in the age of the sagas and of Chaucer; and for an author like Dickens, who was peculiarly susceptible to the influence of his readers, this intimate relationship outweighed the inherent disadvantages of the system.

This point deserves emphasis, for it involves something important in any consideration of a genuine popular tradition – an attitude to art in which the audience is seen neither purely as consumer (the commercial relationship) nor as a superior group of like-minded spirits (the highbrow relationship) but in some sense as collaborator. It involves of course a rejection of the extreme individualist attitude in which 'self-expression' as opposed to the organization of social experience is seen as the object of art and in which the whole importance of communication is played down.

(iii) A further point which has undoubted relevance to the position of Dickens in a popular tradition is his relationship to existing forms of popular culture of various sorts. Too little detailed work has yet been done on this subject, but it is not difficult to sense a number of profitable lines of exploration. There is the absorption, for instance, of the fairy-tale imagination. Quilp and Fagin, to say nothing of Squeers or Krook, are ogres; Betsey Trotwood (not to mention Brownlow or John Jarndyce) is a fairy godmother; Miss Havisham partakes of the tradition (given of course a sharp twist) of the sleeping beauty. The novels are full of witches and wicked uncles and Cinderellas and babes in the wood.

It is perhaps worth making the point that such traditional elements in folk culture do not have to be turned into 'archetypes' in order to gain significance and interest. The prevalence of the wicked uncle is quite easily explained in historical terms rather than as the manifestation of some abstract psychological pattern. In a society in which inheritance and primogeniture are important it is naturally uncle, father's younger brother, who has a particular temptation to do the babes out of their rights. Ralph Nickleby needs no Jungian pedigree. The little lost boys of Dickens are an all too natural product of a situation in which the maternity death rate was still something like 20 per cent. Twentieth-century readers are happy to see Dickens's concern with the Little Em'lys and Nancys as evidence of some kind of unresolved personal obsession; in fact his very sensible interest in Miss Burdett Coutt's attempts to do something practical for prostitutes shows that he saw the problem as an objective, though difficult, social one. If many of the typical recurring figures and episodes in Dickens's novels partake of an older popular tradition it is because he moved, both in life and imagination, so deep in the actual experiences of the people, which do indeed recur and form definable and typical patterns, the expression of which in fantastic terms is the basis and function of folk art.

I am not trying, of course, to suggest that Dickens was himself without his psychological problems, eccentricities and worse. He was a complex and in some ways deeply unhappy man. But his acceptance of an active practical and public life, his thoroughgoing commitment not, in the twentieth-century intellectual's manner, to certain *ideas* about reality but to reality itself, to facing the world and changing it, counteracted to a profound extent his personal frustrations.[2] What I would insist is that the sensibility behind the novels is essentially sane, balanced and un-neurotic; the traditional description of Dickens as a comic novelist, though it has sometimes veiled his greatness, is right; the elements of violence and extremity in the books – which are

2. Dickens's capacity to turn to objective use material, often very deeply felt, from his own life is most impressive. *David Copperfield*, the most autobiographical of the novels, is one of the most balanced, certainly the tenderest. An episode like the rediscovery of Mary Beadnell, about whom he had nursed deeply romantic illusions, is used in *Little Dorrit* with remarkable poise and control.

immensely important – involve no more than an imaginative penetration into the realities of the life he knew. If they are not 'nice' books it is because he did not live in a nice world. I think the fairy-tale tradition greatly helped Dickens to encompass artistically (perhaps fantastically is a richer word) the life he was faced with and one of the marks of his triumphant absorption of this tradition is the fact that he has himself added so many characters and episodes to popular mythology. You do not have to read *Martin Chuzzlewit* to know the significance of Mrs Gamp.

Then there is his closeness to contemporary manifestations like the melodrama and the music-hall. Lady Dedlock is, in one sense, a stock figure of nineteenth-century melodrama. She is an ancestress of the heroine of *East Lynne* and of the smart bad women with a 'past' who move in and out of the plays of Pinero and Oscar Wilde. Dickens's own passion for the theatre and his love of acting were not mere sidelines or exhibitionism. It is hard to imagine any twentieth-century major novelist visiting the provinces for the sheer love of it in some ephemeral contemporary farce. And it is just as hard to imagine a modern author describing *in the same tone* George Rouncewell's visit to Astley's Music Hall in *Bleak House*:

He stops hard by Waterloo Bridge, and reads a playbill; decides to go to Astley's Theatre. Being there, is much delighted with the horses and the feats of strength; looks at the weapons with a critical eye; disapproves of the combats, as giving evidences of unskilful swordsmanship; but is touched home by the sentiments. In the last scene, when the Emperor of Tartary gets up into a cart and condescends to bless the united lovers by hovering over them with the Union Jack, his eyelashes are moistened with emotion.

The point here is that the tone is neither ironical, patronizing nor sentimental though there is a whiff of both the first and last, a whiff which it is easy to blow up into a gale, but which represents, it seems to me, an *acceptance,* neither an ignoring nor a sophisticated savouring, of George's experience. It has nothing in common for instance with Mr T. S. Eliot's self-conscious discovery of the significance of Marie Lloyd.

(iv) Associated with this point one should mention the interesting fact, brought only recently to general notice by the success of Mr Emlyn Williams's 'readings', that the best *milieu* for the appreciation of Dickens is reading *aloud*. The novelist's own performances, so phenomenally successful in his later years, have been used by recent critics to illustrate elements of his personal desperation (his need for money to maintain his extravagant way of life; the psychological need he is alleged to have tried to satisfy by the repeated reading of the blood-curdling murder of Nancy) rather than to illuminate the nature of the novels. Public readings of the sort Dickens himself went in for are of course a special case, involving careful pruning and choice of subject-matter, but they do usefully remind us that novels *can* be read aloud and indeed were. In fact this habit of reading aloud, which Victorian families went in for much more than their descendants of the television age, needs to be considered seriously by anyone trying to define the level of communication at which Dickens was aiming. It also underlines, incidentally, the dilemma involved in the need to avoid bringing a blush to the cheek of the young person. I would suggest that the texture of Dickens's prose is, whether through conscious effort or not, perfectly adapted for reading aloud. At this level his wit, which is apt, in the demanding silence of private reading, to seem a bit heavy-handed, the repetitiousness and underlining which the more sophisticated reader often finds tiresome, turn out to be just right. I think this is an observation worth making because it throws light on the rather basic question of the level of sensibility on which Dickens was working. Before we speak of the effects of a scene like the death of Jo in *Bleak House* as 'crude' – let alone 'sentimental' – we need to remind ourselves of two things: in the first place that, just as the texture of dramatic dialogue is bound to be, for the sake of immediate comprehension, less subtly suggestive than, say, the conversations in a Henry James novel, so will the semi-dramatic medium of a public, or fireside, reading impose on the author a style in which the effects are likely to be somewhat 'broad'. In the second place the very adjective 'public' has important implications: it involves communication, not just on a writer's own terms, but on the terms of the outside world. The tendency of modern western criticism is to resent any such intrusion on the idealized communication between the individual artist and the perfectly attuned reader and to feel the need to explain away as a conscious 'concession' any broadening of effect which an admired artist goes in for. It is time we realized that Dickens's vulgarity – though no doubt it raises its problems – is on the whole an incomparable element of strength.

I have mentioned a number of points – the width of his reading public, his attitude to it, his closeness to what remained or had been adapted after the industrial revolution of an older folk culture, his implicit attitude to art as a public activity – all of which, I believe, inevitably lead us to the word 'popular' when we consider Dickens's art; but I do not think any or all of these considerations, however important, is the chief reason for calling Dickens a great popular writer. For that we must look at the actual nature and content of the novels themselves. By this I do not mean of course simply their subject-matter – the material *on which* Dickens worked – but the total complex that he created, which includes inextricably subject-matter (abstractable only in the sense that the fantastic world of a novel can and must *in the end* be related to the real world), organization, rhetoric, and the writer's personal, controlling point of view. While insisting that art is not life I do not think that we should take at all a purist attitude to the question of subject-matter. I do not think it fortuitous that the greatest English writer of the mid-nineteenth century should have written about London, slums, prisons, railways, factories, dustheaps, the docks, workhouses, and lawcourts, as well as about well-to-do mansions, financial speculators and comfortable middle-class homes. I do not doubt that the novelist who deals really well with a relatively small and even unpromising social area (like Jane Austen) is of more value in every important sense than one who (like Disraeli) deals trivially with a much larger one; but to extend this thought to a defence of limitation almost for its own sake is not, I think, helpful, and I do not doubt that the sheer breadth of Dickens's social interests and his passionate concern with what an historian must call the major issues of his day are one of the essential elements of his greatness.

His novels are fantasies, a series of images, complex but clear, difficult and at the same time simple, of significant areas of life in mid-nineteenth-century England, of human situations within that area which combine into a total situation or pattern or image which is the book. Sometimes the book is dominated by a single visualized image to which all else adheres – the image of the Law (made concrete in the Court of Chancery) in *Bleak House*, of the prison in *Little Dorrit*, of the Thames in *Our Mutual Friend*. Sometimes the image is best described in more abstract terms – the title of *Great Expectations* or *Hard Times* is self-revelatory, bearing as much consideration as the visual pattern of a picture. The content of each book can be thought of only in terms of the total image or pattern which fuses all the component parts which go to make it up – subject-matter, style, the author's controlling point of view. The total image or pattern of a Dickens novel is always concrete not theoretic, many-sided not flat, developing not static, historical not metaphysical. And the content is popular.

4

It is necessary to indicate as clearly as possible the sense in which the words *people* and *popular* are used in these pages. It will not be easy to do so within a short space, without laying oneself open to the charge of a somewhat abstract dogmatism. Fortunately Dickens himself has given us a good starting-point. In a well-known passage which concludes a speech given at the Annual Inaugural Meeting of the Birmingham and Midland Institute on 27 September 1869, he announced that he would discharge his conscience of his political creed 'which is contained in two articles, and has no reference to any party or persons' and proceeded: 'My faith in the people governing, is, on the whole, infinitesimal; my faith in the People governed, is, on the whole, illimitable.'

The remark caused, at the time, quite a rumpus, especially among Liberals who, assuming that by 'the people governing' Dickens was referring to Mr Gladstone's government, thought Dickens must have turned Tory. The novelist himself did his best to clarify his meaning by insisting on a small 'p' for the first people and a capital letter for the second and returned to the subject next time he was in Birmingham, adding for good measure an interesting quotation from Buckle's *History of Civilisation in England* which develops the theme that 'lawgivers are nearly always the obstructors of society rather than its helpers'.

That contemporary politicians and political theorists should have misunderstood Dickens's statement, despite his clear denial that he was referring to any party or persons, is not surprising, for what he said by-passes in two sentences the essential assumptions on which the political thinking of bourgeois democracy is based. The bourgeois democrat, who believes that the British parliamentary system as developed since 1832 is the apogee of democracy, cannot accept that there is a fundamental and insuperable division in his society between those who govern and those who are governed. For, after all, he will argue, the governed *elect* those who govern them. If the People choose as their rulers people who rule against them, or those whose interests are different from their own, then either they are very foolish (and probably not fit to govern anyway) or else they will discover their error and in the course of time correct it. That they *cannot* correct it within the framework of political assumption imposed by the socio-economic system as at present operating is to the average bourgeois democrat literally unthinkable, for it involves passing beyond the very assumptions on which his own thinking is based. For the theory of bourgeois democracy of the type developed in Britain in the last hundred and fifty years is in fact dependent on the contention that there are within that society no *insuperable* class divisions, that is to say no basic divisions of interest which cannot, within the existing social order, be modified to the point of elimination. To put it another way, the bourgeois democrat cannot (without ceasing to be a bourgeois democrat) accept the proposition that the ruling class in his society, by virtue of its ownership of the productive forces and its control of the state and propaganda apparatus of society, is able to rule against the interests of the overwhelming majority of the People, despite the democratic rights the people have won.

The force of Dickens's statement of his political creed lies precisely in the recognition implicit in it of two separate and conflicting forces: the people governing and the People governed. That he was quite well aware, on a pretty deep level of political understanding, of what he was saying and doing is made clear by a letter he wrote to James Fields, a few days after his second appearance at Birmingham in January 1870:

I hope you may have met with a little touch of Radicalism I gave them at Birmingham in the words of Buckle? With pride I observe that it makes the regular political traders, of all sorts, perfectly mad. Such was my intention, as a grateful acknowledgement of having been misrepresented.

Now the recognition of a fundamental division between People and rulers does not necessarily imply an analysis of the class basis of this division of the sort that Marx and Engels, contemporary citizens of Dickens's England, developed. Dickens was not a systematic political thinker. The very speech which ended with his profession of Radical faith reveals an extraordinary mixture of paternalism, radicalism, belief in self-help, religious idealism, anti-clericalism and straightforward practical business-sense. The ambiguous attitudes towards philanthropy, embedded so deep in *Bleak House*, and expressed so interestingly in the complexities of his actual relationship with Miss Burdett Coutts, exemplify the sort of dilemma which was never resolved in his life. One would not wish to give the impression that Dickens was an unconscious Marxist or even a pre-Marxian socialist. He was, as he himself recognized, a Radical, with a good deal of the ambiguity that word implies in the mid-nineteenth century. But we are less interested in Dickens as a political thinker than in Dickens as a novelist. It is the emotional force and the imaginative imagery behind his confession of political faith rather than its abstract significance or its precise connection with Buckle's (or Carlyle's) philosophy that is important. And the test of Dickens's status as a popular writer lies not in his opinions but in his novels. If one stresses, then, this particular political statement it is because it does so remarkably draw together a number of threads, impressions and emphases which, especially in the later novels, become more and more dominant.

Dickens, then, sees the People not as a vague or all-inclusive term – an indiscriminate 'everybody' – but as a specific force in contradistinction to those who rule. And he sees them hopefully, confidently. That is all. But it is enough, both for his purpose as a creative writer and for a general clarification of the use of the word 'popular'. That capital letter on which he set so much store is indeed of great significance. For what it indicates is a recognition of the People not simply as a passive mass but as an active force. This is fundamental. The People, in a society in which the essential property and power is in the hands of a small exploiting class, are those who are exploited as opposed to those who exploit them. There is, of course, no absolute merit in being exploited; but there is a specific de-merit in being an exploiter, because the maintenance of the exploitation by which you live is bound, whatever your personal character or motives or auxiliary good deeds, to lead you to actions and attitudes and ideas which hold back the necessary development of human beings as a whole. In a class society like modern Britain the virtue of the People is that, unlike the ruling class, they are capable of solving constructively the fundamental problems with which society as a whole is faced and in doing so are able to raise themselves and the whole society to a new level of achievement and potentiality, to a new freedom. This advance is neither automatic nor inevitable, except in the general sense that history shows that up till now human beings as a whole have in fact (with whatever difficulties, setbacks and errors) tended to choose to solve their essential problems and to develop rather than to deteriorate. The struggle for power in modern British society is to be seen therefore not just as a struggle between two main and morally equal class groupings, of which the chief virtue of the larger is that it comprises more numbers than the smaller, but as a struggle between people and anti-people. The concept of the People, in fact, is inextricably bound up with questions of value and questions of value can be discussed only in relation to the People. Since there are no values but human values (the whole concept of what is valuable meaning what is good for human beings) it is impossible to judge or evaluate any manifestation of human culture, whether it is *Bleak House* or the latest television serial, except in terms of its part in, and contribution to, human development. To state this general principle is not, of course, to imply that one has done more than to state a general principle. The problems of its application are extremely complex and certainly defy dogmatic treatment. But the principle is nevertheless true and it is for this reason that the question of Dickens's attitude to the People is so closely associated with the value of his novels.

'Popular' does not – if we are to use the word thoughtfully – mean simply pertaining to the people in a passive sense. On the contrary, to use the word in such a sense is to debase it and, in doing so, further debase the people. To refer to the *Daily Mirror* as a 'popular' paper or a trashy television serial as 'popular' culture is a betrayal not only of words but of human dignity itself, for it implies that the worst is good enough for the People. Of course millions of men and women read the *Daily Mirror* and of course the act of buying it is, strictly speaking, voluntary. So no doubt was the act of the Indian women who used to commit suicide when their husbands died and of tens of thousands of young Germans who enlisted in the Nazi armies. If the pressures are strong enough people can be conditioned to take almost any action willingly. Human progress consists in the slow and often painful overcoming of those pressures and attitudes which, however widely accepted and even gloried in for a time, in fact prevent human beings from enlarging their realm of freedom. Popular culture, if the phrase is not to become a mockery, is the culture which helps and strengthens the people, increases their self-confidence and clarifies their problems and potentialities.

A popular tradition in literature implies, then, a literature which looks at life from the point of view of the People seen not passively but actively. Such a literature will not, of course, except at its peril, gloss over the weaknesses, the corruptions, the unpleasantness or the degradation of the People : it will not, except at its peril, see life as it *wants* to see it. If its spectacles are rose-tinted it must be with the reflection of Blake's rose, not the rose on the chocolate box. Blake's or Dickens's London is not the less terrible for being seen from the point of view of the People, nor is Hardy's Oxford or Sholokhov's Ukraine. The essential characteristic of a popular tradition is not that it should be optimistic but

BIRKBECK COLLEGE LIBRARY

that it should be true: and because it is true it will in fact be optimistic. But these large and generous words like true and optimistic are not as a rule the best to use in discussion and analysis. More modest ones serve us, on the whole, best. To use as a touchstone for the products of a popular tradition the question: is it true? may be in practice less helpful and have less to do with truth than the question: does it serve the People? And though this touchstone, too, like any other, can be abused, its abuses are at least more discussable and therefore more corrigible than the sort of inhumanity which defends itself in terms of high abstractions and absolute values.

5

I should like to demonstrate from *Bleak House* what I mean when I suggest that it was the popular point of view from which Dickens's novels were written that determined their essential nature and significance as works of art. I shall have time only to mention three points but perhaps they will serve to show what I am trying to get at.

(i) The central importance of the Law in *Bleak House* and Dickens point of view in relation to it.

At the heart of *Bleak House* is the Court of Chancery. It is, most obviously, at the centre of the plot of the novel, for it is the case of Jarndyce and Jarndyce that links the various essential characters and groupings of the book and brings them into contact. But it is also the dominating image of the book, the very core of its pattern, sensuous and intellectual. It is the heart of the geography of the novel in the sort of way that London is at the centre of modern industrial England, and the Court of Chancery is embedded in London. It is presented with complete concreteness as a man-made institution physically and economically bound up with the development of a particular society, and the insinuating fog, so famously and graphically called up in the opening paragraphs of the book, creeps deep into the very texture of the novel, not merely colouring it but extending its dimensions. For the fog in *Bleak House*, like that of T. S. Eliot's *Prufrock* and indeed a real London fog, has a many-sided physical presence, cruelly pinching the toes and fingers of the shivering little 'prentice boy; and though, through the image of the megalosaurus, it recalls a past of primitive mud, barbarism and uncontrol, it combines this vision with the actual soot-flakes of the coal age so that the fog becomes associated at once with early Victorian London and with how much and how little man has made of man.

Everything in *Bleak House* is linked together by the Law. It is the Law that has ruined Miss Flite and Gridley and will ruin Richard. Tom-All-Alone's, the foul slum which spews up Jo, is 'in Chancery of course'. Lady Dedlock's sin and Esther's stigma is to have offended the Law at a point in which legal and social sanctions come together, for Esther is *illegitimate*. The Law brings almost nothing but misery and it is revealed as being inextricably bound up with the British state, and that state is shown (though Dickens himself would not have used the phrase) as an organ of class domination. To indicate how far Dickens's view of the state had developed by 1852 it is only necessary to compare *Oliver Twist* with *Bleak House*. While *Oliver Twist* is a novel which attacks certain abuses within bourgeois society, *Bleak House* strikes at the very foundations of that society.

The Law then in *Bleak House* is revealed as a vital and integral part of the social fabric as a whole. It is continuously associated in extremely complex but entirely concrete ways with money and power. The poor, like Jo, are at its mercy because they are poor; and it is the power of money that gives Mr Tulkinghorn his hold, via the Smallweeds, over an upright man like George Rouncewell. The Law is, in fact, a business: Mr Vholes is the extreme instance but by no means an isolated one. And Dickens makes his general point when he writes: 'The one great principle of the English Law is to make business for itself. There is no other principle directly, certainly and consistently maintained through all its narrow turnings. Viewed by this light it becomes a coherent scheme, and not the monstrous image the laity are apt to think it.' The Law is administered by people who are at best, like Conversation Kenge and Guppy, absurdly, at worst, like Tulkinghorn and Vholes, wickedly inhuman. Mr Tulkinghorn may not have a very coherent personal motive for his vendetta against Lady Dedlock but the point is that he is the agent of an impersonal system more potent and more sinister in its motivation than any expression of personal spite or hatred. Lady Dedlock implies this when she describes him to Esther as 'mechanically faithful without attachment, and very jealous of the profit, privilege and reputation of being master of the mysteries of great houses'. It is this very impersonality that makes Mr Tulkinghorn so formidable. It is not his personal wickedness that Lady Dedlock is up against any more than it is the personal kindliness of the Lord Chancellor that determines the workings of the Court of Chancery. This sense of the Law as a force in itself, an independent business, self-perpetuating within its own closed circles of privilege and procedure, is basic to the meaning of *Bleak House*.

And yet it is also basic that the Law is not in the last analysis independent. It has, like every bureaucracy, its inner circular logic, an almost infinitely frustrating image which breaks the spirit of those who get trapped in it; yet this apparent self-sufficiency is in the end illusory. Mr Tulkinghorn's power is great but it is dependent on the great houses which employ him. He is Sir Leicester Dedlock's man. That is why the old baronet is so furious when he is killed. In *Bleak House* it is Sir Leicester, despite his personal anachronistic honourability, who is shown as the fountain-head of the Law. The Law is Sir Leicester's Law, the law of the ruling class. To present it in this way was possible to Dickens only because his own artistic point of view was diametrically opposed to Sir Leicester's. Because he saw British society from the point of view of the People, *Bleak House* is conceived and constructed in the way it is.

(ii) The presentation of character in *Bleak House*.

The characters in *Bleak House* are conceived and presented in relation to the central pattern of the book – the revelation of the working of the Law. Dickens habitually gives his characters *general* characteristics, associated with their work, their social position, the sort of lives they lead, before he establishes their more individual features or endows them with their individual, idiosyncratic note or rhetoric. Notice the first presentation of

Lady Dedlock: '... there is this remarkable circumstance to be noted in everything associated with my lady Dedlock as one of a class – as one of the leaders and representatives of her little world; she supposes herself to be an inscrutable being, quite out of the reach and ken of ordinary mortals ...' There is, of course, no contradiction between this general presentation of a character as a type and his presentation as a unique and even eccentric individual. Those readers who think that such a phrase as 'my lady Dedlock as one of a class' denotes in the author a lack of respect for the individual peculiarity of a character are in fact themselves victims of the illusion from which Lady Dedlock suffers. She thinks she is inscrutable but in fact it is she who is most deceived.

It is usual to talk of Dickens's novels as though the characters, so rich and individual as they are, were simply invented casually, if prodigally, with no purpose beyond the expression of their own idiosyncratic vitality. But in fact in *Bleak House* there is scarcely a single character who does not contribute to the central pattern of the book. One or two, like Mr and Mrs Bayham Badger, with whom Richard lodges, do seem to be thrown in gratis for sheer good measure, but they are the exceptions. Take for instance a figure like Mrs Pardiggle, the lady who takes Esther and Ada to the brickworkers. At first it might seem that her sole functions in the novel are to provide a necessary link in the plot and, incidentally, an amusing extra figure. But in fact Mrs Pardiggle is an essential specimen in the exhibition Dickens has prepared. She, the Puseyite philanthropist, not only contrasts with and sets off the significance of Mrs Jellyby but contributes to the consideration of the whole question of philanthropy which is one of the main themes of the book. John Jarndyce's tolerance of the ghastly Mrs Pardiggle becomes a comment on his own philanthropy and quality of feeling, just as his toleration of Skimpole, which at first seems an amiable generosity, in fact nullifies his efforts to help Jo and redeem his connection with Tom-All-Alone's. And, at the same time, Mrs Pardiggle's religious affiliations do more than add a side to her personal character; they contribute to the working-out of the connection between religious bigotry and the working of an unjust Law which is a central theme of the novel.

It is the religious fanaticism of Lady Dedlock's sister which, allied to the legal stigma of illegitimacy, sets in motion the story of Esther. Mr Chadband (connected by marriage with Esther's aunt and through Mrs Snagsby with the world of the Law) contributes also to this important theme.

What I would wish to emphasize here, besides hoping to stress the tightness and consistency of the organization of *Bleak House*, is that the attitude which such a treatment of character involves is something quite outside the province of a bourgeois sensibility. The superb *individuality* of Dickens's creations should not lead us to imagine that his approach to them is an *individualist* one. On the contrary it is because he sees the workings of capitalism as the determining and significant factor in the lives and personalities of his individual characters that he is able to allow them so much freedom of development. It is because a figure like old Beau Turveydrop is so firmly conceived as a *social* phenomenon, an anachronism surviving from the Regency period, that his idiosyncrasy is so rich. It is because the horrible Smallweeds are indeed seen as part of a system, parasites of the oppressive Law, that they can be at the same time repulsive and funny, degraded human beings yet still human. I think this is very important. Because Dickens's artistic point of view is truly popular it is able to be truly inclusive. Even the most degenerate characters in *Bleak House* preserve a quality which makes the reader not ashamed to laugh. It is not quite a case of Baudelaire's '*hypocrite lecteur, mon semblable, mon frère*' (a sentiment which despite its apparent sense of equality and humility has in fact still a suspect residue of individualism); but somehow in a Dickens novel we are all, including the reader, equals. Because there is no exclusion there is no contempt and no superiority. We look degradation in the face and see humanity there. So that we can judge and enjoy at the same time. Our partisanship enlarges our comprehension and our inclusive sympathy strengthens our partisanship. To understand all is to pass beyond limiting class judgements, but it is not to pardon all. This is the sort of thing I mean when I stress the effects of Dickens's popular point of view.

(iii) Imagery.

One of the key scenes and images in *Bleak House* is the famous 'spontaneous combustion' episode in which Krook, the horrible old 'Lord Chancellor', is found dead.

It is an astonishing scene, of a power and intensity which anyone reading *about* it, as opposed to reading it in context, must find hard to imagine. Naturalistically, of course, the idea of the old man literally burning himself out is absurd and it was foolish of Dickens to have attempted a defence of it in such terms. But in terms other than the purely naturalistic the conception of the scene is completely right. It 'works' as infallibly as Gloucester's fall from the cliffs or Don Giovanni's confrontation by the commendatore. It is, in the first place, most carefully prepared for: the final sentence of the first chapter of the novel with its image of Chancery burnt away in a great funeral pyre opens up the idea. Then the presentation of Krook as the 'Lord Chancellor' is done with a wealth of detail of the most convincing sort. The oppressiveness, physical as well as psychological, of that ghastly house with its limitless junk, its sacks of human hair, its creaking staircase and the wicked old cat, is established with tremendous realistic as well as imaginative force. There is a wonderful moment when Jarndyce notices that Krook is trying with great difficulty to teach himself to read and write and suggests that it might be easier for him to be taught by someone else. 'Ay, but they might teach me wrong!' is the old man's immediate reply. In that second the almost schizophrenic horror of the *Bleak House* world is glimpsed. At the most obvious level Krook's reply is wonderfully funny, off-centre, full of eccentric 'character': but beneath the laughter there opens up an abyss of alienation which is far more than eccentric. The horror is not that Krook's distrust should have reached such a point but that he is, in an awful sense, quite right. In the world of Chancery in which every human being fights every other with any weapon of deceit and cunning he can muster, there *is* no security, no possibility of common trust. Language itself becomes a mode of deception and prevarication; the lawyer is there to catch you out. It is only those like John Jarndyce who withdraws from the whole set-up, or Mrs Bagnet, who lives in a different world, who can risk the human emotions of trust and generosity. The rest are like Mr Guppy whose language is indeed self-expression.

It is entirely right that it should be Mr Guppy who discovers what has happened to Krook. The pages leading up to the discovery are technically superb in their building up horror and suspense. A detailed analysis of them would show both the depth and the nature of Dickens's debt to Shakespeare. *Macbeth* is obviously the source of much of the imagery and treatment, especially the scenes around Duncan's murder and its discovery. But if Dickens has learned from Shakespeare, he has learned well, transforming as well as using, so that there is nothing derivative in the limiting sense about the scene. Indeed the climax of it is so uncompromisingly Dickensian and raises so sharply so many of the issues which divide those who admire and those who dislike Dickens that one cannot well avoid a rather long quotation.

They advance slowly, looking at all these things. The cat remains where they found her, still snarling at the something on the ground before the fire and between the two chairs. What is it? Hold up the light.

Here is a small burnt patch of flooring; here is the tinder from a little bundle of burnt paper, but not so light as usual, seeming to be steeped in something; and here is – is it the cinder of a small charred and broken log of wood sprinkled with white ashes, or is it coal? Oh, horror, he is here! and this, from which we run away, striking out the light and overturning one another into the street, is all that represents him.

Help, help, help! come into this house for Heaven's sake!

Plenty will come in, but none can help. The Lord Chancellor of that Court, true to his title in his last act, has died the death of all Lord Chancellors in all Courts, and of all authorities in all places under all names soever, where false pretences are made, and where injustice is done. Call the death by any name Your Highness will, attribute it to whom you will, or say it might have been prevented how you will, it is the same death eternally – inborn, inbred, engendered in the corrupted humours of the vicious body itself, and that only – Spontaneous Combustion, and none other of all the deaths that can be died.

The spontaneous combustion image, examined in the cold light of day, can be seen to express very completely the peculiar quality of the view of British society which is embodied in *Bleak House*. It has three essential features. In the first place it is an image dependent on natural processes as opposed to metaphysical concepts. The process that finishes Krook may not be scientifically accurate but it is nevertheless conceived in scientific, not mystical, terms. The corruption that destroys him is presented not as some quality of being but is specifically associated with dirt, gin, grease and old paper; with rags and bottles; with sordid acquisitiveness.

In the second place the spontaneous combustion image is a revolutionary image, as opposed to a reformist one. No one could cure Krook; he could not have been saved by charity or even by social services. The whole implication is that processes are involved which can culminate only in explosion and that such explosions are not exceptional and unnatural but the inevitable consequences of the processes themselves.

Thirdly, the image emphasizes spontaneity as opposed to planned action. No specific act has caused the explosion. No match has been struck, no chain of powder prepared; indeed no outside agent is involved.

It does not take much perspicacity to see the general significance of all this. The death of Krook, the Lord Chancellor, represents in *Bleak House* the extreme possibility, the ultimate culmination of the processes at work at the very core of the novel. It is in this sense absolutely central to the novel's meaning and nothing that happens afterwards does in fact cancel or even modify the significance of the episode. It is the high point of what is best described as the revolutionary feeling of the book and this quality is not peripheral to *Bleak House* but at the very heart of its power and profundity.

Yet it is a revolutionary feeling of a curious kind, for, though *Bleak House* is in this deep undeniable sense a revolutionary novel, there are no revolutionaries in it. Obviously this contradiction corresponds to the actual contradiction in Dickens's own attitude to capitalism. He hated it and wanted to see it destroyed but had very little idea as to how this could be done. And so in

Bleak House, having expressed half way through the book with unforgettable power the revolutionary implications of his vision, he is faced with the problem of what to do with a real Lord Chancellor whose habits of life make spontaneous combustion less imaginatively plausible than in the case of old Krook.

The second half of *Bleak House* is by no means a failure, but it undoubtedly lacks something of the controlled intensity and relaxed artistry of the earlier reaches of the book. The murder of Tulkinghorn, brilliantly effective as it is on the theatrical level, is, compared with the death of Krook, a bit of a fraud; for whereas there is, despite the naturalistic implausibility of the means, a deep artistic inevitability in Krook's death, the manner of Tulkinghorn's removal is arbitrary, dictated only by the needs of the plot. And because there is no adequate motivation for Mademoiselle Hortense's action the affair is reduced to a 'mystery' in the detective-story sense and Inspector Bucket takes over. And though in one sense the Inspector is a good deal more plausible as *deus ex machina* than the process of spontaneous combustion, in a more important sense he is a good deal less adequate.

The world of *Bleak House* does not, like Krook himself, go up in smoke. The case of Jarndyce and Jarndyce, it is true, burns itself out and the fiasco of it destroys Richard. And the case of Lady Dedlock, too, smoulders relentlessly on to the inevitable, tragic flare-up, destroying not only the lady herself but Sir Leicester and all he stands for. And around these central tragedies the stage is littered with subsidiary corpses, some dead indeed like Jo and Gnadley, some metaphorically dead like Beau Turvey-drop and the Chadbands and Harold Skimpole who are destroyed within the book as inexorably as Miss Flite is deprived of her wits. Each of these characters becomes a sort of living horror: when Mrs Pardiggle walks into a room humanity is squeezed out of it; the ancient Smallweeds live on, but the degradation they embody is more appalling than any death.

The imagery and significance of the spontaneous combustion episode embody both the strength and the limitations of Dickens's sensibility and correspond to the strengths and weaknesses of the popular forces in 1852.

6

I have placed a good deal of emphasis on the Birmingham speech in which Dickens defined his attitude to the people because it seems to me to give an important clue to his significance as an artist. It ties up, so to speak, the gathering impressions made by his later novels and illuminates the essential unity between his artistic and his personal point of view. It shows that, for example, the linking of utilitarianism with the interests of the capitalist class, of Gradgrind with Bounderby (an insight far less obvious in the 1850s, when the Benthamite tradition of philosophic radicalism still wore progressive colours, than it is today), was no casual hunch; that the devastating exposure of the Law as an institution of class domination in *Bleak House* was what Dickens in every sense *meant*; it shows that the revelation of the character of acquisitiveness in *Great Expectations* and of the whole force and horror of Podsnappery in *Our Mutual Friend* were indeed no side-issues but central artistic insights. As I hope I have demonstrated from an analysis of *Bleak House*, it is from his popular point of view that the actual overwhelming artistic energy of the books springs.

Perhaps the most remarkable of the many extraordinary things about *Bleak House* is that it should have been begun in 1851, the year of the Great Exhibition, that symbol of expanding capitalism and of the economic boom which succeeded the miseries of the forties. It is not astonishing that the appalling conditions of the thirties and forties and the strength of the great popular Chartist movement should have produced in this period not only novels like *Oliver Twist* but *Sybil* and *Mary Barton* and *Alton Locke*. What is more remarkable is that *Bleak House* should go on from where *Oliver Twist* left off and that in the fifties and sixties the tone of Dickens's novels becomes ever more uncompromising. It is interesting that whereas the socialist Charles Kingsley was much impressed by the Great Exhibition in the Crystal Palace, Dickens loathed it. And he loathed it, fundamentally, because he hated nineteenth-century capitalism even more when it was working successfully than when it was working badly.

This is a point which repays the deepest consideration, for it reveals the nature of Dickens's moral and artistic sensibility in contrast to that of almost all his contemporaries among the writers. He was not less outraged than a Kingsley or a Mrs Gaskell by the conditions of life of the poor, not less touched in ways which it is no shame to call humanitarian; but in his humanitarianism there was less tinge of superiority, less tendency to look on the people as 'less fortunate than ourselves' with the reservations such a phrase applies. The condition of the poor aroused in Dickens not just pity, but indignation, and his indignation was based on something more solid than a general sense that such things must not be. Dickens was not uttering an empty phrase when he talked about his illimitable confidence in the People : he was expressing the very quality of mind that made it possible for him to be not just a good but a supreme writer.

It is not by chance that in the very speech at Birmingham in which he defined his attitude to the people he had already had occasion to express his views on 'materialism'. What had, appparently, particularly riled him was a sermon, delivered only a few days previously, by Dr Francis Close, Dean of Carlisle, who had delivered himself of the sentiment that 'There is no question that there is in the present day an evil spirit of the "bottomless pit" rising up among us, ... and he was bound to say he laid a large portion of it at the door of science.' Dickens took up the point with splendid gusto :

I cannot forbear from offering a remark which is much upon my mind. It is commonly assumed – much too commonly – that this age is a material age, and that a material age is an irreligious age. I have been pained lately to see this assumption repeated in certain influential quarters for which I have a high respect, and desire to have a higher. I am afraid that by dint of constantly being reiterated and reiterated without protest, this assumption – which I take leave altogether to deny – may be accepted by the more unthinking part of the public as unquestionably true; just as certain caricaturists and painters professedly making a portrait of some public man, which was not in the least like him, to begin with, have gone on repeating it and repeating it, until the public came to believe that it must be exactly like him, simply because it was *like itself*, and really have at last, in the fullness of time, grown almost to resent upon him their tardy discovery that he was not *like it*. I confess, standing here in this responsible situation, that I do not understand this much-used and much-abused phrase a 'material age'. I cannot comprehend – if anyone can; which I very much doubt – its logical signification. For instance, has electricity become more material in the mind of any sane, or moderately insane, man, woman or child, because of the discovery that in the good providence of God it was made available for the service and use of man to an immeasurably greater extent than for his destruction? Do I make a more material journey to the bedside of my dying parents or my dying child, when I travel there at the rate of sixty miles an hour, than when I travel thither at the rate of six? Rather, in the swift case, does not my agonized heart become overfraught with gratitude to that Supreme Beneficence from whom alone can have proceeded the wonderful means of shortening my suspense? ... When did this so called material age begin? With the invention of the art of printing? Surely it has been a long time about; and which is the more material object, the farthing tallow candle that will not give me light, or that flame of gas that will?

I have quoted the speech at length, not only because it is in some of its incidental aspects so splendidly Dickensian, but because it reminds us that Dickens, unlike so many of his contemporaries and successors, was not an intellectual Luddite. And this, as C. P. Snow has recently emphasized, is something significant. An important aspect of the rise of a 'highbrow' as opposed to a popular culture in the last hundred years has been the sharp division among intellectuals between a scientific and a literary culture. Literary intellectuals have, by and large, been not only ignorant of science but have adopted an attitude of self-conscious superiority to it. This attitude is, I feel certain, due less to the increasing complexity and specialization involved in modern scientific knowledge (though obviously this is a real problem), than to what is at bottom a fear of losing a privileged position. The modern literary intellectual is afraid of science for the same reasons that he is afraid of the people: both threaten, though in different ways, his security as a member of an *élite*. The nature of the sensibility developed by the literary intelligentsia of the western world during the last hundred and fifty years, their ideas about freedom, their most sacred and most deeply ingrained modes of feeling, the assumptions of value so deeply assumed that a questioning of them is too agonizing to be even seriously considered: all this is a consequence of a fundamental division between People and ruling class. The significance of the passage from Dickens I have just quoted is that in it he boisterously and yet carefully avoids so many pitfalls. Science he sees not as a danger but as a blessing: it is its potentialities 'for the service and use of man' that attract him, and his illustrations have all the homely practical effectiveness of a man used to thinking not in terms of abstraction but in those of the real world in which theory and practice have to be united.

Even more significant is Dickens's attitude to the word 'material' and his refusal to be drawn into a way of thinking which sees 'material' and 'spiritual' as opposites. This is not, it must be stressed, a mere matter of verbal juggling. It is, as far as the development of a unified popular culture is concerned, an absolutely essential issue. For idealism, the refusal to recognize that spiritual values have a material basis, is in its various forms the mental sustenance of class division. The modern intellectual's posing of spiritual values in some sort of opposition to material values often proceeds (as far as his subjective development is concerned) from a humane and healthy reaction against the actual operation of capitalist society in which spiritual and human decencies are indeed subordinated to mercenary considerations and the perpetuation of class domination; but the posing is nevertheless fatal, for by removing spiritual values or indeed 'thought' of any kind into some kind of 'special' realm so that they become the property of the 'enlightened', their actual application in practice is made more difficult. For it is only when intellectuals have a *respect* for material reality that they are able to help change anything, material or spiritual.

Dickens had such respect for material reality. And because he had it he was able to develop a sensibility that was in so deep a sense popular. I am not suggesting that Dickens's sensibility was completely unified, that there were no areas of weakness, no loose ends or unresolved conflicts in his make-up. But I am suggesting that – perfection excluded – he had an astonishingly unified sensibility – an ability to face, absorb and cope with a remarkably wide area of reality, certainly a good deal wider than that of any succeeding British writer. And I am not posing width here against depth. His art is deep because it is broad and tough and balanced.

He was able to achieve this unified sensibility because he looked at life from the point of view not of the ruling class or of some sort of intellectual *élite,* but from that of the people. One of the sources of his artistic greatness in his capacity to look degradation in the face and see humanity there. This was possible because he looked not from above but from the level. It is easier for an artist in class society to share the People's aspirations in a general, somewhat abstract, way than for him to share their way of looking at life. Dickens was not without his complacencies, but they did not include the basic complacency of evolving an outlook 'better' than the People's or of imagining – as even the most sincere and tormented of middle-class reformers imagine – that the world will be changed by the middle class. The very vulgarity of him, his enjoyment of the material pleasures, the lack of what the petty-bourgeois sensibility calls 'good taste': all this is not a limitation but a colossal strength, a product of an inclusiveness of sympathy which is the opposite of insensitivity.

Looked at in artistic terms this meant that his point of view and hence his artist's poise, his capacity to release and control and organize artistic energy was not only inclusive but at once sufficiently firm and sufficiently flexible to permit of continuous growth and development. When one calls him a popular writer what is primarily involved is not his opinions or his success but the quality of his sensibility.

I have tried, in my analysis of *Bleak House,* to show in concrete terms how this quality of sensibility asserts itself in art. If one were to attempt to summarize in a more general sense the principal features of that sensibility one would have to say that it was:

(i) realistic (in the sense that the fantasy-world which the artist creates bears a humanly helpful relation to the real world, i.e. makes us see the real world more realistically when we look at it again and thereby helps us to cope with the real world),

(ii) critical (as opposed to a view which accepts and records passively. The popular novelist, just because his point of view is popular, sees art actively as a challenge. He is not afraid of being accused of propaganda, for he knows that all writing has an effect and he knows the sort of effect – a strengthening of the people – he wants to make),

(iii) non-abstract (as compared with the work of the 'Condition-of-England' novelists or of the Godwinian Radicals who were in certain respects Dickens's ancestors),

(iv) non-metaphysical (in the sense that the characters are not seen as metaphysical entities but as interdependent social creatures, historically placed, and that there is no tendency towards an underlying metaphysical pattern or interpretation),

(v) inclusive (seeing society from below rather than from above and thus avoiding the exclusiveness of the ruling-class or *élite* sensibility),

(vi) optimistic (basically confident of the capacity of men and women to make their world better),

(vii) historically and linguistically based in existing manifestations of popular culture. Necessarily therefore national (as opposed to cosmopolitan) and linked with the folk-imagination of the peasantry under feudalism.

Dickens is a supreme realist artist. To describe him as a critical realist rightly emphasizes his critical relationship to the bourgeois society he inhabits; to insist on his place in a popular tradition elucidates the nature and quality of his critical realism.

11. JACK MITCHELL

Aesthetic Problems of the Development of the Proletarian-Revolutionary Novel in Nineteenth-Century Britain *

What strikes one when analysing working-class literature in Britain prior to the appearance of our first mature proletarian novel, *The Ragged Trousered Philanthropists*, in the 1900s, is the gap in aesthetic achievement between the lyrical poetry and the imaginative prose. The poetry of Ernest Jones, Massey, Linton, Robert Brough, Francis Adams, Jim Connell, William Morris, Tom Maguire, etc. preserves and continues the best in the revolutionary-romantic tradition and at times attains and even surpasses the achievements of contemporary bourgeois poets; the *novels* of Jones, Wheeler, Bramsbury and others, on the other hand, while making tremendously important historical contributions to the subject-matter of the novel, are, aesthetically, on an immeasurably lower level than the poetry (in the case of Jones written by the same man!) or the contemporary bourgeois novel.

I have both read and heard certain attempts at explaining this. Critics often attribute the early rise to pre-eminence of the lyrical genres by the fact that lyrical poetry, by its nature, is *tactical*, able quickly and effectively to deal with the day-to-day questions as they arise, to enter directly into the struggle. While this is doubtlessly *one* reason for the dominance of the lyrical genres (though I think not the only one) it does not explain why the novel *failed* to develop earlier than the imperialist era. After all, by the end of the forties, when the best Chartist poetry appeared, the modern proletariat had already been in existence for decades and had gathered a rich and varied fund of experience, more than enough to provide both the basis and the need for the novel as a *strategic* literary genre. In conversation I have often been pre-

* From *Zeitschrift für Anglistik und Amerikanistik*, 1963, No. 3.

sented with the argument that in poetry the workers already had a long popular-democratic and revolutionary-romantic tradition to build on, that verse by its very nature is far nearer to the popular folk-culture and therefore does not need the relatively high level of literacy and formal cultural background needed both for the production and reception of novels. There is no doubt some truth in the first part of this argument, but here one should be careful – after all there were the popular-democratic novels of the utopian socialists at the end of the eighteenth century, and there was the great tradition of the realist novel from Defoe to Dickens, which could then have provided a fruitful basis as it did in fact later for Robert Tressell. As for the second part of the above statement, Marx and Engels again and again pointed to the rich and varied cultural activities of the workers in their clubs, discussion groups and unions where the newest developments in culture and science were picked up with a fearlessness which put the bourgeoisie to shame. One last example. In discussion with colleagues I have been told that the reason why Jones and his nineteenth-century successors did not write good novels was because they looked upon the novel form only as a convenient dress for their philosophical and political ideas. True! but it is really begging the question – which is *why* did they have this narrow formalistic relationship to the novel.

I propose that it was because of the relative poverty of their grasp of the new working-class reality as a relatively permanent, historically 'right', humanly valid mode of human existence; that is, that intimate, positive aesthetic subject–object relationship between the worker as subject and existing working-class reality as object, which would have forced the appearance of true novels as the dialectical unity of a special kind of aesthetic content and the corresponding kind of aesthetic form, did not come into existence until the era of imperialism. (See the almost simultaneous break-through of the proletarian-revolutionary novel in the works of Gorky, Nexö, Tressell, etc.)

What do we mean by the aesthetic subject and object and the *relation* between the two? Hans Koch, in his *Marxism and Aesthetics*, follows Anton Burov[1] in emphasizing that since art

1. Anton Burov, *Das ästhetische Wesen der Kunst* (Berlin, 1958).

is a relatively independent branch of the human consciousness it, like science, philosophy, etc., must have its own specific object-of-knowledge in reality. Koch, while agreeing that 'man' (as a concrete, all-sided totality) is the main aesthetic object-of-knowledge, takes a wider view, within this context, than Burov. He says that the whole of reality is the aesthetic object of art, not any certain group of phenomena. But at the same time he empha-sizes that it is a certain *aspect* of the whole of reality, its phenomena seen from a special point of view. All processes, rela-tionships, phenomena are the object of art, not as processes, etc. *as such*, but in their *Bezug auf die Menschen*,[2] in their impor-tance, meaning, value (or vice versa) for man, as a concrete, all-sided subject under concrete historical conditions. Basing himself on the thesis put forward by Hegel and developed by Marx (*Economic and Philosophic Manuscripts*) that every product of human labour, as well as being a use-value or an exchange-value, represents an externalization or objectification of man's speci-fic human quality (*'Vergegenständlichung der menschlichen Wesenskräfte'*[3]), an expression of the historical level of his human universality, Koch defines this last aspect of phenomena as the 'channel' through which the aesthetic relationship between man and his world functions. Nor should this be seen narrowly as applying only to the direct products of social man; as man in his historical development comes to press the whole of nature more and more universally into his service, so more and more sectors of reality come directly or indirectly to take on the stamp of man, to present him with an 'open book' of his own human powers and potentials, his universality. As an example Koch shows that in man's dawn the stars and other heavenly bodies did not seem beautiful to him and only became so when he entered into a conscious, positive relation with them – for in-stance, to find his way through deserts or to foretell the dates of the Nile floods. They became objects of aesthetic curiosity, there-fore, when they began 'to give practical and objective expression to the strength, power and ability of the human race'.[4] Thus

2. Hans Koch, *Marxismus und Ästhetik* (Berlin, 1961), p. 221, etc.
3. ibid., p. 127, etc. (quoted from Marx).
4. ibid., p. 111.

sectors of reality which were at best neutral and often seemingly presenting an alien, independent, threatening power *against* man, came with time to be objects of aesthetic curiosity and appreciation.

From the foregoing it is clear that it is not enough for a phenomenon to exist *objectively* as a 'manifestation of man's essential human qualities': 'But that there is an object there for the subject is not enough; there must also be a subject there for the object in order to transform the latter from a potential to an actual object of aesthetic appreciation. The object needs the subject, as the Sleeping Beauty needed the Prince's kiss, in order to awake into reality.'[5] Koch continues: the situation of man in class society, and above all in industrial capitalist society, means that huge sectors of natural and social reality remain only potential aesthetic objects for man. Alienation in its different forms of existence creates a distorting lens between man and large areas of reality, making them appear neutral or turning them into something against man, alien, uncontrollable, enemy forces.

Now the novel as a form of aesthetic reflection of man in society, with its peculiarly close, intimate, 'empirical', universal and (at least under the conditions of its birth) positive relationship between the subject (the writer and the reader) and the object (existing man in existing society), demands, I propose, much more than the lyrical genres, an extremely high degree of realization on the part of the aesthetic subject of the *human validity*, the importance *for* man of the sector of human reality seen as aesthetic object – despite all contradictions and difficulties in which this object, seen on the 'short-term' social time-scale, may be caught up.

Thus, for the novel to arise in the first place man's attitude to himself must be one of *humanism*. There was no novel in the Middle Ages because the prevalent attitude to man was antihumanist. It was only when, on the basis of the huge strides made in the sphere of material production, man began to doubt if he was indeed a worthless worm, hopelessly crushed by his burden of sin, began to doubt if the point of reference of true

5. ibid., p. 156. (Translations mine – JM.)

validity and worth indeed lay not in the realm of man but in the supernatural realms of the Catholic religion, when he began to explain, judge, evaluate man in terms of *man*, and not of God, when he began to recognize his own essential human qualities and universality for what they really were, only then could the 'curiosity about men and women',[6] the interest in the 'how' as well as the 'what' of human character and action, which is a pre-requisite of the novel, arise. Fox points out that Chaucer and Boccaccio, at the dawn of the Renaissance, showed first this most important feature of the novelist.

Thus, for a *popular* tradition in the novel to exist, the novelist must see the common people, to a lesser or greater degree, as, even in their existing form, in the midst of their misery and degradation, humanly valid, in the last resort containing within themselves the only ultimate yardsticks of human value. In a word, modifying the above definition of humanism, the truly popular novelist must express a *popular humanism*. This strategic belief in and self-confidence of the common people is, to a varying degree, present in the novels of Defoe, Fielding and Dickens. It is the central core of what Arnold Kettle defines as the decisive element in Dickens's greatness – his 'popular sensibility',[7] a popular point of view which is not confined to his *ideas* (in fact it sometimes contradicts these ideas) but is the essential quality of his whole consciousness as a totality of his intellectual, emotional, moral and sensual perspectives and attitudes. And it is this that is decisive for an artist. If we accept that art addresses itself to man as a totality of his intellectual, emotional, moral and sensual aspects, then we must accept that the process of creation also works along the same unified totality of channels. Marx points out that man recognizes a phenomenon as a 'manifestation of man's essential human qualities' with his whole sensibility: 'Thus man is affirmed in the objective world not only in the act of thinking, but with *all* his senses.'[8]

Therefore it was not enough for the artist on the side of the

6. Ralph Fox, *The Novel and the People* (Cobbett Press, 1948), p. 53.
7. Arnold Kettle, 'Dickens and the Popular Tradition', in *Zeitschrift für Anglistik und Amerikanistik* (Berlin, 1961), No. 3.
8. Marx, *Economic and Philosophic Manuscripts of 1844* (Moscow, 1961).

workers to be 'for the people', to affirm their aims and aspirations at the conscious level of his views (though this was enough, I propose, to 'carry' the lyrical *romantic* genres); to be a true proletarian novelist, to be *driven* to write novels by an inexhaustible intellectual, emotional, moral and sensual curiosity about the actual, concrete, existing life of the working class, this reality had to be apprehended by the aesthetic subject as the chief social 'manifestation of man's essential human qualities' at the level of his *whole* sensibility, at the effortless level of second nature. I propose that this kind of mature, intimate, *positive* aesthetic subject–object relationship between the worker as artist and existing, actual working-class reality, despite all its over-layers of degradation, only matured with the general maturing of the international revolutionary proletariat in the age of imperialism, that only then did a true, mature working-class sensibility, that is a proletarian humanism *in our sense*, become relatively fully developed.

Dickens, as Kettle points out, did not represent a working-class sensibility or humanism (using the term in our modified sense of working class = humanity), but a *popular* sensibility. Dickens expresses the point of view of the London plebeian masses – a conglomeration of small traders, dwarf-bourgeoisie, hawkers, semi-proletarian elements, craftsmen, etc., i.e. a form of popular life which in comparison to the industrial proletariat already in existence in the north represented an archaic society whose days were already numbered. Dickens, whose London novels live through their popular point of view, did not understand and partly feared the new People in the north (see *Hard Times*). The social basis for a fully valid tradition of the popular novel of the Dickensian type was finally destroyed with the collapse of the 'old' popular London way of life in the 1860s. The new stage in the popular tradition would have to be built on the strategic self-confidence of the revolutionary proletariat. We have already mentioned the names of certain English proletarian-revolutionary novelists in the nineteenth century. These writers were unable to pick up where Dickens had left off. This was first achieved by Tressell in the 1900s. *Objectively*, of course, the proletariat, with its rich history and experience, was already in the nineteenth century a potential aesthetic object of unparalleled richness and complexity. But the worker-writer as aesthetic subject was not, it would seem, yet ready to give this 'Sleeping Beauty' the Prince's kiss which would awaken it into life in the form of the novel. For the worker in both the great periods of proletarian literary activity in the nineteenth century (Chartism and the second half of the 1880s) the forces *alienating* him from a proper grasp of himself and the life of his class as, even in its existing form, aesthetically an object 'for man', were still stronger than his developing healthy grasp of its true human validity and importance. Certainly no other class had entered history under less favourable conditions for recognizing themselves as the chief social 'manifestation of man's essential human qualities'. Engels put his finger on the crux of the matter: 'In European countries, it took the working class years and years before they fully realized the fact that they formed a distinct and, under the existing social conditions, a permanent class of modern society.'[9]

I would like now to examine a typical novel of the Chartist period and relate its central aesthetic weaknesses to certain concrete conditions of the time which hindered the development of a mature aesthetic subject–object relationship, a proletarian *humanism* in our sense. With only slight modifications my remarks on this novel apply to all our proletarian-revolutionary novels prior to *The Ragged Trousered Philanthropists*.

The novel I want to deal with here is *Sunshine and Shadows* by the worker-writer Thomas Martin Wheeler, a leading Chartist militant, who in the years following 1848, when he wrote this book, was moving rapidly towards the left wing of the movement dominated by the Chartist leader and Wheeler's fellow-writer Ernest Jones. *Sunshine and Shadows* appeared in the Chartist newspaper the *Northern Star* from 1849 to 1850.

This is one of a group of works by Wheeler and Jones, written after 1848, which represent the highest achievement by the Chartists in the field of the novel. As a result of the sobering effect of the defeat of 1848, which revealed the strength and relative 'permanence' of both capitalism and the proletariat, a

9. Engels, *The Condition of the Working Class in England* (Moscow, 1953; Preface to the American Edition, 1887).

new urge is noticeable to analyse more painstakingly the existing society in its own terms. The publication of *The Manifesto of the Communist Party*, showing the historical destiny of the working class as the inheritors of humanity, was also an important inspiration for the sharp move in these years from romanticism to the *beginnings* of realism in the proletarian novel.

The story of *Sunshine and Shadows* is as follows: Arthur Morton and Walter North are school friends. Arthur is from a worker's family; Walter's father is a 'self-made man', a successful wine merchant. Walter has a sister, Julia, a rose among the philistine thorns. Arthur is apprenticed to a Liberal newspaper after he leaves school. At this period the world appears to him as a topsy-turvy mass of arbitrary injustice. Arthur is a rebel, but his revolt is vague. At the end of his apprenticeship he goes to London and is appalled at the luxury and misery which rub shoulders there. He cannot find a job anywhere. Meanwhile Walter has succeeded to his father's business. If Arthur's conscience has been awakened, Walter has smothered his. He has two ambitions – to marry into the aristocracy and to get into Parliament. He forces his sister Julia to marry old Sir Jasper Baldwin, the aristocratic governor of one of the Windward Islands, to further the first of these ends.

Starvation drives Arthur to Birmingham where he arrives at the height of the early Chartist agitation. Here he comes in contact with ideas that give concrete shape to his own vague discontent. He becomes a Chartist. In showing Arthur's motives here to be of the highest, Wheeler is (as throughout the book) polemicizing against the calumny showered on the Chartist workers by the propagandists of the ruling class. Arthur is under the impression that the pure reasonableness of the Charter will sweep all before it.

As a result of internal bickering, the National Convention in London collapses and Birmingham now becomes the centre of the progressive core of the Convention. At a mass rally in the Bull Ring Arthur makes his first public political speech – which we are told was impassioned – and he is filled with joy at his ability to move the listeners. The police attack the Convention. The Chartists hit back and fire houses in the Bull Ring. Arthur disapproves but, inevitably, is arrested and charged with arson. He manages to escape and flees to America. On board ship he is deeply impressed by the beauty of the sea. During a storm Arthur's courage is contrasted to the abject terror of the rich passengers. Shipwreck. Arthur is picked up by the *Esmeralda* bound for the West Indies. On board he meets Julia on her way to her husband. They fall in love. Once in the West Indies, Arthur soon realizes that the freed slaves have only exchanged one kind of slavery for another. Julia languishes in the prescribed romantic manner in her luxurious house-prison. In a delirium she speaks of her love for Arthur and is overheard by Sir Jasper. During an absence of Sir Jasper's Arthur arrives to find her dying. A 'pathetic' but perfectly 'innocent' love scene follows. Arthur is thrown into jail by Sir Jasper – which gives Wheeler the chance to declare the class nature of the law. Julia dies and Sir Jasper suffers a Gradgrindian change of heart.

Meanwhile Walter North has, by devious devices, secured, in Clarence Fitzherbert, the aristocratic wife he had been aiming at and soon procures his seat in Parliament through shady dealings with the Anti-Corn Law League. Having gained his life ambitions Walter sinks into comfortable obscurity – but he fails to win happiness. Here Wheeler declares the ineffectuality of Parliament in the grip of party monopoly – it should be filled with revolutionary representatives of the people.

Sir Jasper releases Arthur and they become something like 'brothers in grief'. Arthur settles in America. He is disappointed; it is not the Promised Land but there still appears to be more hope for it than for England.

1842. Arthur is in England again, in the industrial north, which is in the grip of slump, misery and revolutionary ferment. The unrest boils over. The middle-class Anti-Corn Law League try to use the mass movement to frighten the landed aristocracy into conceding their demands. To this end they convince the workers round Manchester to start a general strike. In the midst of all this the Chartist leadership remains passive. The masses soon shake themselves free of middle-class control and turn the strike into a weapon for the winning of the Six Points. A thoroughly frightened middle class loose the full force of the state against the workers. The Chartist Convention meets too late and the movement is crushed.

Arthur is sent as an envoy from the northern leaders to London. There he meets the great Negro Chartist leader Cuffay. In London he falls in love with a Chartist working girl called Mary Graham. She is beautiful, without false modesty, deeply political and intelligent, but she is more suited to the domestic fireside than to the public platform. Now follows two years of idyllic family life complete with cottage, lawn, geraniums and cultural evenings round the fireside. Calamity smashes the idyll. Slump and unemployment result in the death of their oldest child and a serious illness for Mary. Arthur is driven to desperation. He attacks a rich man in the street and robs him. This money, which he told Mary he found, sets them up again a little, but his peace of mind, like that of Walter (the man he robbed, now Lord Maxwell), is lost for ever.

Winter 1847. Arthur is now much less romantic – a hardened working-class politician. Yet he still believes (like Wheeler) in the power of practical experiment and example. Thus he supports the utopian National Land Company. According to Wheeler the Company failed, not because the basic idea was wrong, but because of the imperfections of the people involved.

1847–8. Mass upheaval. The Chartist leaders are again split and fail to act at the decisive movement. A witch hunt follows. Arthur is given the job of touring the north to gauge the temper of the people. He sees the failure of the land settlements but still believes them to be the yeast that will activate the surrounding mass of agricultural labourers. The Whigs use spies to provoke the Chartist remnants to secret plotting and then to denounce them. Their hero-leader, Ernest Jones, is flung into jail. Arthur escapes by the skin of his teeth and flees abroad, where he lives on a see-saw of wild anticipation and black despair. Walter North on the other hand has a more even existence – unrelieved boredom. Arthur's wife and child keep up their spirits and are supported in England by the democratic grape-vine.

Here, for the first time, we are dealing with the Chartist movement under its own name. The basic content of the novel is the actual history of Chartism from the first National Petition to the

last. Its general themes are for the most part those already introduced by Ernest Jones (in his case indirectly):

(i) an evaluation of the whole of the Chartist experience with
special reference to its mistakes and weaknesses;

(ii) a polemic against the slanderous picture of the Chartists
given in bourgeois propaganda in general and the bourgeois
novel in particular;

(iii) a polemic against the ideas of class collaboration which
were then being peddled more and more by the ruling class;

(iv) the open championing of revolutionary struggle;

(v) the problem of human happiness under capitalism.

When Wheeler wrote *Sunshine and Shadows* his idealist
Owenite past still exercised a certain influence on his ideas. Yet
because he was (unlike Jones) himself a worker who had *experienced* the fate of the workers and the whole rise and fall of
the movement 'on his own back', he was able to make an
original contribution to the development of the proletarian-
revolutionary novel which, despite his ultimate aesthetic failure,
must be taken into account.

In certain important points *Sunshine and Shadows* might be
said to sketch out in rough the general shape which the international proletarian-revolutionary novel was to take.

As with Jones, much of Wheeler's attention is given to a
critique of the weaknesses of the Chartist movement which led to
its defeat. But whereas Jones concentrated on the theoretical
weaknesses and confusion of the Chartist workers and the resulting squabbles which paved the way for the success of *agents
provocateurs*, Wheeler concentrates on the strategy and tactics of
the *leadership*, the National Convention and the National
Charter Association, which failed to give the revolutionary
masses adequate leadership at the moments of crisis. Wheeler
makes it clear that 'Whatever the reasons for the ultimate defeat
of Chartism, lack of fighting spirit among the masses was not

255

one of them.'[10] Thus Wheeler is the first to bring in as a general theme the policy and activity of the working-class party.

But perhaps his greatest historical contribution was to create the broad prototype of the proletarian hero of the future. In contrast to Jones, where the main interest still lies with the bourgeois anti-hero, Wheeler makes the career of the worker-hero the backbone of his book. At the outset Arthur Morton is an ordinary class-conscious British worker with many of the typical illusions. From here we follow his intellectual and spiritual development in conjunction with his broadening social experience and his activity in the developing mass movement. In relating the human development of his hero in this way to the development of the organized mass political movement, Wheeler is the first real forerunner of the modern proletarian novel.

Arthur's character is to a large extent a polemic against the slanderous picture of the revolutionary worker-leader as a sub-human animal. Wheeler it was who first, in Arthur, gives a true picture of the working-class militant of the day. When Arthur makes his first public speech in the Bull Ring he is shown as being inspired by the highest emotions. As the incorruptible voice and teacher of the masses he is the forerunner of a whole series of proletarian propagandists in our literature of which Tressell's Owen is perhaps the outstanding example.

Another aspect of Wheeler's polemic is his attempt to show Arthur as a deeply *human*, many-sided personality. There is some attempt therefore to show Arthur not only in his directly political 'public' aspects, but also in his 'private', inner life, in his love for a woman, his high sensitivity to beauty and the poetry of wild nature.

In his portrait of the working-class woman, too, Wheeler is a pioneer. His Mary Graham is a huge step forward from Jones who is at his weakest in his female characters. Jones's women stand outside everyday problems and struggles as something to be romantically worshipped whatever their class position may be. Wheeler gives his women class characteristics. Mary Graham is politically conscious to a high degree, intelligent and with a role

10. Morton and Tate, *The British Labour Movement* (Lawrence & Wishart, 1956), p. 81.

(even if subordinate) to play alongside man in the struggle. She is an ancestor of the two Paulines in *The Revolution in Tanner's Lane*, of the woman hero in Morris's *Pilgrims of Hope* and many others. Above all, in her steadfastness, intelligence, realism and devotion to her family she already sketches in all the chief characteristics of Nora Owen in *The Ragged Trousered Philanthropists*.

These are the important historical contributions we owe to Thomas Martin Wheeler. But when all is said and done they are no more than contributions of undigested raw material. A further advance to the final conquering of the realistic novel was blocked by the insurmountable fact that these early writers were not yet really writing as novelists at all. The initial starting point for Wheeler as for Jones is that of the political publicist. His object of study is the Chartist movement, its mistakes, strengths and weaknesses *as a movement per se*. He starts from this point of view and invents his artistic framework, his characters and situations as *illustrations* of this. As Plekhanov says – 'If instead of depicting character the writer makes use of logical arguments, or his characters are invented only to drive home an argument, then he is not an artist but a pamphleteer.'[11] This was to a greater or lesser extent true of all the proletarian-revolutionary novels in England before Tressell. Tressell's statement in his preface to *The Ragged Trousered Philanthropists* that his book 'is not a treatise or essay, but a novel', the main object being 'to write a readable story full of human interest and based on the happiness of everyday life', represents nothing less than an aesthetic revolution in the proletarian-revolutionary novel. This becomes clear if we compare it with what the Soviet scholar Dogel says about Wheeler : 'As with the other Chartists Wheeler's views on the relationship between form and content in a work of art were unsound, and this fact reacted on the structure of his novel. In Wheeler's opinion any work of art consists of two elements existing independently of each other; the basis of the work is made up of "actual facts", "truth", while the "realm of romance", the "artistic fantasy", serves only to ornament these facts so as to make them interesting and attrac-

11, Plekhanov, *Art and Social Life* (Lawrence & Wishart, 1953), p. 183.

tive for the readers. The "facts" contain the educative, didactic core of the book, its ideological-political content, whereas the "fantasy" acts only as a frame, as an artistic form for the presentation of the ideas, the "facts".' [12]

As in Jones the artistic form remains separate from the content because the content itself is not yet an aesthetic content!

Now because Jones, Wheeler and the others were still using art (at least in the novel) as 'sugar for the pill', it was only natural that they should turn to the kind of sugar which they thought would sell their message most easily, that is, the kind of fashionable techniques which were generally accepted as 'artistic'. Thus they tended to attach themselves to the fashionable love, mystery and adventure plot of the third-rate literature of the day rather than to those elements in the great realist tradition which could have provided them with a fruitful foundation. Although Wheeler was freer of 'romantic' elements than Jones, we see the same tendency in the way he takes over certain techniques from the contemporary petty-bourgeois moralizing novel. This is above all true of his 'philosophical' digressions, his Purple Passages narrated in a grandiose 'poetic' prose. Thus Arthur's thoughts appear as 'noble' apostrophes beginning 'O thou Ocean' (or 'London', etc.). Because the basic material itself, as apprehended by Wheeler, does not contain the Beautiful it is *added* on in this way from the outside, in the form alone.

Under these circumstances Wheeler's characters (despite his attempt to give us Arthur in the round) are flat types, differentiated from each other only at the level of their political opinions and social-economic activity. We are told much about the 'what' of what they do, but almost nothing about the 'how'.

Thus there can be no question yet of the worker-writer producing a novel from a 'spontaneous', positive aesthetic *need* – the need to express the life of the workers as, despite all alienation and misery, a positive, valid *life*, as the only social 'manifestation of man's essential human qualities', and *from this point of view* to depict the capitalist class as Anti-Humanity hindering the free development of this way of life whose potentials *we*

12. *Iz Istorii Demokraticheskoi Literaturi v Anglii* (Leningrad, 1955), p. 185. My translation – JM.

already grasp in the concrete form of their beginnings in capitalist society. Wheeler wishes to show that man's life as at present constituted is *totally* unnatural, that it must be wholly eradicated and a return made to a natural life based on the free cultivation of the land. To this end (or rather because of this poverty of his grasp of the true, positive nature of working-class life) his picture of this life is one-sided, flat, and therefore abstract – a picture confined, after all, to its 'public', 'official' level – an unrelieved hell-on-earth misery, oppression, unemployment, starvation and death, relieved only by the desperate efforts of the workers to free themselves at the 'public', 'official' level. We get some idea of what they seek to free themselves *from*, but *what*, in human terms, they seek to *free* is totally absent. We do not experience their rich, manifold, indestructible, creative *life*, illuminated from the inside.

The best socialist realists and popular writers, from Dickens, through Tressell, Gorki and Barbusse to Fadeyev, Bruno Apitz and the rest, have always been able to recognize under the misery, alienation and degradation of the present such 'moments of synthesis', where we glimpse in the concrete, *existing* features of popular or proletarian life and struggle in the broadest, most all-sided sense the essential features, the 'first buds' of the future of free humanity. The greatness of a book like *The Young Guard* lies to no small degree in the way the author does not only show the kind of existence the young Soviet patriots are fighting *against* plus the fight at the highest most organized level, but, through revealing to us 'moments of synthesis' in the midst of the Fascist occupation, when the young people meet together, where the forces of oppression are for the moment pushed to the sidelines, when the lads and girls fleetingly live their own kind of lives on their own terms, we are made aware of the kind of life that they are fighting *for*. In this way their struggle at the highest level gains tremendously in pathos, in emotional content; their heroism at this level is seen as the logical conclusion of their all-sided humanity.

Marx was able to recognize, in the life and activity of the proletariat, even in the Chartist period, the first buds of the future of humanity:

When communist *workmen* associate with one another, theory, propaganda, etc. is their first end. But at the same time, as a result of this association, they acquire a new need – the need for society – and what appears as a means becomes an end. You can observe this practical process in its most splendid results whenever you see French socialist workers together. Such things as smoking, drinking, eating, etc. are no longer means of contact or means that bring together. Company, association and conversation ... are enough for them; the brotherhood of man is no mere phrase with them, but a fact of life.[13]

As a result of their failure to grasp this forward-pointing beauty in its concrete, manifold, universal, everyday forms, the worker-heroes and the struggle itself, in these nineteenth-century novelists, tend to be flat, abstract, cut off from the real vitality of the workers and therefore lacking in sufficient emotional content.

It is a sign of immaturity of a working-class humanism in our sense in the Chartist era that they do not yet have a clear, continuous grasp of the class struggle as 'us' *versus* 'them', as Humanity *versus* Anti-Humanity. It was this immaturity which allowed Owenite utopian ideas of a higher humanity above the bounds of classes to hold their ground in the thinking of the workers for so long. The proletarian novel was not yet ready to do as the popular realist Dickens had done – to look degradation in the face and see Humanity there.[14] They still recognized, it would seem, certain points of 'general human' reference outside the bounds of the working class, a supra-class morality in relation to which the worker-writer felt obliged to *defend* the proletariat to some 'general human' public. Thus, much of Wheeler's time is taken up with a defence of the moral excellence of the workers against the slander of the propagandists of the ruling class. For this reason the element of self-criticism which these books certainly contain remains a *tactical* criticism of their methods and organization, not a deep-going self-criticism of the worker as a Man.

In his moral defence of the workers, therefore, Wheeler actually *suppresses* the problems of spiritual and mental degradation, which, although not the main part, is an important part of the truth about the masses under capitalism.

13. Karl Marx, *Economic and Philosophic Manuscripts*, pp. 124-5.
14. *Zeitschrift für Anglistik und Amerikanistik* (1961), No. 3, p. 244.

This assumption of a common bond of humanity, of oppressors and oppressed being equally crippled in their happiness by the cursed system, affected also the picture given of the ruling class and the general shape of the plot. Writing towards the end of his life Engels once said of the theory of the class struggle in his early *Condition of the Working Class*: 'Thus great stress is laid on the dictum that Communism is not a mere party doctrine of the working class, but a theory compassing the emancipation of society at large, including the capitalist class, from its present narrow conditions. This is true enough in the abstract, but absolutely useless, and sometimes worse, in practice.'[15] This reflected the weakness of the early proletariat as a whole in their grasp of the true nature of their class as Humanity with a capital 'H'. Whereas Tressell, with his view of the bosses as Anti-Humanity, 'didn't care a damn' whether the capitalists were happy or unhappy, but showed them primarily in their social-political and economic activity, the Chartist novelists tended, defensively, to concentrate on the moral-spiritual degradation of the bosses and their inability to find happiness in spite of their wealth. Thus we have again, as in the case of the workers, a one-sided, undynamic view of the ruling class, a view which could not really help the proletariat as it should to acquaint themselves with the really dangerous features of their enemy. We are even expected to feel a certain amount of pity for Walter North and Sir Jasper, miserable in the midst of their riches.

In the field of the plot this assumption of a common humanity, of a 'pan-human' morality and emotions leads naturally to the type of plot which involves members of the two enemy classes in *personal* relationships. In Wheeler's *Sunshine and Shadows* Arthur Morton, the worker, and Walter North, the future capitalist, start off as school friends where the qualities of the one are shown as complementing the opposite qualities of the other. This kind of thing, which puts the members of the two classes in a *personal* relationship untypical of the *cash-nexus* relationship of reality, is Wheeler's way of saying that, where the narrowing and twisting pressures of capitalism are absent (here in the school), the differing human qualities which (according to

15. *Marx and Engels on Britain* (Moscow, 1953), p. 22.

Wheeler) are possessed by the middle class ('worldly influence', 'business habits') and by the workers ('strong sense', 'sturdy independence' and 'generous enthusiasm') come together to form a unity of complementary opposites, which guarantees real freedom to both sides. Later, when the former friends take their places in the 'wide world', as exploiter and exploited, this non-antagonistic contradiction turns into an antagonistic one and the happiness of both is ultimately ruined.

The almost universal appearance of the, in reality, highly untypical 'love-triangle' involving a worker, a man from the ruling class and a woman (from either class) in our pre-Tressell proletarian novel is also, I propose, conditioned by this defensive, moral approach. In the present case there is the Arthur–Julia–Sir Jasper theme plus the 'complication' of Walter's behaviour to his sister. By this means the actions and motives of the three principal characters are measured and contrasted against the same woman-yardstick. Up to Tressell, where, for the first time, man's relationship to his labour comes into its own as (alongside the love-relationship) the chief expression of the level of his human qualities, the English working-class novel (like the bourgeois novel) relied almost entirely on the love-relationship to epitomize the human quality of their heroes. Thus the highly developed humanity of Arthur Morton is epitomized in his pure and poetic love for Julia. This is contrasted to the behaviour towards her of her brother and husband; the first uses her as a mere pawn to further his selfish ambitions, the second to satisfy his lust and pride. She is the common measuring rod against which the morality of the ruling class and the working class are compared and contrasted.

How is this lack of a real aesthetic content, this lack of the inexhaustible curiosity about working men and women, which must be the basis of the true proletarian novel, this lack of a mature aesthetic subject–object relationship to be explained in the light of the actual state of development of the working class and society as a whole in the Chartist era?

Dona Torr defines the character of Chartism thus: 'The important thing ... is that Chartism coincided precisely with the point of transition between the pre-history and the history of the British working class.' [16] Morton and Tate have pointed out that huge sections of the Chartist army were composed of desperate hand-weavers: 'They reflected in a most striking way the fact that the British working class was still a new class, still in the process of formation *and still often hoping for a reversal of history by which the handworker could regain his lost prosperity.*' [17]

And indeed, this new proletariat, still in the process of formation, entered upon its career under conditions peculiarly inauspicious for the development of a proletarian humanism in our modified sense. The life of the masses in the first two thirds of the eighteenth century could hardly be called enviable, yet the proletariat of the early nineteenth century often looked back to it with a nostalgic longing. The industrial revolution and the social revolution which accompanied it replaced the old People with the Proletariat, washed away the old life with its established traditions and familiar land-marks.

Objectively the life of the masses in the thirties and forties of the nineteenth century was indeed more miserable than it had been before and, perhaps, has been since. There is no need here to go into the frightful conditions under which the new proletariat had to exist. They are well known. The 1840s were a period when young industrial capitalism really seemed to be staggering on its feet under the weight of its glaring contradictions. Thus the material misery, as such and alone, was not the only cause of the spiritual misery and confusion of the masses at that time. Their material misery seemed part of a whole world gone crazy, stood on its head. Their fate seemed to be in the grip of an *inhuman power over which men had lost control*. One must remember in this connection that the classical defensive and offensive organizations of the proletariat were, throughout the period, at best fleeting and immature. The Hammonds say: 'The men and women of Lancashire and Yorkshire felt of this new power that it was inhuman, that it disregarded all their instincts

16. Dona Torr, *Tom Mann and his Times* (Lawrence & Wishart, 1956), p. 146.
17. *The British Labour Movement*, p. 82. Italics mine – JM.

and sensibilities, that it brought into their lives an *inexorable force*, destroying and scattering their customs, their traditions, their freedom, their ties of family and home, their dignity and character as men and women.' [18]

In this crazy world everything was turned into its opposite. The more wealth the people produced (and there had never been so much material wealth in the country before), the poorer they themselves became, the harder and longer they worked the more surely they were doomed to be thrown onto the streets by the inexplicable economic crashes which burst in on capitalist and worker alike with a diabolical regularity. Last but not least the vaunted freedom of contract had turned into the most complete and inescapable slavery of modern times. The proletariat had been stripped of all property except their labour power, and even this was only in the most formal sense their own. No longer had they even the semblance of freedom in the labour-process itself. For the first time in modern society, alienation had encompassed the actual process of production, man's central human life-activity. Human industry, which Marx defines as 'the *open book of man's essential powers*',[19] was now a *shut* book to the producers themselves. Thus this great avenue for recognizing their human validity, for self-expression, and therefore for the old art, was closed to them and had become an endless torture. Alienation now seemed universal, the workers were only just beginning to develop their own organized revolutionary activity as a defence against it and counter to it. Thus they were not yet able to see their own peculiar type of human power and universality externalized, embodied in their great political-cultural achievements in union organization, etc. This was only to occur universally and dramatically in the age of imperialism.

While the people had not yet had enough time to develop a new type of understanding of their own nature and worth, the attitude of the ruling class to them served to underline the feeling that they were a helot population outside the bounds of the fully human community: 'For the first time there existed a vast

18. *The Town Labourer*, Vol. 1 (Guild Books, 1949), p. 48. Italics mine – J M.

19. Marx, *Economic and Philosophic Manuscripts*, p. 109.

proletariat, with no property but its labour, and therefore in the eyes of its rulers bound by no ties to the society in which it lived except by the ties that discipline could create.'[20]

This was epitomized in the new Poor Law, which summed up, in its ferocious denial of all social responsibility for the distressed, in its branding of the poor man as a criminal, the total repudiation by the ruling class of the People as Humanity.

As we have said, the proletariat was not yet really aware of its new type of revolutionary human validity. The science of historical materialism, which laid bare the necessary but passing nature of capitalist industrialism and the historical perspectives of the proletariat in which the right of the workers to the title of Humanity was proved beyond all gainsay, only appeared at the very end of the period. Thus they still tended to think of human validity in the traditional terms of property. As Engels remarks, these early workers had an 'inherent respect for the sacredness of property'.[21] In this way the fact that the bourgeosie locked them out from the 'human family' on this very basis certainly had a strong demoralizing effect. Thus the world as a whole, including the proletariat itself and all it stood for, was looked upon as an *alien, independent, threatening power*, something to be abolished lock, stock, and barrel.

For the Chartist workers with little understanding of the nature of capitalism and the essential nature of their own class, the whole of their world seemed to them one huge misunderstanding, a mistake of history, something totally 'against man'. Furthermore, it was so illogical that sooner or later the patent common-sense and humanity of the Charter must be recognized by all and the whole silly system swept away. It was only temporary, a passing nightmare of which the proletariat, in all its ramifications, was just one part among many and should, like the rest, disappear without trace. Thus, although, in Chartism, the pre-1850 proletariat had a working-class Idea to set against the bourgeois Idea, it was a partly utopian Idea which misunderstood and underestimated the present and future role of the working class in history. In their hypothetical revolutionary

20. *The Town Labourer*, p. 68.
21. Engels, *Condition of the Working Class*, p. 248.

solutions to the Great Mistake, their eyes were too often turned away from the proletariat as it actually was – the chief and central social 'manifestation of man's essential human qualities'.

Under these conditions of 'alienation from themselves' the curiosity about men and women, which Ralph Fox saw as the most important pre-supposition for the realistic novel, that complex, intimate, positive aesthetic subject–object relationship based on the recognition in the object of aspects of man's power and universality, could not yet mature. A fully-fledged proletarian-revolutionary novel was therefore a historical impossibility in the age of Chartism – and, indeed, remained so until the dawn of the twentieth century.

Letter to Minna Kautsky*

London, 26 November 1885

... I have now also read the *Old Ones and the New*, for which I sincerely thank you. The life of the salt-mine workers is described with as masterly a pen as were the portraits of the peasants in *Stefan*. The scenes depicting Vienna society are for the most part very beautiful. Vienna is indeed the only German city which has a society; Berlin can boast only of 'certain circles', and of uncertain ones, of which there are more. For this reason the only novel that will take root there is one whose hero is a man of letters, an official or an actor. Whether the plot in this part of your work does not develop too hastily in spots may be left to your better judgement. Many things that to our kind of people appear to be rushed may look quite natural in Vienna considering the city's peculiar international character and its intermixture with Southern and East-European elements. In both spheres the characters exhibit the sharp individualization so customary in your work. Each of them is a type but at the same time also a definite individual, a '*Dieser*', as old Hegel would express himself, and that is how it should be. And now, to be impartial, I have to find fault with something, which brings me to Arnold. He is really much too worthy a man and his being killed in a landslide can be reconciled with poetic justice only on some such assumption as that he was too good for this world. But it will never do for an author to put his own hero on too high a pedestal and this is the error which to some extent you seem to me to have fallen into here. In Elsa there is still a certain individualization, though verging on idealization, but in Arnold the personality merges still more in the principle.

* From Marx and Engels, *Selected Correspondence* (Moscow, n.d.).

The novel itself reveals the origins of this shortcoming. You obviously felt a desire to take a public stand in your book, to testify to your convictions before the entire world. This has now been done; that you are through with and need not repeat in this form. I am by no means opposed to tendentious poetry as such. Both Aeschylus, the father of tragedy, and Aristophanes, the father of comedy, were highly tendentious poets, Dante and Cervantes were so no less, and the best thing that can be said about Schiller's *Intrigue and Love* is that it represents the first German political problem drama. The modern Russians and Norwegians, who produce excellent novels, all write with a purpose. I think however that the solution of the problem must become manifest from the situation and the action themselves without being expressly pointed out and that the author is not obliged to serve the reader on a platter the future historical resolution of the social conflicts which he describes. To this must be added that under our conditions novels are mostly addressed to readers from bourgeois circles, i.e., circles which are not directly ours. Thus the socialist problem novel in my opinion fully carries out its mission if by a faithful portrayal of the real relations it dispels the dominant conventional illusions concerning these relations, shakes the optimism of the bourgeois world, and inevitably instils doubt as to the eternal validity of that which exists, without itself offering a direct solution of the problem involved, even without at times ostensibly taking sides. Here your exact knowledge and admirably fresh and lifelike presentation of both the Austrian country folks and Vienna 'society' are offered ample material, and in *Stefan* you have demonstrated that you are capable of treating your characters with the fine irony which attests to the author's dominion over the beings he has created...

Letter to Margaret Harkness*

London, beginning of April 1888

Dear Miss Harkness,

I thank you very much for sending me your *City Girl* through Messrs Vizetelly. I have read it with the greatest pleasure and avidity. It is indeed, as my friend Eichhoff your translator calls it, *ein kleines Kuntswerk*, to which he adds, what will be satisfactory to you, that consequently his translation must be all but literal, as any omission or attempted manipulation could only destroy part of the original's value.

What strikes me most in your tale besides its realistic truth is that it exhibits the courage of the true artist. Not only in the way you treat the Salvation Army, in the teeth of supercilious respectability, which respectability will perhaps learn from your tale, for the first time, *why* the Salvation Army has such a hold on the popular masses. But chiefly in the plain unvarnished manner in which you make the old, old story, the proletarian girl seduced by a middle-class man, the pivot of the whole book. Mediocrity would have felt bound to hide the, to it, commonplace character of the plot under heaps of artificial complications and adornments, and yet would not have got rid of the fate of being found out. You felt you could afford to tell an old story, because you could make it a new one by simply telling it truly.

Your Mr Arthur Grant is a masterpiece.

If I have anything to criticize, it would be that perhaps after all, the tale is not quite realistic enough. Realism, to my mind, implies, beside truth of detail, the truth in reproduction of typical characters under typical circumstances. Now your characters are typical enough, as far as they go; but the circumstances which

* From Marx and Engels, *Selected Correspondence* (Moscow, n.d.).

surround them and make them act are not perhaps equally so. In *City Girl* the working class figures as a passive mass, unable to help itself and not even showing [making] any attempt at striving to help itself. All attempts to drag it out of its torpid misery come from without, from above. Now if this was a correct description about 1800 or 1810, in the days of Saint-Simon and Robert Owen, it cannot appear so in 1887 to a man who for nearly fifty years has had the honour of sharing in most of the fights of the militant proletariat. The rebellious reaction of the working class against the oppressive medium which surrounds them, their attempts – convulsive, half-conscious or conscious – at recovering their status as human beings, belong to history and must therefore lay claim to a place in the domain of realism.

I am far from finding fault with your not having written a point-blank socialist novel, a '*Tendenzroman*', as we Germans call it, to glorify the social and political views of the authors. That is not at all what I mean. The more the opinions of the author remain hidden, the better for the work of art. The realism I allude to may crop out even in spite of the author's opinions. Let me refer to an example. Balzac, whom I consider a far greater master of realism than all the Zolas *passés, présents et à venir*, in *La Comédie humaine* gives us a most wonderfully realistic history of French 'Society', describing, chronicle-fashion, almost year by year from 1816 to 1848 the progressive inroads of the rising bourgeoisie upon the society of nobles, that reconstituted itself after 1815 and that set up again, as far as it could, the standard of *la vieille politesse française*. He describes how the last remnants of this, to him, model society gradually succumbed before the intrusion of the vulgar moneyed upstart, or were corrupted by him; how the *grande dame*, whose conjugal infidelities were but a mode of asserting herself in perfect accordance with the way she had been disposed of in marriage, gave way to the bourgeoise, who horned her husband for cash or cashmere; and around this central picture he groups a complete history of French Society from which, even in economic details (for instance the re-arrangement of real and personal property after the Revolution), I have learned more than from all the professed historians, economists and statisticians of the period together. Well, Balzac was politically a Legitimist; his great work is a constant elegy on the irretrievable decay of good society; his sympathies are all with the class doomed to extinction. But for all that his satire is never keener, his irony never bitterer, than when he sets in motion the very men and women with whom he sympathizes most deeply – the nobles. And the only men of whom he always speaks with undisguised admiration, are his bitterest political antagonists, the republican heroes of the Cloître Saint Merry,[1] the men who at that time (1830–36) were indeed the representatives of the popular masses. That Balzac thus was compelled to go against his own class sympathies and political prejudices, that he *saw* the necessity of the downfall of his favourite nobles, and described them as people deserving no better fate; and that he *saw* the real men of the future where, for the time being, they alone were to be found – that I consider one of the greatest triumphs of Realism, and one of the grandest features in old Balzac.

I must own, in your defence, that nowhere in the civilized world are the working people less actively resistant, more passively submitting to fate, more *hébétés* than in the East End of London. And how do I know whether you have not had very good reasons for contenting yourself, for once, with a picture of the passive side of working-class life, reserving the active side for another work? ...

1. Refers to the uprising of the left wing of the republican party, the Society of the Rights of Man and the Citizen, which took place in Paris on 5 and 6 June 1832.

On 'Art for Art's Sake'*

The belief in art for art's sake arises wherever the artist is out of harmony with his social environment.

It might be said, of course, that the example of Pushkin is not sufficient to justify such a conclusion. I will not controvert or gainsay this. I will give other examples, this time borrowed from the history of French literature, that is, the literature of a country whose intellectual trends – at least down to the middle of the last century – met with the broadest sympathy throughout the European continent.

Pushkin's contemporaries, the French romanticists, were also, with few exceptions, ardent believers in art for art's sake. Perhaps the most consistent of them, Theophile Gautier, abused the defenders of the utilitarian view of art in the following terms :

'No, you fools, no, you goitrous cretins, a book cannot be turned into gelatine soup, nor a novel into a pair of seamless boots ... By the intestines of all the Popes, future, past and present : No, and a thousand times no ! ... I am one of those who consider the superfluous essential; my love of things and people is in inverse proportion to the services they may render.'[1]

In a biographical note on Baudelaire, this same Gautier highly praised the author of the *Fleurs du mal* for having upheld 'the absolute autonomy of art and for not admitting that poetry had any aim but itself, or any mission but to excite in the soul of the reader the sensation of beauty, in the absolute sense of the term' (*'l'autonomie absolue de l'art et qu'il n'admettait pas que la poésie eût d'autre but qu'elle même et d'autre mission à remplir que d'exciter dans l'âme du lecteur la sensation du beau; dans le sens absolue du terme'*).

* From *Unaddressed Letters and Art and Social Life* (Moscow, 1957).
1. Preface to *Mlle de Maupin* (1835).

How little the 'idea of beauty' could associate in Gautier's mind with social and political ideas may be seen from the following statement of his:

'I would very gladly [*très joyeusement*] renounce my rights as a Frenchman and citizen for the sake of seeing a genuine Raphael or a beautiful woman in the nude.'

That, surely, is the limit. Yet all the Parnassians (*les parnassiens*) would probably have agreed with Gautier, though some of them may have had certain reservations concerning the too paradoxical form in which he, especially in his youth, expressed the demand for the 'absolute autonomy of art'.

What was the reason for this attitude of mind of the French romanticists and Parnassians? Were they also out of harmony with their social environment?

In an article Theophile Gautier wrote in 1857 on the revival by the Théâtre Français of Alfred de Vigny's play *Chatterton*, he recalled its first performance on 12 February 1835. This is what he said:

'The parterre before which Chatterton declaimed was filled with pallid, long-haired youths, who firmly believed that there was no dignified occupation save writing poems or painting pictures ... and who looked on the "*bourgeois*" with a contempt hardly equalled by that which the fuchses of Heidelberg and Jena entertain for the philistine.'[2]

Who were these contemptible 'bourgeois'?

'They included', Gautier says, 'nearly everybody – bankers, brokers, lawyers, merchants, shopkeepers, etc. – in a word, everyone who did not belong to the mystical *cénacle* [that is, the romanticist circle – G P] and who earned their living by prosaic occupations.'[3]

And here is further evidence. In a comment to one of his *Odes funambulesques*, Theodore de Banville admits that he too had been afflicted with this hatred of the 'bourgeois'. And he too explains who was meant by the term. 'In the language of the romanticists, the word "bourgeois" meant a man whose only god was the five-franc piece, who had no ideal but saving his own

2. *Histoire du romantisme* (Paris, 1895), pp. 153-4.
3. ibid., p. 154.

skin, and who, in poetry, loved sentimental romance, and in the plastic arts, lithography.'[4]

Recalling this, de Banville begs his reader not to be surprised that his *Odes funambulesques* – which, mark, appeared towards the very end of the romantic period – treated people as unmitigated scoundrels only because they led a bourgeois mode of life and did not worship romantic geniuses.

These illustrations are fairly convincing evidence that the romanticists really were out of harmony with their bourgeois social environment. True, there was nothing dangerous in this to the bourgeois social relationships. The romanticist circles consisted of young bourgeois who had no objection to these relationships, but were revolted by the sordidness, the tedium and the vulgarity of bourgeois existence. The new art with which they were so strongly infatuated was for them a refuge from this sordidness, tedium and vulgarity. In the latter years of the Restoration and in the first half of the reign of Louis Philippe, that is, in the best period of romanticism, it was the more difficult for the French youth to accustom themselves to the sordid, prosaic and tedious life of bourgeoisdom, as not long before that France had been living through the terrible storms of the Great Revolution and the Napoleonic era, which had deeply stirred all human passions.[5] When the bourgeoisie assumed the predominant position in society, and when its life was no longer warmed by the fire of the struggle for liberty, nothing was left for the new art but *to idealize negation of the bourgeois mode of life*. Romantic art was indeed such an idealization. The romanticists strove to express their negation of bourgeois 'moderation and conformity' not only in their artistic work, but even in their own external appearance. We have already heard from Gautier that

4. *Les Odes funambulesques* (Paris, 1858), pp. 294–5.
5. Alfred de Musset describes this disharmony in the following words: 'Two camps, as it were, formed: on one side, exalted and suffering minds, expansive souls who yearn for the infinite, bowed their heads and wept, wrapped themselves in morbid dreams, and one saw nothing but frail reeds in an ocean of bitterness. On the other, men of the flesh remained erect, inflexible, giving themselves over to positive pleasures and knowing no care but the counting of their money. Nothing but sobs and bursts of laughter – the former coming from their soul, the latter from the body.' (*La Confession d'un enfant du siècle* [Paris, 1836], p. 10.)

the young men who filled the parterre at the first performance of *Chatterton* wore long hair. Who has not heard of Gautier's own red waistcoat, which made 'decent people' shiver with horror? For the young romanticists, fantastic costume, like long hair, was a means of drawing a line between themselves and the detested bourgeois. The pale face was a similar means: it was, so to speak, a protest against bourgeois satiety.

Gautier says: 'In those days it was the prevailing fashion in the romantic school to have as pallid a complexion as possible, even greenish, almost cadaverous. This lent a man a fateful, Byronic appearance, testified that he was devoured by passion and remorse. It made him look interesting in the eyes of women.'[6] Gautier also tells us that the romanticists found it hard to forgive Victor Hugo his respectable appearance, and in private conversation often deplored this weakness of the great poet, 'which made him kin with mankind, and even with the bourgeoisie'.[7] It should be observed, in general, that the effort to assume a definite outward appearance always reflects the social relationships of the given period. An interesting sociological inquiry could be written on this theme.

This being the attitude of the young romanticists to the bourgeoisie, it was only natural that they were revolted by the idea of 'useful art'. In their eyes, to make art useful was tantamount to making it serve the bourgeoisie whom they despised so profoundly. This explains Gautier's vehement sallies against the preachers of useful art, which I have just cited, whom he calls 'fools, goitrous cretins' and so on. It also explains the paradox that in his eyes the value of persons and things is in inverse proportion to the service they render. Essentially, all these sallies and paradoxes are a complete counterpart of Pushkin's:

> Begone, ye pharisees! What cares
> The peaceful poet for your fate?

The Parnassians and the early French realists (the Goncourts, Flaubert, etc.) likewise entertained an infinite contempt for the bourgeois society around them. They, too, were untiring in their abuse of the detested 'bourgeois'. If they printed their writings,

6. *Histoire du romantisme*, p. 31.
7. ibid., p. 32.

it was not, they averred, for the benefit of the general reading public, but for a chosen few, '*pour des amis inconnus*' ('for unknown friends'), as Flaubert puts it in one of his letters. They maintained that only a writer who was devoid of serious talent could find favour with a wide circle of readers. Leconte de Lisle held that the popularity of a writer was proof of his intellectual inferiority (*signe d'infériorité intellectuelle*). It need scarcely be added that the Parnassians, like the romanticists, were staunch believers in the theory of art for art's sake.

Many similar examples might be given. But it is quite unnecessary. It is already sufficiently clear that the belief in art for art's sake arises wherever they are out of harmony with the society around them. But it would not be amiss to define this disharmony more precisely.

At the close of the eighteenth century, in the period immediately preceding the Great Revolution, the progressive artists of France were likewise out of harmony with the prevailing 'society' of the time. David and his friends were foes of the 'old order'. And this disharmony was of course hopeless, because reconciliation between them and the old order was quite impossible. More, the disharmony between David and his friends and the old order was incomparably deeper than the disharmony between the romanticists and bourgeois society: whereas David and his friends desired the abolition of the old order, Theophile Gautier and his colleagues, as I have repeatedly said, had no objection to the bourgeois social relationships; all they wanted was that the bourgeois system should cease producing vulgar bourgeois habits.[8]

8. Theodore de Banville says explicitly that the romanticists' attacks on the 'bourgeois' were not directed against the bourgeoisie as a social class (*Les Odes funambulesques*, p. 294). This *conservative* revolt of the romanticists against the 'bourgeois', but not against the foundations of the bourgeois system, has been understood by some of our present-day Russian theoreticians (Mr Ivanov-Razumnik, for instance) as a struggle against bourgeoisdom which was far superior in scope to the social and political struggle of the proletariat against the bourgeoisie. I leave it to the reader to judge the profundity of this conception. In reality, it points to the regrettable fact that people who undertake to expound the history of Russian social thought do not always go to the trouble of acquainting themselves preliminarily with the history of thought in Western Europe.

But in revolting against the old order, David and his friends were well aware that behind them marched the serried columns of the third estate, which was soon, in the well-known words of Abbé Sieyès, to become everything. With them, consequently, the feeling of disharmony with the *prevailing order* was supplemented by a feeling of sympathy with the *new society* which had matured within the womb of the old and was preparing to replace it. But with the romanticists and the Parnassians we find nothing of the kind: they neither expected nor desired a change in the social system of the France of their time. That is why their disharmony with the society around them was quite hopeless.[9] Nor did our Pushkin expect any change in the Russia of his time. And in the period of Nicholas, moreover, it is probable that he no longer wished for any change. *That is why* his view of social life was similarly tinged with pessimism.

Now, I think, I can amplify my former conclusion and say:

The belief in art for art's sake arises when artists and people keenly interested in art are hopelessly out of harmony with their social environment.

But this is not the whole matter. The example of our 'men of the sixties', who firmly believed in the early triumph of reason, and that of David and his friends, who held this belief no less firmly, show that *the so-called utilitarian view of art, that is, the tendency to impart to its productions the significance of judgements on the phenomena of life, and the joyful eagerness, which always accompanies it, to take part in social strife, arises and spreads wherever there is mutual sympathy between a considerable section of society and people who have a more or less active interest in creative art.*

How far this is true, is definitely shown by the following fact.

When the refreshing storm of the February Revolution of 1848 broke, many of the French artists who had believed in the theory of art for art's sake emphatically rejected it. Even Baude-

9. The attitude of mind of the German romanticists was marked by an equally hopeless disharmony with their social environment, as is excellently shown by Brandes in his *Die romantische Schule in Deutschland*, which is the second volume of his work, *Die Hauptströmungen der Litteratur des 19-ten Jahrhunderts*.

laire, who was subsequently cited by Gautier as the model example of an artist who believed inflexibly that art must be absolutely autonomous, began at once to put out a revolutionary journal, *Le Salut public*. True, its publication was soon discontinued, but as late as 1852 Baudelaire, in his foreword to Pierre Dupont's *Chansons*, called the theory of art for art's sake infantile (*puérile*), and declared that art must have a social purpose. Only the triumph of the counter-revolution induced Baudelaire and artists of a similar trend of mind to revert to the 'infantile' theory of art for art's sake. One of the future luminaries of 'Parnassus', Leconte de Lisle, brought out the psychological significance of this reversion very distinctly in the preface to his *Poèmes antiques*, the first edition of which appeared in 1852. He said that poetry would no longer stimulate heroic actions or inculcate social virtues, because now, as in all periods of literary decadence, its sacred language could express only petty personal emotions (*mesquines impressions personnelles*) and was no longer capable of instructing (*n'est plus apte à enseigner l'homme*).[10] Addressing the poets, Leconte de Lisle said that the human race, whose teachers they had once been, had now outgrown them.[11] Now, in the words of the future Parnassian, the task of poetry was 'to give an ideal life' to those who had no 'real life' (*donner la vie idéale à celui qui n'a pas la vie réelle*).[12] These profound words disclose the whole psychological secret of the belief in art for art's sake. We shall have many an occasion to revert to Leconte de Lisle's preface from which I have just quoted.

To conclude with this side of the question, I would say, in addition, that political authority always prefers the utilitarian view of art, to the extent, of course, that it pays any attention to art at all. And this is understandable : it is to its interest to harness all ideologies to the service of the cause which it serves itself. And since political authority, although sometimes revolutionary, is most often conservative and even reactionary, it will be seen that it would be wrong to think that the utilitarian view of art is shared principally by revolutionaries, or by people of

10. *Poèmes antiques* (Paris, 1852), vii.
11. ibid., ix.   12. ibid., xi.

advanced mind generally. The history of Russian literature shows very clearly that it has not been shunned even by our 'protectors'. Here are some examples. The first three parts of V. T. Narezhny's novel, *A Russian Gil Blas, or the Adventures of Count Gavril Simonovich Chistyakov*, were published in 1814. The book was at once banned at the instance of the Minister of Public Education, Count Razumovsky, who took the occasion to express the following opinion on the relation of literature to life:

'All too often authors of novels, although apparently campaigning against vice, paint it in such colours or describe it in such detail as to lure young people into vices which it would have been better not to mention at all. Whatever the literary merit of a novel may be, its publication can be sanctioned only when it has a truly moral purpose.'

As we see, Razumovsky believed that art cannot be an aim in itself.

Art was regarded in exactly the same way by those servitors of Nicholas I who, by virtue of their official position, were obliged to have some opinion on the subject. You will remember that Benkendorf tried to direct Pushkin into the path of virtue. Nor was Ostrovsky denied the solicitous attention of authority. When, in March 1850, his comedy, *Our Own Folks – We'll Settle It Among Ourselves*, was published and certain enlightened lovers of literature – and trade – conceived the fear that it might offend the merchant class, the then Minister of Public Education (Count Shirinsky-Shikhmatov) ordered the guardian of the Moscow Educational Area to invite the young dramatist to come and see him, and

make him understand that the noble and useful purpose of talent consists not only in the lively depiction of ludicrous or evil manners, but in justly condemning them; not only in caricature, but in inculcating lofty moral sentiments; consequently, in offsetting vice with virtue, the ridiculous and criminal with thoughts and actions that elevate the soul; lastly, in strengthening the faith, which is so important to social and private life, that evil deeds meet with fitting retribution already *here on earth*.

Tsar Nicholas himself looked upon art chiefly from the

'moral' standpoint. As we know, he shared Benkendorf's opinion that it would be a good thing to tame Pushkin. He said of Ostrovsky's play, *Don't Get Into Another's Sleigh*, written at the time when Ostrovsky had fallen under the influence of the Slavophiles and was fond of saying at convivial banquets that, with the help of some of his friends, he would 'undo all the work' of Peter – of this play, which in a certain sense was distinctly didactic, Nicholas I said with praise : *'Ce n'est pas une pièce, c'est une leçon.'* Not to multiply examples, I shall confine myself to the following two facts. When N. Polevoi's *Moskovsky Telegraf* printed an unfavourable review of Kukolnik's 'patriotic' play, *The Hand of the All-Highest Saved Our Fatherland*, the journal became anathema in the eyes of Nicholas's ministers and was banned. But when Polevoi himself wrote patriotic plays – *Grandad of the Russian Navy* and *Igolkin the Merchant* – the Tsar, Polevoi's brother relates, was delighted with his dramatic talent. 'The author is unusually gifted,' he said. 'He should write, write and write. Yes, write (he smiled), not publish magazines.'[13]

And don't think the Russian rulers were an exception in this respect. No, so typical an exponent of absolutism as Louis XIV of France was no less firmly convinced that art could not be an aim in itself, but must be an instrument of moral education. And all the literature and all the art of the celebrated era of Louis XIV was permeated through and through with this conviction. Napoleon I would similarly have looked upon the theory of art for art's sake as a pernicious invention of loathsome 'ideologists'. He, too, wanted literature and art to serve moral purposes. And in this he largely succeeded, as witnessed for example by the fact that most of the pictures in the periodical exhibitions (*Salons*) of the time were devoted to the warlike feats of the Consulate and the Empire. His little nephew, Napoleon III, followed in his footsteps, though with far less success. He, too, tried to make art and literature serve what he called morality. In November 1852, Professor Laprade of Lyons scathingly ridiculed this Bonapartist penchant for didactic art in a satire called *Les Muses d'État*. He predicted that the time would soon come when the

13. *Memoirs of Xenofont Polevoi* (St Petersburg, 1888), p. 445.

'state muses' would place human reason under military discipline; then order would reign and not a single writer would dare to express the slightest dissatisfaction.

> *Il faut être content, s'il pleut, s'il fait soleil,*
> *S'il fait chaud, s'il fait froid: 'Ayez le teint vermeil.*
> *Je déteste les gens maigres, à face pâle;*
> *Celui qui ne rit pas mérite qu'on l'empale.' etc.*[14]

I shall remark in passing that for this witty satire Laprade was deprived of his professional post. The government of Napoleon III could not tolerate jibes at the 'state muses'.

14. One must be content in sunshine and rain, in heat or cold: 'Be of ruddy countenance; I detest lean and pallid men. He who does not laugh deserves to be impaled.'

Tolstoy and the Development of Realism *

The evolution of bourgeois society after 1848 destroyed the subjective conditions which made a great realism possible. If we
regard the problem of this decline from the subjective viewpoint
of the writer, we see in the first place that in this period the
writers of Europe were increasingly turning into mere spectators
and observers of the social process, in contrast to the old realists
who had themselves experienced this process and participated in
it. Their conclusions were the results of their own life-struggle
and constituted only one part of the resources they had at their
disposal in depicting reality.

The question whether the writer must experience or need
merely observe what he describes is by no means an isolated
question limited to the sphere of art – it embraces the writer's
entire relationship to social reality. The old writers were partici-
pants in the social struggle and their activities as writers were
either part of this struggle or a reflection, an ideological and
literary solution, of the great problems of the time. In reading
the biographies of the great realists of old, from Swift and Defoe
to Goethe, Balzac and Stendhal, we see that none of them were
writers throughout their life and writers only, and their multiple
and combative ties with society are richly reflected in their
works.

But this mode of life was not a consequence of their personal
preferences. Zola was by instinct certainly a more active and
combative type than Goethe. But it is the social surroundings
which determine the degree to which intricate and combative
relationship can arise between the writer and society, such as
those which resulted in a life so rich in experience as that of
Goethe. It depends on whether the society in which the writer

* From *Studies in European Realism* (1950).

lives contains historically significant social and ideological trends to which the writer can dedicate himself with all the fervour of his personality.

On capitalist society reaching its apologetic stage, such possibilities grew increasingly rare for the great bourgeois writers. Of course there were plenty of writers who experienced the evolution of the bourgeoisie in the period following upon 1848 with a complete engagement of their personality. But what was this evolution like and what literary results could a dedication to it bring a writer? Gustav Freytag and Georges Ohnet experienced the development of the German and French petty bourgeoisie respectively and owe their ephemeral popularity to the 'warmth' of their experience. But they depicted a debased, narrow, trivial life full of concealments and hypocrisy, and they did so by correspondingly narrow, trivial, untruthful means. Only in very few cases did an experience related to reactionary tendencies result in literarily valuable (even though historically insignificant) products, as for instance the experience of the problems of British imperialism in the works of Rudyard Kipling.

The really honest and gifted bourgeois writers who lived and wrote in the period following upon the upheavals of 1848 naturally could not experience and share the development of their class with the same true devotion and intensity of feeling as their predecessors. They were far more likely to repudiate with hatred and loathing the way of life now thrust on the world by that development. And because in the society of their time they found nothing they could support wholeheartedly (for the proletarian class struggle and its implications were beyond their understanding) they remained mere spectators of the social process, until the new humanist movement which began at the end of the nineteenth century, and to which the best of the now living writers belonged, posed the problem of a new democracy and thereby put the whole matter in a different light; but there is no room here to deal with this.

The change in the writer's position in relation to reality led to the putting forward of various theories, such as Flaubert's theory of impartiality (*impassibilité*) and the pseudo-scientific theory of Zola and his school. But much more important than the theories are the realities on which they are based. If the writer merely occupies an observation post in relation to reality, that means that he regards bourgeois society critically, ironically, and often turns away from it in hatred and disgust.

The new type of realist turns into a specialist of literary expression, a virtuoso, an 'armchair scientist' who makes a 'speciality' of describing the social life of the present.

This alienation has for its inevitable consequence that the writer disposes of a much narrower and more restricted life-material than the old school of realism. If the new realist wants to describe some phenomenon of life, he has to go out of his way specially to observe it. It is clear that he will first take into account the superficial traits which meet the eye. And if the writer is really gifted and original, he will seek for originality in the observation of detail and will attempt to carry the literary expression of such originally observed detail to ever higher levels.

Flaubert advised the young Maupassant, who was his personal disciple, that he should observe a tree until he discovered the traits which distinguished it from all other trees and then seek for the words which would adequately express this unique quality of that particular tree.

Both master and disciple often achieved this aim with great artistry. But the task itself was a narrowing of the purpose of art itself, and a blind alley so far as realism was concerned. For – to consider only this particular example – the task set by Flaubert isolated the tree from nature as a whole and from its relationship with man. One may thus discover in what the unique character of the tree consists, but this uniqueness amounts to nothing more than the originality of a still-life.

But when Tolstoy in *War and Peace* describes the leafless gnarled oak which the despondent Andrey Bolkonski contemplates and which later, on his return from the Rostovs, he at first cannot find at all and afterwards discovers transformed and covered with fresh leaves, then, although Tolstoy has given the tree no 'originality' in the Flaubert–Maupassant still-life sense, he has thrown light in a flash and with great poetic vigour on a very intricate psychological process.

We cannot give here a detailed theory and critique of the

realist literary development in Europe after 1848 and must confine ourselves to merely touching in principle on its basic features. We then see that the social evolution which forced the most sincere, upright and gifted bourgeois writers into the position of observers, at the same time inevitably drove them to fill the place of the missing essentials with literary substitutes.

Flaubert recognized this new position of the realist writer very early and with tragic clarity. In 1850 he wrote to Bouilhet, a friend of his youth:

'We have a many-voiced orchestra, a rich palette, varied sources of power. As for tricks and devices, we have more of those than ever. But we lack inner life, the soul of things, the idea of the writer's subject.'

This bitter confession should not be regarded as the expression of a mood, of a transient fit of despair. Flaubert saw only too clearly the true position of the new realism.

Let us consider so important a modern novel as Maupassant's *Une Vie*, which Tolstoy regarded as one of the best works, not only of Maupassant, but of newer literature as a whole. In this book Maupassant took his subject from the past. The novel begins in the time of the restoration of the Bourbons and ends shortly before the revolution of 1848. Thus it depicts mainly the same period of which Balzac was the great historian. But – to point out only one important feature – the reader, although the scene of the novel is set among the nobility, is never made aware of the fact that the July revolution has come and gone and that the position of the nobility in French society is totally different at the end of the novel from what it was at the beginning.

Let no one say that what Maupassant *wanted* to depict was, after all, not this change but the disappointment of his heroine in her marriage and in the child born of it. But the fact that Maupassant posed the problem in this way shows that he considered love, marriage and mother-love separately from the historical and social foundations on which alone they could be realistically depicted. He isolated the psychological problems from the social problems. For Maupassant society was no longer a complex of vital and contradictory relationships between human beings, but only a lifeless setting.

The social being of the nobility, which in Balzac's works is a great, varied process rich in tragedies and comedies, is narrowed to a 'still-life' in Maupassant. He describes the castles, parks, furniture, etc., of the aristocracy with the most consummate skill, but all this has no real, live connection with his subject proper. And this subject proper, too, is relatively meagre, shallow and unilinear.

If then we wish to summarize the principle negative traits of western European realism after 1848 we come to the following conclusions:

First, that the real, dramatic and epic movement of social happening disappears and isolated characters of purely private interest, characters sketched in with only a few lines, stand still, surrounded by a dead scenery described with admirable skill.

Secondly, the real relationships of human beings to each other, the social motives which, unknown even to themselves, govern their actions, thoughts and emotions, grow increasingly shallow; and the author either stresses this shallowness of life with angry or sentimental irony, or else substitutes dead, rigid, lyrically inflated symbols for the missing human and social relationships.

Thirdly (and in close connection with the points already mentioned): details meticulously observed and depicted with consummate skill are substituted for the portrayal of the essential features of social reality and the description of the changes effected in the human personalities by social influences.

This transformation of the writer from a champion of social progress and a participant in the social life of his time into a mere spectator and observer was of course the result of a long development. The connection between the last great realists of the nineteenth century and the social life of their time was already paradoxical and full of contradictions. We need only think of Balzac and Stendhal and compare them with the English and French realists of the preceding century in order to see how contradictory the former's experience of the social life of their time necessarily was. Their relation to society was not only critical – we find a critical attitude in the older realists as well, although their connection with the bourgeois class was far less problematic – but profoundly pessimistic and replete with hatred and loathing.

Sometimes only very loose threads, very transparent illusions, very fragile Utopias connect these writers with the bourgeois class of their day. With advancing age Balzac's foreboding of the collapse of both aristocratic and bourgeois culture throws an ever darker shadow on his outlook. But for all that Balzac and Stendhal still gave an extensive and profoundly conceived picture of the bourgeois society of their time, and the reason for this is that they both had a deep and extensive experience of every important problem and stage in the development of bourgeois society between the first revolution and 1848.

In Tolstoy this relationship is even more paradoxical and contradictory. His development shows a growing aversion from the Russian ruling classes, an increasing loathing and hatred of all oppressors and exploiters of the Russian people. At the end of his life he sees them as a mere gang of scoundrels and parasites. Thus, at the terminal point of his career, Tolstoy comes very close to the western realities of the second half of the nineteenth century.

How is it then that in spite of this Tolstoy the writer never turned into a Flaubert or a Maupassant? Or, if we want to extend the question to the earlier stage of Tolstoy's development, to the time when he still believed or wished to believe that the conflict between landowner and peasant could be solved by patriarchal methods: how is it that not even in this earlier Tolstoy is there any trace of the provincialism so evident in the later realists, even the most gifted ones? How is this to be explained, since Tolstoy understood the socialist movement of the working classes as little or even less than most of his western contemporaries?

It is on this point that Lenin's admirable analysis provides a key to the understanding of Tolstoy.[1]

The vulgar sociologists compiled statistics of the characters depicted by Tolstoy and on the basis of these figures they proclaimed that Tolstoy had depicted mainly the life of the Russian landowner. Such an analysis can at best facilitate the understanding of quite uninspired naturalists, who, when they depict

1. See Text 16 below.

something, describe only what lies immediately in front of them, without any relation to the sum of social reality. When great realists depict social evolution and the great social problems, they never do so in so simple and immediate a fashion.

In the works of a great realist everything is linked up with everything else. Each phenomenon shows the polyphony of many components, the intertwinement of the individual and social, of the physical and the psychical, of private interest and public affairs. And because the polyphony of their composition goes beyond immediacy, their *dramatis personae* are too numerous to find room on the playbill.

The great realists always regard society from the viewpoint of a living and moving centre and this centre is present, visibly or invisibly, in every phenomenon. An instance is Balzac. Balzac shows how capital, which he – correctly at that time – saw incarnated in financial capital, takes over power in France. From Gobseck to Nucingen, Balzac creates a long procession of the immediate representatives of this demoniacal force. But does this exhaust the power of financial capital in Balzac's world? Does Gobseck cease to rule when he leaves the stage? No, Balzac's world is permanently saturated with Gobseck and his like. Whether the immediate theme is love or marriage, friendship or politics, passion or self-sacrifice, Gobseck is ever present as an invisible protagonist and his invisible presence visibly colours every movement, every action of all Balzac's characters.

Tolstoy is the poet of the peasant revolt that lasted from 1861 to 1905. In his life-work the exploited peasant is this visible-invisible ever-present protagonist. Let us look at the description of Prince Nekhlyudov's regimental life in *Resurrection*, one of Tolstoy's late works :

He had nothing else to do than to don a beautifully pressed and brushed uniform, which not he but others had made and brushed, put on a helmet and gird on weapons which were also made, cleaned and put into his hands by others, to mount a fine charger which had again been bred, trained and groomed by others, and ride to a parade or an inspection . . .

Such descriptions, which we find in great numbers in Tolstoy's

288

writings, of course also contain many details. But these details are not meant to throw light on the specific qualities of the objects described but to stress the social implications which determine the use of such objects. And the social implications point to exploitation, the exploitation of the peasants by the landowners.

But in Tolstoy's life-work the exploited peasant is visibly or invisibly present not only in every greater or lesser phenomenon of life – he is never absent from the consciousness of the characters themselves. Whatever their occupation, every implication of this occupation and everything human beings think of it hinges consciously or unconsciously on problems which are more or less immediately linked with this central problem.

It is true that Tolstoy's characters and Tolstoy himself raise these issues on an almost purely individual ethical basis: how can life be arranged in a way that men should not ruin themselves morally by exploiting the labour of others? In his own life and out of the mouth of many of his characters, Tolstoy has given plenty of incorrect and reactionary answers to this question.

But what is important in Tolstoy is the putting of the question and not the answer given to it. Chekhov said quite rightly, in connection with Tolstoy, that putting a question correctly is one thing and finding the answer to it something quite different; the artist absolutely needs to do only the first. Of course the term 'putting the question correctly' should not be taken too literally in the case of Tolstoy. What is important are not the muddled and romantic ideas put forward by, say, the hero of one of his early novels; what is essential are not his fantastic and Utopian plans for the salvation of the world, or at least not only these are important and essential. They are organically linked with the reaction of the peasants to these plans of salvation, their hostile distrust, their instinctive fear that the squire's new plan cannot possibly be anything but some new way of cheating them and the better it sounds the more cunning the deception must be – only in connection with these things can we speak, with Chekhov, of Tolstoy's 'correct putting of the question'.

Tolstoy's correct putting of the question consists among other things in this: no one before him ever depicted the 'two nations' as vividly and palpably as he. There is a paradoxical greatness in the fact that while his conscious striving was constantly directed towards the moral and religious overcoming of this rigid division of society into two hostile camps, in his literary production the reality which he depicted with relentless fidelity constantly exposed the impracticability of this the author's favourite dream. Tolstoy's development followed very tortuous paths; he lost many illusions and found new ones. But whatever Tolstoy wrote, as the truly great poet that he is, he always depicted the inexorable division between the 'two nations' in Russia, the peasants and the landowners.

In the works of his youth, for instance in *The Cossacks*, this implacability manifested itself in as yet idyllic, elegiac form. In *Resurrection* Maslova gives this answer to Nekhlyudov's words of remorse: 'So you want to save your soul through me, eh? In this world you used me for your pleasure and now you want to use me in the other world to save your soul!'

In the course of the years Tolstoy changed all his internal and external means of expression, he made use of and discarded all sorts of philosophies, but the portrayal of the 'two nations' remained the backbone of his life-work from start to finish.

Only if we have discovered this central problem in Tolstoy's art does the contrast in presentation between Tolstoy and the contemporary western realists become evident, in spite of the common affinity of subject. Like all honest and gifted writers of the period, Tolstoy grew more and more estranged from the ruling class and found their life to an increasing degree sinful, meaningless, empty and inhuman.

But the writers of the capitalist west, if they took this attitude towards the ruling class and took it seriously, were forced into the position of isolated observers, with all the artistic drawbacks attendant on such a position – for only an earnest understanding of the struggle of the working classes for their freedom could have shown them the way out of this isolation. Tolstoy, the Russian, lived in a country in which the bourgeois revolution was still the order of the day and in depicting the revolt of the peasants against their exploitation by both landowners and apitalists, in depicting the 'two nations' of the Russian scene ⟨h⟩e could become the last great bourgeois realist of the age.

*

The true artistic totality of a literary work depends on the completeness of the picture it presents of the essential social factors that determine the world depicted. Hence it can be based only on the author's own intensive experience of the social process. Only such experience can uncover the essential social factors and make the artistic presentation centre round them freely and naturally. The hallmark of the great realist masterpiece is precisely that its intensive totality of *essential* social factors does not require, does not even tolerate, a meticulously accurate or pedantically encyclopedic inclusion of all the threads making up the social tangle; in such a masterpiece the most essential social factors can find total expression in the apparently accidental conjunction of a few human destinies.

In contrast to this, the exact copying of reality by a mere onlooker offers no principle of grouping inherent in the subject matter itself. If artistic presentation goes on further than the reproduction of such superficial visible traits of everyday life as meet the eye, the result is a 'bad infinity' (to use the Hegelian phrase), i.e. a chaotic mass of observations the beginning, sequence and end of which are left entirely to the arbitrary choice of the author. Should the author, on the other hand, introduce into the world of observed fact a system originating in his own mind and in nothing else, he may bring some order into the chaos, but the order would be an order determined by abstract considerations, an order external to the material it marshals, an order foreign to real life. The resulting literary work would inevitably be dry and unpoetic and this will be the more obvious the greater the efforts the author makes to counterfeit, by means of descriptions, lyrical passages, symbolism, and the like, a mysticized link between the human destinies depicted in the work and the social forces that rule them. The more superficial the author's observation, the more abstract must be the connections which aim to conjure *a posteriori* some sort of order and composition into such a work.

The inner truth of the works of the great realists rests on the fact that they arise from life itself, that their artistic characteristics are reflections of the social structure of the life lived by the artist himself. The history of the structure of the great realistic novel – from Le Sage's loose sequence of adventures, through Walter Scott's attempts at dramatic concentration to Balzac's partly novelistic-dramatic, partly cyclically intricate compositions – is the literary reflection of a process in which the categories of capitalism as forms of human living gradually penetrate bourgeois society. In the dramatic concentration which Balzac built into his all-embracing cycle we can already discern the beginnings of the crisis into which triumphant capitalism plunges the arts. The great writers of our ages were all engaged in a heroic struggle against the banality, aridity and emptiness of the prosaic nature of our bourgeois life. The formal side of the struggle against this banality and insipidity of life is the dramatic pointing of plot and incident. In Balzac, who depicts passions at their highest intensity, this is achieved by conceiving the typical as the extreme expression of certain strands in the skein of life. Only by means of such mighty dramatic explosions can a dynamic world of profound, rich and many-hued poetry emerge from the sordid prose of bourgeois life. The naturalists overcame this 'romanticism' and by so doing, lowered literary creation to the level of the 'average' of the banality of everyday life. In naturalism capitalist prose triumphed over the poetry of life.

Tolstoy's life-work embraces several phases of this literary process, which runs parallel to the stages of social evolution in Russia. He began his career as an author in a pre-Balzacian stage, in terms of western literary development, and the work of his old age extended into the period of the decline of great realism.

Tolstoy himself was well aware that his great novels were genuine epics. But it was not only he himself who compared *War and Peace* with Homer – many known and unknown readers of the book had the same feeling. Of course the comparison with Homer, while it shows the profound impression made by the truly epic quality of this novel, is more an indication of the general trend of its style than an actual characteristic of the style itself. For in spite of its epic sweep, *War and Peace* is still from first to last a true novel although of course not a novel with the dramatic concentration found in Balzac. Its loose, spacious composition, the cheerful, comfortable, leisurely relationships between the characters, the calm and yet animated abundance of the epic episodes indispensable to the true story-teller – all these are related more to the great provincial idylls of the eighteenth-century English novel than to Balzac.

But this affinity expresses an opposition to the general line of development of the nineteenth-century European novel more than anything else. The old society, only just beginning to submit to capitalist domination, still possessed in its daily life the variety and interest of the pre-capitalist era. Tolstoy's great novels differ from those of his English predecessors in the specific nature of the social reality which they mirror and are superior to their English parallels in artistic richness and depth precisely because of this specific character of the reality presented. The world depicted by Tolstoy is a world much less bourgeois than the world of the eighteenth-century English novelists, but – especially in *Anna Karenina* – it is a world in which the process of capitalist development is more strongly apparent than in the English novels which nearly always depict only one particular phase of it. In addition, the great English novelists of the eighteenth century lived in a *post-revolutionary* period, and this gave their works (especially those of Goldsmith and Fielding) an atmosphere of stability and security and also a certain complacent shortsightedness.

In contrast to this, Tolstoy's literary career began and ended in a period of approaching revolutionary storms. Tolstoy is a *pre-revolutionary* writer. And precisely because the central problem in his works was the Russian peasant problem, the decisive turning-point in the history of western literature, i.e. the defeat of the 1848 revolutions, left no traces on them. In this connection it matters little how far Tolstoy himself, in the various phases of his development, was aware or unaware of this cardinal issue. What is important is that this issue is at the core of all his works, that everything he wrote revolves around this issue; it is only for this reason that he still remained a pre-revolutionary writer even after the disaster of the European revolutions of 1848.

But the village idylls of Tolstoy's great novels are always threatened idylls. In *War and Peace* the financial disaster of the Rostov family is enacted before our eyes as the typical disaster of the old-fashioned provincial nobility; the spiritual crises of Bezukhov and Bolkonski are reflections of the great current which broadened politically into the Decembrist rising. In *Anna Karenina* even darker clouds menace the village idyll and the enemy has already openly shown its capitalist countenance. Now it is no longer a question of financial disaster alone – here one can already feel the undertow of capitalism, against which Tolstoy makes so passionate a protest.

Constantine Levin, who really takes up the problems where Nikolai Rostov left them in *War and Peace*, can no longer solve them as simply and light-heartedly. He fights not only to recover his material prosperity as a landowner (without falling a victim to the capitalization of the land) but has to carry on an incessant inner struggle, a struggle moving from crisis to crisis in trying to convince himself that his existence as landowner is justified and that he has the right to exploit his peasants. The incomparable epic greatness of Tolstoy's novels is based on the illusions which caused him to believe that this was not a tragic conflict from which there was no way out for the honest representatives of the class, but a problem capable of solution.

In *Anna Karenina* these illusions were already shaken to a much greater extent than in *War and Peace*. This manifests itself among other things in the fact that the structure of *Anna Karenina* is much more 'European', much more closely knit and the unfolding of the story far less leisurely. The closer assimilation of the theme to those of the European novels of the nineteenth century is a further, even though external, indication of the approaching crisis; although the style of *Anna Karenina* still has the characteristics of Tolstoy's early period, certain traits of his later critical period are already showing themselves. *Anna Karenina* is far more novel-like than *War and Peace*.

In *The Kreutzer Sonata* Tolstoy takes another long step in the direction of the European novel. He creates for himself a great form of *novella* which resembles the perfected form produced by European realism and which is both broad and dramatically concentrated. He inclines more and more towards presenting the great catastrophes, the tragically ending turning-points in human destinies by a detailed portrayal of all their manifold inner motives, i.e., in the most profound sense of the word, epically.

Thus Tolstoy approaches to some extent the form of composition used by Balzac. Not that Balzac had influenced his literary style; but the reality which they both experienced and the manner in which they experienced it drove both of them by an inner necessity to create such forms. *The Death of Ivan Ilyich* marks the culminating point of this later style of Tolstoy, but its effects can also be traced in his last great novel *Resurrection*. It is no accident that Tolstoy's dramatic works were also written in this period.

But the thematic assimilation to European literature does not mean artistic assimilation to the prevalent literary trends there, the very trends which broke up the artistic forms of the epic and the drama. On the contrary, to the end of his life Tolstoy remained, in all questions relating to art, a great realist of the old school, and a great creator of epic form.

The epic presentation of the totality of life – unlike the dramatic – must inevitably include the presentation of the externals of life, the epic-poetic transformation of the most important objects making up some sphere of human life and most typical events necessarily occurring in such a sphere. Hegel calls this first postulate of epic presentation 'the totality of objects'. This postulate is not a theoretical invention. Every novelist instinctively feels that his work cannot claim to be complete if it lacks this 'totality of objects', that is, if it does not include every important object, event and sphere of life belonging to the theme. The crucial difference between the genuine epics of the old realists and the disintegration of form in the declining newer literature is manifested in the way in which this 'totality of objects' is linked with the individual destinies of the characters.

The modern writer, the looker-on, can very well achieve such an awareness of this totality of objects. And if he is a great writer, he may conjure it up before us by the force, the suggestive power of his descriptions. Every reader will remember, for instance, Zola's markets, stock exchanges, underworld haunts, theatres, racetracks, etc. So far as the encyclopedic character of his contents and the artistic quality of his descriptions is concerned, Zola, too, possessed this 'totality of objects'. But these objects have a being entirely independent of the fate of the characters. They form a mighty but indifferent background to human destinies with which they have no real connection; at best they are the more or less accidental scenery among which these human destinies are enacted.

How different are the classics!

Homer tells us about the weapons of Achilles, weapons made by the gods. But he does not do so as soon as Achilles takes the stage. Only when Achilles has angrily retired to his tent, when the Trojans have triumphed, when Patrocles has been killed in the borrowed armour of Achilles, when Achilles himself is preparing for the mortal combat with Hector – a combat mortal in every sense of the word, for Achilles knows that he himself must die soon after Hector's death – it is just before this dramatic moment of the combat with Hector, when the weapons of the two champions decide the fate of two nations and the better weapons of Achilles, apart from his god-like strength, become a factor deciding the outcome of the duel – only then does Homer describe how Hephaistos forged these weapons for Achilles.

Thus the description of the weapons of Achilles is truly epic, not only because the poet describes their *making* and not their *appearance* (Lessing points this out in the famous chapter in his *Laokoon*), but also from the point of view of the composition as a whole, for it occurs exactly where these weapons of Achilles play a decisive part in the story, in the characterization and fate of the heroes. Thus these arms of Achilles are not objects independent of the characters in the story but an integrating factor of the story itself.

The really great novelists are in this respect always true-born sons of Homer. True, the world of objects and the relationship between them and men has changed, has become more intricate, less spontaneously poetic. But the art of the great novelists manifests itself precisely in the ability to overcome the unpoetic nature of their world, through sharing and experiencing the life and evolution of the society they lived in. It is by sending out their spontaneously typical heroes to fulfil their inherently necessary destinies that the great writers have mastered with such sovereign power the changeful texture of the external and internal, great and little moments that make up life. Their heroes set out on their career and encounter quite naturally the specific objects and events of their sphere of life. Precisely because the characters are typical in the most profound sense of the word, they must of necessity meet the most important objects of their sphere of life more than once in the course of their typical career. The writer is free to introduce these objects when and where they have become typical and necessary requisites in the drama of life he is describing.

There is perhaps no other modern author in whose works the 'totality of objects' is so rich, so complete as in Tolstoy. We need not only think of *War and Peace* in which every detail of the war is shown, from the court and the general staff down to the guerrilla fighters and prisoners of war and every phase of peaceful private life from birth to death. We can recall the dances, clubs, parties, social calls, conferences, work in the fields, horse-races and card games described in *Anna Karenina* and the court and prison scenes in *Resurrection*. But if we subject to a closer analysis any of these pictures – which Tolstoy paints with such pleasure, so broadly and in such detail that each of them becomes a separate picture within the framework of the whole – we cannot fail to see how different they are from the pictures painted by modern realists and how similar to those we find in the old epics.

These pictures of Tolstoy are never mere scenery, never merely pictures and descriptions, never merely contributions to the 'totality of objects'. The Christmas fancy-dress procession in *War and Peace* marks a crisis in the love of Nikolai Rostov and Sonia; the victorious cavalry charge signals a crisis in the life of Nikolai Rostov; the horse-race is a turning-point in the relations between Anna Karenina and Vronski; the trial of Katyusha leads to the fateful meeting between her and Nekhlyudov; and so on. Each such separately presented section of the 'totality of objects' contains some decisive point which makes it a necessary factor in the evolution of one or more of the characters in the novel.

In reality the interconnections and relationships in Tolstoy's novels are much more intricate and varied than merely such points of contact between objective happenings and the subjective experiences of the characters as have been referred to in the foregoing; such points of intersection also mark more or less important turning-points of the whole story. Every phase of such crises, every thought and emotion of the characters is inseparably intertwined with the turning-point, with the event which provides the opportunity for the crisis in the story. For instance: when it is already inevitable that a crisis in the relationship of Anna and Vronski to Karenin should arise, the race and Vronski's accident is nevertheless not merely an opportunity for the crisis to become manifest, it also determines the nature of the crisis. It reveals traits in each of the three characters which in other circumstances would not have manifested themselves in the same way and with the same typicality. Because of the internal threads which link the horse-race with the characters and the plot, the race entirely ceases to be a mere picture – it grows into the fateful culminating scene of a great drama, and the fact that riding in races is a typical pastime of Vronski, that attending horse-races at which royalty is present is a typical habit of the bureaucrat Karenin, renders the manifold relationships between individual destinies and the 'totality of objects' even more manifold and typical by the intervention of social factors.

Such a presentation of the 'totality of objects' dispenses Tolstoy – like every truly great epic poet – from giving dry and tedious descriptions of a setting the connection between which and individual destinies is always general and abstract and hence always remains coincidental. The 'totality of objects' in Tolstoy always expresses, in immediate, spontaneous and palpable form, the close bond between individual destinies and the surrounding world.

*

Such a manner of presenting the 'totality of objects' is a condition *sine qua non* of depicting truly typical characters. Engels stressed the importance of typical circumstances in close connection with the typicality of characters, as a prerequisite of true realism. But typical circumstances may be depicted abstractly or concretely, even if they are correctly described, so far as their social nature is concerned. In the works of the newer realists such descriptions increasingly tend to be abstract. If the characters in a work of art, their mutual relationships, the stories of their lives, etc., cannot be shown in such a manner that the relationships between them and their environment appear as the natural results of the characterization; if the settings and instruments of the story are from the viewpoint of the individual merely accidental (i.e. if artistically they make the impression of mere scenery), then it is impossible for the artist to depict typical circumstances in a really convincing manner. For it is one thing for the intelligence to admit that a certain *milieu*, complete with all the phenomena pertaining to it, has been perfectly described, and quite another to become a participant in the profoundly moving experience of seeing how the destinies of individual men and women grow out of an infinite wealth of circumstances they have encountered and how the turning-points in their lives are indissolubly linked with the typical conditions prevailing in their sphere of life.

It is obvious that changes in the style of presentation are reflections of the changes in social reality itself, that they mirror the fact that capitalism is increasingly becoming the dominant factor in every form of human existence.

Hegel very clearly recognized the harmful effect of this change, on art in general and on epic literature in particular. He says about this:

What man requires for his external life, house and home, tent, chair, bed, sword and spear, the ship with which he crosses the ocean, the chariot which carries him into battle, boiling and roasting, slaughtering, eating and drinking – nothing of all this must have become merely a dead means to an end for him; he must feel alive in all these with his whole sense and self in order that what is in itself merely external be given a humanly inspired individual character by such close connection with the human individual. Our present-day machinery and factories together with the products they turn out and in general our means of satisfying our external needs would in this respect – exactly like modern state organization – be out of tune with the background of life which the original epic requires.

With this Hegel has accurately stated the central problem of style confronting the modern bourgeois novel. The great novelists have ever fought a heroic battle to overcome, in the sphere of art, that coldness and harshness in bourgeois existence and in the relationships of men with each other and with nature, which opposes such a rigid resistance to poetic presentation. But the poet can overcome this resistance only by seeking out the surviving live elements of these relationships in reality itself, by culling from his own rich and real experience and expressing in concentrated form the moments in which such still living tendencies manifest themselves as relationships between individuals. For the mechanical and 'finished' character of the capitalist world, described by Hegel and so often repeated after him, is, it is true, an existing and growing evolutionary tendency in capitalism, but it must never be forgotten that it is still only a tendency, that society is objectively never 'finished', fulfilled, dead, petrified reality.

Thus the decisive artistic problem of bourgeois realism was this: is the writer to swim against the current or should he allow himself to be carried by the stream of capitalism?

In the first case he may create live images, which it is of course extremely difficult to hew out of the refractory material but which are nevertheless true and real, for they depict the still existing spark of life, the struggle against the 'finished' world. Their truth rests on the fact that what they depict, in an extremely exaggerated form, is substantially correct in its social content.

In the second case – and this is the method followed by newer realism since Flaubert – there is less and less swimming against the current. But it would be quite wrong and superficial to say that this brought literature into closer contact with daily life; that it was the way of life that had changed and literature had merely adapted itself to the change. For writers who, in their own literary activity, yield to the undeniably existing social evolutionary tendency referred to in the foregoing must in their works inevitably turn what is merely a tendency into a generalized, all-embracing reality. Their writings, which cannot strike a spark of life from capitalist reality, thus become even more petrified, even more 'finished' than reality itself and are even more dull, hopeless and commonplace than the world they purport to depict.

It is naturally impossible to preserve among the realities of capitalist society the Homeric intensity of the relations between men and the outer world. It was a piece of good fortune quite exceptional in the history of the modern novel that Defoe, in his *Robinson Crusoe*, succeeded in turning all the tools required for the satisfaction of elementary human needs into components of a thrilling story and by means of this vital connection with human destinies endowed them with a significance poetic in the highest sense of the word. And although *Robinson Crusoe* is an isolated, unrepeatable instance, it is yet most instructive because it indicates the *direction* in which the imagination of the writer should move if he is to find an artistic solution to the problem of overcoming the prose of capitalist reality. It is futile for a writer to adorn his descriptions with the choicest, most brilliant, most adequate words, futile to make his characters feel the deepest sorrow and the greatest indignation at the emptiness, hopelessness, inhumanity and 'petrification' of reality. It is all in vain, even if this sorrow is expressed with the greatest sincerity and in the most beautiful lyrical form. The example of *Robinson Crusoe* shows that the struggle against the prose of capitalist reality can be successful only if the author invents situations which are not in themselves impossible within the framework of this reality (although they may never really occur) and then, given this invented situation, allows his characters to develop freely all the essential factors of their social existence.

Tolstoy's unique epic greatness rests on such a power of invention. His stories roll on with apparent slowness, without vehement turnings, seemingly following in a straight line along the track of the ordinary lives of his figures. But always and everywhere along this track Tolstoy invents situations arising with internal poetic necessity from the concrete stage of development reached by the characters, situations in which they are brought into a living relationship with nature. *War and Peace* in particular is full of such significant and magnificently living pictures. Think for instance of the splendid hunting party organized by the Rostov family and the idyllic evening with the old uncle with the sequel to it. In *Anna Karenina* the relationship to nature has already become much more problematic. All the more admirable is the genius with which Tolstoy creates such pictures as Levin's mowing of a field, letting them grow out of the problematic nature of Levin's relationship with his peasants and his sentimental attitude to physical labour.

It would be a mistake, however, to limit this problem of the poetic animation of the world depicted by Tolstoy to the relationship between man and nature. The increasing division of labour between town and countryside, the growing social weight of the towns necessarily shifts the action more and more to the urban scene and to the modern great city, and even in such cities no poetic invention can restore a Homeric relationship between man and nature, between man and the objects now turned into commodities. That does not imply, of course, that the realist writer must surrender without a battle to the 'finished' prose of this urban world. The great realists have never capitulated, on this point least of all. But here again the writer is compelled to invent situations in which the world of the great city is endowed with life and poetry. Such poetry can here be born only if the human figures themselves are deeply imbued with life and their relationships with each other are rendered profoundly dramatic. If the writer succeeds in inventing such situations, situations in which the struggles and mutual relationships between the characters widen into a great dramatic spectacle, then the objects in which these mutual human relationships find expression and which are the vehicle for them will – precisely as a result of this their function – be endowed with a poetic magic. How conscious the great realists were of this is shown by a passage in Balzac's *Splendeur et misère des courtisanes*, where the duel between Vautrin, 'the Cromwell of the hulks', and Corentin, the greatest police spy of his time, has reached its culminating point. Corentin's assistant, Peyrade, feels that he is in constant danger.

Thus the terror, which is spread in the depths of the American forests by the ruses of hostile tribes and from which Cooper has derived so much advantage, enveloped with its glamour the tiniest details of Parisian life. Passers-by, shops, carriages, some man at a window – all this aroused in the human numbers entrusted with protecting old Peyrade (for whom this was a matter of life and death) the same engrossing interest which the trunk of a tree, a beaver lodge, a pelt, a buffalo robe, a motionless boat or an overhanging tree at the water's edge possesses in Cooper's novels.

Naturally this glamour is no longer the clear, bright, simple magic of the infancy of the human race, such as we find in Homer. The striving of the great realists to remain true to the realities of life has for its inevitable result that when they portray life under capitalism and particularly life in the great cities, they must turn into poetry all the dark uncanniness, all the horrible inhumanity of it. But this poetry is real poetry: it comes poetically to life precisely because of its unrelieved horror. This discovery and revelation of poetic beauty in the dreadful ugliness of capitalist life is worlds apart from those photographic copies of the surface which use the hopelessness and desolation of the subject as the medium of presentation. An instance of this is the masterpiece of Tolstoy's late period *The Death of Ivan Ilyich*. Superficially, what is painted here is the everyday story of an average human being, such as any modern realist might have painted. But Tolstoy's gift of invention turns the inevitable isolation of the dying Ivan Ilyich into an almost Robinson Crusoe-like desert island – an island of horror, of a horrible death after a meaningless life – and inspires with a terrible dark poetry all the figures and all the objects through which the human relationships are conveyed. The fading world of court sittings, card-parties, visits to the theatre, ugly furniture, down to the nauseating filth of the dying man's bodily functions, is here integrated to a most vivid and animated world in which each object eloquently and poetically expresses the soul-destroying emptiness and futility of human life in a capitalist society.

In this their poetic quality the late works of Tolstoy have strong affinities with the creative methods of the great realists of the nineteenth century, although the artistic and historical differences are very considerable. Balzac and Stendhal got over the 'finished' unpoetic nature of bourgeois society by resolving social life into a struggle, an interplay of mutual passionate relationships between individuals; thus society does not confront the human beings living in it as a 'finished' force, as a dead machine, as something fateful and inalterable. Not only is society – objectively as well as in the picture given of it in these writings – undergoing constant change (the period in question is that between 1789 and 1848) but the characters depicted by Balzac and Stendhal do actually 'make their own history'. In a Balzac novel a court of law is not simply an institution with certain social functions, as in the books written after 1848. It is a battlefield of various social struggles, and every interrogation of a suspect, every drawing-up of a document, every court sentence is the result of intricate social tugs-of-war whose every phase we are invited to witness.

One of the principal themes of Tolstoy's *œuvre* is the transformation of the social scene. In writing about Tolstoy Lenin quotes these words of Levin: 'How everything has been turned upside down with us now, and is only just getting settled again.' One could scarcely describe the period between 1861 and 1905 more strikingly. Everyone – or at least every Russian – knows what was 'turned upside down' then. It was serfdom and the whole old regime tied up with it. But what is 'only just getting settled again' is quite unknown, strange, and incomprehensible to the masses of the people! The extraordinary poetic sensitivity to all the human implications connected with this 'turning upside down' of old Russia was one of the essential elements of Tolstoy's greatness as a writer. However wrong or reactionary his political and other opinions about this development may have been, he had certainly seen with extraordinary clarity the changes wrought in the various strata of society by this transformation of old Russia and seen them in motion, in all their mobility, never as an established condition, as a static, rigid state.

Let us consider the figure of Oblonski in *Anna Karenina*. Tolstoy shows him, not as a naturalistically conceived landowner-bureaucrat who has reached a certain level of capitalist development; what he shows is the increasing degree of capitalist transformation as it affects Oblonski's own personal life. As a human type, Oblonski is much more of an old-world country squire, who much prefers a comfortable, leisurely, broad foundation for a life of ease and pleasure to however brilliant a career at court, in the administration, or in the army. That is why his metamorphosis into a half-capitalist, capitalistically corrupted type is so interesting. Oblonski's officialdom has purely material motives: on the income of his estates alone he can no longer live the life he wants to live. The transition to closer ties with capitalism (a seat on a board of directors, etc.) is the natural consequence of his evolution, the natural widening of the new parasitic foundations of his life. On this basis the old pleasure-loving outlook of the landowner evolves in Oblonski into a superficially good-natured, superficially epicurean Liberalism. He takes over from a modern bourgeois world-view all that can ideologically justify and support his undisturbed enjoyment of life. But he still remains the old country gentleman when he instinctively despises the ruthless place-seeking of his colleagues-in-office and interprets and practises the Liberal *laissez-faire* in his own good-humouredly egoistic way as 'live and let live', '*après moi le déluge*', and the like.

But what is decisive for the difference between Tolstoy's last principles of composition and the great realists of the early nineteenth century is that the social formations, institutions and the like are much more 'finished', lifeless, inhuman and machinelike in Tolstoy than they ever were in either Balzac or Stendhal. The essential reason for this conception springs from the very fountain-head of Tolstoy's genius: that he regards society from the viewpoint of the exploited peasantry. In Balzac's world, too, the social and political institutions are transformed into militant mutual relationships solely for the representatives of the classes immediately participating in the struggle for power; for the plebeian social groups these institutions, too, are a 'finished' world, complete in itself and confronting them with machinelike apathy. Only the gigantic figure of Vautrin rises up to fight, with changing fortunes, a battle against the powers of the state; the other criminals lead a miserable existence in the pores of society and the police confronts them as an impersonal and irresistible force. Naturally this applies even more to the peasants and the lower middle class. Hence, needless to say it is obvious that Tolstoy, who regarded the world from the angle of the Russian peasant, could not but have a similar conception of society and the state.

But this does not completely explain the attitude of Tolstoy to all these problems. For even the members of the ruling class take up a different attitude to state and social institutions in Tolstoy and in Balzac. Tolstoy's characters, even if they belong to the upper classes, regard these institutions as a 'finished' objectivized world in itself. The reasons for this are obvious enough. The first of them was the character of Tsarist autocracy, which permitted intervention by individuals in social and political events only in the form of intrigue, corruption, backstairs influence – or revolt. No one of any high intellectual and moral quality could regard the Tsarist state as something in which he had a part, not even to the extent to which the characters of Balzac and Stendhal could do so in respect of the several states of their time. This 'finished', this dead quality of the Tsarist state and its social institutions assumed ever greater rigidity in Tolstoy's writings, running parallel in this with the increasing estrangement between the forces of the state and the life of Russian society. From the remote distance of the historic past single figures still protrude into Tolstoy's world, figures of whom he thinks that they might possibly still have some influence over the state. Such is old Prince Bolkonski in *War and Peace*. But even he has retired, angry and disappointed, to his estates and the career of his son already consists of nothing but a chain of disappointments, a progressive destruction of the illusion that a decent and gifted man might actively participate in the military or political life of Tsarist Russia. This chain of disillusionment is shown by Tolstoy not merely as the individual destiny of Andrey Bolkonski or Pierre Bezukhov. On the contrary it very clearly reflects the ideological repercussions in Tsarist Russia of the French revolution and of the Napoleonic period, i.e. those human and psychological motives, those human and psychological conflicts, which drove the flower of the Russian nobility of the time to the Decembrist insurrection. Whether

Pierre Bezukhov's road would have led to such a consummation is a point left open by Tolstoy. But the fact that for some length of time Tolstoy considered the plan of writing a novel about the Decembrists shows that the perspective was at least not foreign to his conception of such aristocratic rebels.

True, the political and social world, as Tolstoy saw it in his youth and early manhood, was a fairly loose structure. The semi-patriarchal form of bondage existing in the world of *War and Peace* gave elbow-room enough for free movement, for independence and autonomy in the local and personal sphere. One need only think of the life led by the independent country squires, the activities of the partisans and the like. There can be no doubt that Tolstoy observed and reproduced these traits with complete historical fidelity. But the eyes with which he regarded them were themselves conditioned by the level of his own development, and by the stage reached in the evolution of Russian society at the time when he wrote these books. With the transformations brought about by historical development and hence with the change in Tolstoy's views on the state and on society, his manner of presentation changes too. His *The Cossacks* and other early Caucasian stories show, in their central conception of society, traits very similar to those found in *War and Peace*, while the late and unfinished *Hadji Murat*, although related to the previous in subject, has a much firmer structure, with less opportunities for private human activities.

The driving force in this transformation of reality was the growth of capitalism. But in order to understand Tolstoy's world it is very important to see clearly that capitalism in the form in which it emerged in Russia was – in Lenin's words – an Asiatic, an 'Octobrist' capitalism.

This form of capitalist development aggravated even further the social conditions unpropitious to art and literature and increased the deadness and rigidity of the resulting social formations. What Marx had in his time said of German developments applied no less to the Russia of Tolstoy's later years:

In all other spheres we are tormented ... not only by the development of capitalist production but also by the lack of its development; side by side with modern troubles we are oppressed by many inherited troubles arising from the survival of ancient and antiquated methods of production with their accompaniment of out-of-date social and political conditions. We suffer not only from the living but also from the dead.

Precisely because Tolstoy's immediate attention was directed mainly towards describing the upper classes, he expressed in the most vivid and plastic fashion this 'Asiatic' character of nascent Russian capitalism and its tendency not to destroy or eliminate the worst aspects of an autocracy already superseded by historical development but merely to adapt them to the requirements of capitalist interests. In *Anna Karenina* Tolstoy already created superb types showing this 'capitalization' and corresponding bureaucratization of the Russian nobility. Here is Oblonski, in whom Tolstoy has painted a wonderfully rich and subtly modelled picture of the Liberal tendencies at work within this social group; here, also, we find the type of the modern aristocrat in the person of Vronski. Vronski changes his mode of life as a result of his passion for Anna; he gives up his military career and develops into a capitalist landowner, who transforms the traditional husbandry of his estates into a capitalist enterprise, champions Liberalism and progress in the political counsels of the nobility and attempts to revive the 'independence' of the nobles' way of life on a capitalist basis. Thus the effect, from the social point of view, of an accidental passion is to induce in Vronski a typical evolution proper to his class. To round off the picture, there is a third character, the type of the already completely bureaucratized, reactionary, obscurantist, hypocritical and empty administrative official in the person of Karenin. Capitalist division of labour increasingly permeates all human relationships, it becomes the way of life, the decisive determinant of thoughts and emotions; Tolstoy depicts with an increasingly bitter irony how in this world of divided labour human beings are transformed into parts of an inhuman machine. This division of labour is a most suitable instrument for the oppression and exploitation of the working masses and Tolstoy hates it precisely because it is an instrument of oppression and exploitation. But as the great and universal genius that he is, Tolstoy presents this *whole* process as it affects *all* classes of the population; he reveals its inner dialectic, the way in which this capitalist-bureaucratic division of labour not only dehumanizes and transforms into mere malignant robots the human beings (even those of the ruling class) which it has enmeshed, but also how this whole process turns against these same human beings at every point in their lives, whenever they attempt to defend their own elementary vital interests or manifest a remnant of humanity still surviving within themselves.

An instance of this is the wonderful scene between Ivan Ilyich and his doctor. Ivan Ilyich has become the complete bureaucrat, a paragon of a judge, who strips his cases of all humanity with consummate bureaucratic skill and who has turned himself into a perfectly functioning cog in the great Tsarist machinery of oppression. In vain do the accused, caught in the wheels of this machine, plead the special, the human implications of their case – the expert judge calmly and politely shepherds them back to the path of the paragraphs on which they are crushed by the juggernaut of the law in accordance with the requirements of the Tsarist system. But now Ivan Ilyich himself is dangerously ill and wants to find out from his doctor what his condition and expectations are. The doctor, however, is just such another superior bureaucrat, just such another perfect piece of machinery as Ivan Ilyich himself; he treats Ivan Ilyich exactly as Ivan Ilyich treats the accused who come before him.

All this was exactly the same as what Ivan Ilyich had himself so brilliantly performed in front of the accused a thousand times. The summing-up of the doctor was just as brilliant and he looked as triumphantly, even cheerfully, at the accused over his spectacles ... The doctor looked at him severely with one eye, over his spectacles, as if to say: 'Prisoner, if you will not restrict yourself to answering the questions put to you, I shall be constrained to order your removal from this courtroom.'

What is so horrible in the death of Ivan Ilyich is precisely that he is confronted with this sort of rigidity in every human contact, when in the face of approaching death he first becomes aware of an urge to establish human relationships with human beings and overcome the futile senselessness of his life.

The development of Russian society deepens the double

hideousness, an autocracy combined with 'Asiatic' capitalism. As this objective development drives inexorably on towards the revolution of 1905, Tolstoy's hatred and contempt of the dehumanized nature of such a society grows rapidly. In Karenin's figure this dehumanization is already put before us in completed form. Karenin and his wife are at a party when Karenin becomes aware of the nascent love between Anna and Vronski. He prepares to have it out with her.

... And everything that he would now say to his wife took clear shape in Alexey Andreyevich's head. Thinking over what he would say, he somewhat regretted that he should have to use his time and mental faculties for domestic consumption, with so little to show for it; but nevertheless the form and train of thought of the speech he would make shaped itself clearly and distinctly, like an official report.

In Tolstoy's later works, particularly in *Resurrection*, his hatred of this inhumanity has deepened. The main reason for that is that in his later years Tolstoy saw much more clearly the connection between the dehumanization of the state machine and the oppression and exploitation of the common people. In Karenin's bureaucratic careerism this tendency was present only implicitly, in the complete indifference with which Karenin, concerned only with his own career, decides the fate of millions of human beings as if it were a mere piece of paper. (From the point of view of Tolstoy's own development it is interesting to note that in some passages of *War and Peace*, e.g. in the figure of Bilibin, he still treats this inhumanity, which manifests itself in a formal-bureaucratic attitude to all problems, with a certain good-natured irony.) But in *Resurrection* he already brings the whole inhuman machinery into relation with the sufferings of its victims and gives a comprehensive, many-sided and accurate picture of the machinery of oppression in the Tsarist form of capitalist state – a picture nothing comparable with which can be found in the bourgeois literature of any country. Here the ruling class is already shown as a gang of vicious imbeciles who carry out their functions either with unsuspecting stupidity or malicious careerism and who are by now nothing but cogs in a horrible machine of oppression. Perhaps never since Swift's

Gulliver's Travels has capitalist society been depicted with such powerful irony. As Tolstoy grew older, his presentation of characters belonging to the upper classes increasingly took this satirical, ironical form. The representatives of the ruling class show an increasing resemblance, for all their polite and polished exterior, to the stinking Yahoos of Jonathan Swift.

The fact that Tolstoy depicts the specific Tsarist form of capitalist machinery detracts nothing from the universal validity of the picture – on the contrary the resultant concrete, full-blooded, lifelike quality enhances this universal validity, for both the hideous tyranny of the oppressors and the utter helplessness of the victims is deeply and universally true. The specific form in which this tyranny manifests itself at the hands of the Tsarist bureaucracy is merely a concrete aggravation of its universal qualities. For instance, Tolstoy's Prince Nekhlyudov intervenes in the interest of an imprisoned woman revolutionary and for this purpose goes to see one of the Yahoos who wears the uniform of a general. Because the general's wife would like to have an *affaire* with Nekhlyudov, the revolutionary is released.

As they were starting, a footman met Nekhlyudov in the ante-room and handed him a note from Mariette: '*Pour vous faire plaisir, j'ai agi tout à fait contre mes principes et j'ai intercédé auprès de mon mari pour votre protégée. Il se trouve que cette personne peut être relâchée immédiatement. Mon mari a écrit au commandant. Venez donc* disinterestedly. *Je vous attends. M.*' 'Think of that,' said Nekhlyudov to the lawyer. 'Why, this is dreadful. A woman has been kept in solitary confinement for seven months and then turns out to be quite innocent and a word suffices to get her released.' 'That is what always happens.'

This is of course no isolated instance in *Resurrection*. Tolstoy shows with an extraordinary fertility of imagination how the fate of a great many people immediately depends entirely on such personal matters of chance, on such arbitrary personal interests of some member of the ruling class. But the sum of all these arbitrary happenings and actions constitutes a clear and coherent system; through all these chances and accidents the main purpose of the dehumanized machinery emerges – it is the protection, by any and every means, even the most brutal, of the private property owned by the ruling classes.

Thus Tolstoy in his later years created a hideous 'finished' world of increasing horror. The pores of society in which human beings could act with some measure of independence have been gradually stopped up. Nekhlyudov can no longer harbour any illusions regarding life on the land, regarding a compromise between the interests of the landowners and the interests of the peasants, such as Konstantin Levin could still harbour, even though in a tormenting, problematic form. Nor does the private safety-valve of family life, the possibility of an escape like that of Nikolai Rostov or Levin exist any longer for Tolstoy in his later years. From the *Kreutzer Sonata* onwards he sees love and marriage, too, in its modern form; he sees in them all the specific forms of lies, hypocrisy and dehumanization which are brought about by capitalism. He once said to Gorki: 'Men must suffer earthquakes, epidemics, dreadful diseases and all the torments of the soul, but the worst tragedy in life was at all times, is now and ever will be the tragedy of the bedroom.' Here, as nearly everywhere else, Tolstoy expresses his thoughts in a timeless form; but when he gives such thoughts *artistic* expression he is incomparably more concrete and historical. His later *descriptions* of the 'tragedy of the bedroom' may have been conceived as documents of his ascetic philosophy, but his earlier *artistic presentations* of the problem burst through this abstract-dogmatic frame and depict the specifically capitalist hideousness of modern bourgeois love, marriage, prostitution and two-fold exploitation of women.

Where is there in such a world any room for action? The world Tolstoy sees and depicts is to an increasing degree a world in which decent people can no longer find any opportunity for action. As capitalistically developing Russia, despite the 'Asiatic' character of its capitalism, approaches ever closer to the normal forms of fully developed capitalism, the material of life on which Tolstoy draws must also approach ever closer to the material of life, the literary mirroring of which led to the naturalist disintegration of the great school of realism in western Europe. There was, of course, one objective possibility of action in the Russia depicted by Tolstoy: but only for democratic and socialist re-volutionaries, and to depict such action was precluded for Tolstoy by his philosophy. When together with the strong and hopeful features of the approaching peasant revolt he also gives poetic expression to its half-heartedness, its backwardness, its hesitations and lack of courage, he leaves his characters no other possibility save the old dilemma of capitulation or flight. And we have seen that such a capitulation must of necessity take increasingly infamous and inhuman forms, and we have also seen that even the possibilities of flight are progressively narrowed for Tolstoy by the objective evolution of society and his own deepening poetical and philosophical insight into the structure of the society thus born.

It is true that Tolstoy also preached the need for good deeds, for individual non-participation in sin and the like and wrote many things in which reality, despite all the magnificent accuracy of detail, is manipulated in such a way as to provide evidence for the possibility and efficacy of such good deeds (*The Forged Coupon*, etc.). But the poetic greatness of the older Tolstoy manifests itself precisely in the fact that when he *writes*, he cannot help presenting the true circumstances of real life with inexorable fidelity, irrespective of whether they corroborate or refute his own favourite ideas. For instance, the impossibility of an active life in this world of which we have just spoken is clearly expressed in *The Living Corpse* by Fedia into whose mouth Tolstoy, without mentioning his own favourite theory at all, even as a possibility, puts these words:

A man born in the sphere in which I was born has only three possibilities to choose from. Either he can be an official, earn money and increase the filth in which we live – that disgusted me, or perhaps I didn't know how to do it, but above all it disgusted me. Or else he can fight this filth, but for that he must be a hero and I have never been that. Or finally and thirdly he tries to forget, goes to the dogs, takes to drink and song – that is what I have done and this is to what it has brought me.

In Nekhlyudov's figure Tolstoy did of course attempt to present the individual good deed itself. But his inexorable truthfulness produces a quite different, bitterly ironical result.

Only because Nekhlyudov himself belongs to the very ruling class he hates and despises, only because in his own social sphere he is regarded as a good-natured fool, as a harmless eccentric bitten by the bug of philanthropy, only becaue he can make use of old family and other connections, can he accomplish his 'good deeds' at all. And objectively all these good deeds are mere insignificant trifles; they are as nothing in comparison with the horrible inexorability of the machine, and they fit easily into the amorous or ambitious intrigues of those who are part of the machine. Subjectively Nekhlyudov himself is forced – often unwillingly, often full of self-contempt, but sometimes also yielding to a temptation – to wear the mask of the courtier in order to be able to accomplish at least a few of his 'individual good deeds'. And where Nekhlyudov draws the Tolstoyan con-clusions from the earlier critical vacillations of Konstantin Levin, he is faced with the hatred and distrust of the peasants who regard every 'generous' proposal of their landlord as a new cunning attempt to deceive them and take advantage of them.

Tolstoy thus pictures a world in which the relationships of human beings to each other and to society approach very closely the relationships depicted by western post-1848 realism. How is it then that Tolstoy, in spite of this necessary link with the newer realism, is yet a great realist of the old type and an heir to the tradition of the old great realists?

*

The crucial difference of style between the old and the new realism lies in the characterization, i.e. in the conception of the typical. The older realism presented the typical by concentrating the essential determinants of a great social trend, embodying them in the passionate strivings of individuals, and placing these personages into extreme situations, situations devised in such a way as to demonstrate the social trend in its extreme conse-quences and implications. It is clear that such a method of presentation was possible only in conjunction with a plot full of movement and variety. Such a plot is not, however, an arbitrary formal principle, a mere technical vehicle which the writer can handle according to his pleasure or his ability. The plot is a poetic form of reflecting reality, i.e. that essential pattern which the relationships of human beings to each other, to society and to nature form in real life. The poetic reflection of reality cannot be mechanical or photographic. We have already pointed out that poetic concentration, the poetic form of reflecting reality, can move in more than one direction and follow more than one trend of development and that as a result it can either surpass or fall short of reality in depicting the animated surface of social existence. We have also pointed out that the static presentation of average characters in surroundings conceived as 'finished' must of necessity cause literature to fall short of reality.

This has been the fate of the realist writers after 1848. The lack of action, the mere description of *milieu*, the substitution of the average for the typical, although essential symptoms of the decline of realism, have their origins in real life and it is from there that they crept into literature. As writers grew more and more unable to participate in the life of capitalism as their own sort of life, they grew less and less capable of producing real plots and action. It is no accident that the great writers of this period, who reproduced important features of social evolution more or less correctly, almost without exception wrote novels without plots, while most of the novels of this time which had intricate and colourful plots were full enough of sound and fury, but signified nothing so far as social content was concerned. It is no accident that the few significant characters produced by this literature were almost still-life-like, static portraits of average people, while the figures pretending to above-the-average stature in the literature of this period could not be anything but caricature-like pseudo-heroes, empty phrase-mongers in a grandiloquent and hollow opposition to capitalism or an even hollower hypocritical vindication of it.

Flaubert recognized early and clearly the difficulties besetting the writer in this period. During the writing of *Madame Bovary*, he complained that the book was not interesting enough:

I have filled fifty pages without recording a single event; it is a continuous picture of a bourgeois life and of a non-active love, a love all the more difficult to depict as it is both timid and deep, but alas!

without internal crises, for my *monsieur* has a placid temperament. I have had something similar in the first part: my husband loves his wife somewhat in the same manner as my lover – they are two mediocrities in the same surroundings, who must nevertheless be distinguished from each other...

Flaubert, as a true artist, consistently followed his road to the end. He attempted to lend artistic colour and movement to his dreary, dull scene by descriptive differentiation and an even more subtle *milieu*-painting and psychological analysis of his average people. This attempt was doomed to fail. For the average man is mediocre precisely because the social contradictions which objectively determine his existence are not given their supreme expression by him and in him, but on the contrary mutually blunt each other and seem to level each other out to a superficial equilibrium. This produces an immobility, a monotony in the essential problems of artistic presentation, which Flaubert admitted with severe self-criticism, but attempted to overcome by mere technical artifices. But the increased refinement of artistic technique only created a new problem, which Flaubert also admitted at times: a contradiction between the subtly artistic presentation of the subject itself and the dreary tedium of the subject. The newer western literature, Flaubert's much less gifted successors, trod the same path, hanging ever more magnificent purple mantles woven of words around the shoulders of ever more lifeless, ever more mass-produced lay-figures.

There can be no doubt that the development of Russian society and of Tolstoy's philosophy, which we have just described very briefly, drove Tolstoy in the same direction, i.e. towards making his characters somewhat more mediocre, more like the average. The rigid, 'finished' world in which they lived, the impossibility of living full and purposeful lives in which their being could manifest itself in appropriate action, had to bring these characters to a certain extent within the range of the average and deprive them of some of the typicality which the characters of Balzac or Stendhal possessed through the colourful flurry of action in which they could develop their qualities.

This problem of style faced not only Tolstoy but every prominent Russian writer of the time. The Russian literature of the second half of the nineteenth century marks a new phase in realism as a whole, not only in Tolstoy's writings. The common problem of style facing all these writers was determined by a reality most unfavourable to the portrayal of passionate characters and even more completely permeated by the social trends which in western Europe had given rise to naturalism and the practice of portraying the average instead of the typical. They did their best to find artistic means enabling them to swim against the current; to find, even in a world such as the one in which they lived, that extreme expression of clearly revealed social determinants which make possible a true typicality, far beyond the merely average.

The great achievement of the Russian realists of this period was that they succeeded in finding such possibilities and giving their characters a typicality mirroring all the social contradictions of their time. The primary, essential means of transcending the average is to create extreme situations in the midst of a humdrum reality, situations which yet do not burst through the narrow framework of this reality so far as social content is concerned, and which, by their extreme character, sharpen rather than dull the edge of social contradictions.

I have already mentioned Goncharov's *Oblomov* and contrasted its qualities with the mediocrity of the contemporary western realists. In this example it is obvious that it is precisely the extreme exaggeration of a trait in Oblomov (which if treated naturalistically would result in the dreariest, most humdrum, average, i.e. his torpid inactivity) that provides the starting-point for this magnificently realistic presentation. By this 'exaggeration' all the mental conflicts engendered by Oblomov's sloth are thrown into bold relief on the one hand and on the other hand it is thus made possible to show this trait in Oblomov against a background of wide social implications.

In all concrete details of poetic presentation Tolstoy has nothing in common with Goncharov's method, but he shares with him the great historical principle of overcoming the unpoetic nature of a society ever more strongly permeated by capitalism. Tolstoy very often tells stories which on the surface contain not a single trait going beyond the everyday average.

But he builds these stories on the foundation of situations, makes his events centre around situations which expose with elemental force the lies and hypocrisy of everyday life. I again refer to the admirable *The Death of Ivan Ilyich*. It is precisely because Tolstoy here presents the life of a commonplace, average bureaucrat that he can, by sharply contrasting this drearily meaningless life with the stark fact of imminent and inevitable death, put before us all the features of middle-class life in a bourgeois society. In its content the story never oversteps the limits of the commonplace and average and yet gives a complete picture of life as a whole and is not commonplace or average in any of its moments.

It is in this connection that the difference in the function of detail in the works of Tolstoy and in those of the western realists should be dealt with. Tolstoy always gives a dazzling mass of brilliantly observed small detail; but his presentation never lapses into the empty triviality of his western contemporaries. Tolstoy devotes much attention to describing the physical appearance of his characters and the physical processes evoked in them by psychological influences, but yet never lapses into the psycho-physiological pedestrianism so prevalent in the writings of his contemporaries.

In Tolstoy details are always elements of the plot. The necessary result of this method of composition is that the plot is always dissected into small, apparently insignificant sections which follow each other minute by minute and in which these details play a decisive part; they provide, in fact, the vehicles for the plot. If the extreme situation is externally as well as intrinsically extreme, as in Balzac, then the plot can consist of a dramatic chain of great and decisive crises which the writer can present with a dramatic concentration sometimes bordering on the drama. But Tolstoy's extreme situations are extreme only intrinsically and intensively, not externally. And this intensity can be conveyed only step by step, minute by minute, in a ceaseless play of moods in which the dramatic fluctuation of the contradictions of life ripple under the motionless surface of the commonplace. The meticulous detail with which the death of Ivan Ilyich is described is not the naturalist description of a process of physical decay – as in the suicide of Madame Bovary

– but a great internal drama in which approaching death, precisely through all its horrible details, tears the veils one after the other from the meaningless life of Ivan Ilyich and exposes this life in all its appalling bleakness. But bleak and devoid of all inner movement as this life is, the process of its exposure is most exciting and vivid in its artistic presentation.

Naturally this is not the only method Tolstoy used in his writings. He created many characters and situations which are extreme even by the standards of the old realists, i.e. externally. Where his material permitted, Tolstoy was even inclined to favour such themes. His artistic temperament revolted against depicting the merely commonplace, as was so widely accepted in western literature. Wherever Tolstoy found it possible to create extreme situations of this kind, he did so quite in the manner of the old realists. The hero who acts extremely is only consistently following to its end the same path which the others treated hesitatingly, half-heartedly or hypocritically. The character and fate of Anna Karenina is an instance of this type of Tolstoyan creation. Anna Karenina lives – with a husband whom she does not love and whom she has married for conventional reasons, and with a lover whom she loves passionately – a life just like the life of other women of her own sphere. The only difference is that she follows this road consistently to the end, ruthlessly drawing every conclusion and not permitting insoluble contradictions to blunt their edges on the banality of everyday life. Tolstoy stresses more than once that Anna is no exceptional case, that she is doing the same as other women do. But the average society lady, like Vronski's mother, is nevertheless scandalized by her conduct: 'No, you can say what you like, she was a bad woman. What sort of desperate passions are these! Just to show that she was something special!' The average bourgeois simply cannot understand the tragedies which arise from the contradictions of bourgeois life itself and which cannot become tragic for him personally because he is too cowardly and base not to find a humiliating compromise as a way out of every situation.

Almost exactly as Anna Karenina is judged by the women of her sphere is Balzac's Viscomtesse de Beauséant judged by the average aristocrats of her circle. But the similarity of the basic artistic conception of these two characters, the similarity of the deep social truth revealed in the portrayal of an extreme individual passion, provides an opportunity to show up clearly the great difference in the methods of Balzac and Tolstoy, those greatest representatives of two different periods of realism. Balzac depicts with the greatest dramatic-novelistic concentration the two catastrophes in the loves of Madame de Beauséant (in *Le Père Goriot* and *La Femme abandonnée*). But he concentrates his interest on these great catastrophes. When Mme de Beauséant's first romance collapses, Balzac describes nothing but the tragic turning-point of the story. Although in the second case he does describe in some detail the birth of a new love, the rupture and catastrophe again occur with dramatic 'suddenness', although, as ever with Balzac, with great inner truth. Tolstoy, on the contrary, depicts in greatest detail every stage in the development of the love between Anna and Vronski, from their first meeting to the tragic catastrophe. He is much more epic than Balzac, in the classical sense of the word. The great turning-points, the catastrophic crises in the destiny of the lovers are always given a wide and broad epic background and only very rarely appear as dramatically concentrated catastrophes. Tolstoy stresses the epic character, in addition, by the even less dramatic and catastrophic parallel story of the destinies of Levin and Kitty.

In this novel, too, the inimitably realistic treatment of detail is an important medium of Tolstoy's creative method. He reproduces the attractions and estrangements in this love as a continuous although clearly articulated process, and the junctions at which the changes occur are most distinctly underlined. But as these points of junction can rarely be dramatic in the external sense of the word, as they might often pass unnoticed if regarded externally, and yet must be shown as real turning-points, they are given prominence by picking some detail out of the flow of mental processes, some apparently small incident in the mental and physical life of the characters, and accenting it so that it acquires a pointed dramatic significance. Thus Anna Karenina, when after the ball in Moscow she tries to escape from Vronski's love for her and her own budding love for him, looks out of the window of the railway carriage at the St Petersburg station after her nightly conversation with Vronski, and suddenly becomes aware of the fact that Karenin has unusually prominent ears. In the same way, at a later time, in the period of the dramatic climax to the dying love between Anna and Vronski, after many bitter and angry quarrels which until then had always ended in a reconciliation, the hopeless rupture between the lovers is revealed by an apparently insignificant detail: 'She lifted her cup, with her little finger held apart, and put it to her lips. After drinking a few sips she glanced at him and by his expression she saw clearly that he was repelled by her hand and her gesture and the sound made by her lips.'

Such details are 'dramatic' in the most profound sense of the word: they are sensually visible and vehemently experienced objectivations of decisive emotional turning-points in the lives of people. That is why they have none of the triviality found in the ever-so-faithfully observed details in the writings of the newer writers – details which are merely well observed but play no real part in the story. But Tolstoy's specific manner of concentration enables him to insert such internally dramatic scenes in the broad, calm flow of his narration, enlivening and articulating the flow without hindering its broad, calm movement.

This renewal of the original epic character of the novel, after the dramatic-novelistic stage of its development in the early nineteenth century (as represented by Balzac), necessarily follows from the nature of the life-material which Tolstoy had to work on and out of the essential traits of which he crystallized his principles of form. We have already discussed the reasons which had compelled Tolstoy to keep, on the whole, within the outer framework of the commonplace, but within this framework there is one more new possibility open to Tolstoy in addition to those already described: his specific method of extreme intensification, which brings out the extreme possibilities latent in his characters. Balzac presents the extreme as the actual pursuit of some course to its end, as a tragic realization of extreme possibilities which represent the contradictions of capitalist society in the purest form. He was still in the position to make this pursuit-to-the-end of extreme possibilities the typical fate of his heroes, precisely because, as we have already shown, his heroes were not as yet living in a 'finished world' – their world was one in which they could still play active parts in the great drama of society. For Tolstoy, as we have also shown, this possibility no longer existed. But because everything he wrote was set against a background representing an important phase in the history of mankind, and was part of a drama of world-wide historical importance and because this great social drama formed the backdrop to the private fortunes of all his characters, he, too, had to make the purest, most extreme forms of social contradictions the focal point of his presentations.

But only in the form of possibilities. This new and specific form of presenting the great social contradictions follows from that specific attitude of Tolstoy to revolutionary developments in Russia which Lenin analysed so brilliantly. Like the works of the older great realists, so Tolstoy's works mirror a great social and historical change; but, regarded from the viewpoint of the characters depicted, they do so indirectly. The characters of the older realists were direct representatives of the motive forces and decisive trends and contradictions of the bourgeois revolution. They represented these trends in immediate form, and the connection between their individual passions and the problems of the bourgeois revolution was an immediate one; characters like Goethe's Werther or Stendhal's Julien Sorel show very clearly this direct connection between individual passion, social necessity, and the general representative significance of just such individual passions. The specific character, so well analysed by Lenin, of the bourgeois revolution in Russia, and Tolstoy's own attitude to the peasant problem, that central question of that bourgeois revolution, make such direct presentation in the manner of the old bourgeois realists impossible for him. We know with what profound understanding and generosity Tolstoy has presented the Russian peasant. But his own specific attitude to the whole peasant movement had the necessary result that the central theme of his main works was always the reflection of the development of the peasant movement in the lives of that ruling class who were the owners and beneficiaries of the ground-rents.

This choice of subject again forms a socially and historically necessary link between Tolstoy and the newer realism. After the end of bourgeois-revolutionary movements in central and western Europe, after the shifting of the core of social conflict to the clash between bourgeoisie and working class, the bourgeois realists could present only indirect echoes of this central problem of the bourgeois society of their time. If they were writers of talent, they observed and described the emotional reflexes, the human problems and realizations arising from social conditions. But as most of them were unable to understand the social problem which was the objective basis of the human conflicts they described, they unconsciously separated these human conflicts from the social basis with which they were objectively connected. Hence they were forced – again without knowing or wishing it – to leave the most decisive social determinants out of their plots and characters and place these, without any serious historical background, into a merely 'sociologically' or impressionistically-psychologically conceived *milieu*. This separation from the historical background created a dilemma for the newer realists: they could either make their characters commonplace, average men and women of bourgeois everyday life, in whom the great objective contradictions of social life appeared in blunted form and often paled into unrecognizability; or else, if they wanted to transcend this humdrum average, they could resort to a purely individual intensification of personal passions, thus making their characters hollow and eccentric or – if a psychological explanation was attempted – pathological figures.

In connection with the brief analysis of Anna Karenina's figure we have already pointed out how Tolstoy's method of presenting passions by their extreme poetic intensification overcame this dilemma. What is outside the average in Anna Karenina's figure and fate is not some individually pathological exaggeration of a personal passion but the clear manifestation of the social contradictions inherent in bourgeois love and marriage. When Anna Karenina breaks through the limits of the commonplace, she merely brings to the surface in tragically clear intensification the contradictions latently present (although their edges may be blunted) in every bourgeois love and marriage.

It is not too difficult to understand why Tolstoy's presentation of passion and personal fate could not always take the form it has in *Anna Karenina*. The presentation of the men and women of the ruling classes and their destinies was to an increasing extent and with increasing consciousness conceived by Tolstoy as a function of their connection with the exploitation of the peasantry. The poetic starting-point in the presentation of each character by Tolstoy was the question: in what way was their life based on the receipt of ground-rents and on the exploitation of the peasants and what problems did this social basis produce in their lives? As a truly great poet and worthy successor to the greatest realists of the past, Tolstoy saw these interconnections in all their intricacy and was never satisfied with the uncovering of the mere immediate link between exploiter and exploited. His genius as a realist expresses itself rather in the fact that he sees the whole intricate life of each character of the ruling class as an integral whole and reveals as the foundation of this unity the character's social passion as an exploiter, as a parasite. In individual traits which on the surface seem to have nothing to do with exploitation – in what his characters think of the most abstract problems, in the fashions in which they make love and in many other such things, Tolstoy demonstrates with admirable realist artistry – which instead of merely analysing and commenting, renders palpably obvious the true existential interconnections – the link between such traits in his characters and the parasitic nature of their existence.

This extraordinary concreteness of poetic vision enables Tolstoy to avoid all stereotyped presentation of either the social foundations of life or their reflections in men's souls. He carefully distinguishes between large and small landowners, between those who cultivate their land themselves and the absentee landlords living on their ground rents, between traditional and capitalist husbandry, between landowners and such bureaucrats or intellectuals who are landowners by origin and still live wholly or in part on ground rents but no longer live on the land. Tolstoy sees very clearly that the same social causes can produce very different human reactions and shape very different human destinies in different individuals, according to the differences in their natural inclinations, education, and the like.

The profound realism of Tolstoy's world thus rests on his ability to present an extremely intricate and differentiated world and yet to make it quite clear, by poetical means, that underlying all this intricate diversity of manifestations there is a coherent, unified foundation to all human destinies. This connection between all the human traits and destinies of his characters and the great social and historical background raises Tolstoy's realism far above the level of the commonplace. He has the same richness and the same natural, organic, non-artificial unity between man and fate which is found in the old realists and none of the meagreness smothered in a spate of superficial and unconnected detail that is characteristic of the new realists.

Tolstoy devised a concrete, creative method of overcoming the unpropitiousness of his essential life-material, the life lived by the parasitic landowners in capitalistically developing Russia; this method was to create types based on the mere possibility of an extreme attitude, an extreme passion, an extreme fate. The contradictions on which the life of these ground-rent-owning parasites rested could not, given such human material, find expression in directly extreme action; and could do so the less, the closer their connection was with exploitation as the decisive human relationship. But it is precisely this relationship between exploiter and exploited and its echoes in the lives of the exploiting class which is one of Tolstoy's main themes. In his essay on art Tolstoy declares 'dissatisfaction with life' to be the characteristic trait of the newer art. This applies to his own work as much as to any other, but in his writings this 'dissatisfaction with life' is always based on the fact that the life of a parasite, of an exploiter, can never permit him to be in harmony with himself and with others, unless he is a complete fool or a complete scoundrel.

It is this 'dissatisfaction with life' which Tolstoy translates into reality by the method of 'extreme possibilities'. In seeking to bring harmony into their lives, eliminate the conflict between their opinions and their actual way of life, and find a satisfactory occupation for themselves in the community, his Bezukhov and Bolkonski, Levin and Nekhlyudov and others strikingly expose the contradiction between the social basis of their lives and their desire for harmony and an adequate occupation.

This contradiction drives them from one extreme to the other. As Tolstoy, on the one hand, chooses subjectively honest representatives of this class as his heroes and, on the other hand, cannot and does not wish to bring them to the point of rupture with their own class, the vacillations due to the contradictions referred to remain within the sphere of the ruling class. 'Extreme possibilities' crop up and are earnestly considered; serious steps are taken towards their translation into reality; but before the decisive step is taken, contrary tendencies appear, which are in part nothing but the same contradictions on a higher level, in part leanings that drag the heroes down to a compromise with reality. This produces a ceaseless movement in which all the important determinants of this life find expression in all their richness, but which very rarely leads to a really dramatic crisis, to a clean break with the previous phase. The lifelike quality, the inner richness of the characters rests on the fact that such extreme possibilities arise again and again, that the thorn of the conflict between social existence and consciousness never ceases to prick. But the movement is always almost a continuous circle or at best a spiral, never the rapid dramatic upheaval we see in the fortunes of Balzac's and Stendhal's heroes.

Every 'extreme possibility' always reveals some stark contradiction between social being and consciousness and is always closely bound up with the great problems of Russian social evolution, although not always in a directly visible form. For this reason the vain searchings and groupings of these heroes, their inactivity or abrupt abandonment of intentions scarcely born, never degenerate into the triviality and banality which inescapably awaits the heroes of western naturalism in their purely private destinies. It is because Tolstoy conceives his problems so broadly, because he follows the echoes of social conflicts deep into the innermost recesses of personal life, that his world is so rich and full of interest. Tolstoy makes his favourite heroes share his own misconception that a man can withdraw from public life and individually escape from participation in its guilt and vileness. But the way Tolstoy depicts such a withdrawal and its various stages, the vacillations on the road and the deviations from it, the way in which all problems of personal life become involved in this movement – all this tends to show precisely the inescapably social quality of all personal, private, individual life.

Thus 'extreme possibilities' in Tolstoy are not *real* and sudden turning-points, but a sort of power station, a centre of attraction around which the lives of individual characters revolve. Nevertheless, the posing of social problems on so high a level of their contradictory quality suffices to raise Tolstoy's world to a great height of realistic presentation which, however, differs considerably in its artistic methods from the great realist literature of the past. In brief it might be said that after the dramatically novelistic phase of Balzac's time, Tolstoy restored to the novel its original epic quality. For if the characters move to and fro within a determined and socially strictly limited sphere of life, as they do in Tolstoy, a much greater epic calm and stability can be achieved, in spite of all the movement, than was possible for Balzac.

Goethe in *Wilhelm Meister* distinguishes thus between the novel and the drama.

In a novel it is pre-eminently mental attitudes and events that are to be presented, in the drama characters and deeds. The novel should proceed slowly and the mental attitudes of the principal character in it should by whatever means available hold back the progress and development of the whole. The drama should hurry and the character of the protagonist should urge matters to a climax and be hampered in this. The hero of the novel should be a sufferer, or at least not highly active; of the dramatic hero one demands activity and deeds.

This definition of the novel, which applied perfectly to *Wilhelm Meister*, was in many respects no longer valid for the later *Elective Affinities* and even less for the novels of the great French realists. But it is not a bad description of the Tolstoyan manner. One should not, of course, interpret Goethe's contrasting of mental attitude and character in the sense that what he had in mind were blurred, outlineless creatures, emotionally swayed by, and merging with, their *milieu*. Wilhelm Meister himself shows clearly that this was not Goethe's idea at all. What Goethe meant by 'mental attitude' and 'character' were differing degrees of density and concentration in the characterization. 'Mental attitude' contrasted with 'character' thus means an almost unlimited breadth of characterization, a great wealth of seemingly incompatible traits, which are nevertheless welded together – by some great social trend, by human aspirations, by the moral and spiritual self-development of the character – into an organic and mobile unity. Dramatic characterization, on the other hand, means the concentration of the essential determinants of social conflicts and contradictions in a compressed passion which explodes in one or more catastrophes into which all the rich material of life must be condensed. After what has been said, it is scarcely necessary to explain at length how closely Tolstoy's epic works approach this Goethean ideal.

This difference between Tolstoy and the great realists of the early nineteenth century emerges most clearly perhaps in the presentation of the moral and spiritual life, the intellectual aspect of their characters. One of the reasons why Tolstoy is a worthy successor to the earlier great realists is that the presentation of this moral and spiritual side plays a decisive part in his portrayal of human beings. But the manner of presentation is again all his own and differs radically from that of the earlier realists.

In Balzac, and in many cases in Stendhal, great dialogues which throw light on the mental make-up of the characters are at the same time great duels of *Weltanschauung*, in which the quintessence of the great social problems is uncovered and which result in dramatic decisions that determine the fate of the characters. When Vautrin and Rastignac discuss social and moral problems, a few such conversations rapidly following each other – and naturally supported by the dramatic weight of the events which provoke them and which they raise to an abstract level – lead to a complete and irrevocable change in Rastignac's whole life.

The great and important dialogues and monologues in Tolstoy can have no such function. They always illustrate, with great acumen and ruthlessness, the 'extreme possibilities' around which the development of the hero revolves. Such are for instance the conversations of Konstantin Levin with his brother and later with Oblonski about the justification of private property and the moral and spiritual justification of that compromise between the interests of the landowners and peasants of which Levin dreams. These conversations cannot bring about any dramatic crisis, because neither a break with the system of private property nor a transformation into a ruthless exploiter with a good conscience are within the range of Levin's social and human possibilities. But they show up with merciless sharpness the central problem, the decisive sore spot in Levin's whole way of life and world-view. They show the focal point around which all his thoughts and emotions ceaselessly revolve, irrespective of whether he loves or is loved, whether he devotes himself to science or escapes into public activities. Thus they, too, are in a more general sense turning-points in a life, but on a very high level of abstraction, turning-points of a very special kind, in which the 'extreme possibilities' of a human life emerge most clearly, which unmistakably outline the specific make-up of the man, but nevertheless remain mere possibilities and are not transformed into deeds, into realities. And yet they are not abstract artificial possibilities, but rather the very concrete central life-problems of a well-defined character.

In Tolstoy these intellectual utterances, these manifestations of the moral and spiritual life of the characters acquire a novel and fateful significance which again constitutes a radical difference between Tolstoy and the newer realists. That the characters of these newer realists lack spiritual life, and that their intellectual physiognomy is blurred and colourless, is known well enough. The reason for this is, above all, that the extinction or blunting of the great objective social contradictions in the portrayal of individuals makes it impossible to portray them on a really high spiritual and intellectual level. Conversations or monologues raised to the level of abstraction can be concrete and alive only if they express the specific abstraction of a specific social contradiction as it manifests itself in one particular person. Detached from this foundation they remain abstract inventions. It is therefore no accident that the newer realists in the western countries increasingly avoid such spiritual or intellectual manifestations or depress them to the level of the average and commonplace.

This is of course at the same time a reflection, in the sphere of thought, of that 'finished' capitalist world which these writers depict. In such a 'finished' world all manifestations of the average human being are increasingly transformed into a tedious, endlessly repeated routine. It goes without saying that Tolstoy, having himself to devote considerable attention to depicting just such a world, could not himself dispense with depicting this tedious routine. In *War and Peace* we already find many conversations the sole object of which is to demonstrate the boring routine which governs social life in the highest spheres. But firstly, for Tolstoy this is only one side of the world he has to show and he uses it as a foil to provide a satirical contrast, and by ironically emphasizing the machine-like character of its functioning (Tolstoy repeatedly compares such conversations with the clacking of a loom), to stress the more vital quality of other manifestations. Secondly, Tolstoy often involves characters who are outside the routine (Bezukhov, Levin, etc.) in conversations of this sort, again in order that they may serve as a foil and by their 'clumsiness' damage the artfully woven threads of the machine. Thus it can be seen even in the smallest details that Tolstoy, even where a similar subject-matter seems to bring him close to the newer realities, in fact represents a diametrically opposed artistic method.

There is, however, a considerable external resemblance between them which we must stress. The great dialogues in the works of the older realists, although they have a background of very concrete circumstances, yet rise so rapidly to great dramatic heights that the outer circumstances and environment have very little influence on the conversations themselves. The dramatically intensified concrete situation, the dramatic concretization of the characters in and through the conversation, make such an intervention of external circumstances almost completely unnecessary. In the modern realists the momentary, external, accidental and impermanent circumstances and factors nearly always blot out the content of the conversations. The more trivial the latter are and the closer they approach the commonplace, the more they need such interaction with the momentary setting in order to show some animation, at least on the surface.

Tolstoy's great dialogues are always closely bound up with the time and place in which they occur. Even the external features of the accidental place and the accidental time constantly crop up in the conversation itself. One need think only of the dialogue between Levin and Oblonski in the barn after the hunt. But the very concrete and ever-present quality of place and time in these conversations is with Tolstoy never a mere device to introduce more life into the scene. Precisely the stressing of such concrete and accidental circumstances shows that what is discussed is a permanent problem in the life of Levin; for instance, it is so actual in every instant of his life that he may burst into a discussion of it at any moment. In the instance quoted the subject happens to crop up in connection with the hunt. The emphasis placed on the concrete circumstances underlines precisely this quality at the same time necessary and accidental, this 'extreme possibility' of a permanent crisis which is always latently present but nevertheless never brings about a real change.

The same purpose is served by the mostly abrupt breaking-off of such conversations in Tolstoy, a device which again underlines their seemingly accidental, commonplace quality. Balzac's conversations must be carried on to the end, for only thus can the dramatic turn be brought about and motivated. The conversations of the modern realists mostly have neither beginning nor end. They are just chance fragments of an, in the poetic sense, incoherent slice of life. But the breaking-off of Tolstoy's conversations is not really accidental, only apparently so. The conversations are carried on with the greatest skill to a point at which the contradictions and the impossibility of eliminating them are stated by the hero with merciless clarity and thoroughness. A conversation apparently evoked by some chance occasion leads to such a culminating point and then breaks off or runs out, again apparently by chance. But by then it has already fulfilled its specific object; for its object was merely to revolve around a specifically Tolstoyan possible turning-point.

Thus the apparently accidental beginning and end of a conversation are intentional devices in Tolstoy's method of epic presentation. They lead out of the quiet flow of life and then lead back into it again after having thrown a bright light on what is constantly going on under the surfaces of this calm stream of life. Here as elsewhere, Tolstoy with extraordinary inventiveness creates new elements of form, elements still capable of raising his unfavourable subject-matter to the level of a great realist epic.

*

Thus Tolstoy's continuation of the work of the great realists rested to a considerable extent on an increased flexibility of characterization and plot-unfolding; superficially seen, this method often recalls the devices used by modern realists (thereby greatly facilitating Tolstoy's great success in western Europe) but its formal purpose is the exact opposite of that of the superficially similar features of the newer realism, which here are symptoms of the disintegration of the great realistic forms, while in Tolstoy's writings they are elements of their further evolution.

Tolstoy did not develop such tendencies of form under the influence of the newer realists, although he knew their works well and studied them carefully. As early as in the sixties of the nineteenth century, immediately after the publication of Tolstoy's first writings, in which these tendencies were as yet only embryonic, the great Russian critic Chernyshevsky had already clearly recognized this feature in Tolstoy's art. He spoke of Tolstoy's preoccupation with the way in which one thought or emotion develops out of another. He made a distinction between the psychological analysis of Tolstoy and of nearly every other writer. He says of the latter, as contrasted with Tolstoy:

Usually it [i.e. the psychological analysis] has a descriptive character, so to speak – it seizes on some static emotion and breaks it up into its component parts – it gives us what may be called an anatomical table. The works of great poets usually show the great dramatic changes from one emotion and one thought to another. But we are mostly given only the two extreme links of the chain, the beginning and end of the psychological process... The peculiarity of Count Tolstoy's gift consists in that he does not restrict himself to the presentation of the results of a psychological process, but is interested in the process itself...

How consciously Tolstoy later developed these tendencies,

which Chernyshevsky had recognized so early, is shown by the following passage in *Resurrection*:

One of the most widespread superstitions is that every man has his own specific definite qualities: that he is kind, cruel, wise, stupid, energetic, apathetic, and so on. But men are not like that at all. We may say of a man that he is more often kind than cruel, more often wise than stupid, more often energetic than apathetic, or the reverse; but it would not be true to say of one man that he is kind and wise, of another that he is bad and stupid. And yet we always classify people in this way. And that is quite wrong. Men are like rivers: the water is the same in all of them, but every river is narrow and rapid in some places and broader and slower in others, sometimes clear, sometimes troubled, sometimes cold and sometimes warm. It is the same with men. Every man carries in himself the germs of every human quality, but sometimes it is one quality that manifests itself and sometimes another; sometimes a man is quite unlike himself, while still remaining the same man.

A similar opposition to the rigid conception of human character, to the allegedly rigid presentation of characters in older literature can be very frequently found in the writings of modern naturalists. But when two say the same (or similar) things, they are not the same. The modern naturalists' opposition to rigidity in characterization contained a tendency to do away with the creation of characters altogether. In literature a character cannot be given a face, an outline, save in motion, save in active conflict with the outer world, save in action. As long as a character is described only in repose, in some *milieu,* its essential traits can only be stated, but not created. In other words there is no poetic means by which it is possible to distinguish creatively between essential traits and fleeting moods. Hence, if the naturalists protested against the superficial tricks with which a writer attempted in these circumstances to stress permanent characteristics (e.g. by means of constantly recurring expressions or gestures) they were right from their point of view and at any rate consistent. But for this very reason consistent naturalists were forced to let their characters dissolve into an incoherent, chaotic tangle of impermanent moods.

With Tolstoy the case is different. His characters do not, any more than the personages of the naturalists, develop dramatically, as did Balzac's; but their movement through life, their conflicts with the external world nevertheless give them very well-defined outlines. These outlines, however, are by no means as strictly monolinear and clear-cut as those of the characters drawn by the old realists. Tolstoy's plots revolve around the 'extreme possibilities' of the characters, possibilities which never become reality but which come to the surface again and again, thus affording each character many opportunities of expressing their thoughts and emotions. Tolstoy describes the fleeting moods of his characters at least as sensitively and accurately as the most gifted of the newer realists, but nevertheless the figures never dissolve into mere clouds of moods, for they are placed within a precisely circumscribed space, a field of force within which all their moods must oscillate.

Thus Konstantin Levin sometimes leans towards a straightforward reactionary conservatism, while at other times he finds the arguments against private ownership of the land irrefutable. But as these two poles represent the extreme pendulum-swings of the thoughts with which he approaches the problems of his time and as the solution of his life-problem, the compromise that he seeks, lies in the middle between these two extremes, such swings of the pendulum do not turn him into a bundle of moods (in the manner of the newer realists) but mark with accuracy, variety and a wealth of detail the socially inevitable zig-zag path men like Levin must necessarily follow. Tolstoy, as we have already seen, never presents the various manifestations of his characters in isolation from each other, and the relationships between Levin and his brothers, his wife, his friends and other people are very closely linked with his decisions on the most important problems of his life. Thus the swings of the pendulum only enrich his image and far from blurring its outlines, make them all the more clear-cut.

This presentation by means of a certain spread, a latitude for the play of thoughts, moods and emotions, enabled Tolstoy to give a very rich and poetic – because contradictory and indirect – picture of human relationships.

This richness and animation are increased even more by the

fact that the latitude Tolstoy allows his characters is not im-mutable. He shows very carefully how through changes in ex-ternal circumstances or in the internal growth or deterioration of the characters themselves this latitude can decrease or increase, sometimes even acquire new contents or completely shed old ones. But as Tolstoy always depicts these changes as a continuity, as we are always invited to observe the cause and manner of such changes and as in spite of such changes many of the most im-portant social and individual determinants of the character re-main the same, this device further increases the richness of Tol-stoy's world and far from blurring the outlines of the characters, traces them even more subtly and intricately.

This method of characterization is an important step forward in the development of realism. Naturally such tendencies were already present in rudimentary form in the old realists. Any character without such oscillation within prescribed limits would always lack flexibility to some extent. What matters here is how important a part this method of presentation played in the crea-tion of characters by various authors. In the writings of the old realists, particularly those who had adopted a dramatic-novelistic manner, the presentation of such a latitude was necessarily merely accessory; on the other hand, the *whole* life of the characters was enacted within such a latitude. But their several movements and hesitations are depicted with dramatic vehemence, sudden-ness and directness. Remember for instance such a vacillating character as Lucien de Rubempré and recall with what dramatic suddenness, without detailed pendulum-swings, he is converted by Vautrin or decides to commit suicide after his examination by the magistrate.

What is new in Tolstoy is that he made this method the centre around which his characterization revolves. That he did so quite deliberately and that his method was closely linked with his own problems of world-view is shown among other things by the fact that the width and flexibility of the latitude accorded each charac-ter are closely connected with the importance of the part played by the character in the whole composition. Episodic figures, par-ticularly those who serve Tolstoy to demonstrate the inhuman rigidity of the society of his time, have comparatively few oscillations of mood. In order that a character may attract the central interest of the writer and reader, its latitude of oscillation must be comparatively great and varied. This applies even to figures whose world-view Tolstoy rejects or criticizes, like Vronski, Karenin or Ivan Ilyich.

The writer's own position is very clearly expressed in the way in which he presents the primary starting-point of these oscillations. Figures whom Tolstoy wants to represent as living human beings are always made to experience a lively interaction between their internal evolution and the external circumstances into which they are placed and with which they must deal. Tolstoy's conception of life has for its natural result that every figure for whom he feels human sympathy must necessarily take up a problematic attitude to society. It can never accept without a struggle the way of life into which it was born and the tasks imposed on it by circumstances. On the other hand Tolstoy's deepest poetic sympathy is always with the characters who by the social and ideological secession from their original way of life are involved in bitter internal struggles. From Olenin to Nekhlyudov Tolstoy drew a whole gallery of such portraits. The greater the tension arising within them, the more Tolstoy is interested in them, but at the same time (and here Tolstoy reveals himself as the great poet of an important transitional period) he shows the more starkly and palpably, in the oscillation of such characters, the extent to which the Russia of his time was 'turned upside down' even in respect of the smallest, most intimate details of life.

When Tolstoy chooses as a central figure a personage to whom he gives a mainly negative characterization, he makes such figures appear from the start as rigid, straight-lined, and bound by convention even in their vacillations. Then he places them in situations which shake their apparently safe, conventional life-basis, force new problems on them and thus bring motion into the figure. This can be observed very clearly in the figure of Karenin. In spite of his real – although naturally at bottom conventional – love for Anna, her estrangement from him and her adultery with Vronski produces in Karenin even more rigidity, an even more complete transformation into a bureaucratic machine. Not until he stands beside Anna's sick-bed and her profound suffering affects him with physical directness are the rigid, mechanized, automatically functioning elements of his personality loosened to some extent; in his deeply buried human core something like real life begins to stir. But as this stirring is much too weak to establish new human relations between him and Anna, he soon sinks back into an increased rigidity; the 'human' traits of his later days are mere hypocrisy, a mere religious mask on the face of this internally petrified bureaucrat. The case of Vronski is somewhat different. He is often genuinely dissatisfied with his own mode of life, although this dissatisfaction never opens new perspectives for him, and in him passion unleashes more vigorous human energies. Tolstoy shows with consummate artistry to what extent changes in his external circumstances (retirement from the army, free life abroad) contribute to the loosening-up of Vronski's rigidity. But even here the dominant factors are the conventional barriers imposed by his position in life. His liberated energies cannot carry him beyond a dilettantism which cannot satisfy him for any length of time. When he returns to Russia the inverse process begins at once : his reconversion into a pleasant average aristocrat with perfect manners in whom a great passion is something 'eccentric' and not organically linked with the central interests of his life. The conventional hardening that results does not go so far in Vronski as in Karenin, but it is sufficient to lead inevitably to Anna's tragic catastrophe.

This original and fruitful method of characterization shows that despite all the profound connection with the old realists and all the divergence from the new, Tolstoy yet has certain basic principles in common with the latter. This fact must necessarily be reflected in his style, for a great realist writer cannot close his eyes to social truths, to real changes in the structure of society. Nor can his presentation be concerned only with their content; it must also reflect them in form, even if they are in their innermost essence inimical to art, even if they contain a threat of destruction, dissolution, or petrification to the forms of art themselves. The swimming-against-the-current of the great realists is always concrete. They strive to discover, in the concrete material before them, the tendencies which enable them artistically to master and bring to life this same material together with all its anti-artistic traits. Writers whom the ugliness of modern capitalist life inspires with a perfectly justified and understandable horror, but a merely abstract horror, must fall victims to an empty formalism if they take this horror for their starting-point. The forms of great realistic art always come into being as the reflections of the essential traits of reality and their material is the concrete fabric of a certain society in a certain period, even though the main trend of social evolution in it is as inimical to art as is that of fully developed capitalism. Realist literature reflects human beings *in action*. The more vigorously the social and individual character of men finds expression in their deeds, or rather in the mutual interaction of their external circumstances, their emotions and their deeds, the greater the scope of realistic presentation. In classical aesthetics it is often pointed out that powerful, vigorous, active evil-doers and criminals provide far more suitable subjects for literature than insipid, pedestrian mediocrities, those average human beings whose character always manifests itself only in actions which are broken off as soon as begun. But the levelling power of 'finished' capitalism produces just such mediocrities in ever-increasing numbers. Thus life itself brings forth an obstacle to the development of a great realist literature. But there is a considerable difference between writers who insistently stress this tendency of life in their writings (as most western realists of this period did) and writers who strive to swim against the current, who do not accept the effects of capitalism simply and directly as accomplished facts (or what is worse, go so far as to generalize them and represent them as 'laws of nature') but who depict the *struggle* the final result of which (as a rule, but by no means always) is the coming into being of such prosaic, anti-poetic mediocrity.

Thus behind certain formal and technical similarities between Tolstoy and the newer realists we find real social problems: the problem of the possibility of action for the individual in a developed bourgeois society, the problem of the inevitable discrepancy between ideology and reality for all who live in capitalist society, except the class-conscious section of the working class.

The contrast between the imagined and the real is, of course, a very ancient problem in literature. It is the central problem, for instance, of such an immortal book as *Don Quixote*. But what we are concerned with here is the specifically modern form in which this contrast manifests itself – the form which, as disappointment with reality, as disillusionment, has increasingly grown to be the central problem of the newer realism. True, Balzac had already given one of his major works the title *Lost Illusions*, but in his book the illusions are shattered by social realities in the form of a desperate struggle, a tragic, at times tragi-comic, battle with the exigencies of social evolution. The typical novel of disillusionment of the newer realism, Flaubert's *Education sentimentale*, no longer contains a real struggle. In it an impotent subjectivity faces the meaningless objectivity of the external world. With concealed lyricism the poet takes sides with the impotent dreams of his characters and against the sordid but overwhelming power of social reality. He can, of course, like Flaubert, cover up this attitude with a veil of ironical objectivism. Disappointment and disillusionment as the principal theme of literature is the poetic reflection of the situation in which the best and most honest representatives of the bourgeois class find themselves. Reality irresistibly forces upon them the recognition of the senselessness of life in a capitalist society; they see through the falseness, the inner unsubstantiality of bourgeois ideology, but are unable to find a solution to this contradiction and remain entangled in the false dilemma of impotent subjectivity and senseless objectivity. The lifelike quality of some such works of art – however problematic they may be from the philosophical and artistic viewpoint – rests on the fact that they express a real social and historical issue, even though by inadequate artistic means.

For Tolstoy, too, the fact that reality is always different from what human beings dream and hope, was a central problem. The Caucasian idyll contradicts the imaginings of Olenin, politics and war those of Bolkonski, love and marriage those of Levin. For Tolstoy, too, it is an axiom that men and women of any value must inevitably be disappointed by life, that for them the discrepancies between ideology and reality are the deepest. The closer a Tolstoyan character approaches stupidity or dishonesty, the narrower is this discrepancy, and that is only natural, for stupidity and dishonesty express themselves psychologically above all in the ease with which the thoughts and emotions of fools and scoundrels adapt themselves to the vileness of social reality. Only here and there, in certain periods of Tolstoy's life, can one find episodic figures who, although not portrayed as fools or scoundrels, yet live in emotional and intellectual harmony with their social *milieu* (e.g. old Prince Shcherbatski in *Anna Karenina*).

But disappointment, the fact that reality must differ from the ideas men have about it, has a very different flavour in Tolstoy and in the newer realists, and such disappointments are presented in a totally different manner by Tolstoy and by the modern realistic school. In the first place, for Tolstoy this disappointment is not always a purely negative thing. He very often uses the disappointment of his characters as a means of exposing the subjective narrowness and shallowness of their conception of reality. He shows that reality is in fact different, but immeasurably richer, more multifarious and alive, than their subjective and romantic conception of it; that what reality can give men is something different from what they imagine, but is for that very reason much more than their lame imagination could conceive. This richer reality is always presented by Tolstoy as 'natural' life. Already in his early story *The Cossacks* he caused all romantic conceptions of Olenin about the Caucasus to be shattered by the reality of the rich life of the Caucasian peasants. Olenin is 'disappointed' but this disappointment at the same time enriches him, raises him to a higher level. In a similar way Levin is disappointed in love and marriage; Bezukhov's evolution runs on the same lines.

Here already the social contrast between Tolstoy and the newer realists is clearly visible. The deep connection of Tolstoy's outlook and art with the incipient revolt of the Russian peasantry preserved him from seeing social reality as a dreary desert, as the newer realists did. For the lack of social perspective caused the latter to identify the social realities of their immediate environment with reality in general and to regard the meaninglessness of life in a capitalist society as the metaphysical senselessness of life as such. It is thus that justified criticism of capitalist society degenerated into a despairing misrepresentation of objective reality itself.

But Tolstoy the writer never identified capitalist society with reality as such. He always saw capitalist society as a world of distortion, as a befouling of human reality proper; he therefore always contrasted it with another, natural and hence human reality. And although his conceptions of this natural, human reality may have been romantically imaginary or utopian reactionary, his basic attitude – which was to side with the peasantry – gave him a deeper insight into the realities of life, a more just and correct appreciation of this conflict between subjective conception and objective reality.

Hence the disillusionment of Tolstoy's characters is always an exposure of the incompleteness, utopianism and inconclusiveness of their ideas. This is expressed most clearly whenever Tolstoy contrasts his own utopian plans of 'making the peasants happy' with reality itself. From *The Morning of a Country Squire* to *Resurrection* and the play *The Light Shineth in the Darkness* Tolstoy has presented this problem in a variety of forms. But the *motif* running through each of them is the shattering of utopian ideas by the realities of peasant life, the deep and irreconcilable hatred of the peasants for all 'well-intentioned' exploiters and parasites. Here again Tolstoy always shows that the disappointed have only themselves and not reality to blame for their disappointment, that reality is in the right when it contradicts utopian ideas and that reality expresses a higher and richer truth.

Where Tolstoy appears to be in closest contact with the newer realists is in the portrayal of the life of the exploiters and of the disappointments which necessarily arise among them. But it is precisely here that the difference between Tolstoy and the newer realists is the greatest. Because Tolstoy presents the life of the ruling class as that of exploiters and parasites (although he sees exploitation in the main only in the form of ground-rent) his exposure of the bestiality and senselessness of such a life is not only more profound and correct than that of the newer realists, it is also free from the inflexible, metaphysical quality inherent in the latter. In Tolstoy there is none of the futile jeremiads and empty ironies of the modern realists. His exposure of this reality has its origin in a healthy, vigorous and violent indignation. When his favourite heroes suffer a disappointment in this world, Tolstoy represents them more or less as silly dupes who were unable to see through or tear away even so threadbare a mask. With advancing age this indignation of Tolstoy grows increasingly violent. (An example is the episode between Nekhlyudov and Mariette in *Resurrection*.)

But even in his earlier periods Tolstoy saw nothing fateful or tragic in these typical 'tragedies' of the ruling class. He always thought of these conflicts that they could be overcome with a little common sense and a sound conception of right and wrong. Of course it is part of Tolstoy's philosophy that the ruling class lack this sound conception of right and wrong and can at best acquire it only with great difficulty, after a bitter internal struggle, after hard lessons from life and many disappointments (e.g. the marriage between Bezukhov and Helen).

Tolstoy never loses sight of this principle even where the disappointment is of a more fundamental nature and where more serious and intricate conflicts between ideology and reality come to the surface. He harbours a deeply rooted peasant disbelief in the genuine sincerity and consistence of even the 'loftiest' feelings and resolutions of members of the ruling class. When he brings such 'loftiness' into contact and contrast with everyday life and causes it to be shattered by its hard little facts, he seemingly comes very close to the disappointments found in the works of the newer realists. But here again the resemblance is superficial and the basic character the exact opposite. For here again the 'lofty' emotion is every time exposed as futile, weak and not serious, and the real cause of failure is in Tolstoy's eyes not its 'loftiness', its humanly valuable moral content, but the insignificance of those who harbour it. The 'lofty' feelings harboured by Karenin and Anna in connection with the latter's illness cannot alter the fact that the former is a shrivelled bureaucrat and the latter a blindly infatuated society lady. For all the 'loftiness' of their emotions this tragic highlight must necessarily be followed by the real tragi-comedy, i.e. the continuation of their old life, the reversion to the rule of their former, not at all 'lofty', but quite genuine feelings and the return to their normal level of life.

This perspective, which follows from his acceptance of the peasant point of view, enables Tolstoy to avoid, even in his tragedies of love and marriage, both the trivial pathology and the inflated sham fatality found in the newer realists. Behind every such tragedy of love and marriage – in *Anna Karenina* as in *Kreutzer Sonata* or *The Devil* – the fact that this form of tragedy has its origin in an idle parasitic life is always kept before our eyes.

Thus Tolstoy's hope of the moral regeneration of mankind raises him above the petty narrowness of the newer realists' philosophy. And because he is never concerned primarily with art, but uses art as a means of spreading a gospel for the regeneration of humanity, he is preserved even in his quality of artist from the formless insubstantiality of the moderns. It is a similar faith, a similar gospelling fervour that makes his contemporary Ibsen superior, even from the artistic viewpoint, to so many other writers of the same period. But we have already seen how great the social difference was between the gospels of Ibsen and Tolstoy. What matters here is not whether the content of these gospels was true or false – Tolstoy preached at least as much reactionary nonsense as Ibsen – what matters is the social movement of which this gospel, for all the falseness of its content, was yet the ideological expression.

Tolstoy's world-view is deeply permeated by reactionary prejudices. But they are indivisibly bound up with that healthy, hopeful and progressive popular movement of which they represent the weak points and defects. Tolstoy's case is not the only case in the literature of the world when a great artist creates immortal masterpieces on the basis of an entirely false philosophy. But in spite of the intricate interaction between a possibly erroneous philosophy and a great realistic creative activity, it is not of course any and every erroneous philosophy which can serve as the foundation for the creation of realistic masterpieces. The illusions and errors of great realist writers can be artistically fruitful only if they are historically necessary illusions and errors bound up with a great social movement. Lenin, the only critic who discovered this connection in Tolstoy, thereby provided the key to Tolstoy's real greatness as a writer. Tolstoy understood little of the nature of capitalism and nothing of the revolutionary movement of the working class, but nevertheless he gave us admirably lifelike and true pictures of Russian society. He could do so because he looked at it from the viewpoint of the revolting peasantry, with all the faults and limits of that movement; but these faults and limits were historically determined and hence could in part become artistically fruitful and in part at least did not hamper the creation of a great artistic world. Lenin said of the peasants before the revolution of 1905: 'In their opposition to serfdom, to the feudal lords and to the state which serves their ends, the peasants still remain a *class*, but a class, not of capitalist society, but of a society based on serfdom.' The reactionary limitations and illusions in Tolstoy's world-view stem from this pre-capitalist character of its social basis.

This complicated positive and negative interaction between world-view and creative work in Tolstoy could be traced in every artistic feature throughout his whole *œuvre*. We wish here only to point out one more feature in which Tolstoy differs sharply from his European contemporaries and by which, in a time of a general decline of the arts, he not only preserved the great realist tradition but carried it worthily on. We are thinking in the first place of the fact that Tolstoy never practised art for art's sake.

For him art was always the communication of certain contents and the artistic form the means of winning over his readers to his views. It was this trait in his art – condemned as tendentious by western aesthetics – which enabled him to save the great tradition of the art of narration. For the great forms of narration were originally plastic presentations of human destinies, and their purpose was to achieve social and moral effects by artistic means. The clear and ordered grouping of events, the gradual uncovering of their causes and origins are always very closely connected with the intentions of the author, which transcend the artistic in the modern, specialized, craft sense of the word.

When the trend of social evolution made the realization of such intentions impossible, when writers were transformed into mere observers of social reality, they necessarily lost this ability of purposefully marshalling the events they narrate. To an increasing degree it came to be the chance interest attaching to certain details which determined the accentuation of the event narrated, rather than the social significance of the event in connection with the general intentions of the author.

By remaining 'old-fashioned' in this respect to the end of his life, Tolstoy was able to preserve a style of narration found only in the very greatest of the old realists. In western Europe it has often been said that after the great crisis in his world-view, Tolstoy's artistic creativeness had declined. It is quite true that the change in his philosophy brought about an essential change in his style – that the naïve epic magnificence, the almost Homeric breadth and uninhibitedness of *War and Peace* could not but be lost. It would, however, be a great mistake to underrate the new, splendid, purely artistic qualities of Tolstoy's late works. Even if looking at it merely from the formal-artistic angle, modern western European literature can boast of few stories so perfect in form (in the classical sense) as Tolstoy's *After the Ball*. And in the whole of modern western literature there is not a single novel that could match *Resurrection* in all-embracing epic greatness. Tone, manner and style of Tolstoy's presentation changed very considerably; but in his completed writings the aged Tolstoy remained to his last breath the incomparably greatest artist of his epoch.

Articles on Tolstoy*

LEO TOLSTOY AS THE MIRROR OF THE
RUSSIAN REVOLUTION

To identify the name of a great artist with the revolution, which he has obviously failed to understand and from which he has obviously alienated himself, may at first sight seem strange and artificial. How, indeed, can one describe as a mirror that which does not reflect things correctly? But our revolution is an extremely complex thing. Among the mass of those who are directly making and participating in it there are numerous social elements which have obviously failed to understand what is taking place and have also alienated themselves from the real historical tasks with which the course of events has confronted them. And if the artist we are discussing is really a great artist, he must have reflected at least some of the important aspects of the revolution in his works.

The permitted Russian press, whose pages teem with articles, letters and comments on Tolstoy's eightieth birthday, is least of all interested in analysing his works from the standpoint of the character of the Russian Revolution and its motive forces. The whole of this press is replete to nausea with hypocrisy, hypocrisy of a double kind, official and liberal. The former is the crude hypocrisy of the venal hack who yesterday had been ordered to hound Leo Tolstoy, and today – to show that Tolstoy is a patriot, and to try to observe the rules of convention before Europe. That the hacks of this kind have been paid for their secrets is common knowledge and they cannot deceive anybody. Much more refined and, therefore, much more pernicious and dangerous is liberal hypocrisy. To listen to the Cadet Balalaikins of *Rech*, one would think that their sympathy for Tolstoy is most complete and ardent. Actually, their calculated declamations and pompous

* From *Articles on Tolstoy* (Moscow, 1971 ed.).

phrases about the 'great god-seeker' are false from beginning to end, for the Russian liberal does not believe in Tolstoy's god, and does not sympathize with Tolstoy's criticism of the present social order. He associates himself with a popular name in order to increase his political capital, in order to play the role of a leader of the nationwide opposition; he strives with the thunder of rattling phrases to *drown* the demand for a straight and clear answer to the question: what are the crying contradictions of 'Tolstoyism' due to, and what defects and weaknesses of our revolution do they express?

The contradictions in Tolstoy's works, views, doctrines, in his school, are indeed crying. On the one hand, we have the great artist, the genius who has not only drawn incomparable pen pictures of Russian life, but has made first-class contributions to world literature. On the other hand we have the crazy landlord obsessed with Christ. On the one hand we have his remarkably powerful, forthright and sincere protest against social falsehood and hypocrisy; and on the other hand we have the 'Tolstoyan', i.e. the jaded, hysterical sniveller called the Russian intellectual, who publicly beats his breast and wails: 'I am a dreadful, wicked sinner, but I am engaging in moral self-perfection; I don't eat meat any more, I now eat rice pudding.' On the one hand we hear ruthless criticism of capitalist exploitation, denunciation of governmental violence, the farcical courts and the state administration, and utter exposure of the profound contradiction between the growth of wealth and the achievements of civilization and the growth of poverty, degradation and misery among the toiling masses; on the other hand we have the crazy preaching of 'resist not evil' with violence. On the one hand we have the most sober realism, the tearing down of all and sundry masks; on the other hand we have the preaching of one of the most odious things on earth, namely, religion, the striving to replace the government-official priests by priests who will serve from moral conviction, i.e. to cultivate the most refined and, therefore, particularly disgusting clericalism. Verily:

> Thou art wretched, thou art abundant,
> Thou art mighty, thou art impotent –
> Mother Russia!

That owing to these contradictions Tolstoy could not possibly understand either the working-class movement and its role in the struggle for Socialism, or the Russian Revolution, goes without saying. But the contradiction in Tolstoy's views and doctrines are not fortuitous; they express the contradictory conditions of Russian life in the last third of the nineteenth century. The patriarchal countryside, only recently emancipated from serfdom, was literally given over to be sacked and looted to rapacious capital and the tax collector. The ancient foundations of peasant economy and peasant life, foundations that had really held for centuries, were scrapped with extraordinary rapidity. And so, the contradictions in Tolstoy's views must be appraised not from the standpoint of the present-day working-class movement and present-day Socialism (such an appraisal is, of course, needed, but it is not enough), but from the standpoint of that protest against approaching capitalism, against the ruination of the masses and their divorcement from the land, which had to arise from the patriarchal Russian countryside. Tolstoy looks ridiculous as a prophet who has discovered new prescriptions for the salvation of mankind – and therefore, utterly wretched are the foreign and Russian 'Tolstoyans' who wanted to convert into a dogma precisely the weakest side of his doctrine. Tolstoy is great as the expresser of the ideas and sentiments that took shape among the millions of Russian peasants at the time the bourgeois revolution was approaching in Russia. Tolstoy is original, because the sum total of his views, taken as a whole, expresses what is precisely the specific features of our revolution as a *peasant* bourgeois revolution. From this point of view, the contradictions in Tolstoy's views are indeed a mirror of those contradictory conditions under which the peasantry had to play their historical part in our revolution. On the one hand, centuries of feudal oppression and decades of accelerated post-reform ruination piled up mountains of hate, anger and desperate determination. The striving completely to sweep away the official church, the landlords and the landlord government, to destroy all the old forms of landownership and land tenure, to clear the ground, to replace the police-class state by a community of free and equal small peasants – this striving runs like a red thread through every historical step the peasantry have taken in our revolution; and, undoubtedly, the ideological content of Tolstoy's writings conforms to these peasant strivings far more than they do to abstract 'Christian Anarchism', as his 'system' of views is sometimes appraised.

On the other hand, the peasantry, while striving towards new forms of social intercourse, had a naïve, patriarchal, religious idea of what kind of intercourse this should be, of what struggle they must wage to win freedom for themselves, of what leaders they can count on in this struggle, of the attitude the bourgeoisie and the bourgeois intelligentsia take towards the interests of the peasant revolution, of why the forcible overthrow of tsarist rule is needed in order to abolish landlordism. The whole past has taught the peasantry to hate the landlords and the government officials, but it has not and could not teach them where to find an answer to all these questions. In our revolution a minor part of the peasantry really did fight, did organize to some extent for this purpose; and a very small part rose in arms to exterminate their enemies, to destroy the tsar's servants and protectors of the landlords. The major part of the peasantry wept and prayed, moralized and dreamed, wrote petitions and sent 'solicitors' – quite in the spirit of Lev Nikolaich Tolstoy! And, as always happens in such cases, the effect of this Tolstoyan abstention from politics, this Tolstoyan renunciation of politics, this lack of interest in and understanding of politics was that only the minority followed the class-conscious, revolutionary proletariat, whereas the majority became the prey of the unprincipled, servile, bourgeois intellectuals who under the name of Cadets hastened from a meeting of Trudoviki to Stolypin's anteroom and begged, haggled, reconciled and promised to reconcile – until they were kicked out with a military jackboot. Tolstoy's ideas are a mirror of the weakness, the shortcomings of our peasant revolt, a reflection of the flabbiness of the patriarchal countryside and of the hidebound cowardice of the 'thrifty *muzhik*'.

Take the mutinies among the armed forces in 1905–6. In social composition these men who fought in our revolution were partly peasants and partly proletarians. The proletarians were in the minority; therefore, the movement among the armed forces does not even approximately show the same nationwide solidarity, the same party consciousness, as was displayed by the proletariat, which became Social Democratic as if by the wave of a hand. On the other hand, there is nothing more mistaken than the opinion that the mutinies among the armed forces failed because no officers had led them. On the contrary, the enormous progress the revolution had made since the time of the People's Will Party was shown precisely by the fact that the 'ignorant brutes' rose in arms against their superiors independently, and it was this independence that so frightened the liberal landlords and the liberal officers. The common soldier fully sympathized with the peasants' cause; his eyes sparkled at the very mention of land. There was more than one case when authority among the armed forces passed to the mass of the rank and file, but determined use of this authority was scarcely made; the men wavered; after a couple of days, in some cases after a few hours, after killing some hated superior, they released the rest of the arrested officers, opened negotiations with the authorities and then some faced the firing squad, others bared their backs for the birch, and then put on the yoke again – quite in the spirit of Lev Nikolaich Tolstoy!

Tolstoy reflected seething hatred, a mature striving for a better lot, a desire to get rid of the past – and also immature dreaming, political ignorance and revolutionary flabbiness. Historical and economic conditions explain both the necessary rise of the revolutionary struggle of the masses and their unpreparedness for the struggle; their Tolstoyan non-resistance to evil, which was a very serious cause of the defeat of the first revolutionary campaign.

It is said that beaten armies learn well. Of course, revolutionary classes can be compared with armies only in a very limited sense. The development of capitalism is hourly changing and intensifying the conditions which roused the millions of peasants – united by their hatred for the feudal landlords and their government – for the revolutionary-democratic struggle. Among the peasantry themselves, the growth of exchange, of the rule of the market and the power of money is more and more ousting ancient patriarchalism and the patriarchal Tolstoyan ideology. But there is one gain from the first years of the revolution and the first reverses in the mass revolutionary struggle about which there can be no doubt, namely, the mortal blow that was struck at the former softness and flabbiness of the masses. The lines of demarcation have become more distinct. Classes and parties have defined their positions. The hammer of Stolypin's lessons and the undeviating and consistent agitation of the revolutionary Social Democrats will inevitably bring to the forefront, not only among the socialist proletariat, but also among the democratic masses of the peasantry, more and more steeled fighters who will be less and less capable of falling into our historical sin of Tolstoyism!

Proletarii, No. 35.
11 [24] September 1908

L. N. TOLSTOY

Leo Tolstoy is dead. His world significance as an artist and his world fame as a thinker and preacher, each in its own way, reflects the world significance of the Russian Revolution.

L. N. Tolstoy stood out as a great artist already in the period of serfdom. In the series of masterly works he wrote in the course of over half a century of literary activity he depicted mainly old, pre-revolutionary Russia, which even after 1861 had remained in a state of semi-serfdom; rural Russia; landlord and peasant Russia. In depicting this period in the historical life of Russia, L. Tolstoy was able to raise so many great problems in his works, was able to rise to such a height of artistic power, that his works occupied a place in the front rank of world fiction. Thanks to the light thrown upon it by Tolstoy's genius, the epoch of preparation of the revolution in one of the countries that are groaning under the yoke of the feudal landlords presented itself as a step forward in the artistic development of the whole of mankind.

Tolstoy the artist is known to an insignificant minority even in Russia. To make his great works really accessible to *all*, it is necessary to fight and fight against the social system which has condemned millions and tens of millions to ignorance, oppression, slavish toil and poverty; a socialist revolution is needed.

351

And Tolstoy not only wrote works of fiction which will always be prized and read by the masses when they have created human conditions of life for themselves after throwing off the yoke of the landlords and capitalists, but he was able with remarkable power to convey the sentiments of the broad masses who are oppressed under the present order, to describe their conditions, to express their spontaneous feelings of protest and indignation. Belonging mainly to the epoch of 1861–1904, Tolstoy, in his works, brought out in amazing relief – as an artist and as a thinker and preacher – the specific historical features of the whole of the first Russian Revolution, its strength and its weakness.

One of the chief distinguishing features of our revolution was that it was a *peasant* bourgeois revolution in the epoch when capitalism is very highly developed all over the world and relatively highly developed in Russia. It was a bourgeois revolution because its immediate aim was to overthrow the tsarist autocracy, the tsarist monarchy, and to abolish landlordism, but not to overthrow the rule of the bourgeoisie. The peasantry in particular were unconscious of this latter aim, they failed to see where it differed from the more immediate and direct aims of the struggle. And it was a peasant bourgeois revolution because the objective conditions had brought into the forefront the question of changing the peasants' fundamental conditions of life, of smashing the old, medieval system of landownership, of 'clearing the ground' for capitalism; the objective conditions had brought the peasant masses into the arena of more or less independent historical action.

Tolstoy expressed in his works the strength and weakness, the might and restrictedness of precisely the peasant mass movement. His ardent, passionate and often ruthlessly sharp protest against the state and the police-official church conveys the sentiments of primitive peasant democracy in which centuries of serfdom, bureaucratic tyranny and robbery, the jesuitism, deception and knavery of the church had piled up mountains of anger and hatred. His unswerving repudiation of the private ownership of land conveys the mentality of the peasant masses at the historical moment when the old, medieval system of landownership, both the landlord estates and the official 'allotments', has definitely become an intolerable hindrance to the country's further development, and when the old system of land-ownership must inevitably be thoroughly and ruthlessly shattered. His unceasing denunciation of capitalism, prompted by the most deep-felt sentiments and most passionate anger, conveys all the horror felt by the patriarchal peasant, against whom a new, inevitable and mysterious enemy was advancing from somewhere in town, or from somewhere abroad, smashing all the 'foundations' of rural life, bringing unprecedented ruin, poverty, death from starvation, degradation, prostitution and syphilis – all the evils of the 'epoch of primitive accumulation' intensified a hundredfold by transplanting to Russian soil the very latest methods of robbery devised by Mr Coupon.

But at the same time, the ardent protestant, passionate denunciator and great critic revealed in his works a failure to understand the causes of the crisis and the means of escape from the crisis that was advancing on Russia such as is characteristic only of the patriarchal, naïve peasant and not of the European-educated writer. For him, the struggle against the feudal and police state, against the monarchy, became the repudiation of politics, led to the doctrine of 'resist not evil', and resulted in complete divorcement from the revolutionary struggle of the masses in 1905–7. He combined the struggle against the official church with the preaching of a new, purified religion, that is, a new, refined and more subtle poison for the oppressed masses. His repudiation of the private ownership of land led not to the concentration of the entire struggle on the real enemy, on landlordism and its political instrument of power, i.e. the monarchy, but to dreamy, vague and impotent longing. He combined denunciation of capitalism and the misery it caused the masses with utter apathy towards the world struggle for emancipation waged by the international socialist proletariat.

The contradictions in Tolstoy's views are not only the contradictions in his own thinking; they are a reflection of those extremely complex, contradictory conditions, social influences and historic traditions which had moulded the mentality of the different classes and different strata of Russian society in the *post*-reform but *pre*-revolutionary epoch.

353

Consequently, a correct appraisal of Tolstoy can be made only from the standpoint of that class which, by the political role it played, and by the struggle it waged at the time of first denouement of these contradictions, during the revolution, proved that it was its mission to be the leader of the struggle for the people's freedom and for the emancipation of the masses from exploitation – proved its selfless devotion to the cause of democracy and its ability to combat the narrowness and inconsistency of bourgeois (including peasant) democracy – such an appraisal can be made only from the standpoint of the Social-Democratic proletariat.

Look at the appraisal of Tolstoy given in the governmental newspapers. They are shedding crocodile tears and vowing respect for the 'great writer' and at the same time are defending the 'Holy' Synod. But the 'holy fathers' have only just played the exceptionally loathsome and abominable trick of sending priests to a dying man in order to fool the people and say that Tolstoy had 'repented'. The Holy Synod excommunicated Tolstoy. All the better. This feat will be put to its account on the people's day of reckoning with these government officials in cassocks, these gendarmes in Christ, these black inquisitors who encouraged the anti-Jewish pogroms and other feats of the tsarist Black-Hundred gang.

Look at the appraisal of Tolstoy given in the liberal newspapers. They make shift with the very vapid, official-liberal, threadbare academic phrases like 'the voice of civilized mankind', 'the unanimous opinion of the world', the 'ideas of truth and virtue', etc., for which Tolstoy so fiercely castigated – and rightly castigated – bourgeois learning. They *cannot* frankly and clearly express their opinion of Tolstoy's views on the state, on the church, on the private ownership of land, and on capitalism, but it is not because of the censorship; on the contrary, the censorship helps them out of their difficulty! They cannot do so because every thesis in Tolstoy's criticism is a slap in the face of bourgeois liberalism; because the fearless, open and ruthlessly sharp *presentation* by Tolstoy of the most burning, of the most vexed questions of the present day is in itself a *glaring exposure* of the stock phrases, the threadbare rhetoric and the evasive 'civilized' falsehood of our liberal (and liberal-Narodnik) journalism. The liberals staunchly support Tolstoy, they are staunchly opposed to the Synod – but at the same time they are for ... the Vekhi-ists, with whom one 'may enter into dispute', but with whom one 'must' get on within one party, 'must' collaborate in literature and in politics. And yet the Vekhi-ists receive the blessing of Anthony of Volhynia.

The liberals put in the forefront the idea that Tolstoy was the 'great conscience'. Is this not an empty phrase which is also repeated in a thousand keys by *Novoye Vremya* and by all of that ilk? Is this not an evasion of all the *concrete* problems of democracy and Socialism which Tolstoy *raised*? Does not this put into the forefront that which expresses Tolstoy's prejudices and not his reason; that about him which belongs to the past and not to the future; his repudiation of politics and preaching of moral self-perfection and not his impassioned protest against all class rule?

Tolstoy has passed away, and pre-revolutionary Russia, whose weakness and impotence are expressed in the philosophy and depicted in the works of the artistic genius, has retreated into the past. But the heritage he has left us contains something which has not retreated into the past, which belongs to the future. This heritage is accepted and is being worked on by the Russian proletariat. The proletariat will explain to the toiling and exploited masses the significance of Tolstoy's criticism of the state, of the church, of the private ownership of the land not in order that the masses should restrict themselves to self-perfection and to sighing for a righteous life, but in order that they should rise to strike a new blow at the tsarist monarchy and landlordism which were only slightly shaken in 1905, but which must be entirely swept away. It will explain Tolstoy's criticism of capitalism to the masses not in order that they should restrict themselves to cursing capital and the money power, but in order that they should learn in every step they take in their life and struggle to lean on capitalism's technical and social achievements, should learn to unite in a single, millions-strong army of socialist fighters who will overthrow capitalism and create a new society in which there will be no poverty among the people and no exploitation of man by man.

Sotsial-Demokrat, No. 18,
16 (29) November 1910

L. N. TOLSTOY AND THE PRESENT-DAY
WORKING-CLASS MOVEMENT

The Russian workers in nearly all the big cities of Russia have already reacted to the death of L. N. Tolstoy and in one way or another have expressed their attitude towards the writer who produced the finest works of fiction that placed him among the great writers of the world – towards the thinker who with tremendous power, conviction and sincerity *raised* a number of questions concerning the fundamental features of the present political and social order. On the whole, this attitude is expressed in the telegram of the workers' deputies in the Third Duma that is published in the newspapers.

L. Tolstoy began his literary activities when serfdom still existed, but at the time when it was already obviously living its last days. Tolstoy conducted his activities mainly in that period of Russia's history that lies between two of its turning points, between 1861 and 1905. During this period the vestiges of serfdom, direct survivals of it, thoroughly permeated the whole of the economic (particularly rural) and the whole of the political life of the country. At the same time, it was precisely this period that witnessed the rapid growth of capitalism from below and the promotion of its development from above.

In what way did the survivals of serfdom make themselves felt? Most of all, and most clearly of all, in that during this period agriculture in Russia, mainly an agricultural country, was in the hands of ruined and impoverished peasants who conducted an obsolete and primitive husbandry on the former serf allotments which had been curtailed for the benefit of the landlords in 1861. On the other hand, agriculture was in the hands of the landlords who, in Central Russia, had their land cultivated by the peasants, working with peasant wooden ploughs and peasant horses, in payment for the use of the 'enclosed lands', meadowland, watering places for cattle, etc. Actually this was the old serf system of husbandry. The political system in Russia was also thoroughly permeated with serfdom during this period. This was evident from the structure of the state until the first steps to alter it were taken in 1905, from the predominating influence on state affairs exercised by the landed nobility, and from the omnipotence of the bureaucracy, which also, particularly the higher ranks, consisted mainly of the landed nobility.

After 1861, this old, patriarchal Russia began rapidly to break up as a result of the influence of world capitalism. The peasants starved, died, were reduced to ruin as they had never been before, and, abandoning the land, they fled to the towns. There was an acceleration in the building of railways, factories and works thanks to the 'cheap labour' of the ruined peasants. In Russia big finance capital, large-scale trade and industry developed.

It was this rapid, painful and abrupt collapse of all the old 'foundations' of old Russia that found reflection in the works of Tolstoy the artist, in the views of Tolstoy the thinker.

Tolstoy knew rural Russia, the life of the landlords and peasants, perfectly. The pictures of this life that he drew in his works of fiction belong to the best productions of world literature. The abrupt breakdown of all the 'old foundations' of rural Russia sharpened his power of observation, intensified his interest in what was going on around him and caused a change in his whole world outlook. By birth and education, Tolstoy belonged to the higher landed nobility of Russia, but he abandoned the habitual outlook of this milieu and in his last works hurled impassioned criticism at the whole of the present-day state, ecclesiastical, social and economic order based on the enslavement of the masses, on their poverty, on the ruin of the peasants and of small proprietors generally, on the violence and hypocrisy which permeate the whole of present-day social life from top to bottom.

There was nothing new in Tolstoy's criticism. He did not say anything that had not been said long before him in both European and Russian literature by those who were on the side of the toilers. But the peculiar feature of Tolstoy's criticism and its historical significance was that it expressed with an artistic power of which only a genius is capable the drastic change in the outlook of the broadest masses of the people of Russia in the period we are discussing, namely, rural, peasant Russia. For Tolstoy's criticism of the present order differs from the criticism of the same order by the representatives of the present-day working-class movement precisely in that Tolstoy took the standpoint of the patriarchal, naïve peasant; he incorporated this peasant's mentality in his criticism, in his doctrines. Tolstoy's criticism was distinguished for its power of feeling, passion, conviction, freshness, sincerity and fearlessness in the striving to 'get down to the roots', to find the real cause of the misery of the masses, precisely because this criticism really reflected the change in the outlook of millions of peasants who had only recently been emancipated from serfdom and who saw that this emancipation meant new horrors of ruin, death from starvation, a homeless life in the 'doss houses' in the towns, etc. Tolstoy reflected their sentiments so faithfully that he incorporated in his doctrine their naïveté, their divorcement from politics, their mysticism, their striving to escape from the everyday world, their 'non-resistance to evil', the impotent imprecations they hurl at capitalism and at the 'power of money'. The protest of millions of peasants and their despair – this is what merged in Tolstoy's doctrine.

The representatives of the present-day working-class movement are of the opinion that they have something to protest against, but that there is no reason for despair. Despair is characteristic of moribund classes, but the wage-working class inevitably grows, develops and gains strength in every capitalist society, including that in Russia. Despair is characteristic of those who fail to understand the causes of evil, who see no way out, who are incapable of fighting. The present-day industrial proletariat is not one of these classes.

Nash Put, No. 7,
28 November 1910
Signed: *V. I—in*

The epoch to which L. Tolstoy belonged and which is reflected in such remarkable relief in his masterly works of fiction and in his doctrine is the epoch that set in after 1861 and lasted until 1905. True, Tolstoy commenced his literary activities before and ended them after this period commenced and ended, but he fully developed as an artist and thinker precisely in this period, the transitional character of which gave rise to *all* the distinguishing features of Tolstoy's works and of 'Tolstoyism'.

The words L. Tolstoy put in the mouth of K. Levin in *Anna Karenina* very vividly express the nature of the turn in Russia's history that took place during this half-century.

... Talk about the harvest, hiring labourers, and so forth, which, as Levin knew, it was the custom to regard as something very low, ... now seemed to Levin to be the only important thing. 'This, perhaps, was unimportant under serfdom, or is unimportant in England. In both cases the conditions are definite; but here in Russia now, when everything has been turned upside down and is only just taking shape again, the question as to how these conditions will shape is the only important question in Russia,' mused Levin.

'Here in Russia everything has now been turned upside down and is only just taking shape' – it is difficult to imagine a more apt characterization of the period of 1861–1905. What was 'turned upside down' is familiar, or at least is well known, to every Russian. It was serfdom, and the whole of the 'old order' that corresponded to it. What is 'just taking shape' is totally unknown, alien and incomprehensible to the broad masses of the population. Tolstoy conceived this bourgeois order which was 'only just taking shape' vaguely in the form of a bogey – England. Precisely a bogey, because Tolstoy rejected, on principle, so to speak, every attempt to investigate the chief features of the social system in this 'England', the connection between this system and the domination of capital, the role played by money, the rise and development of exchange. Like the Narodniks, he refused to see, shut his eyes to, dismissed the thought that it was none other than the bourgeois system that was 'taking shape' in Russia.

It is true that if not the 'only important' then certainly one of the most important questions from the standpoint of the immediate aims of all social-political activities in Russia in the period of 1861–1905 (and in our times too) was the question as to 'what shape' would be taken by this order, the bourgeois order which had assumed extremely diverse forms in 'England', Germany, America, France, and so forth. But such a definite concrete-historical presentation of the question was something entirely alien to Tolstoy. He reasoned in the abstract, he recognized only the standpoint of the 'eternal' principles of morality, the eternal truths of religion, failing to realize that this standpoint is merely the ideological reflection of the old ('overturned') order, the feudal order, the order of the life of Oriental nations.

In *Lucerne* (written in 1857), L. Tolstoy declares that to regard 'civilization' as a boon is 'imaginary knowledge' which 'destroys the instinctive, most blissful primitive requirement of good in human nature'. 'We have only one infallible guide,' exclaims Tolstoy '– the Universal Spirit that permeates us.'

In *The Slavery of Our Times* (written in 1900), Tolstoy, repeating still more zealously these appeals to the Universal Spirit, declares that political economy is a 'pseudo science' because it takes as the 'pattern' 'little England, where conditions are most exceptional', instead of taking as a pattern 'the conditions of men in the whole world throughout all historical time'. What this 'whole world' is like is revealed to us in the article 'Progress and the Definition of Education' (1862). Tolstoy counters the opinion of the 'historians' that progress is 'a general law for mankind' by referring to 'the whole of the so-called Orient'. There is no general law of human progress,' says Tolstoy, 'and this is proved by the quiescence of the Oriental nations.'

It is precisely the ideology of the Oriental order, the Asiatic order, that is the real historical content of Tolstoyism. Hence, asceticism, non-resistance to evil with violence, the deep note of pessimism, and the conviction that 'everything is nothing, all that is material is nothing', and belief in the 'Spirit', 'the beginning of everything', in relation to which man is merely a 'labourer' 'appointed for the work of saving his soul', and so forth. Tolstoy is faithful to this ideology also in his *Kreutzer Sonata*, when he says: 'the emancipation of woman lies not in colleges and not in parliaments, but in the bedroom,' and in the article written in 1862 in which he says that universities train only 'irritable, debilitated liberals' for whom 'the people have no use at all', who are 'uselessly torn from their former environment', 'find no place in life', and so forth.

Pessimism, non-resistance, appeals to the 'Spirit' is the ideology that inevitably appears in an epoch when the whole of the old order is 'turned upside down', and when the masses who have been brought up under this old order, who imbibed with their mother's milk the principles, the habits, the traditions and beliefs of this order, do not and cannot see *what kind* of a new order is 'taking shape', *what* social forces are 'shaping' it, and how they are doing it, what social forces are *capable* of bringing release from the incalculable and exceptionally acute distress that is characteristic of epochs of 'upheaval'.

The period of 1862–1904 was precisely such a period of upheaval in Russia, when, in the sight of all, the old order collapsed, never to be restored, whereas the new order was only just taking shape, and the social forces that were shaping it manifested themselves for the first time on a broad, nationwide scale in mass, public action in the most diverse fields only in 1905. And the 1905 events in Russia were followed by analogous events in a number of countries in that very 'Orient' to the 'quiescence' of which Tolstoy referred in 1862. 1905 marked the beginning of the end of 'Oriental' quiescence. Precisely for this reason that year brought with it the historical end of Tolstoyism, the end of the epoch which could and had to give rise to Tolstoy's doctrine, not as something individual, not as a caprice, or a fad, but as the ideology of conditions of life under which millions and millions actually found themselves for a certain period of time.

Tolstoy's doctrine is certainly utopian and in content is reactionary in the most precise and most profound sense of the term. But this does not mean in the least that this doctrine was not socialistic or that it did not contain critical elements capable of providing valuable material for the enlightenment of the advanced classes.

There is socialism and socialism. In all countries where the capitalist mode of production prevails there is socialism which expresses the ideology of the class that is going to take the place of the bourgeoisie; and there is socialism that expresses the ideology of the classes whose place the bourgeoisie is going to take. Feudal socialism, for example, is socialism of the latter type, and the character of *this* socialism was appraised long ago, over sixty years ago, by Marx, simultaneously with his appraisal of other types of socialism.

Further. Critical elements are characteristic of L. Tolstoy's utopian doctrine, just as they are of many utopian systems. But we must not forget Marx's profound observation that the significance of the critical elements in utopian socialism 'bears an inverse relation to historical development'. The more the activities of the social forces which are 'shaping' the new Russia and bringing release from present-day social evils develop and assume a definite character, the more rapidly is critical-utopian socialism 'losing all practical value and all theoretical justification'.

A quarter of a century ago, the critical elements in Tolstoy's doctrine might have been of practical value sometimes for some strata of the population *in spite of* the reactionary and utopian features of Tolstoyism. This could not have been the case during the last decade, say, because historical development had made no little progress from the eighties to the end of the last century. And in our days, *after* the series of events mentioned above has put an end to 'Oriental' quiescence, in our days, when the consciously reactionary ideas of the Vekhi-ists – reactionary in the narrow class, selfishly class sense – have become so enormously widespread among the liberal bourgeoisie – when these ideas have infected even a section of the quasi-Marxists and have created a 'liquidatorist' trend – in our days, every attempt to idealize Tolstoy's doctrine, to justify or to mitigate his 'non-resistance', his appeals to the 'Spirit', his exhortations for 'moral self-perfection', his doctrine of 'conscience' and universal 'love', his preaching of asceticism and quietism, and so forth, causes the most direct and most profound harm.

Zvezda, No. 6,
22 January 1911
Signed: *V. Ilyin*

The Formalist School of Poetry and Marxism*

Leaving out of account the weak echoes of pre-revolutionary ideologic systems, the only theory which has opposed Marxism in Soviet Russia these years is the Formalist theory of Art. The paradox consists in the fact that Russian Formalism connected itself closely with Russian Futurism, and that while the latter was capitulating politically before Communism, Formalism opposed Marxism with all its might theoretically.

Victor Shklovsky is the theorist of Futurism, and at the same time the head of the Formalist school. According to his theory, art has always been the work of self-sufficient pure forms, and it has been recognized by Futurism for the first time. Futurism is thus the first conscious art in history, and the Formalist school is the first scientific school of art. Owing to the efforts of Shklovsky – and this is not an insignificant virtue! – the theory of art, and partly art itself, have at last been raised from a state of alchemy to the position of chemistry. The herald of the Formalist school, the first chemist of art, gives a few friendly slaps in passing to those Futurist 'conciliators' who seek a bridge to the Revolution, and who try to find this bridge in the materialistic conception of history. Such a bridge is unnecessary; Futurism is entirely sufficient unto itself.

There are two reasons why it is necessary to pause a little before this Formalist school. One is for its own sake; in spite of the superficiality and reactionary character of the Formalist theory of art, a certain part of the research work of the Formalists is useful. The other reason is Futurism itself; however unfounded the claims of the Futurists to a monopolistic representation of the new art may be, one cannot thrust Futurism out of that process which is preparing the art of the future.

*From *Literature and Revolution* (Ann Arbor Press, 1960).

What is the Formalist school?

As it is represented at present by Shklovsky, Zhirmunsky, Jacobson and others, it is extremely arrogant and immature. Having declared form to be the essence of poetry, this school reduces its task to an analysis (essentially descriptive and semi-statistical) of the etymology and syntax of poems, to the counting of repetitive vowels and consonants, of syllables and epithets. This analysis which the Formalists regard as the essence of poetry, or poetics, is undoubtedly necessary and useful, but one must understand its partial, scrappy, subsidiary and preparatory character. It can become an essential element of poetic technique and of the rules of the craft. Just as it is useful for a poet or a writer to make lists of synonyms for himself and increase their number so as to expand his verbal keyboard, so it is useful, and quite necessary for a poet, to estimate a word not only in accord with its inner meaning, but also in accord with its acoustics, because a word passed on from man to man first of all by acoustics. The methods of Formalism, confined within legitimate limits, may help to clarify the artistic and psychologic peculiarities of form (its economy, its movement, its contrasts, its hyperbolism, etc). This, in turn, may open a path – one of the paths – to the artist's feelings for the world, and may facilitate the discovery of the relations of an individual artist, or of a whole artistic school, to the social environment. In so far as we are dealing with a contemporary and living school which is still developing, there is an immediate significance in our transitional stage in probing it by means of a social probe and in clarifying its class roots, so that not only the reader but the school itself could orientate itself, that is, know itself, purify and direct itself.

But the Formalists are not content to ascribe to their methods a merely subsidiary, serviceable and technical significance – similar to that which statistics has for social science, or the microscope for the biological sciences. No, they go much further. To them verbal art ends finally and fully with the word, and depictive art with colour. A poem is a combination of sounds, a painting is a combination of colour spots and the laws of art are the laws of verbal combinations and of combinations of colour spots. The social and psychological approach which, to us, gives a meaning to the microscopic and statistical work done in connection with verbal material is, for the Formalists, only alchemy.

'Art was always free of life, and its colour never reflected the colour of the flag which waved over the fortress of the City' (Shklovsky). 'Adjustment to the expression, the verbal mass, is the one essential element of poetry' (R. Jacobson, in his 'Recent Russian Poetry'). 'With a new form comes a new content. Form thus determines content' (Kruchenikh). 'Poetry means the giving of form to the word, which is valuable in itself' (Jacobson), or, as Khlebnikov says, 'The word which is something in itself,' etc.

True, the Italian Futurists have sought in the word a means of expressing the locomotive, the propeller, electricity, the radio, etc., for their own age. In other words, they sought a new form for the new content of life. But it turned out that 'this was a reform in the field of reporting, and not in the field of poetic language' (Jacobson). It is quite different with Russian Futurism; it carries to the end 'the adjustment to verbal mass'. For Russian Futurism, form determines content.

True, Jacobson is compelled to admit that 'a series of new poetic methods finds application [?] for itself in urbanism' (in the culture of the city). But this is his conclusion: 'Hence the urban poems of Mayakovsky and Khlebnikov.' In other words: not city culture, which has struck the eye and the ear of the poet and which has re-educated them, has inspired him with new form, with new images, new epithets, new rhythm, but, on the contrary, the new form, originating arbitrarily, forced the poet to seek appropriate material and so pushed him in the direction of the city! The development of the 'verbal mass' went on arbitrarily from the 'Odyssey' to 'A Cloud in Trousers'; the torch, the wax candle, the electric lamp, had nothing to do with it! One has only to formulate this point of view clearly to have its childish inadequacy strike the eye. But Jacobson tries to insist; he replies in advance that the same Mayakovsky has such lines as these: 'Leave the cities, you silly people.' And the theorist of the Formalist school reasons profoundly: 'What is this, a logical contradiction? But let others fasten on the poet thoughts expressed in his works. To incriminate a poet with ideas and feelings is just as absurd as the behaviour of the medieval public which beat the actor who played Judas.' And so on.

It is quite evident that all this was written by a very capable high-school boy who had a very evident and quite 'self-significant' intention to 'stick the pen into our teacher of literature, a notable pedant'. At sticking the pen, our bold innovators are masters, but they do not know how to use their pen theoretically or grammatically. This is not hard to prove.

Of course Futurism felt the suggestions of the city – of the tram-car, of electricity, of the telegraph, of the automobile, of the propeller, of the night cabaret (especially of the night cabaret) much before it found its new form. Urbanism (city culture) sits deep in the subconsciousness of Futurism, and the epithets, the etymology, the syntax and the rhythm of Futurism are only an attempt to give artistic form to the new spirit of the cities which has conquered consciousness. And when Mayakovsky exclaims: 'Leave the city, you silly people,' it is the cry of a man citified to the very marrow of his bones, who shows himself strikingly and clearly a city person, especially when he is outside the city, that is, when he 'leaves the city' and becomes an inhabitant of a summer resort. It is not at all a question of 'incriminating' (this word misses something!) a poet with the ideas and feelings which he expresses. Of course the way he expresses them makes the poet. But after all, a poet uses the language of the school which he has accepted or which he has created to fulfil tasks which lie outside of him. And this is even true also when he limits himself to lyricism, to personal love and personal death. Though individual shadings of poetic form correspond to individual make-up, they do go hand in hand with imitation and routine, in the feeling itself, as well as in the method of its expression. A new artistic form, taken in a large historic way, is born in reply to new needs. To take an example from intimate lyric poetry, one may say that between the physiology of sex and a poem about love there lies a complex system of psychological transmitting mechanisms in which there are individual, racial and social elements. The racial foundation, that is, the sexual basis of man, changes slowly. The social forms of love change more rapidly. They affect the psychologic superstructure of love, they produce new shadings and intonations, new spiritual demands, a need of a new vocabulary, and so they present new demands on poetry. The poet can find material for his art only in his social environment and transmits the new impulses of life through his own artistic consciousness. Language, changed and complicated by urban conditions, gives the poet a new verbal material, and suggests or facilitates new word combinations for the poetic formulation of new thoughts or of new feelings, which strive to break through the dark shell of the subconscious. If there were no changes in psychology produced by changes in the social environment, there would be no movement in art; people would continue from generation to generation to be content with the poetry of the Bible, or of the old Greeks.

But the philosopher of Formalism jumps on us, and says it is merely a question of a new form 'in the field of reporting and not in the field of poetic language'. There he struck us! If you will, poetry is reporting, only in a peculiar, grand style.

The quarrels about 'pure art' and about art with a tendency took place between the liberals and the 'populists'. They do not become us. Materialistic dialectics are above this; from the point of view of an objective historical process, art is always a social servant and historically utilitarian. It finds the necessary rhythm of words for dark and vague moods, it brings thought and feeling closer or contrasts them with one another, it enriches the spiritual experience of the individual and of the community, it refines feeling, makes it more flexible, more responsive, it enlarges the volume of thought in advance and not through the personal method of accumulated experience, it educates the individual, the social group, the class and the nation. And this it does quite independently of whether it appears in a given case under the flag of a 'pure' or of a frankly tendentious art. In our Russian social development tendentiousness was the banner of the intelligentsia which sought contact with the people. The helpless intelligentsia, crushed by Tsarism and deprived of a cultural environment, sought support in the lower strata of society and tried to prove to the 'people' that it was thinking only of them, living only for them and that it loved them 'terribly'. And just as the 'populists' who went to the people were ready to do without clean linen and without a comb and without a toothbrush, so the intelligentsia was ready to sacrifice the 'subtleties' of form in its art, in order to give the most direct and spontaneous expression to the sufferings and hopes of the oppressed. On the other hand, 'pure' art was the banner of the rising bourgeoisie, which could not openly declare its bourgeois character, and which at the same time tried to keep the intelligentsia in its service. The Marxist point of view is far removed from these tendencies, which were historically necessary, but which have become historically *passé*. Keeping on the plane of scientific investigation, Marxism seeks with the same assurance the social roots of the 'pure' as well as of the tendentious art. It does not at all 'incriminate' a poet with the thoughts and feelings which he expresses, but raises questions of a much more profound significance, namely, to which order of feelings does a given artistic work correspond in all its peculiarities? What are the social conditions of these thoughts and feelings? What place do they occupy in the historic development of a society and of a class? And, further, what literary heritage has entered into the elaboration of the new form? Under the influence of what historic impulse have the new complexes of feelings and thoughts broken through the shell which divides them from the sphere of poetic consciousness? The investigation may become complicated, detailed or individualized, but its fundamental idea will be that of the subsidiary role which art plays in the social process.

Each class has its own policy in art, that is, a system of presenting demands on art, which changes with time; for instance, the Maecenas-like protection of court and grand seigneur, the automatic relationship of supply and demand which is supplemented by complex methods of influencing the individual, and so forth, and so on. The social and even the personal dependence of art was not concealed, but was openly announced as long as art retained its court character. The wider, more popular, anonymous character of the rising bourgeoisie led, on the whole, to the theory of 'pure art', though there were many deviations from this theory. As indicated above, the tendentious literature of the 'populist' intelligentsia was imbued with a class interest; the intelligentsia could not strengthen itself and could not conquer for itself a right to play a part in history without the support of the people. But in the revolutionary struggle, the class egotism of the intelligentsia was turned inside out, and in its left wing it assumed the form of highest self-sacrifice. That is why the intelligentsia not only did not conceal art with a tendency but proclaimed it, thus sacrificing art, just as it sacrificed many other things.

Our Marxist conception of the objective social dependence and social utility of art, when translated into the language of politics, does not at all mean a desire to dominate art by means of decrees and orders. It is not true that we regard only that art as new and revolutionary which speaks of the worker, and it is nonsense to say that we demand that the poets should describe inevitably a factory chimney, or the uprising against capital! Of course the new art cannot but place the struggle of the proletariat in the centre of its attention. But the plough of the new art is not limited to numbered strips. On the contrary, it must plough the entire field in all directions. Personal lyrics of the very smallest scope have an absolute right to exist within the new art. More-over, the new man cannot be formed without a new lyric poetry. But to create it, the poet himself must feel the world in a new way. If Christ alone or Sabaoth himself bends over the poet's embraces (as in the case of Akhmatova, Tsvetaeva, Shkapskaya and others), then this only goes to prove how much behind the times his lyrics are and how socially and aesthetically inadequate they are for the new man. Even where such terminology is not a survival of experience so much as of words, it shows psychological inertia and therefore stands in contradiction to the consciousness of the new man. No one is going to prescribe themes to a poet or intends to prescribe them. Please write about anything you can think of! But allow the new class which considers itself, and with reason, called upon to build a new world, to say to you in any given case: It does not make new poets of you to translate the philosophy of life of the seventeenth century into the language of the Acméists. The form of art is, to a certain and very large degree, independent, but the artist who creates this form, and the spectator who is enjoying it, are not empty machines, one for creating form and the other for appreciating it. They are living people, with a crystallized psychology representing a certain unity, even if not entirely harmonious. This psychology is the result of social conditions. The creation and perception of art forms is one of the functions of this psychology. And no matter how wise the Formalists try to be, their whole conception is simply based upon the fact that they ignore the psychological unity of the social man, who creates and who consumes what has been created.

The proletariat has to have in art the expression of the new spiritual point of view which is just beginning to be formulated within him, and to which art must help him give form. This is not a state order, but an historic demand. Its strength lies in the objectivity of historic necessity. You cannot pass this by, nor escape its force.

The Formalist school seems to try to be objective. It is disgusted, and not without reason, with the literary and critical arbitrariness which operates only with tastes and moods. It seeks precise criteria for classification and valuation. But owing to its narrow outlook and superficial methods, it is constantly falling into superstitions, such as graphology and phrenology. These two 'schools' have also the task of establishing purely objective tests for determining human character; such as the number of the flourishes of one's pen and their roundness, and the peculiarities of the bumps on the back of one's head. One may assume that pen-flourishes and bumps do have some relation to character; but this relation is not direct, and human character is not at all exhausted by them. An apparent objectivism based on accidental, secondary and inadequate characteristics leads inevitably to the worst subjectivism. In the case of the Formalist school it leads to the superstition of the word. Having counted the adjectives, and weighed the lines, and measured the rhythms, a Formalist either stops silent with the expression of a man who does not know what to do with himself, or throws out an unexpected generalization which contains five per cent of Formalism and ninety-five per cent of the most uncritical intuition.

In fact, the Formalists do not carry their idea of art to its logical conclusion. If one is to regard the process of poetic creation only as a combination of sounds or words, and to seek along these lines the solution of all the problems of poetry, then the only perfect formula of 'poetics' will be this: Arm yourself with a dictionary and create by means of algebraic combinations and permutations of words, all the poetic works of the world which have been created and which have not yet been created. Reasoning 'formally', one may produce *Eugene Onegin* in two ways: either by subordinating the selection of words to a pre-conceived artistic idea (as Pushkin himself did), or by solving the problem algebraically. From the 'Formal' point of view, the second method is more correct, because it does not depend upon mood, inspiration, or other unsteady things, and has besides the advantage that while leading to *Eugene Onegin* it may bring one to an incalculable number of other great works. All that one needs is infinity in time, called eternity. But as neither mankind nor the individual poet have eternity at their disposal, the funda-mental source of poetic words will remain, as before, the pre-conceived artistic idea understood in the broadest sense, as an accurate thought and as a clearly expressed personal or social feeling and as a vague mood. In its striving towards artistic materialization, this subjective idea will be stimulated and jolted by form and may be sometimes pushed onto a path which was entirely unforeseen. This simply means that verbal form is not a passive reflection of a preconceived artistic idea, but an active element which influences the idea itself. But such an active mutual relationship – in which form influences and at times entirely transforms content – is known to us in all fields of social and even biological life. There is no reason at all for rejecting Darwinism and Marxism and for the creation of a Formalist school either in biology or sociology.

Victor Shklovsky, who flits lightly from verbal Formalism to the most subjective valuations, assumes a very uncompromising attitude towards the historical-materialist theory of art. In a booklet which he published in Berlin, under the title of *The March of the Horse*, he formulates in the course of three small pages – brevity is a fundamental and, at any rate, an undoubted merit of Shklovsky – five (not four and not six, but five) ex-haustive arguments against the materialist conception of art. Let us examine these arguments, because it won't harm us to take a look and see what kind of chaff is handed out as the last word in scientific thought (with the greatest variety of scientific references on these same three microscopic pages).

'If the environment and the relations of production,' says Shklovsky, 'influenced art, then would not the themes of art be tied to the places which would correspond to these relations? But themes are homeless.' Well, and how about butterflies? According to Darwin, they also 'correspond' to definite relations, and yet they flit from place to place, just like an unweighted littérateur.

It is not easy to understand why Marxism should be supposed to condemn themes to a condition of serfdom. The fact that different peoples and different classes of the same people make use of the same themes merely shows how limited the human imagination is, and how man tries to maintain an economy of energy in every kind of creation, even in the artistic. Every class tries to utilize, to the greatest possible degree, the material and spiritual heritage of another class. Shklovsky's argument could be easily transferred into the field of productive technique. From ancient times on, the waggon has been based on one and the same theme, namely, axles, wheels, and a shaft. However, the chariot of the Roman patrician was just as well adapted to his tastes and needs as was the carriage of Count Orlov, fitted out with inner comforts, to the tastes of this favourite of Catherine the Great. The waggon of the Russian peasant is adapted to the needs of his household, to the strength of his little horse, and to the peculiarities of the country road. The automobile, which is undoubtedly a product of the new technique, shows, nevertheless, the same 'theme', namely, four wheels on two axles. Yet every time a peasant's horse shies in terror before the blinding lights of an automobile on the Russian road at night, a conflict of two cultures is reflected in the episode.

'If environment expressed itself in novels,' so runs the second argument, 'European science would not be breaking its head over the question of where the stories of *A Thousand and One Nights* were made, whether in Egypt, India, or Persia.' To say that man's environment, including the artist's, that is, the conditions of his education and life, find expression in his art also does not mean to say that such expression has a precise geographic, ethnographic and statistical character. It is not at all surprising that it is difficult to decide whether certain novels were made in Egypt, India or Persia, because the social conditions of these countries have much in common. But the very fact that European science is 'breaking its head' trying to solve this question from these novels themselves shows that these novels reflect an environment, even though unevenly. No one can jump beyond himself. Even the ravings of an insane person contain nothing that the sick man had not received before from the outside world. But it would be an insanity of another order to regard his ravings as the accurate reflection of an external world. Only an experienced and thoughtful psychiatrist, who knows the past of the patient, will be able to find the reflected and distorted bits of reality in the contents of his ravings. Artistic creation, of course, is not a raving, though it is also a deflection, a changing and a transformation of reality, in accordance with the peculiar laws of art. However fantastic art may be, it cannot have at its disposal any other material except that which is given to it by the world of three dimensions and by the narrower world of class society. Even when the artist creates heaven and hell, he merely transforms the experience of his own life into his phantasmagorias, almost to the point of his landlady's unpaid bill.

'If the features of class and caste are deposited in art,' continues Shklovsky, 'then how does it come that the various tales of the Great Russians about their nobleman are the same as their fairy tales about their priest?'

In essence, this is merely a paraphrase of the first argument. Why cannot the fairy tales about the nobleman and about the priest be the same, and how does this contradict Marxism? The proclamations which are written by well-known Marxists not infrequently speak of landlords, capitalists, priests, generals and other exploiters. The landlord undoubtedly differs from the capitalist, but there are cases when they are considered under one head. Why, then, cannot folk-art in certain cases treat the nobleman and the priest together, as the representatives of the classes which stand above the people and which plunder them? In the cartoons of Moor and of Deni, the priest often stands side by side with the landlord, without any damage to Marxism.

'If ethnographic traits were reflected in art,' Shklovsky goes on, 'the folklore about the peoples beyond the border would not be interchangeable and could not be told by any one folk about another.'

As you see, there is no letting up here. Marxism does not maintain at all that ethnographic traits have an independent character. On the contrary, it emphasizes the all-determining significance of natural and economic conditions in the formation of folklore. The similarity of conditions in the development of the herding and agricultural and primarily peasant peoples, and the similarity in the character of their mutual influence upon one another, cannot but lead to the creation of a similar folklore. And from the point of view of the question that interests us here, it makes absolutely no difference whether these homogeneous themes arose independently among different peoples, as the reflection of a life-experience which was homogeneous in its fundamental traits and which was reflected through the homogeneous prism of a peasant imagination, or whether the seeds of these fairy tales were carried by a favourable wind from place to place, striking root wherever the ground turned out to be favourable. It is very likely that, in reality, these methods were combined.

And finally, as a separate argument – 'The reason (i.e. Marxism) is incorrect in the fifth place' – Shklovsky points to the theme of abduction which goes through Greek comedy and reaches Ostrovsky. In other words, our critic repeats, in a special form, his very first argument (as we see, even in so far as formal logic is concerned, all is not well with our Formalist). Yes, themes migrate from people to people, from class to class, and even from author to author. This means only that the human imagination is economical. A new class does not begin to create all of culture from the beginning, but enters into possession of the past, assorts it, touches it up, rearranges it, and builds on it further. If there were no such utilization of the 'second-hand' wardrobe of the ages, historic processes would have no progress at all. If the theme of Ostrovsky's drama came to him through the Egyptians and through Greece, then the paper on which Ostrovsky developed his theme came to him as a development of the Egyptian papyrus through the Greek parchment. Let us take another and closer analogy: the fact that the critical methods of the Greek Sophists, who were the pure Formalists of their day, have penetrated the theoretic consciousness of Shklovsky does not in the least change the fact that Shklovsky himself is a very picturesque product of a definite social environment and of a definite age.

Shklovsky's destruction of Marxism in five points reminds us very much of those articles which were published against Darwinism in the magazine *Orthodox Review* in the good old days. If the doctrine of the origin of man from the monkey were true, wrote the learned Bishop Nikanor of Odessa thirty or forty years ago, then our grandfathers would have had distinct signs of a tail, or would have noticed such a characteristic in their grandfathers and grandmothers. Second, as everybody knows, monkeys can only give birth to monkeys... Fifth, Darwinism is incorrect, because it contradicts Formalism – I beg your pardon, I meant to say the formal decisions of the universal church conferences. The advantage of the learned monk consisted, however, in the fact that he was a frank *passéist* and took his cue from the Apostle Paul and not from physics, chemistry or mathematics, as the Futurist Shklovsky does.

It is unquestionably true that the need for art is not created by economic conditions. But neither is the need for food created by economics. On the contrary, the need for food and warmth creates economics. It is very true that one cannot always go by the principles of Marxism in deciding whether to reject or to accept a work of art. A work of art should, in the first place, be judged by its own law, that is, by the law of art. But Marxism alone can explain why and how a given tendency in art has originated in a given period of history; in other words, who it was who made a demand for such an artistic form and not for another, and why.

It would be childish to think that every class can entirely and fully create its own art from within itself, and, particularly, that the proletariat is capable of creating a new art by means of closed art guilds or circles, or by the Organization for Proletarian Culture, etc. Generally speaking, the artistic work of man is continuous. Each new rising class places itself on the shoulders of its preceding one. But this continuity is dialectic, that is, it finds itself by means of internal repulsions and breaks. New artistic needs or demands for new literary and artistic points of view are stimulated by economics, through the development of a new class, and minor stimuli are supplied by changes in the position of the class, under the influence of the growth of its wealth and cultural power. Artistic creation is always a complicated turning inside out of old forms, under the influence of new stimuli which originate outside of art. In this large sense of the word, art is a handmaiden. It is not a disembodied element feeding on itself, but a function of social man indissolubly tied to his life and environment. And how characteristic it is – if one were to reduce every social superstition to its absurdity – that Shklovsky has come to the idea of art's absolute independence from the social environment at a period of Russian history when art has revealed with such utter frankness its spiritual, environmental and material dependence upon definite social classes, subclasses and groups!

Materialism does not deny the significance of the element of form, either in logic, jurisprudence or art. Just as a system of jurisprudence can and must be judged by its internal logic and consistency, so art can and must be judged from the point of view of its achievements in form, because there can be no art without them. However, a juridical theory which attempted to establish the independence of law from social conditions would be defective at its very base. Its moving force lies in economics – in class contradictions. The law gives only a formal and an internally harmonized expression of these phenomena, not of their individual peculiarities, but of their general character, that is, of the elements that are repetitive and permanent in them. We can see now with a clarity which is rare in history how new law is made. It is not done by logical deduction, but by empirical measurement and by adjustment to the economic needs of the new ruling class. Literature, whose methods and processes have their roots far back in the most distant past and represent the accumulated experience of verbal craftsmanship, expresses the thoughts, feelings, moods, points of view and hopes of the new epoch and of its new class. One cannot jump beyond this. And there is no need to make the jump, at least, for those who are not serving an epoch already past nor a class which has already outlived itself.

The methods of formal analysis are necessary, but insufficient. You may count up the alliterations in popular proverbs, classify metaphors, count up the number of vowels and consonants in a wedding song. It will undoubtedly enrich our knowledge of folk art, in one way or another; but if you don't know the peasant system of sowing, and the life that is based on it, if you don't know the part the scythe plays, and if you have not mastered the meaning of the church calendar to the peasant, of the time when the peasant marries, or when the peasant women give birth, you will have only understood the outer shell of folk art but the kernel will not have been reached. The architectural scheme of the Cologne cathedral can be established by measuring the base and the height of its arches, by determining the three dimensions of its naves, the dimensions and the placement of the columns, etc. But without knowing what a medieval city was like, what a guild was, or what was the Catholic Church of the Middle Ages, the Cologne cathedral will never be understood. The effort to set art free from life, to declare it a craft self-sufficient unto itself, devitalizes and kills art. The very need of such an operation is an unmistakable symptom of intellectual decline.

The analogy with the theological arguments against Darwinism which was made above may appear to the reader external and anecdotal. That may be true, to some extent. But a much deeper connection exists. The Formalist theory inevitably reminds a Marxist who has done any reading at all of the familiar tunes of a very old philosophic melody. The jurists and the moralists (to recall at random the German Stammler, and our own subjectivist Mikhailovsky) tried to prove that morality and law could not be determined by economics, because economic life was unthinkable outside of juridical and ethical norms. True, the formalists of law and morals did not go so far as to assert the complete independence of law and ethics from economics. They recognized a certain complex mutual relationship of 'factors', and these 'factors', while influencing one another, retained the qualities of independent substances, coming no one knew whence. The assertion of complete independence of the aesthetic 'factor' from the influence of social conditions, as is made by Shklovsky, is an instance of specific hyperbole whose roots, by the way, lie in social conditions too; it is the megalomania of aesthetics turning our hard reality on its head. Apart from this peculiarity, the constructions of the Formalists have the same kind of defective methodology that every other kind of idealism has. To a materialist, religion, law, morals and art represent separate aspects of one and the same process of social development. Though they differentiate themselves from their industrial basis, become complex, strengthen and develop their special characteristics in detail, politics, religion, law, ethics and aesthetics remain, none the less, functions of social man and obey the laws of his social organization. The idealist, on the other hand, does not see a unified process of historic development which evolves the necessary organs and functions from within itself, but a crossing or combining and interacting of certain independent principles – the religious, political, juridical, aesthetic and ethical substances, which find their origin and explanation in themselves. The (dialectic) idealism of Hegel arranges these substances (which are the eternal categories) in some sequence by reducing them to a genetic unity. Regardless of the fact that this unity with Hegel is the absolute spirit, which divides itself in the process of its dialectic manifestation into various 'factors', Hegel's system, because of its dialectic character, not because of its idealism, gives an idea of historic reality which is just as good as the idea of a man's hand that a glove gives when turned inside out. But the Formalists (and their greatest genius was Kant) do not look at the dynamics of development, but at a cross-section of it, on the day and at the hour of their own philosophic revelation. At the crossing of the line they reveal the complexity and multiplicity of the object (not of the process, because they do not think of processes). This complexity they analyse and classify. They give names to the elements, which are at once transformed into essences, into sub-absolutes, without father or mother; to wit, religion, politics, morals, law, art. Here we no longer have a glove of history turned inside out, but the skin torn from the separate fingers, dried out to a degree of complete abstraction, and this hand of history turns out to be the product of the 'interaction' of the thumb, the index, the middle finger, and all the other 'factors'. The aesthetic 'factor' is the little finger, the smallest, but not the least beloved.

In biology, vitalism is a variation of the same fetish of presenting the separate aspects of the world-process, without understanding its inner relation. A creator is all that is lacking for a super-social, absolute morality or aesthetics, or for a super-physical absolute 'vital force'. The multiplicity of independent factors, 'factors' without beginning or end, is nothing but a masked polytheism. Just as Kantian idealism represents historically a translation of Christianity into the language of rationalistic philosophy, so all the varieties of idealistic formalization, either openly or secretly, lead to a God, as the Cause of all causes. In comparison with the oligarchy of a dozen sub-absolutes of the idealistic philosophy, a single personal Creator is already an element of order. Herein lies the deeper connection between the Formalist refutations of Marxism and the theological refutations of Darwinism.

The Formalist school represents an abortive idealism applied to the questions of art. The Formalists show a fast ripening religiousness. They are followers of St John. They believe that 'In the beginning was the Word.' But we believe that in the beginning was the deed. The word followed, as its phonetic shadow.

Franz Kafka or Thomas Mann? *

Franz Kafka is the classic example of the modern writer at the mercy of a blind and panic-stricken *angst*. His unique position he owes to the fact that he found a direct, uncomplex way of communicating this basic experience; he did so without having recourse to formalistic experimentation. Content is here the immediate determinant of aesthetic form – that is why Kafka belongs with the great realistic writers. Indeed, he is one of the greatest of all, if we consider how few writers have ever equalled his skill in the imaginative evocation of the concrete novelty of the world. Never was the quality of Kafka's achievement more striking or more needed than at the present day, when so many writers fall for slick experimentation. The impact of Kafka's work derives not only from his passionate sincerity – rare enough in our age – but also from the corresponding simplicity of the world he constructs. That is Kafka's most original achievement. Kierkegaard said, 'The greater a man's originality, the more he is at the mercy of *angst*.' Kafka, original in the Kierkegaardian sense, describes this *angst* and the fragmented world which – it is incorrectly assumed – is both its complement and its cause. His originality lies not in discovering any new means of expression but in the utterly convincing, and yet continually startling, presentation of this invented world, and of his characters' reaction to it. 'What shocks is not the monstrosity of it,' writes Theodor W. Adorno, 'but its matter-of-factness.'

The diabolical character of the world of modern capitalism, and man's impotence in the face of it, is the real subject-matter of Kafka's writing. His simplicity and sincerity are, of course, the product of complex and contradictory forces. Let us consider

* From *The Meaning of Contemporary Realism* (1963).

only one aspect. Kafka wrote at a time when capitalist society, the object of his *angst*, was still far from the high mark of its historical development. What he described and 'demonized' was not the truly demonic world of Fascism, but the world of the Habsburg Monarchy. *Angst*, haunting and indefinable, is perfectly reflected in this vague, ahistorical, timeless world, steeped in the atmosphere of Prague. Kafka profited from his historical position in two ways. On the one hand, his narrative detail gains from being rooted in the Austrian society of that period. On the other hand, the essential unreality of human existence, which it is his aim to convey, can be related to a corresponding sense of unreality and foreboding in the society he knew. The identification with the *condition humaine* is far more convincing than in later visions of a diabolical, *angst*-inspiring world, where so much has to be eliminated or obscured by formal experimentation to achieve the desired ahistorical, timeless image of the human condition. But this, though the reason for the astonishing impact and lasting power of Kafka's work, cannot disguise its basically allegorical character. The wonderfully suggestive descriptive detail points to a transcendent reality, to the anticipated reality – stylized into timelessness – of fully developed imperialism. Kafka's details are not, as in realism, the nodal points of individual or social life; they are cryptic symbols of an unfathomable transcendence. The stronger their evocative power, the deeper is the abyss, the more evident the allegorical gap between meaning and existence.

The counterpart to this fascinating, though ill-starred, development in modern bourgeois literature is the work of Thomas Mann. I have examined Thomas Mann's work extensively elsewhere, and shall be brief. It is only important for our purposes to work out the contrast with Kafka. Let us begin with the artistic presentation. The world of Thomas Mann is free from transcendental reference: place, time and detail are rooted firmly in a particular social and historical situation. Mann envisages the perspective of socialism without abandoning the position of a bourgeois, and without attempting to portray the newly emergent socialist societies or even the forces working towards their establishment (in the context of realism, Thomas Mann's mature attitude of acceptance and resignation, and Roger Martin du Gard's heroic failure, form an interesting opposition).

This apparently limited perspective is nevertheless of central importance in Thomas Mann's work : it is the main reason for the harmony of its proportions. Each section of a portrayed totality is placed in a concrete social context; the significance of each detail, its meaning for the evolution of society, is clearly defined. It is our world that Thomas Mann describes, the world in whose shaping we play a part, and which in turn shapes us. The deeper Thomas Mann probes into the complexity of present-day reality, the more clearly we come to understand our position in the complex evolution of mankind. Thus Thomas Mann, despite his loving attention to detail, never lapses into naturalism. For all his fascination with the dark regions of modern existence, Thomas Mann always shows up distortion for what it is, tracing its roots and its concrete origins in society.

In his study of Dostoyevsky, André Gide wrote, 'Beautiful feelings make bad art,' and 'without the devil's help there would be no art'. Some of Thomas Mann's writings are based on not dissimilar views; there are parallels in his early story *Tonio Kröger*. Yet, in the same story, Mann also gives us the opposing view. The problem treated is familiar in the modern world. Thomas Mann is concerned to investigate the demonic, the underworld of the human mind, within the context of present-day society. Early in his career he realized that the artist himself is one of the main mediators of this experience. It is therefore natural that he should have followed up this early insight with increasingly rigorous studies of the problem in its social context. The examination begun with *Tonio Kröger* ended with *Dr Faustus*. With Adrian Leverkühn, Mann's Faustus, the inquiry is concentrated on the present time, though it is a present seen in the perspective of history. The devil has to confess that, with Goethe, his assistance was strictly unnecessary, but that the social conditions of Leverkühn's time compelled the composer to seek guidance from the underworld. Yet Leverkühn's final monologue reveals the perspective of a new society, of socialism, under which the artist will be freed from his former enslavement. Indeed, the mere struggle for the social reformation of mankind may of itself suffice to break the power of the underworld.

Gide's attitude to the problem, as we saw from the above remarks, was 'naïve', uncritical. He surrendered to the supremacy of the underworld, greeted it even with a certain intellectual relish, and with the customary contempt for the trivial philistinism of bourgeois existence. Gide's notion of the *action gratuite* reflects the same view,- as does his doctrine of 'sincerity'. What in Mann is simply one legitimate theme among others – legitimate even where it is the main theme of a novel or story – becomes with Gide a doctrine governing all life and all art – and thus distorting both. This is the crossroads where critical realism not only parts ways with modernism, but is even forced into opposition to it.

Between these methods, between Franz Kafka and Thomas Mann, the contemporary bourgeois writer will have to choose. There is no necessity for a writer to break with his bourgeois pattern of life in making this choice between social sanity and morbidity, in choosing the great and progressive literary traditions of realism in preference to formalistic experimentation. (Of course, there are many writers who will choose socialism as a way of solving their personal dilemma. I only want to emphasize that this is not the only possible choice for the contemporary writer.) What counts is the personal decision. Chekhov's 'reasonable question' implies, above all, a choice of direction. And today that is determined by the question: acceptance or rejection of *angst*? Ought *angst* to be taken as an absolute, or ought it to be overcome? Should it be considered one reaction among others, or should it become the determinant of the *condition humaine*? These are not primarily, of course, literary questions; they relate to a man's behaviour and experience of life. The crucial question is whether a man escapes from the life of his time into a realm of abstraction – it is then that *angst* is engendered in human consciousness – or confronts modern life determined to fight its evils and support what is good in it. The first decision leads then to another: is man the helpless victim of transcendental and inexplicable forces, or is he a member of a human community in which he can play a part, however small, towards its modification or reform?

These problems could well be expanded and generalized; but it is not necessary to do so here. The implications of our basic question – acceptance of *angst* or rejection – are clear enough. We see here, ideologically and artistically, the root of our modern dilemma. However passionately, however sophistically, the historical origins of *angst* may be obscured, no work of art based on it can avoid – objectively speaking – guilt by association with Hitlerism and the preparations for atomic war. It is, indeed, of the nature of literature's social significance that it reflects the movements of its age even when it is – subjectively – aiming to express something very different. (This opposition between subjective intention and objective compulsion is at the root of the modernist dilemma: modernism is in revolt against the anti-aestheticism of capitalism, and yet in the process revolts against art itself.)

Earlier, I quoted Adorno's remark that modern music had lost the original authenticity of *angst*. This, and similar instances, being interpreted, could well be taken as an admission of defeat in the field of nuclear war preparations, an admission of loss of ground in the Cold War, as new perspectives for peace begin to open up. Modernism, based on nihilism, is losing that suggestive power which contrived to invest Nothingness with a false objectivity. The experience of Nothingness, though distorting reality when made use of in literature, did possess a certain subjective authenticity. This authenticity, however, has diminished with time. Thus, as the crisis of modernism deepens, critical realism grows in importance.

Let me repeat: these changes are primarily changes in human behaviour, in ideological attitude; only by this route can they affect literature. Moreover, I would like the reader to recall what I said earlier about the peculiar ideological pattern underlying the Peace Movement: how it allows great ideological divergencies, even contradictions, holding together different approaches by a certain community of opinion on human, social, and international problems. Chekhov's 'reasonable question', which we found to be the basis of all realistic literature, is the theoretical link between a community of opinion of this kind and the creative process itself.

It is evident that changes of this sort must be complex and contradictory. They may involve the gradual transformation of a writer's understanding of the social and historical reality of his time (Thomas Mann, for instance, during and after the First World War). A writer's earlier views will not necessarily be abandoned in their entirety, even if these views are really inseparable from the abandoned intellectual position (e.g. Thomas Mann's continued attachment to Schopenhauer and Nietzsche). One result, in the field of theory, is likely to be the partial break-up of the earlier ideology – as with Sartre, whose political views are often inconsistent with his unrevised existentialist premises. A writer faced with this dilemma may yet succeed in formulating his 'reasonable question' on the basis of his new position. The problems he leaves unsolved may appear in his work as truthful reflections of contradictions actually present in society. Sartre's work provides evidence of this.

Apparent inconsistencies in a writer's view of the world, reflected in his work, should never be treated dogmatically. The main thing – and it is no small thing – is whether the writer's view is able to include – or, better, demands – a dynamic, complex, analytical rendering of social relationships, or whether it leads to loss of perspective and historicity. We are confronted once again with an alternative – acceptance of *angst* or rejection – and with all the consequences flowing from that alternative. This dilemma is the key to the assessment of modern literature.

It is applicable, not least, in matters of style. Earlier, in talking of the historical and aesthetic significance of certain stylistic phenomena, I rejected any rigid distinction, on formal principles alone, between bourgeois realism and decadent anti-realism. In a period of transition, when the rejection of old beliefs and the formulation of new beliefs is a continuous process, this negative principle of judgement becomes more, rather than less, important. Crucial, for the critic, is the determination of the direction in which a writer is moving, not the detection of stylistic idiosyncrasies. This is not to say that style is unimportant. On the contrary, I maintain that the more closely we combine an examination of the ideology informing a writer's work with an examination of the specific form given to a specific content, the better our analysis will be. That is to say, the critic must establish by examination of the work whether a writer's view of the world is based on the acceptance or rejection of *angst*, whether it involves a flight from reality or a willingness to face up to it.

The more *angst* predominates, the greater will be the levelling effect. We have seen this in the case of abstract and concrete potentiality. But the loss of any concern for ethical complexity, for the problems of society, is part of the same process. The question of the 'authenticity' of human behaviour is no longer important. Particularly in modernist writing, the differing reactions of human beings come to seem insignificant in the face of 'metaphysical' *angst* (and of the increasing pressures of conformity). The fact that in the midst of this 'permanent revolution', this endless 'revaluation of all values', there were writers of major talent who clung to the standards of nineteenth-century realism is, therefore, of ethical as much as of artistic significance. These writers' attitudes sprang from the ethical conviction that though changes in society modify human nature, they do not abolish it. Once again, Roger Martin du Gard is the classic example. The conviction is evident, not only in his thinking about literature, but also in the values inherent in his work. We have only to contrast the tragic authenticity of his Jacques Thibault with the inauthenticity of his Fontanin, who embodies the Gidean ethic.

But Martin du Gard is by no means the only example. The best work of Eugene O'Neill, an experimentalist from his expressionist period onward, was done under the influence of nineteenth-century, Ibsenite drama. I am not implying that O'Neill, either philosophically or artistically, was an imitator of Ibsen. On the contrary, he does away with Ibsen's moralizing and his weakness for romantic symbolism. The tragi-comedy of Ibsen's stern imperatives, too, is foreign to O'Neill's drama. O'Neill's tragi-comedy has been through the school of Chekhov. The ethical-dramatic dialectic is no longer that between absolute imperatives and the impossibility of their realization. We are now concerned with the scope and possibilities of human action as such; O'Neill's subject is man himself, his subjectively tragic and yet objectively comic situation. Again, to say that O'Neill drew inspiration from Chekhov is not to accuse him of imitation. The America he portrays is, sociologically, that described by his contemporaries – though he often, to win dramatic distance, sets the scene in the America of the past. But he is interested not so much in the way human beings can be manipulated in the name of 'Freedom', as in whether, and how, the human substance can survive such a process. O'Neill wishes to know whether a man is in the last analysis responsible for his own actions or is the plaything of psychological and social forces over which he has no control. His American Electra acknowledges responsibility for her actions with tragic pride; the integrity of human personality is preserved, though at great cost. But such a situation is unusual in O'Neill. More often, the authentic and the inauthentic are inextricably interwoven in his characters – the accent falling more and more frequently on the latter. That is O'Neill's originality. Seeing the situation as he does, he is yet able to affirm, with is own brand of tragi-comic defiance, a basic integrity in human personality. For all the apparent gloom, this is the message of later dramas like *A Moon for the Misbegotten* or *A Touch of the Poet*. In other words, O'Neill's return to Ibsen and Chekhov is at the same time a protest against the dominance of modernism and a confession of faith in the future of humanity.

Stylistically, Elsa Moranti, the Italian novelist, might seem a far cry from O'Neill. Her technique is very much of the present day; little would seem to associate her with the literature of the nineteenth century. All the more striking, then, the philosophical and ethical affinities apparent in her treatment of motive and perspective. Life and its turmoils, in her work, are the threshing-floor where the authentic is winnowed from the inauthentic. Her best-known novel is entitled, significantly, *Lies and Magic*. The plot is intelligent, finely symbolic, excellently suited to the problems she examines. She describes in the opening chapters the inner revolt of a human being, caught in a net of magic and unreality, against these entangling forces. The '*recherche du temps perdu*' is here no more than a prelude, an introductory evocation of the past – but of the past as it really was, and as none of the characters in the story could have known it from personal experience. Thus, the true subject-matter of the story, the world of *temps retrouvé*, is not reduced to a mere *état d'âme*. The motives are derived from actual life; they are the passions, though informed by 'false consciousness', that are at the root of men's actions. The reader – as in the traditional epic – is granted an omniscience allowing him to see the totality of the world portrayed. The winnowing of the authentic from the inauthentic is not effected by the personal intervention of the author. It is the concrete contradictions embodied in her characters, their complex interrelations, that accomplish the process. The novel becomes, in fact, a grandiose parable of modern man's ethical condition. This parabolic quality might seem to yield a point of contact with modernism. But the resemblance does not go very deep; it is confined to the depiction of general background rather than to the portrayal of individuals. The social pressures on the individual are never abstractly conceived – the chief temptation of the parabolic form. The characters' rootedness in their milieu is rendered with remarkable skill. Purely individual and purely class characteristics, carefully distinguished, are yet fused in a unity rarely found outside classical realism. The parabolic quality of the whole is *'aufgehoben'*, in the Hegelian sense, in three ways: it is 'cancelled out', yet also preserved; and at the same time it is raised to a higher level – a level where life, and philosophical reflection upon it, form a dialectical unity.

Thomas Wolfe's novel *You Can't Go Home Again* deserves a brief mention here, since it illustrates the turning-point in his life so well. Wolfe has described how he began his career as a disciple of Joyce; but his substitution of the *monologue intérieur* for the formal rigours of plot has, in actual fact, a quite different character. It is never a mere stream of consciousness behind which objective reality disappears. The real subject-matter, even of the young Thomas Wolfe, is the reality of modern America; and the stream of consciousness is no more than a part of this objectively rendered whole. Wolfe's early style, still Joycean but already pointing beyond Joyce, must be seen in relation to his general philosophical stance. Wolfe was passionately involved in the life of his time; but his hates and enthusiasms were on a level of pure emotion. Joyce's technique enabled him to react to and record, emotionally and subjectively, the life around him. But he went beyond Joyce in that he was not the uninvolved spectator of his age. Rather, he was impelled by – admittedly largely unconscious – ethical and social motives either furiously to reject or furiously to affirm what he saw. In his last novel, this unawareness of his own motives has gone. The experience of the Depression, and later of Nazi Germany, revealed to him the makeup of the society of which he was a member. This new understanding enabled him to order and clarify his emotions. The result is the magnificent portrait – particularly in the first half of the book – of America on the eve of the 1929 disaster. But the second half of the book shows that the awareness was not yet complete. By giving his fictive hero certain features obviously taken from Sinclair Lewis, Wolfe attempts to set up a new ideal of what the writer should be. His hero achieves what the young Wolfe had longed for – fame. But fame, when found, is not enough to slake his ambition. Wolfe offers, then, a somewhat abstract solution – he argues that 'one can and should better the human lot', that there is a greater wisdom than the wisdom of Ecclesiastes. This enables him to give, for instance, splendidly realized descriptions of conditions in the Third Reich. But the second half of the novel is artistically chaotic and leans far too heavily, towards the end, on mere discussion. It must be said, nevertheless, that Thomas Wolfe's death robbed us of a realistic writer of the first promise.

In Brecht's development, too, traditional realism played an important role. I have no space here to examine Brecht's work at length. We must begin with Brecht's middle period, the period of his turning towards communism, of *The Measures Taken* and of his adaptation of Gorky's *Mother*. Brecht's political didacticism, his attempt to impose intellectual schemata on the spectator, turned his characters into mere spokesmen. He based his new aesthetic on a contempt for cheap theatrical emotionalism. The full blast of his hatred was directed towards the 'culinary' aspects of the contemporary bourgeois theatre. And he seized on the theory of *Einfühlung* as the source of much of the bad art of the time. Now there is no doubt that Brecht, despite his exaggerations, was right to reject this particular theory. But he made the then not uncommon mistake – implicit in Wilhelm Worringer's

389

original formulation of the theory – of assuming that *Einfühlung* was fundamental to traditional aesthetics. The boss's secretary may 'identify', through *Einfühlung*, with her opposite number on the screen; and the young man about town may identify with, say, Schnitzler's Anatol. But no one surely has ever, in this sense, 'identified' with Antigone or King Lear. The truth is, Brecht's dramatic theories were the product of an – at the time, quite justified – local polemic. Brecht's actual dramatic practice changed radically after the rise to power of Hitler, during his long years of exile. But he never subjected his theories to revision. I have no space to investigate the problem in detail. But two poems, written during that exile, may serve to indicate the change I have in mind:

> A wooden Japanese mask hangs on my wall,
> The mask of an angry demon, covered with gold.
> With fellow-feeling I see
> The swollen veins in the forehead, showing
> What a strenuous business it is to be angry.

Or these lines from the marvellous poem 'To Posterity':

> Yet we know too well,
> Hatred of evil
> Can distort the features,
> Rage at injustice
> Make the voice hoarse. Alas, we
> Who wished to make room for friendliness
> Could not ourselves be friendly.

We see here how ethical preoccupations, a concern for the inner life and motivation of his characters, began to loom larger in Brecht's mind. Not that his central political and social pre-occupations were displaced. On the contrary, the effect of this change was to give them greater depth, range and intensity. And even the greatest admirers of Brecht's dramaturgy must admit that many plays of this period – *The Rifles of Señora Carrar* or *The Life of Galileo* – evidence a partial return to despised Aristotelean aesthetics. Be that as it may, let us briefly turn our attention to those plays – *Mother Courage, The Caucasian Chalk Circle, The Good Woman of Setzuan* – which do not thus return to traditional norms. These plays are indeed *Lehrstücke*, products of epic theatre; the anti-Aristotelean intention, the calculated use of alienation-effects, is undeniable. But if we compare these plays with, say, *The Measures Taken*, we see that the over-simplified schema of that play has given way to a complex dialectic of good and evil. Problems of society have become problems of humanity, subsuming the inner conflicts and contradictions of the warring parties. Where Brecht's characters had once been spokesmen for political points of view, they are now multi-dimensional. They are living human beings, wrestling with conscience and with the world around them. Allegory has acquired flesh and blood; it has been transformed into a true dramatic typology. Alienation-effect ceases to be the instrument of an artificial, abstract didacticism; it makes possible literary achievement of the highest order. All great drama, after all, must find means to transcend the limited awareness of the characters presented on the stage. It must express the general philosophical theme, represented in concrete terms by the action, in adequate poetic form (this is the function of the chorus in Aeschylus and Sophocles, and of the monologue in *Hamlet, Othello*, and *Lear*). It is this aspect that predominates in the later Brecht, a direct consequence of his new concern for ethical complexity, of his search for a multi-dimensional typology. That Brecht clung to his earlier theories should not conceal from us this fundamental change. Even the scenic structure of Brecht's plays begins to approximate to the Shakespearean model. The break with the '*milieu*-theatre', with the 'atmospheric' ambience of the older stage, is really a break with naturalism. It is a return to a dramaturgy aiming both at a typology that displays the full range of human complexity and at the creation of living human beings grappling with the forces of their environment. The mature Brecht, by overcoming his earlier, one-sided theories, had evolved into the greatest realistic playwright of his age. And the most influential, too, for good and for bad. Indeed, Brecht's influence shows once again how misleading it is to argue from the theory to the work and not from the work, its structure and intellectual content, to the theory. For Brecht's theories lead both to the pretentious, empty experimentation of Ionesco and to topical, realist drama like

Dürrenmatt's *The Visit*. The confusion to which this gave rise – the result of a formalistic over-emphasis on one element abstracted from literature – is still remarkably widespread and influential. (That Brecht was a socialist writer, both in personal ideology and literary practice, in no way contradicts what I have said here. His influence has been, and is, chiefly effective in the struggle between critical realism and modernist anti-realism.)

The critic today must put aside his personal preferences and use all his tact, energy and discretion in evaluating those works of literature which fight against old-established prejudices and strive to open up new areas of experience. To take one example: it is true to say that naturalism represents – compared with true realism – a decline and an impoverishment. In existing conditions, however, a naturalistic novel like Norman Mailer's *The Naked and the Dead* marks a step forward from the trackless desert of abstractions towards a portrayal of the actual suffering of actual people during the Second World War. Arbitrary though much of the detail is, and retrograde though the author's subsequent artistic development has been, the merits of that achievement, tentative as it was, should not be overlooked. The same may be true even where at first glance there is little evidence of realism. A case in point is *Kimmerische Fahrt*, a novel by the German writer, Werner Warsinsky. Stylistically, this is a competent exercise in the Kafka manner, using techniques evolved by Joyce and Beckett. Formally, the subject would appear to be the *condition humaine* of modernist ideology: there are the same forces working towards man's degradation and ultimate destruction. But the real focus of the book is the hero's experience of the collapse of Nazism; his fate is representative of the fate of a whole generation. The mist and darkness occluding the *angst*-ridden mind of the hero, who is running away from himself and from all contact with the outside world, are the true subject-matter of the book, not a mere stylistic device (though the opposite would seem to be true, if the book is approached from a formal angle). Again, through this mist we catch sight, from time to time, of living human beings, realistically portrayed. As an account of an historical catastrophe the book is excellent. Not dissimilar is the use of dream sequences in Wolfgang Koeppen's

Treibhaus. Here, the dream-like atmosphere helps to establish a definite historical atmosphere, while implying a judgement on the dreamlike world of Bonn politics. In his *Tod in Rom* Koeppen goes further in the realism of his treatment of human situation and character. Many other examples, of course, could be found; but the scope of this study does not permit us to take further examples. I want only to point out that these works are the products of a period of transition, and should be investigated as such.

It is a difficult and complex task, yet it is perfectly possible, for a writer to change his attitude to himself, to his fellow human beings, and the world at large. The forces employed against him, admittedly, are enormously powerful. Nihilism and cynicism, despair and *angst,* suspicion and self-disgust are the spontaneous product of the capitalist society in which intellectuals have to live. Many factors, in education and elsewhere, are arrayed against him. Take, for example, the view that pessimism is aristocratic, a worthier philosophy for an intellectual *élite* than faith in human progress. Or the belief that the individual – precisely as a member of an *élite* – must be a helpless victim of historical forces. Or the idea that the rise of mass society is an unmitigated evil. The majority of the press, highbrow and lowbrow, tends to minister to prejudices of this kind (it is their role in the campaign for the continuation of the Cold War). It is as if it were unworthy of the intellectual to hold other than dogmatic modernist views on life, art, and philosophy. To support realism in art, to examine the possibilities of peaceful coexistence among nations, to strive for an impartial evaluation of communism (which does not involve allegiance to it), all this may make a writer an outcast in the eyes of his colleagues and in the eyes of those on whom he depends for a livelihood. Since a writer of Sartre's standing has had to endure attacks of this kind, how much more dangerous is the situation likely to be for younger, less prominent writers.

These, and much more, are hard facts. But we must not forget that strong counter-forces are at work, particularly today; and that they are growing in strength. The writer who considers his own basic interests, those of his nation and of mankind as a whole, and who decides to work against the forces prevailing in the capitalist world, is now no longer alone. The further his explorations take him, the firmer his choice will be, and the less isolated will he feel, for he will be identifying himself with those forces in the world of his time which will one day prevail.

The period during which Fascism rose to power, like the period of Fascist ascendancy and the subsequent Cold War period, were hardly favourable to the growth of critical realism. Nevertheless, excellent work was done, neither physical terror nor intellectual pressure succeeded in preventing it. There were always critical realist writers who opposed war – in both its cold and hot manifestations – and the destruction of art and culture. Not a few works of high artistic merit emerged from the struggle. Today, the imminent defeat of Cold War policies, the new perspective of peaceful coexistence among the nations, should allow wider scope for a critical and realistic bourgeois literature. The real dilemma of our age is not the opposition between capitalism and socialism, but the opposition between peace and war. The first duty of the bourgeois intellectual has become the rejection of an all-pervading fatalistic *angst*, implying a rescue operation for humanity rather than any breakthrough to socialism. Because it is these perspectives that confront him, the bourgeois writer today is in a better position to solve his own dilemma than he was in the past. It is the dilemma of the choice between an aesthetically appealing but decadent modernism and a fruitful critical realism. It is the choice between Franz Kafka and Thomas Mann.

Some Thoughts on our New Literature *

A talk given to the Chinese Literature Society of Yenching University on 22 May 1929.

For more than a year now I have spoken very seldom to young people, because since the revolution there has been very little scope for talking. You are either provocative or reactionary, neither of which does anyone any good. After my return to Peking this time, however, some old friends asked me to come here and say a few words and, not being able to refuse them, here I am. But owing to one thing and another, I never decided what to say – not even what subject to speak on.

I meant to fix on a subject in the bus on the way here, but the road is so bad that the bus kept bouncing a foot off the ground, making it impossible to concentrate. That is when it struck me that it is no use just adopting one thing from abroad. If you have buses, you need good roads too. Everything is bound to be in-fluenced by its surroundings, and this applies to literature as well – to what in China is called the new literature, or revolu-tionary literature.

However patriotic we are, we probably have to admit that our civilization is rather backward. Everything new has come to us from abroad, and most of us are quite bewildered by new powers. Peking has not yet been reduced to this, but in the International Settlement in Shanghai, for example, you have foreigners in the centre, surrounded by a cordon of interpreters, detectives, police, 'boys' and so on, who understand their languages and know the rules of foreign concessions. Outside this cordon are the common people.

When the common people come into contact with foreigners, they never know quite what is happening. If a foreigner says

* From *Selected Works of Lu Hsun*, III (Peking, 1959).

'Yes,' his interpreter says: 'He told me to box your ears.' If the foreigner says 'No,' this is translated as 'Have the fellow shot.' To avoid such meaningless trouble you need more knowledge, for then you can break through this cordon.

It is the same in the world of letters. We know too little, and have too few materials to help us to learn. Liang Shih-chiu has his Babbitt, Hsu Chih-mo has his Tagore, Hu Shih has his Dewey – oh yes, Hsu Chih-mo has Katherine Mansfield too, for he wept at her grave – and the Creation school has revolutionary literature, the literature now in vogue. But though a good deal of writing goes with this, there is not much studying done. Right up to today, there are still some subjects which are the private preserve of the few men who set the questions.

All literature is shaped by its surroundings and, though devotees of art like to claim that literature can sway the course of world affairs, the truth is that politics comes first, and art changes accordingly. If you fancy art can change your environment, you are talking like an idealist. Events are seldom what men of letters expect. That is why the so-called revolutionary writers before a great revolution are doomed. Only when the revolution is beginning to achieve results, and men have time to breathe freely again, will new revolutionary writers be produced. This is because when the old society is on the verge of collapse you will very often find writing which seems rather revolutionary, but is not actually true revolutionary literature. For example, a man may hate the old society, but all he has is hate – no vision of the future. He may clamour for social reforms, but if you ask what sort of society he wants, it is some unrealizable utopia. Or he may be tired of living, and long for some big change to stimulate his senses, just as someone gorged with food and wine eats hot pepper to whet his appetite. Then there are the old campaigners who have been spurned by the people, but who hang out a new signboard and rely on some new power to win a better status for themselves.

There have been cases in China of writers who look forward to revolution but fall silent once the revolution comes. The members of the South Club at the end of the Ching dynasty are an example. That literary coterie agitated for revolution, lamented the sufferings of the Hans, raged at the tyranny of the Manchus and longed for a return to the 'good old days'. But after the establishment of the Republic they lapsed into utter silence. I fancy this was because their dream had been for 'a restoration of ancient splendour' after the revolution – the high hats and broad belts of the old officials. As things turned out differently and they found the reality unpalatable, they felt no urge to write. Even clearer examples can be found in Russia. At the start of the October Revolution many revolutionary writers were overjoyed and welcomed the hurricane, eager to be tested by the storm. But later the poet Yesenin and the novelist Sopoly committed suicide, and recently they say the famous writer Ehrenburg is becoming rather reactionary. What is the reason for this? It is because what is sweeping down on them is not a hurricane, and what is testing them is not a storm, but a real, honest-to-goodness revolution. Their dreams have been shattered, so they cannot live on. This is not so good as the old belief that when you die your spirit goes to heaven and sits beside God eating cakes.[1] For they died before attaining their ideal.

Of course China, they say, has already had a revolution. This may be so in the realm of politics, but not in the realm of art. Some say 'the literature of the petty bourgeoisie is now raising its head'. As a matter of fact, there is no such literature; this literature has not even a head to raise. Judging by what I said earlier – little as the revolutionaries like it – there has been no change or renaissance in literature, and it reflects neither revolution nor progress.

As for the more radical revolutionary literature advocated by the Creation Society – the literature of the proletariat – that is simply empty talk. Wang Tu-ching's poem, which has been banned here, there and everywhere, was written in the International Settlement in Shanghai whence he looked out towards revolutionary Canton. But his

PONG, PONG, PONG!

in ever larger type merely shows the impression made on him by

1. A reference to Heine's poem 'Mir träumt: ich bin der liebe Gott' (I dreamt I was the Lord Himself) in *Die Heimkehr* (*The Journey Home*).

Shanghai film posters and advertisements for soya sauce. He is imitating Blok's *Twelve*, but without Blok's force and talent. Quite a number of people recommend Kuo Mo-jo's *Hand* as an excellent work. This tells how a revolutionary lost a hand after the revolution, but with that remaining to him could still hold his sweetheart's hand – a most convenient loss, surely! If you have to lose one of your limbs, the most expendable certainly is a hand. A leg would be inconvenient, a head even more so. And if all you expect to lose is one hand, you do not need so much courage for the fray. It seems to me, though, a revolutionary should be prepared to sacrifice a great deal more than this. The *Hand* is the old, old tale about the trials of a poor scholar who ends, as usual, by passing the palace examination and marrying a beautiful girl.

But actually this is one reflection of conditions in China to-day. The cover of a work of revolutionary literature recently published in Shanghai shows a trident, taken from the cover of *Symbols of Misery*,[2] with the hammer from the Soviet flag stuck on its middle prong. This juxtaposition means you can neither thrust with the trident nor strike with the hammer, and merely shows the artist's stupidity – it could well serve as a badge for all these writers.

Of course, it is possible to transfer from one class to another. But the best thing is to say frankly what your views are, so that people will know whether you are friend or foe. Don't try to conceal the fact that your head is filled with old dregs by pointing dramatically at your nose and claiming: 'I am the only true proletarian!' Folk are so hypersensitive today that the word 'Russia' almost makes them give up the ghost, and soon they will not even allow lips to be red. They are scared of all sorts of publications. And our revolutionary writers, unwilling to introduce more theories or books from abroad, just point dramatically at themselves, till in the end they give us something like the 'reprimands by imperial decree' of the late Ching dynasty – no one has the least idea what they are about.

I shall probably have to explain the expression 'reprimands by

2. A book of literary criticism by Haxon Kuriyagawa, translated by Lu Hsun from the Japanese.

imperial decree' to you. This belonged to the days of the empire when, if an official committed a mistake, he was ordered to kneel outside some gate or other while the emperor sent a eunuch to give him a dressing-down. If you greased the eunuch's palm, he would stop very soon. If not, he would curse your whole family from your earliest ancestors down to your descendants. This was supposed to be the emperor speaking, but who could go and ask the emperor if he really meant all that? Last year, according to a Japanese magazine, Cheng Fang-wu was elected by the peasants and workers of China to go and study drama in Germany. And we have no means of finding out if he really was elected that way or not.

That is why, as I always say, if we want to increase our understanding we must read more foreign books, to break through the cordon around us. This is not too hard for you. Though there are not many books in English on the new literature and not many English translations of it, the few that we have are fairly reliable. After reading more foreign theoretical works and literature, you will feel much clearer when you come to judge our new Chinese literature. Better still, you can introduce such works to China. It is no easier to translate than to turn out sloppy writing, but it makes a greater contribution to the development of our new literature, and is more useful to our people.

A Glance at Shanghai Literature*

A talk given to the Social Science Study Group on 2 August 1929

Shanghai literature began with the *Shun Pao*. This paper started sixty years ago, but I know nothing of those times. I can merely cast my mind back to thirty years ago, when the *Shun Pao* still used Chinese bamboo paper printed on one side only, and most of its contributors were 'talented scholars' from elsewhere.

The educated men of those days could be divided roughly into two categories: orthodox scholars and talented scholars. The orthodox scholars confined their reading to the Four Books and Five Classics, wrote *paku* essays, and were extremely correct. The talented scholars read novels like the *Dream of the Red Chamber* too, and wrote poems in different classical metres which were not required for the examinations. That is, they read the *Dream of the Red Chamber* openly, while whether or not the orthodox scholars read it in secret I have no means of knowing. Once there were foreign concessions in Shanghai – sometimes called 'western settlements' or 'barbarian settlements' – talented scholars started flocking here, because such men are broad-minded enough to go anywhere. Since orthodox scholars rather look down on things foreign and are set on winning rank and fame through the proper channels, they never rush about lightly. Confucius said, 'If the Way makes no progress, I shall get upon a raft and float out to sea.'[1] Talented scholars are rather partial to this viewpoint, which is why they think the way of orthodox scholars 'folly'.

These talented scholars were delicate, sensitive souls, enraged by a cock's crow and upset by moonlight. Once in Shanghai, they met prostitutes. When they went whoring they could surround themselves with ten or twenty girls, much as in the

* From *Selected Works of Lu Hsun*, III (Peking, 1959).
1. A quotation from *The Analects*.

Dream of the Red Chamber, till they fancied themselves the young hero of that novel. Since they were talented scholars, the prostitutes of course were beautiful girls – and so were born the books about scholars and beauties. The general thesis was that only scholars could sympathize with fallen beauties, and only beauties could appreciate ill-fated scholars; but after many, many trials they would marry happily or become immortals.

These men helped the *Shun Pao* to publish certain essays and articles of the Ming and Ching dynasties, formed literary groups, and wrote lantern riddles; and as they used anthologies of these as gifts, they had a wide circulation. They published long works too, like *The Scholars, Cheng Ho's Travels* and *Pleasant Stories*. These small volumes are still to be found on second-hand book-stalls, with the announcement on the title page: 'Published by the *Shun Pao* Press, Shanghai.'

These books about beauties and scholars remained in vogue for many years, till by degrees talented scholars began to change. They discovered that it was money alone, not 'a passion for talent', that made beauties turn prostitute. But how could a beauty covet a scholar's money? Then the talented scholars devised clever means to deal with the prostitutes, so that far from being cheated themselves they could take advantage of the girls; and stories describing their tactics were highly popular as textbooks for whoring. The hero of such books was no longer a scholar-cum-simpleton, but a brave gallant who got the better of drabs – a scholar-cum-hooligan.

Prior to this had appeared the *Tien-shih-chai Pictorial* edited by Wu Yu-ju, with pictures of men and immortals, domestic and foreign news. But since Wu was rather hazy about foreign affairs, he depicted a battleship as a cargo boat with cannon on the deck, and 'a duel' as two uniformed soldiers fighting with swords in a sitting-room till all the vases were broken. Still, his 'Bawd Beats a Strumpet' and 'Hooligan Assaults a Girl' were excellent drawings, doubtless because he had seen so many cases in real life. Even today in Shanghai, we can see many faces just like those he painted. This pictorial was extremely influential in its time, selling in every province and considered required reading for all who wished to understand 'current events' – the equivalent of our present-day 'new learning'. Some years ago it was reprinted under the title *Wu Yu-ju's Album*, and the extent of its influence was fantastic. We need not mention illustrations in novels; even textbook illustrations often have children with caps askew, slant eyes, fleshy jowls and the look of hooligans.

Among our new hooligan artists is Yeh Ling-feng. Mr Yeh has plagiarized the drawings of Aubrey Beardsley, who believed in 'art for art's sake' and owed much to the Ukiyoe school of painting in Japan. Though Ukiyoe was a popular art, most of the artists belonging to this school drew plump prostitutes and actors with slant-set, erotic eyes. But Beardsley's figures are thin because he belonged to the decadent school, and since most decadents are cadaverous, they dislike robust women who give them a sense of inferiority. Now that our Mr Yeh's new slant-eyed drawings are crossing with Wu Yu-ju's old slant-eyed drawings, they should be popular for quite a few years. Mr Yeh does not draw hooligans only, however. At one time he also drew proletarians, though his workmen were slant-eyed too and held out huge fists. I personally think proletarians should be drawn realistically, just as they are – there is no need to make their fists bigger than their heads.

Modern Chinese films are still much influenced by the scholar-cum-hooligan, and their heroes – supposed to be 'good characters' – are all slick types like the sleek young Shanghai fellows who are adepts in 'sowing wild oats', 'finding pickings' or 'getting girls into trouble'. These films give you the impression that to be a hero or good fellow you must be a hooligan.

But the novel of the scholar-cum-hooligan gradually died out. For one thing, I think, they harped too long on the same old theme – the prostitute wanted money but the scholar tricked her – and you could not write on that for ever. Another reason was that only natives of Shanghai or Chekiang could understand the Soochow dialect in which those books were written.

Then another novel of the scholar-and-beautiful-girl type appeared which was all the rage for a time. That was the translation of Rider Haggard's *Joan Haste*. Only the first half appeared, though. According to the translator, he bought it on a second-hand bookstall and found it excellent, but unfortunately could not get the second volume. Sure enough, this story touched the sensitive hearts of scholars and beauties, and was very widely read. Later on it even touched the heart of Mr Lin Chin-nan,[2] who translated the whole book, using the same title. But he was violently abused by the first translator for bringing it out in full, thereby detracting from Joan's worth and upsetting the readers. And only then did we learn that the reason for publishing only one half before was not because the second half was missing, but because in it Joan had an illegitimate child. In fact, they would not print a medium-sized novel like this in two volumes abroad. But this gives us a good idea of Chinese views on marriage at that time.

Next new scholar-and-beauty novels circulated, but the beauty was a girl of good family who shared the scholar's pleasures and would not leave him. Under the willows and blossoming trees they were like two butterflies or love birds; but because their parents were cruel or fate unkind, they sometimes came to an unhappy end instead of living happily ever after – and we must admit that this was a great advance. When not long ago the magazine *Innuendo* appeared, edited by Mr Tien-hsu-wo-sheng, who also manufactures tooth powder which can be used as face powder, that was the heyday of this 'scholar-and-beauty' writing. Later, though *Innuendo* was banned, its influence remained as strong as ever until *New Youth* grew powerful enough to attack it. Then the appearance of a new form of writing – translations of Ibsen's plays and Hu Shih's *Marriage*[3] – made an end of that school whose basic theme was marriage.

After that appeared the new talented men's Creation Society. They laid emphasis on individual genius, believed in art for art's sake and the value of the individual, worshipped original writing and detested translation – especially translation at second-hand. These men opposed the Shanghai Literary Research Society. Their very first announcement declared that some people – meaning this society – were 'monopolizing' the literary arena. In fact, the reverse was true. The Literary Research Society believed in art for life, encouraged translation as well as writing, and did

2. One of the earliest translators of western novels who lived during the early days of the Republic.

3. A play published in *New Youth* in March 1919.

what it could to introduce the literature of oppressed peoples. Because these belonged to small countries and no one in China understood their languages, they nearly all had to be translated at second-hand. Moreover because the society expressed its support for *New Youth*, there was old and new enmity, and it was attacked on three sides. First the Creation Society, which believed in art for art's sake, naturally ran down the officious Literary Research Society which believed in art for men's sake, considering it 'vulgar' as well as incompetent, and even writing long articles expressly to point out one mistake in translation. Secondly there were the gentlemen-scholars who studied in America, who thought art the prerogative of ladies and gentlemen. Apart from ladies and gentlemen they considered all other characters must be men of letters, scholars, artists, professors or débutantes – they must speak English – so as to show the dignity of the *élite*. At that time Mr Wu Mi[4] wrote an article saying he could not understand why some people liked to write only about the lower orders. The third side was the scholar-and-beauty school already mentioned. I do not know what means they used to get the publishers to dismiss the member of the Literary Research Society who edited *Story Monthly* and to bring out *Story World* to print their articles. This journal only stopped coming out last year.

On the face of it, the Creation Society seemed to have won this battle. Many of their writings appealed to the taste of those who used to style themselves scholars, and with help from the publishers their strength increased. Once this happened, big firms like the Commercial Press started publishing translations by its members – I refer to the works of Kuo Mo-jo and Chang Tzu-ping. After that, as far as I can remember, the Creation Society stopped writing articles on the translation mistakes they had discovered in Commercial Press publications. Here I seem to detect traces of the scholar-cum-hooligan. But 'new Shanghai' is no match for 'old Shanghai'. While chanting songs of triumph, members of the society suddenly realized that they were providing commodities for their publishers and that all their efforts, from the bosses' point of view, were no better than the blinking

4. A professor of western literature who held conservative views.

dummy which serves merely as an advertisement in an oculist's window. When they wanted to publish independently the publisher sued them, and after they won independence, though they said all their books would be re-edited and printed elsewhere, their old boss went on using the old types, printing, selling and slashing prices every year in honour of some anniversary or other.

Able neither to go on providing commodities nor living independently, naturally their only path was to Canton, 'the cradle of revolution' where the prospects seemed a little brighter. Hence the appearance in Canton of the expression 'revolutionary literature' – unaccompanied by any works – while in Shanghai not even this expression was used.

Only the year before last did this 'revolutionary literature' begin to flourish here, sponsored by some veterans of the Creation Society newly back from the 'cradle of revolution' and a few newcomers. It flourished naturally owing to the situation, because ordinary people and young folk wanted it. When the Northern Expedition set out from Canton, most young enthusiasts rushed into action, and there was no definite revolutionary movement in literature. But when the sudden change in the political situation and the setback to the revolution caused a clear differentiation between classes, and to 'purge the party' the Kuomintang killed so many Communists and revolutionaries, the young people who survived found themselves in oppressive surroundings again. Then revolutionary writers became extremely active in Shanghai. So the upsurge of revolutionary literature here looks different on the face of it from that in other countries, being due not to a high tide of revolution but to a setback. Some of these writers, it is true, were old literati who put down their batons to take to their old trades again. Some were youngsters who had to write for a living because they were squeezed out of real jobs. But as revolutionary literature had a genuine mass foundation, among the new recruits were some who were firm and clear-headed. As I see it, however, lack of planning caused many mistakes in the revolutionary literary movement. For instance, no detailed analysis of Chinese society was made, and methods suited only for use under Soviet political power were mechanically applied. Again, many of these writers, notably Mr Cheng Fang-wu, created the impression that revolution is a fearful thing and behaved in an utterly leftist, threatening manner, as if to show that once the revolution came all non-revolutionaries must die, making everyone afraid of revolution. In fact, revolution is not to make men die but live. This 'I'll give you a taste of the terrors of revolution' for the personal satisfaction of the teller also showed the bad influence of the scholar-cum-hooligan school.

Quick to kindle, quick to calm down, and even quick to grow decadent, men of letters can always find reasons and precedents from the classics to justify their shifts of allegiance. For instance, if they need help they quote Kropotkin's doctrine of mutual aid, while when they want to fight they use Darwin's theory of the survival of the fittest. All those from ancient times till now who hold no definite views and have no guiding principle for the changes they advocate, but make use of the arguments of different schools, deserve to be called hooligans. Take a Shanghai hooligan. If he sees a man and woman from the country walking together, he calls out: 'Hey! You're immoral – you've broken the law!' Here he uses Chinese law. If a peasant makes water by the roadside, he shouts: 'Hey! That's not allowed. You've broken the law, and deserve to be locked up!' Here he is using foreign law. But in the end the law can go by the board – if you grease his palm he will let the matter drop.

There is quite a difference in China between last year's revolutionaries and the ones of the year before. Of course this is due to the changed circumstances, yet some 'revolutionary writers' have the root of disease in themselves. 'Revolution' and 'literature' seem distinct and yet connected, like two boats close together. One boat is 'revolution', the other 'literature', and the writer stands with one foot on each. When conditions are fairly good, he puts more weight on the revolutionary boat, and is clearly a revolutionary; but when the revolution is being crushed, he shifts his weight to the boat of literature, and becomes a simple man of letters. So the men who were so radical two years ago in clamouring for a clean sweep of all non-revolutionary literature last year recalled how Lenin liked to read the works of

Goncharov, and decided non-revolutionary writing could be highly significant too. Even that out-and-out revolutionary writer Mr Yeh Ling-feng, who gave that out-and-out description of revolutionaries who used my *Call to Arms* as toilet paper, is now tagging along, Heaven knows why, behind the so-called writers of nationalist literature.

Mr Hsiang Pei-liang is a similar case. When the star of revolution was in the ascendant, he was very revolutionary. It was he who said young people should not merely clamour but show their teeth like wolves. This was not a bad idea, but we should be careful, because wolves are the ancestors of dogs, and once tamed by men they become dogs themselves. Today Mr Hsiang Pei-liang is all for human art, and opposes class art; he divides men into good and bad, and considers art as a weapon in the 'struggle between good and evil'. Dogs divide men into two kinds too: the good are the masters who feed them, while all poor people and beggars are bad in their eyes, to be either barked at or bitten. But this is not a bad idea either, because it shows they still have some wildness in their nature. If they were to turn into pug dogs, which work hard for their masters for all their air of detachment, they would be like those famous men who say they are not concerned with mundane affairs but believe in art for art's sake – all they are fit for is to adorn some university classroom.

Such petty-bourgeois intellectuals keep turning somersaults like this. Even when they become revolutionary writers and write revolutionary works, they are liable to distort the revolution. And since this does no damage to the cause, their shifts in allegiance need not upset us at all. When the revolutionary movement was going strong many petty-bourgeois writers suddenly came over to us, describing their *volte-face* as a mutation. But we knew that a mutation means that when all necessary conditions but one exist, the appearance of the last condition will lead A to turn into B. For water to freeze, for instance, the temperature must be zero and there must be some movement of air. Without the latter, water will not freeze even if the temperature drops to zero; but with it, it will suddenly turn into ice. Though such mutations look sudden, in reality they are not. And until all the necessary conditions exist, even if you claim to have changed, that will not

407

be true. This is why some of those petty-bourgeois revolutionary writers who professed to have changed overnight changed back again so quickly.

The establishment of the League of Left-Wing Writers in Shanghai last year was an important event. As the theories of Plekhanov, Lunacharsky and others had been introduced by then, they enabled us to study them and become firmer and stronger. But precisely because of this, we were oppressed and persecuted in a way scarcely ever known in the world. And this being so, those so-called revolutionary writers who had thought left-wing writing was going to be all the fashion and authors would be offered bread and buttter by the workers immediately changed again – some recanted, while others turned to attack the League of Left-Wing Writers to show how much wiser they were this year. Though the League did not take the initiative in this, it still served as a sort of house-cleaning; for those authors, whether they change back or not, are incapable of good writing.

But can the left-wing writers who remain write good proletarian literature? I think it is very hard. For all our left-wing writers today are still educated people – intellectuals – hence it is difficult for them to write the truth about the revolution. H. Kuriyakawa of Japan once posed this question: 'Must an author write solely about his own experience?' His answer was: 'No, because he can study other people's experience. To describe a thief he need not steal himself; to describe illicit love he need not have an affair.' But to my mind, an author can understand all these things, because, living in the old society, he is acquainted with the things and people in it. He cannot do this, though, in connection with the working class and characters with which he has had no contact, or he will paint a wrong picture. So revolutionary writers must at least share in the life of the revolution or keep their fingers closely on its pulse. (The Left-Wing League's recent slogan to 'Proletarianize the writers!' shows a very correct understanding of this.)

In a society like China today, the best we can hope for is the appearance of works showing the revolt of the petty-bourgeoisie against their own class, or works of exposure. For a writer who has grown up in this dying class has a deep understanding of and hatred for it, and so he can deal a most powerful, mortal blow. Of course some seemingly revolutionary writers do not really desire the overthrow of their class or of the bourgeoisie, but are angry or disappointed because they cannot carry out reforms to maintain their position any longer. From the working-class point of view, this is simply 'brothers at loggerheads' fighting inside the enemy's camp. These books are like bubbles on the revolutionary tide. I see no need to call works like this proletarian literature, nor need such authors – with an eye to future fame – style themselves proletarian writers.

Even those writers who merely attack the old society may do harm to the revolution unless they see abuses clearly and understand the root of the trouble. The pity is that so many of our present authors – including revolutionary writers and critics – are incapable of this, or dare not look society in the face to find out its real nature, the enemy's nature in particular. Let me give an example at random. An article on modern Chinese literature in the old *Lenin Youth* said that Chinese writers could be divided into three camps. First it described the Creation Society at great length as the literary group of the proletariat; then it dealt briefly with the *Tatler* group representing the petty bourgeoisie; and thirdly it dealt even more briefly – in less than one page – with the Cresent Moon Society representing the bourgeoisie. Apparently that young critic had the least to say about those he hated most. In other words he had not studied them.

Of course it is less comfortable, amusing and profitable to read books by our opponents than by our friends; but to my mind a fighter who wants to understand the revolution and the enemy should make the closest analysis of the foe confronting him. The same applies to literature. Not only must we know the facts about revolution; we need a thorough knowledge of the enemy and all aspects of the situation today before we can foresee the future of the revolution. The sole hope of development for our literature lies in understanding the old and seeing the new, in comprehending the past and deducing the future. I believe it is possible for writers in present-day conditions to do this, if they will make the effort.

Today, as I mentioned earlier, literature and art are being

oppressed and persecuted as seldom before, and a general dearth is the result. Literature voicing any protest or attacking old abuses is being suppressed just as often as revolutionary work or work criticizing present conditions. This shows that so far the revolution of the ruling class has been nothing more than a tussle for an old chair. When they try to knock it over the chair looks odious, but once in their hands it turns into a treasure, and they realize how much they have in common with the old. Twenty years ago everyone called the first emperor of Ming a national revolutionary, when in fact this was not true. As soon as he ascended the throne he addressed the Mongol court as 'the great Yuan court' and killed more Chinese than ever the Mongols had. When a slave becomes a master, he insists on being addressed as 'sir' and generally gives himself greater, more ridiculous airs than his former master. It is the same with some Shanghai workers who have made a little money and started a small factory – they treat their workers worse than anyone else.

In an old collection of anecdotes – I forget its title – I read that during the Ming dynasty a military officer called in a story-teller who told the tale of Tan Tao-chi, a general of the Tsin dynasty. At the end the officer ordered the story-teller to be beaten, and when questioned said: 'If he tells me about Tan Tao-chi, he's bound to go and tell Tan Tao-chi about me.' Our rulers today are as neurotic as that officer – afraid of everything. So they have introduced improved hooligans into the publishing world, who cannot be recognized as hooligans yet use the most vicious tactics: advertisements, libel and blackmail. Some men of letters have actually put themselves under the protection of hooligans for profit or safety's sake. So revolutionary writers should be on their guard not only against open enemies but also against the turn-coat spies on their own side. This is much more difficult than the simple battle of books, and hence its effect on art and literature.

Though piles of so-called literary magazines are still published in Shanghai, they actually have no content. To steer clear of trouble, those printed by publishers out for a profit choose the most innocuous articles they can on such subjects as 'Revolution is necessary – but it must not be too radical.' The unique thing about them is that you may read them from beginning to end, but will find nothing in them. As for the government-owned magazines and those published to please the authorities, the contributors are a mixed lot whose one aim is to make money. They themselves think nothing of their writing and do not believe their own arguments in such articles as 'English Literature of the Victorian Age' or 'Why Sinclair Lewis Received the Nobel Prize'. That is why I say all literary magazines in Shanghai have no content. Revolutionary writing is being suppressed, and the magazines sponsored by those doing the suppressing contain no literature either. Do the oppressors really have no literature then? They have, but not here. It is contained in telegrams, decrees, news items, nationalist 'literature', court sentences and the like. A few days ago, for instance, the *Shun Pao* carried a story of a woman who accused her husband of buggering her and beating her black and blue. The court replied that there was no law forbidding a husband to bugger his wife, and although she was bruised from her beating that did not count as a physical injury, so her charge could not be accepted. Now the man is suing his wife for making a 'false charge'. I know nothing of the law, but I have studied a little physiology. When the skin is black and blue, though the lungs, liver and kidney are not necessarily impaired, physical injury is done to the place bruised. This is common enough in China today – nothing out of the ordinary – yet I think this gives us a better picture of society than the average novel or long poem.

In addition to the foregoing, I should have analysed what passes by the name of nationalist literature and the adventure stories which have been popular so long. But as there is no time left, I must wait for another occasion. This is all I shall say today.

Theatre for Pleasure or Theatre for Instruction*

A few years back, anybody talking about the modern theatre meant the theatre in Moscow, New York and Berlin. He might have thrown in a mention of one of Jouvet's productions in Paris or Cochran's in London, or *The Dybbuk* as given by the Habima (which is to all intents and purposes part of the Russian theatre, since Vakhtangov was its director). But broadly speaking there were only three capitals so far as modern theatre was concerned.

Russian, American and German theatres differed widely from one another, but were alike in being modern, that is to say in introducing technical and artistic innovations. In a sense they even achieved a certain stylistic resemblance, probably because technology is international (not just that part which is directly applied to the stage but also that which influences it, the film for instance), and because large progressive cities in large industrial countries are involved. Among the older capitalist countries it is the Berlin theatre that seemed of late to be in the lead. For a period all that is common to the modern theatre received its strongest and (so far) maturest expression there.

The Berlin theatre's last phase was the so-called epic theatre, and it showed the modern theatre's trend of development in its purest form. Whatever was labelled '*Zeitstück*' or '*Piscatorbühne*' or '*Lehrstück*' belongs to the epic theatre.

The Epic Theatre

Many people believe that the term 'epic theatre' is self-contradictory, as the epic and dramatic ways of narrating a story are held,

* This and the following two texts are from *Brecht on Theatre*, ed. John Willett (1964).

following Aristotle, to be basically distinct. The difference between the two forms was never thought simply to lie in the fact that the one is performed by living beings while the other operates via the written word; epic works such as those of Homer and the medieval singers were at the same time theatrical performances, while dramas like Goethe's *Faust* and Byron's *Manfred* are agreed to have been more effective as books. Thus even by Aristotle's definition the difference between the dramatic and epic forms was attributed to their different methods of construction, whose laws were dealt with by two different branches of aesthetics. The method of construction depended on the different way of presenting the work to the public, sometimes via the stage, sometimes through a book; and independently of that there was the 'dramatic element' in epic works and the 'epic element' in dramatic. The bourgeois novel in the last century developed much that was 'dramatic', by which was meant the strong centralization of the story, a momentum that drew the separate parts into a common relationship. A particular passion of utterance, a certain emphasis on the clash of forces are hallmarks of the 'dramatic'. The epic writer Döblin provided an excellent criterion when he said that with an epic work, as opposed to a dramatic, one can as it were take a pair of scissors and cut it into individual pieces, which remain fully capable of life.

This is no place to explain how the opposition of epic and dramatic lost its rigidity after having long been held to be irreconcilable. Let us just point out that the technical advances alone were enough to permit the stage to incorporate an element of narrative in its dramatic productions. The possibility of projections, the greater adaptability of the stage due to mechanization, the film, all completed the theatre's equipment, and did so at a point where the most important transactions between people could no longer be shown simply by personifying the motive forces or subjecting the characters to invisible metaphysical powers.

To make these transactions intelligible the environment in which the people lived had to be brought to bear in a big and 'significant' way.

This environment had of course been shown in the existing drama, but only as seen from the central figure's point of view, and not as an independent element. It was defined by the hero's reactions to it. It was seen as a storm can be seen when one sees the ships on a sheet of water unfolding their sails, and the sails filling out. In the epic theatre it was to appear standing on its own.

The stage began to tell a story. The narrator was no longer missing, along with the fourth wall. Not only did the background adopt an attitude to the events on the stage – by big screens recalling other simultaneous events elsewhere, by projecting documents which confirmed or contradicted what the characters said, by concrete and intelligible figures to accompany abstract conversations, by figures and sentences to support mimed transactions whose sense was unclear – but the actors too refrained from going over wholly into their role, remaining detached from the character they were playing and clearly inviting criticism of him.

The spectator was no longer in any way allowed to submit to an experience uncritically (and without practical consequences) by means of simple empathy with the characters in a play. The production took the subject-matter and the incidents shown and put them through a process of alienation: the alienation that is necessary to all understanding. When something seems 'the most obvious thing in the world' it means that any attempt to understand the world has been given up.

What is 'natural' must have the force of what is startling. This is the only way to expose the laws of cause and effect. People's activity must simultaneously be so and be capable of being different.

It was all a great change.

The dramatic theatre's spectator says: Yes, I have felt that too – Just like me – It's only natural – It'll never change – The sufferings of this man appal me, because they are inescapable – That's great art; it all seems the most obvious thing in the world – I weep when they weep, I laugh when they laugh.

The epic theatre's spectator says: I'd never have thought it – That's not the way – That's extraordinary, hardly believable –

It's got to stop – The sufferings of this man appal me, because they are unnecessary – That's great art : nothing obvious in it – I laugh when they weep, I weep when they laugh.

The Instructive Theatre

The stage began to be instructive.

Oil, inflation, war, social struggles, the family, religion, wheat, the meat market, all became subjects for theatrical representation. Choruses enlightened the spectator about facts unknown to him. Films showed a montage of events from all over the world. Projections added statistical material. And as the 'background' came to the front of the stage so people's activity was subjected to criticism. Right and wrong courses of action were shown. People were shown who knew what they were doing, and others who did not. The theatre became an affair for philosophers, but only for such philosophers as wished not just to explain the world but also to change it. So we had philosophy, and we had instruction. And where was the amusement in all that? Were they sending us back to school, teaching us to read and write? Were we supposed to pass exams, work for diplomas?

Generally there is felt to be a very sharp distinction between learning and amusing oneself. The first may be useful, but only the second is pleasant. So we have to defend the epic theatre against the suspicion that it is a highly disagreeable, humourless, indeed strenuous affair.

Well : all that can be said is that the contrast between learning and amusing oneself is not laid down by divine rule; it is not one that has always been and must continue to be.

Undoubtedly there is much that is tedious about the kind of learning familiar to us from school, from our professional training, etc. But it must be remembered under what conditions and to what end that takes place.

It is really a commercial transaction. Knowledge is just a commodity. It is acquired in order to be resold. All those who have grown out of going to school have to do their learning virtually in secret, for anyone who admits that he still has something to learn devalues himself as a man whose knowledge is inadequate. Moreover the usefulness of learning is very much limited by factors outside the learner's control. There is unemployment, for instance, against which no knowledge can protect one. There is the division of labour, which makes generalized knowledge unnecessary and impossible. Learning is often among the concerns of those whom no amount of concern will get any forwarder. There is not much knowledge that leads to power, but plenty of knowledge to which only power can lead.

Learning has a very different function for different social strata. There are strata who cannot imagine any improvement in conditions : they find the conditions good enough for them. Whatever happens to oil they will benefit from it. And : they feel the years beginning to tell. There can't be all that many years more. What is the point of learning a lot now? They have said their final word : a grunt. But there are also strata 'waiting their turn' who are discontented with conditions, have a vast interest in the practical side of learning, want at all costs to find out where they stand, and know that they are lost without learning; these are the best and keenest learners. Similar differences apply to countries and peoples. Thus the pleasure of learning depends on all sorts of things; but none the less there is such a thing as pleasurable learning, cheerful and militant learning.

If there were not such amusements to be had from learning, the theatre's whole structure would unfit it for teaching.

Theatre remains theatre even when it is instructive theatre, and in so far as it is good theatre it will amuse.

Theatre and Knowledge

But what has knowledge got to do with art? We know that knowledge can be amusing, but not everything that is amusing belongs in the theatre.

I have often been told, when pointing out the invaluable services that modern knowledge and science, if properly applied, can perform for art and specially for the theatre, that art and knowledge are two estimable but wholly distinct fields of human activity. This is a fearful truism, of course, and it is well to agree quickly that, like most truisms, it is perfectly true. Art and science work in quite different ways: agreed. But, bad as it may sound, I have to admit that I cannot get along as an artist without the use of one or two sciences. This may well arouse serious doubts as to my artistic capacities. People are used to seeing poets as unique and slightly unnatural beings who reveal with a truly godlike assurance things that other people can only recognize after much sweat and toil. It is naturally distasteful to have to admit that one does not belong to this select band. All the same, it must be admitted. It must at the same time be made clear that the scientific occupations just confessed to are not pardonable side interests, pursued on days off after a good week's work. We all know how Goethe was interested in natural history, Schiller in history: as a kind of hobby, it is charitable to assume. I have no wish promptly to accuse these two of having needed these sciences for their poetic activity; I am not trying to shelter behind them; but I must say that I do need the sciences. I have to admit, however, that I look askance at all sorts of people who I know do not operate on the level of scientific understanding: that is to say, who sing as the birds sing, or as people imagine the birds to sing. I don't mean by that that I would reject a charming poem about the taste of fried fish or the delights of a boating party just because the writer had not studied gastronomy or navigation. But in my view the great and complicated things that go on in the world cannot be adequately recognized by people who do not use every possible aid to understanding.

Let us suppose that great passions or great events have to be shown which influence the fate of nations. The lust for power is nowadays held to be such a passion. Given that a poet 'feels' this lust and wants to have someone strive for power, how is he to show the exceedingly complicated machinery within which the struggle for power nowadays takes place? If his hero is a politician, how do politics work? If he is a business man, how does business work? And yet there are writers who find business and politics nothing like so passionately interesting as the individual's lust for power. How are they to acquire the necessary knowledge? They are scarcely likely to learn enough by going round and keeping their eyes open, though even then it is more than they would get by just rolling their eyes in an exalted frenzy. The foundation of a paper like the *Völkischer Beobachter* or a business like Standard Oil is a pretty complicated affair, and such things cannot be conveyed just like that. One important field for the playwright is psychology. It is taken for granted that a poet, if not an ordinary man, must be able without further instruction to discover the motives that lead a man to commit murder; he must be able to give a picture of a murderer's mental state 'from within himself'. It is taken for granted that one only has to look inside oneself in such a case; and then there's always one's imagination ... There are various reasons why I can no longer surrender to this agreeable hope of getting a result quite so simply. I can no longer find in myself all those motives which the press or scientific reports show to have been observed in people. Like the average judge when pronouncing sentence, I cannot without further ado conjure up an adequate picture of a murderer's mental state. Modern psychology, from psychoanalysis to behaviourism, acquaints me with facts that lead me to judge the case quite differently, especially if I bear in mind the findings of sociology and do not overlook economics and history. You will say: but that's getting complicated. I have to answer that it *is* complicated. Even if you let yourself be convinced, and agree with me that a large slice of literature is exceedingly primitive, you may still ask with profound concern: won't an evening in such a theatre be a most alarming affair? The answer to that is: no.

Whatever knowledge is embodied in a piece of poetic writing has to be wholly transmuted into poetry. Its utilization fulfils the very pleasure that the poetic element provokes. If it does not at the same time fulfil that which is fulfilled by the scientific element, none the less in an age of great discoveries and inventions one must have a certain inclination to penetrate deeper into things – a desire to make the world controllable – if one is to be sure of enjoying its poetry.

Is the Epic Theatre Some Kind of 'Moral Institution'?

According to Friedrich Schiller the theatre is supposed to be a moral institution. In making this demand it hardly occurred to

Schiller that by moralizing from the stage he might drive the audience out of the theatre. Audiences had no objection to moralizing in his day. It was only later that Friedrich Nietzsche attacked him for blowing a moral trumpet. To Nietzsche any concern with morality was a depressing affair; to Schiller it seemed thoroughly enjoyable. He knew of nothing that could give greater amusement and satisfaction than the propagation of ideas. The bourgeoisie was setting about forming the ideas of the nation.

Putting one's house in order, patting oneself on the back, submitting one's account, is something highly agreeable. But describing the collapse of one's house, having pains in the back, paying one's account, is indeed a depressing affair, and that was how Friedrich Nietzsche saw things a century later. He was poorly disposed towards morality, and thus towards the previous Friedrich too.

The epic theatre was likewise often objected to as moralizing too much. Yet in the epic theatre moral arguments only took second place. Its aim was less to moralize than to observe. That is to say it observed, and then the thick end of the wedge followed: the story's moral. Of course we cannot pretend that we started our observations out of a pure passion for observing and without any more practical motive, only to be completely staggered by their results. Undoubtedly there were some painful discrepancies in our environment, circumstances that were barely tolerable, and this not merely on account of moral considerations. It is not only moral considerations that make hunger, cold and oppression hard to bear. Similarly the object of our inquiries was not just to arouse moral objections to such circumstances (even though they could easily be felt – though not by all the audience alike; such objections were seldom for instance felt by those who profited by the circumstances in question) but to discover means for their elimination. We were not in fact speaking in the name of morality but in that of the victims. These truly are two distinct matters, for the victims are often told that they ought to be contented with their lot, for moral reasons. Moralists of this sort see man as existing for morality, not morality for man. At least it should be possible to gather from the above to what degree and in what sense the epic theatre is a moral institution.

Can Epic Theatre be Played Anywhere?

Stylistically speaking, there is nothing all that new about the epic theatre. Its expository character and its emphasis on virtuosity bring it close to the old Asiatic theatre. Didactic tendencies are to be found in the medieval mystery plays and the classical Spanish theatre, and also in the theatre of the Jesuits.

These theatrical forms correspond to particular trends of their time, and vanished with them. Similarly the modern epic theatre is linked with certain trends. It cannot by any means be practised universally. Most of the great nations today are not disposed to use the theatre for ventilating their problems. London, Paris, Tokyo and Rome maintain their theatres for quite different purposes. Up to now favourable circumstances for an epic and didactic theatre have only been found in a few places and for a short period of time. In Berlin Fascism put a very definite stop to the development of such a theatre.

It demands not only a certain technological level but a powerful movement in society which is interested to see vital questions freely aired with a view to their solution, and can defend this interest against every contrary trend.

The epic theatre is the broadest and most far-reaching attempt at large-scale modern theatre, and it has all those immense difficulties to overcome that always confront the vital forces in the sphere of politics, philosophy, science and art.

The Popular and the Realistic

When considering what slogans to set up for German literature today [1938] one must remember that anything with a claim to be considered as literature is printed exclusively abroad, and with few exceptions can only be read there. This gives a peculiar twist to the slogan of *Volkstümlichkeit* [or *Popularity*] *in literature*.

The writer is supposed to write for a people without living among it. When one comes to look closer, however, the gap between the writer and the people has not grown so wide as might be thought. All the same, it would be wrong, i.e. unrealistic, to see this growth as purely 'external'. Certainly a special effort is needed today in order to write in a popular way. But at the same time it has become easier : easier and more urgent. The people has clearly separated from its top layer; its oppressors and exploiters have parted company with it and become involved in a bloody war against it which can no longer be overlooked. It has become easier to take sides. Open warfare has, as it were, broken out among the 'audience'.

Nor can the demand for a realist way of writing any longer be so easily overlooked. It has become more or less self-evident. The ruling strata are using lies more openly than before, and the lies are bigger. Telling the truth seems increasingly urgent. The sufferings are greater and the number of sufferers has grown. Compared with the vast sufferings of the masses it seems trivial and even despicable to worry about petty difficulties and the difficulties of petty groups.

There is only one ally against the growth of barbarism : the people on whom it imposes these sufferings. Only the people offer any prospects. Thus it is natural to turn to them, and more necessary than ever to speak their language.

The words *Popularity* and *Realism* therefore are natural companions. It is in the interest of the people, the broad working masses, that literature should give them truthful representations of life; and truthful representations of life are in fact only of use to the broad working masses, the people, so that they have to be suggestive and intelligible to them, i.e. popular. None the less these conceptions need a thorough clean-up before being thrown into sentences where they will get smelted and put to use. It would be a mistake to treat them as fully explained, unsullied, unambiguous and without a past. ('We all know what's meant by that, no need for hair-splitting.') The German word for 'popular', *Volkstümlich*, is itself none too popular. It is unrealistic to imagine that it is. A whole series of words ending in *tum* need handling with care. One has only to think of *Brauchtum, Königstum, Heiligtum*, and it is well known that *Volkstum* too has a quite specific ceremonious, sacramental and dubious ring which we cannot by any means overlook. We cannot overlook it, because we definitely need the conception of popularity or *Volkstümlichkeit*.

It is part of that supposedly poetic way of wording, by which the '*Volk*' – more folk than people – is presented as particularly superstitious, or rather as an object of superstition. In this the folk or people appears with its immutable characteristics, its time-honoured traditions, forms of art, customs and habits, its religiosity, its hereditary enemies, its unconquerable strength and all the rest. A peculiar unity is conjured up of tormentor and tormented, exploiter and exploited, liar and victim; nor is it by any means a simple matter of the many, 'little' working people as against those on top.

The history of all the falsifications that have been operated with this conception of *Volkstum* is a long and complex story which is part of the history of the class war. We shall not embark on it but shall simply keep in mind the fact of such forgery whenever we speak of our need for popular art, meaning art for the broad masses of the people, for the many oppressed by the few, 'the people proper', the mass of producers that has so long been the object of politics and now has to become its subject. We shall remind ourselves that powerful institutions have long prevented this 'folk' from developing fully, that it has been artificially or forcibly tied down by conventions, and that the conception *Volkstümlich* has been stamped as a static one, without background or development. With this version of the conception we shall have no dealings, or rather we shall have to fight it. Our conception of 'popular' refers to the people who are not only fully involved in the process of development but are actually taking it over, forcing it, deciding it. We have in mind a people that is making history and altering the world and itself. We have in mind a fighting people and also a fighting conception of 'popularity'.

'Popular' means intelligible to the broad masses, taking over their own forms of expression and enriching them/adopting and consolidating their standpoint/representing the most progressive section of the people in such a way that it can take over the leadership: thus intelligible to other sections too/linking with tradition and carrying it further/handing on the achievements of the section now leading to the section of the people that is struggling for the lead.

We now come to the concept of 'Realism'. It is an old concept which has been much used by many men and for many purposes, and before it can be applied we must spring-clean it too. This is necessary because when the people takes over its inheritance there has to be a process of expropriation. Literary works cannot be taken over like factories, or literary forms of expression like industrial methods. Realist writing, of which history offers many widely varying examples, is likewise conditioned by the question of how, when and for what class it is made use of: conditioned down to the last small detail. As we have in mind a fighting people that is changing the real world we must not cling to 'well-tried' rules for telling a story, worthy models set up by literary history, eternal aesthetic laws. We must not abstract the one and only realism from certain given works, but shall make a lively use of all means, old and new, tried and untried, deriving from art and deriving from other sources, in order to put living reality in the hands of living people in such a way that it can be mastered. We shall take care not to ascribe realism to a particular historical form of novel belonging to a particular period, Balzac's or Tolstoy's, for instance, so as to set up purely formal and literary criteria of realism. We shall not restrict ourselves to speaking of realism in cases where one can (e.g.) smell, look, feel whatever is depicted, where 'atmosphere' is created and stories develop in such a way that the characters are psychologically stripped down. Our conception of *realism* needs to be broad and political, free from aesthetic restrictions and independent of convention. *Realist*[1] means: laying bare society's causal network/ showing up the dominant viewpoint as the viewpoint of the dominators/writing from the standpoint of the class which has prepared the broadest solutions for the most pressing problems afflicting human society/emphasizing the dynamics of development/concrete and so as to encourage abstraction.

It is a tall order, and it can be made taller. And we shall let the artist apply all his imagination, all his originality, his sense of humour and power of invention to its fulfilment. We will not stick to unduly detailed literary models or force the artist to follow over-precise rules for telling a story.

We shall establish that so-called sensuous writing (in which everything can be smelt, tasted, felt) is not to be identified automatically with realist writing, for we shall see that there are sensuously written works which are not realist, and realist works which are not sensuously written. We shall have to go carefully into the question whether the story is best developed by aiming at an eventual psychological stripping-down of the characters. Our readers may quite well feel that they have not been given the key to what is happening if they are simply induced by a combination of arts to take part in the inner emotions of our books' heroes. By taking over the forms of Balzac and Tolstoy without a thorough inspection we might perhaps exhaust our readers, the people, just as these writers often do. Realism is not a pure question of form. Copying the methods of these realists, we should cease to be realists ourselves.

For time flows on, and if it did not it would be a poor look-out for those who have no golden tables to sit at. Methods wear out, stimuli fail. New problems loom up and demand new techniques.

1. To G. Lukács in particular *Das Wort* owes some most notable essays, which shed light on the concept of realism even if, in my opinion, they define it rather too narrowly.

Reality alters; to represent it the means of representation must alter too. Nothing arises from nothing; the new springs from the old, but that is just what makes it new.

The oppressors do not always appear in the same mask. The masks cannot always be stripped off in the same way. There are so many tricks for dodging the mirror that is held out. Their military roads are termed motor roads. Their tanks are painted to look like Macduff's bushes. Their agents can show horny hands as if they were workers. Yes: it takes ingenuity to change the hunter into the quarry. What was popular yesterday is no longer so today, for the people of yesterday were not the people as it is today.

Anybody who is not bound by formal prejudices knows that there are many ways of suppressing truth and many ways of stating it: that indignation at inhuman conditions can be stimulated in many ways, by direct description of a pathetic or matter-of-fact kind, by narrating stories and parables, by jokes, by over- and understatement. In the theatre reality can be represented in a factual or a fantastic form. The actors can do without (or with the minimum of) make-up, appearing 'natural', and the whole thing can be a fake; they can wear grotesque masks and represent the truth. There is not much to argue about here: the means must be asked what the end is. The people knows how to ask this. Piscator's great experiments in the theatre (and my own), which repeatedly involved the exploding of conventional forms, found their chief support in the most progressive cadres of the working class. The workers judged everything by the amount of truth contained in it; they welcomed any innovation which helped the representation of truth, of the real mechanism of society; they rejected whatever seemed like playing, like machinery working for its own sake, i.e. no longer, or not yet, fulfilling a purpose. The worker's arguments were never literary or purely theatrical. 'You can't mix theatre and film': that sort of thing was never said. If the film was not properly used the most one heard was: 'that bit of film is unnecessary, it's distracting'. Workers' choruses spoke intricate rhythmical verse parts ('if it rhymed it'd all slip down like butter, and nothing would stick') and sang difficult (unaccustomed) compositions by Eisler ('it's got some guts in it'). But we had to alter particular lines whose sense was wrong or hard to arrive at. When there were certain subtleties (irregularities, complexities) in marching songs which had rhymes to make them easier to learn and simple rhythms to 'put them across' better, then they said: 'that's amusing, there was a sort of twist in that'. They had no use for anything played out, trivial, so ordinary that one doesn't need to think ('there's nothing in it'). If an aesthetic was needed, here it was. I shall never forget how one worker looked at me when I answered his request to include something extra in a song about the USSR ('It must go in – what's the point otherwise?') by saying that it would wreck the artistic form: he put his head on one side and smiled. At this polite smile a whole section of aesthetic collapsed. The workers were not afraid to teach us, nor were they afraid to learn.

I speak from experience when I say that one need never be frightened of putting bold and unaccustomed things before the proletariat, so long as they have to do with reality. There will always be educated persons, connoisseurs of the arts, who will step in with a 'The people won't understand that.' But the people impatiently shoves them aside and comes to terms directly with the artist. There is highly cultured stuff made for minorities, designed to form minorities: the two-thousandth transformation of some old hat, the spicing-up of a venerable and now decomposing piece of meat. The proletariat rejects it ('they've got something to worry about') with an incredulous, somewhat reflective shake of the head. It is not the spice that is being rejected, but the meat; not the two-thousandth form, but the old hat. When they themselves took to writing and acting they were compellingly original. What was known as 'agit-prop' art, which a number of second-rate noses were turned up at, was a mine of novel artistic techniques and ways of expression. Magnificent and long-forgotten elements from periods of truly popular art cropped up there, boldly adapted to the new social ends. Daring cuts and compositions, beautiful simplifications (alongside misconceived ones): in all this there was often an astonishing economy and elegance and a fearless eye for complexity. A lot of it may have been primitive, but it was never primitive with the kind of primitivity that affected the supposedly varied psychological portrayals of bourgeois art. It is very wrong to make a few misconceived stylizations a pretext for rejecting a style of representation which attempts (so often successfully) to bring out the essential and to encourage abstraction. The sharp eyes of the workers saw through naturalism's superficial representation of reality. When they said in *Fuhrmann Henschel*, 'that's more than we want to know about it,' they were in fact wishing they could get a more exact representation of the real social forces operating under the immediately visible surface. To quote from my own experience: they were not put off by the fantastic costumes and the apparently unreal setting of *The Threepenny Opera*. They were not narrow; they hated narrowness (their living quarters were narrow). They were generous; their employers were stingy. They thought it possible to dispense with some things that the artists felt to be essential, but they were amiable enough about it; they were not against superfluity: they were against certain superfluous people. They did not muzzle the threshing ox, though they saw to it that he threshed. 'The universally applicable creative method': they didn't believe in that sort of thing. They knew that they needed many different methods in order to reach their objective. If you want an aesthetic, there you are.

So the criteria for the popular and the realistic need to be chosen not only with great care but also with an open mind. They must not be deduced from existing realist works and existing popular works, as is often the case. Such an approach would lead to purely formalistic criteria, and questions of popularity and realism would be decided by form.

One cannot decide if a work is realist or not by finding out whether it resembles existing, reputedly realist works which must be counted realist for their time. In each individual case the picture given of life must be compared, not with another picture, but with the actual life portrayed. And likewise where popularity is concerned there is a wholly formalistic procedure that has to be guarded against. The intelligibility of a work of literature is not ensured exclusively by its being written in exactly the same way as other works which people have understood. These other works too were not invariably written just like the works before them. Something was done towards their understanding. In the same way we must do something for the understanding of the new works. Besides *being popular* there is such a thing as *becoming popular*.

If we want a truly popular literature, alive and fighting, completely gripped by reality and completely gripping reality, then we must keep pace with reality's headlong development. The great working masses of the people are on the move. The activity and brutality of their enemies proves it.

On Rhymeless Verse with Irregular Rhythms

Sometimes on publishing unrhymed verse I was asked how on earth I could present such stuff as verse; this happened most recently with my 'German Satires'. It is a fair question, as it is usual for verse which does without rhyme to offer at least a solid rhythm. Many of my most recent works in verse have had neither rhyme nor any regular solid rhythm. The reason I give for labelling them verse is: because they have a kind of (shifting, syncopated, gestic) rhythm, even if not a regular one. My first book of poems contained virtually nothing but songs and ballads, and the verse forms were fairly regular; they were nearly all supposed to be singable, and in the simplest possible way: I set them to music myself. There was only one poem without rhymes, and it was rhythmically regular; the rhymed poems on the other hand nearly all had irregular rhythms. In the nineteen stanzas of the 'Ballad of the Dead Soldier' there were nine different scansions of the second line: [The examples quoted are from stanzas 1–6, 14, 15 and 18].[1] After that I wrote a play (*Im Dickicht der Städte*) making use of Arthur Rimbaud's heightened prose (from his *Une Saison en Enfer*).

For another play (*Edward II*) I had to tackle the problem of iambics. I had been struck with the greater force of the actors' delivery when they used the almost unreadable 'stumbling' verses of the old Schlegel and Tieck Shakespeare translation rather than Rothe's smooth new one. How much better it expressed the tussle of thoughts in the great monologues! How much richer the structure of the verse! The problem was simple: I needed elevated language, but was brought up against the oily smooth-

1. See the German text with an English translation by H. R. Hays in *Selected Poems* (New York, 1959), pp. 56–60.

ness of the usual five-foot iambic metre. I needed rhythm, but not the usual jingle. I went about it like this. Instead of:

> I heard the drumbeats ring across the swamp
> Horses and weapons sank before my eyes
> And now my head is turning. Are they all
> Now drowned and dead? Does only noise still hang
> Hollow and idle on the air? But I
> Should not be running ...

I wrote:

> After those drumbeats, the swamp gulping
> Weapons and horses, all turns
> In my mother's son's head. Stop panting! Are all
> Drowned and dead, leaving just noise
> Hanging on the air? I will not
> Run further.

This gave the jerky breath of a man running, and such syncopation did more to show the speaker's conflicting feelings. My political knowledge in those days was disgracefully slight, but I was aware of huge inconsistencies in people's social life, and I didn't think it my task formally to iron out all the discordances and interferences of which I was strongly conscious. I caught them up in the incidents of my plays and in the verses of my poems; and did so long before I had recognized their real character and causes. As can be seen from the texts it was a matter not just of a formal 'kicking against the pricks' – of a protest against the smoothness and harmony of conventional poetry – but already of an attempt to show human dealings as contradictory, fiercely fought over, full of violence.

I could be still freer in my approach when I wrote opera, *Lehrstück* or cantata for modern composers. There I gave up iambics entirely and applied firm but irregular rhythms. Composers of the most varied schools assured me, and I myself could see, that they were admirably suited for music.

After that, alongside ballads and mass choruses with rhymes and regular (or almost regular) rhythms, I wrote more and more poems with no rhymes and with irregular rhythms. It must be remembered that the bulk of my work was designed for the theatre; I was always thinking of actual delivery. And for this delivery (whether of prose or of verse) I had worked out a quite definite technique. I called it 'gestic'.

This meant that the sentence must entirely follow the gest of the person speaking. Let me give an example. The Bible's sentence 'pluck out the eye that offends thee' is based on a gest – that of commanding – but it is not entirely gestically expressed, as 'that offends thee' has a further gest which remains unexpressed, namely that of explanation. Purely gestically expressed the sentence runs 'if thine eye offends thee, pluck it out' (and this is how it was put by Luther, who 'watched the people's mouth'). It can be seen at a glance that this way of putting it is far richer and cleaner from a gestic point of view. The first clause contains an assumption, and its peculiarity and specialness can be fully expressed by the tone of voice. Then there is a little pause of bewilderment, and only then the devastating proposal. The gestic way of putting things can of course quite well apply within a regular rhythm (or in a rhymed poem). Here is an example showing the difference.

Haven't you seen the child, unconscious yet of affection
Warming and cherishing him, who moves from one arm to
    another
Dozing, until the call of passion awakens the stripling
And with consciousness' flame the dawning world is illumined?
              (Schiller: *Der philosophische Egoist*)

And:

Nothing comes from nothing; not even the gods can deny it.
So constrained by fear our poor mortality, always;
So many things it sees appearing on earth or in heaven,
Moved by some basic cause that itself is unable to compass,
That it assumes some Power alone can be their creator.
But when we've seen for ourselves that nothing can come out of
    nothing,
Then we shall understand just what we are asking: the reason
Why all these things arose without divine intervention.
              (Lucretius: *De Rerum Naturae*)

The lack of gestic elements in Schiller's poem and the wealth of them in Lucretius's can be easily confirmed by repeating the verses and observing how often one's own gest changes in the process.

I began speaking of the gestic way of putting things for the reason that, although this can be achieved within our regular rhythmical framework, it seems to me at present that irregular rhythms must further the gestic way of putting things. I remember two observations helping me to work out irregular rhythms. The first related to those short shouted choruses at workers' demonstrations, which I first heard one Christmas Eve. A band of proletarians was marching through the respectable Western districts of Berlin shouting the sentence 'We're hungry': *'Wir haben Hunger.'* The rhythm was this:

$$\overline{Wir}\ \overline{haben}\ \overline{H\breve{u}ng\breve{e}r}$$

I subsequently heard other similar choruses, just with an easily spoken and disciplined text. One of them ran 'Help yourselves: vote for Thälmann'.

$$\overline{Helft}\ \overline{euch}\ \overline{s\breve{e}lb\breve{e}r},\ w\breve{a}hlt\ \overline{Th\ddot{a}lmann}.$$

Another experience of rhythm with a popular origin was the cry of 'Textbook for the opera *Fratella* to be given on the radio tonight' which I heard a Berlin streetseller calling as he sold libretti outside the Kaufhaus des Westens. He gave it the following rhythm:

$$\overline{Textb\breve{u}ch}\ f\breve{u}r\ di\breve{e}\ \overline{Op\breve{e}r}\ Fr\breve{a}t\breve{e}ll\breve{a}\ w\breve{e}lch\breve{e}\ h\breve{e}ut\breve{e}\ \overline{\Ah\breve{e}nd}\ im\ \overline{Rundf\breve{u}nk}$$
$$g\breve{e}h\ddot{o}rt\ wird$$

He continually varied the pitch and the volume, but stuck inflexibly to the rhythm.

The newspaper-seller's technique of rhythmical cries is easily studied. But irregular rhythms are also used in written matter, whenever it is a question of more or less dinning something in.

[Two advertising slogans are then quoted and scanned]

These experiences were applied to the development of irregular rhythms. What do these irregular rhythms look like, then? Here is an example from the 'German Satires': the two last verses from 'Die Jugend und das Dritte Reich'. First

Ja, wenn die Kinder Kinder blieben, dann
Könnte man ihnen immer Märchen erzählen
Da sie aber älter werden
Kann man es nicht.
[Ah yes, if children only remained children, then
One could always tell them stories
But since they grow older
One cannot.]

How does one read that? We start by superimposing it on a
regular rhythm.

Ja, wenn die Kinder Kinder blieben, dann
Könnte man ihnen immer Märchen erzählen
Da sie aber älter werden
Kann man es nicht.

The missing syllables [Brecht says 'feet', but clearly syllables are
meant] must be allowed for when speaking either by prolonging
the previous syllable ['foot'] or by pauses. The division into lines
helps that. I picked this particular verse because if one splits its
second line in two:

> *Könnte man ihnen*
> *Immer Märchen erzählen*

it becomes still easier to read, so that the principle can be studied
in a borderline case. The effect on sound and emphasis of this
division can be seen if the last verse:

When the regime rubs its hands and speaks of Youth
It is like a man, who
Looking at the snowy hillside, rubs his hands and says:
How cold it'll be this summer, with
So much snow,

is divided differently, thus:

When the regime rubs its hands and speaks of Youth
It is like a man
Who, looking at the snowy hillside, rubs his hands and says:
How cold it'll be this summer
With so much snow.

This way of writing it can in fact be read rhythmically too. But the qualitative difference hits the eye. In general, it must be admitted, this free way of treating verse strongly tempts the writer to be formless: rhythm isn't even guaranteed to the same extent as with a regular rhythmical scheme (though with this the right number of feet does not necessarily produce rhythm). The proof of the pudding is simply in the eating.

It must also be admitted that at the moment the reading of irregular rhythms presents one or two difficulties. This seems to me no criticism of it. Our ear is certainly in course of being physiologically transformed. Our acoustic environment has changed immensely. An episode in an American feature film, when the dancer Astaire tap-danced to the sounds of a machine-room, showed the astonishingly close relationship between the new noises and the percussive rhythms of jazz. Jazz signified a broad flow of popular musical elements into modern music, whatever our commercialized world may have made of it since. Its connection with the freeing of the Negroes is well known.

The extremely healthy campaign against Formalism has made possible the productive development of artistic forms by showing that the development of social content is an absolutely essential precondition for it. Unless it adapts itself to this development of content and takes orders from it, any formal innovation will remain wholly unfruitful.

The 'German Satires' were written for the German Freedom Radio. It was a matter of projecting single sentences to a distant, artificially scattered audience. They had to be cut down to the most concise possible form and to be reasonably invulnerable to interruptions (by jamming). Rhyme seemed to me to be unsuitable, as it easily makes a poem seem self-contained, lets it glide past the ear. Regular rhythms with their even cadence fail in the same way to cut deep enough, and they impose circumlocutions; a lot of everyday expressions won't fit them; what was needed was the tone of direct and spontaneous speech. I thought rhyme-less verse with irregular rhythms seemed suitable.

The Writer's Conscience*

I wish to consider this problem only under the most formidable aspects of immediate reality. These notes are by a writer who has the feeling of having fought for twenty years in the middle of events which are more and more suffocating, and where continually, and in various ways, he saw men (and works) perish whose essential vocation was to express responsibility.

I have recently received from afar, and by circuitous means, two simultaneous messages which complement each other in their tragic significance. The literature of our time of cessation of war without peace, that is to say, without reconciliation of the victims, without impulse towards a reconstruction of the world, without renewal of our confidence in man, reflects, more than anything else, anguish. It shows what a narrow margin of creative freedom is left by social reality to the intellectual, even when the latter, in order to give himself a vivifying illusion and doubtless to raise himself to the height of nightmare, is pleased to affirm, like certain French authors, 'a vertiginous freedom'. If today, however, there were sufficiently sincere exchanges, if we did not live isolated by immense imprisoning partitions, we should perceive the singular apparition, in Russo-Soviet literature, of a beneficent clarity. Amid the crowd of war books, sometimes written with an undeniable talent, but whose general theses, furnished by the relevant Bureaus, are known in advance, a few poems have arisen which carry the official stamp only in the same way as a soldier bears his uniform. It so happens that one suddenly perceives the man under the uniform, and that this man has an intense face, a personal silhouette. The Regime of Directed Thought has reasonably decided that in the times of the blackest sufferings it would be necessary to accord some relief to the human soul; and it has authorized on one hand a religious

* From *Now*, No. 7.

renaissance suitably supervised, on the other a lyrical poetry strictly limited to the great theme of love. Love is indeed more dangerous to tyrannies than one would believe at first sight. They know it. The man and woman must not find, in the exaltation of the couple, absorbing evasions likely to lessen their zeal for work, their obedience to the supreme orders of the state, their devotion to the Leader ... I remember a young worker 'tired of ideology' who wrote to the old Maxim Gorky: 'I would like the peasant, instead of embracing his tractor, to embrace the peasant woman, I would like fields where not nails would grow but grass, I would like to amuse myself!' And the great writer, having become official, replied in an angry tone, 'To amuse oneself – that is the oldest slogan of the parasites: Let others work, while we amuse ourselves' (*Pravda*, 20 December 1931). The most remarkable lyrical poet of Russia, Sergei Yessenin, lived, for precisely that reason, under a galling reprobation which led him finally to suicide in 1925. Some years later, the same internal conflict brought to suicide the poet of hope in the dictatorship, Vladimir Mayakovsky ... But in times of war, perils less psychological than lyricism menace the absolute state. It thus becomes wise, since all youth is frustrated of the right to life, to permit the song of love which, if it helps to live, can also help to fight and die. The fact is that, by the side of a patriotic prose overwhelming with its monotony, the Russo-Soviet literature has just produced some poems of love of a noble vigour and of a freshness of sentiment and thought which would suffice to show that the Russian man continues to live deeply, even under the heaviest constraints. I have before me the 9th number of the review *Znamia* (the *Standard*) for 1945, which contains the poem of Margarita Aliguer, *Your Victory*, in 6,700 lines. The author was yesterday only a young unknown. The work is simple, written in the classic tongue of the Russian poets of the nineteenth century, and it reaches at certain moments the heights of a lyricism packed with lived experience, with lucid passion, with emotional intelligence, proper to the greatest emotional radiance.

> Let him who falls on the reddened dust,
>   His helmet pierced with lightning,
> Let him who falls pardon the two who live
> Their holy right in earthly caresses.

As a whole, in spite of inevitable and probably sincere concessions to the ideological phraseology of the moment, this work appeared to be of the first order; and I see nothing to compare with it in the four European languages in which I try to follow literary production.

At the same moment as I received the official literary review containing this poem, I learnt after some years of delay, for secrecy is the rule, of the death (one should say the assassination) of one of the most significant Russian poets of the last thirty years: Osip Emilievitch Mandelstam. He would have been a little more than fifty, had he lived. He founded, round about 1913, with Nicholas Stepanovitch Gumilev, the school of Acmeism, which exerted a wide and fertile influence. Acmeism made its object to express the 'immediate truth' in perfectly complete forms. (N. S. Gumilev, one of the four or five Russian poets of the first magnitude at the outbreak of the revolution, professed openly counter-revolutionary opinions and was shot in 1921.) I remember an evening at Mandelstam's home in Leningrad during 1932. The poet had collected a number of writer friends to read us a work in prose which he had brought back from a journey in Armenia. I will not name here any of those present, my comrades and friends, in order not to compromise the survivors. A Jew, rather small, with a face of concentrated sadness and restless and meditative brown eyes, Mandelstam, highly appreciated in the literary world, lived poorly and with difficulty. He was published hardly at all, he produced little, not daring to struggle against the condemnation of the censors and the diatribes of the orators of the Associations of Proletarian Writers. The chiselled text which he read to us made me think of Giraudoux at his best, but here was no question of the vast dream of Suzanne before the Pacific; instead, it was secretly the question of the poet's resistance to the strangler's cord. The visions of the lake of Erivan and of the snows of Ararat raised in the murmur of a breeze a demand for liberty, a subversive praise of the imagination, an affirmation of ungovernable thought ... Mandelstam, his reading finished, questioned us: 'Do you believe that this will be publishable?' It was not forbidden to admire landscapes. But would the censors penetrate the protesting language of these landscapes? I do not know if these pages saw the light of day for, not long after that, I was shut away in the Internal (and secret) Prison of Moscow (for an offence of opinion). I learnt that Mandelstam tried later to commit suicide; that he wrote during the terror an epigrammatic quatrain in which one could see an allusion to the Leader, and committed the imprudence of letting it be known to several people; that he was arrested; that since 1942 his few friends considered him as deceased in captivity, in unknown circumstances.

It is allowed to publish a great poem of love. It is mortally forbidden to ask of the state what has happened to poets and prose writers who have disappeared. Even love must hold its tongue on the threshold of the dungeons.

The history of the massacre of Soviet writers in 1936–9 has not been written. No account of it has been published. What publisher, what review, would have accepted that account? All having passed into the darkness, it could only be fragmentary. But, published or not, this drama constitutes one of the fundamental events of culture in the present age. A friend, who was one of the most remarkable writers of the revolutionary generation, said to me in Moscow: 'Our consciousness as Soviet writers is very different from that of Western men of letters. Not one of us escapes the anguish of possible execution. Not one of us does not exclaim bitterly in his solitude: Ah! if I could create freely!' The anguish of this extraordinary creator has been fully justified: nobody knows what has happened to him. His fifteen powerfully valuable novels have been withdrawn from the libraries. His colleagues no longer dare to pronounce his name. Such has been the fate of several master-writers of the first order, in whom should be recognized the true founders of Soviet literature. Boris Pilniak, the author of *Ivan de Maria,* of *The Naked Year,* of *Wood of the Isles,* of *The Volga Throws Itself into the Caspian Sea*; Babel, author of *Red Cavalry (Konarmia)* and *Tales of Odessa*; Voronski, a former revolutionary convict, who was the animator of Soviet literature from 1918 onwards (*Art and Life, Beyond the Dead and Living Waters, The Eyes of the Hurricane*), certainly shot because he was of the Left Opposition; the old Ivanov-Razumnik, philosopher and historian, one of the intellectual guides of the generation of 1917 (Ivanov-Razumnik had just published a biography of Shchedrin when he disappeared. I had news of him in prison, through a young poet, my cell companion for a night, who did not know for sure why he himself was shut away; I thought I could discern that the master and his pupils were reproached with maintaining a hidden attachment to the idealist philosophy of Mikhailovsky and Pierre Lavrov); the producer Meyerhold whose audacities renewed the Russian theatre between 1902 and 1936; Riazanov, the historian of Marxism, who died in exile at the beginning of the war.

Naturally I do not know enough to compile the list of lesser known writers, of the young, of authors of revolutionary memoirs, who disappeared in hundreds. No one knows that list, except perhaps the directors of the Secret Service of the Political Police. And the *perhaps* which I place there is opaque, for the police chiefs who made the purges have themselves disappeared. The rule is that once the man is suppressed, his works are eliminated, his name is no longer pronounced; it is erased from the past and even from history. I have just read the very beautiful memoirs of Konstantin Fedin on Maxim Gorky. They refer to an epoch during which I knew Maxim Gorky fairly well; he then maintained a courageous independence, did not hesitate to criticize the 'revolutionary' power and finished by receiving from Lenin a friendly invitation to go into foreign exile. It is possible for me to verify the astonishing exactitude of the notes of Konstantin Fedin, the care which he has put into gathering the customary discourses of Gorky, whose gesture and voice I seem to find again. In each page, meanwhile, I discover the omission of ideas often expressed, of historical facts, of names. I admire the ability, the tenacity, the paralysed honesty of the writer who succeeds in tracing a truthful and powerfully living portrait while conforming without fault (but not without distress, I imagine) to the rule of obedience.

None of these vanished writers whom I have just named, except Riazanov, was made the object of an openly declared accusation. (And Riazanov was accused in the press of having conspired with the Socialist International to prepare war against the USSR, which was the height of delirium; he was condemned in secret, by an administrative measure. In reality, he had shown several outbursts of indignation and some gestures of generosity towards persecuted Marxists.) None was the object of a condemnation motivated by anything that was made the least public. Several, like Pilniak, Babel, Meyerhold, Riazanov, were personally known in both hemispheres. They had works translated into English, French, German, Spanish, Catalan, Czech, Yiddish, Chinese. No PEN Club, even of those who had offered them banquets, posed the least question on their cases. No literary review, to my knowledge, commented on their mysterious end. Books on Soviet literature have been published abroad, which pass them over in silence, or only mention them incidentally and evasively. A universal complicity surrounds their sufferings.

On the attitude of the reviews, that is to say of the intellectuals who make the reviews, before these mysteries and crimes, I will allow myself to cite one example. When the old German Marxist, Otto Ruhle, biographer of Karl Marx, author of many works of recognized importance, militant of the German revolution of 1918, died in Mexico in 1943, I offered to write an essay on him for an important South American review, where there were numbers of his friends. My proposition was at first received with interest, although my heretical reputation aroused a certain inquietude. As soon as I expressed the intention of mentioning, among the struggles upheld by Otto Ruhle, his participation in the John Dewey Commission which proclaimed, after the Moscow Trials, the innocence of Trotsky, I received the categorical reply: 'No. Impossible.'

From a rational point of view, I have never well understood why it was impossible, unless it was that an unjustifiable fear warped the conscience of the review's editors. The same evil is today diffused at both ends of the map of the world. A new Parisian review, popular and sympathetic, called *Maintenant*, published in last January a study of the poet Marcel Martinet, who died under the occupation (*Les Temps maudits*, 1918; *La Nuit*, 1920; *Une Feuille de hêtre*, 1935). The author of these warmhearted pages passes entirely in silence the struggles which the poet upheld for twenty years for the integrity of revolutionary thought. An omission touching on impiety: Marcel Martinet, whose moral courage never flinched, would have repulsed it like a treason. I understand, however, that it is practically impossible to publish today in Paris a hundred clear lines on the problem which I treat here. And I understand that the friends of the poet, having to choose between total silence on his death and his work and this mutilated *in memoriam*, have preferred to erect a provisional monument which will lack his true greatness.

The civilized person who sees a crime committed under his window, in full daylight, without allowing himself to intervene or even to make an audible shout, will he afterwards retain his own full self-esteem, his clarity of judgement, critical spirit, the capacity to create, if he is an artist? The writer informed of what passes in the world – and I hold that it is a duty of the writer thus to be informed – is often in the uncomfortable position of this civilized person. His conscience wounded, he can only escape the oppressive contamination of directed thought, directed all the more by terror and by psychological perversion, if he confronts the whole inhumanity of the problem with a firm decision of disapproval. Here are posed, it is true, the complex questions of faith, inseparable from the social environment and from personal interest. Yet we should demand of religious or political faith that it does not obliterate the conscience. The faith of modern man should be compatible with clear knowledge, with loyalty, with that simple mental hygiene, the sense of the dignity of oneself and others; otherwise it becomes a regression to mentalities anterior to our culture considered in its superior forms. It happens too frequently under our eyes that the writer (in more general terms, the intellectual) gives proof of a blindness which borders sometimes on imbecility, sometimes on knavery. We thus behold the disintegration of universal values by the insecurity imposed by the double game towards oneself and others. That such insecurity can be pushed back into the unconscious and that the writer believes himself, in abandoning himself to it, perfectly sincere, or devoted to a supreme *reason of state*, is a no less disquieting feature of the situation.

I would not dream of underestimating the importance of the literary work of the French resistance, to which so many of my friends have given so many deaths and so much suffering. That work obviously attests a precious vitality. And that is why I feel in reading certain of its texts a sensation of asphyxia. That poetry should arise to scourge the executioners, to exalt the heroism of the tortured, to guard the proud memory of the shot, is undoubtedly one of its most human missions in the present time. But that such poetry should often be signed by poets who elsewhere praise the hangman, praise the torturer, insult the shot, speak untruths over the tombs of another Resistance inspired by the same motives – the defence of man against tyranny – that leads us, by a terrible alchemy, to the negation of all affirmed values. Pure gold is no longer better than stirred-up mud. The conscience of the writer shows itself full of black shadows. The impassioned voice of song is nothing more than that of the false witness. The poetic quality of the work of Aragon has sometimes appeared to me moving and even excellent; but how many men from whom he sought instruction, whom he has loved or pretended to love in Russia and in the Third International, have suffered torture and death by shooting without his having been moved by it? Without his having posed in their cases the elementary question of innocence or guilt? Without his having questioned himself on the sinister gravity of the repressions paradoxically justified by 'revolutionary humanism'? Aragon wrote at another time, in 1937 I believe, in *Commune*, some incredible pages on the accused of the Moscow Trials.

The Poet of the Communist Resistance was among others the friend of Bruno Jaszinski, the Polish communist writer whose novels were published by *Humanité*, whom I knew in Moscow timidly faithful to the 'general party line', and who was to die in a concentration camp in the Far East. Aragon was the friend of the Secretary General of the Association of Proletarian Writers, Leopold Averbach, the most official of the directors of Soviet literature, shot where, when, how? But certainly shot, because he was the nephew of the People's Commissar for the Interior and chief of the Political Police, Yagoda, who was himself shot.

The allegiance of the writer to the party of a great power accustomed to shoot many people is in this precise case a sufficient explanation. But beyond this, how can one understand these verses on the 'traitors', written by another poet of the same party (Paul Eluard):

Ils nous ont vanté nos bourreaux
Ils nous ont detaillé le mal
Ils n'ont rien dit innocemment –

yes, how can one understand them? Let us grant the psychological disintegration. Let us grant that the poem, perfect as it may be in its flow, gives a false note. The reader expects to hear the voice of a defender of freedom, of an enemy of the murderers of the innocent, and the reader is deceived. And one asks uneasily: But what is then happening in the soul of these poets? The poet is suddenly stripped of his clarity. 'What is truth?' asked Pontius Pilate of the condemned. Thousands of men formed by the intellectual disciplines of scientific thought – it seems – reply in fact: 'It is the commandment of the Leader of my party.' This is the death of intelligence, the death of ethics.

In lesser degrees, numbers of other writers of the Resistance, less clearly classified, suffering from an intoxication of the environment, incur the same criticism. They seem to have discovered the annihilation of man by totalitarian machineries only by having suffered it for several years. Have they not seen it before, elsewhere? Do they not know that this drama is not national, that Europe, that our whole civilization is riddled with it? It is abundantly a question, under these beautiful pens, of 'engaged thought', of 'participation in action', of 'making up one's mind', of 'responsible literature' and even of consenting to perish for the just causes of our time ... But what exactly do these formulas mean? Does one wish to apply them only in the narrow circle of the patriotism of an already past movement? Is it intended to confer on these words an esoteric sense to the detriment of their universal sense? 'Engaged thought' – is it permitted here, and there effaced humbly before directed thought? 'Participation in action' – is it legitimate against one oppression and to be condemned against another? That would be only a return to the tribal mentality of past ages: 'Thou shalt not kill' the man of the same tribe, but it is praiseworthy to kill the man of the neighbouring tribe. 'Responsible literature', rightly extolled by Jean-Paul Sartre – will it limit its own responsibility to certain determined historical cases in order to renounce it before certain others? It is necessary to say that the conscience of the writer cannot elude these questions without betraying itself. And these questions today interest the conscience alone, I would say, of all men for whom the old magic of words, and of living works created with words, remains a means of clarifying and ennobling life.

What is 'Littérature Engagée'? *

The concept of 'littérature engagée' emerged as a result of the impact of modern ideologies on literature. These ideologies, in spite of their diversity, have one thing in common – they reflect the deep and rapid social changes of our time. Because of this, they compel each one of us to re-examine critically his position in the world and his responsibility to other men. Under their influence the writer in particular approaches his work in a new way, he commits himself. This simply means that he becomes aware that the real nature of his art is to focus attention on an aspect of reality and thus, inevitably, to pass judgement on it. The greatest originality of the modern conception of commitment is that it claims to be inseparable from literature itself. It does not merely repeat the pious platitude that there should be room in art for the big world of reality outside, but asserts almost aggressively that a writer is great only to the extent that he can provide society in general (or the reading public of the time) with a true mirror of itself, of its conflicts and its problems. His success in this respect is determined by the fact that he himself is no mere spectator in the drama he depicts, he is also an actor. What is required of him is that he should be a conscious actor.

The idea is not specifically French, but if it received its first coherent expression in post-war France, it is probably because the years of Occupation and Resistance had made Frenchmen more keenly aware of the need for a complete reassessment of all values. In the late forties, the part which literature could play in the world came in for particular attention, and the idea of commitment arose quite naturally, both as an answer to the problems of art and as a contribution to the requirements of society. That the movement survived those specific circumstances and moreover spread to other lands is proof enough that its vitality does

* From *Commitment in Modern French Literature* (1967).

BIRKBECK COLLEGE LIBRARY

not rest on the conditions which helped to give it birth. The emergence of commitment in the twentieth century rather suggests that it corresponds to the needs of the present age. There are two main reasons for this. We are faced today with a reality which is moving so fast that it is difficult to understand it, even partly, without being to some extent involved in it. Standing by the wayside condemns one to missing the essence of life. It may not necessarily spell the doom of art (for native talent usually finds more than one way of asserting itself), but it almost certainly limits its appeal and its human greatness. In the past, it was possible for artists to delude themselves into believing that their art was a thing apart. If in fact very few of them did, it was precisely because they had genius and could see beyond superficial appearances. Today, no one can hide even behind such appearances. We know only too well that the province of art is not a so-called unchangeable human nature but a contemporary situation which has its own unique features, and that it is only through this highly original situation that one can express the lasting and universal emotions which give art its permanent appeal. The paradox that eternal issues have a temporal shell has ceased to be a paradox for our generation because life has repeatedly proved it in practice. To ignore the temporal shell is to deal with lifeless abstractions.

Closely connected with a sense of the present is another objective factor peculiar to our age – the profound crisis of modern civilization. Not only have two world wars shattered most of our illusions, but we are now compelled to choose between life and death for our species. In the age of nuclear energy this is the dilemma which faces us. How can sensitive men escape from it? Some writers affect to be quite cynical about it, others tend to dismiss the issue as too big and too remote for them, but both their attitudes could well be a form of protest or an expression of suffering and anxiety. Moreover, their refusal to face reality, whether it is deliberate or cowardly, does not make contemporary reality disappear. Far from it! The latter manages to sneak in through the back door and leave its mark on thinkers and artists who think they have turned their backs on it. For example, it is doubtful whether an age less given to turmoil and violence could have witnessed such movements as the revolt of the 'angry young men', the theatre of the absurd, or the impersonal objectivity of the Robbe-Grillet type of '*nouveau roman*', this last feature being almost certainly an echo of the inhuman world in which individuals are crushed. Committed writers do not despise any of those trends, but they believe that an open acknowledgement of the links between the writer and society would be more honest and more profitable. This is the path of commitment, a path bristling with hardships and setbacks, but difficult to avoid.

The Case against Commitment

As the committed writer must begin by discarding many cherished notions and habits, it may not be a bad idea to examine very briefly some of the most important objections which have been put forward against commitment. This will clarify the true nature of committed literature and help us to avoid possible misconceptions about its aims. A frequent criticism is that '*littérature engagée*' gives too big a place to politics. The objection has been expressed time and again and it is not uncommon to find that people reduce committed writing to political writing or, at best, to books whose main interest is political. Even a subtle critic like R. Albérès complains that committed writers have paid too much attention to politics.[1]

The committed reply would start by pointing to the fact that the political crisis is the most acute expression of the general crisis of our time. Our moral and ideological conflicts all have a political background and there are hardly any aspects of our private lives which are not tangled with the political battle, in one way or another. Aragon and Sartre often illustrate the point in their novels. For example, in Aragon's *Passengers of Destiny* the central character is a man who prides himself on deliberately ignoring the political events of his day, refusing even to read the newspapers except for the financial columns. In the end, however, as a result of an accident, he finds himself partly paralysed. By a supreme irony of fate, he loses the use of speech, except for one word which is now the only one he can utter:

1. cf. his *Bilan Littéraire du vingtieme siècle*.

'*politique*'! And so it is with the help of this one word that he makes all his wants known to the woman who looks after him – hunger, thirst, sleep, etc. This is a particularly forceful allegory to suggest that in the twentieth century human destiny is decided through politics. (Napoleon called politics '*la forme moderne du destin*'.) The same lesson emerges from Sartre's novel *Reprieve*. The action takes place at the time of the Munich crisis in 1938, and the fate of each character is influenced by Hitler's decisions and by Chamberlain's and Daladier's capitulation before his demands. A really pathetic figure is that of Gros Louis, an illiterate peasant who would do no harm to anyone and yet finds himself, very much against his will, transported from place to place and finally locked up in jail, all because of 'politics' of which the poor fellow is quite ignorant. The inescapable moral is that even if we ignore politics, politics will not ignore us.

This does not mean that politics is the only theme, or even the most important one, in committed works of art. In some of them, it seems to be almost absent, as for example in the lyrical poems of Péguy and Aragon. In '*engagé*' novels, particularly in those of Aragon, the story concerns private individuals, busily trying to solve their personal problems and usually unaware of the part played by politics in shaping their destinies. Most of the heroes of Sartre's *Roads to Freedom* are in the same position. But the novelists themselves never forget that their characters are firmly rooted in the society of their time, with the result that the message about the importance of political problems is conveyed precisely by showing the little impact they make on the heroes' conscious minds. The political moral is seldom artificially or pompously laid down – it is implied without being openly suggested. One can say that in committed fiction, politics is literally the background – a vital one, but only a background.

Moreover, '*littérature engagée*' does not believe that complete individual freedom is achieved outside or against society. It rather takes the view that outside society man ceases to be a human being altogether and is reduced to the level of the brute, and, as such, subject to the most relentless determinism. Human freedom is a social conquest. Neither is it true, committed writers would add, that society cripples the free instincts of the individual. Social institutions may, and often do, stand in the way of individual self-expression, but the remedy is to attack and abolish those institutions; simply to ignore them does not remove their harmful effects, any more than the ostrich kills its enemy by pretending not to see him.

What applies to the characters of committed literature applies with even greater force to the committed artist himself. There is a reciprocal and fruitful exchange between his creative activity and his life as a man of action. The latter provides him with rich material for his art; as he mixes with people, he shares their difficulties and learns about their feelings. In return, his works can help his fellow men to understand themselves. Péguy probably provides the most convincing illustration of this fact because the spiritual truths which he discovered were the result of his deep involvement in the struggles of his time : it was in the course of fighting for the innocence of Dreyfus that he came face to face with the issues involving 'the eternal salvation' of man.

Lastly, according to Sartre, 'metaphysical anguish' (i.e. the attempt to grasp the full meaning of life) is a 'luxury' in which the vast majority of mankind can ill afford to indulge so long as their social problems still clamour for solution, but he adds that the search for the ultimate significance of existence will eventually become the main concern of man 'when men have made themselves truly free'.[2] As for commitment, it involves giving 'a complete picture of the human condition'.[3] In fact, we shall see that Péguy, Aragon and Sartre have always endeavoured not to 'mutilate' man in any essential respect. For example, Péguy held that 'spiritual salvation' was an extension of 'temporal' (i.e. political) salvation; Aragon always links the quest for personal happiness with political activity, and sees in love the

2. Sartre makes this point in an essay devoted to the Jewish question in which he explains why modern Jews are more prominent in the field of politics than in philosophy. This, according to him, is due to their feeling of insecurity, for, he adds, 'one must be quite sure of one's rights in society to be able to concern oneself with the fate of man in the universe', so that, for the time being, metaphysics is bound to remain 'the privilege of an Aryan ruling class'. (*Réflexions sur la question juive*, 1947, p. 174.)

3. Sartre, *Situations II* (Paris, 1947), p. 251.

finest *individual* expression of the committed approach because in love each partner prefers the other to himself; and Sartre attaches great importance to the study of 'mediations', i.e. of the concrete specific ways in which society exerts an influence on individuals (e.g. family relationships, etc.).

A second objection is that modern society has made commitment obsolete, for there are supposedly no causes left to which it is worth committing oneself. This is the really sophisticated objection against commitment, the one which is usually accompanied by the condescending admission that the idea could have been useful in the thirties, a bygone era for our critics, but that today no serious literature can be based on such primitive notions. The rejection of the traditional novel which is basically constructed around the conflict between the individual and society, and its replacement by the *objective* type of fiction, are advanced as proof that commitment is dead.

The commited reply is that this objection is not really 'literary' but is based on a very debatable assessment of the present time. There is no doubt that life in the sixties is very different from what it was twenty or thirty years ago, but the work of committed writers illustrates the change remarkably well. The Sartre who wrote the autobiographical essay *Words* in 1963 has obviously learnt from his own mistakes and he can describe his childhood as well as his early illusions with greater lucidity. As for Aragon, the majority of the books he has published in the last ten years give a privileged place to subjective elements, much to the surprise and chagrin of some of his friends. Actually, this new approach, far from being accidental or due to the author's personal whims, corresponds much better to the stage our society has reached: on the one hand, the increased complexity of life makes greater demands on personal initiative whereas, on the other, the danger of technology reducing us to mere robots is sufficiently real to warrant a vigorous reaction from the artist – in *Les Poètes* (1960), Aragon tries to visualize the new world which is being built and he makes the following passionate plea:

In that world I claim room for poetry.[4]

4. '*Je réclame dans ce monde-là une place pour la poésie*': *Les Poètes*, p. 145.

With regard to the assumption that there are no suitable conflicts to inspire today's writers, it is contradicted by the existence of at least four major sources of tension. First, writers and artists are the last people who should be taken in by the assertion that we've 'never had it so good'. Whether this is true on the purely material level or not, the sad fact is that modern life is dull and oppressive. Against such a background it may be difficult to write the type of poignant fiction which was inspired by the Spanish Civil War, for example, but for a sensitive artist there is rich material to be found in a society which has manifestly failed to provide its members with a sense of purpose and a true appreciation of the joys of life. And as the remedy involves more than strictly cultural measures, as it is bound up with political and moral decisions, it requires commitment. A two-way process is involved here: on the one hand, modern man needs artists to depict his life to him without illusions or complacency and suggest a way out; but on the other hand, the artist can find in the tragedy of modern man a challenging source of inspiration precisely because so much of contemporary life is vulgar and cheap.

This is closely connected with another conflict peculiar to our age, the acute and disturbing contrast between 'pop' culture and traditional culture. Without examining all the implications of this issue, perhaps a few questions should at least be raised. Is 'pop' culture the inevitable price we have to pay for the extension of political and social democracy, i.e. is it the only type of culture one can expect the broad masses to enjoy – or does it rather illustrate the fact that we are still very far from having achieved democracy and that the tendency of our modern masters is to prevent most of us from engaging in the eternally dangerous activity of thinking clearly and deeply? Is 'pop' culture entirely negative, or does it, in spite of all efforts to commercialize it, express in its own way the anguish of our generation and its pathetic search for new values? What, in any case, is the real dividing line between the two cultures? These and similar questions are the concern of all those who feel that 'man does not live by bread alone' and that cultural and ideological poverty is at least as bad as material poverty, if not worse. They affect each one of us, and not just a handful of 'intellectuals'. As one of Arnold Wesker's heroines says, 'The whole stinkin' commercial world insults us and we don't care a damn ... – it's our own bloody fault.'[5] Commitment does not claim to have all the answers to the above questions, nor does it suggest there cannot be more than one answer. What it does say is that they are bound up with one's philosophy of life and that the writers and artists whose obvious right and duty it is to contribute to their solution can hardly do so without taking sides in the political and moral debates of their times, in other words *without committing themselves!*

Another aspect of modern culture is the frightening increase of pornography. I use the word 'frightening', not in a puritanical sense, but because there is a real danger of losing one's sense of perspective in approaching this issue. Very few people would deny that the open and frank discussion of sex by present-day writers is a welcome reaction against Victorian prudery and hypocrisy and, moreover, that an artist worthy of the name should not recoil from describing all aspects of human behaviour, including those which bring into play our most primitive and animal instincts. Such an approach is rightly regarded as realistic art and not as pornography at all. The difference between the two lies in the intention of the artist and consequently in the effect produced. It is one thing to describe sex without any squeamish disgust, and as *part*, but only part, of human life, and quite another to aim simply at being crude for no other reason than the belief that most of us are sure to like it anyway. This cheapens sex and insults man; it degrades both author and public instead of producing an uplifting effect, as genuine art usually does. It is necessary to emphasize that the uplifting effect is not achieved by the convenient suppression of what is sordid and crude in human life, nor even by relegating these aspects to a secondary place. Paradoxical though it may sound, it can be achieved by giving pride of place to such elements, provided the object is to increase our human understanding and sympathy. Once again, this requires more than mere technical skill, it

5. Beatie Bryant in *Roots*, Act III : *The Wesker Trilogy* (Penguin ed., 1964), p. 148.

requires a definite philosophy to which the writer is genuinely *committed*. The novels of Sartre are a case in point. There is much in his trilogy *Roads to Freedom* which could rival any 'Fanny Hill' type of fiction when it comes to crudity and obscenity, but these aspects are never isolated and presented for their own sake. It is impossible, for example, not to be genuinely moved (as opposed to morbidly excited) after reading the pathetic scene where two cripples attempt to make love and can only achieve an orgasm by the combined use of their hands and imagination. The luxury of details has the effect of increasing the poignancy of the situation and certainly not of titillating our sexual hunger.

A third modern conflict is provided by the contrast between the potential advantages and the real dangers of scientific advances. The discovery of nuclear energy has given this issue an urgent and compelling character and made the question of war and peace one of the most vital questions of our time. That it has not left artists indifferent is shown by the number of songs, plays and novels which actually deal with the topic, to say nothing of all those which would be unintelligible if one did not take this background into account. Furthermore, at the time of writing, the war in Vietnam is eliciting in the West the same kind of responses as did the struggle against Fascism thirty years ago in the sense that it is providing a comparable polarization of opinions and attitudes[6] – this tends to disprove the supposedly outmoded character of commitment, for there are still many vital choices before us, and we still need the inspiring help of art and literature in facing them. Aragon's poem 'Les Yeux et la mémoire' ('Eyes and Memory'), which appeared in 1954, was written as a sort of counterpoint to one of his wife's novels (Elsa Triolet's *Le Cheval roux – The Red Horse*)[7] in which she

6. This does not mean that we can, or should, expect to be flooded with books dealing directly with the Vietnam conflict. It means rather that the Vietnam war, like the Spanish Civil War before it, is one of those concrete issues which compel us periodically to re-examine our basic principles. So long as this war continues, and threatens to turn into a world war, the whole question of man's inhumanity to man remains an acute, practical problem.

7. An allusion to the Red Horse in the Book of Revelation, which is a symbol of war.

visualized the destruction of mankind by H-bombs. Not that the novel was pessimistic: it was rather intended to make us aware of the nuclear threat so that we should act in time. The poet supplements the lesson by showing with great simplicity and sincerity all the things it is worth preserving and fighting for. He concludes with a poem on peace (inspired by the end of another Vietnam war, the war between the Vietnamese and the French) of which the last two lines read:

> Be silent ye atoms and ye guns cease spluttering
> Cease fire on every front on every front cease fire[8]

Lastly, there is the eternal conflict between ideals and reality, the kind of conflict which led Péguy to remark bitterly at the beginning of this century that a *'mystique'* usually degenerates into a *'politique'*, by which he meant, as we shall see later, that it is a normal fate for a pure ideal to deviate from its original noble purpose and become exploited for selfish ends. Such a conflict is particularly acute for those who are politically committed because the world of politics is often a world of 'dirty hands', as the title of a Sartrian play suggests. A recent example was afforded by the shock in Communist ranks after the Twentieth Congress of the CPSU had revealed the mistakes and the crimes of Stalin. But it is not only for Communists that there are rude awakenings in the modern world. All those who seek to improve conditions for others are bound to realize sooner or later that the pace of change is seldom as fast as they had hoped; and it is not very long before they discover that as soon as an ideal begins to be translated into practice, there are many unexpected difficulties which suddenly spring up and call for an 'agonizing reappraisal'. The danger in such cases is that people tend to hide their disappointment behind a blasé and cynical façade. Great committed art can save us from this fruitless attitude, because the artist's vision helps us to see beyond temporary setbacks and defeats. Another of Wesker's heroines comes to mind, the valiant Sarah

---

8. *'Tais-toi l'atome et toi canon cesse ta toux / Partout cessez le feu cessez le feu partout'* – Les Yeux, p. 163. Aragon's lack of punctuation is intentional. Its aim is to compel the reader to regard each line of poetry as a complete unity where no artificial divisions can be made.

Kahn who stubbornly refuses to follow her friend Monty along the road of betrayal and her son Ronnie along the path of despair:

> If the electrician who comes to mend my fuse blows it instead, so I should stop having electricity? I should cut off my light? Socialism is my light, can you understand that? A way of life. A man can be beautiful.[9]

In a recent poem ('Elégie à Pablo Neruda', 1966) Aragon described poets as 'creatures of the night' who nevertheless 'carry the sun within themselves'.[10] The background to the poem is the 1965 earthquake in Chile which destroyed Pablo Neruda's house. After expressing sympathy for his friend, Aragon went on to accuse the earth itself of betraying the poets, and he widened his theme by showing that there is an even worse calamity for an artist when he realizes the gap between his generous dreams of justice and happiness and the obstacles which must be overcome before men turn those dreams into realities. The poet's message is not that we should give up the struggle, but fight with our eyes open and be vigilant:

> Oh what did we allow Pablo my friend
> Pablo my friend what of our dreams what of our dreams [11]

The above examples do not seem to bear the contention that the days of commitment are numbered because there are no real conflicts in modern society. Committed writers believe that present-day conflicts are less 'obvious' and probably more 'sophisticated' than those of two or three decades ago; this simply means that commitment must express itself differently, not that it is obsolete. It would be a great pity if the conflicts of our time found their sole expression in the modern protest songs and failed to inspire the writer. It would be a tragedy, not for the writer 'as a citizen', but 'as a writer'!

We owe the above distinction to George Orwell. According to him,

9. *Chicken Soup with Barley*: Trilogy, pp. 73-4.
10. '*Nous sommes les gens de la nuit qui portons le soleil en nous*'.
11. '*Qu'avons-nous permis Pablo mon ami/Pablo mon ami nos songes nos onges*' – Aragon, op. cit., p. 26.

When a writer engages in politics he should do so as a citizen, as a human being, but not AS A WRITER... He should make clear that his writing is a thing apart.[12]

This is the 'liberal' objection to commitment. It does not refuse commitment as such – for Orwell admits that '...to lock yourself up in the ivory tower is impossible and undesirable' – but it insists that there is no place for it in literature, for the latter is 'a thing apart'. The French 'new novelists' take the same view. Robbe-Grillet, in particular, repeats Orwell almost word for word when he writes,

It is not reasonable ... to claim to serve a political cause in our novels, even a cause that seems to us a just one, even if, in our political life, we fight for its triumph.[13]

For the writers of the '*nouveau roman*', there is only one possible commitment – literature itself, and Robbe-Grillet adds,

...commitment for the writer is a full awareness of the problems of his own language, his conviction of their extreme importance, and his determination to resolve them from within.[14]

According to '*littérature engagée*', such an opinion rests on the fallacy that artistic problems arise outside society and can be looked upon as technical issues exclusively. A committed writer like Aragon, without in the least playing down the importance of language and the need to master it, stresses that language is a means of communication and that all creative attempts aimed at improving such a medium have been linked with a philosophy of life. In literature, 'technical' change is never an end in itself, but a way of conveying more adequately, more powerfully, the artist's experiences and views. Robbe-Grillet himself admits that the 'new novel' is a valid experiment because it can express the realities of the modern age better than traditional fiction. Does not this contradict his own assertion that a work of art has no purpose and that an artist creates 'for nothing'?

12. 'Writers and Leviathan', in *England, Your England* (Secker & Warberg, 1953), p. 25.
13. Article in *Revue de Paris* (Paris, September 1961), p. 121.
14. Alain Robbe-Grillet, *Pour un nouveau roman* (Paris, 1960), pp. 46–7.

Moreover, if Orwell is right in thinking that there is a Chinese wall between art and life, one would have to assume that the same individual is entitled to get out of his ivory tower when he behaves 'as a citizen', but should immediately return to it when he is about to perform his duty 'as a writer', and presumably forget all he has learnt in the course of his brief encounter with lesser mortals. Admittedly, Orwell himself never went to such ridiculous lengths, but does not his statement lend itself to a treatment of this kind? The expression 'a thing apart' is, to say the least, very vague and can be made the excuse for all sorts of irresponsible attitudes which Orwell would certainly condemn. If he simply meant that one cannot issue orders in art as one does in politics, no committed writer would disagree with him. (Mistakes made by religious and political leaders represent a distortion rather than a genuine application of the committed outlook.) But if Orwell or anyone else is prepared to go further and assert that a writer is independent from all authority, he is, in the view of *littérature engagée*, treading on dangerous ground. The writer's so-called independence is a myth because no literature can avoid being, implicitly or explicitly, a critical evaluation of contemporary values. Sartre even says that abstention is a form of commitment because it implies acceptance of the status quo. Moreover, does the idea of independence mean that an author is not accountable to anyone for what he writes because it is his privilege as an artist to be above normal human restrictions? Committed writers would strongly criticize this view. Irresponsibility, they would point out, is not an indispensable ingredient of art, and few masterpieces, if any, have been produced by disregarding the needs of society. What Orwell feared is that the writers would be *told* of those needs instead of discovering them for themselves, and it cannot be denied that his fears strike a sympathetic chord in all those who have been pained and horrified by past events in the Soviet Union and more recently in China. But because Orwell was right to sound the alarm, does it mean that he found the correct solution to the problem? Committed writers do not think so.

They admit that there are dangers in their approach and that it is not enough to dismiss sensitive critics as 'petty bourgeois'.[15] Sticking a label on your opponent is not the best way of silencing him. The real answer is not to deny that one is taking risks, but to ask oneself if they are worth taking and the extent to which they can be minimized. No great task can be accomplished without taking certain risks, and commitment does not claim it is an insurance policy against all dangers. It rather feels that it contains the seeds of its own purification because it generally implies greater acceptance on the writer's part of the opinions of other people. The committed writer is not alone, he is a 'man among men', as Sartre repeatedly emphasizes.

The main danger he must guard against is that of bias, one-sidedness and dogmatism. It is a very real one, but it is inherent in any human enterprise, and no writer has ever been free from it. In fact, the non-committed writer, who tends to recognize no other authority than himself, is more vulnerable to the danger. One of the cardinal requirements of commitment, on the other hand, is that a writer should not regard himself as the sole judge of truth, but should be willing to seek the truth alongside the members of a wider group, a church or a party. Will this lead to the 'regimentation' which Orwell feared so much? Here, we touch upon one of the dangers which is most frequently associated with commitment, although, in fact, it does not constitute a criticism of commitment at all. It may be a valid criticism of the Communist Party (or of any other group for that matter), but not

15. Incidentally, there is little doubt that Orwell himself approached politics in a 'petty bourgeois' way, if by this one means that he had more faith in the middle classes than in the organized workers. But these pages are not an attempt to discuss, however briefly, Orwell's personal contribution (his views have been mentioned simply because they sum up rather well what I termed the 'liberal' standpoint), particularly as such a discussion exists already in John Mander's *The Writer and Commitment* (Secker & Warberg, 1961). The reader will find that 'Orwell's thinking is frequently contradictory. He is quite capable of saying that propaganda is the ruin of art one day, and on the next that all art must have a political purpose' (p. 84). As for the meaning attached to the expression 'art is a thing apart', Mr Mander thinks that for Orwell, 'a writer can never become a good party-liner; if he introduces politics into his writing he will become a pamphleteer' (p. 112). May I add that no serious reader of Péguy, Aragon and Sartre could possibly describe them as 'pamphleteers'.

of commitment as such. The regimentation of writers is detrimental to art and, in the long run, to the cause one serves. It gives an entirely distorted image of what commitment really is by confusing two vastly different things, the desirability of the writer's descending into the arena (which is a personal decision for him to make), and the administrative measures which a ruling party or an established church may take against him if he does not toe the line. The latter must be thoroughly condemned, but it cannot be done effectively by retiring into the wilderness. Whether the writer decides to combat narrow-mindedness inside his own party, like Aragon,[16] or to retain the critical independence of the friendly outsider, like Sartre,[17] or to give up for ever 'the god that failed', the fact is that each of these positive stands represents more commitment, not less. One could venture to express the following paradox: in order to present a thorough case against commitment as it is being practised, one has to be thoroughly committed!

Moreover, the excesses of what came to be known as Zhdanovism in the Stalin era were due to an abusive interpretation of a correct principle, in this case the principle that the writer has a responsibility towards society. The Zhdanov mistake, it is worth stressing, was to approach the issue of responsibility in an *administrative* way and to forget that the methods which work in the field of politics do not necessarily apply to the field of aesthetics. (Lenin himself had a much healthier view of the matter when he wrote that 'literature is the last thing in the world to lend itself to mechanical levelling and uniformity, to the subjection of

16. Aragon's independence of mind was recently brought to the attention of a large public when he roundly condemned the Soviet decision to sentence two writers for publishing their books abroad, but this does not represent a new departure for him. In the post-war era, particularly, he has associated himself with the fight against 'dogmatism' and 'sectarianism'.

17. Sartre's refusal to join a political party is not regarded by him as a virtue but as a regrettable necessity so long as he feels unable to endorse the methods of the French Communist Party. He realizes that his position is neither fully consistent nor comfortable, but he believes it is the only one open to him at the moment. Sartre's Communist critics naturally stress the weakness of his stand and some even accuse him of having produced a 'non-militant' version of literary commitment. Does not this betray a rather restrictive conception of militancy?

the minority by the majority ... in this field, great freedom must be assured to individual initiative'.)[18] This does not excuse social or political irresponsibility in the writer, but the point is that a correct approach cannot be imposed on him. Administrative measures lead to an impoverishment of art; literature which is written 'to order' is a caricature of committed literature, if only because it utterly fails to achieve its object. Instead of instilling enthusiasm in the reader, it leaves him cold and unmoved. An artist must listen to the voice of his own conscience, not because he is always sure to be right, but because if he does not, his work would immediately reveal the presence of a foreign, spurious element and would cease to be *effective*. It is on behalf of commitment itself rather than in the name of 'pure' art that regimentation must be opposed. '*Littérature engagée*' has always emphasized that an ideology cannot be artificially introduced into a work of art. It should come from within the artist himself and be inseparable from his own personality. Although it believes that all art is a form of 'propaganda' in the sense that it is a criticism of life and expresses a particular point of view,[19] if propaganda is superimposed on the work of art, the artist has failed. Péguy never allowed anyone, not even the Church, to tell him how or what to write, and when he could not publicly defend a Catholic decision, he either kept quiet or courted ecclesiastical disapproval by speaking his own mind. (The Church's attitude to Bergson is a case in point: Péguy, always a great admirer of Bergson, continued to express his support for the master even when there were moves denouncing him from Rome.) Sartre goes further than Péguy and refuses to join any political party, although this is not really consistent with his understanding of a committed writer's duty. As for Aragon, who cannot be suspected of any 'individualistic deviation' in view of his unbroken membership of the French Communist Party over a period of forty years, he utterly rejects the idea of

18. *Party Organization and Party Literature* (1905).

19. People usually call 'propaganda' (in a derogatory sense) the defence of ideas with which they disagree, but they would never dream of describing their own unquestioned assumptions or their own acceptance of certain values as 'propaganda'!

'directives' in literature and speaks instead of an 'inner necessity' which makes the artist echo in his work ideas and trends with which he is in agreement. His own war-time poetry, which constitutes a vivid illustration of the Communist 'line' in those days, manages at the same time to retain an unmistakable personal flavour, without which it would have failed to move millions of Frenchmen from all parties.

In spite of all this, it would be idle to deny that the greatest danger facing '*littérature engagée*' is that of forgetting 'literature' for the sake of 'engagement'[20] or to claim that the correct relationship between these two aspects has either been successfully established in practice or easily defined in theory. We are dealing here with one of the most difficult issues connected with commitment. All that one can add to what committed writers have said on the subject is that the idea of commitment is still a young idea; as it matures, it will be enriched by experience and gradually discard excesses and misconceptions. Already, the personal evolution of Péguy, Aragon and Sartre is instructive in this respect. The unexpected autobiographical revelations made by Aragon and Sartre in very recent years[21] show that neither of them has been entirely free from '*mauvaise foi*' (i.e. self-deception), but also that both of them place sincerity and truth above everything else – to use a favourite expression of Aragon's, they are determined to leave of themselves '*une image vraie*', a true image.

The Case for Commitment

The case for commitment rests on two simple propositions. One is that interest in one's own time is a great source of inspiration

20. cf. Sarte's famous dictum: '*Dans la littérature engagée*, l'engagement *ne doit en aucun cas faire oublier* la littérature' (*Situations II*, p. 30). Cf. also his article on 'Nationalisation de la littérature' (op. cit., pp. 35–53) where he warns that a novel, committed or not, is primarily an individual work, '. . . *l'enterprise hasardeuse d'un homme seul*' (p. 43). Readers and critics must agree to be mutually involved – literature is a gamble, and without this element of risk, art dies.

21. esp. Aragon, *La Mise à mort* (Paris, 1965); Sartre, *Les Mots* (1964–Penguin ed., 1967).

for art, and the other that creative freedom for the writer is inseparable from a sense of social responsibility. With regard to the first point, the example of the past tends to show that the lasting value of a literary masterpiece often derives from its topical character at the time of publication and that the greater the artist's involvement in his own age, the deeper is his understanding of permanent human characteristics, and consequently, the more lasting and universal his appeal. This illustrates a thesis which is common to Péguy, Aragon and Sartre and can be summed up by saying that eternal issues express themselves through concrete and specific circumstances. According to Aragon, great poetry is eternal *because* it is dated, '*éternelle d'être datée*', as he puts it.[22] Sartre extends this to all literature, claiming that eternity is the reward of those who take sides in the 'peculiarity of our time' ('*la singularité de notre époque*').[23] Finally, Péguy puts the matter in a nutshell when he writes,

And Eternity itself belongs to the temporal world.[24]

If we leave aside the theological aspect of the notion of *eternity*, what men, as finite beings, call 'eternal' is that which survives passing circumstances; but according to '*littérature engagée*', the paradox of human affairs is that this lasting quality demands, in addition to artistic genius, that one should enter into the concrete life of a transient epoch. Although love, hatred, anger, etc., are of all times, they move us only when they are embodied in creatures of flesh and blood, in men and women who belong to a real human age and are rooted in a real corner of the planet. For example, before Romeo and Juliet could symbolize, as they do, the lovers of all time, they had first to be lovers of their own day and age; in Shakespeare's play, their love is not thwarted by vague 'eternal' obstacles, but by contemporary social values, and although these have long ceased to have any meaning for us, it is in the course of their fight against such *dated* values that Romeo and Juliet are able to express those basic human emotions in which men and women of all ages

22. *Chronique du bel canto* (Geneva, 1947), p. 25.
23. *Situations II*, p. 15.
24. *Œuvres poétiques completes* (Paris, 1948 ed.), p. 813.

recognize their kith and kin. Another example is provided by the patriotic poetry written in France during the years of German Occupation.[25] There is little doubt that future generations will forget the precise incidents which aroused the anger of Resistance poets, but so long as there are national tragedies, their protest will keep a permanent quality and inspire those who are waging the unending battle against injustice. Aragon remarks that such was indeed the fate of Hugo and Péguy, whose patriotic writing took on a special significance in 1940 although they had been inspired by other defeats and other circumstances.

But the crux of the matter, so far as commitment is concerned, lies in the relationship between creative freedom and social responsibility. Broadly speaking, the opinion of *'littérature engagée'* is that the writer is entitled to expect freedom from any given society, but that society is entitled to expect a sense of social responsibility in the writer. *The recognition of this double demand and of this dialectical process is at the heart of commitment.* It is important to insist on the social aspect of responsibility in French *'littérature engagée'* because in his book on English committed writers, John Mander, after rightly saying that 'commitment is grounded ... in responsibility', suggests that it is nothing more than a 'moral concept'. This is either too wide or too restrictive a view. It is too wide in so far as there is no work of art which does not display *some* moral attitude, so that all one has to do, as Mander puts it, is to determine, in each case, 'the quality' of the writer's commitment. I believe that to talk of commitment in such broad terms is misleading and that INVOLVEMENT would be a much better word, a point to which I intend to return when I discuss Sartre's definition of commitment. But involvement is not a literary method at all – it is simply a fact from which no writer (and no man) can escape. On the other hand, Mr Mander's definition means too little because it reduces commitment to devotion to an *idea*, whereas French *'engagés'* insist on the militant and practical character of their writing. Péguy, for example, was never content with gener-

25. A good account of Aragon's contribution in those years may be found in *Aragon, Poet of Resurgent France*, by Hannah Josephson and Malcolm Cowley (Pilot Press, 1946).

alities of a socialist or a Christian nature; his works untiringly discuss the events of the day as seen by a Socialist and a Christian, and more particularly the Dreyfus Affair. One critic describes him as 'a journalist who looks upon current happenings *"sub specie aeterni"* '.[26] Most of Sartre's works also have this militant character. Sometimes the author intervenes directly in topical controversies, and sometimes he raises fundamental moral issues *in the light of present-day problems*. As for Aragon, he described his work as a permanent song to help us keep our faith in human happiness:

> To sing to sing to sing
> So that the shadow becomes human
> As Sunday blesses the week
> And as hope sweetens truth[27]

All this represents much more than a vague 'moral concept'. It involves a definite social point of view, not necessarily a right one, but one which is inseparable from commitment and without which the latter simply does not make sense. It should be stressed that social responsibility is not synonymous with the defence of a social system, even when one happens to agree with it, as this often leads to the type of insipid and nauseating literature which unconvincingly sings the praises of the Establishment, such as the happily forgotten edifying fiction written in Victorian England or in Third Republic France, or more recently in Stalinist Russia. A sense of social responsibility should be, according to *'littérature engagée'*, a *critical* sense, for the aim of commitment is not to foster illusions but rather to destroy them. The debunking of false values is an important characteristic of its approach. In this respect, Aragon's attitude to changing cultural developments in the Communist Movement is not without significance. To his credit, he did not wait until Stalin's death in order to support the timid but genuine attempts to bring more

26. *Il peut apparaître comme un journaliste qui examinerait les faits du jour "sub specie aeterni".* (Maurice David, *Initiation à Charles Pèguy* [Paris, 1946], pp. 21–2).

27. '. . . *chanter chanter chanter/Pour que l'ombre se fasse humaine/ Comme un dimanche à la semaine/Et l'espoir à la vérité*' – *Les Poètes*, p. 161.

constructive criticism into Soviet art instead of confining it to the stereotyped glorification of the system. In more recent years, he went much further and openly sided with the more daring and unorthodox Soviet trends. In a speech he made in 1959 to a group of Young Communists, he reminded his audience that 'there is no light without a shadow' and that a book in which there are no conflicts or in which they are conveniently settled at the end 'does not deserve to be opened'. Then he went on to say,

If you expect to be supplied with beautiful and reassuring pictures which do not raise any problems in your minds and with which you are bound to agree beforehand, don't rely on me. The kind of literature which settles all the hard issues of life in a few hundred pages belongs to the kind of activity generally known as *utopia*. Nothing is so dangerous as utopia. It lulls people to sleep and when they are awakened by reality, they are like sleep-walkers on the top of a roof – they suddenly find themselves tumbling down to the ground.[28]

Lastly, is it true that in order to maintain his integrity the artist must refuse to 'compromise' and have no truck whatever with non-literary bodies? This point of view, with which we have become increasingly familiar since the second half of the last century, arose in a divided society, torn by class conflicts, and it contains within itself contradictory features. On the one hand, it expresses a critical refusal of the world as it is, an honest reluctance to become the accomplice of a lying, ruling clique; but on the other hand it represents an individualistic protest which is, at best, highly ineffectual. By stressing the close relationship between literature and the public for whom it is meant, commitment helps to overcome the contradiction : the committed writer knows that in modern society he must side *with* certain social forces *against* injustice. He refuses to compromise with the Establishment, but his rebellion is part of a wider movement.

28. *J'abats mon jeu*, p. 136. Cf. also his forceful denunciation of utopia at the end of *History of the USSR*, and in particular the passage where he states that utopia 'is noxious because of the possibilities of disillusionment it carries within it, because at every step it holds up a false image in contrast to reality, because it leads to discouragement through the want of proportion between the hoped-for prospect and the work to be done; it might be said that utopia is "a terrible strike-breaker" and even more a terrible seducer of the working class' (1963 ed.), p. 647.

For him, literature becomes what Sartre calls an *'integrated and militant function'* (*'une fonction intégrée et militante'*).[29]

Sartre's Definition of Commitment

According to Mr Mander, we in England 'have adopted Sartre's term, and largely ignored its theoretical basis'. I am not sure that I agree with him when he adds that our neglect '... may prove to have been a blessing in disguise'.[30] Although Sartrian theories are often debatable, and although the 'theoretical basis' is not as fixed as the phrase suggests – for it is being modified by Sartre all the time, sometimes in a dramatic fashion – it is not good enough to be content with what Mr Mander calls 'Anglo-Saxon empiricism'. One of the purposes of the present essay is to suggest that commitment is not a haphazard or instinctive reaction but a valid and challenging *method* of approaching artistic creation and that we can learn a good deal from the French example, both from the literary theories, for what they are worth, and from the works which endeavour to illustrate them.

According to Sartre, commitment is inherent in the act of writing. To write, he says, is to talk, and to talk is to reveal an aspect of the world, in order to change it. Literature is therefore the result of an attitude, conscious or unconscious, towards the world. The committed writer is different from others, not because he is involved in the world, but because he is aware of it, because '... he endeavours to acquire the most lucid, most complete awareness of being involved,[31] i.e. because he transfers his commitment from the level of the immediately spontaneous to the level of consciousness'.[32]

29. *Situations II*, p. 185.
30. *The Writer and Commitment*, p. 11.
31. The French word which Sartre uses is *'embarqué'*, as he has just been discussing Pascal's famous saying, *'Nous sommes embarqués'* ('We're all in the same boat'). I have translated *'embarqué'* by 'involved' (not a great liberty in this context, I believe) in order to introduce the important distinction between involvement and commitment which is made in the next paragraph.
32. *'Je dirai qu'un écrivain est engagé quand il cherche à prende la conscience la plus lucide et la plus entière d'être embarqué, c'est à dire quand il fait passer . . . l'engagement de la spontanéité immédiate au réfléchi'* (*Situations II*, p. 124).

466

The main weakness of this otherwise excellent definition is that it does not draw a sufficiently clear distinction between INVOLVEMENT (which no writer can avoid) and COMMITMENT proper (which is the conscious acknowledgement of the involvement). The distinction is all the more important inasmuch as it helps to explain an apparently strange contradiction in the crusade undertaken by Sartre and others in favour of commitment : if the latter is so common, so 'inevitable', why waste ink and energy to preach about it? The answer, of course, is that it is involvement, not commitment, which is inevitable, and furthermore that writers are not automatically aware of their involvement (hence the need to remind them of it). Sartre lays the blame at their door and speaks of 'mental laziness', refusal to face facts, etc. That may be true in some cases, but by and large confusion on this issue has precise historical roots. It is part of the general onslaught on the critical character of literature which began in the nineteenth century and is based on the fallacy, no matter how differently expressed, and no matter how sincerely accepted by many, that art is 'a thing apart'. Those who fear the effects of a truthful portrayal of reality would like nothing better than to spread the notion that art moves in a province of its own. The value of the committed concept is that it rejects this facile and escapist explanation and reminds writers that they cannot help belonging to the world of men. Commitment thus implies the debunking of a hypocritical lie as well as the acceptance of an obvious truth, deliberately blurred or hidden away by certain social forces. The practical consequence is that the writer looks upon his activity 'as a citizen' as an essential part of his job 'as a writer', and is in a better position to will the effect of his work instead of leaving it to chance. (It does not necessarily mean that he will invariably be successful; it will depend on the degree and on the quality of his commitment.) The 'project' of writing becomes a lucid project.

The originality of Sartre's concept of commitment is not that it puts forward a new definition of literature but rather that it claims to be the only form of literature devoid of self-deception. It is an impressive challenge. For the writer, the challenge implies a new approach to his responsibility and to the issue of liberty. Sartre believes that the committed writer openly faces the two basic questions implied in literary creation – namely, *why* does one write? *for whom* does one write? Incidentally, these are the titles of two sections in *What is Literature?* Moreover, because he speaks to free men, the committed writer, according to Sartre, can have only one theme – Liberty. Not Liberty in general (which is a meaningless abstraction), but the concrete liberties which men try to win and preserve at each stage of their historical development. To illustrate his meaning, Sartre gives an example which is probably more topical today than when he first gave it: he says that a good book cannot be written to justify lack of liberty and that, consequently, a good novel against the Jews or the Negroes is impossible. Iris Murdoch takes him to task for this statement. She thinks he has been carried away by his own enthusiasm when he implies that only a 'progressive' writer can produce good literature. It is true that Sartre has often tended to overstress his case and that he did, at one time, hold the extreme view ascribed to him by Miss Murdoch. But it is not necessary to go to the same lengths in order to grant that an avowedly anti-Semitic or anti-Negro novel can hardly be a great work of art. Whatever the theoretical value of the Sartrian analysis, his *practical* challenge ('... show me a single good novel written against the Jews,' etc.) has never been successfully taken up. Furthermore, although a writer may well be an arch-reactionary, his artistic work is certain to give the lie to his one-sided private opinions: a novelist who would describe Jews or Negroes as mere villains would fail *on aesthetic grounds* because his characters would be crude caricatures, devoid of any credibility; on the other hand, if he depicts them as real human beings, with their virtues as well as their faults, he is *ipso facto* destroying the case for racialism which rests on the irrational belief that 'inferior' races have no virtues at all.

Iris Murdoch's criticism does, however, help to remind us that there are two ways of interpreting *'littérature engagée'*: a narrow one, which consists in denying that art can have any real value unless it carries 'good' ideas, and a broader one, which stresses that art, by its very nature, has the positive effect of making us think and look at reality in a different way, and that committed art has only one superiority – that of fulfilling the function of *all art* in a conscious way. Sartre himself began with the former outlook, but there has been in recent years a very significant and, in my opinion, very welcome change in his approach.[33] *Commitment is no longer looked upon as a categorical imperative which all writers are in duty bound to embrace, but rather as a quality which adds awareness and lucidity to literature.*

From 'What is Literature?' *to* 'Words'

No introduction to *'littérature engagée'* would be adequate if it did not attempt a brief discussion of Sartre's *What is Literature?*, for despite its many faults and the partial rejection of some of its theses by the author, this essay is rightly regarded as the Bible of French commitment. Even if some of its answers are unsatisfactory or insufficiently worked out, the book has the merit of being the first serious attempt to define 'engagement'. To regard it as final, however, is to forget that Sartre is still alive and can, at any time, enlarge upon it, if not disown it altogether, and – more important still – to ignore his plea that each of his works must be seen as a stepping-stone on the path to further progress.[34] It is therefore necessary to examine *What is Literature?*, first as it stands, and then in the light of later works on the subject, the most important of which is *Words*. Although commitment is by no means an exclusively Sartrian concept, its changes of meaning in the course of Sartre's own development reveal its living character – for it is under the influence of life that Sartre has

33. As usual with him, one should not speak of change but of a radical shift of emphasis. For example, his present open-minded attitude is already contained in embryo in *What is Literature?*, particularly in such statements as those which assert that the description of *any* aspect of human behaviour increases our understanding and thus has a 'liberating effect'. (Cf. *Situations II*, pp. 143 and 185.)

34. He says in *Words*, 'My best book is the one I am in the process of writing', and he defines his aim as 'doing better tomorrow, and better still the day after tomorrow'. (French ed., pp. 200 and 201.)

Cf. Aragon's statement that each of his new books disappoints some of his friends. 'It is against them that I write,' he adds; 'my purpose is not so much to write a new book, but rather to make people forget the books I have written'. (*Entretiens avec Francis Crémieux*, p. 141.)

amended and enriched his views – as well as its practical quality – for it is as the result of his own commitment that Sartre has made new discoveries.

What is Literature? can be divided into two parts, theoretical and historical, of which the former is by far the more stimulating. Its first major argument is that writing is a social act because it rests on the will to communicate with other people and on the resolve to change the world. It is difficult to disagree with the first part of the statement, which is almost an elementary truism. In fact, Sartre often bases his whole argument on such apparently axiomatic truths, with the object of drawing the logical and practical consequences which are implied in them. Therein lies his genius. He compels us to go back to first principles, as it were, and to make a permanent reassessment of what is involved in the truths which we take for granted. In the present case, the reminder that language is a means of communication naturally leads to the question of content (what to communicate?) and of responsibility, both of which are of crucial importance for '*littérature engagée*'.

The aim of language [Sartre writes] is to communicate ... to impart to others the results one has obtained ... As I talk, I reveal the situation ... I reveal it to myself and to others *in order* [Sartre's italics] to change it.[35]

Unfortunately, it is not enough to appreciate this point in order to disclose the nature of writing. Is it really true, as Sartre suggests, that literature communicates 'results', or should one look upon it as a writer's *appeal*, as his defence of certain *values*? Later in the book, we are told that

A work of art is an end in itself ... a work of art is a value because it is an appeal.[36]

There is perhaps a slight contradiction between the two statements quoted, and the ambiguity of Sartre's position leads him to assert, rather one-sidedly, that prose alone can be committed, all other arts, including poetry, being declared unfit to fulfil a revolutionary function because they approach reality through obscure and devious ways, instead of directly coming to grips

35. *Situations II*, pp. 72–3.   36. *Situations II*, p. 98.

with it through the medium of words. (It is ironic that the title of the book in which Sartre radically criticizes his former views should be just *Words*!) According to this argument, when the poet uses words, he treats them as ends in themselves, just as the musician handles sounds, or the painter colours and shapes. For the prose writer, on the other hand, words are merely *signs* which help us to stick labels on the objects around us so that we may easily act upon them. Prose alone can lead to action, because it is a rationalization of human activity (which Sartre often likes to endow with the Greek name of '*praxis*'); it clarifies the issues which modern man has to face, with the result that our will to act is considerably increased. In subsequent articles, as we shall see later, Sartre modified his views, and described the art of painting as a form of human '*praxis*'. This constitutes a remarkable advance on *What is Literature?*

As for the claim that the purpose of writing is 'to change the world', it might have gained, I feel, from a more precise formulation.[37] Would it not be better to speak of the impact of literature instead of its aim, and to state that the *effect* of great art is that it compels us to remould our lives?[38] Such a proposition could be proved both inductively and deductively. The inductive proof is that history provides us with convincing examples. Sartre himself mentions the writers of the Enlightenment, whose influence on their time was so obvious and so direct that it constitutes almost too good an illustration of the point; but in dealing with other periods, he seems more intent on passing wholesale condemnation on his predecessors than on making an objective assessment of the part they actually played in reflecting and criticizing their time. His description of the French seventeenth century in particular is based on the traditional notion of

37. The expression 'to change the world' which Sartre often uses is an echo of Marx's famous saying that 'philosophers have hitherto interpreted the world in various ways – the point, however, is to change it'. By 'change', Sartre occasionally means a political and social revolution in the Marxist sense, and sometimes a more modest and partial reform.

38. The *aim* of committed literature is certainly to 'change the world', but this is not true of all art. The point which Sartre himself makes is that '*littérature engagée*' sets itself the *conscious* purpose which is always *implied* in a work of art.

the period as one of order and stability, a view which no one accepts today. Similarly, his accusation that the nineteenth century no less than 'betrayed' literature (he graciously makes an exception in the case of Victor Hugo!) cannot be taken seriously. In both cases, his opinion rests on inadequate historical knowledge (a really unforgivable sin in a thinker who never tires of talking of the importance of history), and on the debatable view that unless commitment takes at all times the same form of direct and militant participation in political events, it is not commitment at all.[39] The historical part of *What is Literature?* is one of the weakest (the author is not unaware of this [40]) and it would be wrong to regard it as the perfect example of committed literary criticism. Sartre's own study of Flaubert (in which he shows the various ways in which the individual Flaubert was influenced by the ideology of his time), Aragon's study of Stendhal (in which the political character of *Le Rouge et le Noir* is particularly well brought out), and, in a different way, Péguy's remarks on Corneille (whom he regards as one of the few great poets who managed to mix philosophy and poetry) are, fortunately, among the many interesting illustrations of the way in which a committed critic can arrive at a better understanding of the authors he is studying.

As for the deductive proof, it is also Sartre who supplied it – but much later, when he said at an International Writers' Congress that the artist is a witness of his time to the extent that he reflects the *totality* of its problems.

In such conditions [he added], it matters little whether literature calls itself committed, for committed it is bound to be inasmuch as *totality* nowadays consists, among other things, in the fact that we are

39. Commitment, one must repeat, is a twentieth-century concept because it corresponds to the specific conditions of our time. It is quite unrealistic to expect the writers of previous epochs to have developed such a concept, for which conditions were far from ripe. The similarities between the eighteenth century and the present are due precisely to the fact that both epochs are epochs of great changes.

40. He admits that his historical analyses are hasty and superficial, but claims that this is because he had a more *urgent* task – that of *defining* literature. (Notice how this unwittingly proves that Sartre's approach is basically *not* historical.)

all threatened with the possibility of dying in a nuclear war ... This does not mean that the writer must necessarily deal with nuclear war; it rather means that a man who is afraid of dying like a rat cannot be wholly sincere if he confines himself to writing poems about birds. Some aspects of the times must, in one way or another, be reflected in a work of art.[41]

The notion of *totality* enables Sartre to make commitment implicit in all literature instead of restricting it to an explicit ideological point of view as he did in 1947.

But the main theoretical argument in *What is Literature?* is that there is no literature without a public.[42] The character of a work of art is determined by its public, and if we do not write today as in the time of Shakespeare or Racine, it is because the twentieth-century public is different, both historically and socially. Moreover, the writer, Sartre reminds us, is a consumer, not a producer. He is maintained by society, which, in class societies, means that he is maintained by the ruling class. He comes into conflict with the latter when he reveals the truth about the world. It is therefore imperative for him to decide *for whom* he is going to write. This choice is forced upon him, not by moral or ideological considerations, but by the requirements of his art. When the social conflict is particularly acute and when the alternatives are far from clear (at least for the writers themselves), literature inevitably reflects the tension by acquiring a tragic character. (The nineteenth-century Romantics are a case in point.)

But even in 1947 the choice of public presented difficulties, according to Sartre, and he spoke of a 'virtual public' for the committed writer. This represented a rationalization of his own uneasy position at the time as a critic of the bourgeois order who could not bring himself to support the Communist Party. If neither exploiters nor exploited, he argued, are ready to hear the committed message, then *'littérature engagée'* must speak to an imaginary public, the public it hopes will exist some day,

41. Statement made at the International Writers' Congress, Leningrad, 1963.

42. Once again, we have here an apparent truism from which Sartre is able to draw practical and logical conclusions.

either when the working class has given up Communist indoctrination, or when the exploiting class has been abolished. The necessarily utopian character of such a 'virtual public' led Sartre to evolve a predominantly speculative conception of commitment, which he was later to modify as he grew more involved in social and political struggles without losing his independence in any way. In a recent interview, he expressed pleasure at being read by the common people:

> I have changed my public . . . Now, I receive letters from workers, from secretaries. They are the most interesting ones.[43]

The main weakness of *What is Literature?*, in my opionion, is that the approach is often based on an abstract conception of the nature of writing, or, to put it in Sartrian terminology, that essence seems to precede existence. Although Sartre's starting-point is the social character of literature, he tends to deduce the literary 'project', not from the writer's concrete social situation, but from the ideal essence of literature. This leads him to over-estimate its value. He rightly says that writing is a 'social function', but one has the impression at times that he is not far from believing that it is *the* social function *par excellence*. The danger of such an approach is, firstly, that it weakens the value of commitment by implying that the writer does not have to change his whole life, since the main thing for him is to handle words successfully, and, secondly, that it can easily lead to the opposite extreme of thinking that literature has no value at all, as soon as its real limitations are discovered in practice. It is just what happened to Sartre. There have been times when, not content with denouncing the illusion of literature as a *priesthood*, as he does specifically in *Words*, he has allowed himself to be carried away much further, even to the point of asserting that in a world where hunger prevails, most of Western art and literature is a waste of time.[44] It is piquant to find a Marxist like Ernst

43. Interview in *Le Monde*, reprinted in *Encounter*, No. 129 (June 1964), pp. 61–3.
44. cf. his statement that 'over against a dying child *La Nausée* [Sartre's first major novel] cannot act as a counterweight', and his challenge, 'Do you think I can read Robbe-Grillet in an under-developed country?' (*Encounter*, No. 129, June 1964.)

Fischer replying indirectly to this outburst when he states in *The Necessity of Art* that although literature cannot side-step such issues as famine, poverty and ignorance, it would be wrong to expect a purely aesthetic attitude towards these problems, for it would amount to either an over-estimation or an under-estimation of the power of art. What Fischer means is that the solution to the world's problems is the concern of all men, writers included, but that theirs is not a privileged role. It is not merely 'as writers' that they will change the world (this is the over-estimation Fischer has in mind), but as writers who *add* their contribution to a wider struggle; neither is their job an idle game with words (here we have the under-estimation Fischer denounces), because the task of changing the world requires many-sided activities, including talking, singing, writing and painting. It is no less piquant to find under the pen of another Marxist critic the accusation that Sartre is guilty of 'aesthetic leftism', an expression which recalls that of political 'leftism' which was coined by Lenin to describe an over-simplification of reality and a narrow-minded condemnation of all those who do not follow the 'right' path. The critic in question is Christine Glucksmann who writes in *Nouvelle Critique* [45] that Sartre's leftism lies in his confusion of the *deed* with the *literary* deed and in his naïve belief that revolution will take place through language. This, she claims, led him to base commitment on avowed ideological content exclusively and to dismiss as unworthy all art which is not consciously *'engagé'*. It is probably unfair to suggest that Sartre was ever as naïve and sectarian as that, even in *What is Literature?*, but when the critic goes on to state that he remains fundamentally a 'leftist' despite the real changes which have taken place in his thought, it is hard to agree with her. [46] Is she not making too much of Sartre's occasional, but uncharacteristic, moods of despair, in the course of which he condemns literature

45. Nos. 173–4 (March 1966).
46. She accuses him, for example, of not having really changed because although his answers are no longer the same, he continues to ask the same questions (e.g. what is the place of literature in an under-developed world?). But are not Sartre's questions inescapable, and is it not the very opposite of 'leftism' to have the courage to heed the lessons of experience and life?

to being 'nothing', as a reaction against his former belief that it was 'everything'? Above all, is she not underestimating the significance of *Words*?

This little booklet, which came out as a literary bombshell at the end of 1963,[47] dramatically destroys the image of Sartre as a High Priest of Commitment, and reveals instead his bitter scepticism concerning the all-powerful character of words and his ironical onslaught on the so-called 'mandate' of literature. Although it is largely an account of the author's childhood, the last few pages are a mercilessly frank commentary on the relationship between his childish illusions and his adult attitude until quite recently. He shows that little Jean-Paul's faith in the magical revolutionary power of words was not really given up by Sartre the man but was merely endowed with a new look. His presentation of Commitment as a Moral Absolute was due to the persistence of a deeply religious outlook, now subtly disguised as a social and political philosophy. He had given up God the Father and God the Son, but the Holy Spirit had managed to keep a hold on him and inspire him with false ideas about a special 'mandate' and the 'priesthood' of literature. After describing how long he remained a prisoner of these fallacies, Sartre says quite simply, 'I have changed.' Then he adds the significant explanation,

> I have given up the priesthood of literature, but not the frock ... I am still writing books and I shall go on doing so; they are needed; they have their uses after all. Culture does not save anything nor anybody, one cannot be justified through it. But it is a product of man ... in this critical mirror alone does he find his own image.[48]

This shows that commitment has not been thrown overboard but has been purified of illusions in order to become more effective. (It is impossible not to be struck by the fact that the

47. First published in *Les Temps modernes*, October and November issues, 1963; in book form, 1964.
48. The French text (p. 211) actually says, '*J'ai désinvesti mais je n'ai pas défroqué.*' Notice Sartre's intentional retention of religious terminology. His wording suggests that he has given up all ideas of wearing the 'vestment' of a High Priest of literature, but that he still believes in wearing the ordinary cassock of the rank-and-file clergyman.

shedding of illusions also characterizes Aragon's recent evolution. Although the comparison must not be pushed too far, as the circumstances are different, it does reveal an unmistakable trend towards sober realism in this second half of the twentieth century.) In a recent interview, Sartre emphasized that for him, the writer's duty was still to place his pen at the service of the oppressed, but he added, '... this is the writer's task, and if he fulfils it as he should, he acquires no merit from it. Heroism is not to be won at the point of a pen. What I ask him is not to forget the reality and the fundamental problems that exist.'[49] There is no going back on the essential aspect of *What is Literature?* The value of this early essay can be appreciated all the better in the light of Sartre's further development. In particular, it is no mean achievement to have raised the issue of commitment for the first time and have attempted to define it, to have stressed forcefully the writer's responsibility in the modern world (irrespective of the somewhat weak theoretical foundations on which it is based), to have analysed with great clarity (albeit insufficiently) the social character of literature and the importance of the public, and lastly to have posed a number of questions, whose answers we are still seeking, but without which it is impossible to evolve a modern theory of aesthetics.

Aragon's 'Rejection' of 'Engagement'

It is impossible to close this chapter without mentioning Aragon's attitude to the concept of commitment. In a book published in 1946, he protested, almost laughingly, against the expression *poésie engagée'* on the grounds that poetry was not a maid whom one can 'engage' or dismiss at will. This was not an amusing sally or a facetious pun on the meaning of the word *engagée'*, but a spirited attack on the view which assimilates commitment to the toeing of a 'party line' and the committed writer to a sincere but naïve sycophant. Twenty years later, Aragon was even more specific, and he vigorously called the critic Jean Sur to task for sticking the label *'engagé'* on to his person and his work. He argued that he had done more than

49. Interview in *Le Monde/Encounter* cited above.

477

'escape from' the Sartrian challenge that literature must be either *'engagée'* or *'dégagée'* (committed or detached), for he had denied that such a dilemma existed :

> It is not so much that I escape from it, but that I violently deny its necessity ... One generally says that people like myself are *committed*, to signify that they say what they really think. I find this neologism quite unnecessary.[50]

When, later in the book, Jean Sur described him again as a 'committed man', he hastened to assert that he would always categorically reject 'not only the word but the concept of commitment', and he warned against the danger of using meaningless 'labels'.[51]

In the face of such unambiguous statements, has one the right to speak of Aragon as a committed writer and to take no notice of what he says? I suggest that one may do so, without necessarily rejecting his warning. Of course, commitment is only a label, and all labels are limiting, but can the literary critic do without them altogether? Aragon's own admission that he 'says what he really thinks' is both a valid description of commitment and of his own approach, so that, in spite of his understandable reluctance to be labelled, it is legitimate to go on considering him as a committed writer. One should, however bear in mind that commitment, whether it is an awful 'neologism' or not, does not involve giving up the writer's freedom but rather represents that rare and valuable quality of telling the truth as one sees it, a quality which Aragon shares with Péguy and Sartre. We may, and indeed we must, accept his criticism of the narrow conceptions with which commitment was unfortunately associated in its early years; but this should lead, not to the outright rejection of the label (unless a better one is substituted) but to a permanent attempt on the part of committed writers to seek a broadening of the concept. There is every indication that this is taking place, and Aragon's own effort is among the most valuable in this respect.

Moreover, Aragon is a man who would describe himself as a

50. Jean Sur, *Aragon, le réalisme de l'amour* (Paris, 1966).
51. ibid., p. 147.

'socialist realist', a phrase which indicates that his literary activity is guided by Marxism. We shall examine later his specific contribution to the issues raised by socialist realism, but what can be stressed immediately is that he takes a passionate interest in the problems of his time and that his work is openly coloured by his philosophy of life. The concept of commitment implies nothing more – and nothing less.

Lastly, it was none other than Elsa Triolet, Aragon's wife, who stated in a little book published in 1948 that it was permissible to use the word 'committed' in the case of Mayakovsky, for example, because such a word 'corresponds to something real in the minds of people today'.[52] She emphasized that a committed work of art had value only to the extent that it expressed the 'flesh and blood' of the artist and that it cannot be written to order. It is in this sense that I speak here of Aragon as a committed writer – his realism and his socialism are indeed his 'flesh and blood'.

Some Conclusions

The concept of commitment, although it is particularly well illustrated in the field of literature, is not in itself a purely literary concept but a philosophical one. In broad terms, commitment is the acceptance of an outlook on life, a *Weltanschauung*, which is 'defended and illustrated' to the best of one's ability in everything one undertakes.[53] Although Sartre has given it an atheistic content and has even measured the progress of his own commitment by his ability to discard religious patterns of thought, it does not necessarily follow that there is no such thing as a Christian commitment – the example of Péguy disproves such a contention. A committed man is primarily a man who feels a sense of responsibility to his fellow men and who takes practical

52. *L'Ecrivain et le livre* (Paris, 1948), pp. 38–9.

53. The difference between a worker and a writer in this respect is that the former cannot express his commitment in his actual job – there is no committed way of making tools, for example – but that the latter finds his creative work acquires new meaning in the light of commitment. (Cf. *Que peut la littérature?*, p. 34.)

steps to help them. No single ideology can claim that it alone is capable of arousing such an attitude among its followers. One of the most encouraging trends in recent years is the gradual breaking down of barriers of mistrust and incomprehension among people of the most diverse ideologies, and, more particularly, between believers and unbelievers. Neither side is giving up its own principles, but each has agreed to join in a *dialogue* in order to find possible areas of agreement, both on the theoretical and on the practical levels. This welcome way of interpreting 'peaceful co-existence' in the field of ideas is still in its infancy, but it *is* taking place, in England as well as in many other countries. In France, the dialogue has already had important internal repercussions within the two most important ideological groups involved, the Catholic Church and the Communist Party. Some Christians have been re-examining in a new light the old question of whether man can lead a good life without believing in God; and a lively debate has started among Marxists concerning the role of religion in society, with one group asserting that progressive Christians are progressive in spite of their faith, and the other suggesting that religious faith can under certain conditions actually inspire and support fighters for justice and liberty.

Perhaps the correct answer to these problems, both for Christians and for Marxists, is to recognize that there are two stages of development. The first stage is the desire to take part in the battle for human betterment, to commit oneself. The second stage is determined by a great number of circumstances, such as background, upbringing, personal experience, etc., and involves embracing a particular ideology. The committed approach is not the result of an ideology, but rather the step which precedes it and leads to it. It is not so much the particular ideology which matters but the *spirit* in which it is taken up. There will always be far more in common between a *committed* Christian and a *committed* Communist than between either of them and the Pharisees of his own church or party. Both Péguy and Aragon divined this important truth and voiced it in their works. For example, Péguy once wrote that 'all is not lost – far from it – in the case of revolutionary atheism', because it contains 'sparks of charity', but he added that 'reactionary, bourgeois atheism' was

480

an 'atheism without charity, ... an atheism without hope'.[54] For his part, Aragon often expressed his respect for genuine Christians, as when he wrote his wartime poem, 'La Rose et le réséda' ('The Rose and the Mignonette'), dedicated to Catholic and Communist patriots who were shot by the Germans. Devotion to the motherland, says the poet, matters more than an ideology:

> It matters little what you call
> The light which guided their steps
> Or that one would go to church
> While the other would stay away
> He who believed in Heaven
> And he who did not
> Both of them were faithful[55]

Péguy and Aragon believe that people are usually better (or worse) than their ideologies. This does not mean that ideologies are not important and that pragmatism is the answer. On the contrary, if commitment is not given solid foundations, it is in danger of remaining vague and ineffectual. It would not be complete unless it were commitment to a specific cause, and it is perfectly legitimate to expect each ideology to state its claim for being a better guide than any other, provided that by doing so it does not close the door upon the possibility of cooperation with other men of good will. I suggest that commitment is the unifying link because, whatever his philosophical or political allegiance, a committed person knows that he is 'a man among men'.[56] Moreover, as commitment requires a realistic approach to life the

54. Significantly, this comes from an essay in which Péguy attacks an orthodox theologian of his time. ('Un Nouveau Théologien' in *Œuvres en Prose* [1909–14], p. 893.)

55. 'La Rose et le réséda' in *La Diane française*.
> Qu'importe comment s'appelle
> Cette clarté sur leur pas
> Que l'un fût de la chapelle
> Et l'autre s'y dérobât
> Celui qui croyait au ciel
> Celui qui n'y croyait pas
> Tous les deux étaient fidèles

56. This favourite expression of Sartre's occurs frequently in his essays as well as in his novels and his plays. It sums up the basically human content of commitment.

better to change it, it can help to discard, not so much religion, as Sartre would have it, but dogmatism, which is – as recent events have shown – a disease which can disgrace any organized ideology. The rejection of routine and the tyranny of convention, which Sartre so eloquently proclaims, is not necessarily the prerogative of atheists and humanists, although it must be admitted they have done more than anybody else to spread these virtues. But a Catholic like Péguy spent his whole life denouncing the '*bien-pensants*'[57] and drawing a radical distinction between 'respectable' Christianity – which accepts things ready-made ('*du tout fait*') – and 'revolutionary' Christianity – which is based on things in the making ('*du se faisant*').

'*Littérature engagée*' is the application of commitment to the special field of literature. Its one and only requirement is that the writer should take part in the struggles of the age, and it urges him to do so, not because it is presumptuous enough to decree where his artistic duty lies, but, more modestly, because it knows the value of such a source of inspiration. Committed literature has no special themes, styles or methods – it is distinguished only by greater realism and by the author's attitude to life. These do not, by themselves, create a work of art, but they do enhance its quality. They help literature to make us aware of our true condition and to increase our sense of responsibility. In addition to providing aesthetic enjoyment, '*littérature engagée*' fulfils a 'social function'. Is not the blending of these two aspects characteristic of all great art? This is probably what Bernard Shaw had in mind when he ridiculed 'the parrot-cry that art should never be didactic' and defiantly proclaimed that 'great art can never be anything else'.[58]

POSTSCRIPT (1973)

Five years after writing the above, I realize that the differences between the Sartrian and the Marxist concepts of commitment

57. This expression describes 'right-thinking' people who are uncritical in their acceptance of convention and orthodoxy. Péguy always hinted that the '*bien-pensants*' were smug, self-satisfied Pharisees, and he attacked them bitterly both before and after his own return to Christianity.

58. Preface to *Pygmalion* (Penguin, 1941), ix.

could have been made clearer and sharper. Sartre deduces commitment from the *nature* of literature: thus an ideal essence constitutes his starting-point, rather than the class role of literature at any given stage of social development. The result is that his famous definition of commitment as *awareness* of being committed fails in three respects. First, it does not sufficiently stress that 'awareness' is not general or neutral and that this particular kind of awareness depends on a definite social practice. By *identifying* the forces he supports and those he fights, the committed writer becomes more conscious of his involvement – as a man; and of his responsibility – as a writer. He also realizes that the two are inseparable. Brecht puts the matter in his usual straightforward way:

> There was little I could do. But without me
> The rulers would have been more secure. This was my hope.

Secondly, action (to which awareness must lead) cannot be individual action, the noble deed of a Hamlet, of an Orestes in *The Flies*. For a Marxist, commitment implies fellow-feeling and cooperation with a wider group. In 1947 (at the time of writing *What is Literature?*) Sartre was honest enough to concede that a committed writer who is outside a working-class party lays himself open to the criticism of intellectual irresponsibility, but he pleaded that 'it was not his fault' if the Communist Party was not revolutionary enough. If that is the way he felt, he should not have shrunk from the consequence that commitment is impossible *today*, that it can only thrive in the future. There can be no commitment if the writer remains in a state of splendid, though principled, opposition.

Finally, Sartre does not account for the fact that commitment emerged in the twentieth century. In fact, one gets the impression that, according to him, it *ought* to have emerged earlier – if only the writers had been 'aware' of their true function. A Marxist, on the other hand, explains that commitment has arisen today, in the first place, because of the increased intensity of the class struggle, the sharpening of the contradictions between the aims of opposed sections of society which has made it more and more difficult to remain indifferent. (Many who reject commitment feel the need to justify their stand.) Furthermore, as the social basis of monopoly capitalism is getting even narrower, the alliance between intellectuals and the working class is no longer confined to a few individuals, as it was when Marx and Engels wrote the *Manifesto of the Communist Party*, but is now a social phenomenon. Commitment reflects these social changes and, to the extent that it reflects them accurately, it can contribute to further changes.

With regard to the other ideas in my chapter, I think that today I would deal more explicitly with the standard objection against commitment, namely that it is neither good nor bad because it has no direct bearing on literary form. My reply would involve stressing that an artist's whole experience and personality may be drawn upon when he writes, so that the choice he makes 'as a citizen' is bound to affect what he does 'as a writer'.

Three further points occur to me after a critical re-reading of the above text. First, it is misleading to say, as I do at the beginning of the section entitled 'Some Conclusions', that the concept of commitment is not 'purely literary' but 'philosophical'. The phrase 'purely literary' is unfortunate because it suggests that there is such a thing as 'pure' literature, which can be studied independently from the rest of life. The whole of my approach shows that I reject this 'phantom' (as T. S. Eliot calls 'pure poetry'), but in order to avoid confusion, I should have said, more simply, that the concept of commitment is not *confined* to literature – which is what I really meant. As for the word 'philosophical' it is also unfortunate as it appears to link commitment with philosophical categories, as is the case with Sartre (Being Freedom for, The Other, etc.). For a Marxist, commitment is not so much the product of Freedom, conceived in existential terms, as an activity which leads to freedom through struggle.

Secondly, I am not very happy about the formulation that 'the committed approach is not the result of an ideology, but rather the step which precedes it and leads to it'. Again, I think that the idea itself is sound, but is badly expressed. This is because I used the word 'ideology' too loosely in this context. What I was trying to suggest is that commitment to a *ready-made* ideology is not a *necessary pre*-condition of commitment itself. In this sense, it is true that the writer first commits himself to his fellow men and subsequently to a *particular* outlook which he feels provides the best guide to action. But ideology must not be confused with *Weltanschauung*. Ideology is more than just ideas, it is a system which corresponds to the interests and practice of a given class. We always have to choose between supporting and opposing the ideology of the exploiters; in so far as the idea of commitment, arising out of a desire to improve conditions, implies commitment to social change, it represents, in practice, an opposition to the exploiters' ideology. This amounts to more than a 'dissenting view' (which the ruling class can always live with), for it leads to practical steps against the system. To commit oneself, under present conditions, is therefore to fight the ideology of the *status quo* (which does not rely on an idealist crusade for its maintenance!) and, in effect, to embrace the ideology being built by the masses of the people, by the majority.

Lastly, I feel I should clarify my point about the 'spirit' in which an ideology is taken up being more important than the ideology itself. Without any qualification, this smacks of sheer idealism. I should have said that the acid test is not the *belief you hold*, but the *deeds you perform*: the importance of wrong ideas is that, though they are determined by definite social practice, they lead in turn to further wrong practice, so that 'spirit' or no spirit, an objectively progressive philosophy is always a more reliable guide to action.

The Loss and Discovery of Reality*

Ludwig Tieck, the German Romantic, first spoke of the 'loss of reality' in the preface to his edition of Heinrich von Kleist's works. This 'loss of reality', only dimly sensed in the Romantic age, has grown into a central problem in the highly industrialized capitalist world.

The industrialized, commercialized capitalist world has become an *outside world* of impenetrable material connections and relationships. The man living in the midst of that world is alienated from it and from himself. Modern art and literature are often reproached with 'destroying reality'. Such tendencies exist; but really it is not the writers or the painters who have abolished reality. A reality belonging to the day before yesterday, a reality that long ago became its own ghost, is being conserved in a rigid framework of phrases, prejudices, and hypocrisy. The end-product of a vast machinery of research, investigations, analyses, statistics, conferences, reports, and headlines is the comic strip, the embodiment of an illusory world of Everyman and No-man. Illusion displaces contradiction. The outcome of a multitude of 'points of view' is a hideous uniformity of minds. The answer precedes the question. A few dozen clichés, some of which were once reflections of reality, are served up again and again. Today they are as much like reality as an oil king is like a holy picture.

'I am convinced', wrote the Austrian satirist Karl Kraus, 'that happenings no longer happen; instead, the clichés operate spontaneously.' Things have become too much for people, the means too much for the ends, the tools too much for their producers.

Once again [Karl Kraus wrote about the Press] a tool has got out of our control. We have set the man who is meant to report the fire –

* From *The Necessity of Art* (1963).

a man who should surely play the most subordinate part in the whole State – above the State, above the fire and the burning house, above fact and above our imagination.

That was written half a century ago. Since then the process of 'destroying reality' has made alarming advances.

Many of the sincerest and most gifted artists and writers in the capitalist world are conscious of this loss of reality. They refuse to be led astray by outdated formulas and catchpenny phrases. They refuse to accept the system forced upon them by the ruling 'public opinion' as reality; they insist on seeing things 'as they are'. They detest all forms of propaganda, distrust all ideologists, they go out in search of reality beyond the illusory world of pseudo-facts, phrases, and conventions. They are determined to speak only of what they can see, hear, touch, or directly perceive. They cling to the smallest detail, the visible, audible, unchallengeably 'real' detail. Anything that goes beyond such details is suspect to them. Out of them they try, cautiously and without comment, to reconstruct reality. The widespread movement of neo-positivism is not wholly negative: it corresponds in part to a wish for unprejudiced sincerity.

In this fight against the fulsomeness of the late bourgeois novel and in his search for economy, purity, and lightness of form, Franz Kafka developed a narrative method whereby tiny details are linked together to make faint contours that hint at reality. Kafka once wrote of a woman he loved: 'Outwardly – at least sometimes – all I can see of F. are a few small details, so few that they could easily be counted. That is what makes her image so clear, pure, spontaneous, defined yet airy at the same time.' That is the principle according to which he drew his characters and situations.

This principle of allowing the status of reality only to the small true fact, the true detail', as Nathalie Sarraute never tires of repeating, has been carried to an extreme in the French 'anti-novel'. Detail follows detail, two-dimensionally, without perspective, without ever going beyond the Here and Now. Consider this passage from Camus's *L'Étranger*:

In the evening Marie came to fetch me and asked whether I wanted to marry her. I said I didn't mind and we could do it if she wanted. Then she wanted to know whether I loved her. I replied, as always, that this meant nothing, but that probably I didn't love her. Why marry me then? she asked. I explained that this was of no significance and that we could marry if she wished. Anyway she was the one who was asking; all I was doing was saying yes. She then remarked that marriage was a serious thing. I answered: no. She was silent for a moment and looked at me.

This emphasized detachment and coldness are a refusal to recognize any priority among objects, feelings, or events. The consequence of such understatement is, however, that material relationships acquire exaggerated power (almost as in the Romantic 'tragedies of fate' where human destinies were governed by mysterious objects). The world is neither meaningful nor absurd, says Robbe-Grillet, it is just *there*. 'All around us and in spite of all our objectives meant to endow them with soul and purpose, things are *there*. Their surface is clean and smooth, it is intact, but without ambiguous brilliance or transparence.'

This principle leads to a state of torpor, a series of images jerkily strung together, not a continuum but a fragmentary discontinuity: the passing moment is unreal, and only in recollection do situations freeze into reality. Nathalie Sarraute wrote of Proust that he had 'observed psychological processes from a great distance when they were already completed: frozen in tranquillity and, as it were, in the memory'. Robbe-Grillet's novel *Le Voyeur* represents the quintessence of this method: people are merely objects among objects, a murder means no more than the sale of a watch, crime no more than the screech of a seagull; an event is no more than a confusing dream or a witness's false evidence: reality without perspective, value, or measure.

In several respects, the method of the 'anti-novel' seems to be connected with the rise of cybernetics, the study of self-regulating dynamic systems. The existence of 'learning', 'thinking', self-improving machines has given encouragement to behaviourism and neo-positivism. The difference between human beings and these dialectical machines must now be formulated, the *nature* of man must now be grasped afresh, and dialectical materialism must now be expanded and made more precise. Machines which, it has been calculated by cybernetics, are possible and which, in part, have already been made, frequently behave as though they had consciousness, although in fact conscious machines cannot and do not exist. Leading cyberneticists therefore consider consciousness to be irrelevant or even fictitious; what they describe is solely the *behaviour* of a system. W. Ross Ashby, who with Norbert Wiener is the leader of modern cybernetics, writes in *Design for a Brain* (1960):

> Throughout the book, consciousness and its related subjective elements are not used, for the simple reason that at no point have I found their introduction necessary... Vivid though consciousness may be to its possessor, there is as yet no method known by which he can demonstrate his experience to another.

I do not wish to recapitulate here all the arguments between neo-positivism and dialectical materialism, but only to point out how closely the 'anti-novel' corresponds to these neo-positivistic ideas and to what a striking extent the people in these novels are reduced to the 'black box' of cybernetics, where only the relations of input and output matter and never the nature and essence of man. False philosophical conclusions from the revolutionary discoveries of cybernetics have linked up with a literary method which, in certain individual instances, may be as useful as behaviourism is in science but which, as a whole, not only describes the dehumanization of man but actually invests this dehumanization with the character of inescapable finality.

The method of the 'anti-novel' does not regain lost reality. In place of empty phrases and prefabricated conventional associations it puts forward details drained of all meaning and entirely disconnected sensory impressions. In rejecting the pseudo-facts of newspaper headlines, this literature has discarded facts altogether. All that is concrete dissolves; figures grope in a chaotic primeval fog, and there is for them no forwards nor backwards but only a timeless, directionless 'existence'. The official illusory world has been replaced by a private yet no less ghostly one. The intention is to represent uncomprehended being, the 'timeless' being of man in a timeless darkness. But 'being in itself is not yet real', wrote Hegel; 'only what has been comprehended is real'. And Marx: 'Only the comprehended world as such is reality.' *A literature which deliberately rejects comprehension lacks the decisive edge of reality.* The unreality that is its content may have come out of protest against the standardized illusory world: but in fact it is only the shadow of that world.

Some writers who also set out from the precisely observed detail nevertheless go beyond a world where everything has been frozen into an object or a fixed state. J. D. Salinger is such a writer. He too uses the behaviourist method, portraying the behaviour of people through a sequence of petty details. Here is a passage taken at random from *Franny and Zooey* (1962):

Ten-thirty on a Monday morning in November 1955, Zooey Glass, a young man of twenty-five, was seated in a very full bath, reading a four-year-old letter. It was an almost endless-looking letter, type-written on several pages of second-sheet yellow paper, and he was having some little trouble keeping it propped up against the two dry islands of his knees. At his right, a dampish-looking cigarette was balanced on the edge of the built-in enamel soap-catch, and evidently it was burning well enough, for every now and then he picked it off and took a drag or two, without quite having to look up from his letter. His ashes invariably fell into the tub water, either straightaway or down one of the letter pages. He seemed unaware of the messiness of the arrangement. He did seem aware, though, if only just, that the heat of the water was beginning to have a dehydrating effect on him. The longer he sat reading – or re-reading – the more often and the less absently he used the back of his wrist to blot his forehead and upper lip...

Yet out of such a mosaic of details, gestures, snatches of conversation, faintly outlined situations, Salinger creates a maximum of atmosphere and discovers fresh aspects of psycho-logical and social reality. His stories are without comment and without propaganda, yet they are exciting and gripping in an unusual way, perhaps for that very reason. In Salinger reality is newly discovered through the medium of young people sickened by the world that surrounds them and engaged, in one way and another, in a search for the meaning of life. It is this new and extraordinarily subtle form of social criticism, going far outside and beyond the behaviourism of the 'anti-novel', that makes Salinger's work so valuable and attractive. The world is seen through the eyes of children or very young people: that is why it appears, not as a conventional system to be circumscribed by ready-made phrases, but as an unexpected and shocking reality. A similar example is the film *Zazie dans le Métro* (based on Raymond Queneau's novel), where a little girl from the provinces discovers the grown-up world of Paris, the ghastly reality of a system where a toy turns into a bomb, a match can blast the ground sky-high, house-fronts collapse, and Fascist terror, murder, and fear creep out of the ruins. And when, at the end, the mother returning from a rendezvous with her lover asks the little girl how she has spent the day, Zazie replies with bitter scorn: '*J'ai vieilli*.' The positive, unforgettably beautiful counterpart to this bitter film showing a child's discovery of the capitalist world with all its fantastic antagonisms is the Soviet film *A Man Goes Towards the Sun*, in which another child discovers the world of growing socialism. These two films should be shown together all over the world. They would provide the strongest possible proof of two things: of the colossal contrast between the two worlds, seen unconventionally, without propaganda or false pathos; and of the overwhelming possibility of presenting both worlds with similar methods of modern art.

Many modern artists and writers share the belief that modern reality has nothing whatever to do with the available range of cliché images: that it is necessary to discover new situations characteristic of our time, and to build up a supply of new, powerful, unhackneyed images. Eisenstein, Mayakovsky, Chaplin, Kafka, Brecht, Joyce, O'Casey, Makarenko, Faulkner, Léger, Picasso, all those are among the outstanding researchers. I have deliberately mingled the names of socialist and non-socialist artists and writers because the rejection of clichés and the search for a new 'world picturebook' is common to them all. Where they differ is not in their method but in their perspective.

Walter Benjamin's *Theses on the Philosophy of History* includes the following passage:

There is a picture by Klee called *Angelus Novus*. It shows an angel looking as though it were recoiling from something it is staring at.

Its eyes are wide open, its mouth agape, its wings outstretched. The angel of history must look like that. It has turned its face towards the past. Where we distinguish a chain of events, it sees a single catastrophe incessantly piling ruins upon ruins and hurling them down at its feet. It would surely like to stay there, awaken the dead and make the murdered ones whole again. But a storm is blowing from paradise, a storm that has caught the angel's wings and is so strong that the angel can no longer fold them. This storm drives it inexorably towards the future, to which it turns its back, whilst the heap of ruins before it grows sky-high. That storm is what we call progress.

The same angel inspired Proust and Joyce, Kafka and Eliot: the shattered fragments of the past, the past as reality, grew vast before the eyes of their creative imagination. In the film *L'Année dernière à Marienbad*, for which Robbe-Grillet wrote the script, the present is composed of masks, ghosts, and the sound of footsteps in the sand, the future is shrouded in complete darkness, and only the stony images of memory are real. The angel of Mayakovsky and Brecht is different. It has a second face, turned forward. This different 'Angelus Novus' sees not only what lies in ruins but also what is as yet incomplete, sometimes scarcely discernible, sometimes obscure, sometimes strange. This other, different angel's range of reality is not only what has already become fact but whatever is possible. The realities and the essential situations it discovers are not idyllic but they are encouraging; they are not soothing, but they show the way forward.

Kafka dreamed of an angel that suddenly turned into a dead thing, 'not a live angel but only a painted wooden figure from the bow of a ship such as you see hanging from the ceiling in sailors' taverns. Nothing further ...' It was a ghastly dream about all living things turning into objects. Eisenstein, in *The Battleship Potemkin*, discovered the opposite situation. When the guns that are pointed at the rebel ship unexpectly change aim, the victory of men over the power of these lifeless things overwhelms the onlooker. The free decision of men communicates itself to objects. One of the great functions of art in an age of immense mechanical power is to show that free decision exists and that man is capable of creating the situations he wants and needs. Chaplin, too, in his grotesque parodies of everyday life, hints at this victory: not a revolutionary event like Eisenstein's but a victory all the same, the victory of man enslaved by the machine over the machine itself. Picasso, using the painter's means, showed a world blown into a million pieces, not as an expression of anonymous fate or as a cosmic event, but as *Guernica*, as human existence threatened by Fascist dictatorship. This magnificent painting does not merely represent reality in its most concentrated form: it sides with tortured humanity, writing its accusation in the light. If this were a case of so-called 'formalism', Picasso would not have called his work *Guernica* but *Explosion, Destruction, Under the Sign of the Bull*, or something of that kind. No anti-Fascist should ask, 'What is there to understand in this picture?' The question is better left to Fascists as they guiltily look away. When hundreds of genre paintings and academic historical canvases that hope to pass as realistic have long been forgotten, our great-grandchildren will recognize a chronicle of our times in the bitter, extreme realism of this tremendous work.

And then Brecht. In his work, the new situation is often the very reverse of the old, familiar one. In *The Caucasian Chalk Circle*, for instance, the judgement of Solomon that belonged to a patriarchal age is changed into a more humane one: the child is not awarded to its mother but to the woman who is truly motherly. Or the situation in *Galileo*: the man who knows yet who refuses to be a hero, the opponent of intolerant superstition who is willing to cower in the dirt in order that his work may outlive him. These portrayals of new, essential situations will increasingly create a total image of the new reality as it struggles against clichés, dogmas, phrases, the illusory world of files and pseudo-facts, prejudices, conventions, and everything officially celebrated as 'reality'.

This total image cannot be attained without the dialectical philosophy of Marxism. But non-Marxist artists and writers are also taking part in the discovery of the world in which we live and in the artistic expression of many of its aspects. Every effort to present reality without prejudice – that is to say, with all sincerity – helps us all to advance. Not that sincerity alone can represent the complex reality of our age in anything but a fragmentary way. But without it nothing can be done at all.

Art and the Masses

The efforts of socialist literature and art to discover new social realities were temporarily inhibited by bureaucracy, and even today these efforts are liable to run into bureaucratic opposition from time to time. The problematic nature of the transitional stage through which we are living today has deeper causes, however, than simple bureaucratic interference. The decisive task of contemporary socialist literature and art – that of representing the new reality through the means of expression appropriate to it – is intimately linked with another contemporary problem : the entry of millions of people into cultural life.

When Goethe wrote *Faust*, ninety per cent of the inhabitants of the Grand Duchy of Weimar were illiterate. Art and literature were the privilege of a narrow *élite*. Industrialized society, however, needs people who are able to read and write. Knowledge, and with it the need for further knowledge, grew together with industry. 'It has always been one of the most important functions of art', wrote Walter Benjamin, 'to create a demand for the complete satisfaction of which the hour has not yet struck.' And André Breton has written : 'A work of art has value only if tremors from the future run through it.' But apart from this anticipation of future needs by the *avant-garde*, there also exists a present need to cover lost ground, and this chiefly takes the form of a demand for entertainment. The deriving of profit from this demand is the main object of the producers and distributors of 'mass art' in the capitalist world. The immense possibilities of mechanical reproduction allow good books to be distributed on a mass scale, good pictures to be printed in large quantities, good works of music to be 'canned', and good films to be shown to millions of people. But on the other hand, the capitalist world has discovered rich possibilities of profit through the production of artistic opiates. The producer of these opiates starts with the assumption that most consumers are troglodytes whose barbarian instincts he must satisfy. And on this assumption he actually arouses those instincts, keeps them awake, and systematically stimulates them. The dream-image is commercialized: the poor girl marries the millionaire; the simple boy overcomes, through sheer brute strength, all the obstacles and opponents of a hostile, sophisticated world. The fairy-tale motif is brought up to date and mass-manufactured. And all this at a time when artists and writers are struggling against the cliché and painfully experimenting for means of reproducing a new reality!

The discrepancy is alarming: on the one hand, the necessary search for new means of expressing new realities, an awareness that 'our artistic means are worn out and exhausted; we are bored with them and we probe for new ways' (Thomas Mann); on the other hand, masses of human beings for whom even old art is something wholly new, who have yet to learn to distinguish between good and bad, whose taste must still be formed, and whose capacity to enjoy quality must still be developed. The composer Adrian Leverkühn in Thomas Mann's *Doctor Faustus* believes that all art needs to be set free 'from being alone with an educated *élite*, called "the public", for this *élite* will soon no longer exist, indeed it already no longer exists, and then art will be completely alone, alone unto death, unless it finds a way to "the people", or, to put it less romantically, to human beings'. If that happened, art would 'once more see itself as the servant of a community, a community welded together by far more than education, a community that would not *have* culture but which would perhaps *be* one ... an art on intimate terms with mankind'.

In the Soviet Union there is an intensive striving to achieve this. In the late bourgeois world, art is regarded as a kind of hobby, a distraction, unworthy of the attention of people occupied with matters as grave as business and politics. The socialist world takes art seriously. I have discussed Yessenin, Blok, Mayakovsky, Yevtushenko, and Voznessensky with young workers in Moscow, and have admired their intelligence and understanding. New books, films, plays, and musical works are not only consumed by hundreds of thousands, by millions of people, they also stimulate them to passionate discussion. The social, educational, formative force of words and images is taken for granted. A work of art is regarded, not as an ephemeral event, but as an action with far-reaching consequences. Born of reality, it acts back upon reality. Young people will argue a whole night long over a poem. Poetry has come out into the streets. A discussion about the characters and situation in a novel stirs up decisive problems of social life and philosophy. Art and the discussion of art are a forward-thrusting part of life in the socialist world.

This 'taking art seriously', splendid as it is, has also led to various mistakes and excesses. The way from art to man – 'putting art on intimate terms with mankind' – is not the shortest distance between a Party Secretary's office and an organization. It is bound to be a long road, not a short one, leading through many and varied experiments by artists and through the large-scale, generous education of the masses. What is alarming in the capitalist world is not 'formalism', not abstract paintings or poems, not serial music or the anti-novel. The real and terrible danger lies in the highly concrete, down-to-earth, 'realistic' if you will, productions of idiotic films and comics, commodities for the promotion of stupidity, viciousness, and crime. Anti-Communism does not use 'abstract' methods. War is not prepared by subtle works of art but by a very coarse diet indeed. In the Soviet Union one finds boring plays, boring books, and boring films side by side with excellent ones, tastelessness side by side with art, sticky sentimentality side by side with passionate truthfulness; but not the corrupting, evil filth of capitalist 'pulp' art. This great difference cannot be valued too highly. The negative element in the Soviet Union – the conservative clinging to forms of expression no longer appropriate to the times – is only a problem of transition.

The first motor-cars were designed like horse-drawn carriages. But the new core – the engine – was stronger than the old shell; new forms developed out of the demands of increasing speed; technology became the midwife to a new kind of beauty. The taste of every victorious class usually starts where that of the fallen class has left off, and tends to build a new life behind an old façade. The rise of the English bourgeoisie in the eighteenth century meant that Gothic architecture suddenly became 'modern' and ruins a sought-after attraction. The bourgeois wanted to disguise his capital in fancy dress, to own a castle – more than that, the ruins of a castle – as a symbol of a noble past. In 1760 a merchant by the name of Sterling had a ruin renovated with such consummate art that 'you believed it was going to collapse over your head'. A hundred years later, the rise of the German and Austrian bourgeoisie led to similar phenomena. An architecture of triumphant hypocrisy, a pastrycook's Neo-Gothic, came into existence. Banks postured as castles, railway stations as cathedrals. Adolf Loos, one of the pioneers of modern architecture, called such ornamentation a 'crime' and saw in the pretentious stuccoed house-fronts of gloomy offices and dwellings the architectural expression of the bourgeoisie's inherent hypocrisy.

Similarly, many workers, having achieved political victory, begin by adopting the taste of the petty bourgeoisie. As a result there is at first a discrepancy between the artistic ideas of many progressive intellectuals and those of most of the working class. It can even happen that the gap between what is socially progressive and that which is modern in the arts becomes so absurdly large that the very word 'modern' becomes a term of abuse on the lips of certain officials. The younger generation gradually overcomes this curious contradiction; it wants to be not only progressive but also truly modern; it looks for a modern style of living – that is to say a style appropriate to the times – and watches out for innovations of all kinds. A struggle between the old and the new thus begins in the sphere of culture, and apologists of the old may frequently invoke the 'healthy instincts of the simple man'. I must confess that such talk makes me thoroughly uncomfortable; I cannot help hearing overtones of condescension in it. Does he still exist, this much-praised 'simple' man, this ordinary, unsophisticated reader, listener, or gallery visitor? And if he does, is he really the highest court of appeal, the full and many-sided personality that Communism sets out to form? The 'simple man' belonged to primitive social conditions which produced works of art compounded of instinct, intuition, and tradition. Such people are becoming increasingly rare in our industrialized, town-dominated civilization. The combination of spontaneity and custom characteristic of the bards of feudal times has been lost; industry and the town have had a disintegrating effect. Man in industrial society is exposed to many different stimuli and sensations. His taste is not *tabula rasa* – it has been affected by all the mass-produced commodities that have flooded his life since childhood. His artistic judgement is in most cases a prejudice. The Viennese operetta would triumph over Mozart in almost any plebiscite.

The 'simple man' belongs to an illusory world of clichés. He exists as little as 'the worker' or 'the intellectual'. Even in the capitalist world with its commercial tendency to level out all cultural differences, the differences are in fact infinitely greater than simplifiers allow. The effect of inferior mass-produced commodities is great, but spontaneous opposition is by no means lacking. An exhibition of drawings and paintings by Austrian railway workers was held in Vienna recently. Contrary to all expectation, only about a third of the items shown were the familiar mixture of naturalism and false sweetness; two thirds showed the influence of Van Gogh, Gauguin, Cézanne, Picasso, and modern Austrian artists. It would be quite wrong to assume that 'the workers' or 'simple people' instinctively reject modern art; the percentage of workers who prefer conventional art is probably no higher than that of businessmen, company directors, or politicians.

The major task of a socialist society, where the 'art market' is no longer supplied with commodities mass-produced by capitalist speculators, is therefore twofold: to lead the public towards a proper enjoyment of art, that is to say, to arouse and stimulate their understanding; and to emphasize the social responsibility of the artist. That responsibility cannot mean that the artist accepts the dictates of the dominant taste, that he writes, paints, or composes as so-and-so decrees: but it does mean that, instead of working in a vacuum, he recognizes that he is ultimately commissioned by society. There are many cases, as Mayakovsky pointed out long ago, when this general social commission does not coincide with the explicit commission of any particular social institution. A work of art does not have to be understood and approved by everyone from the start. It is not the function of art to break down open doors but rather to open locked ones. But when the artist discovers new realities, he does not do so for himself alone; he does it also for others, for all those who want to know what sort of a world they live in, where they come from, and where they are going. He produces for a community. This fact has been lost sight of in the capitalist world, but it was taken for granted in ancient Athens and in the age of Gothic art. The desirable synthesis – freedom of the artist's personality in harmony with the collective – cannot be achieved all at once; it requires much undogmatic thought and experimentation. Every great revolution is an explosive synthesis; but disturbances in the dynamic equilibrium always occur again and again, and new syntheses have to be re-established under changing conditions. The romantic and individualistic revolt of the young Mayakovsky drew its great content from the Revolution; personal and collective experiences were merged into one. Such unity is not static and cannot be preserved, least of all by decree. But socialist art must always draw strength from this very task of re-establishing unity, so that finally, through a slow and painstaking process, all the symptoms of alienation are eradicated.

All kinds of misunderstanding are liable to arise. The demand for art in the Soviet Union and the People's Democracies cannot be fully satisfied either by enormous editions of the classics or simply by the works of outstanding socialist artists and writers. The desire for an art that simply 'entertains' is legitimate, and side by side with the more original innovators there is bound to be a large number of 'average' artists. The boundary between entertainment and serious art cannot be clearly drawn, nor is it unalterable, least of all in a society that deliberately sets out to educate the entire people towards knowledge and culture. Entertainment should not mean silliness any more than serious art should mean boredom; both the public's education and the artist's social consciousness should prevent this. A society moving towards Communism needs many books, plays, and musical works that are entertaining and easy to grasp, yet at the same time also serve to educate both emotionally and intellectually. But this need carries with it the danger of hackneyed over-simplification and crude propaganda disguised under a high moral tone. Stendhal wrote as a young man: 'Any moral intention, that is to say any self-interested intention of the artist's, kills the work of art.' No socialist artist can work without moral intention, but he should always endeavour not to allow it to become 'self-interested', not to over-simplify it in terms of propaganda, but to elevate and purify it in terms of art. This should be the motto, too, of artists producing 'entertainment', i.e. working purely for the needs of the day. In a socialist world, works of entertainment, like all other art, are addressed to mature human beings. They are entirely failing in their purpose if they patronize their public.

It would be foolish to denigrate those who produce decent, unobjectionable literary or musical works by the dozen. But it would be a much more serious error to set them up as an example to those who are trying to express new realities with new artistic means. We can understand why many socialist artists cling to old styles during difficult transitional periods; even a socialist society, whose very essence is novelty, has need of certain conservative tendencies, if only so that, in the struggle against them, the new should grow stronger and more resolute. But it is the original artists who create new styles – artists like Mayakovsky, Eisenstein, Brecht, or Eisler – and it is they who will live on in the future. Even today, and not only in the socialist but also in the capitalist world, the new proves itself more effective than imitations of the old. For although the two economic systems are fundamentally antagonistic to each other, and although the struggle and competition between them is one of the central problems of the new social reality, nevertheless many elements of modern life are common to both systems: industrialization, technology, science, large cities, speed, rhythm, many modern experiences, sensations, and stimuli. Life in a large city demands to be expressed in a different way from life in a sleepy provincial town. A skier's or motor-cyclist's experience of nature is different from a peasant's or a rambler's. The content and style of life of the modern working class and its intelligentsia are no longer directly related to the poetic methods of the last century. We see, hear, and associate differently from our ancestors. The things that shocked them in art – the Impressionists' use of colour or the dissonances of Wagner – no longer worry us in the least. The average public today is thoroughly familiar with such things and no longer thinks of them as 'modern'.

Cybernetics envisages the possibility of machines giving theoretical answers to questions concerning as yet unexplored areas of reality, these answers being beyond the powers of comprehension of the human brain. Science does not capitulate before such a staggering possibility, nor will it scornfully reject the answers supplied by such computers because the human brain cannot yet cope with them. On the contrary, cyberneticists say that it may become necessary to design 'brain amplifiers' in order to equip the brain with the means for coping with the new concepts. Science and art are two very different forms of mastering reality, and any direct comparison would be misleading. Yet it is equally true of art that it also discovers new areas of reality, making visible and audible what had been invisible and inaudible before. Artistic comprehension, too, is not a constant; it too can be expanded and more finely adjusted by means of 'amplifiers'. Socialism, convinced of man's infinite capacity for development, should therefore not reject the new in any field just because it is new: instead, it should use 'amplifiers' in order to grasp what at first seems incomprehensible, and, having grasped it, submit it to close examination and analysis.

Often all the artistic means of expression discovered since the middle of the last century are lumped together and dismissed as 'decadent'. It is certainly true that the late bourgeois world is a declining world and therefore by its very nature decadent. But it is by no means homogeneous – on the contrary, it is exceedingly rich in contradictions, not only between the bourgeoisie and the working class but also within each social stratum; the struggle between the new and the old rages with particular violence among the intelligentsia. What is new is not of course *ipso facto* on the side of the working class. It is more complicated than that. On the one hand, many workers have been infected by the decadence of the bourgeoisie; on the other hand, the capitalist world is incessantly influenced by the existence of the socialist world, and this influence itself is full of contradictions in that it not only provokes anti-Communism but also stimulates intellectual inquiry. The protests of artists against the capitalist world, their direct or indirect reactions to the fact of Communism, their discovery of a highly complex reality, all give rise to new forms and means of expression in which the decay of what is old is inseparable from the fermentation of what is new. In many cases it is impossible for us to distinguish between what is useless and what may be of future value. But to dismiss all modern elements in the literature and arts of the capitalist world as 'rotten' is like Lassalle's idea, condemned by Marx, that the working class confronts a uniformly reactionary mass. Such compact uniformity does not exist in politics – still less in the arts of any period, let alone ours.

The insistence of conservative elements in the socialist world on the idealized figure of the 'simple' man as the final arbiter in all artistic matters is a retrograde tendency. It is part of the irresistible advance of socialism that the 'simple' man gradually turns into a subtle and highly differentiated man. The structure of a people can change more quickly than the minds of certain administrators. Already the dividing line between the qualified worker and the intellectual technologist is beginning to blur; the working class and the intelligentsia are beginning to overlap; the highly educated sons and daughters of the working class are acquiring a taste for intellectual adventure, for daring artistic experiment. They smile when their fathers shudder at the names of Moore, Léger, Picasso, or when they dismiss Rimbaud, Yeats, and Rilke as 'obscure', or say that twelve-tone music is the work of the devil. The younger generation in the socialist world will not be deprived of their right to know these things. Nor will they stop there. There are new Soviet films and the works of certain young writers, sculptors, and painters which justify the belief that we are about to see a flowering of Soviet art in which socialist content will be triumphantly expressed in a truly modern form.

Between Rise and Decline

The late bourgeois world is still capable of producing art of importance (and the existence and challenge of the socialist world, the moral and intellectual issues which it poses, are of considerable help here). But in the long-term view socialist art has the advantage over late bourgeois art. The latter, although it has much to offer, lacks one thing: a large vision of the future, a hopeful historical perspective. Despite disappointments, this vision still belongs to the socialist world. It is far more than a question of bread and space rockets, prosperity and technical perfection: it is a matter of the 'meaning of life', a meaning that is not metaphysical but humanist.

Despite all the conflicts it has undergone, socialism remains convinced of the unlimited possibilities that exist for man. The vision of the future expressed by many of the most gifted and sincere artists and writers in the late bourgeois world is negative, indeed apocalyptic. Superficial optimism cannot provide a counterweight to these gloomy views, for it is true that, for the first time in history, the suicide of the human race has become a possibility. Many years ago, one of Karl Kraus's aphorisms anticipated this: 'The modern end of the world will come about when machines become perfect and, at the same time, man's inability to function reveals itself.' Human consciousness has lagged far behind technical progress. Socialist artists and writers cannot, therefore, argue lightly against the grim vision of the future depicted in bourgeois art and literature. Even if there were life left after an atomic war, this life, the infected air of a moon landscape, would have nothing whatever to do with the vision of a socialist world.

To prevent war is therefore the duty of all reasonable men under all social systems. Those who despair of the power of reason believe the catastrophe to be unavoidable; and the pale shadow of destruction falls on their work. Against this *possibility* of the end of the world, the socialist artist sets another *possibility*, that of a rational and therefore humane world. The second possibility is not predetermined any more than the first is inescapable. The choice, as never before, lies with the individual, and Hebbel's lines are truer than ever:

> *Du has vielleicht*
> *gerade jetzt dein Schicksal in den Händen*
> *und kannst es wenden, wie es dir gefällt.*

Für jeden Menschen kommt der Augenblick
in dem der Lenker seines Stern ihm selbst
die Zügel übergibt ...

(Your fate perhaps is in your hands at this very moment, and you can turn it as it pleases you. For every human being comes the moment when he who guides his star passes the reins into his own hands ...)

In a world in which the concentration of power is so great and the workings of that power so obscure, many people are inclined to think that their personal decision does not matter and, therefore, they surrender to 'fate'. In such a situation, the central problem of socialist art is to portray the men behind the nameless objects and to present the possibility of man's victory over them – without grand phrases or over-insistent optimism. William Faulkner's tremendous novel *Sanctuary* – a tragedy about the impotence of human beings who, when they try to break out of their allotted social situation, are destroyed in the attempt or driven back into the past – has not yet found its socialist counterpart. Alexey Tolstoy's *Road to Calvary* deals with a corresponding theme, but it is set in the special emergency situation of a revolution. A writer tackling the same theme today would need to have, apart from a talent comparable with Faulkner's, unerring sincerity and the determination to ignore all tactical considerations, however worthy. The theory (originating in Stalin's time) which ordered the 'conflict-free' novel, which claimed the existence of non-tragic solutions to all problems that could arise in a socialist society, and which consequently demanded a happy ending to every story, has fortunately been cast aside – along with the equally false theory of increasing class differences under socialism. But there is still a tendency to sidestep the portrayal of conflicts and to substitute wish-fulfilments for reality.

The less socialist art confuses its vision of the future with idealization of the present, the more it gains in authority and conviction. The genuine despair of serious artists and writers in the late bourgeois world cannot be dismissed by being labelled 'decadent', nor by the argument that, in the grand scheme of world history, everything is really going according to plan. The apocalyptic contingency must be recognized as *conceivable*, yet shown to be *avoidable*. This does not mean that the struggle for peace must now be the exclusive theme of all socialist art. What it does mean is that the argument of 'inevitable' disaster so common in late bourgeois art must be answered by works which show how it is possible to avoid disaster; but these works must be real, they must not be trimmed to propagandist aims.

If saving peace is the one great common task – and everything suggests that it is – then socialist art should not concentrate its attention wholly on internal problems of the socialist countries, but should speak to the world at large as an essential contribution to world art. The works of Gorky, Mayakovsky, Isaak Babel, Alexey Tolstoy, Eisenstein, and Pudovkin have meant a great deal to a vast non-Socialist public; conversely, Chaplin, de Sica, Faulkner, Hemingway, Lorca, and Yeats have a large following in the socialist countries. Though we belong to different social systems and pursue different aims and ideas, we live, after all, in one world. And our world needs Russian as well as American literature, Russian as well as French and Austrian music, Japanese as well as Italian, British, and Soviet films. It needs the modern Mexican painters as well as Henry Moore, Brecht as well as O'Casey, Chagall as well as Picasso. The political struggle between the two social systems will continue. That it should take place in peace, not war, is a condition of the existence of us all. And that men on both sides should not speak in a vacuum but should understand each other's problems, aims, and desires has become one of the greatest functions of contemporary literature and art.

The Dream of the Day after Tomorrow

An opposite line of argument might go something like this: 'What confidence! What makes you so certain of the necessity of art? Art is on its last legs. It has been driven out by science and technology. When the human race can fly to the moon, is there any real need of moonstruck poets? The aeroplane is swifter than the gods, the car more efficient than Pegasus. The astronaut can see what the poet merely dreamed of. Remember Byron's Cain flying through space with Lucifer:

> 'CAIN: Oh god, or demon, or whate'er thou art,
> Is yon our earth?
> LUCIFER: Dost thou not recognize
> The dust which form'd your father?
> CAIN: Can it be?
> Yon small blue circle, swinging in far ether
> With an inferior circlet near it still,
> Which looks like that, which lit our earthly night? ...
>   As we move
> Like sunbeams onward, it grows small and smaller
> And as it waxes little, and then less,
> Gathers a halo round it, like the light
> Which shone the roundest of the stars, when I
> Beheld them from the skirts of Paradise ...

'Are not Gagarin's, Titov's, or Glenn's prose reports even more overwhelming than this vision in verse? Is art not something that belonged to the childhood and puberty of mankind? Can it not be dispensed with now that we have reached maturity?

'It is clear that capitalism is no longer capable of producing a new renaissance of the arts. But socialism? Is it conceivable that another Homer or Shakespeare, Mozart or Goethe will be born? And if he is, will society need him? Is art not an enchanting substitute, a magic invocation of reality by men and for men who cannot cope with it? Does it not presuppose a mental passivity that is prepared to accept the dream for the deed, shadow for existence, and a cloud for Juno? Within the foreseeable future we shall have perfect cybernetic machines capable of handling reality with mathematical precision. No feeling will lead them astray, no passion will tempt them into error. What use is art, what use is Helen's ghostly veil in an age of total automation, unlimited productive forces, and unlimited consumption?'

In future, machines will eventually relieve men of all mechanical labour, which will come to be regarded as unworthy of human effort. But as machines become more and more efficient and perfect, so it will become clear that *imperfection is the great-*

ness of man. Like cybernetic machines, man is a dynamic, self-perfecting system – but never sufficient unto himself, always open towards infinity, never capable of becoming a creature of pure reason obeying only the laws of logic. '*Quod nunc ratio est, impetus ante fuit,*' wrote Ovid. This passion, this *impetus*, this creative imperfection will always distinguish man from the machine.

'Agreed,' my invisible opponent may say. 'The perfect machine will have no urge to express its suffering, because it will not suffer; outside joy or suffering, it will carry on with solving the mysteries of reality. But even if man will never possess the absolute infallibility of the machine, why should he need art in a Communist society? You have said that the mission of art is to help us, half-men that we are, fragmentary, wretched, lonely creatures in a divided, incomprehensible, terrifying class society, towards a fuller, richer, stronger life – to help us, in other words, to be men. But what happens when society is itself the safeguard of a truly human life? All true art has always invoked a humanity that did not yet exist. When once we have attained it, what is the use of all the Faustian magic?'

Questions of this kind are prompted by naïve hopes – or fears – that human development will one day reach a final goal : universal happiness, the fulfilment of every dream, the accomplishment of the cycle of history. But only the pre-history of mankind will have been accomplished then; man will never be condemned to the immobility of paradise, but will always continue to develop. He will always want to be more than he can be, will always revolt against the limitations of his nature, always strive to reach beyond himself, always struggle for immortality. If ever the desire to be all-knowing, all-powerful, all-embracing vanished, man would no longer be man. And so man will always need science in order to prise every possible secret and privilege out of nature. And he will always need art in order to be at home not only in his own life but in that part of reality which his imagination knows to be still unmastered.

In the first collective period of human development art was the great auxiliary weapon in the struggle against the mysterious power of nature. Art in its origins was magic, essentially one with religion and science. In the second period of development – the period of the division of labour, of class distinction, and the beginning of every kind of social conflict – art became the chief means of understanding the nature of these conflicts, of imagining a changed reality by recognizing existing reality for what it was, of overcoming the individual's isolation by providing a bridge to what all men shared. In the late bourgeois world of today, when the class struggle has become more intense, art tends to be divorced from social ideas, to drive the individual still further into his desperate alienation, to encourage an impotent egoism, and to turn reality into a false myth surrounded by the magic rites of a bogus cult. And in the Socialist world today art tends to be subordinated to specific social requirements and to be used as a simple means of enlightenment and propaganda. But when the third, Communist, period is reached – when the individual and the collective are no longer in conflict, when classless society exists in an age of abundance – the essential function of art will consist in neither magic nor social enlightenment.

We can only dimly imagine such an art, and our visions of it may well be mistaken. Marxism rejects any ideal utopia with all the severity of science; yet utopia is its golden background. And so we may be allowed, as we dream of the future, to evoke a picture of a world where human beings, no longer exhausted by labour, no longer weighed down by today's cares and tomorrow's duties, have time and leisure to be 'on intimate terms' with art.

We need not fear that a prosperous and highly differentiated society will mean an impoverishment of the arts. The differentiation will be between personalities, not classes; between individuals, not social masks. Everything will encourage the interplay of the intimate and the universal, the fanciful and the problematic, reason and passion. Highly developed means of art reproduction will allow the 'public' to become individuals, each becoming familiar with art in his own home. At the same time public festivals and competitions of all kinds will encourage direct participation. It may well happen that apart from the novel, whose essential function is to analyse and criticize society, there will be a revival of the epic, for the epic is the literary form that affirms social reality. Tragedy will doubtless continue to exist, because the development of any society – even a classless one – is inconceivable without contradiction and conflict, and perhaps because man's dark desire for blood and death is ineradicable. Our own appetite today for the grotesque and scurrilous in art may not only be the consequence of the juxtaposition of the terrible and the comic in modern life; it may also be the forecast of a rebirth of comedy. Hitherto comedy has generally meant criticism – destructive laughter, or, as Marx put it, 'a merry farewell to the past'; in a distant future it may reflect the life of sovereign man, his freedom, gaiety, and spirit.

Perhaps it is more than personal taste that links the names of Homer, Aristophanes, Villon, Giotto, Leonardo, Cervantes, Shakespeare, Brueghel, Goethe, Stendhal, Pushkin, Keller, Brecht, Picasso, and above all Mozart, always and always Mozart. The differences between these artists only emphasize one thing they all have in common: a triumphant rejection of all that is heavy, puritan, oppressive. In many of their works reality has been distilled by the imagination to such a point that it seems altogether weightless: the gravity of things vanishes, suspended between nothingness and infinity. Terror is not toned down, causes for fear are not denied, but everything is touched with grace and nothing is a stranger to gaiety. On the island of Caliban and Ariel, Prospero transforms cruelty, darkness, and blood into comedy, into clouds suffused with light. The magic of art blends *seeming* into *being* and beauty into nothingness.

> ... These our actors,
> As I foretold you, were all spirits, and
> Are melted into air, into thin air:
> And, like the baseless fabric of this vision,
> The cloud-capp'd towers, the gorgeous palaces,
> The solemn temples, the great globe itself,
> Yea, all which it inherit, shall dissolve,
> And, like this insubstantial pageant faded,
> Leave not a rack behind. We are such stuff
> As dreams are made on ...

Prospero's wand also wields a tragic power:

> ... the strong-based promontory
> Have I made shake, and by the spurs pluck'd up
> The pine and cedar: graves at my command
> Have waked their sleepers, oped, and let 'em forth
> By my so potent art. But this rough magic
> I here abjure ...

Prospero's magic finally transforms itself into 'heavenly music', into 'airy charm' and gaiety full of wisdom. Leonardo's smile is of the same essence; so is the bright sky against which Stendhal lightly draws outlines of passion, failure, and death; so too is the blend of enlightenment and romanticism, reason and jest in Brecht. And Mozart is the epitome of such art, Mozart in whose music tension is so delicately adjusted that the slightest variation produces a *non plus ultra* of delight. The magic wand that Prospero dropped is passed on from generation to generation. The abundance of life (not only of consumer goods) promised by Communism will affirm, gladly, without sadness, that 'we are such stuff as dreams are made on'.

The Romantic yearning for the 'universal' work of art – itself the expression of a deeper longing for man's unity with the world and with himself – may find fulfilment (in contrast to Wagner's theories) in a new kind of comedy that will make use of all the possibilities of the theatre and create a synthesis of word and image, dance and music, logic and harlequinade, sensuality and reason. Martyrdom and sacrifice, the smell of blood and incense, the tying of art to religion, all this belongs to the pre-history of mankind. And it may be that comedy will be the most apt expression of man's liberation.

In one of his dialogues entitled *On Stupidity in Art*, Hanns Eisler writes: 'The whine of the disappointed petty bourgeois, of the hard-done-by shopwalker – *that* exists in music, too. And in music under capitalism it seems to be the typical characteristic.' We can expect that music in a Communist future will free itself of all romantic whimpering and smug silliness, all hysteria and all ham-handed propaganda: that it will presuppose listeners who are neither nervously over-stimulated nor sentimentally flabby; that its effect will be to refresh rather than to stun, to illuminate the mind instead of dimming it – and that, although it will use many new means of expression and never try to imitate the past, it will nevertheless have something of Mozart's serene richness and Mozart's wise audacity.

The function of painting and sculpture will no longer be to fill museums. There will be patrons, both public and private; and halls, squares, stadiums, swimming pools, universities, airports, theatres, and blocks of flats will each have sculptures and paintings to fit their character. The visual arts will probably not conform to a uniform style as they did in previous periods of class and imperial domination : the idea of a uniform style being the distinguishing feature of a culture may well prove to be old-fashioned. It is more likely that a wide variety of styles will be the new characteristic of a culture and age in which nations will merge into one, new syntheses will destroy all that is parochial and static, and no centre, either of class or nation, will predominate. In a classless society we are likely to find a *multiplicity of styles*.

Man, being mortal and therefore imperfect, will always find himself part of, and yet struggling with, the infinite reality that surrounds him. Again and again he must face the contradiction of being a limited 'I' and at the same time part of the whole. Mystics have striven towards another state where man would be 'beside himself' and at one with a totality mysteriously called God. We are not mystics and we do not yearn for that paradoxical state where man, by maximum concentration upon himself, succeeds in blotting out that very self; where, by totally denying reality, he hopes to lose himself in the reality he destroys and so achieve communion with an infinity drained of life. Our aim is not unconsciousness but the highest form of consciousness. But even the highest attainable consciousness of the individual will not be able to reproduce the totality in the 'I' – will not be able to make one man encompass the whole human race. And so, just as language represents the accumulation of the collective experience of millennia in every individual, just as science equips every individual with the knowledge acquired by the human race as a whole, so the permanent function of art is to re-create *as every individual's experience* the fullness of *all that he is not*, the fullness of humanity at large. And it is the magic of art that by this process of re-creation it shows that reality can be transformed, mastered, turned into play.

All art has to do with this identification, with his infinite capacity of man for metamorphosis so that, like Proteus, he can assume any form and lead a thousand lives without being crushed by the multiplicity of his experience. Balzac used to imitate the gait and movements of people walking ahead of him in the street in order to absorb them, even as unknown strangers, into his own being. He was so obsessed with the characters in his novels that they were more real to him than the reality surrounding him. Those of us who simply enjoy art do not often run such a risk; but our limited 'I' is also marvellously enlarged by the experience of a work of art; a process of identification takes place within us, and we can feel, almost effortlessly, that we are not only witnesses but even fellow creatures of those works that grip us without permanently tying us down. And so it is a little true to say that what art offers us is a substitute for life. But let us try to realize how much the unsatisfied man of today, identifying his sad ego with princes, tough gangsters, and irresistible lovers, differs from the free and self-aware man of a future society. This man will no longer need primitive mass-produced ideals but, because his life will be full of content, will strive for a content that is grander and richer still. Art as the means of man's identification with his fellow men, nature, and the world, as his means of feeling and living together with everything that is and will be, is bound to grow as man himself grows in stature. The process of identification, which originally covered only a small range of beings and natural phenomena, has already extended beyond recognition, and will eventually unite man with the whole human race, the whole world.

In his novel *Wilhelm Meister* Goethe created the marvellous and enigmatic character of Makarie, the strange woman who identifies herself with the solar system and whose magic unity with the universe is watched and verified by a matter-of-fact astronomer. Goethe wrote:

Makarie stood in a relationship to our solar system that one hardly dares to name. She does not merely contemplate and cherish it in her mind, her soul, her imagination – no, she is, as it were, a very part of it; she believes herself to be drawn along in those heavenly cycles, but in a very special way; since her childhood she has been travelling round the sun, and more precisely, as we have now discovered, in a spiral, moving further and further away from the centre and circling towards the outer regions ...

This property of hers, glorious though it is, was nevertheless imposed upon her from her earliest years as a heavy task ... The superabundance of this condition was in some degree mitigated by the fact that she, too, seemed to have her night and day, for when her inner light was dimmed she strove most faithfully to fulfil her outward duties, but when the inner light blazed afresh, she yielded to a blissful rest.

This curious description, reminiscent of the reports of certain mystics, expresses Goethe's pantheism. Makarie is a symbol for the world unity of creative man, and the astronomer at her side is a personification of science. True, the 'superabundance of her condition' lacks a social element, that of the creative human being's unity not only with the natural world but also with the rest of mankind. Such 'superabundance' in society as we have known it until now has been the lot and the heavy burden of only very few men and women; but in a truly human society the springs of creative power will gush forth in many, many more; the artist's experience will no longer be a privilege but the normal gift of free and active man; we shall achieve, as it were, *social genius*.

Man, who became man through work, who stepped out of the animal kingdom as transformer of the natural into the artificial, who became therefore the magician, man the creator of social reality, will always stay the great magician, will always be Prometheus bringing fire from heaven to earth, will always be Orpheus enthralling nature with his music. Not until humanity itself dies will art die.

From Report on the Journals *Zvezda*
and *Leningrad*, 1947

It is clear from the Central Committee's decision that *Zvezda's* worst mistake has been that of allowing the writings of Zoshchenko and Akhmatova to appear in its pages. It is, I think, hardly necessary for me to instance Zoshchenko's 'work' *The Adventures of a Monkey*. You have certainly all read it and know it better than I do. The point of this 'work' of Zoshchenko's is that in it he portrays Soviet people as lazy, unattractive, stupid and crude. He is in no way concerned with their labour, their efforts, their heroism, their high social and moral qualities. He never so much as mentions these. He chooses, like the cheap philistine he is, to scratch about in life's basenesses and pettinesses. This is no accident. It is intrinsic in all cheap philistine writers, of whom Zoshchenko is one. Gorky often used to speak of this; you will remember how, at the 1934 Congress of Soviet Writers, he stigmatized the so-called *literati* who can see no further than the soot on the kitchen range and in the boiler room.

The Adventures of a Monkey is not a thing apart from the general run of Zoshchenko's stories. It is merely as the most vivid expression of all the negative qualities in his 'literary work' that it has attracted the critics' attention. Since he returned to Leningrad after the evacuation, he has, we know, written several things demonstrating his inability to find anything positive whatever in the life of Soviet people or any positive character among them. He is in the habit of jeering at Soviet life, ways and people, as he does in *The Adventures of a Monkey*, and of concealing his jeers behind a mask of empty-headed entertainment and pointless humour.

If you take the trouble to read his *Adventures of a Monkey* more closely you will find that he makes the monkey act as a supreme judge of our social customs, a dictator of morality to

Soviet people. The monkey is depicted as an intelligent creature capable of assessing human behaviour. The writer deliberately caricatures the life of Soviet people as unattractive and cheap, so as to have the monkey pass the judgement, filthy, poisonous and anti-Soviet as it is, that living in the zoo is better than being at liberty, that you can draw your breath more freely in a cage than among Soviet people.

Is it possible to fall morally and politically lower than this? How can the people of Leningrad tolerate such rubbish and vulgarity in the pages of their journals?

The Leningraders in charge of *Zvezda* must indeed be lacking in vigilance if a 'work' of this sort is offered to the journal's Soviet readers, if it is found possible to publish works steeped in the venom of bestial enmity towards the Soviet order. Only the scum of the literary world could write such 'works', and only the blind, the apolitical could allow them to appear.

Zoshchenko's story is said to have gone the rounds of Leningrad's variety halls. The leadership of educational work in Leningrad must have fallen to a low level indeed for such a thing to be possible.

Zoshchenko has managed to find a niche for himself in the pages of an important Leningrad journal and to popularize his loathsome 'moral lessons' there. And yet *Zvezda* is a journal purporting to educate our young people. Is that a task to be coped with by a journal that has taken a low un-Soviet writer like Zoshchenko to its heart? Is *Zvezda*'s editorial board unaware of what he is?

It is not so long ago – early 1944, in fact – that *Bolshevik* published an article sharply critical of Zoshchenko's book *Before Sunrise*, which was written at the height of the Soviet people's war of liberation against the German invaders. In this book Zoshchenko turns his low, cheap little self inside out, and delights to exhibit himself to the public gaze; indeed, he does it with gusto, crying: See what an oaf I am!

It would be hard to find in our literature anything more revolting than the 'lesson' Zoshchenko teaches in this book, *Before Sunrise*, where he portrays himself and others as lewd and repulsive beasts with neither shame nor conscience. Such was the the 'lesson' he offered Soviet readers when our people were shedding their blood in an unprecedentedly bitter war, when the life of the Soviet state hung by a thread, when the Soviet people were making countless sacrifices to defeat the Germans. Far in the rear, entrenched in Alma-Ata, Zoshchenko was doing nothing to help. *Bolshevik* publicly castigated him, and rightly, as a low slanderer having no place in Soviet literature.

But he snapped his fingers at public opinion. Less than two years later, friend Zoshchenko struts back to Leningrad and starts making free use of the pages of the Leningrad journals. Not only *Zvezda* but *Leningrad*, too, welcomed his stories. Variety concert halls were rapidly made available. Moreover, he was allowed to occupy a leading position in the Leningrad section of the Union of Soviet Writers and to play an active part in the literary affairs of Leningrad.

What grounds have you for letting him roam at will through the parks and gardens of Leningrad literature? Why have Leningrad's active Party workers and the Leningrad Writers' Union allowed such shameful things to occur?

Zoshchenko's thoroughly rotten and corrupt social, political and literary attitude does not result from any recent transformation. There is nothing accidental about his latest 'works'. They are simply the continuation of his literary 'legacy' dating from the twenties.

Who was he in the past? He was one of the organizers of the literary group known as the Serapion Brothers. And when the Serapion Brothers group was formed, what was he like socially and politically? Let me turn to *Literaturniye Zapiski* (3, 1922) where the founders of this group expounded their creed. This journal contains, among other things, Zoshchenko's *credo*, in an article entitled 'About Myself and a Few Other Things'. Quite unashamed, he publicly exposes himself and states his political and literary 'views' with the utmost frankness. Listen to what he says:

... It is very difficult to be a writer, on the whole. Take this business of ideology... Writers are expected to have an ideology nowadays ... What a bore! How can I have any 'definite ideology', tell me, when no Party really attracts me? From the Party members' point of view I am not a man of principle. What of it? For my part, I may say: I am not a Communist, nor a Socialist-Revolutionary, nor a Monarchist, but merely a Russian, and a politically amoral one, at that ... Honest to God, I don't know to this day what Party, well, Guchkov ... say, belongs to. Heaven knows what party he's in; I know he isn't a Bolshevik, but whether he's a Socialist-Revolutionary or a Cadet I neither know nor care.

And so on and so forth.

What do you make of that sort of 'ideology'? Twenty-five years have passed since Zoshchenko published this 'confession' of his. Has he changed since? Not so that you would notice it. Not only has he neither learned anything nor changed in any way in the last two and a half decades, but with cynical frankness he continues, on the contrary, to remain the apostle of empty-headedness and cheapness, a literary slum-rat, unprincipled and conscienceless. That is to say, now as then he cares nothing for Soviet ways, now as then he has no place in Soviet literature and opposes it.

If he has nevertheless become something approaching a literary star in Leningrad, if his praises are sung on Leningrad's Parnassus, we can but marvel at the lack of principle, of strictness, of discrimination, in the people who paved the way for him and applauded him.

Allow me to instance one more illustration of what the Serapion Brothers, so-called, were like. In the same issue of *Literaturniye Zapiski* (3, 1922) another Serapionist, Lev Lunts, also tried to expound the ideological basis of the harmful trend represented by the Serapion Brothers, which is alien to the spirit of Soviet literature. Lunts wrote:

We gathered together at a time of great political and revolutionary tension. 'He who is not with us is against us,' we were told on all hands. 'Who are you with, Serapion Brothers,' we were asked, 'with the Communists or against them, for the revolution or against it?' And so, who are we with, Serapion Brothers? We are with the hermit Serapion. Officialdom has ruled Russian literature too long and too painfully. We do not want utilitarianism. We do not write for propaganda purposes. Art is real, like life itself, and like life it exists because it must, without purpose or meaning.

Such was the role allotted to art by the Serapion Brothers, depriving it of all ideological content or social significance; they proclaimed the non-ideological nature of art, demanding art for art's sake, without purpose or meaning. This is nothing but a plea for philistinism, superficiality and lack of political belief.

What conclusion does this lead to? Zoshchenko does not like Soviet ways: so what would you advise us to do? Adapt ourselves to him? It is not for us to change our tastes. It is not for us to alter our life and our order to suit him. Let him change; and if he will not, let him get out of Soviet literature, in which there can be no place for meaningless, cheap, empty-headed works.

This was the Central Committee's starting point in adopting its decisions on *Zvezda* and *Leningrad*.

I will now turn to the literary 'work' of Anna Akhmatova. Her works have been appearing in the Leningrad journals recently as an example of 'increased output'. This is as surprising and unnatural as it would be if someone were to start issuing new editions of the works of Merezhkovsky, Vyacheslav Ivanov, Mikhail Kuzmin, Andrei Bely, Zinaida Hippius, Fyodor Sologub, Zinovyeva-Annibal, and so on and so forth; that is, of all the writers whom our advanced public and literary circles have always considered to be representatives of reactionary obscurantism and perfidy in art and politics.

Gorky once said that the ten years from 1907 to 1917 might well be called the most shameful, the most barren decade in the history of Russian intellectuals; in this decade, after the 1905 Revolution, a great many of the intellectuals spurned the revolution and slid down into a morass of pornography and reactionary mysticism, screening their perfidy with the 'pretty' phrase: 'I too have burned all I revered and have revered what I burned.'

It was during these ten years that there appeared such perfidious works as Ropshin's *The Pale Horse* and the writings of Vinnichenko and other deserters from the camp of revolution to that of reaction, hastening to dethrone the lofty ideals that the best and most progressive representatives of Russian society were fighting for. It was then that there rose to the surface Symbolists, Imagists and decadents of every shape and hue, disowning the people and proclaiming the thesis of 'Art for Art's sake', preaching the meaninglessness of literature and screening their ideological and moral corruption behind a pursuit of beauty of form without content. All of them were united in their brutish fear of the coming workers' revolution. Suffice it to recall that one of the most notable 'theoreticians' in these reactionary literary movements was Merezhkovsky, who called the coming workers' revolution 'the approaching rabble' and greeted the October Revolution with bestial malice.

Anna Akhmatova is one of the representatives of this idea-less reactionary morass in literature. She belongs to the 'Acméist' literary group, who in their day emerged from the ranks of the Symbolists, and she is one of the standard-bearers of the meaningless, empty-headed, aristocratic-salon school of poetry, which has no place whatever in Soviet literature. The Acméists represented an extremely individualistic trend in art. They preached 'Art for Art's sake', 'Beauty for Beauty's sake', and had no wish to know anything about the people and the people's needs and interests, or about social life.

This was a bourgeois-aristocratic trend in literature, appearing at a time when the days of the bourgeoisie and of the aristocracy were numbered, when the poets and theoreticians of the ruling classes were trying to hide from harsh reality in the mists and clouds of religious mysticism, in paltry personal experiences and in absorption in their own petty souls. The Acméists, like the symbolists, decadents and other representatives of the disintegrating bourgeois-aristocratic ideology, were preachers of defeatism, pessimism and faith in a hereafter.

Akhmatova's subject-matter is individualistic to the core. The range of her poetry is sadly limited; it is the poetry of a spoilt woman-aristocrat, frenziedly vacillating between boudoir and chapel. Her main emphasis is on erotic love-themes interwoven with notes of sadness, longing, death, mysticism, fatality. A sense of fatality (quite comprehensible in a dying group), the dismal tones of a death-bed hopelessness, mystical experiences shot with eroticism, make up Akhmatova's spiritual world; she is a left-over from the world of the old aristocracy now irrevocably past and gone, the world of 'Catherine's good old days'. It would be hard to say whether she is a nun or a fallen woman; better perhaps say she is a bit of each, her desires and her prayers intertwined.

> But I vow by the garden of angels,
> By the miraculous icon I vow,
> I vow by the child of our passion ...
> – from 'Anno Domini', by Anna Akhmatova

Such is Akhmatova, with her petty, narrow personal life, her paltry experiences, and her religiously mystical eroticism.

Her poetry is far removed from the people. It is the poetry of the ten thousand members of the *élite* society of the old aristocratic Russia, whose hour has long since struck and left them with nothing to do but sigh for 'the good old days', for the country estates of Catherine's time, with their avenues of ancient lime trees, their fountains, their statues, their arches, their greenhouses, summer-houses and crumbling coats of arms, for aristocratic St Petersburg, for Tsarskoye Selo, for the railway station in Pavlovsk, and for other relics of the nobility's culture. All of these have vanished into the irredeemable past. The few representatives of this culture, so foreign to the spirit of the people, who have by some miracle lived on into our own times, can do nothing but shut themselves up in themselves and live with chimeras. 'All has been plundered, betrayed and sold,' writes Akhmatova.

Osip Mandelstam, a prominent Acméist, wrote this, not long before the revolution, on the social, political and literary ideals of this little group : 'The Acméists share their love of organism and organization with the physiologically perfect Middle Ages ...' 'The Middle Ages, with their own peculiar way of estimating a man's relative weight, felt and recognized it in every individual irrespective of merit ...' 'Yes, Europe once passed through a labyrinth of filigree-fine culture, when abstract being, personal existence, wholly unadorned, was valued as an outstanding achievement. This gave rise to the aristocratic intimacy binding everybody, so foreign to the spirit of "equality and fraternity" of the great revolution ...' 'The Middle Ages are dear to us because they had so highly developed a sense of boundaries and dividing lines ...' 'A noble mixture of rationality and mysticism, and a perception of the world as a living equilibrium, make us feel a kinship with this age and prompt us to draw strength from the works that appeared on Romance soil about the year 1200.'

These statements of Mandelstam's contain the Acméists' hopes and ideals. 'Back to the Middle Ages' was the social idea of this aristocratic-salon group. 'Back to the monkey' choruses Zoshchenko. Incidentally, the Acméists and the Serapion Brothers are of the same descent. Their common ancestor was Hoffman, one of the founders of aristocratic-salon decadence and mysticism.

Where was the need to popularize Akhmatova's poetry all of a sudden? What has she to do with Soviet people? What need is there to offer a literary pulpit to all these defeatist and un-Soviet literary trends?

We know from the history of Russian literature that the reactionary literary trends to which the Symbolists and the Acméists belonged tried time and time again to start a crusade against the great revolutionary-democratic traditions of Russian literature and against its foremost representatives, tried to deprive literature of its high ideological and social significance and to drag it down into the morass of meaninglessness and cheapness.

All these 'fashionable' trends have been engulfed and buried with the classes whose ideology they reflected. What, in our Soviet literature, has remained of all these Symbolists, Acméists, Yellow Shirts, Jacks-o'-Diamonds and *Nichevoki* ('Nothingers')? Nothing whatever, though their crusades against the great representatives of Russian revolutionary-democratic literature, Belinsky, Dobrolyubov, Chernyshevsky, Herzen, Saltykov-Shchedrin, were launched noisily and pretentiously and just as noisily failed.

The Acméists proclaimed it their motto 'not to improve life in any way whatever nor to indulge in criticism of it'. Why were they against improving life in any way whatever? Because they liked the old bourgeois-aristocratic life, whereas the revolutionary people were preparing to disturb this life of theirs. In November 1917 both the ruling classes and their theoreticians and singers were pitched into the dustbin of history.

And now, in the twenty-ninth year of the socialist revolution, certain museum specimens reappear all of a sudden and start teaching our young people how to live. The pages of a Leningrad journal are thrown wide open to Akhmatova and she is given *carte blanche* to poison the minds of the young people with the harmful spirit of her poetry.

One of the issues of *Leningrad* contains a kind of digest of the works written by Akhmatova between 1909 and 1944. Among the rest of the rubbish, there is a poem she wrote during evacuation in the Great Patriotic War. In this poem she describes her loneliness, the solitude she has to share with a black cat, whose eyes looking at her are like the eyes of the centuries. This is no new theme: Akhmatova wrote about a black cat in 1909, too. This mood of solitude and hopelessness, which is foreign to the spirit of Soviet literature, runs through the whole of Akhmatova's work.

What has this poetry in common with the interests of our state and people? Nothing whatever. Akhmatova's work is a matter of the distant past; it is foreign to Soviet life and cannot be tolerated in the pages of our journals. Our literature is no private enterprise designed to please the fluctuating tastes of the literary market. We are certainly under no obligation to find a place in our literature for tastes and ways that have nothing in common with the moral qualities and attributes of Soviet people. What instructive value can the works of Akhmatova have for our young people? They can do them nothing but harm. These works can sow nothing but gloom, low spirits, pessimism, a desire to escape the vital problems of social life and turn away from the broad highway of social life and activity into a narrow little world of personal experiences. How can the upbringing of our young people be entrusted to her? Yet her poems were readily printed, sometimes in *Zvezda* and sometimes in *Leningrad,* and were published in volume form. This was a serious political error.

It is only natural, in view of all this, that the works of other writers, who were also beginning to adopt an empty-headed and defeatist tone, should have started to appear in the Leningrad journals. I am thinking of works such as those of Sadofyev and Komissarova. In some of their poems they imitate Akhmatova, cultivating the mood of despondency, boredom and loneliness so dear to her.

Needless to say, such moods, or the extolling of them, can exert only a negative influence on our young people and are bound to poison their minds with a vicious spirit of empty-headedness, despondency and lack of political consciousness.

What would have happened if we had brought our young people up in a spirit of despondency and of disbelief in our cause? We should not have won the Great Patriotic War. It is precisely because the Soviet State, and our Party, with the help of Soviet literature, had brought our young people up in a spirit of optimism and with confidence in their own strength, that we were able to surmount the tremendous difficulties that faced us in the building of socialism and in defeating the Germans and the Japanese.

What does this mean? It means that by printing in its pages cheap and reactionary works devoid of proper ideas, side by side with good works of rich content and cheerful tone, *Zvezda* became a journal having no clear policy, a journal helping our enemies to corrupt our young people. The strength of our journals has always lain in their optimistic revolutionary trend, not in eclecticism, empty-headedness and lack of political understanding. *Zvezda* gave its full sanction to propaganda in favour of doing nothing.

To make matters worse, Zoshchenko seems to have acquired so much power in the Leningrad writers' organization that he even used to shout down those who disagreed with him and threaten to lampoon his critics in one of his forthcoming works. He became a sort of literary dictator surrounded by a group of admirers singing his praises.

Well may one ask, on what grounds? Why did you allow such an unnatural and reactionary thing as this to occur?

No wonder Leningrad's literary journals started giving space to cheap modern bourgeois literature from the West. Some of our men of letters began looking on themselves as not the teachers but the pupils of petty-bourgeois writers, and began to adopt an obsequious and awestruck attitude towards foreign literature. Is such obsequiousness becoming in us Soviet patriots who have built up the Soviet order, which towers higher a hundredfold, and is better a hundredfold, than any bourgeois order? Is obsequiousness towards the cheap and philistine bourgeois literature of the West becoming in our advanced Soviet literature, the most revolutionary in the world?

Another serious failing in the work of our writers is their ignoring of modern Soviet subjects, which betrays on the one hand a one-sided interest in historical subjects and on the other an attempt to write on meaningless, purely amusing subjects. To justify their failure to keep pace with great modern Soviet themes, some writers maintain that the time has come to give the people meaningless and 'entertaining' literature, to stop bothering about literature's ideological content.

This conception of our people, of their interests and requirements, is entirely wrong. Our people expect Soviet writers to understand and integrate the vast experience they gained in the Great Patriotic War, to portray and integrate the heroism with which they are now working to rehabilitate the country's national economy.

A few words on the journal *Leningrad*: Zoshchenko's position is even stronger here than in *Zvezda*, as is Akhmatova's too. Both of them have become active powers in both journals. Thus *Leningrad* is responsible for having put its pages at the disposal of such cheap writers as Zoshchenko and such salon poetesses as Akhmatova.

The journal *Leningrad* has, however, made other mistakes also.

For instance, take the parody of *Evgeny Onegin* written by one Khazin. This piece is called *The Return of Onegin*. It is said to be frequently recited on the variety concert platforms of Leningrad.

It is hard to understand why the people of Leningrad allow their city to be vilified from a public platform in such a way as Khazin vilifies it. The purpose of this 'satire' is not simple ridicule of the things that happen to Onegin on finding himself in modern Leningrad. The point is that Khazin essays to compare our modern Leningrad with the St Petersburg of Pushkin's day, and for the worse. Read just a few lines of this 'parody' attentively. Nothing in our modern Leningrad pleases the author. Sneering in malice and derision, he slanders Leningrad and Soviet people. In his opinion, Onegin's day was a golden age. Everything is different now: a housing department has appeared, and ration cards and permits. Girls, those ethereal creatures so much admired by Onegin, now regulate the traffic and repair the Leningrad houses and so on and so forth. Let me quote just one passage from this 'parody':

> Our poor dear Evgeny
> Boarded a tram.
> Never had his benighted age known
> Such a means of transportation.
> But fate was kind to Evgeny;
> He escaped with only a foot crushed,
> And only once, when someone jabbed him
> In the stomach, was he called an idiot.
> Remembering ancient customs,
> He resolved to seek satisfaction in a duel:
> He felt in his pocket, but
> Someone had taken his gloves,
> A frustration that reduced
> Onegin to silence and docility.

That is what Leningrad was like before, and what it has turned into: a wretched, uncouth, coarse city; and that is the aspect it presented to poor dear Onegin. It is in this vulgar way that Khazin describes Leningrad and its people.

The idea behind this slanderous parody is harmful, vicious and false.

How could the editorial board of *Leningrad* have accepted this malicious slander on Leningrad and its magnificent people? How could Khazin have been allowed to appear in the pages of the Leningrad journals?

Take another work, a parody on a parody by Nekrasov, so written as to be a direct insult to the memory of the great poet and public figure Nekrasov, an insult that ought to arouse the indignation of every educated person. Yet *Leningrad*'s editorial board did not hesitate to print this sordid concoction in its columns.

What else do we find in *Leningrad*? A foreign anecdote, dull and shallow, apparently lifted from hackneyed anecdote-books dating from the late nineteenth century. Is there nothing else for *Leningrad* to fill its pages with? Is there really nothing to write about in Leningrad? What about such a subject as the rehabilitation of the city? Wonderful work is being done in Leningrad; the city is healing the wounds inflicted during the siege; the people of Leningrad are imbued with the enthusiasm and emotion of post-war rehabilitation. Has anything on this appeared in *Leningrad*? Will the people of the city ever live to see the day when their feats of labour are reflected in the pages of this journal?

Further, let us take the subject of Soviet woman. Is it permissible to cultivate in Soviet readers the disgraceful views on the role and mission of women that are typical of Akhmatova, and not to give a really truthful concept of modern Soviet woman in general and the heroic girls and women of Leningrad in particular, who unflinchingly shouldered the heavy burden of the war years and are now self-sacrificingly working to carry out the difficult tasks presented by the rehabilitation of the city's economic life?

The situation in the Leningrad section of the Union of Soviet Writers is obviously such that the supply of good work is now insufficient to fill two literary journals. The Central Committee of the Party has therefore decided to cease publication of *Leningrad*, so as to concentrate all the best literary forces in *Zvezda*. This does not mean that Leningrad will not, in suitable circumstances, have a second or even a third journal. The question will be settled by the supply of notable literary works. Should so many appear that there is no room for them in one journal, a second and even a third may be started; it all depends on the intellectual and artistic quality of the works produced by our Leningrad writers.

Such are the grave errors and failings laid bare and detailed in the resolution of the Central Committee of the Communist Party on the work of *Zvezda* and *Leningrad*.